Process
Philosophy
and
Christian
Thought

Process Philosophy and Christian Thought

Edited by

Delwin Brown

Ralph E. James, Jr.

Gene Reeves

The Bobbs-Merrill Company, Inc.

Indianapolis and New York

Copyright © 1971 by The Bobbs-Merrill Company, Inc.

Printed in the United States of America
Library of Congress Catalog Card Number 74–127586

ISBN 0-672-60799-9 (pbk)
ISBN 0-672-51529-6
Third Printing

Design by: Anita Duncan

Preface

"Process philosophy" is basically a metaphysical position, the view that reality is fundamentally both temporal and creative, and therefore that "becoming" is more fundamental than "being." It can be contrasted effectively with the metaphysics of Being which has dominated Western philosophy and Christian theology. Defined very broadly, process philosophy can be detected in much of Buddhism, at least in Theravada, in the obscure fragments of Heraclitus, and in the sixteenth-century philosophical theology of Faustus Socinus. Some would find it coming to bloom in the idealistic philosophies of Hegel and Schelling. Certainly Bergson, Alexander, Peirce, and James can be called process philosophers. More recently Berdyaev and Teilhard de Chardin have developed views that belong in this category.

In recent years, however, process philosophy has come to mean especially, though not exclusively, the philosophy of Alfred North Whitehead and his intellectual descendants, most notably Charles Hartshorne. It is this narrower sense of process philosophy—Whiteheadian process philosophy—that provides one pole of the title and content of this book.

Besides the prejudices of the editors, there are at least two reasons for limiting this anthology to Whiteheadian process philosophy. For one, no one has created a process metaphysics as complete, comprehensive, and as suggestive for future developments as Whitehead's. The sheer greatness of *Process and Reality* necessarily makes his philosophy the primary locus of modern process philosophy. Secondly, though other process philosophers have been influential within Christian theology, in recent years Whiteheadian process philosophy has generated increasing interest and excitement as a philosophical basis for Christian thought. In America at least, it has become one of the few major options for contemporary theology, and perhaps the only genuine philosophical option.

The reasons for this new interest in Whiteheadian thought are not hard to find. On the negative side it has to do with the general demise of neo-orthodoxy and the relative absence of other theologically relevant philosophical options. On the positive side it can be attributed chiefly to the rise in philosophical stature of Charles Hartshorne and to the growing theological prominence of two of his students, Schubert M. Ogden and John B. Cobb, Jr.

Thus, when process theology is talked about in American (and to some extent British) theological schools today, Bergson, Berdyaev and Teilhard may be in the background, but the work of Whitehead, Hartshorne, Ogden and Cobb is primarily in mind. To us it seems eminently timely and appropriate, therefore, to publish a selection of major works by twentieth-century Whiteheadian process philosophers and theologians.

In the Introduction we have attempted to present a brief historical account of the rise of this point of view, including the place in the movement of the contributors to this volume. Since all of Whitehead's theologically relevant works are readily available in inexpensive editions, there is very little from them in this book. Victor Lowe's piece is the best brief introduction to Whitehead's metaphysics available. Hartshorne's contribution is an abridged version of the very important first chapter of his *Man's Vision of God*. It contains much of both the substance and method of his approach to theological problems and issues. Most of the remaining chapters are a selection from the works of Christian theologians who have been strongly influenced by Whiteheadian philosophy. A few are critical examinations of this approach or aspects of it.

The contributors are philosophers and theologians, young and old, American and British, Protestant, Roman Catholic, Jewish, and secular. All in all they provide a sound introduction to the variety and scope of Whiteheadian process theology and its place in contemporary Christian thought. The book will be very useful in courses dealing, either exclusively or in part, with process theology. It can also be read with profit by clergymen seeking to know what this "new" option in theology has to offer, or by anyone interested in what happens to a philosophy when it is used by theologians and intimately related to Christian thought.

Credit for the idea of this book belongs to Ralph James. He recruited the other editors for collaboration in what has proved to be an enjoyable and intellectually rewarding effort. All editorial responsibilities and decisions have been shared equally.

All three of us owe a note of appreciation to those who have given financial support to our research for this book: Mr. Brown to Anderson College; Mr. James to the Knapp Fund; and Mr. Reeves to Tufts University. Above all we must express our appreciation to the authors. They have been wise consultants as well as cooperative contributors. Without their work, in some cases presented here for the first time, such a volume on process philosophy and Christian thought could not exist.

Delwin Brown
Ralph E. James, Jr.
Gene Reeves

The Contributors

George Allan holds degrees from Union Theological Seminary, New York, and Yale University. He is Associate Professor of Philosophy at Dickinson College.

Delwin Brown holds degrees from Union Theological Seminary, New York, and Claremont Graduate School. He is Associate Professor of Philosophy and Religion at Anderson College, and Lecturer in Philosophy of Religion at the School of Theology.

Don S. Browning was educated at the University of Chicago where he is now Professor of Pastoral Theology in the Divinity School.

John B. Cobb, Jr., attended Emory University and the University of Chicago. He is Ingraham Professor of Theology, the School of Theology at Claremont.

Malcolm L. Diamond was educated at Yale, Cambridge, and Columbia Universities. He is Associate Professor in the Department of Religion at Princeton University. Among his publications is Martin Buber: Jewish Existentialist.

Lewis S. Ford holds undergraduate and graduate degrees from Yale University. He is Associate Professor of Philosophy and Religion at Pennsylvania State University.

David Griffin was educated at Claremont Graduate School. He is Assistant Professor of Theology at the University of Dayton.

Peter N. Hamilton was educated at Cambridge University. Having previously taught mathematics and divinity at Marlborough College, he is now engaged in research at Trinity Hall.

Charles Hartshorne received his degree from Harvard University, where he was Whitehead's assistant. He has taught at Harvard, Chicago, and Emory Universities and he is now Ashbel Professor of Philosophy at the University of Texas.

Ralph E. James, Jr. attended Emory and Drew Universities. He is Associate Professor of Philosophy and Religion at North Carolina Wesleyan College.

Bernard M. Loomer was educated at the University of Chicago where
he taught and was Dean for several years in the Divinity School.
Now he teaches at Berkeley Baptist Divinity School.

Victor Lowe was educated at Harvard University, where he studied
with Whitehead. He is Professor of Philosophy at Johns Hopkins
University.

Bernard E. Meland, educated at the University of Chicago, was Professor of Constructive Theology at the Divinity School for eighteen
years prior to his retirement in 1964.

Schubert M. Ogden attended the University of Chicago. Formerly Professor of Theology at Perkins School of Theology, he now teaches
at the University of Chicago Divinity School. He has written *Christ
Without Myth.*

Thomas W. Ogletree attended Garrett Theological Seminary and Vanderbilt University. He is Assistant Professor of Constructive Theology at Chicago Theological Seminary and has published *Christian
Faith and History* and *The Death of God Controversy.*

Gene Reeves holds degrees from Boston and Emory Universities. He
has taught at Tufts University and is now Professor of Philosophy
at Wilberforce University.

Donald W. Sherburne attended Oxford and Yale Universities. He is
Professor of Philosophy at Vanderbilt University.

Walter E. Stokes, S. J., was educated at St. Louis University and Cambridge. Until his death in 1969, he was Assistant Professor of
Philosophy at Fordham University and Loyola College and Seminary.

Daniel Day Williams attended the University of Chicago, Chicago Theological Seminary and Columbia University. He is Roosevelt Professor of Systematic Theology at Union Theological Seminary in
New York.

Contents

TWO God

THREE Christ

FOUR   *Man and Society*

Abbreviations

Throughout this text the following abbreviations are used to refer to the principal works of Alfred North Whitehead.

AE   *The Aims of Education and Other Essays.* Macmillan, 1929.

AI   *Adventures of Ideas.* Macmillan, 1933.

CN   *The Concept of Nature.* Cambridge University Press, 1920.

Dial   *Dialogues of Alfred North Whitehead,* as recorded by Lucian Price. Little, Brown, 1954.

ESP   *Essays in Science and Philosophy.* Philosophical Library, 1947.

FR   *The Function of Reason.* Princeton University Press, 1929.

IS   *The Interpretation of Science: Selected Essays.* Edited, with an Introduction, by A. H. Johnson. Bobbs-Merrill, 1961.

MT   *Modes of Thought.* Macmillan, 1938.

PNK   *An Inquiry Concerning the Principles of Natural Knowledge.* Cambridge University Press, 1919; Second Edition, 1925.

PR   *Process and Reality, An Essay in Cosmology.* Macmillan, 1929.

RM   *Religion in the Making.* Macmillan, 1926.

S   *Symbolism, Its Meaning and Effect.* Macmillan, 1927.

SMW   *Science and the Modern World.* Macmillan, 1925.

Introduction

Whitehead's Metaphysical System   1

Victor Lowe

I

... Whitehead's amazing philosophical achievement is the construction of a system of the world according to which the basic fact of existence is everywhere some process of self-realization, growing out of previous processes and itself adding a new pulse of individuality and a new value to the world. So far as familiar classifications of metaphysical systems are concerned, then, I should first of all classify Whitehead's as pluralistic; it denies that ultimately only one individual (God, or the Absolute) exists. But no one-sentence characterization, not even of the roughest kind, is possible for this system. Whitehead the pluralist saw the great monistic metaphysicians as endeavoring to exhibit the unity and solidarity which the universe undoubtedly has, while failing to do justice to the equally evident plurality of individual existents. He saw Spinoza the monist, equally with Leibniz the pluralist, as having made valuable depositions. It is not that their systems, however, should be reconciled (at some cost to each). It is that their insights, along with those of Plato and others, should be reconciled—or better, used—in a new system. It will have its own elements and its own structure. For reasons which will appear, Whitehead named it "the philosophy of organism."

Taken as a whole, this deposition of Whitehead's can neither be subsumed under any movement of the twentieth century nor accurately represented as the joint influence of recent thinkers on its author. It must be understood in its own terms. But it is so complex and elaborate that all but the main concepts will be omitted in the one-chapter summary which follows. These concepts will be presented sympathetically, with some fullness and a little comment, as a bald statement of them would be unintelligible.

From Victor Lowe, *Understanding Whitehead*. Copyright 1962, The Johns Hopkins Press. Originally published in *Classic American Philosophers*, Max H. Fisch, ed., copyright 1951, Appleton-Century-Crofts, Inc. Used by permission of The Johns Hopkins Press, Appleton-Century-Crofts, Inc., and Victor Lowe.

II

By way of initial orientation, let us say that Whitehead's universe is a *connected* pluralistic universe. No monist ever insisted more strongly than he that nothing in the world exists in independence of other •hings. In fact, he repeatedly criticizes traditional monisms for not carrying this principle far enough; they exempted eternal being from dependence on temporal beings. Independent existence is a myth, whether you ascribe it to God or to a particle of matter in Newtonian physics, to persons, to nations, to things, or to meanings. To understand is to see things together, and to see them as, in Whitehead's favorite phrase, "requiring each other." A system which enables us to do this is "coherent."

Each pulse of existence—Whitehead calls them "actual entities" —requires the antecedent others as its constituents, yet achieves individuality as a unique, finite synthesis; and when its growth is completed, stays in the universe as one of the infinite number of settled facts from which the individuals of the future will arise. "The many become one, and are increased by one." The ultimate character pervading the universe is a drive toward the endless production of new syntheses. Whitehead calls this drive "creativity." It is "the eternal activity," "the underlying energy of realisation." Nothing escapes it; the universe consists entirely of its creatures, its individualized embodiments. Accordingly, Whitehead's Categoreal Scheme begins with the three notions, "creativity," "many," and "one," which comprise the "Category of the Ultimate." This category is presupposed by all his other metaphysical categories.

Creativity is not to be thought of as a thing or an agency external to its actual embodiments, but as "that ultimate notion of the highest generality" which actuality *exhibits.* Apart from that exhibition it does not exist. Like Aristotle's "matter," creativity has no character of its own, but is perfectly protean: "It cannot be characterized, because all characters are more special than itself." Nor can its universal presence be explained in terms of anything else; it must be seen by direct, intuitive experience.

The doctrine that all actualities alike are in the grip of creativity suggests a general principle which Whitehead thinks every metaphysical scheme, so far as it is coherent, must follow. The principle is that there is ultimately but one kind of actuality.

> 'Actual entities'—also termed 'actual occasions'—are the final real things of which the world is made up. There is no going behind actual entities to find anything more real. They differ among themselves: God is an actual entity, and so is the most trivial puff of existence in far-off

empty space. But, though there are gradations of importance, and diversities of function, yet in the principles which actuality exemplifies all are on the same level.—*PR 27f.*

This statement represents an ideal which Whitehead, so far as the concept of God is concerned, does not entirely achieve. But he is distinguished by his conscious adoption and pursuit of it, in place of the more traditional, dualistic doctrine of inferior and superior realities.

Our experience of the universe does not, at first glance, present any obvious prototype of actual entities. Selves, monads, material atoms, and Aristotelian substances have been tried out in the history of philosophy. Whitehead develops a theory of a different entity—an *experience.* The doctrine that experience comes in drops or pulses, each of which has a unique character and an indivisible unity, is to be found in the writings of William James; but James never outlined a metaphysics on this basis. In any case, Whitehead had motives of his own for adopting the working hypothesis that "all final individual actualities have the metaphysical character of occasions of experience."

There was the antidualistic motive: belief that some such actualities are without any experience of their own, when joined to the fact that the human existence with which philosophic thought must begin is just a series of experiences, makes it impossible to think of these extremes as contrasting but connected instances of one basic kind of actuality. But on Whitehead's hypothesis, "the direct evidence as to the connectedness of one's immediate present occasion of experience with one's immediately past occasions, can be validly used to suggest categories applying to the connectedness of all occasions in nature" (*AI* 284).

Secondly, we instinctively feel that we live in a world of "throbbing actualities"; and such "direct persuasions" are the ultimate touchstones of philosophic theory.

Thirdly, Whitehead does not wish to think that intrinsic value is an exclusive property of superior beings; rather it belongs to even "the most trivial puff of existence." In human life, he finds value not far off, but at hand as the living essence of present experience. If every puff of existence is a pulse of some kind of immediate experience, there can be no final dualism of value and fact in the universe.

A fourth reason why Whitehead chose occasions of experience for his "actual entities" emerges as a reader becomes familiar with his thought. It is his love of concrete immediacy. An immediate experience, in its living occurrence at this moment—that, to this rationalist's way of thinking, is a full fact, in comparison with which all other things are pale abstractions. It is a mistake for philosophers to begin with substances which appear solid or obvious to them, like the material body or the soul, and then, almost as if it were an afterthought, bring in transient experiences to provide these with an adventitious historical filling. The transient experiences *are* the ultimate realities.

But experience is not restricted to consciousness. "We experience the universe, and we analyze in our consciousness a minute selection of its details." Like most psychologists today, Whitehead thinks of consciousness as a variable factor which heightens an organism's discrimination of some part of its world. Consciousness is no basic category for him, because it is so far from being essential to every drop of experience in the cosmos, that it is not even present in every human experience. The same remark applies—the tradition of modern philosophy to the contrary notwithstanding—to thought and sense-perception.

The chief meaning intended by calling every actual entity a pulse of *experience* is that the entity is conceived as having an immediate existence in and for itself. "Experience" is "the self-enjoyment of being one among many, and of being one arising out of the composition of many." Each appropriation of an item of the many into the arising unity of enjoyment is a "feeling" or "prehension" (literally, a grasping) of that item, and the process of composition is a "concrescence" (growing together) of prehensions. The appropriated "many" are "objects," existing before the process begins; the "one" is the privately experiencing "subject." Thus "the subject-object relation is the fundamental structural pattern of experience."

A good way to continue our exposition now is to connect it with the challenge which William James, who had championed "psychology without a soul," issued to philosophers in his famous essay of 1904, "Does 'Consciousness' Exist?" He there attacked the notion, then current in various forms, that the existence of a conscious subject, if not of a soul, must be assumed in the discussion of experience. Is Whitehead trying to resuscitate the notion which James led many twentieth-century philosophers to reject? No. He does think it obvious that experience is a relation between private centers of experience and public objects experienced. But there are three big differences between his theory of this relation and the views which James attacked.

1. In the earlier views this was a cognitive relation of a conscious mind to objects known. Whitehead's fundamental relation of prehension is something broader and more elemental, the generally unconscious emotional feeling by which one bit of life responds to other realities. An essential factor in every prehension is its "subjective form"—the affective tone with which that subject now experiences that object. An example is the unconscious annoyance with which you experienced this page when you turned to it and saw another solid mass of

print. Everything in your environment contributes something both to the tone of your experience and to its content.

2. A prehension is not so much a relation as a relating, or transition, which carries the object into the makeup of the subject.[1] Whitehead's "feelings" are not states, but " 'vectors'; for they feel what is *there* and transform it into what is *here*" (PR 133).[2] He was writing a theoretical transcript of the fact that you feel this moment of experience to be your very own, yet derived from a world without. By taking that elemental assurance at its face value, he was able to accept a primary rule of modern philosophy—that the evidence for an external world can be found only within occasions of experience—without being drawn into solipsism.

Prehensions, like vectors, should be symbolized by arrows. The arrows run from the past[3] to the present—for the "there" is antecedent, however slightly, in time as well as external in space to the "here"— and *from* objects *to* a subject. The method is realistic, not idealistic: Whitehead remarks that instead of describing, in Kantian fashion, how subjective data pass into the appearance of an objective world, he describes how subjective experience emerges from an objective world.

3. For Whitehead the subject which enjoys an experience does not exist beforehand, neither is it created from the outside; it creates itself in that very process of experiencing. The process starts with the multitude of environmental objects awaiting unification in a fresh perspective, moves through stages of partial integration, and concludes as a fully determinate synthesis, effected by a concrescence of feelings. "The point to be noticed is that the actual entity, in a state of process during which it is not fully definite, determines its own ultimate definiteness. This is the whole point of moral responsibility" (PR 390). It is also the point of the descriptive term, "organism," which Whitehead applies to actual entities, and which supplies the very name of his philosophy. He means that an organism determines the eventual character and integration of its own parts. Its growth is motivated by a living—if generally unconscious—aim at that outcome. So the brief course of each pulse of experience is guided by an internal teleology.

Many philosophers consider Whitehead's doctrine of a self-

[1]Thus there is some analogy between "prehension" and the "felt transition" of which James wrote.

[2]Vectors, in physical theory, are quantities which have direction as well as magnitude: e.g., forces or velocities. Although it is evident from Whitehead's language, here and in the several other passages where he refers to prehensions as "vectors," that this is the analogy he intends, the meaning of "vector" in biology (the carrier of a microorganism) also provides an appropriate analogy. I owe this observation to Prof. Nathaniel Lawrence.

[3]Except in the case of "conceptual prehension," which will be explained shortly.

creating experiencer unintelligible. It certainly contradicts the mode of thought to which we are accustomed—*first* a permanent subject, *then* an experience for it. But how did the subject originally come into being? Whitehead looks upon process as not only the appearance of new patterns among things, but the becoming of new subjects, which are completely individual, self-contained units of feeling. "The ancient doctrine that 'no one crosses the same river twice' is extended. No thinker thinks twice; and, to put the matter more generally, no subject experiences twice." "The universe is thus a creative advance into novelty. The alternative to this doctrine is a static morphological universe" (PR 43; 339f).

Whitehead pictures reality as cumulative. When, upon the completion of an actual occasion, the creativity of the universe moves on to the next birth, it carries that occasion with it as an "object" which all future occasions are obliged to prehend. They will feel it as an efficient cause—as the immanence of the past in their immediacies of becoming. The end of an occasion's private life—its "perishing"—is the beginning of its public career. As Whitehead once explained:

> If you get a general notion of what is meant by perishing, you will have accomplished an apprehension of what you mean by memory and causality, what you mean when you feel that what we are is of infinite importance, because as we perish we are immortal—ESP 117.

Part of the appeal of Whitehead's metaphysics lies in this, that through his conception of pulses of experience as the ultimate facts, he invests the passage of time with life and motion, with pathos, and with a majesty rivaled in no other philosophy of change, and in few eternalistic ones.

Our experience does not usually discriminate a single actual entity as its object, but rather a whole nexus of them united by their prehensions. That is how you experience your body or your past personal history. "The ultimate facts of immediate actual experience," then, "are actual entities, prehensions, and nexūs.[4] All else is, for our experience, derivative abstraction." In Whitehead's cosmology, however, some types of derivative abstractions are constituents in every actual entity. Propositions are such; in every experience, conscious or unconscious, they function as "lures proposed for feeling." (Whitehead cites "There is beef for dinner today" as an example of a "quite ordinary proposition.") Because human beings think it important to consciously judge some propositions true or false, all propositions have traditionally been treated as units of thought or discourse, and supposed to be the concern of logicians alone. But we have no space for

---

[4]Plural of "nexus." The quotation is from *PR* 30.

Whitehead's highly original theory of propositions as factors in natural processes.

We shall confine attention in this chapter to the simplest type of abstract entity. The entertainment of propositions is but one of the ways in which "eternal objects" are ingredients in experience. These entities, uncreated and undated, are his version of Plato's timeless ideal Forms. They are patterns and qualities like roundness or squareness, greenness or redness, courage or cowardice. The fact that every actual occasion in its process of becoming acquires a definite character to the exclusion of other possible characters is explained as its selection of *these* eternal objects for feeling and its rejection ("negative prehension") of *those*. (This is not as fantastic as it sounds; actualities inherit habits of selection, and these habits are so strong that scientists call them laws of nature.)

For Whitehead as for Aristotle, process is the realizing of selected antecedent potentialities, or it is unexplainable. "Pure potentials for the specific determination of fact"—that is what eternal objects are. And that is all they are. The ideal is nothing more than a *possibility* (good *or* bad) *for* the actual. Whitehead so emphatically repudiates the Platonic tendency to think of the realm of forms as constituting a superior, self-sufficient type of existence, that he interprets even the propositions of mathematics as statements about certain possible forms *of process*.

As an antidualist, Whitehead rejects the doctrine that mind and body are distinct, disparate entities. He generalizes the mind-body problem, and suggests that a certain contrast between two modes of activity exists within every actual occasion. An occasion is a throb of experience, so of course its "physical pole" cannot consist of matter, in the sense of a permanent unfeeling substance; and consciousness is too slight and occasional to define the "mental pole."[5] The physical activity of each occasion is rather its absorption of the actual occasions of the past, its direct *rapport* with the environment from which it sprang; and its mental side is its own creativeness, its desire for and realization of ideal forms (including its own terminal pattern) by means of which it makes a novel, unified reaction to its inheritance. (So there are two species of prehensions in Whitehead's system: "physical prehensions" of actual occasions or nexūs, and "conceptual prehensions" of eternal objects.) Each occasion is a fusion of the already actual and the ideal.

The subjective forms of conceptual prehensions are "valuations," up or down; this or that possibility is felt to be important or trivial or

[5]These terms are prominent in *Process and Reality*. Whitehead privately regretted that he had used them; too many readers thought they referred to substantially separate parts of each actual occasion.

irrelevant, or not wanted. We see again how, in trying to make theory correspond to the character of immediate experience, Whitehead insists that emotional feeling, not pure cognition of a neutral datum, is basic. Except for mathematical patterns, the data are not neutral either: red is a possibility of warmth, blue of coolness.

An eternal object as a form of definiteness, may be realized in one actual occasion after another, through each prehending that form in its predecessor. A nexus composed of one, or simultaneously of many, such strands, Whitehead aptly calls a "society of occasions," which has that eternal object for its "defining characteristic." Such a process of inheritance seems to be the essence of every human "society," in the usual meaning of the word. But the general principle has a much wider application; through it, a metaphysics of drops of experience can define personal identity, and a philosophy of process can account for things— for frogs and mountains, electrons and planets—which are certainly neither becomings nor forms. They are societies of becomings—of "atoms of process," . . . . Thus personal minds (each with its history of experiences) and enduring bodies finally appear in the philosophy of organism, but as variable complexes rather than metaphysical absolutes.

Though Whitehead's philosophy is very much a philosophy of change, we must notice that according to it the ultimate members of the universe do not, strictly speaking, change—i.e., alter some of their properties while retaining their identities. Because it is a process of self-realization, an actual occasion can only become itself, and then "perish." Whatever changes is a serial "society" of such occasions, and its persistence during the change is not due to any underlying substance —Whitehead eliminates that notion—but to retention of one form (the defining characteristic) while others vary.

The differences between the kinds of things in nature then go back to the different contrasts, repetitions, divisions, or modes of integration involved in the chains of prehensions by which actual occasions make up societies with different defining characteristics. Whitehead sketched the main principles involved.[6] His universe exhibits societies arising and decaying, societies within other societies which sustain them (consider the animal body), societies on all scales of magnitude. The structure of Nature comes out well—in fact beautifully—in this philosophy of the flux.

The bare statement of Whitehead's theory of actual entities, apart from its elaboration, takes the form in Process and Reality (I 2) of thirty-six principles—twenty-seven "Categories of Explanation" and nine "Categoreal Obligations." Many of his Categories of Explanation

[6]It is not only readers interested in natural science who should find the chapters in Process and Reality on "The Order of Nature" and "Organisms and Environment" fascinating.

have appeared, unnamed, in our exposition. Before we go farther, we must draw attention to three others. The nature of the Categoreal Obligations will be explained in the next section.

The principle that "no two actual entities originate from an identical universe" is one that we should expect in a philosophy of process. An actual occasion's "universe"—also called its "actual world"—is the nexus of all those occasions which have already become and are available for feeling.[7] This nexus is *its* past, and is not quite the same as the past of any other occasion. The part that is the same for both, each will absorb into its unique perspective from its unique standpoint in the cosmos.

The "principle of relativity" applies the doctrine of the relativity of all things to the very definition of "being." The being of any kind of entity is its potentiality for being an element in a becoming. That means: for being felt in an occasion of experience. So, according to Whitehead's cosmology, "There is nothing in the real world which is merely an inert fact. Every reality is there for feeling: it promotes feeling; and it is felt" (PR 472). In this consists the reality even of spatio-temporal relations (see pp. 17–19, below). But there is danger of reading too much into the term, "feeling." Its technical definition is "positive prehension"; thus to be "felt" means to be included as a prehended datum in an integrative, partly self-creative atom of process.

It should now be evident that Whitehead's metaphysical concepts are intended to show the interpenetration of "being," "becoming," and "perishing." Becoming draws on being (or "process" on "reality"); and what becomes, perishes. Becoming is the central notion; for the universe, at every moment, consists solely of becomings. Only actual entities *act*. Hence the "ontological principle":

> Every condition to which the process of becoming conforms in any particular instance, has its reason *either* in the character of some actual entity in the actual world of that concrescence, *or* in the character of the subject which is in process of concrescence. . . . This ontological principle means that actual entities are the only *reasons;* so that to search for a *reason* is to search for one or more actual entities.—*PR* 36f., Category xviii.

The effect of this fundamental doctrine is to put all thought into an ontological context. In the last analysis, there is no such thing as a disembodied reason; no principles of order—in logic, science, epistemology, even in ethics or aesthetics—have any reality except what they derive from one or more actualities whose active characters they express.

[7]Contemporary occasions are precisely those, neither of which can feel the other as a cause.

Then what of the realm of eternal objects in Whitehead's system? By the ontological principle, there must be an eternal actual entity whose active character that realm expresses. Whitehead naturally calls this entity "God"; more exactly, this consideration defines the "primordial" side of God's nature, which is "the unconditioned actuality of conceptual feeling at the base of things." Thus "the universe has a side which is mental and permanent." Whitehead's God is not a creator God, and is "not *before* all creation, but *with* all creation"—i.e., immanent in every concrescence at its very beginning. His envisagement of the infinite multiplicity of eternal objects—he does not create them either—bestows a certain character upon the creativity of the universe. Here is how Whitehead asks us to conceive this character:

> Enlarge your view of the final fact which is permanent amid change. . . . This ultimate fact includes in its appetitive vision all possibilities of order, possibilities at once incompatible and unlimited with a fecundity beyond imagination. Finite transience stages this welter of incompatibles in their ordered relevance to the flux of epochs. . . . The notion of the one perfection of order, which is (I believe) Plato's doctrine, must go the way of the one possible geometry. The universe is more various, more Hegelian.—ESP 118; IS 219.[8]

Whitehead seems never to have considered atheism as a serious alternative in metaphysics. An atheist would naturally suggest that all the potentialities for any occasion are derived from its historic environment. A "society," in Whitehead's cosmology, is built on this sort of derivation. Why then need the occasion also draw upon a God? The answer is that if the past provided everything for the present, nothing new could appear. Novelty and adventure were too real to Whitehead to permit him to say, like the materialists, that the apparently new is a reconfiguration of the old. Yet his thoroughgoing rationalism did not permit him to say that novelty just happens. His religious humility told him whence it came.

Throughout his philosophy, Whitehead contrasts the compulsion of what is with the persuasive lure of what might be. God's action on the world is primarily persuasive: he offers to each occasion its possibilities of value. The theory that each occasion creates itself by realizing an aim internal to it, however, requires that the germ of this aim be initially established at that spot in the temporal world by God; otherwise the occasion's self-creation could never commence, since nothing can come from nowhere. Whitehead's position is that the initial aim partially defines the goal which is best in the given situation, and that the temporal occasion itself does the rest. God thus functions as the

---

[8]On the meaning of "flux of epochs," see the end of Sect. III, below.

"Principle of Concretion," in that he initiates the move toward a definite outcome from an indeterminate situation.

III

Whitehead calls actual occasions the "cells" of the universe. As in biology, the "cells" are organic wholes which can be analyzed both genetically and morphologically. These two analyses make up the detailed theory of actual occasions in *Process and Reality*.

The genetic analysis is the analysis of the self-creation of an experiencing "subject." In the first phase of its self-genesis an actual occasion merely receives the antecedent universe of occasions as data for integration. None of these can be absorbed in its entirety, but only so far as is consistent with present prehension of the others. In a continuing chain of occasions the past progressively fades, but, like energy radiated from afar, never disappears. Thus the datum for physical feeling by a new occasion consists of some of the constituent feelings of every occasion in its "actual world." The first phase of the new occasion's life is an unconscious "sympathy"[9] with its ancestors. The occasion then begins to put the stamp of its developing individuality on this material: the intermediate phase is "a ferment of qualitative valuation" effected by conceptual feelings, some of them automatically derived from the physical feelings of the first phase, others introduced because of their contribution toward a novel unification. All these are integrated and reintegrated with each other until at the end of the concrescence we have but one complex, integral feeling—"the 'satisfaction' of the creative urge." This final phase includes the occasion's anticipatory feeling of the future as necessarily embodying this present existence.

The difference between the universe as felt in the first phase and as felt in the last is the difference, for that occasion, between the plural public "reality" which it found and the integral, privately experienced "appearance" into which it transformed that reality. Since the difference is the work of the "mental pole," we may say that Whitehead has

[9]As we would say "in the language appropriate to the higher stages of experience" (*PR* 246). But the word fits Whitehead's technical meaning, namely, feeling another's feeling with a similar "subjective form." This is prominently illustrated in the relation between your present drop of experience and that which you enjoyed a second earlier.

The concept of sympathy is emphasized in Prof. Charles Hartshorne's reading of Whitehead, and in his own metaphysical work. It is more severely treated in Prof. William A. Christian's interpretation of Whitehead.

Among books in print, attention should also be called to Prof. Ivor Leclerc's and Prof. A. H. Johnson's accurate expositions of Whitehead's philosophy.

generalized the modern doctrine that mentality is a unifying, transforming agency. He also makes it a simplifying agency. By an actual entity
with a strong intensity of conceptual feeling, the qualities common to
many individual occasions in its immediate environment can be "fused
into one dominating impression" which masks the differences between
those occasions. That is why a world which is really a multitude of
atoms of process appears to us as composed of grosser qualitative
objects.

In the language of physics, the simplest "physical feelings" are
units of energy transference; or, rather, the physicist's idea that energy
is transmitted according to quantum conditions is an abstraction from
the concrete facts of the universe, which are individual occasions of
experience connected by their "physical feelings." Whitehead's principles governing the integration of physical and conceptual feelings,
and the way in which an actual occasion's conceptual feelings are
physically felt by that occasion's successors in a "society" (so that
appearance merges into reality), constitute an original treatment of
the interaction of the physical and the mental, which has been such a
problem for modern philosophy.

Taken as a whole, this theory of the internal course of process is remarkable in three respects. Efficient causation and teleology are nicely
linked in Whitehead's cosmology: the former expresses the transition
from completed to nascent becomings, while the latter is the urge
toward self-completion, and toward a future career, within each becoming. Nevertheless the system is first and foremost a new teleology,
for it makes every activity, in its immediate occurrence, purposive.
The main postulates of the genetic theory—the "Categoreal Obligations"—are the conditions to which every concrescence must conform
to achieve a fully determinate end as a unity of feeling. These conditions are very general[10] and do not specify the content of this unity.
Each occasion has its own aim, and that is what renders it an individual
in a pluralistic universe.

In this concept of existences as teleological processes, Whitehead
thought, we find the proper way for the philosopher to perform his
task, now that the basic idea of physics has become the flux of energy

---

[10]E.g., that the feelings which arise in various phases of a concrescence be
compatible for integration; that no element in a concrescence can finally (in the
"satisfaction") have two disjoined roles; that no two elements can finally have the
same role; that every physical feeling gives rise to a corresponding conceptual
feeling; that there is secondary origination of variant conceptual feeling; and that
the subjective forms (valuations) of the conceptual feelings are mutually determined by their aptness for being joint elements in the satisfaction aimed at. For
the sake of brevity, no attempt at accuracy is made in this list, and three principles
are omitted because their gist has been already given.

rather than the particle of Newtonian matter. It is obvious that "physical science is an abstraction"; but to say this and nothing more would be "a confession of philosophic failure." Whitehead conceives physical energy as "an abstraction from the complex energy, emotional and purposeful, inherent in the subjective form of the final synthesis in which each occasion completes itself" [AI 239].

Second, this teleology is evidently a universal quantum-theory of *growth*. Whitehead, though sympathetic with Bergson's reaction against materialism, was teaching by example that it *is* possible for theoretical concepts to express the inner growth of things. His conception of growth has points of similarity with Hegel's, but differs in having no use for "contradiction," and in presenting a hierarchy of categories of feeling rather than a hierarchy of categories of thought.

Third, the principles of this teleology are, broadly speaking, aesthetic principles. The culmination of each concrescence, being an integrated pattern of feeling, is an aesthetic achievement. "The ultimate creative purpose" is "that each unification shall achieve some maximum depth of intensity of feeling, subject to the conditions of its concrescence" [PR 381]. God's immanence in the world provides novel possibilities of contrast to this end. The conditions of synthesis are not the dialectical antagonism of opposites, but aesthetic contrast among ideal forms, and between these forms and the occasion's inheritance. The latter contrast is exhibited at its simplest in the wave-vibration which is so prominent in nature. The superiority of a living over an inanimate nexus of occasions is that it does not refuse so much of the novelty in its environment, but adapts it to itself by a massive imposition of new conceptual feeling, thus transforming threatened incompatibilities into contrasts. The very notion of "order" in an occasion's environment is relative to the syntheses which that environment permits; adaptability to an end is what makes the difference between order and disorder. (*Regularity* is a secondary meaning of order, definable by reference to "societies.")

The distinctive character of occasions of *human* experience, to which we now turn, is the great difference between "appearance" and "reality." The genetic process is based on feelings of the causal efficacy of the antecedent environment, and more especially of the body; it generates the appearance called "sense-perception." Of sense-data Whitehead says:

> Unfortunately the learned tradition of philosophy has missed their main characteristic, which is their enormous emotional significance. The vicious notion has been introduced of mere receptive entertainment, which for no obvious reason by reflection acquires an affective tone. The very opposite is the true explanation. The true doctrine of sense-perception is that the qualitative characters of affective tones inherent in the

bodily functionings are transmuted into the characters of [external] regions.—*AI* 276.

Our developed consciousness fastens on the sensum as datum: our basic animal experience entertains it as a type of subjective feeling. The experience starts as that smelly feeling, and is developed by mentality into the feeling of that smell.—*AI* 315.

According to this fresh treatment of an ancient philosophic problem, the data of sense are indeed received from the external world, but only in the form of innumerable faint pulses of emotion. The actual occasions in the various organs of the animal body, acting as selective amplifiers, gather these pulses together and get from them sizeable feelings; and these—e.g., the eye's enjoyment of a reddish feeling— are intensified and transmuted by the complex occasions of the brain into definite colors, smells, and other instances of qualitative eternal objects, definitely arranged in a space defined by prolongation of the spatial relations experienced inside the brain. In this process the original physical feelings of causal efficacy are submerged (not eliminated) by an inrush of conceptual feelings, so that the throbbing causal world of the immediate past now appears as a passive display of qualities "presented" to our senses. Whitehead calls this new kind of experience "perception in the mode of presentational immediacy."

The higher animals have learned to interpret these sense-qualities, thus perceived, as symbols of the actualities in the external world— actualities which are themselves perceived only by vague feelings of their causal agency. The epistemology of sense-perception is the theory of this "symbolic reference." The recognition of these two levels of perception distinguishes Whitehead's epistemology from other realistic ones.

The practical advantage of sense-perception over causal feeling lies in its superior clarity and definiteness. And of course natural science would be impossible without it. For Whitehead scientific theory refers to causal processes, not, as the positivists think, to correlations of sense-data; but science is accurate for the same reason that it is no substitute for metaphysics—its observations are limited to experience in the mode of presentational immediacy; and science is important because it systematically interprets sense-data as indicators of causal processes.

Presentational immediacy, in addition to its practical value, has the aesthetic value of a vivid qualitative display. Although unconscious feeling is the stuff of nature for Whitehead, his theory of "appearance" is one of the things which brings home the splendor of his philosophy —and that even as this theory emphasizes the fusion of conceptual feeling with physical nature. We cannot go into his discussion of the aesthetics of appearance. This passage will suggest what is meant:

> The lesson of the transmutation of causal efficacy into presentational immediacy is that great ends are reached by life in the present; life novel and immediate, but deriving its richness by its full inheritance from the rightly organized animal body. It is by reason of the body, with its miracle of order, that the treasures of the past environment are poured into the living occasion. The final percipient route of occasions is perhaps some thread of happenings wandering in "empty" space amid the interstices of the brain. It toils not, neither does it spin. It receives from the past; it lives in the present. It is shaken by its intensities of private feeling, adversion or aversion. In its turn, this culmination of bodily life transmits itself as an element of novelty throughout the avenues of the body. Its sole use to the body is its vivid originality: it is the organ of novelty.—PR 515f.

In his theory of appearance Whitehead also shows how truth-relations, types of judgment, and beauty are definable within the matrix provided by his general conception of prehensions and their integrations. And he advances a striking thesis about consciousness: it is that indefinable quality which emerges when a positive but unconscious feeling of a nexus as given fact is integrated with a propositional feeling about the nexus, originated by the mental pole. Consciousness is how we feel this contrast between "in fact" and "might be." It is well-developed so far as the contrast is well-defined and prominent; this is bound to be the case in negative perception, e.g., in perceiving a stone as not gray, whereas perception of a stone as gray can occur with very little conscious notice. The difference between these two cases supports Whitehead's conjecture about consciousness, and leads him to say: "Thus the negative perception is the triumph of consciousness. It finally rises to the peak of free imagination, in which the conceptual novelties search through a universe in which they are not datively exemplified" (PR 245).

The morphological analysis of an actual occasion is the analysis of the occasion as completed, no longer having any process of its own; it is only an "object"—a complex, permanent potentiality for being an ingredient in future becomings. Each concrescence is an indivisible creative act; and so the temporal advance of the universe is not continuous, but discrete. But in retrospect and as a potentiality for the future, the physical side (though not the mental) of each atom of process is infinitely divisible. The theory of this divisibility is the theory of space-time—a subject on which Whitehead was expert, original, and involved.

Space-time, he holds, is not a fact prior to process, but a feature of process, an abstract system of perspectives (feeling is always per-spectival). It is no actuality, but a continuum of potentialities—of potential routes for the transmission of physical feeling. (The transmission of purely mental feeling is not bound by it.) "Actuality is incurably atomic"; but potentialities can form a continuum.

Each actual occasion prehends the space-time continuum in its infinite entirety; that, says Whitehead, is nothing but an example of the general principle (also illustrated by prehension of qualitative eternal objects) that "actual fact includes in its own constitution real potentiality which is referent beyond itself." There is a similarity to and a difference from Kant's doctrine of space and time as forms of intuition; each occasion inherits this network of potential relatedness from its past, actualizes a portion of it as its own "region," and (if it has any substantial experience in the mode of presentational immediacy) redefines the network and projects it upon the contemporary world.

We often say that space and time are composed of points and instants; these should be defined as systematic abstractions from empirical facts instead of being accepted as volumeless or durationless entities. Well before he turned to metaphysics, Whitehead had devised a "method of extensive abstraction" for doing this. *Process and Reality* includes his final application of the method (IV 2 and 3), in which he begins with a general relation of "extensive connection" among regions.

There is one "extensive continuum" of potential regions; it is differentiable into space and time according to relativistic principles. When we consider the vastness of the universe, it would be rash to ascribe to the entire continuum anything more than very general properties of extensiveness and divisibility. The dimensional and metric relationships to which we are accustomed (laymen and physicists alike) are only local, characteristic of the particular "cosmic epoch" in which we live—i.e., of "that widest society of actual entities whose immediate relevance to ourselves is traceable" (PR 139). Whitehead also suggests that the "laws of nature" in this epoch are not precisely and universally obeyed; he adopts a broad statistical view of natural law. The "running down" of the physical universe is interpreted as a general decay of the patterns of prehensions now dominant; new societies defined by new types of order, now perhaps sporadically foreshadowed, will arise in another cosmic epoch.—And so on, forever.[11]

[11]If we are tempted to call this view impossible in the light of scientific cosmology, we should notice that "the expanding universe" gets older in every fresh estimate of its age, and that enigmas seem to be multiplied by recent galactic studies. Dr. Jon H. Oort, president of the International Astronomical Union, has been quoted as saying at its 1961 meeting that some galaxies apparently were created "in past and quite different phases of the universe." My point is not that

"This is the only possible doctrine of a universe always driving on to novelty" (*ESP* 119; *IS* 220).

Whitehead does not say what the time-span of an actual occasion is, even in the cosmic epoch in which we live. The theory of actual occasions is a *general way* of thinking about the pluralistic process of the universe; it suggests basic concepts, but does not automatically apply them. The "specious present" of human experience and the quantum events of physics are perhaps the best samples of actual occasions now discernible.

IV

The philosophy of organism culminates in a new metaphysical theology.[12] In Whitehead's view, "The most general formulation of the religious problem is the question whether the process of the temporal world passes into the formation of other actualities, bound together in an order in which novelty does not mean loss" (*PR* 517)—as it does in the temporal world. Whitehead thought anything like proof was impossible here; with great diffidence he sketched the sort of other "order" which his metaphysics suggests.

Evidently the question is one of permanence; but it is not merely that, for permanence without freshness is deadening. And to oppose a permanent Reality to transient realities is to brand the latter as inexplicable illusions. The problem is the double one of conceiving "actuality with permanence, requiring fluency as its completion; and actuality with fluency, requiring permanence as its completion." Whitehead's solution is his doctrine of "the consequent nature of God." God's primordial nature is but one half of his being—the permanent side, which embraces the infinity of eternal forms and seeks fluency. The temporal world is a pluralistic world of activities, creatively arising, then fading away. But "by reason of the relativity of all things," every new actual occasion in that world reacts on God—is felt by him. The content of a temporal occasion is its antecedent world synthesized and somewhat transformed by a new mode of feeling; the consequent nature of God consists of the temporal occasions transformed by an

---

this suggests the possibility of positive support for Whitehead's notion of a variety of cosmic epochs (on his own theory of perception, it must be impossible for us to make observations of another epoch); my point is the negative one that generalizations from available astronomical data to uniformity throughout the universe may be precarious.

[12]*PR* V. This short Part, though often technical, is a fine expression of wisdom and of religious feeling. (The quotation which follows is from 1 iv.) The interaction of God and the World was also the subject of the last philosophical paper Whitehead wrote, "Immortality."

inclusive mode of feeling derived from his all-embracing primordial nature, so as to be united in a conscious, infinitely wide harmony of feeling which grows without any fading of its members. It is a creative advance devoid of "perishing."

> The theme of Cosmology, which is the basis of all religions, is the story of the dynamic effort of the World passing into everlasting unity, and of the static majesty of God's vision, accomplishing its purpose of completion by absorption of the World's multiplicity of effort.—*PR* 529f.[13]

It is essential to note the interdependence of God and the world, and the final emphasis on creativity:

> Neither God, nor the World, reaches static completion. Both are in the grip of the ultimate metaphysical ground, the creative advance into novelty. Either of them, God and the World, is the instrument of novelty for the other.

The story requires a final chapter:

> . . . the principle of universal relativity [or interdependence] is not to be stopped at the consequent nature of God. . . . For the perfected actuality passes back into the temporal world ["according to its grada-tion of relevance to the various concresecent occasions"], and qualifies this world so that each temporal actuality includes it as an immediate fact of relevent experience.—*PR* 532.

Whitehead has evidently been concerned to embody the finer in-tuitions of religion in his cosmology. From these he emphatically ex-cludes the notion of omnipotence. God in his primordial nature is rather "the divine persuasion, by reason of which ideals are effective in the world and forms of order evolve" (*AI* 214). His consequent nature perfects and saves the world. And its passing into the world is God's love, whereby "the kingdom of heaven is with us today."

Any doctrine of an omnipotent God, Whitehead held, would also undermine the assertion of freedom and novelty in the temporal world. And it would be contrary to his basic metaphysical orientation, which is directed toward showing how God and the World, and the poles of every other perennial antithesis, can be reconceived so as to require each other.

---

[13]Whitehead thought his conception of the consequent nature of God was close to F. H. Bradley's conception of Reality (*PR* Preface). Referring to God's primordial nature as "the lure for feeling, the eternal urge of desire" (*PR* 522), Whitehead noticed a similarity there to Aristotle's conception of the Prime Mover.

The Development of Process Theology

2

Gene Reeves and Delwin Brown

The story of the influence of Alfred North Whitehead's process philosophy on British and American theology is much larger, and more complex, multiform, and intricate than can be told in a few pages. It includes the imprecise appropriation of Whitehead's vision of reality and the application of his vision and ideas to a wide variety of cultural and theological problems. It involves the development of Whitehead's major metaphysical ideas into a more complete philosophical theology, and the development and use of those ideas for an understanding of Christian faith. Also involved is the highly technical discipline of interpreting and revising Whitehead's very sophisticated and rigorous metaphysics, an endeavor which was undertaken in a major way only after 1950 but since then has been carried on by an increasingly large number of both secular philosophers and Christian theologians. And this story must also take account of a variety of negative responses to process philosophy, some carefully critical, some emotionally reactionary.

In this paper we will attempt to present the highlights of this story. We hope that a sense of the sweep and variety and significance of what appears to be a growing theological movement will be evident. Some of the detailed argument involved, some of the richness of development, some of the complexities and problems of process theology are present in the chapters which follow this historical introduction.

It is important to realize that, while process theology has recently received considerable attention in both religious and popular journals, this development, though lacking the organization of a movement, has been under way for more than forty years. It has always had its fervid adherents, its warm sympathizers, and its vehement detractors. And, though it has never occupied the central place of popularity among theologians, process theology is a development which over these four decades has shown continued, and increasing vitality, scope, and creativity.

ONE   Developments to 1950

Alfred North Whitehead, after a highly successful career in mathematics at Cambridge and London, left England in 1924 at the age of
sixty-three to settle at Harvard University and begin the most brilliant
and productive part of a career which would make him one of the giants
of modern philosophy. Response to his philosophy by Christian theologians followed soon upon the publication of his early philosophical
works, *Science and the Modern World* in 1925 and *Religion in the
Making* in 1926. Somewhat contrary to Miss Stebbing's prediction that
Religion in the Making would likely be widely quoted in pulpits and
approved by theologians,[1] much of the early reaction was severely
critical and negative. Father Sheen, for example, vigorously attacked
this philosophy which he saw as based exclusively on the new physics
and encumbered with an esoteric vocabulary. In it he found a rejection
of the "true conception of substance," a false view of evil, and a conception of God which does honor neither to God nor logic.[2] And, like
Sheen, Wyndam Lewis in England identified Whitehead's conception
of God with that of Samuel Alexander and found it wholly inadequate
as a resource for Christian thought.[3]

Not all of the negative criticism came from the theological right.
The well-known advocate of atheistic humanism, Corliss Lamont, was
quick to argue that Whitehead's use of "God" in "nonsupernaturalistic
ways" was both deceptive and incomprehensible.[4] And Max Otto raged
at the audacity of Whitehead's attempt to do metaphysics at a time
when "the millions" are concerned about human suffering and need
a restructuring of society.[5]

Some early theological response to Whitehead was complimentary.
Reinhold Niebuhr, for example, wrote an exuberant review of *Science
and the Modern World* in which he saw Whitehead's philosophy as
"exactly the emphasis which modern religion needs to rescue it from
defeat on the one hand and from a too costly philosophical victory on
the other."[6] Indeed, during the decade following publication of Whitehead's major philosophical works, a variety of theologians, both in the
United States and in Great Britain, were responsive to the new views

---

[1] Susan Stebbing, review of *Religion in the Making, Journal of Philosophical
Studies,* II (1927), 238.

[2] F. J. Sheen, "Professor Whitehead and the Making of Religion," *The New
Scholasticism,* I, 2 (April 1927), 147–162.

[3] *Time and Western Man,* (London: Ghatto and Windus, 1927).

[4] "Equivocation on Religious Issues," *The Journal of Religion,* XIV, 4 (April
1934), 412–427.

[5] "A.N. Whitehead and Science," *The New Humanist,* VII, 5 (Autumn 1934),
1–7.

[6] *The Christian Century,* XLIII, 14 (April 8, 1926), 448–449.

articulated by Whitehead and made considerable use of many general features of his philosophy in constructing their own theologies. Categories such as "process" (or "evolution") and "organism," categories which were present in a number of dynamic philosophies similar in many respects to Whitehead's,[7] were seen as the philosophical basis for a new Christian theism consistent with modern science. Indeed, until the Barthian storm broke in America in the form of *The Word of God and the Word of Man* in 1927, this new theism based on evolutionary philosophies was becoming the most influential among British and American theologians and showed considerable promise of sweeping the theological field.

One of the most widely read theological works giving a rather large amount of attention to Whitehead was *Nature, Man and God* by William Temple.[8] Throughout the book, Temple quotes Whitehead extensively in support of a process or organismic conception of the universe. But when it comes to Whitehead's more distinctive notions, such as panpsychism or ultimate atomism, Temple expresses doubts. And, of Whitehead's doctrine of God, he is almost entirely critical, finding that it does not give sufficient importance to "Mind" or "Personality."

The most thoroughgoing early use of Whitehead's philosophy appeared in the context of an attempt to formulate a very supernaturalistic Christology. In *The Incarnate Lord*,[9] British theologian Lionel Thornton made extensive use of Whitehead's categories for framing a view of the world in which the Incarnation of Christ is the culmination of complex evolutionary process. As "the Eternal Object incarnate," Christ is the "source of all revelation," the "goal towards which the universe as a developing system of events had previously moved," and the "starting point from which all its subsequent history flows." For Thornton, the Incarnate Lord is a new order of being in which lower orders of nature are taken up by the incorporation of humanity in the Eternal Order. Writing prior to *Process and Reality,* Thornton made relatively little use of Whitehead's concept of God, but his use of the notions of events and objects in cosmology, his defense of Whitehead's Platonism, his attempt to summarize Whitehead's philosophy, and his use of *Religion in the Making* to defend the melding of philosophy and the "special evidence" of Christianity, all showed him to be an energetic process theologian.

In the United States, Whitehead's closest theological sympathizers

---

[7]Especially important were Henry Bergson, *Creative Evolution* (1907); Samuel Alexander, *Space, Time and Deity* (1920); C. Lloyd Morgan, *Emergent Evolution* (1923), *Life, Mind and Spirit* (1926); Jan C. Smuts, *Holism and Evolution* (1926).

[8]London: Macmillan, 1934.

[9]London: Longmans, Green, 1928.

were at nearly the opposite end of the theological spectrum from Thornton. Several "theological naturalists," centered mainly at the University of Chicago, were favorably inclined toward Whitehead during the thirties. The earliest of these American theologians to begin a dialogue with Whitehead's philosophy was Henry Nelson Wieman. As early as 1927 Wieman had written a sympathetic presentation of Whitehead's view of God as the principle of concretion.[10] When Wieman was brought to the University of Chicago to interpret Whitehead[11] there began a long, and in many respects misleading, identification of Whitehead's philosophy and the empirical and pragmatic style of theology headed by Wieman. Three chapters of Wieman's 1927 work, *The Wrestle of Religion with Truth*,[12] are devoted to a non-critical interpretation of Whitehead for theological purposes. But very early in the book the pattern which would continue to govern Wieman's appropriation of Whitehead's views is evident: Whitehead's philosophy, particularly his views published prior to *Process and Reality*, is transformed into American pragmatism. While conceptual knowledge of God is seen as valuable, Wieman was much more concerned with the method and values of seeking personal and social adjustment to "that character of events to which man must adjust himself in order to attain the greatest goods and avoid the greatest ills."[13] Wholly out of keeping with Whitehead's developed views, Wieman insisted that God is not concrete but only "the principle which constitutes the concreteness of things."[14] Later, Wieman and Meland would argue that for Whitehead it is creativity rather than God that is the ultimate reality and that in proposing that God has a concrete, consequent nature, Whitehead had indulged in unempirical and therefore unwarranted speculation.[15] In much later works Wieman increasingly rejected process metaphysics as idle speculation—"a waste we cannot afford."[16]

Thus, despite the fact that Wieman and others of similar persuasion found elements of Whitehead's philosophy congenial, and de-

[10]"Professor Whitehead's Concept of God," *The Hibbert Journal*, XXV, 4 (1927), 623–630.

[11]See Bernard E. Meland, "Evolution and the Imagery of Religious Thought: From Darwin to Whitehead," in this volume and originally published in *The Journal of Religion*, XL, 4 (October 1960), 229–245.

[12]New York, 1927. In his first book, *Religious Experience and Scientific Method* (1926), Wieman had already begun to make use of Whitehead's philosophy as expressed in *The Concept of Nature*.

[13]*The Wrestle of Religion with Truth*, 15.

[14]*Ibid.*, 185.

[15]H. N. Wieman and B. E. Meland, *American Philosophies of Religion* (New York: Willett, Clark, 1936), 229–241.

[16]"A Waste We Cannot Afford," *Unitarian Universalist Register-Leader*, CXLIII, 9 (November 1962) 11–13.

spite the fact that many others saw Wieman as a Whiteheadian, in retrospect one must conclude that Whitehead's influence on Wieman was very partial and that the influence of John Dewey, with a resultant emphasis on empirical observation and verification, was much more formative for Wieman's distinctively empirical and pragmatic theology.

Despite the views, and perhaps hopes, of some that Whitehead's metaphysics provided an opportunity for theology to rise above empirical naturalism and provide a *via media* between the rationalism of Thomistic theology and the subjectivism of Protestantism,[17] Whitehead's actual influence on American theology during the thirties was very limited. In 1939 some thirty-five participants in a "How My Mind Has Changed In This Decade" series in *The Christian Century* gave scant mention of Whitehead. Only James Luther Adams claimed to have been influenced by him, and he did not demonstrate or discuss this influence. In general, the contributors are preoccupied with a humanism which they see as dead, with the economic depression and war, and with Barthianism in theology. A constructive approach to theology through the use of Whiteheadian metaphysics is nowhere evident.

In the forties, while some were praising Whitehead for providing a basis for a theological defense against positivism, for attacking theological dogmatism, and for envisioning a deity more suitable for religious worship than the aloof Absolute of traditional metaphysics and theology,[18] others were claiming that you cannot pray to a principle of concretion,[19] and that the Whiteheadian conception of divinity, "probably as strange, bizarre and grotesque as can be found in the philosophic literature of modern times," has no connection with the God of historic theism.[20]

This issue—whether the God of the philosopher Whitehead can be the God of religious devotion and worship—has been a persistent one throughout the history of the relation between process philosophy and Christian theology. Interestingly, the charge that Whitehead's conception of God is unsuitable for religion was first given prominent at-

[17]Edwin E. Aubrey, *Present Theological Tendencies*, (New York: Harper and Brothers), 1936), 187; C. C. Morrison, "Thomism and the Re-birth of Protestant Theology," *Christendom*, II, 1 (Winter 1937), 110–125; Randolph Crump Miller, "Theology In Transition," *The Journal of Religion* XX, 2 (April 1940), 160–168; Eugene W. Lyman, *The Meaning and Truth of Religion* (New York: Charles Scribner's Sons, 1933), 269–283.

[18]J. S. Bixler, "Whitehead's Philosophy of Religion" and Charles Hartshorne, "Whitehead's Idea of God," in *The Philosophy of Alfred North Whitehead*, Paul A. Schilpp, ed. (New York: Tudor Company, 1941).

[19]George A. Buttrick, *Prayer* (New York: Abingdon-Cokesbury, 1942), 59.

[20]John A. O'Brien, " 'God' in Whitehead's Philosophy: A Strange New 'Deity'," *The American Ecclesiastical Review*, CX (June 1944), 444–450.

tention not by more conservative theologians but by the columnist, political theorist, and sometime theologian, Walter Lippman. In *A Preface to Morals*, an attempt at humanistic theology, Lippman charged Whitehead with having a conception of God "which is incomprehensible to all who are not highly trained logicians," a conception which "may satisfy a metaphysical need in the thinker," but "does not satisfy the passions of the believer," and for the purposes of religion "is no God at all."[21]

This issue reached a kind of culmination in the publication in 1942 of a little book entitled *The Religious Availability of Whitehead's God*, by Stephen Lee Ely.[22] Though it involved a technically careful and reasonably detailed exposition of Whitehead's view of God, Ely's fundamental thesis was quite simple. It assumed that a conception of God suitable for religious purposes would align the divine purpose with human good. But, Ely argued, in Whitehead's view it is God himself who is the ultimate enjoyer of value, and thus we have no evidence that Whitehead's God is truly good in the sense that he "wishes humanity well." Though all of our experiences may contribute to the divine experience and enjoyment, such objective immortality does not help or comfort the individual worshiper who, presumably, needs assurance that God is on his side. In short, according to Ely, not only is Whitehead's conception of God inadequate, it is positively inimical to "religious availability."

Response to Ely's book was swift and substantial as a number of philosophers and theologians rose to Whitehead's defense. Victor Lowe argued that Ely had not dealt with Whitehead's conception at all, but rather with one of straw built out of a misconception of important aspects of his philosophy. But Lowe admitted that there is an important sense in which God, for Whitehead, is not all good in Ely's sense, i.e., good for us, and that there is a sense in which he is not available for our use.[23]

The most complete response to Ely's book was made by Bernard M. Loomer.[24] Loomer clarifies Whitehead's view of the primordial nature of God as being *with* all creation rather than prior to it. *Process and Reality*, with its notion of the two natures of God, is not as clear as one might like on the relation between the two. Some seized upon the primordial nature either in support of their own views, as in the case of Wieman, or to attack as hopelessly abstract, as in the case of

[21]New York: Macmillan, 1929, pp. 25–27.

[22]Madison: The University of Wisconsin Press, 1942.

[23]*The Review of Religion*, VII, 4 (May 1943), 409–415.

[24]"Ely on Whitehead's God," *The Journal of Religion*, XXIV, 3 (July 1944), 162–179. Reprinted in this volume.

Ely. Loomer shows that according to Whitehead's centrally important "ontological principle" actuality is prior to possibility, the abstract derivative from the concrete, and consequently that Whitehead's mature metaphysics requires that God as the primordial and abstract principle of limitation is only an aspect of God as a consequent, concrete reality. Loomer's article also shed considerable light on the problem of the relation of God and evil. Ely had claimed that God ultimately turns all events into elements of his own satisfaction thereby making evil into good and rendering our acts irrelevant to God. But Loomer shows how this is in important respects the very opposite of Whitehead's views. For Whitehead, "there is tragedy in God even though it be a tragic peace." That is, God's inclusive vision and experience does enable him to relate evil events to others in such a way that some positive value results. But this does not mean that past evils are simply obliterated or that they are no longer evil in any sense. Loomer's article also carefully pointed out that in Whitehead's view there is not the incompatability of human and divine values seemingly presupposed by Ely's argument. God's standards of value are, in principle, compatible with our own. In fact, according to Whitehead all entities pursue the same abstract value—increase in diversity, contrast, and intensity of experience consonant with harmony. That is, God wills our highest good. But this means that his good may not be identical with what men at any particular time hold to be good. "Whatever God wills for man would be recognized by man as good if man . . . were to realize his greatest potentialities." Thus, what is "really" good for man cannot be evil for God.

Another attack on Ely's work came from the philosopher-theologian and member of the University of Chicago faculty who was becoming the foremost advocate of process philosophy and theology, Charles Hartshorne.[25] From the publication of his first book in 1934[26] until the present, no thinker has matched Hartshorne in the detailed elaboration and adaptation of Whitehead's philosophy. Though he claims to have been influenced as much by William Ernest Hocking and Charles S. Pierce as by Whitehead, for thirty-five years Hartshorne has sought to develop and explicate a consistent, Whiteheadian understanding of God.

[25]For a brief but accurate summary of Hartshorne's philosophy, see Andrew J. Reck, "The Philosophy of Charles Hartshorne," *Studies in Whitehead's Philosophy,* Tulane Studies in Philosophy, Vol. X (New Orleans: Tulane University, 1961). For a more recent and much more complete treatment, see Ralph E. James, *The Concrete God* (Indianapolis: Bobbs-Merrill, 1967).

[26]The *Philosophy and Psychology of Sensation* (Chicago: University of Chicago Press, 1934).

In early articles and in *Beyond Humanism*[27] Hartshorne expounded
a view of God which provided a middle way between the absolutism
of traditional theologies and the atheistic humanism of many of his
contemporaries in the thirties. His first theological paper was published
in the journal which a few years earlier had presented the "Humanist
Manifesto" setting forth the major tenets of a new faith based upon
atheism and science. In this article,[28] Hartshorne introduced many of
the key ideas which he would elaborate in future years. Hope for the
future of theology, he argued, lies in seeing that the new metaphysics,
most profoundly enunciated by Whitehead, provides a fresh basis for
raising the old question of the existence or non-existence of God. The
key idea is a new conception of absoluteness or perfection in which
*"whatever is present in some degree in every creature is maximally
present in God"* (excluding self-contradiction of course). That is, in
contrast with traditional views, God is not to be regarded as the negation of positive qualities in creatures nor are creatures to be regarded
as devoid of divine qualities. The difference between the creatures and
God is one of degree, but of a qualitatively different degree respre-
sented by the difference between the logical quantifiers 'some' and
'all.' Thus, for example, while creatures have some knowledge, God
knows all that can be known. The extreme quantitative difference between human knowledge and divine knowledge makes a qualitative
difference, making it possible to conceive of divine omniscience as 'all
that can be known' without resorting to some absolute difference. But,
given the new metaphysics of becoming and creativity, our understanding of 'all that can be known' must also be revised. Consistent with the
freedom of the creatures and the idea of the universe as genuinely
creative process, the future must be regarded as a class without members or as completely nonactual. Thus, future events are in principle
unknowable and therefore excluded from the idea of divine omniscience.

Both in this article and more extensively in *Beyond Humanism,*
Hartshorne argued that in contrast with the new supernaturalism
emerging in European theology the new "theistic naturalism" recognizes that in a certain sense nature is God. But this is not to be construed in Spinoza's pantheistic sense that God and nature are to be
simply identified; rather, nature is an individual with a quality that
is divine. God is not wholly beyond the passing flux of events, but includes them, responds to them, and is himself influenced by them.

[27]Chicago: Willett, Clark, 1937. See also "Ethics and the New Theology," *The
International Journal of Ethics*, XLV, 1 (October 1934), 90–101; and "The New
Pantheism," *The Christian Register*, CXV, 8 (February 20, 1936), 119–120 and 9
(February 27, 1936), 141–143.

[28]"Redefining God," *The New Humanist*, VII, 4 (July-August, 1934), 8–15.

The relationship between God and the creatures which Hartshorne seeks to elucidate is in some important respects a function of
what he calls "panpsychism."[29] Though Whitehead did not use the
term "panpsychism," it is clear that the actual occasions of his metaphysics are significantly homogeneous and that this homogeneity includes an ability to feel the environment and respond creatively and
purposively to it. All occasions are "psychic" in the negative sense
that they are not, to use Whitehead's term, "vacuous." Every actual
entity, from God to the most insignificant physical occasion, is a responding, valuing, creative subject.

In order to avoid the discredited panpsychism of Fechner in which
macroscopic objects such as rocks and plants and planets are said to
have souls, Hartshorne, like Whitehead, defends a cell theory of "compound individuals" wherein macroscopic objects are construed as ag-
gregates of sentient occasions of experience. In this view, while rocks
and such are not sentient, the simplest physical entities of which they
are composed are. Though their level of sentience is much lower than
that of higher animals, this does not preclude their having some degree
of feeling, willing, and mentality.

Panpsychism has theological implications which are both methodological and substantial. Methodologically panpsychism is related
to Hartshorne's apparent anthropomorphism. That is, every occasion
of reality is to be regarded as a momentary experience or specious
present. But only our own specious present is directly experienced with
any vividness; and it is from this direct experience that philosophy
must, according to process philosophy, seek to generalize its understanding of the non-human world. Thus, while we do not know empirically that lower orders of reality have life and subjectivity, there
is no reason to draw some arbitrary line absolutely separating living
and non-living, or subjects and pure objects. But the same is true in
the opposite direction. Just as process philosophy's understanding of
sub-human levels of existence is dependent on analogy with the human,
its understanding of God is based on a similar analogy. The universe,
accordingly, is a vast hierarchy of organisms and non-organic societies
of organisms, from microscopic physical events to God, in which there
is a high degree of continuity between levels because at every level
existence is constituted by *social* relationships. This contrasts sharply,
Hartshorne, believes, with traditional views in which "mere" matter
is regarded as too inferior to be social and God too superior to be truly
social.

[29]Hartshorne's "Panpsychism" in *A History of Philosophical Systems*, V.
Ferm (ed.) (New York: Philosophical Library, 1950) traces the history of panpsychism
and presents Hartshorne's view of it. See also Chapter 11, "Mind and Matter," of
Beyond Humanism.

That reality is social at all levels means, Hartshorne believes, that God, who is the supreme exemplification of all positive universal qualities, is supremely social. He alone is directly related to all other creatures, both as an influence on them and as influenced by them. And, since to prehend others is to include them, God includes all others in a manner such that their freedom is preserved and his responsibility for their acts limited. Thus, in part at least, the doctrine of the relativity of God can be seen as a consequence of process philosophy's panpsychism.

In much of his earliest work on the nature of God, Hartshorne wrote for and to contemporary humanists without giving much attention to Christian faith. But in *Beyond Humanism* and elsewhere he expresses the idea that the new conception of God is not only philosophically superior to that of classical philosophies and theologies, it is also theologically and religiously more adequate in that it is much more compatible with the Biblical idea of God as love. Thus, when Hartshorne criticized Ely's book,[30] he argued that in some important respects Whitehead's view of God is a return to the Gospel conception after a long history of its disappearance in the absolutism of medieval theology. His chief claim in this connection is that only if genuine creaturely freedom is maintained, and with it the logically implied limitations of divine power and knowledge, can the notion of God as love be upheld. It is the idea of God as an unchanging absolute for whom no act of men could possibly make any difference that is inconsistent with religious relevance and availability. "Never before," he wrote, "has a really first-rate philosophical system so completely and directly as Whitehead's supported the idea that there is a supreme love which is also the supreme being."[31]

Hartshorne's most important theological work is perhaps *Man's Vision of God* published in 1941.[32] In it he develops with utmost rigor his new conception of perfection. The strategy here is to set forth a logically complete classification of all possible ideas of God. In this scheme the quantifiers 'all,' 'some,' and 'none' are combined with the ideas of 'absolute perfection,' 'relative perfection,' and 'imperfection' to produce seven different conceptions of deity which are conveniently grouped into three broad types of theism: classical theism, within which God is conceived as absolutely perfect in all respects and in no way surpassable; atheistic views, in which there is no being which is in

[30]"Is Whitehead's God the God of Religion?" *Ethics*, LIII, 3 (April 1943), 219–227; and "Whitehead's Idea of God," *The Journal of Religion*, V, 1 (Summer 1943), 55.

[31]"Is Whitehead's God the God of Religion?" 219.

[32]*Man's Vision of God and the Logic of Theism*, (Chicago: Willett, Clark, 1941). An abridged version of Chapter 1 is reprinted in this volume.

any respect perfect or unsurpassable; and the "new theism," in which God is in some respects perfect and unsurpassable by others but is surpassable by himself. Thus Hartshorne sees his own version of theism as a much improved synthesis of the old alternatives of theism and atheism. Only an extreme intellectual shortsightedness, he holds, could make one believe that the theistic question has or can be settled by the old, pre-process philosophy alternatives. And most of *Man's Vision of God, The Divine Relativity*,[33] and the editorial contributions to *Philosophers Speak of God*[34] is a careful and extensive argument for the philosophical superiority and rational elegance of the "dipolar" conception of God in which the abstract, absolute side of God is balanced by a concrete, relative side.

Hartshorne's dipolar conception of God is compatible with Whitehead's notions of the primordial and consequent natures of God. But it should be emphasized that, while Hartshorne has been a foremost interpreter and defender of Whitehead, he is an original and creative philosopher-theologian in his own right. It is not always easy to sort out the points at which the two men diverge, but, since much of the subsequent development of process theology depends on Hartshorne's conceptions, it is important to at least attempt to set out some of the ways in which Hartshorne has modified and developed the views of God found in Whitehead's works.

In the first place, Whitehead's conception of God was not fully worked out or the various references to God, even within *Process and Reality*, well integrated. While the idea of the primordial nature of God as the principle of limitation is developed through several works, discussion of the consequent nature is almost wholly confined to the last chapter of *Process and Reality*. The relation between the two natures is nowhere discussed, and, in fact, some critics reasoned that for all practical purposes Whitehead might have been speaking of two (or more) different gods. Hartshorne's treatment of this problem, like Loomer's, makes it clear that there is only one God, a concrete individual who has abstract or primordial aspects. Thus, what Whitehead called the primordial nature of God is, in Hartshorne's view, only a very important aspect of a concrete and dynamic reality who is the one God.

Further, it is not entirely clear in Whitehead's writings whether God is to be conceived as a single, eternal actual entity, or whether, after the manner of other personal beings, he is to be regarded as a

[33]*The Divine Relativity: A Social Conception of God* (New Haven: Yale University Press, 1948).

[34]Charles Hartshorne and William L. Reese, *Philosophers Speak of God* (Chicago: University of Chicago Press, 1953).

personally ordered, temporal series of actual entities. Debate over this issue remains prominent among process theologians to this day and will be discussed more fully in the second part of this paper, but it should be remarked here that Hartshorne has consistently attempted to envision God, in this and in some other respects, after the model of the human person. Much more than Whitehead, he emphasizes that God is conscious, that he has memory, that he is influenced in his own development by what finite creatures do. But, at the same time that Hartshorne attributes such anthropomorphic qualities to God, he insists that in God they are perfections qualitatively different from their incarnations in imperfect ways in human beings. Thus, while we are conscious, we are actually conscious of very little; God, in contrast, is fully conscious of all that happens. As Hartshorne has argued, the difference between himself and Whitehead on this matter is not very great, but the clarity with which he has pursued it constitutes a major development of Whitehead's views.

In close relation to this, is Hartshorne's "panentheism." Whereas classical theism had described God as wholly other than the world and classical pantheism had identified God and the world, in Hartshorne's view God includes the world while transcending it. Again, he finds the human model instructive. God transcends the world in much the same manner as I transcend my own body; I am dependent upon it but not identical with it. Thus, according to panentheism, the universe is a compound individual, a society of occasions in relation to which God is both dominant and all inclusive. In the language of *The Divine Relativity*, God is supreme yet indebted to all, absolute yet related to all. While absolute and unchanging in some respects, God is the supremely relative ("surrelative"); he is the only individual who is positively related to every other individual.

Considering its extremely critical stance toward classical Christian theology and its neglect of most of the usual concerns of Christian theologians, response to *Man's Vision of God* within the American theological community was surprisingly favorable. Edgar S. Brightman, who had himself been working for many years on the development of a nontraditional view of God, rejected Hartshorne's panentheism but praised other aspects of his view of God.[35] Reinhold Niebuhr wrote a brief but very sympathetic review,[36] and John Bennett claimed that Hartshorne's was perhaps the best hypothesis about God available to contemporary theology.[37] D. C. Macintosh found the book "exception-

---

[35]*The Journal of Religion*, XXII, 1 (January 1942), 96–99.

[36]*Christianity and Society*, VII, 2 (1942), 43–44.

[37]"Three Levels of Persuasiveness," *Christendom*, VII, 1 (Winter 1942), 102–104.

ally penetrating, stimulating, and instructive," but by accusing Hartshorne of being too rationalistic he touched on what has been one of the
major differences between Hartshorne and most other Whiteheadian
theologians.[38]

Another one-time member of the Federated Theological Faculty
of the University of Chicago, who has attempted to relate the insights
of process philosophy to Christian faith, is Daniel Day Williams. In
"Truth in the Theological Perspective"[39] he uses the notion of "perspectives" to solve the dilemma of the relationship between the particularity of Christian faith and the universality of philosophy. The
notion of perspectives involves the idea that whatever we see or believe, whether as Christians or philosophers, our own particular and
limited perspective is involved. All our views are relative to our own,
historically conditioned, perspective. But, by recognizing the relativity
of our own perspective, we become aware of other perspectives and
thereby create the possibility at least of enlarging our own. This view
is called "objective relativism" because, while recognizing the relativity
of perspectives, it encourages every limited perspective to point beyond itself to something which is not a perspective. Thus Christian
theology not only ought to "walk on its own feet and not ride on the
back of philosophy," it must call to the attention of philosophy the
particular facts about man which its perspective always involves. But,
since theological statements if true must be true for all human experience, no theological statement can be simply exempted from philosophical criticism. Philosophy and Christian theology are, therefore,
only relatively independent; "in the long run each can be completed
only by effecting a final settlement with the other." Such a view, Williams argues, does not mean that some criterion of truth is set above
Christian faith, for all perspectives are relative. The test of their truth
is their capacity "to become more inclusive, more coherent, more adequate through a continuing discussion, criticism, and reformulation in
contact with other interpretations of . . . human experience."

Williams's first major work is *God's Grace and Man's Hope*.[40] In it
he seeks a theological stance occupying a middle ground between the
unrealistic optimism of traditional liberalism and the equally unrealistic
pessimism of the neo-orthodox reaction to liberalism. Both, he claims,
have no place for God's redemptive work in history; liberalism because
it sees no need for it, and neo-orthodoxy because it denies a place for
it within the human enterprise. Throughout the book, the conception

[38]*The Review of Religion*, VI, 4 (May 1942), 443–448.
[39]*The Journal of Religion*, XXVIII, 4 (October 1948), 242–254.
[40]New York: Harper & Brothers, 1949; revised edition, 1965. Chapter 5 is reprinted in this volume.

of God articulated by Whitehead and Hartshorne is utilized to make it possible "for the Living God, the God who acts, the caring, saving God of the Bible to be made intelligible."[41] Further, though not labeled as such, Williams's discussion of "the good earth" can be seen, at least in part, as a practical application of Whiteheadian panpsychism. Finally, by developing a doctrine of divine grace which does not destroy the genuine freedom and responsibility of men, Williams places himself squarely on the side of the new metaphysics of becoming.

The problem of the relation between philosophy and theology which has claimed Williams's attention has also been approached in an essentially similar way by Loomer. Having defended in a previous article[42] a "neo-naturalism" which is based on a naturalistic methodology and many of the principles and categories of Whitehead's metaphysics as well as on the Christian tradition, in "Christian Faith and Process Philosophy"[43] Loomer takes up the problem raised by the prevalent rejection of philosophy by neo-orthodox theologies. Like Williams, he argues that the relation between philosophy and Christian theology must be one of "co-dependents" in tension, for only through the generality of rational metaphysics can the idolatry of narrowness be avoided. Process philosophy offers definite advantages for Christian theology over earlier naturalistic and idealistic philosophies because it recognizes the qualitative discontinuities in human existence and refuses to identify God with any natural process. The assumption by theology of some philosophical perspective is simply unavoidable, regardless of what some theologians may deceive themselves into believing; therefore the most fruitful way for Christian theology to proceed is by recognizing its relative dependence and by adopting the philosophy which will be most fruitful in making Christian faith significant, meaningful and available to contemporary men.

Though it might not have been anticipated from his earlier writings, one of the most highly favorable reviews of Hartshorne's *Man's Vision of God* was penned by Bernard E. Meland.[44] Meland was one of the much-discussed "Chicago school" of "empirical" theologians who in his early writing attempted to bring together many currents of contemporary thought along the lines of Gerald Birney Smith's "mystical naturalism." In the thirties, however, Meland's thought came to be

---

[41] Page 42.

[42] "Neo-Naturalism and Neo-Orthodoxy," *The Journal of Religion*, XXVIII, 2 (April 1948), 79–91.

[43] *The Journal of Religion*, XXIX, 3 (July 1949), 181–203. Reprinted in this volume.

[44] "God, the Unlimited Companion," *The Christian Century*, LIX, 42 (October 21, 1942), 1289–1290.

very closely associated with that of Henry Nelson Wieman. In an almost steady stream of articles and books he attempted to work out aspects of a theological empiricism which was, in fact, based on Whitehead's early book, *The Concept of Nature*, but which rejected the complexities of metaphysics found in *Process and Reality*. But the man who was frequently viewed as the chief disciple of Wieman began during the second world war to find difficulties in that position and moved considerably closer to the philosophy of Whitehead.[45] Much more than Hartshorne, Meland has been concerned with the interpretation of contemporary culture, and more particularly with the interplay of thought and emotion.[46] In Whitehead's thought he increasingly found "the only structure of thought that offers adequate conceptions, both of feeling and knowing, to cope with the problem that confronts us. . . ."[47] Whitehead's metaphysics, he has said, could be as formative for the modern world, and for Christian theology in particular, as the thought of Aristotle, Plotinus and Thomas have been for previous centuries.[48]

While both Meland and Hartshorne can readily be called Whiteheadian process theologians, the thrust of both approach and concern is quite different. Whereas Hartshorne, the philosopher, has devoted himself largely to developing the logic of a theism based on process metaphysics, Meland has sought to balance this rationalistic approach with a heightened sensitivity to depth of feeling based on the aesthetic side of Whitehead's philosophy. Thus Meland's approach is generally not highly systematic but more nearly in the form of explorations into the felt meanings of cultural and religious phenomena. As one sympathetic critic has put it, "Meland's thought is rich in suggestive power and frustrating in its conceptual-theological elusiveness."[49] Meland is convinced that intellectual and emotional sensitivity to culture, to its depth significance, to its transcendent qualities and felt reality can bring one to the realities of faith, to the meaning of realities which cannot be contained within merely rational structures, to realities which have not so much to be defined as to be acknowledged.

[45]"The Religious Availability of a Philosopher's God," *Christendom*, VIII, 4 (Autumn 1943), 495–502. "The Genius of Protestantism," *The Journal of Religion*, XXVII, 4 (October 1947), 273–292. *Seeds of Redemption* (New York: Macmillan, 1947). *The Reawakening of Christian Faith* (New York: Macmillan, 1949).

[46]See especially *Higher Education and the Human Spirit* (Chicago: University of Chicago Press, 1953) and *Faith and Culture* (New York: Oxford University Press, 1953).

[47]"The Genius of Protestantism," 290.

[48]*Ibid.* and *The Reawakening of Christian Faith*, 91.

[49]Gerhard Spiegler, "Ground-Task-End of Theology in the Thought of Bernard E. Meland," *Criterion*, III, 3 (Summer 1964), 34.

TWO   Contemporary Philosophical Discussions

Since 1950, philosophical discussions of Whitehead's view of God have been influenced primarily by Charles Hartshorne and William Christian.[50] Hartshorne has continued to develop and apply the doctrines of panpsychism and panentheism explained in Part One. Against the Barthians and Thomists in theology and the positivists and analysts in philosophy, Hartshorne has urged that neoclassical theism renders obsolete many of the contentions of traditional theology and anti-theology.[51] He believes that process thought now allows for a philosophically respectable and religiously adequate view of God.

Hartshorne's most recent major effort relates the process view of God's perfection to the question of God's existence. The resultant

Portions of Parts two and three of this essay are reprinted from Delwin Brown, "Recent Process Theology," *Journal of the American Academy of Religion,* XXV, 1 (March 1967), 28–41. Copyright 1967 by the American Academy of Religion. Used by permission of the publisher.

[50]In addition to the works of Hartshorne and Christian, the following are major studies of Whitehead's general philosophy published since 1950 which include extensive discussions of Whitehead's idea of God: A. H. Johnson, *Whitehead's Theory of Reality* (Boston: Beacon, 1952; New York: Dover, 1962). A. H. Johnson, *Whitehead's Philosophy of Civilization* (Boston: Beacon, 1958; New York: Dover, 1962). Ivor Leclerc, *Whitehead's Metaphysics: An Introductory Exposition* (New York: Macmillan, 1958). Wolfe Mays, *The Philosophy of Whitehead* (London: George Allen and Unwin, 1959; New York: Collier Books, 1962). Dorothy Emmett, *Whitehead's Philosophy of Organism* (London: Macmillan, 1932; New York: St. Martin's, 1966). Victor Lowe, *Understanding Whitehead* (Baltimore: Johns Hopkins Press, 1962); Edward Pols, *Whitehead's Metaphysics: A Critical Examination of Process and Reality* (Carbondale: Southern Illinois University Press, 1967). Martin Jordan, *New Shapes of Reality: Aspects of A. N. Whitehead's Philosophy* (London: George Allen and Unwin, 1968). Alix Parmentier, *La Philosophie de Whitehead et le Probleme de Dieu* (Paris: Beauchesne, 1968).

Several relevant essays appear in the following symposia: Paul A. Schilpp, ed., *The Philosophy of Alfred North Whitehead* (New York: Tudor, 1951). Ivor Leclerc, ed., *The Relevance of Whitehead* (New York: Macmillan, 1961). *Studies in Whitehead's Philosophy, Tulane Studies in Philosophy, Vol. X* (The Hague: Martinus Nijhoff, 1961). George L. Kline, ed., *Alfred North Whitehead: Essays on His Philosophy* (Englewood Cliffs: Prentice Hall, 1963). William L. Reese and Eugene Freeman, eds., *Process and Divinity* (LaSalle, Ill.: Open Court, 1964). *The Christian Scholar,* L, 3 (Fall 1967), *The Southern Journal of Philosophy,* 7, 4 (Winter 1969–1970).

See also Donald W. Sherburne, ed., *A Key to Whitehead's Process and Reality* (New York: Macmillan, 1966), an invaluable systematic presentation of the most important sections of Whitehead's *magnum opus.*

[51]For statements since 1950, see *passim, Reality As Social Process* (Glencoe: The Free Press, and Boston: Beacon Press, 1953); *Philosophers Speak of God,* edited with William L. Reese (Chicago: University of Chicago Press, 1953); *The Logic of Perfection* (LaSalle: Open Court, 1962); *Anselm's Discovery* (LaSalle: Open Court, 1965); *A Natural Theology for Our Time* (LaSalle: Open Court, 1967).

reformulation of the ontological argument appears in *The Logic of Perfection* and *Anselm's Discovery*.[52] Hartshorne argues that the statement "perfection exists," unlike ordinary propositions, cannot be contingent; either it is necessarily true or necessarily false. To be the latter, however, the idea of perfection must be self-contradictory. The classical idea of God's perfection is indeed problematic. But process philosophy can elaborate a neoclassical idea of perfection free from self-contradiction. Being consistent, it is not false of necessity. Hence the statement "perfection exists" is necessarily true.[53]

This "necessity" is not merely linguistic, Hartshorne argues in a reply to R. L. Purtill, since "the ontological modalities are what language, if properly designed, has to express or reflect."[54] As evidence, Hartshorne reformulates the argument as follows: Whatever we can think of (a) necessarily exists, or (b) contingently exists, or (c) contingently does not exist, or (d) necessarily does not exist. The mere conceivability of a consistent process conception of God renders (d) inapplicable to God. But also, "the ontological conditions for contingency are excluded by the definition of God, as they are for no other individual definition or concept." Therefore, (a) alone is applicable to God. That is, "a most perfect being exists, and must exist necessarily."

Recent expositions of the process view of God are as often indebted to Hartshorne as to Whitehead. A. Boyce Gibson in "The Two Strands of Natural Theology,"[55] for example, analyzes the "two compet-

[52]See *The Logic of Perfection*, chap. two, and *Anselm's Discovery*, part one; cf. also *A Natural Theology*, chaps. 2–4.

[53]The literature relative to Hartshorne's argument is sizable. See the critical reviews by John Cobb in *Religion in Life*, XXXII, 2 (Spring 1963), 294–304; Julian Hartt in *The Review of Metaphysics*, XVI, 4 (June 1963), 747–769; John Hick in *Theology Today*, XX, 2 (July 1963), 295–298; and H. W. Johnstone in *The Journal of Philosophy*, XL, 16 (August 1, 1963), 467–472. Cf. also articles by J. N. Findlay and F. B. Fitch in Reese and Freeman, *Process and Divinity*, 515–527 and 529–532, respectively; J. Hick in Hick and A. C. McGill, eds. *The Many-faced Argument* (New York: Macmillan, 1967), 341–356; J. O. Nelson in *The Review of Metaphysics*, XVII, 2 (December 1963), 235–242; David Platt in *The Journal of Bible and Religion*, XXXIV, 3 (July 1966), 244–252; J. E. Smith in *The Chicago Theological Seminary Register*, LIII, 5 (May 1963), 41–43; and R. J. Wood in *The Journal of Religion*, XLVI, 4 (October 1966), 477–490; and David A. Pailin, "Some Comments on Hartshorne's Presentation of the Ontological Argument," *Religious Studies*, 4, 1 (October 1968), 103–122. Also important are Hartshorne's responses to Hartt in *The Review of Metaphysics*, XVII, 2 (December 1963), 289–295; to Hick in *Theology Today*, XX, 2 (July 1963), 278–283; and to Nelson in *The Review of Metaphysics*, XVII, 4 (June 1964), 608f. (See also next footnote.)

[54]See R. L. Purtill's critique, "Hartshorne's Model Proof," *The Journal of Philosophy*, LXII, 4 (July 14, 1966), 397–409; and Hartshorne's reply, "Necessity," *The Review of Metaphysics*, XXI, 2 (December 1967), 290–296, plus the rejoinder (297–307) and surrejoinder (308f.).

[55]In *Process and Divinity*, 471–492.

ing conceptions of divinity" in Western philosophy—the "self-sufficient" and the "outgoing." Taken alone, he argues, each is inadequate.
But, drawing on the Hartshornian abstract-concrete dichotomy and the
related eternal-temporal distinction in Whitehead, Gibson shows how
process theism consistently combines the two traditions, retaining from
each what is essential to a "working religion." Paul G. Kuntz's interesting study of the motifs of order and chaos in religion follows a
similar pattern.[56] Kuntz uncovers the power and the weakness of each
image. He then claims, following Hartshorne, that "order and disorder
are essentially correlative terms." Hence he concludes that the truths
of the religions based on each must be (and, Kuntz implies, in process
theology can be) "grasped coherently together in a synthesis." Others
equally influenced by Hartshorne's interpretation of Whitehead include
Schubert M. Ogden, John B. Cobb, Jr., and Walter E. Stokes, S. J., whom
we shall discuss below.

William Christian is the other major influence in current philosophical discussions of Whitehead. In "The Concept of God as a Derivative Notion" Christian seeks to clarify the logical status of the
concept of God.[57] Christian concludes, among other things, that Whitehead's view of God is "categoreally contingent, systematically necessary and existentially contingent." The first two conclusions mean that
Whitehead's God is required, not by the metaphysically necessary
categories as such, but by the contingent fact of the temporal character
of the actual world; thus Whitehead's approach rejects an ontological
argument and employs a cosmological argument. Christian's third conclusion means that Whitehead's philosophical theology is in a sense
a confessional theology, i.e., a rational "explanation of an interpretation" of human experience. Indeed Christian maintains that this
uncommon modesty underlies Whitehead's entire speculative endeavor:
Whitehead "does not claim to have deduced his system from premises
which are clear, certain and sufficient. He thinks that no such premises
are available for speculative philosophy." Hence, he will never say
that "all possible alternatives to his system are absurd."

Christian's most influential work, *An Interpretation of Whitehead's
Metaphysics*, is a systematic study of impressive scope and original-
ity.[58] Its challenge to the Hartshornian understanding of Whitehead has
won varying degrees of support from many, including Lewis S. Ford
and Donald W. Sherburne. But more significantly, Christian's *Inter-*

---

[56]"Religion of Order or Religion of Chaos?", *Religion in Life*, XXXV, 3 (Summer
1966), 433–449.
[57]In *Process and Divinity*, 181–203.
[58]New Haven: Yale University Press, 1959, 1967.

pretation marvelously brings before all process thinkers legitimate philosophical questions about Whitehead's theology. For these reasons it remains *the* interpretive study of Whitehead.

The contributions of Christian, Hartshorne and several others to the current philosophical development of process theology are probably best viewed in the context of certain important problems of process theism. We shall now explore four of these: the nature of God, the location of God, the problem of evil, and the coherence of process theism.

The first debate has to do with whether God ought to be considered a single actual entity or a personally ordered society of actual entities. In the succession from one entity or occasion of experience to the next in a society of actual entities, there is always a certain loss of content. The moment of my beginning this paragraph, for example, is considerably less real to me than the present moment. Something has been lost—if nothing more than the "first-handedness" of a moment now in the past. If God is a succession of occasions of experience, there seems to be no metaphysical guarantee that he preserves all values. It is at least possible that some values are lost to God.

It should not be surprising then that Whitehead thought of God as a single actual entity immune to the possibility of loss.[59] At least William Christian sees this as the proper Whiteheadian view.[60] Nevertheless, Christian's position is challenged by Ivor Leclerc, who argues, in agreement with Hartshorne, that Christian's conclusion is incompatible with the categoreal scheme elaborated in chapter two of *Process and Reality*.[61] Here, according to Leclerc, Whitehead "makes clear" that the category of "subjective perishing" is "necessarily applicable to every actual entity whatever, including God."

The theologian John B. Cobb, Jr. sides with Leclerc and Hartshorne, partly however for reasons that are religious.[62] It is essential both to Whitehead's system and to the Christian faith, Cobb thinks, to hold that God influences and is influenced by the temporal world. In Whitehead's writings an actual entity is affected only at the inception and is efficacious only at the completion of its momentary existence. Hence,

---

[59]*PR* 47, 54, 137, 531.

[60]*An Interpretation of Whitehead's Metaphysics,* 393; cf. also pp. 13, 298, 409f., 411. A. H. Johnson, while conceding its difficulties, had held the same view (see *Whitehead's Theory of Reality,* 69.).

[61]*The Journal of Philosophy,* LVII, 4 (February 18, 1960), 138–143. For Hartshorne's statement, see "Whitehead's Novel Intuition" in George L. Kline, ed. *Alfred North Whitehead: Essays on His Philosophy* (Englewood Cliffs: Prentice-Hall, 1963), 23. This view is also favored by D. Emmett, *Whitehead's Philosophy of Organism,* p. xxxiii.

[62]*A Christian Natural Theology* (Philadelphia: Westminster Press, 1965), 188–192.

if God interacts with the world, presumably he too must be a society of successive entities of temporal duration rather than a single actual entity always in concrescence. Cobb claims that although this conclusion fails to require the complete preservation of value in God, philosophically the continuance of value in God does remain a possibility. The religious intuition which affirms that preservation, therefore, need not be set aside.

Lewis S. Ford concedes that Cobb deals successfully with the question of loss in God. Nevertheless Ford maintains that the categoreal scheme requires not perishing, but merely "something determinate in God" in order for God to be objectified by the world.[63] Hence God, to influence the world, need not be a society. But further, God cannot be a society. The subjective aim determines "when and how an actual entity will find its completion." Since God's "aim seeks the physical realization of all potentiality insofar as this is compatible with maximum intensity," it follows that "God's aim . . . requires an everlasting concrescence physically prehending the unending actualization of these possibilities."[64] In "Boethius and Whitehead" Ford argues that the entire multiplicity of temporal (and spatial) experiences can be included within the unity of a single, everlasting divine concrescence. For eternity is an everlasting moment that includes time; it is not, as Aquinas supposed, mere atemporality. Thus God's particular experiences of the world are spatio-temporally localized with respect to their objective data, but they are trans-spatio-temporally unified within the eternity of the one divine concrescence.

The second area of controversy concerns the relation of God to space-time.[65] Einstein's special theory of relativity precludes absolute simultaneity. According to it, any particular meaning of simultaneity can only be specified relative to some particular space-time system. John T. Wilcox argues that this theory poses a problem for any theism which holds that "God's knowledge grows as the universe grows in time, and the moments in his experience form a temporal sequence."[66] For at any particular moment God's experience of the universe would constitute a particular (divine) meaning of simultaneity, thereby relat-

---

[63]"Boethius and Whitehead on Time and Eternity," *International Philosophical Quarterly*, VIII, 1 (March 1968), 65 (cf. pp. 63–67). For a more extensive argument that objectification does not require perishing see Ford's essay, "Whitehead's Conception of Divine Spatiality," *Southern Journal of Philosophy*, VI, 1 (Spring 1968), 8, 9.

[64]"Boethius and Whitehead," 65f.

[65]We wish to acknowledge here our special debt to Lewis S. Ford for his contribution to our discussion of this issue, though responsibility for the final formulation must remain our own.

[66]"A Question from Physics for Certain Theists," *The Journal of Religion*, XLI, 4 (October 1961), 293–300.

ing God to one particular space-time system. Therefore, "to decide which space-time system God utilizes . . . would grant to that system . . . a unique relationship with deity, a relationship discriminatory against other events and their space-time systems." Moreover, says Wilcox, if God is prehended by temporal events, as Whitehead holds, we should be able to catch some trace of his space-time system.

Prior to Wilcox's article, William Christian had proposed what Wilcox admitted was a possible solution.[67] Whitehead's God, according to Christian, is a single, eternally-concrescing actual entity. And since space-time is derivative from temporal succession, Christian concludes that God occupies no spatio-temporal region. God does prehend the world, to be sure. But his syntheses of feelings are only partial, not full satisfactions, each including only the data available to particular space-time locations. The occasions occupying these perspectives in turn prehend in God only the harmonization of the data ingredient in their own past worlds. Thus the particular interactions between God and actual occasions are spatio-temporally localized even though God occupies no spatio-temporal region. God would therefore treat each spatio-temporal region identically. Furthermore no prehensions of alternative divinely entertained space-time systems should be expected. Wilcox rejects this interpretation, however, arguing that its assumption of particularized interactions between God and the world is purely *ad hoc*.[68]

Charles Hartshorne concedes that the special theory of relativity conflicts with the theistic assertion of a "cosmic observer." Hartshorne's rebuttal is twofold:[69] "The assumption of a divine simultaneity need not mean that some actual perspective in the world is 'right' as against others. For the divine perspective might be 'eclectic,' agreeing (approximately) as to some items with one standpoint, as to others with another, and the incidence of agreement might be constantly shifting." Hence the cosmic discrimination Wilcox notes is of no importance. Moreover, Hartshorne observes, the relativity theory may after all be "a deep truth about the world" without being "the whole truth." In fact, the claim that it is not the whole truth cannot be empirically refuted, for the inevitably relative perspective of any scientific observer

<hr />

[67]*An Interpretation of Whitehead's Metaphysics,* 286–289, 294–300, 393–396. Cf. Wilcox, 299.

[68]Wilcox, 299. More recently Lewis Ford challenged Christian at a different point, arguing that if God physically prehends the world, God must occupy spatio-temporal regions because "every physical prehension necessarily includes some extensive standpoint." See Ford, "Divine Spatiality," 7.

[69]See Sidney and Beatrice Rome, eds. *Philosophical Interrogations* (New York: Holt, Rinehart and Winston, 1964), 324f; and Hartshorne, *A Natural Theology for Our Time,* 93–95.

precludes his reception of empirical evidence for a non-relative spatio-temporal perspective.

In *A Christian Natural Theology* John Cobb seeks to understand God's relation particularly to space in terms of a doctrine of regional inclusion. Cobb argues that the individuality of an actual entity resides in the unity of its subjective immediacy, not in the peculiarity of its spatio-temporal region. This means that the region of one actual entity may be included in the region of another without compromising the individuality of either.[70] Hence it would be consistent with Whitehead's principles to hold that God is omnispatial, for "his region includes all other contemporary regions" without his being related to these entities as a whole to a mere part.[71]

Cobb's doctine of regional inclusion has been sharply challenged by Donald Sherburne.[72] Sherburne appeals first to the systematic evidence against regional inclusion complied by William Christian. Secondly, he argues point by point against Cobb's interpretation of Whitehead's statements to which Cobb appeals for implicit support. Finally Sherburne argues: For Whitehead space-time is not a container sitting there waiting to be filled. The region of each actual entity is derivative from the concrescence of the given mass of feelings which is that occasion; each becoming subject specifies and actualizes its own particular region. Hence for every subject there is a different region. Unless God violates the individuality of the entities supposedly included in his region so that he as subject becomes identical with them as subjects (which Cobb rejects), it follows that God's spatio-temporal region cannot include the regions of other entities.

Lewis Ford criticizes Sherburne's claim that each subject must have a different region. In "Divine Spatiality" Ford argues that the standpoint of a physical prehension is part of the objective datum of that prehension and not part of its subjective unity. Therefore two prehensions may have the same spatio-temporal standpoint but still differ if the subjects in question differ in the unity of their subjective immediacies.[73] But though in this he sides with Cobb, Ford faults Cobb on the very point Wilcox raises.[74] For while God, in Cobb's view, is omnispatial, he is not omnitemporal. Each successive omnispatial moment in the divine life is a brief, particular slice of time. As such it specifies a particular, absolute meaning of simultaneity and this result contradicts the relativity theory. Nor does Ford find Hartshorne's al-

---

[70]*Op. cit.*, 86.

[71]192–196.

[72]"Whitehead Without God," *The Christian Scholar*, L, 3 (Fall 1967), 257–264; reprinted in this volume, pp. 311–320.

[73]*Op. cit.*, 4–6.

[74]Ford, "Is Process Theism Compatible with Relativity Theory?" *The Journal of Religion*, 48, 2 (April 1968), 124–135 (esp. 127ff.).

ternative much better: "Hartshorne's theory may account for all the appearances, but at the price of simplicity and elegance."

Ford's own answer to the question of God's location in general and the relativity problem in particular rests upon his Boethian interpretation of Whitehead, discussed above. God experiences the world from every spatio-temporal standpoint, yet these experiences are unified in him eternally. This distinction can be maintained in Whiteheadian thought, Ford argues, because the spatio-temporal standpoints of subjects belong to the objective data of their prehensions, not to the subjects as such; moreover, prehensions are many in terms of their data, but one in terms of their subject. In Ford's view the concept of regional inclusion is extended to embrace time as well as space. God is the single, ever-concrescing actual entity whose "spatio-temporal region is the entire, everlasting extensive continuum."[75]

The third issue is the problem of evil. Doubts about the religious adequacy of Whitehead's treatment of evil were raised very early by critics of process thought. The challenge, however, has nowhere been worded more sharply than in a recent essay by E. H. Madden and P. H. Hare.[76] They argue that process theology is "shipwrecked upon the rock of the problem of evil" because the process God is limited, unable to guarantee the triumph of good, and in pursuit of morally objectionable values.

In separate essays, Charles Hartshorne [77] and Lewis Ford[78] point out the serious misunderstandings of Whitehead at work in this critique, and Ford and others explain the Whiteheadian solution to the problem of evil as follows:[79] God does not wholly determine the course of the temporal process. There is some degree of freedom for self-creation at all levels.[80] But the temporal process is neither a matter of absolute freedom nor of chance. As a part of its data for synthesis, each emergent occasion prehends God's ordered evaluation of its possibilities for becoming. Thus God seeks to "lure" the world toward

---

[75]"Divine Spatiality," loc. cit.

[76]"Evil and Unlimited Power," The Review of Metaphysics, XX, 2 (December 1966), 278–289; reprinted in P. H. Hare and E. H. Madden. Evil and the Concept of God (Springfield: Chas. C. Thomas, 1967), chap 6.

[77]"The Dipolar Conception of Diety," The Review of Metaphysics, XXI, 2 (December 1967), esp. 282–289.

[78]"Divine Persuasion and the Triumph of Good," The Christian Scholar, L, 3 (Fall 1967), 235–250; reprinted in this volume.

[79]Ford, "Divine Persuasion," loc. cit.; Peter Hamilton, The Living God and the Modern World (London: Hodder and Stoughton, 1967), 97–108; and John Cobb, A Christian Natural Theology, 218–220.

[80]Hence the observation of Colin Wilson: "Whitehead has created his own kind of existentialism." Wilson adds, ". . . and it is fuller and more adequate than that of any continental thinker." See Religion and the Rebel (Boston: Houghton Mifflin, 1957), 317.

more desirable forms of order.[81] The power of the divine ideal, however, is not different in kind from the influence of other past actual entities. There always remains freedom—at one level to deviate from dominant patterns of energetic activity, at a higher level to refuse proffered moral ideals. Hence evil is due, not to God, but to finite occasions' rejections of the divine aim.

God is pervasively involved in the emergence of good in this world —first, as he provides ideals for temporal becomings; second, as he in his consequent preservation of temporal values is objectified back into the world.[82] But Whitehead does not claim that God *guarantees* the temporal "triumph of good." Even if cognitively meaningful,[83] this notion, according to Ford, presupposes a morally and religiously objectionable understanding of God's power as being coercive. But God's power is persuasive: it "maximizes creaturely freedom, respecting the integrity of each creature . . . God creates by persuading the world to create itself."[84] Moreover, only persuasive power is consistent with a religious faith that calls its adherents into real battle for the temporal achievement of good. Finally, being able to posit the maximizing and preserving of temporally accrued values in the everlasting divine experience, process theology allows hope for the eternal significance of those values won in our human freedom. God, in this view, is not omnipotent; but his power is unsurpassed, maximal, and sufficient to secure eternally whatever is of worth.

In discussing the fourth issue we shall consider three different attacks upon the coherence of process theology. In the first, "Temporality and Finitism in Hartshorne's Theism," Merold Westphal grants, with process thought, that there must be contingency in God.[85] For if God knows the contingent world, his awareness of that actuality which might not have been, itself might not have been, i.e., his awareness is contingent. But Hartshorne wishes to move from divine contingency to divine temporality. That some divine knowledge might not have been, Hartshorne insists, introduces possibilities into the divine life, some of which *come to be* actualized and others not. So there is successiveness or temporality in God.

---

[81]That which God pursues, Whitehead calls "beauty" which includes "goodness" and "truth." The unique, trans-aesthetic meaning Whitehead attaches to "beauty" has caused much misunderstanding of his value theory. Excellent explanations are provided by Ford, "Divine Persuasion," 240–248, and Cobb, *A Christian Natural Theology*, 98–113.

[82]This is Whitehead's doctrine of "the kingdom of heaven." See Ford, *ibid.*, 250, and Cobb's discussion of "peace," *ibid.*, 131–134 and 220–223.

[83]See Hartshorne's "The Dipolar Conception of Deity," 285.

[84]"Divine Persuasion," 237.

[85]*The Review of Metaphysics*, XIX, 3 (March 1966), 550–564.

Westphal rejects this move, claiming that God's contingent knowledge is a property, not a state. Like other divine properties, such as goodness, this one may be possessed eternally, unless the identity of "eternal" and "necessary" is demonstrated. But in Hartshorne it is not. Therefore, unless we, with the positivists, equate the humanly inconceivable with the meaningless, there is no reason why God cannot be said to know as actual and determinate what is, to us, potential.

Hartshorne replies, first by observing that the brevity of life and human fallibility make it impossible to fix any "observational meaning" upon "eternal."[86] If so, the only epistemic meaning eternity can have for us—thus for us its definition—is "necessary existence." Also Hartshorne asks what Westphal can mean when he says "what God wills (in terms of our discussion, God's decision to know this contingent world rather than another) he wills eternally." Does this not mean that God *first* entertained two possible worlds, one of which he then actualized? In short, even the idea of eternal willing must attribute some form of real successiveness to the life of God.

Westphal also challenges the conclusion that God's contingency involves some measure of divine finitude or dependence upon the world. Hartshorne holds that God's concrete acts of knowing (though not God's abstract essence of perfectly knowing whatever comes to be) depend upon their contingent objects; had they not existed his knowledge of them would not have existed.

In reply, Westphal agrees that "the world is so and so" entails "God knows the world as so and so" (and vice versa). But this, he says, only establishes the logical, asymmetrical dependence of propositions, not the ontological or causal interdependence of individuals. In fact, logical interdependence is wholly compatible with the classical position that God's knowledge constitutes or creates its objects and thus is causally independent of them.

Hartshorne's response is that what follows from logical interdependence is neither the ontological dependence of knower on known (Hartshorne) nor of known on knower (Westphal). "X (ontologically) depends on Y if and only if, without Y, X cannot be; and X is (ontologically) independent of Y if and only if it could be, although Y were not. Logical interdependence . . . (however) excludes this latter possibility a priori." Therefore, logical interdependence entails ontological interdependence—God as knower and the world as known depend, in some respects, on each other.[87]

---

[86]"The Dipolar Conception of Deity," 273–281.

[87]Hartshorne views the interrelationship as follows: Our present moment of existence is dependent upon God's abstract character of inevitably knowing whatever exists, but not vice versa. God's concrete knowing of our present existence is dependent upon our present existence, but not vice versa. See *ibid.*, 277f.

In his essay Westphal argues only that God's temporality and dependence do not follow necessarily from God's contingency; he doubts
the justification for holding the process view, not its possibility or
adequacy. In view of this Hartshorne seeks support in two other arguments. One is that the religious notion of "serving God" is empty unless
this means contributing something to God's concrete states. The other
is that values are mutually incompatible. Since all possible values cannot be realized simultaneously, the most exalted status would be that
which combines the actual possession of realized values with the capacity fully to possess remaining values as they become actual. Thus
though wholly unsurpassable by others, God, to be perfect, must be
capable of surpassing himself in successive states.

The second and most recent challenge to process theology is Robert
Neville's claim that Whitehead's metaphysical theology leaves unanswered the more fundamental questions of ontology, resulting in an
inadequacy that is both philosophical and religious. The basic ontological problem is why there is anything at all and, since what does
exist is a plurality, how the things that do exist are unified into a
world.[88] Neville understands Whitehead's principle of "creativity" (together with "one" and "many," conjointly called the "Category of the
Ultimate" by Whitehead) to be an attempted answer to the ontological
question. But creativity is not a concrete thing; it is a principle—either
a descriptive generalization, or a normative principle derivative from
the primordial decision of God. If it is the former, Neville says, it is a
mere description and not an explanation of the fact that there are
creative actual entities and that they constitute a world. If creativity
is the latter, a normative principle, it still leaves unexplained that
primordial creative act by which it is itself constituted. In sum, we are
not told why there is any creative actuality at all. Thus the question
of being remains unanswered.

Process theology's attempted solution to the problem of the one
and the many depends, according to Neville, on the doctrine that "God
unifies the plurality of particulars by including them in his knowledge,
by prehending them together."[89] But God does not know and hence
cannot unify actual occasions as they are in the subjective immediacy
of their own concrescent becoming. Thus, while God does give oneness
to the world of actual entities as they are for others, the world of things
as they are coming to exist in themselves remains without ontological

---

[88]"Whitehead on the One and the Many," *The Southern Journal of Philosophy*,
7, 4 (Winter 1969–1970), 387–393; *God the Creator* (Chicago: The University of Chicago Press, 1968), esp. chaps. 3, 5 and 7.

[89]"Neoclassical Theology and Christianity: A Critical Study of Ogden's *Reality
of God*," *International Philosophical Quarterly*, IX, 4 (December 1969), 605–624.

unity. Whitehead's system explains neither why there *is* a world (the problem of being) nor why there is *a world* (the problem of the one and the many).

The ontological failing of process philosophy results in serious religious inadequacy in two ways. First, the process God "is in no way the ground or source of the being of finite things."[90] Second, God can know only things as they are objectified, not as they are in concrescence.[91] In this way, God's superiority and his presence, both essential to a religiously viable theology, are seriously undercut. Neville concludes that even if an adequate ontological account could be integrated with Whitehead's metaphysical system, the question of the religious adequacy of the Whiteheadian God would remain.

One may expect varied Whiteheadian responses to Neville, at least two of which are already implicit in present discussions. For one thing, that Whitehead's God is in no sense the ground of finite being, as Neville holds, is by no means undisputed. John Cobb, for example, has suggested that God "is the reason *that* each new occasion becomes" even if *what* it becomes is explained by that occasion, its past and God together.[92] Cobb's contention is that the initial aim of an occasion is the "originating element" of its becoming. Since God is the source of each initial aim, it follows that God is uniquely the ground or source of the origination of each becoming occasion. Gene Reeves, however, has contested bobb's conclusion.[93] Reeves argues in detail that Cobb's theory of the originative function of the initial aim cannot be sustained. Even if correct, however, God would not therefore be "the reason *that*" there is an occasion, nor would God's creative role be more "decisive" than that of eternal objects, the past, or the becoming occasion itself. With respect to Neville's kind of claim, nevertheless, Reeves holds with Cobb that the Whiteheadian God is uniquely creative in the sense that his influence alone is universally effective and infinitely more powerful than that of other actual entities.[94]

---

[90]*God the Creator, op. cit.*, 78.

[91]"Neoclassical Theology and Christianity," *op. cit.*, 618.

[92]*A Christian Natural Theology, op. cit.*, 203–214; see this volume, pp. 235–343.

[93]"God and Creativity," *The Southern Journal of Philosophy*, 7, 4, (Winter 1969–1970), 377–385.

[94]Renewed discussions regarding the explanatory function of the principle of creativity have implications for understanding God's creative role. Charles Hartshorne and William Christian take a minimal view of the explanatory power of creativity in Whitehead's metaphysics. Hartshorne (in "Whitehead on Process," *Philosophy and Phenomenological Research*, XVIII, 2 [June 1958], 517) regards creativity as "a concept" referring to "agency as such." Christian takes creativity to be the "name for a general fact, namely that the universe is made up of novel concrescences" (in *Interpretation, op. cit.*, 403) and proposes to translate statements about creativity into statements about individual actual entities ("Some Uses of Reason"

One may also expect to hear Whiteheadians challenge the philosophical legitimacy and the religious significance of Neville's own ontology. Indeed, Whiteheadians generally have regarded the question, why is there something rather than nothing? to be logically impossible.[95] If, however, Neville's demand for an ontological analysis can be sustained, Whiteheadians may then be forced to deal with the problems of being and the one and the many (perhaps by wedding Neville's Platonic-Augustinian ontology to process metaphysics, a possibility Neville himself entertains).[96] Even so, two of Neville's most crucial claims remain debatable: (1) that indeterminate Being-Itself—without definiteness and beyond description—is supremely deserving of religious devotion,[97] and (2) that the process God—personal, the pervasive source of moral ideals, and the supreme agent in the achievement of these aims— is not.

A third attack upon the coherence of process theology comes from within the circle of leading process thinkers. In "Whitehead Without God"[98] Donald Sherburne contends (a) that the concept "God" is incompatible with the basic principles of the system, and (b) that the roles God plays in the system may be filled in other ways; thus God should be eliminated and coherence restored. Sherburne begins by explaining the "problem of the past" encountered in Whitehead's philosophy. He argues that the different solutions proposed by Christian, Hartshorne, and Cobb, each of whom appeals to the concept of God, in

---

in I. Leclerc, ed., *The Relevance of Whitehead, op. cit.,* and "The Concept of God as a Derivative Notion," *op. cit.*). With this view of creativity, the possibility of ascribing to God a uniquely creative role, as for example Cobb does, would seem to be increased.

A contrasting view, which maximizes the explanatory role of creativity and by implication diminishes the role of God, is that of Walter E. Stokes, S. J. and William Garland. Garland rejects Christian's view and argues that creativity is a unique kind of explanation, the "ultimate explanation" of the world's unity and ongoingness ("The Ultimacy of Creativity," *The Southern Journal of Philosophy,* 7, 4 [Winter 1969–1970], 361–376). Stokes moves exceedingly close to Neville's description of Being-Itself when he characterizes creativity as "indeterminate [having] no character of its own," yet possessing a fundamental reality not reducible to the characteristics of the actual entities ("Recent Interpretations of Whitehead's Creativity," *The Modern Schoolman,* XXXIX, 2 [May 1962], 325f. and 329).

[95]See, e.g., Reeves, "God and Creativity," *op. cit.,* 383f. and Garland, "The Ultimacy of Creativity," *op. cit.,* 367f.

[96]"Whitehead on the One and the Many," *op. cit.,* 393. For an enlightening discussion of the problem of the one and the many as it is treated in Greek and medieval philosophy and in Whitehead, see Ivor Leclerc, "Whitehead and the Problem of God," *The Southern Journal of Philosophy,* 7, 4 (Winter 1969–1970), 447–455.

[97]Precisely this point is raised by Lewis Ford in his recent review of Neville's *God the Creator* in *Journal of the American Academy of Religion,* XXXVIII, 2 (June 1970), 217–219.

[98]*Op. cit.,* 251–272; enlarged and reprinted in this volume.

varying ways leave God's relation to his past an exception to the system's metaphysical requirements. He then claims that Whitehead's doctrine of creativity solves the problem without recourse to God. Finally, Sherburne suggests how other aspects of process attributed to God can be consistently explained by the temporal process itself.

Two types of responses to Sherburne are likely. First, on several issues there is the involved problem of the proper interpretation of the categoreal scheme. But, secondly, even if the systematic necessity of God, e.g., in dealing with the past, can be eliminated, Sherburne has yet to demonstrate incoherence; for if creativity is indeed the solution to the problem of the past, it also consistently explains God's relation to his past. It follows that God's existence would remain possible, even if not required. In this case, Whitehead's philosophy may have the virtue of picturing the theistic issue exactly as it seems to be—with the question of God's existence an open one to be decided on grounds other than those of systematic necessity.[99]

THREE   Contemporary Theological Discussions

Among the theologians discussed in Part One are some who, though earlier greatly indebted to H. N. Wieman, have now moved to positions more closely dependent upon Whiteheadian categories. Those of this group who remain most prominent are Bernard E. Meland and Daniel Day Williams.

In his recent writings Meland has continued to utilize the aesthetic side of Whitehead's thought in an analysis of faith and culture. In *The Realities of Faith* and *The Secularization of Modern Cultures*[100]

---

[99]One description of these "other grounds" was recently provided by David Hall in "The Autonomy of Religion in Whitehead's Philosophy," *Philosophy Today*, XIII, 4 (Winter 1969), 271–283. While not denying the systematic possibility of a "naturalized" Whiteheadian metaphysics, Hall argues that Whitehead grounds rational religion in distinctive aspects of experience which cannot be reduced to ethical modalities, as Sherburne suggests, without greatly impoverishing "the sources of thought, action and feeling to which civilized men refer for self-understanding."

[100]*The Realities of Faith* (New York: Oxford University Press, 1962); *The Secularization of Modern Cultures* (New York: Oxford University Press, 1966). Much of Meland's recent thought is briefly summarized in "Analogy and Myth in Postliberal Theology," *The Perkins School of Theology Journal*, XV, 2 (Winter 1962), 19–27, reprinted in this volume. See also "The Structure of Christian Faith," *Religion in Life*, XXXVII, 4 (Winter 1968), 551–562.

The aesthetic side of Whitehead's thought is developed by others too. See, e.g., Ralph Norman, "Steam, Barbarism and Dialectic: Notations on Proof and Sensibility," *The Christian Scholar*, L, 3 (Fall 1967), 184–196; Stanley R. Hopper, "Whitehead: Redevivus? or Absconditus?" in W. A. Beardslee, ed. *America and the Future of Theology* (Philadelphia: Westminster, 1967), 112–126; and Colin Wilson,

he attempts to comprehend the revolutionary character of the contemporary world and to discern the relevance of Christian faith to it.
Meland frankly recognizes the widespread secularization of modern life
in both Western and Eastern cultures. At the same time, he finds important elements within these cultures which tend to call men toward
what is most elemental and real. But still needed, he argues, is a fuller
acceptance of the vision of reality made possible by modern science
and process philosophies. This vision of reality combined with openness toward revolutionary culture in general enables new vistas of
understanding in which the realities conveyed in the heritage of Christian faith may once again be felt with power.

Crucially important to Meland's enterprise is a recognition of
myth as the felt expression of the depths of human culture. In his view,
religious faith, and more particularly Christian faith, finds embodiment
and expression not only in religious institutions and individual religious
experience, but in the midst of secular cultures as well. The Judeo-
Christian mythos underlies and is formative of the cultural sensibilities
of Western men. This means "there are resources within the culture that
lend a sense of reality to the gospel of grace and judgment to which
the Church bears witness, but which the church as *church,* and Christians as *Christians,* may be but vaguely atuned. . . . What we read about
in Scripture, celebrate in sacrament, and proclaim through the Word,
is a truth of immediate experience, a truth that transpires within every
epochal occasion to visit upon every nexus of relationships, its offering
of grace and judgment."[101]

D. D. Williams reflects the Hartshornian interpretation of Whitehead more than does Meland. In "Deity, Monarchy and Metaphysics"
Williams explains Whitehead's moral and metaphysical objections to
the coercive God of classical theology.[102] In its place Whitehead proposes an idea of God consistent with the biblical insight that "the highest goods are realized only through persuasion." And yet, asks Williams,
must God act only in universally present persuasion? Can he not also
speak? That Whitehead's philosophy can admit God's special activity
is shown by Williams in a later essay, "How Does God Act?"[103] Williams
writes: "The consequent nature acts by being concretely apprehended
in feeling in such a way that God's specific response to the world be-

---

Religion and the Rebel, 303–318. In a nice comparison of process thought and the
death-of-God movement, Richard E. Weingart calls for a similar development of
process theology; see "Process or Deicide?" *Encounter,* XXIX, 2 (Spring 1968), 149–
157.

[101]"How Is Culture a Source for Theology?" *Criterion,* III, 3 (Summer 1964),
10.

[102]In Leclerc, ed. *The Relevance of Whitehead,* 353–372.

[103]In Reese and Freeman, eds. *Process and Divinity,* 161–180.

comes a constituitive function in the world. Here there is specific divine causality . . . (But) verification here can hardly take the form of precise descriptions . . . Verification must take the form of observable results in cosmic history, in human history, and in personal experience."

In *The Spirit and the Forms of Love* Williams analyzes the meaning of love and indicates what this implies about the nature of God.[104] The classical conviction that the immutable is the superior is shown to devalue human love and to conflict with the biblical conception of God's love. In chapter six Williams examines the metaphysical structures revealed in the human experience of love. Loving requires "individuality in relation," mutual freedom and risk, action and suffering, a form of causality responsive to emerging values and possibilities, and "impartial judgment in loving concern for others." Williams then argues that, biblically and philosophically, these categories must also apply to God, even if in special ways. The result is a process doctrine of God's two-fold nature. "The invulnerability of God is the integrity of his being, his creative vision and function which is his sovereign majesty. This is not acted upon, it is not moved or altered. But God in his creativity works in and through creatures who do suffer and who become occasions of his suffering."

Williams's book, as one reviewer has said, is the first major process systematic theology.[105] It deals successively with the doctrines of love, God, man, and Christology, and considers special problems in Christian ethics. The concluding chapter is on theological method.

Younger process theologians have been as significantly influenced by Hartshorne as by Whitehead. The two outstanding members of this third generation, in fact, were both Hartshorne's students: Schubert M. Ogden and John B. Cobb, Jr.

The two major sources of Ogden's thought come together in his essay, "Bultmann's Demythologizing and Hartshorne's Dipolar Theism."[106] Ogden accepts Bultmann's position that theology must speak of man's existential self-understanding. But that is not all; theology, he insists, also must speak of God. While Bultmann in some sense agrees with this, Ogden says, his employment of Heidegger's philosophical system makes the second kind of language virtually impossible. Yet the key to speaking of God without thereby reducing God to a mere object may be found in Bultmann's own work. Following Heidegger, he has always known that while "existential analysis does 'objectify' man's being, . . . it objectifies him precisely as subject and thus makes clear that his actual concrete existence transcends objecti-

[104]New York: Harper and Row, 1968.

[105]John B. Cobb, Jr., "A Process Systematic Theology," *The Journal of Religion*, 50, 2 (April 1970), 199–206.

[106]In Reese and Freeman, eds., 493–513.

fication." Likewise, Ogden maintains, theology can speak of God "without in the least calling into question that God as fully actual can be known only to faith alone." Or rather, it can thus speak of God *if* it can discover a conceptual perspective in which such speaking is possible. Hartshorne's dipolar theism provides precisely this possibility.

Thus does Ogden argue that speaking about God is theologically necessary and, within the framework of a process metaphysics, philosophically possible. Further, he is convinced that process philosophy provides the best vehicle for the expression of Christian beliefs. In traditional philosophical theology, talk about God is either symbolic or self-contradictory; hence today's widespread repudiation of religious belief.[107] But in process theology, Christian statements about God are literally affirmed. For example, in "What Sense Does It Make to Say, 'God Acts in History'?," Ogden shows how the Whiteheadian can speak literally of God's general activity as Creator and Redeemer and of his special action in unique historical events.[108] In "Beyond Supernaturalism," Ogden indicates how God's personality can be maintained with strict philosophical rigor.[109] And in an essay prepared for the Bultmann Festschrift, Ogden deals similarly with the biblical affirmation of the "temporality of God."[110] But Ogden's most attractive apologia for process theism is probably "Toward a New Theism."[111] In it he observes that the basic claim of secular man is the refusal "to consent to that traditional interpretation of the world as a shadow-screen of unreality, masking or concealing the eternal which is the only true reality."[112] The basic claim of Christianity is that God genuinely affects *and is affected by* this temporal world. Ogden then argues that, ironically, modern secularism cannot consistently maintain the secular claim, and classical theism cannot consistently express the Christian affirmation. But process theology, he contends, can coherently and completely express the essential claims of each.

[107]See Ogden, *The Reality of God and Other Essays* (New York: Harper and Row, 1966), 16–20. This analysis of the roots of current disbelief is challenged by Langdon Gilkey, "A Theology in Process," *Interpretation*, XXI, 4 (October 1967), 448–450, and by Shirley C. Guthrie, Jr., "Theology and Metaphysics," in Wm. A. Beardslee, ed., *America and the Future of Theology*, 128f.

[108]*Journal of Religion*, XLIII, 1 (January 1963), 1–19; reprinted in *The Reality of God*, 164–187.

[109]*Religion in Life*, XXXIII, 1 (Winter 1963–1964), 7–18.

[110]"The Temporality of God," in Eric Dinkler, ed. *Zeit und Geschichte* (Tübingen: J. C. B. Mohr, 1964), 381–398; reprinted in *The Reality of God*, 144–163.

[111]Published in this volume from *Theology In Crisis: A Colloquium on the Credibility of 'God'*, 3–18, printed by Muskingum College. An earlier version appeared as "Love Unbounded: The Doctrine of God" in *The Perkins School of Theology Journal*, XIX, 3 (Spring 1966), 5–17.

[112]Quoted from William Hamilton, "The Death of God Theology," *The Christian Scholar*, XLVIII, 1 (Spring 1965), 45.

Two other articles by Ogden suggest the relevance of process theology to the analysis of religious language. In "Myth and Truth" he maintains that the truth of mythical utterances can be shown only by restating them in nonmythical terms.[113] Yet adequately to demythologize Christian myths will require not just any nonmythological language, but one, such as process philosophy provides, which can do justice to the biblical view of God. In "Theology and Objectivity" Ogden holds that theological language, though different from that of science, is objectifying because it is both cognitive and subject to rational assessment and justification.[114] Of course, this view assumes the possibility of metaphysics, a possibility now generally denied. But what is usually overlooked, says Ogden, is that the recent development of process philosophy radically alters the situation in current philosophical thinking. Moreover, this development is a tremendous boon to theology, for Hartshorne and Whitehead have revised metaphysical thinking at precisely the points where heretofore it was found seriously at odds with Christian faith.[115] Indeed Ogden claims in his review of Hartshorne's *Logic of Perfection* that process philosophy is "a generalization of basic principles whose decisive historical representation is undoubtedly the Hebrew-Christian Scripture."[116] Nevertheless he believes that Hartshorne's arguments for God's existence are fully relevant to those outside these traditions because these arguments appeal to faith-

[113]*McCormick Quarterly*, XVIII, Special Supplement (January 1965), 57–75; reprinted in *The Reality of God*, 144–163.

[114]*The Journal of Religion*, XLV 3 (July 1965), 175–195; reprinted in *The Reality of God*, 71–98.

The need to relate process theology to current linguistic philosophy is nicely posed by Malcolm Diamond in "Contemporary Analysis: The Metaphysical Target and the Theological Victim," *The Journal of Religion*, 47, 3 (July 1967), 210–232; reprinted in this volume.

Ogden has offered a critique of one linguistic philosopher, Antony Flew, in "God and Philosophy," *The Journal of Religion*, 48, 2 (April 1968), 161–181 (note Ogden's response to Diamond in footnote 19). Three other essays relating process thought to the problem of religious language are: John B. Cobb, Jr., "Speaking About God," *Religion In Life*, XXXVI, 1 (Spring 1967), 28–39; Donald A. Crosby, "Language and Religious Language in Whitehead's Philosophy"; and Herbert R. Reinelt, "Whitehead and Theistic Language," in *The Christian Scholar*, L, 3 (Fall 1967), 210–221 and 222–234, respectively. The most extensive study in this area, however, is *Language and Natural Theology* by Bowman L. Clarke (The Hague: Mouton, 1966). Clarke defends and clarifies the rules for descriptive discourse about God in both natural and revealed theology. Then he develops an informal and a formal "explicatum" for the neo-classical view of God, utilizing in the latter the linguistic framework of Nelson Goodman.

[115]Ogden refers to Hartshorne's discussion of "the two strands in historical theology" in the latter's *Man's Vision of God*, 85–141.

[116]"Theology and Philosophy: A New Phase of the Discussion," *Journal of Religion*, XLIV, 1 (January 1964), 1–16.

assumptions which are *neutral*, that is, aspects of general secular experience.

Ogden has himself formulated a "neutral" argument for theism in
the title essay of *The Reality of God*.[117] Here he defines God as "the
objective ground in reality itself of our ineradicable confidence in the
final worth of our existence." In the crucial portion of his argument
Ogden seeks to demonstrate that a consistent denial of life's ultimate
significance is wholly impossible, and therefore that a denial of the
objective ground of this significance is equally untenable.[118] Thus
Ogden concludes that "for the secular man of today . . . faith in God
cannot but be real because it is in the last analysis unavoidable."

The idea that any philosophy can be based upon neutral grounds
marks the point where John B. Cobb, Jr. differs from both Ogden and
Hartshorne. More than they, Cobb is profoundly influenced by the
problem of historical relativism and its contemporary derivation, the
death-of-God theology. In Whitehead's philosophical achievement
Cobb sees a way to take relativism seriously and to transform it.

Cobb's treatment of relativism is perhaps best epitomized in his
essay, "From Crisis Theology to the Post-Modern World."[119] Here he
pictures man as having either to accept the modern world and "live
the death of God" it implies, or to refuse modernity and isolate his
faith to preserve it. For theology the former is impossible, but given the
reality of relativism so is the latter. Perhaps the first step toward recovery is to recognize that our sense of what relativism implies,
namely the death of God, is also historically conditioned. If other
options than this one should be opened to us, arbitrarily to reject them
would be to absolutize the very relative sense of God's absence. And
other alternatives are evolving, fully as modern as the one that so

---

[117]*The Reality of God*, chap. one, esp. 21–43. A brief version of the argument is
presented in "How Does God Function in Human Life?" *Christianity and Crisis*,
XXVII, 8 (May 15, 1967), 105–108, and, slightly expanded, in *Theology in Crisis*, *op.
cit.*, pp. 33–39. For a critique and proposed revision of Ogden's view, see Delwin
Brown, "God's Reality and Life's Meaning," *Encounter*, XXVIII, 3 (Summer 1967),
256–262.

For critical discussions of Ogden's argument and the entire book, see Langdon
B. Gilkey, "A Theology in Process," *Interpretation*, XXI, 4 (October 1967), 447–459;
Ray L. Hart, "Schubert Ogden on the Reality of God," *Religion In Life*, XXXVI, 4
(Winter 1967), 506–515; Antony Flew, "Reflections on 'The Reality of God'," *The
Journal of Religion*, 48, 2 (April 1968), 150–161; and Robert C. Neville, "Neoclassical
Metaphysics and Christianity: A Critical Study of Ogden's *Reality of God*," *Interna-
tional Philosophical Quarterly*, IX, 4 (December 1969), 605–624.

[118]Cf. also "The Strange Witness of Unbelief" in *The Reality of God*, 120–143.

[119]*The Centennial Review*, VIII, 2 (Spring 1964), 174–188. See also Cobb's *A
Christian Natural Theology*, 270–277.

For another process analysis of the problem of relativism, see Clark M. Williamson, "God and the Relativities of History," *Encounter*, XXVIII, 3 (Summer
1967), 199–218.

dominates us now. We can and indeed we must share in their development, even without certainty of where they will lead us. Obviously,
to take this course is doubly insecure, for it involves wresting ourselves
from the authority of both past forms of Christianity and present forms
of modernity.

Whitehead's philosophy is one of these developing, new alternatives. What is appealing in it is its full acknowledgment of its own
relativity. All reality is experience from a finite perspective; hence, all
reality is relative. Indeed, it is quite impossible to demonstrate the
truth of any one apprehension of reality. But there is a reality, one "to
which our opinions correspond more or less well." Relativism itself is
therefore relative. Even more important for current theology, the very
ontology that is modern in its openness to historical relativism requires
also, on purely philosophical grounds, the existence of a God who is
very much alive and who is fully as personal as the God of Christian
faith.

In "Christianity and Myth" Cobb again considers the possibility
of Christian theism for the modern mind.[120] The profane spirit of contemporary man finds it impossible to talk about some "reality radically
different from all other reality . . . ," i.e., to speak mythically. But Whitehead's metaphysics is in this sense also profane. In it there are no
degrees of being: "all reality is on the same level, however diverse its
forms may be." Nevertheless, even though it is expressive of this profane consciousness, process philosophy is able to speak of God—a God
indeed who has surprisingly much "in common with the God of the
New Testament."

Cobb believes that Whitehead's philosophy is modern in its acceptance of relativism and post-modern in its avoidance of nihilism.[121]
In addition he is convinced of its internal coherence and its faithfulness
to experience. These are high recommendations for any philosophy,
but what have they to do with theology? In Living Options in Protestant Theology,[122] Cobb attempts to show that every Christian theology makes assumptions about the nature of reality which are not
given in faith itself.[123] Must systematic theology therefore begin by
justifying those assumptions through a philosophical consideration of
neutral or generally accessible facts, as traditional natural theologies
have claimed to do? The reality of historical relativism raises doubt
that any strictly neutral starting point is possible. What is therefore
necessary, according to Cobb, is a Christian natural theology: a co-

[120]The Journal of Bible and Religion, XXXIII, 4 (October 1965), 314–320.

[121]Cobb indicates how Whitehead's philosophy avoids nihilism in an essay
"Nihilism, Existentialism, and Whitehead," Religion In Life, XXX, 4 (Autumn 1961),
521–533.

[122]Philadelphia: Westminster, 1962.

[123]See chap. one of ibid. and Cobb's "Personal Conclusions."

herent statement about the nature of reality that recognizes its interpretation of the facts to be decisively conditioned by the Christian
tradition, yet remains content to rest its case upon purely philosophical
criteria of truth.[124] Cobb offers such a statement in his important book,
A Christian Natural Theology.

A Christian Natural Theology explains and defends Whitehead's
thought philosophically, and it contributes to current scholarly debates
on the interpretation of Whitehead, as we have already seen.[125] Its main
purpose though is to illustrate how Christian thinking is uniquely possible within the framework of process philosophy. Thus in chapters
two and three Cobb develops a Whiteheadian anthropology expressive,
he says, of the Christian view of man. In the interests of both philosophical rigor and his own Christian perceptions, Cobb expands and
corrects the Whiteheadian doctrine of God in chapter five. In chapter
six Cobb discusses the various modes of Christian religious experience
conceivable in process thought. He concludes his effort with an analytical yet remarkably personal chapter on the theological method underlying the book.[126]

What William Christian's *Interpretation* has been to the philosophical debate on Whitehead's theology, John Cobb's *Natural Theology* is
becoming to Christian assessments of Whitehead. It is a creative
achievement in its own right, and on many issues it has already established a consensus. But it also is proving to be a powerful impetus to

[124]Schubert Ogden's critique of the idea of "a *Christian* natural theology"
appeared in *Christian Advocate*, IX, 18 (September 23, 1965), 11f., and is reprinted
in this volume. See also the extensive critical reviews by Langdon Gilkey in *Theology Today*, XXII, 4 (January 1966), esp. 530–535 (Cobb's reply is in *Theology Today*,
XXIII, 1 [April 1966], 140–142) and by Fritz Guy in *Andrews University Seminary
Studies*, IV, 4 (1966), 107–134.

[125]For a less technical statement of Cobb's theological views, see *God and the
World* (Philadelphia: Westminster, 1969).

[126]Cf. also the preface, and the first two sections of "Christian Natural Theology and Christian Existence," *The Christian Century*, XXXII, 9 (March 3, 1965),
265–267.

Because this survey does not include a separate section on theological method,
other discussions of this topic must be noted here. A view of the relation of theology and metaphysics similar to Cobb's is offered in William A. Christian, "The
New Metaphysics and Theology," in Wm. A. Beardslee, ed. *America and The Future of Theology*, 94–111; reprinted in *The Christian Scholar*, L, 3 (Fall 1967), 304–
315. Both volumes contain replies to Christian's essay. The topic is also discussed in
essays by J. Harry Cotton ("The Meaning of 'God' in Whitehead's Philosophy") and
Clark M. Williamson ("A Response to Professor Cotton") in *Encounter*, 29, 2 (Spring
1968), 125–140 and 141–148, respectively. An analysis of a different aspect of the
problem of theological method may be found in Don S. Browning, "Psychological
and Ontological Perspectives on Faith and Reason," *The Journal of Religion*, XLV, 4
(October 1965), 296–308, reprinted in this volume. D. D. Williams's most recent discussion is "Love and the Intellect," chap. 13 of *The Spirit and the Forms of Love, op.
cit.* (For additional material on theological method, see footnotes 100 and 114.)

further discussion and to additional development in Christian process theology.

The work of Williams, Ogden, and Cobb on the doctrine of God has been supplemented by that of other theologians. In four recent essays, for example, Walter E. Stokes, S.J., has maintained that Thomism would be enriched greatly by taking seriously Whitehead's insistence upon God's freedom and his real relatedness to the world.[127] Stokes, contrary to most Whiteheadians, is convinced that classical theism contains within itself the resources for affirming these doctrines. He claims that reemphasizing Augustine's notion of freedom would produce a Thomistic conception of God more consistent with St. Thomas's own Christian intent and parallel to the view of Whitehead. Equally important is the work of an Anglican priest and mathematician, Peter Hamilton. His book *The Living God and the Modern World* is an engaging treatment of several Christian themes from the vantage point of process philosophy. It deals with Christology and the doctrine of God, as well as prayer, the resurrection, heaven, etc. and it provides a general introduction to Whitehead's thought.[128] *The Task of Philosophical Theology* by C. J. Curtis, a Lutheran theologian, is a process exposition of numerous "theological notions" important to the "conservative, traditional" Christian viewpoint.[129] Two very fine semi-popular introductions to process philosophy as a context for Christian theology are *The Creative Advance* by E. H. Peters[130] and *Process Thought and Christian Faith* by Norman Pittenger.[131] The latter, reflecting the concerns of a theologian, provides a concise introduction to the process view of God together with briefer comments on man, Christ, and "eternal life." Peters's book, more philosophically oriented, is a lucid,

---

[127]Stokes's essay "God for Today and Tomorrow" is published in this volume. Earlier related works include "Freedom As Perfection: Whitehead, Thomas and Augustine," *Proceedings of the American Catholic Philosophical Association*, XXXVI (1962), 134–142; "Whitehead's Challenge to Theistic Realism," *The New Scholasticism*, XXXVIII, 1 (January 1964), 1–21; and "Is God Really Related to This World?" *Proceedings* XXXIX, (1965), 145–151. Whereas Stokes relates process thought to Augustinian Trinitarian theology, another Catholic theologian, Ewert Cousins, turns to the Greek model of the dynamic Trinity as, e.g., in St. Bonaventure (see "Truth in St. Bonaventure," *Proceedings* . . . XLIII [1969], 204–210). Both Stokes and Cousins hold that the tradition of a dynamic deity is much stronger in classical theology than is generally supposed.

[128]London: Hodder and Stoughton, 1967. Cf. Hamilton's "The Theological Importance of A. N. Whitehead," *Theology*, LXVIII, 538 (April 1965), 187–195. A Whiteheadian interpretation of prayer may also be found in Robert M. Cooper, "God as Poet and Man as Praying," *The Personalist*, XLIX, 4 (Autumn 1968), 474–488.

[129]New York: Philosophical Library, 1967.

[130]St. Louis: Bethany, 1966.

[131]New York: Macmillan, 1968. Though very brief, Pittenger's more recent book, *Alfred North Whitehead* (Richmond, Va.: John Knox Press, 1969) is a wonderfully sensitive introduction to Whitehead's influence in current theology.

accurate and balanced account, and is enhanced by Hartshorne's concluding comments. Finally, in *Science, Secularization and God* Kenneth
Cauthen seeks to show how a version of process theology (drawn from
Brightman, Tillich and Teilhard, as well as Whitehead) can positively
relate the creative and redemptive God of Christianity to "currents
springing from science and secularization."[132]

Two other books relate the process concept of God to evolutionary
theory. *Nature and God* by L. Charles Birch, a biologist, is an attractive
work for the sophisticated layman.[133] Richard H. Overman's *Evolution
and the Christian Doctrine of Creation* is more extensive. It is a perceptive and original study which, in a key section, defends in Whiteheadian terms the neo-Lamarckian notion that "all new patterns of
efficient causation in animal bodies can be traced to *some* reaction influenced by final causation."[134] The book's general aim is to show how
a Whiteheadian perspective can unite the conclusions of science and
the biblical concept of God as creator and sustainer.

Although the doctrine of God was their initial concern, process
theologians have begun also to deal with other Christian beliefs. We
shall examine two of these: Christology and the concept of man.

Using as his criterion the biblical doctrine of the Incarnation,
Thomas Ogletree recently issued a positive evaluation of process
thought. "Dipolar theism," he judged, is "relevant to the attempt to
think about God christologically" because it "seems to express the
understanding of God that is implied in the distinctive logic of the
Christian confession of Christ."[135] Actually, process theology has been
deemed adequate to express a variety of Christological formulations.
Lionel Thornton's early statement was highly supernaturalistic.[136]
Charles Hartshorne briefly suggested a more naturalistic Christology:
"Jesus appears to be the supreme symbol furnished to us by history of
the notion of a God genuinely and literally 'sympathetic' (incomparably
more literally than any man ever is), receiving into his own experience
the sufferings as well as the joys of the world."[137]

---

[132]Nashville: Abingdon Press, 1969. Mention should also be made here of the
particularly informative comparison of Teilhard and Whitehead by Ian G. Barbour,
"Teilhard's Process Metaphysics," *The Journal of Religion*, 49, 2 (April 1969), 136–
159.

[133]Philadelphia: Westminster, 1965.

[134]Philadelphia: Westminster, 1967, 210.

[135]"A Christological Assessment of Dipolar Theism," *The Journal of Religion*,
47, 2 (April 1967), 87–99; reprinted in this volume.

[136]*The Incarnate Lord*. Cf. Pittenger's criticisms of Thornton in *The Word
Incarnate, op. cit.*, 107.

[137]*Reality As Social Process*, 24. See also pp. 145–154, and Hartshorne's "A
Philosopher's Assessment of Christianity" in Walter Leibrecht, ed. *Religion and
Culture* (New York: Harper & Bros., 1959), 175. Ralph E. James, Jr. develops a Chris-

Yet another process Christology was developed by Norman Pittenger in *The Word Incarnate*. Pittenger shows how, using process categories, one may affirm Jesus' divinity without thereby contradicting his full humanity. He writes, Jesus "is that One in whom God actualized in a living human personality the potential God-man relationship which is the divinely intended truth about every man. . . . Thus the Incarnation of God in Christ is the focal point of the divine action vis-à-vis humanity. . . ." Pittenger's additional opinion, allowed but not required by process philosophy, is that "the difference between our Lord and all other instances of divine operation in manhood is of immeasurable degree, not of absolute kind."[138]

Pittenger's understanding of the relation of God's action in Jesus to other divine actions is basically shared by Schubert Ogden. According to Ogden, God's general activity as Creator and redeemer is literally the ground and destiny of every historical event.[139] But some particular events are properly viewed as special acts of God. They decisively represent God's general activity through symbolic words and deeds. Since these special events must be received and understood as being revelatory, there is of course a subjective element in revelation. But there is an objective element too, for "an event is a decisive revelation of God only insofar as it truly represents God's being and action as existential gift and demand."

While the special and revelatory character of God's act in Jesus is clearly objective in Ogden's view, the uniqueness of this event as compared to other special events is subjective and a matter of degree.[140] The position of Peter Hamilton is somewhat similar in this regard, although Hamilton does introduce additional process categories into this christological analysis. He explains the "christness" of Jesus in terms of the "unreserved" prehensive interrelationship of Jesus and

---

tology along Hartshornian lines in *The Concrete God*, 127–148. See too James's Christology in "A Theology of Acceptance," *The Journal of Religion*, 49, 4 (October 1969), 376–387; and in "Process Cosmology and Theological Particularity," published in this volume. Also Ronald L. Williams, responding to Ogletree, proposes a rather novel christological methodology utilizing Hartshorne's philosophical method and his dipolar theism. Williams's Christology is similar to Hartshorne's, though considerably more elaborate.

[138]*Op. cit.*, 285f. In *Christology Reconsidered* (London, SCM Press, 1970) Pittenger restates and defends his christological position in response to criticisms of his earlier statements.

[139]"What Sense Does It Make to Say, 'God Acts in History'?" and "What Does It Mean to Affirm, 'Jesus Christ is Lord'?" in *The Reality of God*, 164–205.

[140]See David Griffin's essay, "Schubert Ogden's Christology and the Possibilities of Process Philosophy," *The Christian Scholar*, L, 3 (Fall 1967), 290–303; reprinted in this volume. Eugene H. Peters's criticisms of Ogden's Christology are found in *The Creative Advance*, 111–117.

God, and Jesus' adherence to God's initial aim for him: "as Jesus intensified his obedience to the call from God, so . . . God was supremely, yet objectively, immanent in Jesus."[141] Despite these additional features, for "strong religious reasons" Hamilton declines to "affirm a difference in kind between Jesus and other men."[142]

The objective uniqueness of Jesus becomes clearly affirmed in an essay by David Griffin. Fundamental to Griffin's analysis is Whitehead's concept of the ideal aim—in the case of Jesus a peculiar ideal aim which (a) purposes the optimal expression of God's being, and (b) is optimally actualized in Jesus.[143] It is John Cobb, however, who most elaborately works out the concept of Jesus' uniqueness. Cobb discusses the person, the presence, and the work of Christ. Analyzing the person of Christ, Cobb builds upon the Whiteheadian doctrine that one entity may be prehensively present in another without displacing its individuality.[144] In this respect God is present in all actual occasions. But God's presence in Jesus was unique in four ways. First, the content of God's initial aim for Jesus was radically unique. Second, Jesus' adherence to that aim was peculiarly complete. Third, the divine aim for Jesus intended that the source of that aim i.e., God as a concrete entity, be prehended in addition to its content. Finally, "and most uniquely," this prehension of God as God was not experienced as one prehension among others to be synthesized along with them; instead it "constituted in Jesus the center from which everything else in his psychic life was integrated."

Cobb marshals an elaborate argument to demonstrate the possibility of the presence of Christ in the lives of believers.[145] He begins by contending for "the causal efficacy of past events for the present." Then he claims that, despite our Newtonian bias to the contrary, no a priori reason precludes the direct—and even consciously entertained —causal presence of the *distant past* in the present.[146] Nor is there any

---

[141]"Some Proposals For a Modern Christology," in Norman Pittenger, ed. *Christ for Us Today* (London: SCM Press, 1968), 164. See esp. 161–165 of this essay, also published in the present volume (see pp. 367–372) Cf. *The Living God and the Modern World*, chaps. 6 and 7.

[142]"Some Proposals For a Modern Christology," 166f.

[143]"Schubert Ogden's Christology," *loc. cit.*

[144]"A Whiteheadian Christology," published in this volume. Also see Cobb's essays, "The Finality of Christ in a Whiteheadian Perspective," in Dow Kirkpatrick, ed. *The Finality of Christ* (New York: Abingdon Press, 1966), 138–147; "Ontology, History and Christian Faith," *Religion in Life*, XXXIV, 2 (Spring 1965), 270–287; and "Some Thoughts on the Meaning of Christ's Death," *Religion In Life*, XXVIII, 2 (Spring 1959), 212–222.

[145]"The Finality of Christ," 147–154.

[146]For a critique of direct physical prehensions of distantly past occasions see Donald Sherburne, "Whitehead Without God," 265–267; in the present volume, 320–322.

greater philosophical difficulty in conceiving of the direct prehension of the experiences of *other persons* in the remote past. Our experiences of suddenly remembering events long forgotten, as well as alleged instances of mental telepathy between persons who are contemporaries, render such relationships a little less incredible. Hence, however, strange, it is entirely possible that "Jesus is immediately and effectively present" in the lives of some Christians.

Cobb's analysis of the work of Christ is original, indeed astonishing.[147] It includes a psycho-ontological comparison of the evolved structures of human existence—primitive, civilized and axial, and a differentiation of the basic forms of axial existence—Indian, Greek, Hebrew, and Christian. The structure of existence actualized in Jesus is defined as "spiritual existence that expresses itself in love."[148] In spiritual existence the "I" accepts responsibility for what it does, but also for what it is, knowing that it "need not remain itself but can, instead, always transcend itself."[149] Christian existence, in this view, surpasses other forms of existence, transforming the spiritual values they achieve into a still higher synthesis. A part of Christ's finality, therefore, is the unique and unsurpassable structure of existence he accomplished.

A different approach to Christology appears in Don S. Browning's *Psychotherapy and Atonement*.[150] Browning seeks to justify and to practice the procedure of illuminating Christian doctrines of the atonement with findings from psychotherapy. The crucial role of acceptance in psychotherapy raises the question of the real or ontological acceptability of the client. Therapeutic acceptance, Browning contends, has its ground in the divine acceptance universally present to man at a pre-reflective level of experience and specially manifest in Jesus Christ. Dorothy Emmet's Whiteheadian epistemology is employed for explicating the mode in which this divine acceptance is universally intuited, and Hartshorne's doctrine of God is used to elaborate the ontological grounding of that acceptance. Thus all healing, whether atonement or psychotherapy, is fundamentally related, and Browning can use insights provided by each to evaluate and illuminate theories about the other.

What emerges in Browning's book is a process analysis of man and sin, as well as a Christology. The image of God in man is the universal, prerational givenness of God's "unconditioned empathic acceptance" in human experience. Sin, thus, is turning away from this inward reality to outward and conditional bases for one's worth. The incarnation is

---

147*The Structure of Christian Existence* (Philadelphia: The Westminster Press, 1967). There is a brief analysis in "The Finality of Christ," 122–138.

148*The Structure of Christian Existence*, 125.

149*Ibid.*, 124.

150Philadelphia: Westminster, 1966.

necessary since no sinner can "witness *unambiguously* to the *justitia originalis* of another sinner." Jesus is the Christ because his own self-concept conformed completely to the primordial, divine acceptance, and his atoning work is his unambiguous mediation of that acceptance already present to us, but ignored or rejected, in the depth of our life.

John Cobb, too, has discussed aspects of the nature of man, such as freedom, responsibility, and sin, from a Whiteheadian point of view.[151] Like existentialism, he writes, process thought makes subjective categories central to the analysis of man, and it understands subjectivity to be "in a very important sense *causa sui*," that is, self-determinative. Unlike existentialism, however, freedom is placed in the context of personal development and social relationships and is seen as being confronted by an objective oughtness derived from God. Sin consequently is "the self-determination of the actual occasion in such a way as to inhibit the actualization of God's aim for that individual."[152]

George Allan has argued that God provides aims to human societies as well as to individuals.[153] The elements of purposive activity which characterize men singly, according to Allan, also characterize institutions. Societies thus have ends and norms influenced by, but not reducible to, those of their members, and vice versa. The relationship of individuals to societies is one of interdependence. From a Whiteheadian viewpoint, the reality of collective purposes implies that God has aims for nations and institutions as well as for individuals, as the Hebrews insisted. Furthermore, the interdependence of parts and wholes suggests that conformity to the divine will at one level affects that at the other. The salvation of the individual therefore depends in part upon the salvation of society.

The question of man's ultimate destiny is another aspect of the doctrine of man. The minimal claim of process thought is that "by reason of the relativity of all things" each actual entity is preserved everlastingly in the divine experience.[154] "God is immortal," Hartshorne writes, "and whatever becomes an element in the life of God is therefore imperishable . . . I think the idea of omniscience implies that we have such an abiding presence in the mind of God."[155] Peter

---

[151]Cobb discusses the soul, immortality, freedom, and ethical obligation in *A Christian Natural Theology,* chaps. two and three. Immortality and man as a responsible sinner are topics developed in "Whitehead's Philosophy and a Christian Doctrine of Man," *The Journal of Bible and Religion,* XXXII, 3 (July 1964), 209–220.

[152]"Whitehead's Philosophy and a Christian Doctrine of Man," 210–215.

[153]"The Aims of Societies and the Aims of God," *Journal of the American Academy of Religion,* XXXV, 2 (June 1967), 149–158; reprinted in this volume.

[154]*PR* 523ff.

[155]"The Significance of Man in the Life of God," in *Theology In Crisis,* 41. Cf. "Time, Death, and Everlasting Life," in *The Logic of Perfection,* 245–262.

Hamilton holds the same view, and from it he draws three implications:[156] First, while human occasions possess greater significance due to their capacity for a conscious relationship with God, in some measure all entities contribute everlastingly to the divine life. Second, each moment of our lives makes its positive or negative contribution to God *immediately* upon its occurrence, as well as through the cumulative reality we call the "I." Third, since God's consequent nature "passes back into the temporal world and qualifies this world,"[157] our lives, being elements in God, also "reach back to influence the world" even apart from our direct social immortality.

Hamilton personally is dubious about *subjective* immortality, i.e., the continuation of the present stream of consciousness beyond death. But he does not deny it as a logical possibility.[158] John Cobb has sought to defend at least the credibility of subjective immortality against criticisms from anthropology and cosmology.[159] The anthropological objection is that the soul or mind cannot exist apart from the body. Process thought concedes that no entity can exist independently of all societal relationships. But this fact, Cobb notes, would not prevent the psyche from existing apart from the bodily society over which at present it presides. Moreover, the psyche "is the truly personal, the true subject." The continuation of the psyche, therefore, would be the continuation of the person even though in a radically different environment. The cosmological objection stems from the difficulty of conceiving a "place" for the soul's continual existence. Cobb's response is that this problem stems primarily from an outmoded Newtonianism which assumes that all space-time is similar to our own. For process philosophy however space-time is derivative from the relatedness of actual occasions. Diverse forms of relatedness would produce different spatio-temporal dimensions. Hence there may be forms of relatedness other than the four-dimensional system we know. We can but vaguely conceive of them, and from our perspective we are perhaps incapable of describing their relationship to our own space-time continuum. But at least they are possible.

The development of process theology from Whitehead's cautious speculation on religion and theology to the current scene is impressive. Indeed the growing quantity of process literature is quite astounding.

[156]*The Living God*, 108–141.

[157]*PR* 532.

[158]*The Living God*, 128, 137–141. Here he follows the judgment of Whitehead, (*RM* 110f.) and Hartshorne ("Time, Death, and Everlasting Life," 253f. and *Philosophers Speak of God, op. cit.,* 284f.)

[159]*A Christian Natural Theology*, 63–70, and "Whitehead's Philosophy and a Christian Doctrine of Man," 215–220.

Between 1960 and mid-1965, for example, about thirty-five articles and books appeared in English on the topic of process theology. Over four times that number appeared in the following five years. It is hardly less evident that the diversity and sophistication of this movement in theology has increased too. Studies continue to appear examining process theism vis-à-vis biology and physics, art and culture, analytic philosophy and existentialism. Christian proponents continue to deepen their treatments of the entire spectrum of doctrine, and the variation in their views, for example on Christology, reveals both the inherent openness of Whiteheadian categories to manifold Christian sensibilities and the diversity of the theological movement which utilizes these modes of thought. Indeed, except for neo-thomism, process theology is the oldest, strongest and most sophisticated movement in contemporary theology.

While such considerations bear somewhat on the question of worth, the crucial issue is whether process theology is adequate—adequate to the requirement of logical coherence, and to the demands of modern religious perceptions, Christian and otherwise. On the question of coherence, some old problems remain and some new ones appear. What is important here is that process thinkers by and large see the difficulties, often functioning as their own best critics. The other question—whether process theology is able adequately to illumine religious perceptions that are at once faithfully modern and authentically Christian—is more difficult to answer. The meaning of modernity is unsettled and the criteria of theological adequacy vary. But judgment, however tentative, is surely possible. To facilitate such a judgment is in part the aim of this book.

ONE

Philosophy
and Theology

Religion and Metaphysics   3

Alfred North Whitehead

Religion requires a metaphysical backing; for its authority is endangered by the intensity of the emotions which it generates. Such emotions are evidence of some vivid experience; but they are a very poor guarantee for its correct interpretation.

Thus dispassionate criticism of religious belief is beyond all things necessary. The foundations of dogma must be laid in a rational metaphysics which criticises meanings, and endeavors to express the most general concepts adequate for the all-inclusive universe.

This position has never been seriously doubted, though in practice it is often evaded. One of the most serious periods of neglect occurred in the middle of the nineteenth century, through the dominance of the historical interest.

It is a curious delusion that the rock upon which our beliefs can be founded is a historical investigation. You can only interpret the past in terms of the present. The present is all that you have; and unless in this present you can find general principles which interpret the present as including a representation of the whole community of existents, you cannot move a step beyond your little patch of immediacy.

Thus history presupposes a metaphysic. It can be objected that we believe in the past and talk about it without settling our metaphysical principles. That is certainly the case. But you can only deduce metaphysical dogmas from your interpretation of the past on the basis of a prior metaphysical interpretation of the present.[1]

In so far as your metaphysical beliefs are implicit, you vaguely interpret the past on the lines of the present. But when it comes to the

[1]By "metaphysics" I mean the science which seeks to discover the general ideas which are indispensably relevant to the analysis of everything that happens.

primary metaphysical data, the world of which you are immediately conscious is the whole datum.

This criticism applies equally to a science or to a religion which hopes to justify itself without any appeal to metaphysics. The difference is that religion is the longing of the spirit that the facts of existence should find their justification in the nature of existence. "My soul thirsteth for God," writes the Psalmist.

But science can leave its metaphysics implicit and retire behind our belief in the pragmatic value of its general descriptions. If religion does that, it admits that its dogmas are merely pleasing ideas for the purpose of stimulating its emotions. Science (at least as a temporary methodological device) can rest upon a naïve faith; religion is the longing for justification. When religion ceases to seek for penetration, for clarity, it is sinking back into its lower forms. The ages of faith are the ages of rationalism. . . .

In the previous lectures religious experience was considered as a fact. It consists of a certain widespread, direct apprehension of a character exemplified in the actual universe. Such a character includes in itself certain metaphysical presuppositions. In so far as we trust the objectivity of the religious intuitions, to that extent we must also hold that the metaphysical doctrines are well founded.

It is for this reason that in the previous lecture the broadest view of religious experience was insisted on. If, at this stage of thought, we include points of radical divergence between the main streams, the whole evidential force is indefinitely weakened. Thus religious experience cannot be taken as contributing to metaphysics any direct evidence for a personal God in any sense transcendent or creative.

The universe, thus disclosed, is through and through interdependent. The body pollutes the mind, the mind pollutes the body. Physical energy sublimates itself into zeal; conversely, zeal stimulates the body. The biological ends pass into ideals of standards, and the formation of standards affects the biological facts. The individual is formative of the society, the society is formative of the individual. Particular evils infect the whole world, particular goods point the way of escape.

The world is at once a passing shadow and a final fact. The shadow is passing into the fact, so as to be constitutive of it; and yet the fact is prior to the shadow. There is a kingdom of heaven prior to the actual passage of actual things, and there is the same kingdom finding its completion through the accomplishment of this passage.

But just as the kingdom of heaven transcends the natural world, so does this world transcend the kingdom of heaven. For the world is evil, and the kingdom is good. The kingdom is in the world, and yet not of the world.

The actual world, the world of experiencing, and of thinking, and of physical activity, is a community of many diverse entities; and these entities contribute to, or derogate from, the common value of the total community. At the same time, these actual entities are, for themselves, their own value, individual and separable. They add to the common stock and yet they suffer alone. The world is a scene of solitariness in community.

The individuality of entities is just as important as their community. The topic of religion is individuality in community.

Christian Faith
and Process Philosophy

4

Bernard M. Loomer

One of the genuine alternatives in our time to the "dialectical" or "Continental" theology as a constructive advance upon liberalism is the mode of theological thinking which seeks to reinterpret the force and meaning of the Christian faith within the new intellectual framework that is being provided by modern metaphysics. The dominant motif of the new metaphysics is process, since the creative character of events is seen to be a fundamental notion; hence the point of view has come to be referred to as *process philosophy*.

Any effort to restate the insights of the Christian faith within a philosophical framework is bound to awaken protest among many Protestant thinkers for the reason that Protestant theologians have tended to dissociate faith from any consciously conceived rational structure. Such criticisms have been frequently made against efforts within process philosophy to relate faith and philosophy. These objections purport to invalidate from the outset the fitness of process philosophy to be a proper framework within which to interpret the Christian faith. By "process philosophy" I have reference in this case to the general Whiteheadian orientation, although the details of this system are not necessarily subscribed to nor are they of primary importance from the point of view of this discussion. My purpose in this paper is to state and discuss several criticisms of process philosophy that are raised or that can be raised from the standpoint of Christian faith.[1]

From The Journal of Religion, XXIX, 3 (July 1949). Used by permission of The University of Chicago Press and Bernard M. Loomer.

[1]I have made no effort to identify the specific sources of the criticisms with which I shall deal, since they are general in character and have come from a variety of writings and discussions. In this article I have in mind particularly certain questions raised by Niebuhr in his writings and statements made by some of

It should be noticed that these criticisms apply also to liberalism (whether old or new) in so far as liberalism attempts to arrive at some rational understanding of the world of our experience. Rationalism, in the widest sense, involves some kind of system; it emphasizes primarily continuity of explanation. This factor causes it to be suspect from the vantage point of faith. Furthermore, I am inclined to think that these objections constitute several variations of one recurrent theme.

I

The first general and less specific criticism would hold that a philosophical interpretation of Christian faith almost inevitably tends to be inadequate. The explanation for this inadequacy is inherent in the nature of the philosophic enterprise itself. A system of metaphysical categories is concerned with every type of experience at all levels of existence. Therefore, it cannot do full justice to any particular kind of experience or to any specialized inquiry or quest. Continuity takes precedence over discontinuity. Particularity and individuality are swallowed up in universality. The unique is reduced to the common and identical. This is especially true in the relationship between philosophy and a historical religion such as Christianity. Faith is in danger of being resolved, either prematurely or maturely, into reason. The tension that must necessarily exist between faith and reason is broken. System predominates over the adventurous and unsystematic outreaches of faith. The sovereign God of faith is reduced to a manageable idol trapped or caged within a system. The temptation of the philosopher is to treat his system as a constant and the faith as a variable. The result is that he discards all those aspects of the faith which do not fit nicely into the system which he has constructed primarily from sources and data outside the faith.

Whenever theology has become too philosophical in its interpretation, the criticism continues, a reformation has been necessary as well as forthcoming. Theology has had to declare its autonomy from philosophy, and faith has had to assert its independence of reason. These reformations have also been carried out in the interests of rational understanding itself. Furthermore, while the Christian faith has been associated (and even identified) with several philosophical systems, it has outlived them all because it has transcended them all. This association (and identification) has been too often detrimental to the vitality and purity of the faith.

---

my colleagues in the Federated Theological Faculty with whom I have had frequent discussions on this problem. The formulation of the criticisms in each instance, however, is my own and represents a composite statement of specific objections which have seemed to me important and relevant.

Therefore, what would cause one to think that process philosophy is an exception to these considerations? There is evidence, indeed, that would lead one to the opposite conclusion. For example, the language of process thought is derived primarily from scientific disciplines, and this impersonal language is ill suited for religious purposes. "How can one pray to a process? One can pray only to a person, or a conscious personality, or a living and loving father." Furthermore, its use of a rational-empirical methodology for deriving and testing knowledge motivates it to adopt the procedure of standing outside the Christian faith and evaluating that faith in terms of a so-called "objective criterion." But by what marks are its method and criterion of truth to be established as true? The Christian faith is given, and process philosophy must come to terms with this givenness. This faith can be understood only from a standpoint within itself. This faith cannot be "validated" by means of criteria external to itself. There is no "faith in general." Therefore, to stand outside the Christian faith, and to attempt to ascertain its truth-value by measuring it with objective norms, is to judge the Christian faith in terms of another faith. The adequacy of process philosophy as a standpoint for interpreting the Christian faith will be determined, at least in part, by the willingness of process thought to accept the revelation of God in Jesus Christ as the central clue for its metaphysical outlook.

In reply to this criticism one must grant the point that a metaphysical account of experience, taken by itself, does not and cannot give a fully adequate description of the nature of man, especially of man in his religious dimension. This is so because metaphysical categories will only be illustrated in the several sciences and disciplines. Metaphysical categories, if true, are applicable to all individuals at all levels of existence. But they exhaust the total content and structure of no one individual or type of individual at any level. The several more specialized inquiries are needed to supply the more specific knowledge of various types of individuals. It follows, therefore, that the resources of metaphysics are not sufficient in themselves to exhaust the meaning and profundity of the Christian faith and the nature of man and God as interpreted in the light of that faith. This is true even if the metaphysical description should include the results of a philosophy of religion with its persistent concern for value as a category of all experience.

This being the case, what is the relevance of metaphysics for the task of interpreting the Christian faith, for our day or any day? Its relevance and significance, at least in part, are that of a world view in relation to a specialized inquiry. The fact is that all disciplines, intellectual or practical, scientific or religious, presuppose in one form or another some sort of world view, explicit or implicit, total or partial, systematically or incoherently perceived and formulated. This world view is our philosophy.[2] We see with eyes and minds that are, in part at least, colored and shaped by this explicit or implicit philosophic background. Our very language testifies to this fact. The religious interpretations of man and God vary, among other reasons, because of changing world views. It is important, therefore, that we make this larger perspective explicit so that it may be criticized. These world views, criticized or uncriticized, guide our inquiries, be they intellectual or practical.

This critical function of a world view is important further because it enables us to evaluate more adequately the interpretation of man and his world that emerges from any specialized inquiry, such as theology or the Christian life itself. Thus, one function of metaphysics is to evaluate the possible pretensions of restricted modes of thinking and behavior. Stated differently, one function of a metaphysical system is to free us from bondage to systems or structures of thought of less generality than itself. In this regard, Whitehead has underscored the relevance of metaphysics for science. Faith and theology are no necessary exceptions to the evils that befell science.

These considerations are especially pertinent to the problem of interpreting the Christian faith in view of the fact that in some circles a purely kerygmatic theology is said to be possible. This type of theology attempts to state and interpret the fundamental Christian message in dissociation from any philosophical framework. But even if this goal were desirable, it could not be achieved. An approach to this ideal limit might be made, but some philosophic assumptions and implications would be inherent in the interpretation. They might be hidden and obscured, but they would be there. As hidden they may unduly restrict or even corrupt the meaning of the Christian message itself. As a matter of fact, one of the chief difficulties that confronts the Christian theological world today concerns interpretations of the Christian faith which contain hidden and uncriticized philosophical assumptions that operate under the guise of being essential ingredients of the faith. Part of the task of evaluating interpretations of Christian faith consists in the criticism of the philosophical predilections that inevitably accompany these theologies, either as substance or as shadow. This is as true of the biblical interpretation of faith as it is of all later portrayals.

Therefore, the implicit suggestion that the Christian community should distrust equally all philosophic systems of thought because they in turn are restrictive and even corrupting in their religious effects is basically idolatrous in character. To be sure, metaphysics is no guaranty against idolatry or even narrowness of outlook and practice. But a

[2]In this discussion I am using the terms "philosophy" and "metaphysics" synonymously.

persistent and pervasive distrust of all systems is either only another system in itself or the effort is self-defeating. Incurably we are creatures of meanings, and meanings can be grasped fully only in the context of their relationships. An adequate religious life is impossible apart from some degree of interrelated reflective thought. Philosophy is simply the systematization of this kind of thinking and acting.

The necessity of system or coherence is grounded in the intellectual and religious demand for integrity, for unity, for an undivided self. We cannot worship our sovereign Lord if we are divided and compartmentalized selves. Integrity both presupposes and brings about self-consciousness, that is, the awareness of who one is, where one stands and why he stands there, and what God one commits himself to. But we cannot be sufficiently self-conscious without having probed the depths of our cultural and religious presuppositions. We cannot worship the true God unless we are conscious of the extent to which we define the meaning of life in terms of the cultural gods that surround us. We cannot realize the limitations of our cultural gods unless we know the true God. The circle is complete. But philosophic inquiry is one of the means for the achievement of self-consciousness, for the enlargement of the circle. It constitutes one resource for escaping the tyranny of idolatrous viewpoints.

The demand for integrity does not imply that a philosophical system is to be superimposed on studies of lesser scope and generality. Metaphysical generalizations may be derived from any specialized field of inquiry. For example, Whitehead generalized the quantum and relativity theories of physical science into universal propositions. Furthermore, the adequacy of metaphysical categories is ascertained by reference to other specialized disciplines, including the discipline of the Christian faith. The categorial system is derived from and tested by the various areas of specialized inquiry. Thus, the relations between metaphysics and these areas are mutual and interdependent. Consequently, each specialized discipline has a kind of autonomy in that each is free to contribute its basic concepts and insights to the over-all generalized description which is metaphysics. Both the categorical system and the structure of thought of each specialized inquiry are variables, although the former is usually more constant than the latter in the nature of the relationship. Each is modifiable by the other.

This general methodological principle is applicable to the problem of the relationship between philosophy and the interpretation of the Christian faith. Both are variables. It is true that philosophers have treated their own systems as constants and the Christian faith as the variable. It is also true that process thought has probably not been sufficiently informed and modified in terms of basic Christian insights.

The difficulty here is that of philosophically generalizing these religious insights so as to make them relevant to other categorial concepts and applicable to other specialized disciplines, without devitalizing the content of these insights. Yet it must be granted that Whitehead's general orientation has been considerably and consciously shaped in terms of Christian insights, even though much of his general thought has been constructed from the data of science.

Furthermore, this general principle implies that the "givenness" of the Christian faith must be qualified. However this faith is to be interpreted, neither the faith nor its interpretation is simply "given" in the sense that it is given as a constant. Nor is either given as an unalloyed datum. The faith comes to us structured with the matchless wisdom of many prophets and saints. But it also comes to us burdened down with the barnacles of superstition and error. If this faith is given to us as self-evidently true and if it contains its own creative criteria of warranty, it is so and does so only because it has been tested and not found wanting by countless generations of inquiring hearts and minds.

But from the point of view of Christian faith, another dimension must be added to the search for integrity and maturity. True integrity must be realized and lived under "tension." This added quality can be stated in terms of the difference between religious and intellectual integrity or in terms of the relation between faith and reason. Faith is trust, and a mature trust must adventure beyond reason and beyond evidence. An adequate faith must be rooted in evidence, but faith in a God who is wholly evidential is trust in one's own self-sufficiency. Faith is prior to reason, logically, biologically, and religiously.

In stating this point, it is important to consider the fact that a true tension exists between two things only when they are internally and mutually related. A tension does not exist between two externally related elements. There is only dichotomy or compartmentalization. Too often faith and reason have been defined in terms of external relations, so that the tension between them has been broken and not merely resolved. But if a tension exists between faith and reason, then each must modify the other and be modified in turn. As one's intellectual understanding develops, his faith must change accordingly. As one's faith deepens and matures, his understanding must reflect this added penetration.

This means that Christian faith and process philosophy are codependents. They should be in close relationship. In fact, they must be. It also means that they must be held in tension if faith is to remain true to its own genius and insights. Faith and reason are not synonymous. Philosophy is the attempt to arrive at one intellectual world as defined by the systematic relationship of the categories of its system. Christian

faith is a giving of one's self to that reality which is held to be sovereign
over even that one intellectual world. The mutual dependence is intimate, but the tension is abiding.

II

The second criticism is a more specific application of the first. It runs
to the effect that process philosophy, being a type of naturalism and
consequently predisposed in favor of continuity of explanation, neglects
the discontinuous qualities of existence. More particularly, it does an
injustice to that which is peculiarly human, especially to that which
is fundamental from the standpoint of Christian faith: man's capacity
to sin. In attempting to avoid a metaphysical dualism by showing how a
man is an integral child of nature, it vitiates man's understanding of
himself.

A frankly dualistic philosophy, the objection states, has certain
advantages over a monistic outlook that tries to find analogous elements
in man and the sub-human levels. If man is a child of nature, he is a
very strange child who hardly can be recognized by his parents. Nature
knows of a will to live, but only man knows of a will to power. Nature
knows of sex and hunger drives, but in nature these compulsions operate within limits, and satiety has its appointed level. Only man is
capable of defining the total meaning of existence in terms of one of
these natural needs. Nature knows of a hierarchy of weaker and
stronger, but only man is an imperialist who wants to subjugate all
others to his own purposes. Nature knows of consciousness; but only
man is self-conscious, with the capacity to make himself into his own
object. Nature knows of security in terms of biological fulfilment and
parental care and protection, but only man is anxious about his status
in the universe. Nature knows of death, but only man knows that he is
finite and fears death. Only man desires to be infinite; only man has
moral, intellectual, and religious pride. Nature knows of animal intelligence, but only man speculates and constructs alternative mathematical
and logical systems. Only man can transcend himself. Nature knows of
an animal's separation from its mate or children or parents, but only
man is cosmically lonely. Nature knows of the order of the seasons,
but only man worships. Nature knows of physical satisfaction, but only
man knows peace in the midst of tragedy. Nature knows of sacrifice,
but only man knows of justice, mercy, and forgiveness. Only man carries a cross. Nature knows of deception, but only man lies and is in-
sincere. Only man tries to fool himself, and only man knows that he
cannot really deceive himself. Nature, in other words, is governed by
necessity, but only man is free—free to affirm, deny, obey, rebel, corrupt, tyrannize, worship, deify, laugh, suffer, pervert, repress, sublimate,

wonder, to doubt and to transcend his doubts. Only man is made in the image of God, and only man can be demonic and love his own demonic usurpations. Nature knows of animal leaders, the strong who can lead a herd to safety. Only man can be a saint or a messiah.

This criticism is akin to another which contends that all philosophies, in the interests of simplicity and system, tend to deify one aspect of man, either his reason, or his will, or his emotions. This tendency to deify one aspect of man to the neglect of his other essential qualities is an instance of the fallacy of "misplaced concreteness." This inevitable procedure of systematic thought not only breaks down because of its own inadequacy and because of its failure in helping us to understand ourselves but in the long run results in idolatry. We conclude our system by constructing a God in our own image and of our own choosing. Is not this form of the criticism obviously applicable to process philosophy? Does it not subsume everything under "feelings" or "emotions"? How, then, can it give an honest reading of the facts of Christian experience? Does it not become subject to the same criticisms that Niebuhr, for example, has leveled against rationalism, romanticism, and early forms of naturalism?

In answer to this objection, it should be admitted at once that there are discontinuities between the human and the subhuman levels. There are discontinuities between all levels of existence, at least as seen by process philosophy. There are properties or qualities at any designated level of existence which apparently are characteristic of that level alone. A whole is more than the sum of its parts, and there are novel and emergent wholes. Furthermore, the parts of a whole at one level of existence are different from these analogous parts as they function at lower levels. When Whitehead attributes "feeling" and "mind" to the subhuman levels, he does not mean that they are the same as human feelings and human reason. Similarly, time and space cannot be completely the same for the subhuman as they are for us.

Therefore, the metaphysical attempt to find similarity of structures at different levels of existence does not deny the fact of discontinuity. It does not account for the higher in terms of the lower (in a reductionistic sense). It is concerned to see discontinuities in terms of continuous patterns of structure. These patterns of structure can be defined in terms of the categorial elements that constitute a metaphysical system. They are the factors which are present in all experiences of all individuals. Categories are concepts which refer to factors which cause us to exist, not to those things whereby we are peculiarly human. They refer to those things without which existence as we know it would be impossible. Within this total picture of those elements which all individuals share in common in order to exist at all, discontinuities are possible. But discontinuities are qualitative differences along a continuous dimension.

For example, metaphysics as such is not concerned with sin. Yet a metaphysics does attempt to show how sin is possible in terms of organic functionings and mechanisms which are shared in common (in varying degrees, to be sure) by all levels of life. In other words, the fact of discontinuity does not necessarily imply a dualistic philosophic outlook.

Process philosophy does generalize metaphysically the concept of feeling (or prehension). But there is nothing particularly one-sided or psychological about the meaning that is intended. The term "feeling" is attributed to all levels of existence because of Whitehead's insistence that there is no such thing as "vacuous actuality." All events are individuals which become something definite by means of integrating into one unit the several data which are received from other past events. This process of appropriation, which is the self-enjoyment involved in being an actual event, is called "feeling." But the term is devoid of any suggestion of consciousness or of representative perception. Thus "feeling" is an inclusive term that is indicative of the basic feature (i.e., "process") which all events share.

All processes (or processes of appropriation) exemplify two basic kinds of feelings: physical or bodily feelings and conceptual feelings (mentality). Emotions are primarily types of the "how" of feelings, especially of physical feelings. Existence is dipolar. This means that there are no substances which are purely mental or purely physical. Body and mind are inseparable components of each actual entity. Mentality is correlative with form or structure. Therefore, mentality is inherent in nature because there is no process apart from some form or structure illustrated in the process. One function of form or structure (and thus mentality) is to individualize or channelize the fluid and unbounded character of feelings. This function of form is to achieve definiteness and particularity on the part of events. One must be a specific and definite something in order to exist at all. This does not mean that inorganic processes can think (in the human sense), but it does mean that all events are selective. It means that order (in the general sense) is intrinsic to all events.

In saying that body and mind are inseparable in each actual entity, I mean to emphasize also the physical basis of all things. "Physical" means extension and causal efficacy. It connotes habit and compulsion, vitality and process. We are earth-bound, and we are subject to analogous drives, limitations, and necessities that characterize all organic life. We experience our world primarily by means of our bodies. All our ideas are primarily either reflections of or derivations from bodily behavior. It is true that ideas can be derived from other ideas, but in each process mentality originates by a conceptual reproduction of a bodily feeling. Man is a materialist, in the best sense. Our ideas and aspirations, our yearnings, joys and tragedies, are imbedded in and carry the marks of our earthly frames. We are never as free and uncoerced as we like to think we are; our ideas are never as general and unprejudiced as we innocently imagine; and our actions are never as pure and untainted as we pretend.

The basis of life is physical and emotional, blind desire or appetition if you will. But the blindness is not unrelieved, and life is not wholly compulsive in character. There is freedom, novelty. This quality of existence is possible because of another function of mentality whereby we have the power to produce abstractions. Forms and structures can be abstracted from their physical matrix. At the human level, ideas can be lifted out of their emotional rootage. Novel structures and ideas can be envisaged. In process philosophy the factor of form is necessary to account for the fact of abstraction wherein we have the ability to isolate one thing from another. There is freedom, novelty, and abstraction because there is mentality or conceptual feeling. The forms or the "hows" of conceptual feelings, as contrasted with the forms of physical feelings, possess an autonomy whereby novel conceptual reactions are possible. (This is the category of "conceptual reversion.") The "how" of a conceptual reaction is not completely determined by the "what" of its object. This is the continuous dimension along which the discontinuities of different levels appear.

The whole evolutionary process has been looked at in terms of a scale defined in terms of increasing complexity or specialization. From the standpoint of process thought, this evolutionary development can be interpreted along a dimensional scale of increasing conceptual autonomy or abstractiveness. The higher up we go on the evolutionary ladder, the greater the complexity of the physical organism, the more conceptual autonomy we find. Or, alternatively, the greater capacity do we find for abstracting forms from their physical or emotional base. At the inorganic level, the ability to seize upon forms of behavior very different from what has been is practically nonexistent. Causal efficacy is paramount. Thus the greater predictability in the physical sciences. There is tedious sameness and monotony. There is a minimum of freedom.

At the human level the degree of conceptual autonomy is such that it seems to be a difference in kind. The power to abstract forms from concrete processes is so great that mentality emerges into reason. We now have speculations and alternative geometrical systems. Sense-perception, which we share with some of the subhuman species, is itself evidence of this increased capacity for abstraction. Consciousness, which we also share, is likewise an indication of greater conceptual autonomy. Conceptual feelings are abstracted from physical feelings, and consequently reintegrated, in such fashion that finer and more complex contrasts result. Consciousness develops in this kind of process of abstraction and reintegration.

This capacity for greater conceptual autonomy not only makes consciousness possible. It is the same factor which is the basis of our self-consciousness. It is the means whereby we can transcend ourselves and make ourselves our own object. Not only can we abstract a structure from its event-context, but we can abstract ourselves from ourselves.

It is important to note that the process of abstraction takes place in a context of internal relations wherein the presence of our fellowmen furnishes us the data for greater contrasts. The fact of a supporting community or environment makes possible a greater available contrast whereby a greater conceptual autonomy (and thus a more complete self-consciousness) may be realized. And this autonomy makes it possible for us to set ourselves over against our fellows. Here we find the grounds of tyranny, pride, imperialism, demonry, the corruption of natural vitalities and the disruption of natural harmonies. Here is our greater freedom for good or ill.

Conceptual autonomy in itself, however, does not constitute freedom or the misuse of freedom. Conceptual autonomy or increased abstractive capacity means, negatively, that the form of our conceptual feelings (the "how") is not completely deducible from what we physically feel by way of concrete events. Positively, it means that novel forms or structures can be integrated and reintegrated (at levels of increasing complexity) with physical feelings in such a way that the complexity, intensity, inclusiveness, and direction of these feelings can be altered. The realization of freedom is a bodily achievement in which conceptual thought is a necessary but not a sufficient ingredient. There must be the appropriate physical basis for the attainment of freedom. The same qualification applies to the fact of self-consciousness. Thus, freedom is correlative but not strictly synonymous with conceptual autonomy. Freedom is not wholly the product of reason.

In this account, autonomy is dependent upon community; our abstractive capacity is supported by internal relations. The fact of community forms the basis, the material, whereby greater compatible contrasts are possible which may issue in greater conceptual autonomy. One must have a rich background from which to abstract, else the abstraction is thin, unfertile, and impoverished. Conversely, the autonomy must feed back into the community from which it sprang in order to be meaningful and fruitful. The autonomous conceptual feelings must reintegrate themselves with relevant and supporting physical feelings, else the realized novelty and freedom will not endure. True freedom consists in a sensitive balance between autonomy and dependence. The misuse of freedom consists in autonomy's denial of its dependence upon community. Thus sin, or idolatrous autonomy, is a denial of or a rebellion against community.

The organic relation between physical and conceptual feelings, together with the autonomy of the latter, makes possible the sin of sensuality as well as that of pride. Because of his greater autonomy, man is able to subordinate his whole being to an aspect of himself and to define the total meaning of life in terms of this corrupted vitality. The sin of sensuality is a denial of the community which is the individual's whole being or self. The characteristic of man whereby he can transcend himself, and subordinate all others to his own desires, is the same fundamental quality whereby he can define his destiny in terms of his biological necessities. This quality is rooted in the fact of conceptual autonomy and the capacity for abstraction.

I suggest that this process of the reintegration (at levels of increasing complexity) of conceptual and physical feelings resulting in self-consciousness is equivalent to Niebuhr's concept of "spirit," which he apparently conceives of as something more than body and mind. It is the recognition of this factor which he thinks was the contribution of biblical Christianity to the understanding of the nature of man. For Niebuhr, spirit is the ingredient in man whereby man transcends nature and himself, whereby man is free to corrupt nature as well as himself, and whereby man sets himself over against his fellow-men and the God who is the true author of his being. I suggest further that this analysis of man's freedom, of his spirit, has one advantage over Niebuhr's use of the term "spirit": it attempts to locate the "mechanism" of spirit and to relate spirit inherently to organic functioning. This description attempts to tie together body, mind, and spirit and tells of their interdependence.

Therefore, and in summary, process philosophy does try to take account of the discontinuities of existence, and it does not try to explain all of life in terms of one dimension or category of experience.

III

The two following criticisms are in reality two aspects of one basic objection. They should be treated as one unit. The division can be justified only on grounds of convenience of presentation.

The third criticism states that the God of Christian faith cannot be equated with any natural process or vitality, because every natural process is ethically and religiously ambiguous. There is no perfection or absolute to be found within nature or history as such. Christian faith is a trust in the perfect and unambiguous incarnation of God in Jesus Christ. Here the Christian finds the absolute ethical and religious norm in terms of which history is both judged and yet found meaningful. Apart from Christ, there is no adequate ethical and religious norm because history exemplifies only the inextricable intermingling of good and evil. The created world and the creatures who live within it are good because God created them. But man is also a sinner because in his freedom he rebels against his creator, and there is no pure goodness in nature itself. In terms of nature and history alone, there is no resolution of the tension between good and evil. Good and evil are so entertwined in experience that (except by a process of abstraction which does not result in our dealing with a concrete reality) we cannot single out one process and call it the source of human good. Therefore, no natural process can be fully trusted, and no human vitality is adequate to man's ethical and religious needs and insights. The goodness and the perfect love of God revealed in Jesus Christ transcend the norms and ethical tensions of history. Faith in this God is not even justified with reference to historical consequences. The Christian God is a transcendent being who became immanent and took on human form, and no naturalistic account can do justice to this reality revealed in Christian experience.

Another version of this objection to process philosophy from the standpoint of Christian faith concludes that God cannot be identified with any natural process, because man can make any natural vitality subservient to his own ends. All mundane forces are ultimately manageable by man because of his freedom. This does not mean that man can control all natural phenomena or that man is not bound by natural necessities. It means, rather, that man can use any wholly immanental force or process in such a way that he constructs a god in his own image whose nature is subject to man's own wilful and sinful self. In other words, man can create false idols from all kinds of earthy materials. But these idols are no better than their creators. Since man is not adequate for himself (else why the idols before whom he bows?), these created gods lead to man's misunderstanding of himself. Naturalism, therefore, leads to frustration and despair because man in his freedom (whereby he transcends nature) must commit himself to something greater than himself. The God in Christ is not a "natural" God.

In reply to this criticism, it should be noted, first of all, that there seem to be two assumptions involved in this outlook, both of which are incompatible with process philosophy. (a) Nature is interpreted as being essentially uncreative, lifeless, and nonredemptive. At least history and nature are regarded as quite discontinuous. For process thought, "nature" includes the total experienced and experienceable world; it comprises the whole natural order with its power of creating, recreating, and redeeming the human person. (b) There is posited, either by inference, conjecture, or faith, a transcendent absolute which obviously cannot be identified with the natural world. There is this assumption, it seems to me, even though it is asserted that this God has been revealed in Jesus Christ. The fundamental nature of this transcendent God is that of absolute sacrificial love. Since man is made in the image of God, absolute love becomes obligatory for man. Process philosophy knows of no God who is fundamentally transcendent in the epistemological or metaphysical sense. From its point of view, the limits of knowledge are defined in terms of the limits of what is experienceable. The limits of the experienceable are defined in terms of the limits of relationship. This is its world of nature, describable in terms of the categorial system. "Beyond" this world is the unknowable, and "the unknowable is unknown."

A comment may be interjected at this point to the effect that the God revealed in Jesus Christ is transcendent but not primarily in the sense described in the assumption. The God revealed in Christ is religiously and ethically transcendent. Any transcendence of a metaphysical character that is to be ascribed to God is a derivation from this prior type of transcendence. Therefore, the basic meaning of transcendence is concerned with the problem of perfection.

Let us accept the point of this interjection for the moment. What is the understanding of perfection that is to be derived from process philosophy? In the first place, one basic principle of process thought is that all realization is finite. Actuality may be defined as a process of selection. Since not all possibilities can be realized at once, realization of concrete things therefore involves limitation. In this sense, "definition is the soul of actuality."

Second, the process of realization involves selection because of the fact of incompatibility. Selection, limitation, and exclusion are relevant notions for the understanding of perfection because not all things are compossible as contemporaries. Some possibilities are mutually contradictory. The principle of harmony must be exemplified in all actual processes to a greater or lesser degree if there are to be any definite and specific actualities at all. Order is intrinsic in events. Harmony means, in one respect, that contrasts may border on chaos but that they should not reach the stage of mutual destructiveness or incompatibility. Possibilities which may not be mutually realizable as contemporaries because of their incompatibility may be related as past and future events. Because of these considerations it can be seen that the process of realization has a "seasonal" character. ("Insistence on birth at the wrong season is the trick of evil.") This means that process is inherent in the very nature of God. Time is one of his necessary attributes. He is a temporal being with an eternal or changeless character.

Third, the primordial nature of God is the conceptual ordering of all eternal objects and possibilities such that a graded scale of relevance is established between each possibility and each actual entity. Because of this unchanging order in the world, each possibility has a different relevance or significance for each actuality. This ordering of all possibilities constitutes the abstract and not the concrete nature of God. This is Whitehead's "principle of concretion." If the term "absolute" is applied to God, it can refer only to his abstract character.

But some possibilities are "abstract" possibilities, and some are "real" possibilities. That is, some possibilities are not sufficiently relevant to the actual course of history to be considered live options for us. In this sense, "perfection" means the "best possible," where "possible" has reference to live options. There is no abstract perfection in terms of abstract possibilities which have no real relevance to the concrete world of events. God may be conceived of as absolute or as abstractly perfect, but this is abstract and not concrete perfection. Concrete or actual perfection has reference to the actual state of affairs now going on. God does not operate in a vacuum. He works in terms of the conditions which define our temporal existence. Therefore, concrete perfection must be understood in relation to these conditions. "God does the best he can, given that impasse." Perfection is a concept the understanding of which involves such notions as limitation, relevance, and community.

This means that the "best possible" for any individual cannot be defined as though the individual were an isolated and self-sufficient unit. The individual exists only in a community or "society" of individuals. Existence is fundamentally social in character. The individual is sustained by some supporting community of his fellows, even though in certain respects he also transcends this community. Therefore, certain possibilities are relevant for any individual, *relative* to that community of which he is a part. All individuals and all communities have specific characters, and they have specific substantial histories. Relevant possibilities are possibilities which are relevant to the specific characters and histories of definite individuals and groups. Chaos and disintegration ensue if we attempt to actualize possibilities which we are not prepared to realize. What may be abstractly possible for any individual considered apart from his context is qualified when that context is taken into account. Possibilities have an order of relevance appropriate to each individual event considered in its context with its mixture of good and evil. The creative process can aim, at most, only at that realization which is best for that individual event, relative to those forces and conditions which have brought it into being.

The "common good" means that, relative to every particular individual in a specific community or other particular individuals, the creative process offers relevant and novel possibilities for that individual's deepened and enriched fulfilment. The possibilities relevant for that individual are also relevant and relative to other novel possibilities which in turn are relevant to the other individuals in that community.

This is the possible common good, relative to that context. The ideal or greatest possible good for any individual would consist of his realization of the greatest number of diverse and mutually enriching potentialities relevant to his character and history, relative to his community. The best possible communal good is obtained when the several individuals achieve their fullest development in the most mutually sustaining and enhancing community, when "development" and "community" are contextualistically defined. This ideal or perfect good that is offered to us at every moment of our existence is the structure of the creative process. This is at least part of the character of the goodness of God. In this sense God is perfect or absolute, because this pattern of relationships among possibilities relevant to actualities is unchangingly applicable to all events.

This perhaps overlong explanation has been thought necessary in order to emphasize that "perfection" is a relative and seasonal concept. We have no meaning to attach to the idea of absolute perfection in the concrete sense. Whatever perfection may mean, it cannot mean that the course of history is to be evaluated solely in terms of the realm of abstract ideal potentiality. Perfection must be viewed in the context of specific conditions, attitudes, and relevant possibilities. Time, relevance, and community are of the essence in this regard. And, granted the unlimited wealth of potentiality, "there is no perfection beyond which there is no greater perfection."

The "perfect will of God" is synonymous with the "best possible." It is a transcendent demand upon man because relevant perfection represents an enduring standard in terms of which man is continually judged. This basic structure, which is the foundational order of existence, is transcendent because it is autonomous. The fulfillment of man is dependent upon conformity to this autonomous and primordial order —an order descriptive of increased mutuality in due season, an order which is efficacious because it is the structure of the process of creative growth. It is an order of autonomous valuation which is binding on man. That is, Whitehead's primordial nature of God expresses the divine lure, the divine persuasion of order, harmony, and enriched mutuality. But this structure is not merely an ideal or a pretty picture which we may disregard as irrelevant. It is a structure which is a stubborn and unyielding fact that must be taken into account because it is the character of a process of efficient causality.

This structure is autonomous in that man did not create it. Certainly man, if left to his own wilful desires, would not choose it. It is autonomous in the sense that apparently it is uncreated. No matter where or when we look, we find this order impressing itself upon us. God as primordial "is not *before* all creation but *with* all creation." This order partly accounts for our common world. It is the conceptual basis of mutuality and the conceptual criterion of ethics. This structure is also apparently fixed and unalterable. Thus the path of human fulfilment is a narrow one. God is transcendent also in the sense that his is the final autonomy which measures all other types of autonomy, and beyond which there is no appeal.

The unyieldingness of this order is needed to protect man from himself, from his demonic distortions and his defensive escapes and denials. It is needed to coerce man to face himself and to recognize himself for what he is. At the same time, the sometimes gentle working involved in the restructuring of our minds and hearts in faith is necessary to release those burdened down with oppressive pasts. Man in his freedom can attempt to disregard this inevitable presence. But we always encounter this structured process, either as companion or as tormentor, "either in fellowship or in wrath."

God is accessible, but he is not manageable. We cannot twist this order to suit our purposes. We cannot try, with impunity, to domesticate or emasculate this process. God is as much transcendent as man can endure. He is as much immanent as man can gaze upon and not be blinded.

This unmanageable structure is a transcendent and abiding demand. It is the criterion of the best possible. It is the relevant ideal standard. But this obviously is not the whole story of the human situation, for we refuse to be persuaded of the necessity and the rightness of a divine order. Or if some are persuaded at times, others rebel. In either case we realize much less than the best possible. We are sinners, even though we may not sin in every occasion of our experience. We will not realize ourselves sacrificially; that is, we will not allow ourselves to be fulfilled through yielding ourselves to that process which works for the mutual good of all. Or if we will at times, others will not. We try to fulfil ourselves, to find ourselves, by holding to ourselves, by centering attention on ourselves. We will not sacrifice our present selves and values for greater selves and values. We fear the losing of ourselves. Or if at times some do not so fear, others do. We refuse to believe that sacrificial love is that peculiar means necessary to the achievement of the richest mutuality wherein each individual receives his greatest possible maturity. Or if at times we do not, others do. In either case the inevitable result is tragic. It might have been otherwise.

The failure to realize the best possible is the measure of our sin. But the desire on the part of some to realize the perfect will of God in a great social situation may be politically unseasonal and ethically ineffective or even irresponsible; hence the ubiquitous presence of the fact of compromise. Many times ("at all times," some would say) our only relevant political or social choice is that between the lesser of two evils. This decision frequently involves the use of coercion. At best it is a tragic choice. We attempt oft-times to realize a greater good in one respect at the price of greater evil in another respect. The result, however, many times is better than no community at all.

I mention the fact of compromise in order to distinguish it from the "best possible." Compromise is a lower level of achievement than that involved in the transcendent criterion. Compromise represents the sacrifice of some values peculiar to the concerns of the several conflicting interests in order to realize some values which can be shared by all.

Let us assume, someone may interpose, that this autonomous order does constitute (in a sense) an unambiguous working. Even so, can this conception do justice to the revelation of God in Jesus Christ? Christian faith conceives of God as absolute love, as self-sacrificing, as merciful and forgiving as well as judge, as suffering Father, as providential redeemer. Where is the *agape* of God as seen in the context of process philosophy?

The answer, it seems to me, lies in the nature of experience itself. The fact appears to be that reality is fundamentally and intrinsically social in character. We cannot realize ourselves apart from the realization of others. Others cannot be fulfilled if we are not. Also, because we are sinners against both God and our fellow-men, we cannot realize ourselves unless others forgive our sins by restoring our relationship to them. Others cannot be re-created unless we forgive them. But we cannot forgive the sins of others unless we take the sins of others into ourselves. We must sympathetically identify ourselves with them and take into ourselves their burdens. We must suffer with them. We cannot be merciful if we hold ourselves apart from others as though we were self-sufficient and independent beings. Feeling the feelings of others, even their sins, is necessary for our fulfilment.

God, according to the categories of process philosophy, cannot realize himself apart from the fulfilment of his creatures. God and the world are mutually dependent. Therefore, if the finite creatures are to be fulfilled, and if God is to achieve his purpose through his self-realization and the realization of his creatures, God must forgive our sins. In forgiving us, he takes our sins unto himself and identifies himself with our sins. This is the suffering of God. This is also the mercy of God, even though mercy involves more than just the fact of suffering. Mercy indicates the restoration of a broken relationship.

The "sacrifice" of God means that God gives himself to us for his own, as well as our, realization. He fulfils himself through his creatures, even his sinful creatures. God forgives and re-creates us out of his mercy, but this re-creation of us out of God's mercy is necessary for God's own self-fulfilment. Therefore, forgiveness, love, mercy, and redemption are not accidental qualities of God. These are inherent in his very being. The fundamental character of existence is mercy. God's forgiveness of us is different from our forgiveness of others in that God always forgives us, whereas we rarely forgive others. Furthermore, not only should we forgive others because God restores us, but we are motivated to forgive because God forgives. Finally, we should forgive because we ourselves need to be forgiven.

With this as a background for understanding, one might say that the "sacrifice" of God is somewhat metaphorical. It cannot mean that mercy is optional with God. Surely it cannot mean that the self-giving of God revealed in Jesus Christ consisted in God's becoming "incarnate," as an act of condescension, as though God as he is in himself is a being who basically exists apart from the world of process (and thereby fundamentally transcends history), and who out of mercy became immanent and took on human form. As a matter of fact, the doctrine of the incarnation is likewise metaphorical in nature. Surely it cannot mean that God was not always "incarnate." From the perspective of process philosophy, the Word never "became" flesh; God never "became" incarnate or embodied. The world always embodies this divine ordering and this creative process. To speak of God's becoming incarnate in a human person would mean that in Jesus Christ the basic and most intimate attributes of God and existence itself were revealed: the mercy and love of God. By faith in this love we are justified. The idea of historical or special revelation means, it seems to me, not only that God acts in history but also that there is a history of the acts of disclosure of God whereby the character of existence is progressively revealed to man. The disclosure of God in Jesus Christ revealed most fully that the qualities of mercy and sacrificial love are necessary if the living of life is to have its justification.

The revelation of God in Jesus Christ indicates that the path of sacrificial love is the "law of life." God offers himself to us according to the transcendent structure that we have previously discussed. But the cross of Christ also reveals our failure to respond to sacrificial love in like manner. If we had the gratitude, the love, and the courage to respond, the faith to endure, and the wisdom to understand the implications of this love, the fuller workings of this divine order could be realized among us. But we possess neither the love, the faith, nor the wisdom to a sufficient degree. To this extent and for this reason, the fulfilment of this law of life is impossible. However, this does not mean that this transcendent standard is irrelevant.

In the first place, the *agape* of man, deriving as it does from the *agape* of God, does not necessarily mean that "the best possible" is realizable only if an individual or a group literally and biologically gives up its existence. To be sure, this possibility is sometimes the only option or consequence. But the exemplification of sacrificial love should not be so conceived that the "sacrificing" individual does not count for one. The realization of the mutually enhancing community involved in the actualization of "the best possible" includes, normally, the greater good of the "sacrificing" individual. The fact that the individual realizes a greater good because of his "sacrifice" does not necessarily make his act less sacrificial. The cross of sacrificial love usually does not and cannot mean the cross of physical death. Existence is not synonymous with sin. Nor is existence equivalent to the will to power. The pervasiveness, the depth, the subtlety, and the power of sin and evil in human life are not denied. Rather I am insisting on the situational nature of the best possible, the perfect will of God. Even though one finds his life by losing it, by letting go of his present self, and even though one cannot realize his greater fulfilment by attempting to control the process of creative mutuality for his own purposes or by concentrating his attention upon his forthcoming reward, surely the vision of perfect love of man cannot be conceived normatively in terms of extinction.

I do not mean to water down the meaning of the sacrificial love of the cross to the point where human compromise is equated with divine and creative mutuality. I am not consciously equating political and divine possibility. I am trying to recognize the place of sacrificial love and at the same time to avoid the dangers of an absolutely transcendent ethic. There is sin with its destructiveness. There is the cross of Christ which is the price of redemption over sin and spiritual death. There is the brokenness of the self in sin. There is the renewal of the new self in faith and forgiveness. In attempting to live the life of sacrificial love, we cannot set limits to the degree of the brokenness of the old self that may be required of us. We cannot say: only so far will we yield now. But the brokenness, the yielding, and the renewal, like perfection itself, are relative factors. Usually we are not broken completely, and certainly we are renewed (sanctified) only relatively and relevantly. The grace may be absolute in terms of justification, in terms of forgiveness, but our rebirth is always relative to a context. It cannot be otherwise.

These statements may appear to be too cautious, too calculated in tone and intent, too qualified, restricted, and prudential to do justice to the apparent unboundedness and selflessness of Christian love. But I trust that this appearance is due to an attempt to avoid what I think is an excessiveness in other presentations. One need not deny the value of martyrdom in certain instances, or the selflessness of sacrificial death that is sometimes involved in trying to live a life of love, or even at times of pacifism (as a strategy, without believing in it as an absolute principle). The point is that these concrete acts are not necessarily normative. The problem of how far we can realize "the best possible" in any given situation, and the problem of the means to be employed, are partly matters of judgment. In any case, either in the short or in the long run, our act is one of faith. The faithful shall live by his faithfulness.

Second, this divine criterion and self-giving is our inexorable judge. The order of creative mutual love is the law of life, and by that law we are condemned as sinners. We know that we are sinners. It is our measure, our "natural" norm. Without it we would become our own judges and find ourselves innocent, even though the marks of our anxiety, pride, and tyranny would belie our words. The divine order is relevant and needed, in other words, to protect us from ourselves, to prevent us from trying to escape from ourselves. The degree of its relevance as well as its transcendence is measured by the extent to which we rebel against it and flee from it—and by the failure of our rebellion and our flight.

Third, this criterion is relevant because this creative process works in us in spite of our sin. It is the ground of our redemption and fulfilment. The work of God is not exhausted by the ethical striving of man. Over and above, and sometimes in spite of the efforts and sins of men, this process moves in its own determined way. Man is sometimes fulfilled in spite of himself. The working of this process is evidenced in the experience of grace and man's re-creation, in the frustration of sin and its accompanying anxiety, and in the destructiveness visited to man if he attempts to stop the inexorableness of its march.

In summary, then, the reply to this third criticism has involved the thesis that there is an ethically and religiously unambiguous order within nature and that this structure is not corruptible by man. It should be noted that this thesis has involved reference not only to an order or structure but also to a creative process which embodies this structure. The more detailed characterization of this process has been omitted. A discussion of the possible difficulties involved in the "concreteness" of this process are here postponed for a future occasion.

It is quite conceivable that this thesis will not stand examination. It may well be that the ambiguity of the described structure within nature remains. Those who claim that all natural processes are ethically and religiously ambiguous presuppose that there is an unambiguous working of God in history and that this work is to be seen primarily in the revelation of God in Christ. But if there is this unambiguous working of God in history, the character of this working should be identifiable and, I would add, empirically identifiable. If this character or structure is not identifiable, then the solid basis of this view vanishes. If, on the other hand, this structure is identifiable, why is it not available for the general outlook of process thought?

If we start, as many insist we should, with the revelation of God in Jesus Christ as the basic datum, then the notion of an essentially transcendent God who became immanent in the incarnation is an interpretation that is not necessarily warranted by the datum itself (complex though it be). The theologian ends up with a transcendental, nonnatural or nonprocess God (with reference to the datum of Christ) only if he begins there. This is presupposition and not fact. This assertion does not in itself establish the validity or the adequacy of process philosophy as a framework within which to interpret Christian faith. But it purports to point up the idea that the nature of the transcendence of the God revealed in Christ is a matter for inquiry.

IV

The fourth objection to process philosophy makes explicit the other elements that were implicit in the third objection. This criticism states that the system of process thought is an inadequate framework within which to understand the Christian faith because history and nature are not self-redeemable. Admittedly "nature" (within which "history" is lived and made) constitutes the total resources available to process philosophy. The world of nature is not self-explanatory and self-sufficient. This is true, so the criticism asserts, because in the orientation of process thinking there is no final resolution of the conflict between good and evil. History and the processes of nature do not issue in victory, in the ultimate triumph of good over evil. The paradoxes and ambiguities of life are not finally resolved. In terms of this system history is ultimately meaningless.

The criticism, stated somewhat differently, contends that the God of Christian faith and history, as seen through the eyes of process philosophy, is not truly sovereign. He is trapped and domesticated by the system itself. Admittedly the ultimate of ultimates, in this outlook, is creativity and not God. God cannot transcend this frame of reference because he is at the mercy of the conditions inherent in the categorial system. In other words, the sovereignty of the God of Christian faith is given up because the freedom of God is too restricted. The freedom of God as exemplified in his mighty acts, as these are recorded in the Old and New Testaments, does not find a ready place in this system of thought.

Another version of this same fundamental objection states that process thought does not do justice to the eschatological elements of New Testament faith. The fact of the resurrection is central and determinative for our thinking about the meaning of Christian faith. In the resurrection the power of God triumphed over sin and death. (For some "death" means physical death, such that there is the hope of resurrection and not just an "intimation of immortality.") On the basis of the fact of the resurrection, there is ground for trust in the "second coming." The "second coming" is a somewhat "mythical" or metaphorical concept used to indicate the New Testament faith in the power of God (manifested in the resurrection) to conquer the conditions that now define our earthly existence, particularly the condition of man's sinfulness. The "point beyond history" is also a "mythical" concept (to be taken not literally but nonetheless seriously) which connotes the Christian's faith that the power and goodness of God can be made even more manifest in the hearts and minds of men. The "point beyond history" need not connote a nonhistorical and transcendental type of existence. It can refer to a form of historical life wherein the conditions of existence would be radically altered. In this state of affairs, the paradoxes and ambiguities of life would be resolved, man would not be a sinner, the meaning of life would be completely realized, and man would know even as now he is known.

This kind of criticism is an illustration of what some theologians mean when they insist that the revelation of God in Jesus Christ is the central fact that should furnish the basis for Christian theology. All else is a derivation from this fundamental datum. In biblical faith God is the creator of all that exists. He is sovereign over the whole physical universe. But there are no "arguments" in support of this notion. The idea of God as creator, God as philosophically sovereign, seems to be derived from the faith that he is religiously sovereign. The God who has done such wondrous things for the people of Israel, the God who is the rock of our salvation and a very present help in time of trouble, the God who has given his people such sure promises and who has fulfilled them, the God who is our judge and our redeemer, who spoke to prophets, who conquered sin and death in the figure of Christ—surely the power and goodness of this God are such that he is also creator of heaven and earth. Niebuhr, for example, argues that the centrality of the figure of Christ implies the logically absurd doctrine of creation *ex nihilo*. But this doctrine is not clearly biblical in content. The eleventh chapter of Hebrews is hardly adequate and certain support for Niebuhr's contention.

It is clear, however, that the biblical God is creator. This would seem to mean that God is responsible for the conditions that define and limit our existence. All creatures and all conditions are subject to his control. God is also the origin and source of man's freedom. Therefore, all of nature and history testify to God's power and goodness. He transcends his created world and is therefore not to be identified with it, although the created world does reveal the nature of his work. God's freedom is not exhausted by the laws that govern his creation. He reveals himself as he chooses and in his own time. God is not subject to alien forces and material which he did not create. Therefore God is creator, judge, and redeemer. What God has created he judges. What he judges he also redeems in mercy. The paradoxes and ambiguities which baffle us will be ultimately resolved because, in a sense, they are resolved now in the very being of God. He is Lord over even the contradictions and the evil which beset us. We do not see how all this is so, to be sure. We see as through a glass darkly. But for Christian faith the power and love of God manifested in Jesus Christ are the evidence of things not seen, the assurance of things hoped for.

Now in process philosophy, process itself or creativity is the ultimate category. That is, the fact of process cannot be explained in terms of anything more fundamental. It simply is. It is given. Yet process is not possible apart from the primordial structure which is part of God's nature. In a sense this order or structure is the ground of being. Creativity is not possible apart from certain conditions, and the primordial order is the fundamental condition. Likewise this order does not exist apart from the world of creativity. There is a world because there is this order which is the principle of concretion. But the principle does not exist as disembodied. It "exists" only as exemplified in concrete events.

In terms of process philosophy, therefore, in one sense God is not responsible for the character of the conditions through which creativity works. The freedom of man, for example, is a gift of creativity. It is inherent in created things. The creativeness or the energy whereby there is creation is inherent in created events. They are self-creative, and they give rise to other events. The incompatibility of certain possibilities is inherent in the nature of possibility itself. Therefore, process itself is inherent in the being of God if incompatibility is to be surmounted. Furthermore, in process thought God is not (or should not be) an exception to the categorial system. The denial of this principle involves the price of erecting an unknowable God before whom all our honest strivings and seekings are as nothing. The world of our experience, which is what a categorial system defines, would then be a world of illusion, of mere appearance. In this sense God is responsible for at least some of the conditions that define our world. God's primordial nature "at once exemplifies and establishes the categorial conditions."

There is also chance in the world of process thought. There is chance involved in the fact of selection or inclusion. There is adventure, and the outcome is not predetermined. In the realization of some values we exclude the realization of other possible values. Many times these excluded values appear to have been as potentially enriching as the values we actually chose. There are general possibilities, and there are possibilities relevant only to specific individuals at specific moments of history. If those possibilities are not realized by those individuals at those specific moments, they are gone forever. We are filled with the haunting sense of what might have been but never can be. We seemingly illustrate an arbitrariness and an element of chance within the very nature of things. We feel less sure of the justice or the wisdom of our election to our appointed tasks. We reflect an uneasiness within ourselves at being tossed up or down by accidental elements. We wonder. The tormenting sense of vast alternatives is abiding.

God is religiously sovereign. He is the source of good in the sense that the realization of the good is dependent on him. Creation is good because without God there could be no creation. Also we sin in our freedom. God is our judge and the source of our redemption. But beyond this what can we say in regard to the power of God to transcend the conditions of existence that now obtain? What are some of the difficulties?

In the first place, historical experience does not support the claim that evil is gradually being eliminated. On the contrary, there is much evidence that the increase of good increases the possibility for greater evil. The higher good results in a greater sensitivity which in turn offers greater opportunity for the evil of demonic powers. The more far-reaching the brotherhood, the greater the communicability of disease and prejudice. The more delicately balanced the organism, the closer attention it requires. The tension between good and evil seems to be abiding.

Second, creation (in process philosophy) occurs in terms of the emergence of the higher from the lower. This is not reductionistic evolution but emergent evolution. This is the long, arduous, and halting struggle upward. According to process philosophy, God works and labors in terms of this evolutionary development. One of the most remarkable features of much of so-called "neo-orthodox" theological thought is its explicit or implicit attitude that the fact (or the theory) of evolution is not relevant to religious reflection about the nature of God or the meaning of Christian faith. Apparently, evolution is accepted as a scientific fact. But equally apparently this fact has no implications for Christian faith. I find this attitude to be not only remarkable but somewhat fantastic. For Christian faith, God is the creator of the physical and biological world. Surely one implication of this doctrine is that Christian faith and science cannot be dichotomized into separate compartments.

Third, there is the theory of the second law of thermodynamics having to do with the running-down of the available energy of the universe to a dead level. What are the implications of the theory for Christian faith, especially for the doctrine of the sovereignty of God? If one holds to the idea of the complete sovereignty of God, does he say that this physical theory is not true, that it cannot be true, or that it will be found to be false when more evidence is accumulated? But suppose, for the sake of the discussion that the theory comes to assume the proportions of a valid hypothesis? Would not this fact seriously qualify the power of God to alter radically the conditions of existence?

To be sure, the theory of entropy does not account for the fact of "upward" evolution. But where is the evidence that the upwardness of evolutionary development will necessarily continue? From the point of view of process philosophy, the actual realization of entropy would mean the end of creativity itself. There would still remain some kind of order, but the power of God would be reduced to practical negligibility. In process thought the universe is actually "in the making," and God is incomplete in his concrete nature. If there should come a time when there would be no more "making," then the adventure of God would be at an end. The only escape from this conclusion seems to be in terms of a basically transcendental God. This alternative is categorically denied by process philosophy.

One might reply to these questions by stating that for those whose faith is biblical in orientation the fact of the resurrection is supreme over even these difficulties. The weight to be assigned to this consideration depends upon what is meant by "the fact" of the resurrection. In this sphere particularly there is no such thing as a bare uninterpreted fact. The nature of the alleged fact presupposes a whole philosophic orientation. If "resurrection" means the physical resurrection of the human Jesus (even though one adds "the human-divine Christ"), then indeed this miracle might well outweigh the difficulties mentioned above. Then indeed God is Lord not only over sin but physical death as well. Physical entropy then becomes a possibly surmountable obstacle. But if this is what "resurrection" means, then philosophy (at least process philosophy) has nothing to say to faith. Actually in this case there is no "tension" between faith and reason; there is only the complete absence of any relationship. Nothing in the world of either science or philosophy need cause any uneasiness in the devout soul. But the implication of this meaning of "resurrection" is that with this interpretation one has chosen the (or "a") biblical world view in preference to a modern world view. Further, the grounds for this choice need not and may well not be primarily religious in nature.

But if by "the fact of the resurrection" one means not the physical resurrection of the man Jesus but the resurgence of the power of God in Jesus even when evil and death had seemingly triumphed, then this "fact" is not necessarily determinative in regard to the difficulties mentioned—even though it is a "fact" of tremendous importance. It is evidence of the power of God and his love over spiritual death, but it is hardly evidence of God's sovereignty over physical death. God would still seem to be subject to conditions that define our world.

Now it could be asserted that these difficulties may concern what

I have called the "philosophical" sovereignty of God but not his "religious" sovereignty. One might hold that these conditions of the natural world need not be determinative in regard to God's power to make his love more manifest in the hearts and minds of men. Let us assume, for the moment, that Christian faith in the revelation of God in Jesus Christ implies the trust that God will conquer sin to such an extent that the kingdom of God will be fully realized. Will this state of affairs apply only to those generations then living? Or are all the past generations to inherit the kingdom? If the latter, does not this involve the resurrection of the dead of ages past? If so, can one then divide the sovereignty of God into compartments? Are not then the conditions of physical nature relevant considerations?

Why does the full meaningfulness of life and history necessarily demand that good will ultimately triumph over sin and evil so that sin will no longer be a condition of our being? Why must all the paradoxes and ambiguities of life be resolved? Why must every purpose have its completion in order to be a purpose at all? Why is tragedy meaningful and "really redeemed" only if there is a faith that there is a kingdom coming wherein there will be no more tragedy?

One answer is that this is the wrong kind of question. These are not just demands and cravings of our souls which must be satisfied. We have faith in these eschatological eventualities because of the power and love of God revealed in Christ. His love for us is so all-encompassing and his power is so great that neither life, nor death, nor the principalities and powers of this world can separate us from him. It is God in Christ who has brought meaning into history. It is God in Christ who will return to complete this meaning.

Possibly so. Yet we Christians hold that the revelation of God in Christ disclosed the "final" attribute of God: his mercy. In a sense our fulfilment is always broken and incomplete. We sin. We die. But is not the final fulfilment and the ultimate relationship to be found in the peace of forgiveness? Is a more intimate relationship possible? Would participation in a kingdom without the presence of sin make more manifest the love of God?

One might reply that the love and power of God are inseparable. One cannot limit too severely the freedom of God's sovereignty over man. In the history of God's free acts of self-disclosure, culminating in Christ, one finds evidence that God's power over sin increased so that in Christ the power of sin over man was decisively broken. Also there is no reason to assume that God's work is now finished. Wieman, for example, has stated that the revelation of God in Jesus Christ was such as to assure us of the victory of good over evil—much as the victory of Stalingrad assured the Russians of their eventual victory over the Germans. Not that Stalingrad made further fighting unnecessary but that Stalingrad decisively determined the final outcome of the war. I would agree. But this analogy does not rule out the possibility of other wars. The victory of Christ may mean that evil can never be completely victorious, but the victory of good over evil and of God over sin does not necessarily imply the total elimination of evil. In other words, in terms of process thought, there is no end. There are only more battles and more victories to be won. Tragedy is abiding, and forgiveness is a perennial necessity.

In such a world is the life of sacrificial love justified? If the meaning of "justified" in this connection has reference to the final elimination of evil, or the historical and metaphysical permanence of this kind of love, then the answer is "in the making." If "justified" has reference to the validity of sacrificial love, its intrinsic value and goodness, its beneficial consequences (both to the loved and to the lover), its meaningfulness, then the answer is in the affirmative. Socrates' statements about suffering injustice rather than inflicting injustice, Jesus' teachings and Paul's elaborations, and Luther's classic description of the power of the Christian life, to name but a few, are sufficient testimony for those who have the eyes and hearts to see. And the justification is now.

Yet it is true that, although we cannot answer the unanswerable questions, or even know whether they are proper questions, nonetheless we cannot down our wonder. The sense of life's twisted ironies, its unexpected turnings and unlooked-for delights of mind and heart, its vengeful and sometimes unbearable cruelty, its moments of sheer beauty and joy, its hours of stark and soul-shriveling loneliness, its occasions of shared love and community when the heart has almost burst because it could hardly contain its exultation, its times of unappreciated sacrifice and undeserved blessings—these and many other kindred experiences cause us to lift our eyes beyond death. Whitehead has said that one of the deepest longings of the human heart is to experience the new and at the same time to maintain the old. He conceives of the past as preserved in "living immediacy" in the present. Further, all values are saved in their fulness. Possibly so. At least this is the cry of the soul.

But this yearning of the heart cannot be made into a qualification of our faith. We cannot demand its satisfaction as a condition of our self-giving or as a price for our services. The goodness of God is its own value. Its present fulfilment of its own promise is its own benediction.

The meaning of life, the justification of sacrificial love, the redemption of tragedy, the meaningfulness of history, and the resolution of whatever paradoxes there be, are "now." The meaning of life, for good or ill, for those enriched or impoverished, defeated or victorious, just or unjust, slave or free, is here and now. History builds on its past and points to its future. But only the present, which contains the past and envisages the future, is holy ground. Each life is its own reward. Its recompense is in terms of the things, people, and causes it has loved or hated, its feelings of countless qualitative meanings, its joys and sorrows, its defeats and victories, and the God it has known. It has seen God as empty nothingness, or as unbending judge, or as merciful redeemer. Respectively, the experience has contained its own hollow laughter, or its own cry of anguish and rebellion, or its own benediction of religious peace.

Christian Natural Theology   5

John B. Cobb, Jr.

1.   The Task of Natural Theology

In *Living Options in Protestant Theology*,[1] I argued that there is need for a Christian natural theology and that the philosophy of Whitehead provides the best possibility for such a theology. Critics quite reasonably complained that I did not develop such a theology in that book or even provide adequate clues as to what shape it would have. This book is my attempt to fulfill the obligation I imposed on myself by making that proposal. It intends to be a Whiteheadian Christian natural theology. This expression needs clarification.

By theology in the broadest sense I mean any coherent statement about matters of ultimate concern that recognizes that the perspective by which it is governed is received from a community of faith.[2] For example, a Christian may speak coherently of Jesus Christ and his meaning for human existence, recognizing that for his perception of ultimate importance in the Christ event he is indebted to the Christian church. In this case, his speech is theological. If, on the other hand, he speaks of the historic figure of Jesus without even implicit reference to Jesus' decisive importance for mankind, his speech is not theological. Also, if he claims for statements about Jesus' ultimate significance a self-evidence or demonstration in no way dependent upon participation in the community of faith, he would not intend his statements to be theological in the sense of my definition.

Most theological formulations take as their starting point state-

   [1]Philadelphia: Westminster, 1962.

   [2]In this section I am following Tillich in using "faith" and "ultimate concern" interchangeably.

ments that have been sanctioned by the community in which the theologian's perspective has been nurtured, statements such as creeds, confessions, scriptures, or the fully articulated systems of past theologians. But according to my definition of theology, this starting point in earlier verbal formulations is not required. One's work is theology even if one ignores all earlier statements and begins only with the way things appear to him from that perspective which he acknowledges as given to him in some community of shared life and conviction. . . .

The definition of theology here employed is relatively neutral on the question of its virtue or evil. Those who believe that the only fruitful thinking is that which attempts strenuously to clear the slate of all received opinion and to attain to methods that can be approved and accepted by men of all cultures, will disapprove of the continuance of a mode of thought that recognizes its dependence upon the particularities of one community. On the other hand, those who believe that there are questions of greatest importance for human existence that are not amenable to the kind of inquiry we associate with the natural sciences, will be more sympathetic toward theology.

My own view is that theology as here defined has peculiar possibilities for combining importance and honesty. Practitioners of disciplines that pride themselves on their objectivity and neutrality sometimes make pronouncements on matters of ultimate human concern, but when they do so they invariably introduce assumptions not warranted by their purely empirical or purely rational methods. Usually there is a lack of reflective awareness of these assumptions and their sources. The theologian, on the other hand, confesses the special character of the perspective he shares and is therefore more likely to be critically reflective about his assumptions and about the kind of justification he can claim for them. If in the effort to avoid all unprovable assumptions one limits his sphere of reflection to narrower and narrower areas, one fails to deal relevantly with the issues of greatest importance for mankind, leaving them to be settled by appeals to the emotions. The theologian insists that critical reflection must be brought to bear in these areas as well as in the rigorously factual ones.

In the light of my definition of theology, we can now consider what *natural* theology may be. Some definitions of natural theology put it altogether outside the scope of theology as I have defined it. This would be highly confusing, since I intend my definition of theology to be inclusive. However, we should consider such a definition briefly. Natural theology is often identified with that of theological importance which can be known independently of all that is special to a particular community. In other words, natural theology, from this point of view, is all that can be known relative to matters of ultimate human concern by reason alone, conceiving reason in this case as a universal human power. This definition is, of course, possible, and it has substantial continuity with traditional usage. It is largely in this sense that Protestant theologians have rejected natural theology. A consideration of the reasons for this rejection will be instructive.

In principle, natural theology has been rejected on the ground that it is arrogant and self-deceptive. It is argued that reason alone is not able to arrive at any truth about such ultimate questions. When it pretends to do so it covertly introduces elements that are by no means a part of man's universal rational equipment. Every conviction on matters of ultimate concern is determined by factors peculiar to an historically-formed community or to the private experience of some individual. Since no doctrine of theological importance can claim the sanction of universal, neutral, objective, impartial reason, what is called natural theology can only be the expression of one faith or another. If Christian thinkers accept the authority of a natural theology, they are accepting something alien and necessarily opposed to their own truth, which is given them in the Christian community.

The last point leads to a consideration of the substantive or material reason for the rejection of natural theology. The philosophical doctrines traditionally accepted by the church on the basis of the authority of philosophical reason have, in fact, been in serious tension with the ways of thinking about God that grew out of the Old and New Testaments and the liturgy of the church. The philosophers' God was impassible and immutable whereas the Biblical God was deeply involved with his creation and even with its suffering. Brilliant attempts at synthesis have been made, but the tensions remain.

My view is that it is unfortunate that natural theology has been identified substantively with particular philosophic doctrines. There is no principle inherent in reason that demands that philosophy will always conclude that God is impassible and immutable and hence, unaffected by and uninvolved in the affairs of human history. Philosophers may reach quite different conclusions, some of which do not introduce these particular tensions into the relation between philosophy and Christian theology.[3] The modern theological discussion of natural theology has been seriously clouded by the failure to distinguish the formal question from the substantive one.

On the formal question, however, I agree with the rejection of natural theology as defined above. The individual philosopher may certainly attempt to set aside the influence of his community and his own special experiences and to think with total objectivity in obedience to the evidence available to all men. This is a legitimate and worthy

[3]That this is so is fully established by the work of Hartshorne. See especially *The Divine Relativity* (New Haven: Yale University Press, 1948, 1964).

endeavor. But the student of the history of philosophy cannot regard it as a successful one. It is notorious that the ineradicable ideas left in Descartes's mind after he had doubted everything were products of the philosophical and theological work, or more broadly of the cultural matrix, that had formed his mind. There is nothing shameful in this. Descartes's work was exceedingly fruitful. Nevertheless, no one today can regard it as the product of a perfectly neutral and universal human rationality. If one should agree with him, he should recognize that he does so decisively because his fundamental experience corresponds to that of Descartes. He cannot reasonably hope that all equally reflective men will come to Descartes's conclusions.

To put the matter in another way, it is generally recognized today that philosophy has a history. For many centuries each philosopher was able to suppose that his own work climaxed philosophy and reached final indubitable truth. But such an attitude today would appear naïve if the great questions of traditional philosophy are being discussed. Insofar as philosophers now attempt to reach final conclusions, they characteristically abandon the traditional questions of philosophy and limit themselves to much more specialized ones. In phenomenology, symbolic logic, and the analysis of the meaning of language, attempts are still being made to reach determinate conclusions not subject to further revision. These attempts are highly problematic, and in any case questions of ultimate concern cannot be treated in this way. If natural theology means the product of an unhistorical reason, we must reply that there is no such thing.

However, responsible thinking about questions of ultimate human importance continues to go on outside the community of faith. Furthermore, many of the members of the community of faith who engage in such thinking consciously or unconsciously turn away from the convictions nurtured in them by the community while they pursue this thinking. It is extremely unfortunate that the partly legitimate rejection of natural theology has led much of Protestant theology to fail to come effectively to grips with this kind of responsible thinking. Some theologians have idealized a purity of theological work that would make it unaffected by this general human reflection on the human situation. They have attempted so to define theology that nothing that can be known outside the community is relevant to its truth or falsehood, adequacy or inadequacy. I am convinced that this approach has failed.[4]

In almost all cases, the theologian continues to make assumptions or affirmations that are legitimately subject to investigation from other

---

[4]In *Living Opinions in Protestant Theology,* I have tried to show in each case how, whether recognized or not, theological positions depend systematically on affirmations that are not private to theology. I acknowledge the brilliance of Barth's near success in avoiding such dependence.

points of view. For example, he assumes that history and nature can be clearly distinguished, or that man can meaningfully be spoken of as free. He may insist that he knows these things on the basis of revelation, but he must then recognize that he is claiming, on the basis of revelation, the right to make affirmations that can be disputed by responsibly reflective persons. If he denies that science can speak on these matters, he thereby involves himself in a particular understanding of science that, in its turn, is subject to discussion in contexts other than theology. He must either become more and more unreasonably dogmatic, affirming that on all these questions he has answers given him by his tradition that are not subject to further adjudication, or else he must finally acknowledge that his theological work does rest upon presuppositions that are subject to evaluation in the context of general reflection. In the latter case he must acknowledge the role of something like natural theology in his work. I believe that this is indispensable if integrity is to be maintained and esotericism is to be avoided.

The problem, then, is how the theologian should reach his conclusions on those broader questions of general reflection presupposed in his work. The hostility toward natural theology has led to a widespread refusal to take this question with full seriousness. Theologians are likely to accept rather uncritically some idea or principle that appears to them established in the secular world. For example, a theologian may assume that modern knowledge leads us to conceive the universe as a nexus of cause and effect such that total determinism prevails in nature. Conversely, he may seize the scientific principle of indeterminacy as justifying the doctrine of human freedom. Or he may point to the dominant mood of contemporary philosophy as justifying a complete disregard of traditional philosophy. My contention is that most of this is highly irresponsible. What the theologian thus chooses functions for him as a natural theology, but it is rarely subjected to the close scrutiny that such a theology should receive. It suffers from all the evils of the natural theologies of the past and lacks most of their virtues. It is just as much a product of a special point of view, but it is less thoroughly criticized. In many cases it is profoundly alien to the historical Christian faith, and yet it is accepted as unexceptionably authoritative.

If there were a consensus of responsible reflection, then the adoption of that consensus as the vehicle for expression of Christian faith might be necessary. But there is no such consensus that can be taken over and adopted by the Christian theologian. Hence, if natural theology is necessary, the theologian has two choices. He may create his own, or he may adopt and adapt some existing philosophy.

If the theologian undertakes to create a philosophy expressive of his fundamental Christian perspective, we may call his work Christian philosophy in the strict sense. There can be no objection in principle to this undertaking, but historically the greatest philosophical work of theologians has never been done in this way. Many philosophies have been Christian in the looser sense that their starting points have been deeply affected by the Christian vision of reality. But the conscious recognition of this dependence on a distinctively Christian perspective has been rare.

Practically and historically speaking, the great contributions to philosophy by theologians have been made in the modification of the philosophical material they have adopted. Augustine's work with Neoplatonic philosophy and Thomas's adaptation and development both of Aristotle and of Augustinian Neoplatonism are the great classical examples. Both Augustine and Thomas were superb philosophers, but neither undertook to produce a new Christian philosophy. They brought to the philosophies they adopted questions that had not occurred to the philosophers with comparable force. In the process of answering these questions, they rethought important aspects of the philosophies. In doing this they did strictly philosophical work, appealing for justification only to the norms of philosophy. But even in making their philosophical contributions they were conscious that the perspective that led them to press these questions arose from their Christian convictions. This source of the questions does not lessen the value of their work as philosophy, but it does mean that their philosophical work was a part of their work as theologians. Theology is not to be distinguished from philosophy by a lesser concern for rigor of thought!

If, then, we are today to follow in their footsteps, our task will be to adopt and adapt a philosophy as they did. I suggest that in implementing this program the theologian should accept two criteria for the evaluation of available philosophies.

First, he should consider the intrinsic excellence of the structure of thought he proposes to adopt and adapt. The judgment of such excellence may be partly subjective, but it is not wholly so. Despite all the irrationalism of the modern world there remains the fact that consistency and coherence where they are possible, are to be preferred over inconsistency and incoherence. A theory that proposes to explain many things must also be judged as to its success in doing so. If a few broad principles can unify a vast body of data, the employment of many *ad hoc* principles is to be rejected. Criteria of this sort have almost universal practical assent, so that it is always necessary to give special reasons for their rejection. If a particular position that claims philosophical authority is markedly inferior by these criteria, there can be no justification for adopting it to serve as a natural theology.

Second, there is no reason for accepting as a natural theology a position hostile to Christian faith, if another position more congenial to faith is equally qualified according to the norms suggested above. The study of the history of thought suggests that there is a plurality of philosophical doctrines, each of which can attain a high degree of excellence by all the norms on which they agree in common. This does not mean that any of them are wholly beyond criticism, but it does mean that the finally decisive criticisms stem from a perception of the data to be treated in philosophy that is different from the perception underlying the philosophy criticized. Diverse visions of reality lead to diverse philosophies and are, in turn, strengthened by the excellence of the philosophies to which they give birth.

For example, there are persons to whom it is wholly self-evident that sense data are the ultimate givens in terms of which all thought develops and who are equally convinced that the only acceptable explanation of the way things happen follows mechanical models. These convictions will lead to a particular philosophical position. Against this position it is useless to argue that there are data that this philosophy does not illumine, and that mechanical models capable of explaining the processes of thought have not been devised. The philosopher in question does not agree that there are other data and assumes that the lack of adequate models is a function of continuing human ignorance.

The particular position I have described would be a caricature of any major philosophical thinker, but it does point to a type of mentality that is not rare in our culture. When I realize that the particular conclusions generated by the serious reflection that arises from such assumptions have only the authority of those assumptions, then I feel free to turn to another philosophy that includes among its data human persons and their interactions; for my perception of reality is such that these seem to me at least as real and ultimate as sense data and mechanical relations. I cannot prove the truth of my vision any more than the sensationalist can prove the truth of his, but this does not shake me in my conviction. I may well recognize that my way of seeing reality has been nurtured in the community of faith, but this provides no reason for accepting as my natural theology the conclusions derived from the sensationalist-mechanist vision. On the contrary, it provides excellent reasons for choosing the conclusions of a personalistic philosophy, always providing that as a philosophy, measured by the appropriate criteria of that discipline, it is of at least equal merit. Every natural theology reflects some fundamental perspective on the world. None is the pure result of neutral, objective reason. Every argument begins with premises, and the final premises cannot themselves be proved. They must be intuited. Not all men intuit the same premises. The quest for total consensus is an illusion, and indeed there is no reason to accept majority rule in such a matter if the majority does not share one's premises. Hence, a Christian theologian should select for his natural theology a philosophy that shares his fundamental premises, his fundamental vision of reality. That philosophy is his Christian natural theology, or rather that portion of that philosophy is his natural theology which deals most relevantly with the questions of theology. It would be confusing to include under the heading of natural theology all the technical aspects of philosophy, but, on the other hand, no sharp line can be drawn, and the coherence of the whole is of decisive importance for selection.

In the sense now explained, natural theology is the overlapping of two circles, the theological and the philosophical. Natural theology is a branch of theology because the theologian in appropriating it must recognize that his selection expresses his particular perspective formed in a community from which he speaks. On the other hand, it is also philosophy because it embodies thinking that has been done and judged in terms of philosophical norms.

There may seem to be some tension here. Philosophy is critical, imaginative, and comprehensive thinking that strives to free itself from the conditioning of particular traditions and communities, whereas a criterion for the selection of a philosophy by a theologian should be its sharing of a basic vision of reality. But there is no contradiction. The philosopher does not set out to show how the world appears from the perspective of a community of faith, and to some degree, he can free himself from such perspectives. Even if he is a Christian, for example, he can set aside all the particular beliefs about Jesus Christ, God, miracles, salvation, and eternal life that he recognizes as peculiar to that tradition. He can and should refuse to accept as relevant to his philosophical work, any data that do not appear to him to be generally accessible. He will begin with ordinary language, or the findings of science, or widespread experience of mankind, rather than with the special convictions of his community. This starting point will lead the philosopher to the consideration of many questions ordinarily not treated by Christian theology and to the omission of many questions usually treated by theology. It will also lead to the consideration of overlapping questions.

However, beyond this level of conviction, life in a community also produces a primary perspective, a basic way of understanding the nature of things, a fundamental vision of reality. It is at this level that the philosopher cannot escape his perspective.[5] He can, of course, reject

[5]Whitehead saw the work of the creative philosopher in terms of the novelty of his perspective. The philosopher "has looked at the universe in a certain way, has seen phenomena under some fresh aspect; he is full of his vision and anxious to communicate it. His value to other men is in what he has seen" (*Dial* 266). Whitehead also recognized that the philosopher's vision is affected by the historic community in which he stands. "Modern European philosophy, which had its

a perspective that he may have at one time accepted, but he can do so only in favor of some other perspective. And it should be said that changing perspectives in this sense is not simply a voluntary matter. Conscious decisions may affect the process but they do not in themselves constitute it. The decision on the part of the Christian theologian as to where he should turn for his natural theology should involve the judgment as to whether the vision of reality underlying the philosophical system is compatible with that essentially involved in the Christian faith. . . .

2.   The Problem of Relativism

In the preface and elsewhere in [*A Christian Natural Theology*], I have indicated my conviction that a cosmology inspired by the natural sciences has played the dominant role in undermining Christian understanding of both God and man. I have developed at some length aspects of a Whiteheadian cosmology which, I believe, both does more justice to the natural sciences and creates a new possibility of Christian understanding of man, God, and religion. But there is another factor that has contributed to the decline of faith in modern times, which has not yet been seriously considered. This is the historical study of culture and thought. This study has led to the view that every kind of human activity and thought can only be understood as an expression of a particular situation, that all value and "truth" are culturally and historically conditioned, and that this means also that our attempts to find truth must be understood as nothing more than an expression of our conditioned situation.

In the foregoing discussion of Christian natural theology I expressed my own acquiescence in this relativistic understanding to a considerable degree. It is because no philosophy can be regarded as philosophically absolute that the Christian can and should choose among philosophies (so long as they are philosophically of equal merit) the one that shares his own vision of the fundamental nature of things. But if so, then are we not engaged in a fascinating and difficult game rather than in grounding our affirmations of faith? If we can pick and choose among philosophies according to our liking, what reason have we to suppose that the one we have chosen relates us to reality itself? Perhaps it only systematizes a dream that some of us share. The problem of relativism is fundamental to our spiritual situation and to our

---

origins in Plato and Aristotle, after sixteen hundred years of Christianity reformulated its problems with increased attention to the importance of the individual subject of experience, conceived as an abiding entity with a transition of experiences." (RM 140.)

understanding of both theology and philosophy. Before bringing this discussion to a close I want to confront this problem directly, and, though I cannot solve it, perhaps shed some light upon it as Whitehead helps us to see it.

Few philosophers have recognized as clearly as Whitehead did the relativity of their own philosophies.[6] Yet in Whitehead's vision the relativity of philosophies need not have so debilitating an effect as some views of the relativity of thought suggest. He understands the relativity of philosophies as closely analogous to the relativity of scientific theories.[7]

In the field of science the fundamental principles now applied are remote from the fundamental principles of the Newtonian scheme. Nevertheless, the Newtonian scheme is recognized as having a large measure of applicability. As long as we focus attention upon bodies of some magnitude and upon motion of moderate velocity, the laws of science developed by the Newtonians hold true. They have, therefore, real validity, and those who accepted them were not deceived. These laws did not cease to be true when science passed beyond them to the investigation of elements in the universe to which they do not apply. What happened was that heretofore unrecognized limits of their truth came to light. Certainly the Newtonian apprehension of nature was conditioned by history and culture, but it was also substantiated in its partial truth by centuries of patient thought and experimentation. That thought and experimentation are not discredited.

Whitehead believed that the situation in philosophy is similar. No philosophical position is simply false. Every serious philosophy illumines some significant range of human experience. But every philosophy also has its limits. It illumines some portion of experience at the cost of failure to account adequately for others.[8] Also, science and history keep providing new data of which philosophy must take account. The task of the philosopher in relation to the history of philosophy is not to refute his predecessors but to learn from them. What they have shown is there to be seen. A new philosophy must encompass it. Where there are apparent contradictions among philosophers, the goal must be to attain a wider vision within which the essential truth of each view can be displayed in its limited validity.[9]

There are, of course, sheer errors in the work of philosophers. These can and should be detected, but this has nothing to do with the problem of relativism. Indeed the possibility of showing errors presupposes a nonrelativistic principle at work. And no philosophical

[6] ESP 87.
[7] PR 20–21.
[8] FR 70–71.
[9] PR 11–16.

position is built upon sheer error. The more serious problem arises at the point at which philosophers draw inferences based on the assumption that their systematic positions are essentially complete. These inferences will prove erroneous, because in the nature of the case no system of thought is final. All must await enlargement at the hands of the future.

If Whitehead is right, and surely he is not entirely wrong here, then we should employ a philosopher's work with proper caution. We should never regard it as some final, definitive expression of the human mind beyond which thought cannot progress. But we need not suppose that the entire validity of his work depends upon the chance correctness of some arbitrarily selected starting point. What the philosopher has seen is there to be seen or he would not have seen it. His description may be faulty, and what he has seen may have blinded him to other dimensions of reality. He may have drawn inferences from what he has seen that he would not have drawn if he had also seen other aspects of reality—perhaps those other aspects dominating the work of another philosophical school. But when all is said and done, we may trust philosophy to give us positive light on problems of importance.

Whitehead's excellence is impressive when judged by his own principle. . . . But at the same time that I find Whitehead's thought so deeply satisfying, I realize that there are others, more intelligent and sensitive than myself, who see all things in some quite different perspective. Can I believe that they are simply wrong? From my Whiteheadian perspective I can usually understand why they adopt the view they hold, what factors in the whole of reality have so impressed themselves upon them that they allow their vision to be dominated by those factors. But is there not an ultimate and unjustified arrogance in supposing that my perspective can include theirs in a way that theirs cannot include mine? Must I not reckon more radically with the possibility of sheer error in my own vision?

Here I think we must come to terms with an aspect of the modern sensibility that we cannot transcend. Just because we humans can transcend ourselves, we can and must recognize the extreme finitude of all our experiences, all our judgments, all our thoughts. Every criterion we establish to evaluate our claims to truth must be recognized as itself involved in the finitude it strives to transcend. From this situation there is no escape. We must learn to live, to think, and to love in the context of this ultimate insecurity of uncertainty.

This may suggest to some theologians that the whole enterprise of natural theology is, after all that has been said, misguided. It seeks support for theology in a philosophy that cannot transcend relativity and uncertainty. These theologians may hold that Christian theology should remain faithful only to the Word of God that breaks through

from the absolute into the relative. But there is no escape here. I can
be no more sure of the truth of the claim that the absolute has shown
itself than of the truth of the philosophical analysis. However certain
the absolute may be in itself, it is mediated to me through channels
that do not share that absoluteness. If the appeal is to some unmediated
act of the absolute in the believer, there must still be trust beyond certainty that the act has truly occurred and been rightly interpreted. Faith
does not free us from involvement in relativities any more than does
philosophy.

Yet, in another sense, faith is the answer to the human dilemma
of being forced to live in terms of a truth that one knows may not be
true. Perhaps even here Whitehead can help us or at least we can sense
in him a companion in our struggles.

. . . Whitehead's discussion of peace has already been treated twice
in this volume, but it has not been exhausted. One element in particular
remains. Ingredient in peace, for Whitehead, is an assurance that ultimately the vision of the world given in sense experience is true.[10]
This is the assurance that reality does not ultimately deceive. It is an
assurance that exceeds rational demonstration. It is faith.

In the context of the present discussion this faith must be that
the necessity to live and act by a belief whose truth we cannot know is
accompanied by an assurance that as we do so we are not wholly deceived. We will not pretend to a privileged apprehension of reality as
a whole. We will not suppose that those who disagree with us are therefore wrong. We can only witness to the way that our best reflection
leads us to perceive our world. But we can and must believe that in
this witness also, somehow, the truth is served.

[10]*AI* 377ff.

A *Christian* Natural Theology? 6

Schubert M. Ogden

Nothing more characterized the new movement in Protestant theology of the last generation than its exaggerated reaction against so-called "natural theology." Indeed, Karl Barth, whose genius dominated the whole period, claimed that "even if we only lend our little finger to natural theology, there necessarily follows the denial of the revelation of God in Jesus Christ."[1]

Of course, part of the reason Barth's judgment was so extreme was the role "natural theology" played in the church's struggle against Nazism in the thirties. It is clear, for example, that the sharpness of his famous *Nein!* to Emil Brunner (by which writing, incidentally, Americans still know him best) reflected his sense for the possible effect of Brunner's speaking of "nature and grace" on the outcome of that struggle. Still it would be wrong to suppose that Barth's opposition to all natural theology was due entirely or even primarily to the perverse efforts of "German Christians" to give theological sanction to their Nazi ideology. Its real basis was a new vision of Protestant Christianity, which saw, as Barth put it in 1933, that "many roads lead back to Rome" and that Protestantism will fulfill its calling only when it at last "bids farewell to each and every form of natural theology."[2]

In America, as in the English-speaking world generally, this vision never succeeded in fascinating very many Protestant theologians. Liberals (and that includes most "neo-orthodox" theologians as well) were too committed to a broadly empirical and critical approach to

From "A Review of John B. Cobb's New Book: *A Christian Natural Theology*," in the *Christian Advocate*, IX, 18 (September 23, 1965), 11f. Copyright © 1965 by The Methodist Publishing House. Used by permission of the publisher and Schubert M. Ogden.

[1]*Church Dogmatics,* II/1, (Edinburgh: T. & T. Clark, 1957), 173.

[2]"Das erste Gebot als theologisches Axiom," *Zwischen den Zeiten,* XI (1933), 312f.

religious problems to accept a "theology of revelation" without demurrer. Conservatives, on the other hand, while showing an increasing interest in Barth, were not inclined to share his complete repudiation of natural theology. It was probably inevitable, then, that the eclipse of natural theology during the thirties and forties should prove temporary and that it should once again find its English-speaking champions.

Less certain was that the revival, when it came, would be more than an effort to return to business as usual. Its first signs, as they appeared in Britain in the fifties, were hardly encouraging. Although these "new essays in philosophical theology" displayed a certain refinement of analytical tools, the synthesis they were used to build (or to destroy) was by and large the same old natural theology that Barth had repudiated. Lately, however, there have been other signs that the cause of natural theology may have a future as well as a past. The latest of such signs—and the one which so far gives the greatest ground for hope —is the appearance of John Cobb's book, *A Christian Natural Theology.*[3]

As was clear already from his earlier study, *Living Options in Protestant Theology,*[4] Cobb holds that some form of natural theology is unavoidable and that this is evident even from the work of theologians who repudiate it, including Barth himself. No theological statement can be made without certain assumptions, and these assumptions are in most cases legitimately subject to examination from a philosophical standpoint outside the theological circle. Hence, as Cobb shows, the issue can never be *whether* natural theology, but only *what* natural theology—and how exactly we are to conceive its nature and set about deciding between its different forms. I think Cobb would agree that the only alternative to this position leads to a lack of self-consciousness about one's philosophical assumptions and thus induces a false security as to the adequacy of one's theological formulations.

Cobb's deep conviction, which he defends at length in his new book, is that the fortunes of natural theology today depend on Christian theologians appropriating the philosophy of Alfred North Whitehead. Rightly recognizing that the great natural theologies of the past, whether Augustinian or Thomistic, were creative adaptations of independent philosophical systems, Cobb undertakes just such an adaptation of the system of Whitehead. This is not to say that he, any more than his great predecessors, seeks some "hybrid of philosophy and Christian convictions." His intention, at any rate, is to develop a comprehensive vision of man and God which is "philosophically responsible throughout." I do mean to say, however, that Cobb approaches Whitehead's philosophy

[3]Philadelphia: Westminster, 1965.
[4]Philadelphia: Westminster, 1962.

with his own questions as a Christian theologian and then reads it in such a way as to get answers to those questions. For this reason, the subtitle of his book is exactly right: he offers us a natural theology "*based* on the thought of Alfred North Whitehead."

Thus two of the best chapters in the book are those in which he develops, often in a highly original way, what amounts to a Whiteheadian existentialist analysis or doctrine of man. Whitehead himself had very little to offer by way of a formal anthropology or a philosophical ethic. And this may well account for much of the neglect of his philosophy by Protestant theologians. But, as Cobb beautifully demonstrates, this neglect has been unfortunate, since the insights into man's nature and action that abound in all of Whitehead's writings can be made to yield as promising a set of answers as one can find to the theologian's anthropological and ethical questions. As a matter of fact, Cobb goes a long way toward justifying the claim of Colin Wilson "that Whitehead has created his own kind of existentialism; and that it is fuller and more adequate than that of any Continental thinker."[5]

There are many other points as well, in the conception of God and in the general theory of religion, where Cobb creatively elaborates— and, on occasion, corrects—the contributions of Whitehead toward an adequate natural theology. Without commenting further on these points (which, as might be expected, are often involved—and that despite Cobb's always lucid style), I would say simply that this defense of Whitehead's theological significance is throughout impressive and deserves to be taken with the greatest seriousness. This is no doubt the easier for me to say because I so fully share Cobb's conviction about the importance of Whitehead's thought. But Cobb has his own way of being "Whiteheadian," and it is *this* way that I should hope his fellow theologians will recognize and take seriously.

To be sure, there are several places where other students of Whitehead will want to quarrel with Cobb's judgments. His claim, for example, that Whitehead associates God's aim "exclusively with the primordial nature" (p. 183) ignores Whitehead's statement that "the process of finite history is essential for the ordering of the basic vision, otherwise mere confusion."[6] Then, too, Cobb sometimes seems to fail in his intention to avoid falsely theologizing Whitehead's thought. Thus, when he holds that it would be "arbitrary" to deny to God the freedom to "take very particular and decisive initiative" in revealing himself (p. 237), the standard defining this denial as "arbitrary" is not, I believe, a philosophical standard—at least in Whitehead's philosophy. Given the

[5]*Religion and the Rebel* (Boston: Houghton Mifflin, 1957), 317.
[6]*ESP* 89f.

unique relation by which Whitehead conceives God to be related to all other actual entities, such "initiative" would seem to be neither necessary nor possible, and Whitehead himself, so far as I am aware, nowhere suggests anything different.

Yet these points and others that might be mentioned are at most minor failings in a remarkable achievement. Without question, Cobb has succeeded in brilliantly confirming what has long been clearly indicated by the work of Charles Hartshorne and others: that Whitehead's vision of human existence is of the utmost relevance for Christian theology; that it, at last, offers a really serious challenge to the so-called *philosophia perennis*; and that the natural theology it makes possible is excelled by none of the forms now available in the adequacy of its conclusions.

The one place where I have major reservations is Cobb's conception of the nature of natural theology and of how we arrive at a decision between its different forms. I am as unconvinced by his argument in this book as by that in *Living Options in Protestant Theology,* that we can properly speak of "a *Christian* natural theology." I realize, of course, that such speaking often has a legitimate motivation. It lies in the very nature of Christian faith to claim for itself—or for its Lord— the *whole* truth about man's existence before God. Hence, from the standpoint of the theologian, whatever truth can be found in any natural or philosophical theology must somehow be of a piece with what is decisively represented in Jesus Christ. But this does not, I believe, justify our speaking (with the tradition) of "Christian philosophy" or (with Cobb) of "Christian natural theology"—although we *may* say (with Karl Rahner) that any philosophy which is true is to that extent "anonymously" Christian.

One must insist on this because, as Cobb himself recognizes, no philosophy is to be taken seriously as philosophy unless its warrants are those of our common human experience, rather than of the uncommon experience of some special religious tradition. Nor is this requirement altered by the observation, which Cobb seems to me to make rather more of than he should, that the philosopher, too, always stands in a special tradition which shapes his vision. Even if there is no "unhistorical reason," it does not follow, as Cobb sometimes infers, that none of the findings of reason can claim universal validity; nor can one say, as he does, that "the quest for total consensus is an illusion" (p. 266). (Actually, Cobb could be quoted on the other side of both issues— which leaves little doubt that his whole discussion of relativism is unsatisfactory.) The most that follows is the need for the philosopher or natural theologian to remember with Whitehead that "the accurate expression of the final generalities is the goal of discussion and not its origin." But this kind of caution is perfectly compatible with Whitehead's own confidence that "there is no first principle which is in itself unknowable, not to be captured by a flash of insight."[7]

So, too, I cannot share Cobb's judgment that there must be some other standard than its intrinsic philosophical excellence which enables us to decide for a certain form of natural theology. I agree that, if we are to be Christian theologians at all, we must seek the "right" philosophy and that one of the marks of its rightness will indeed be its essential congruence with the claims of Christian faith. But whether there is any such philosophy—and thus whether theology itself is really possible—is a *philosophical* question which must be decided on philosophical terms. The venture of faith as the theologian makes it is that the "right" philosophy is sure to be found. Yet his confidence *is* a venture which only a natural theology, valid by its own standard, is able to confirm.

Analogy and Myth in Postliberal Theology

Bernard E. Meland

This is an occasion for which one can have only gratitude and praise; for it is a time for honoring the achievements of a colleague. But I sense an even more heartening cause for rejoicing as I hear some of the young theologians talk here in the Southwest who recognize a significant thrust toward a new focus of theological thinking in what their colleague, Schubert Ogden, has done. There are intimations of excitement, zeal, and dedication peering out from behind words they use in describing this event to others. There are signs that a movement of life is astir here, and that something of extraordinary importance to many who are present here is being observed and celebrated in this colloquy. This is what gives depth and intensity to this occasion; and we who have been brought in from other centers of learning to participate in this colloquy cannot fail to be caught up in the lure and zest of this creative ferment.

If I may speak personally for a moment, as one who shared in his earlier years of preparation and study, I must say that I enjoy a measure of pride and a great deal of satisfaction in the present attainments and promise of Schubert Ogden. I take this occasion to express my congratulations, and those of my university, his Alma Mater, to him as well as to his colleagues in Perkins School of Theology.

We are gathered here this afternoon, not simply to praise him, but to take seriously the words Schubert Ogden has spoken through this published work *Christ Without Myth*. There is, of course, no greater praise one can give one than to take his words seriously, to be moved by their stimulus, even to react and to resist their incitement, or to counter their claims upon us. It will become obvious to you that I have taken this work seriously, for it speaks to issues which have concerned me deeply in recent years. To illustrate to you how vitally I have re-

From the *Perkins School of Theology Journal*, XV, 2 (Winter 1962). Used by permission of the *Perkins School of Theology Journal* and Bernard E. Meland.

sponded to what Schubert Ogden has to say, I found myself, while reading the galley proof of this book, reading a paragraph and then writing a page, either in response or in reaction to what he had said. I had to give that up, for at that rate I could see that my paper would exceed the length of the book.

This book is more than a presentation and critique of another theologian's method. It is a clarion call to reassert the claims of liberal theology within the range of insights now available to us, and in response to new demands and responsibilities which now make their claim upon us. The sharpness with which Dr. Ogden has focused the alternatives in contemporary theology gives to the present theological task a vividness of purpose and direction which must immediately win our response and gratitude. Even when we take issue with the way he describes some of these alternatives, or the judgment he makes concerning them, we find the clarity of perspective which he has brought to the consideration of these issues significant and helpful.

The patient and meticulous manner in which Ogden delineates the one alternative that is central to his concern, namely, the theological method of Rudolf Bultmann, bespeaks his scholarly temper of mind. There is, to be sure, a vivid display of passion and intensity of feeling as he fends off Bultmann's critics. Like a hard running defensive back, Ogden blocks out one critic after another, enabling Bultmann to come within range of scoring. Then a peculiar thing happens. Just as you expect to see Bultmann crossing the goal line, Ogden turns and blocks him out. This would be strange behavior on the football field. In the theological field, however, this is not unusual. Somehow the critic in us always wins out, as he shall in the paper I am now presenting.

But Professor Ogden's criticisms of Bultmann rest upon so substantial an agreement with the alternative he presents that one must view this final maneuver at the goal line, not as that of negating Bultmann, but of carrying his theological method to a surer victory in establishing a basis for a postliberal theology.

Since I am the first speaker in the colloquy, it is necessary for me to state briefly what is at issue in this book.

The problem centers around the phrase which Bultmann has made famous, "the demythologizing of the New Testament." This problem comes to the front in Bultmann's theology because of his conviction, as Schubert Ogden has said, that "if theological work is properly pursued, it is neither speculative nor scientific in an 'objective' sense, but rather *existentiell*, that is, a type of thinking inseparable from one's most immediate understanding of oneself as a person." Bultmann is concerned "to unfold . . . the *existentiell* self-understanding implicit in Christian faith." Such a self-understanding, says Ogden, has a specific object and content. "It is a self-understanding that is realized . . . in response to the word of God encountered in the proclamation of Jesus Christ. It is always faith in the Kerygma, in the revealed word expressed in the New Testament and made concretely present in the proclamation of the church."

> If this understanding of the nature of theology is taken seriously, however, the contemporary theologian is faced with a fundamental problem. For him, just as for those to whom he speaks, the proclamation of the church in the conceptual form in which it encounters him in the New Testament and in the classical theological tradition, seems unintelligible, incredible, and irrelevant. According to Bultmann, any attempt at the present time to understand and express the Christian message must realize that the theological propositions of the New Testament are not understood by modern man because they reflect a mythological picture of the world that we today cannot share.[1]

We cannot share in this mythological picture, continues Bultmann, because we live and think within "the world-picture formed by modern natural science" and within "the understanding man has of himself in accordance with which he understands himself to be a closed inner unity that does not stand open to the incursion of supernatural powers."[2]

> This sounds very much like the earlier liberal analysis of the situation, but it differs from the earlier liberalism in one fundamental respect. Earlier liberalism saw in the proclamation of the Kerygma itself a stumbling block to modern man, and thus sidled away from its eschatological message, preferring to center upon the ethical dimension of Christian faith as this was expressed in the life and teaching of Jesus. Bultmann, on the other hand, insists that this proclamation of the saving act in Jesus Christ must be retained and restated within existential terms. Thus demythologizing is not a relinquishment of the mystery of kingdom, but a translation of its meaning in terms consonant with man's present self-understanding.

> The issue intensifies as one explores the implications of this last assertion. How does one translate the meaning of the Kerygma in terms consonant with man's present self-understanding? Does one allow the Christian message to coalesce with the philosophy of existence? Or does one hold to the centrality of the historical and saving act of God in Jesus Christ? Although the logic of Bultmann's thought seems to move toward the former, his decision is to affirm the latter. And this gives rise to the claim that inconsistency plagues Bultmann's exposition.

> Now it is with a view to removing this inconsistency, and at the same time to support Bultmann's concern with retaining the Biblical

---

[1]*Christ Without Myth: A Study of The Theology of Rudolf Bultmann* (New York: Harper and Brothers, 1961), 24.
[2]*Ibid.*, 32.

witness, that Schubert Ogden proposes his constructive alternative, based upon the procedure of speaking of God analogically rather than mythologically. In this context, the appeal to the Kerygma becomes an appeal to the act of faith as being *a knowledge of* the universal love of God, concerning which a process metaphysics may provide analogical *knowledge about*. In this way faith and knowledge, Kerygma and the philosophy of existence, are correlated, and the seemingly irreconcilable tension between them is resolved.

II

Before addressing myself directly to questions which are raised in my mind by the analysis of this issue in *Christ Without Myth,* I should like to record certain points at which I find myself heartily in accord with Schubert Ogden. I do this, not simply to soften the barbed sting of the criticism which I shall offer later, but to say as decisively and as positively as I can at the outset that I am mainly sympathetic with the basic thrust and intention of this work. My deviations, I think, are more tactical than substantial; though of this there may be some question when my criticisms are fully stated. But now as to our points of agreement: One is Schubert Ogden's assertion that theology must be postliberal; it cannot be preliberal. It must continue to pursue its task within the critical disciplines that were initiated by liberal scholarship at the beginning of the modern period. Yet it must have a listening ear for voices that speak across the centuries from within more distant perspectives of Christian thought and experience. There are both decisiveness and openness in this scholarly attitude.

A second directive is that theology must be alive to its responsibilities within the culture at large, and be prepared to speak to its contemporary mind as well as to its issues. It cannot be content to withdraw into the sheltered compound of churchanity and to speak a language available only to those initiated into the mysteries of its faith. There are problems here, about which I shall speak later; but the thrust of this concern is one in which I heartily concur.

It follows from this as a third directive that theology will concern itself with the problem of intelligibility in ways that are appropriate to rendering the witness of faith available to modern men and women. There are issues here, too, and I think differences between us in the way we conceive this task, and possibly in the way we understand the claims of intelligibility; but at this stage of my presentation, let me say that with the intention of Professor Ogden's concern with intelligibility in faith, I heartily concur.

Consistent with this note of inclusiveness in matters of faith and culture, I find Dr. Ogden's stress upon the primordial love of God, and what this means for a doctrine of revelation and Christology, singularly valid and refreshing. My own way of speaking of this matter is to insist that the doctrines of redemption and creation must be held together. Any tendency to isolate the doctrine of redemption will appear to set Jesus Christ above the God of creation, and to particularize the faith in Jesus Christ to such an extent that our primordial unity with all men through creation is disavowed. A great deal hinges upon this issue. And with the direction of Ogden's thought on this matter, with certain reservations about which I shall speak later, I find myself in hearty accord.

What this means for our understanding of revelation needs further elaboration than Ogden has been able to give in this book. For various reasons, which I shall make clear, I find it necessary to make more of the spontaneities and depths of history than Ogden has acknowledged, and thus I am led to lift up the notion of the New Creation in Christ with more emphasis than I find Ogden doing in his analysis. That he has not stressed this point is of apiece with his tendency to assimilate the meaning of Christ to the more generalized interpretation of the love of God one finds in metaphysics, particularly that of Charles Harts-horne, wherein neither revelation nor Christ is finally necessary since what is conveyed through them is available through the metaphysical analysis of the meaning of love as it is understood in a fully explicated view of God. This is a point where things begin to pinch more seriously; but I still hold the basic understanding of revelation in Ogden's analysis to be valid, even though his explication and defense of it leave something to be desired theologically.

And finally, I am impressed by the slyness and cogency with which Ogden insinuates the appeal to analogy as an alternative to myth in the constructive argument. I shall have some critical things to say about this proposal, but let it be known that I am impressed by the adversary even as I seek to slay him.

There are other aspects of Professor Ogden's constructive emphasis which lead me to be encouraged by his contributions to what he and I together envisage as directives for a postliberal theology; but these may suffice to express my sense of kinship with what he proposes, and with what he cherishes as a vital concern of Christian faith in the present hour. And now we must turn to the critical phase of this paper wherein I shall designate the points at which I find myself in tension with the theological proposals of this highly significant work, *Christ Without Myth.*

III

It may appear strange to some of you, as you read my paper, that one can concur with another scholar's intention and point of view as heartily as I

claim to concur with that of Schubert Ogden, and yet be so decisive, possibly aggressive, in opposing him on specific issues. It has always been a
conviction of mine that we disagree most intensively on particular issues with those with whom we agree fundamentally. Thus Barth and
Brunner were hotly at one another; and Reinhold Niebuhr and Paul
Tillich, so we are told, made theology interesting and vital at Union
Seminary by the arguments between them, even as they supported and
respected one another deeply. This is because a common vision opens
up common problems upon which there are bound to be differences in
judgment. Because the vision of thought is held in common, the issues
involved in these differences that arise are felt with equal keenness and
intensity. But where differences of this sort exist within a common
vision, it is of the utmost importance that they be stated with candor
and with forthrightness. For the strength and power of any community
of thought lies in the integrity and openness with which basic differences are confronted and with which they are dealt.

I have three questions concerning this work by Schubert Ogden;
they relate both to Ogden's interpretation and defense of Bultmann's
method as an alternative for modern theology, and to Ogden's own constructive effort. All three questions have to do with the adequacy of
the conceptual imagery and presuppositions underlying the method of
demythologizing, particularly as this method addresses itself to the
present task of a postliberal theology.

My first question is, what is the image of the modern mind to which
Bultmann and Ogden would have a postliberal theology address itself?
Lurking behind this question is the further query, has Ogden really
dealt adequately with the criticisms of those who have attacked Bultmann on the scientific imagery which he equates with the modern mind?

When one appeals to "the world-picture formed by modern natural
science" as the common basis for understanding man and his world, do
we not have to be more definitive and discriminating within scientific
imagery itself than either Bultmann or Ogden appear to be? For the fact
is, as modern men, we stand between two scientific visions of man and
his world. As science is commonly understood, even among many sophisticated liberals today, the scientific picture of man and his world
bears the image of a Newtonian form of orderliness in nature which
readily lends itself to observation and description, and to the work of
reason following from such direct apprehension of physical realities.
It is, in fact, a world of orderliness based upon a conception of causality that allows no depth and freedom in nature, no discontinuities, no
unforeseen variations, hence no inexactness or discrepancy in science.
The ways of scientific method are sure and altogether trustworthy.

But the scientific vision of man that informs our most basic research is quite other than this. I refer to relativity physics and quan-

tum theory, and to the revolutionary changes that have come into our scientific estimate of human thinking, and even into areas of experimentation, revising one's understanding of scientific method. Bultmann seems to be making an oblique reference to these changes in saying that "the decisive thing is not the results of scientific thinking but its method." "Has the natural science renounced experimentation?" he asks. And Schubert Ogden adds, by way of amplifying Bultmann's statements, "However much the *results* of scientific research change, the fundamental *method* of science and the picture of the world correlative with it remains constant."[3]

Now we may be looking at different problems here, or have different considerations in mind; but from where I view the matter, Bultmann's own statements seem to evade the crucial aspect of change in scientific thinking affecting the vision of our world; and his position, as amplified by Ogden's comments, seems to me simply not to square with the facts, as one may glean them from hearing scientists talk among themselves. With the change of scientific vision in the present century there has come about a very radical change in the method of science, its being less a description of phenomena and the formulation of universal laws, and more a statistical formulation of probabilities and a venture in determining which of the many probabilities might be taken to be true to fact in this situation. And "the picture of the world correlative with the method of science" which is now in progress is vastly different from that picture of the world which Newtonian science throughout the nineteenth century and well into our own presented. So different is it, in fact, that I would venture to say that the realities of faith which were obscured by human formulations, and thus nonexistent for the liberal mind of the nineteenth and early twentieth centuries, have become remarkably vivid and insistent in our time, thanks in large measure to the new vision of science. This vision has opened up to us the depths and complexities, the discontinuities and indeterminacies of the physical world of nature. I have argued in a forthcoming work, *The Realities of Faith and The Revolution in Cultural Forms,* that the dimension of depth which has appeared in contemporary theology under the discussion of eschatology, has affinities with this new vision of science, if in fact it is not of apiece with it. The mystery of the Kingdom as an intimation of ultimacy in the midst of our immediacies, speaks a language consonant with this new epoch of relational thinking issuing from field theory and the complexity of any description of events that begins with relatedness. A postliberal theology, we have said, must go beyond liberalism, not back of it. But it must go beyond it in scientific imagery as in every other aspect of its thought.

[3]*Ibid.*, 33f.

And now I come to my second question: How adequately have Bultmann and Ogden assessed the capacities of human thought in dealing with the realities of faith? Since a difference in estimating the shift in the vision of science affects one's views concerning the capacity of human observation and its formulations in reporting the realities of experience, one can assume that our views here would diverge somewhat. I sense in Schubert Ogden, especially, a degree of confidence in the formulations of human reason comparable to that of Professor Hartshorne, which I am unable to share. I take my cue here, not only from the critique of reason which the Christian doctrine of man conveys, but from the judgments of relativity science which quite openly place a different estimate upon the powers of human observation and reason in dealing with realities in themselves, than was true of science prior to radiation experiments and subsequent physical theories. The disparity which relativity science finds between man's measure of physical realities and realities in themselves has led to a notion of indeterminacy and depth in experience which would not have occurred to scientists of an earlier period. But it is not indeterminacy in measurement alone that has intruded this notion. The vivid awareness of relationships, arising from field theory, has alerted the modern scientist to the complexity of the phenomena in nature to a degree that has made him cautious about employing his findings for any generalized law beyond the status of a working proposition.

Now the point toward which my remarks are intended to argue is that the canons of reason and observation within a postliberal theology must assume a far humbler role than was observed or exercised by an earlier liberalism. Where depth and complexity are taken seriously, in speaking of history as in speaking of physical realities, something other than appeal to logic, or even to the claims of observation, is involved. The appeals to logic and observation are important to sustain. They represent our most disciplined forms of utterance in dealing with the realities of experience. But they stand under the judgment of the very realities to which they attend. They appeal to these realities as metaphors to recall Whitehead's memorable statement, speaking of the words and phrases which philosophers use: "they remain metaphors mutely appealing for an imaginative leap." As such they are as words listening for a truth that is given, not as one defining or describing that truth.

It is interesting that Schubert Ogden should suggest, by way of finding a means of breaking through Bultmann's dilemma, that we ponder the relation between analogy and myth. I think this has real possibilities: though the danger here, as I see it, is precisely the one that befell Hegel, who assumed that metaphysical thinking was simply mythical thinking grown mature and sure of itself. What happens when this assumption is made is that what was once known as metaphor and as an approximation to meanings apprehended, yet deeper than our recognition of them, become manageable concepts and categories within the human framework of thought. Thus rationality takes over, crowding out the subtle discontinuities hinted at by the word analogy, and the tension between man's thoughts and what is other than man disappears.

This, to my mind, is the crucial problem confronting postliberal theology: How do you employ such a tool of intelligibility as analogy in a way that preserves the tension between what is manageable and unmanageable in the deeper experiences of creaturely existence? Whitehead begins quite boldly declaring his recognition of the limits of human thought in his *Process and Reality,* saying, "Philosophers can never hope finally to formulate these metaphysical first principles"; but by the time his formulation of precise categories has been completed, one feels that confidence in the adequacy of these categories has noticeably risen, almost to the point of taking these forms at face value as being descriptive of the realities to which they point. By the time Whiteheadians begin to distribute this new crop of fundamental notions, process thinking takes on the air of a new rationalism. Thus the demon dogmatism begins to plague us again. I have been a rebel among process theologians, protesting this very tendency to close the gap between manageable and unmanageable aspects of experience. My concern with myth has been motivated, in fact, by the realization that analogy as employed in metaphysics appears unable to hold back the floodwaters of rationalism, once the tenuous "appeal for an imaginative leap" gives way to a more definitive mood of logical analysis. This may be because analogy stresses the note of continuity between thought and being, and does not stress sufficiently the discontinuity that exists. Myth, on the other hand, at least registers the shock of disparity between my thoughts as a human formulation and the reality that is other than my thoughts. I admit it is a weasel word, as Schubert Ogden's discussion in *Christ Without Myth* continually implies. Nevertheless, I would argue that we cannot dispose of it, any more than early man could dispose of it, in so far as we choose to be attentive to that dimension of existence which elicits our sense of creaturehood.

This brings me to my third and final question. Does the discussion in *Christ Without Myth* take adequate account of the nature and status of myth as a cultural form, and thus as an indispensable ingredient of history?

Let me say first that Schubert Ogden seems to me to be perfectly justified in insisting, against Bultmann's critics, that if they are to understand his effort at demythologizing, or to try to interpret it, they must do so within his terms, else confusion follows. Bultmann, says Ogden, employs the terms myth and mythology in the sense of "a language objectifying the life of the gods," or, as we might say, of objectifying the powers of Spirit into a supernaturalism, a super-history transcending or supervening our human history, thus forming a "double history." Now I agree to stay within these bounds of meaning as long as we are simply trying to understand Bultmann, or to interpret him; but the moment we get beyond these tasks to the larger constructive task of a postliberal theology, I want to take issue with this way of dealing with myth. I think Bultmann has adequately defined mythology in its classical sense. But I resist equating myth with mythology.

It may be pertinent to say that Bultmann, when he is speaking of myth, appears to be speaking solely within the context of classical philology and of the historical study of religions that has rested upon its research. Here there is concern with the term only as a conceptual medium for conveying the dramatic logic underlying historic mythologies. What is completely lacking here is the dimension of understanding which cultural anthropology and recent studies in the history of religions has brought to light, namely, that myth is more than a cognitive notion. I would argue that myth provides a deeper orientation in any culture than this kind of analysis assumes.

Myth reaches to the level of the creaturely stance which a people will assume in speaking of their existence. It affects and shapes, not only language, the mode of thinking and speaking, but sensibilities of thought, psychical orientation, thus psychical expectations. One senses this as one moves from one orbit of cultural meaning to another. Different myths have insinuated into the very historical heritage of the respective cultures a continuing fabric of meaning which has immediate and intrinsic intelligibility within that cultural orbit. It directs the way human beings normally think and feel, as one might say; but one really means it is the way human beings normally think and feel within that historic orbit of existence.

Now of this aspect of myth, Bultmann seems oblivious. At least he is indifferent to it, as when he writes that what should disturb his critics is "that philosophy all by itself already sees what the New Testament says."[4] Does this not overlook the fact that all thought occurs within a cultural matrix. Once the revelation of God in Jesus Christ became a concrete historical fact of Western experience, there was no concealing it, not even from philosophers. Or to state it differently, no thinking or feeling of man's being within its orbit of meaning and experience was immune from its shaping. A philosopher may not say, "Jesus Christ is Lord." He may not even acknowledge the name, or think of it. He will still feed upon the sensibilities of thought that issue from its nurturing matrix. Thus to say that a philosopher, even when he is Heidegger, all

[4]Ibid., 69.

by himself sees what the New Testament says, is to appear to have no sense of historical context; certainly not the kind of contextual sensitivity which the cultural anthropologist has come to understand and value.

Now it is possible to come to the Christian understanding of man's existence within the framework of philosophical terms and at the same time to be speaking out of the mythical orientation. Thus when a philosopher like Heidegger or Kamlah "sets forth in purely philosophical grounds a 'secularized' Christian understanding of existence," one should not assume that they are doing so independently of the Christian myth. To be sure, one can say, "But the actualization of the attitude to which they point is not dependent on the event of Jesus Christ"; but it does not follow that "revelation is unnecessary."

The confusion arises here because one assumes that philosophizing occurs in Western culture without benefit of the Judaic-Christian mythos. This I would deny. The very way in which Greek philosophy is read and understood in Western thought is through the imagery and sensibilities of this primal mythos. How else does it happen that the problem of the One and the Many, or any philosophical analysis of the meaning of God, is plagued, or at least challenged by a concern with its implications for a personal deity? The indifference of philosophers to Christianity has nothing to do with their dependence upon a nexus of cultural meaning which, in subtle and unobtrusive ways, permeates every discourse that, of necessity, draws upon a given heritage of accumulative cultural meaning. The philosopher, George Herbert Mead, was acknowledging this when he wrote in *Movements of Nineteenth Century Philosophy* that the notion of Order which looms so importantly in modern science and philosophy was taken over from Christian theology. But in saying that he was not tracing the notion to its source; for back of Christian theology is the Judaic-Christian mythos, the primal source of all our fundamental notions in Western experience.

Now what I am leading up to say is that mythology is expendable. This is the superstructure of myth, the literal and imaginative elaborations of these metaphorical responses issuing in myth. Mythology is expendable; myth is not.

Thus when I observe a meticulous and highly sensitive scholar like Bultmann proceeding with his method of demythologizing to interpret Christian faith exhaustively and without remainder as man's original possibility of authentic historical existence, and then making, as it were, a sharp turn from this procedure in his appeal to the saving event of Jesus Christ, by way of preserving the Kerygma, something demonic in me leaps up with glee, and I want to shout for joy. For it seems to me that, despite his equating of myth and mythology, in the final analysis, his own incurable and inalienable involvement in the Christian mythos impels him to make a distinction between the two. The metaphorical response to the saving act of God in history, that subtle and complex instance of attending to ultimacy in our immediacies, to the mystery of the Kingdom in the midst of historical circumstances, is thus seen to be a persisting and unexpendable witness to the very realities that inform and sustain our authentic existence.

Thus what others have noted and called a great scandal of inconsistency in Bultmann's method strikes me as being singular evidence of his own remarkable sensitivity to the persisting truth of myth, as something *existentiell*, which somehow must stand over against the logic of demythologizing.

The corrective I would like to urge upon Schubert Ogden, then, is not that he abandon his method of process theology based upon analogical thinking, but that he consider some means by which he might avoid the inevitable drift of such thinking toward a closed rationalism, in which only man and his formulations speak forth.

The only concern I have here, really, is that we do not obscure the realities of faith or block them out of view by our human formulations —formulations which depend so exclusively upon resources drawn from present forms of experience for their intelligibility. Something that will continually register the shock of *reality over reason* is needed to keep reasonable men from becoming victims of their own mental enclosures, and thus open to the judgment and grace of the living God.

Psychological and Ontological Perspectives on Faith and Reason

8

Don S. Browning

This essay will attempt to discuss the relation of faith and reason. At the outset, it recognizes as fundamental the Protestant idea that reason, starting from outside the circle of faith, cannot work its way to an affirmation of the central Christian truths. This is so, not because reason is without access to sufficient data that point to these truths, but because reason is never unencumbered by sin so that it can appropriately handle the data available to it. Our discussion will be guided by the following question: If Jesus Christ overcomes the distortions of sin, at least to the point that reason can acknowledge the grace and providence of God, is it then possible to move beyond the confines of the circle of faith for further witness to and verification of the faith?

It is the intent of this essay to bring together resources from psychology and ontology in an effort to clarify the relation of faith and reason. Although the ontological resource will be more the fundamentally clarifying tool, there are two psychological constructs that I intend to set into the context of my onto-epistemological position as supplemental. These constructs deal with the "self-concept" and the structure and dynamics of the "therapeutic relation."

The problem of the relation of faith and reason can be stated as follows: What is the relation between those certitudes man gains through his ability to specify, abstract, and manipulate reality through certain publicly verifiable symbolic forms and those certitudes man gains through commitment to truth claims, be they religious or otherwise, which do not readily submit to clear and distinct symbolic specification or easily attainable public verification? Truth claims that seem to be specifiable in that they lend themselves to public verification are often called matters of reason. Truth claims that do not readily submit to public verification are often called matters of faith.

In the context of Christian theology, the problem of faith and rea-

Reprinted from *The Journal of Religion*, XLV (October 1965). Used by permission of the University of Chicago Press and Don S. Browning.

son asks this question: What is the relation between the certitude that
God enters into a saving relationship with man (most effectively and
uniquely in the historical existence of Jesus of Nazareth) and those
certitudes that seem tc spring from man's commonly held ability to abstract and verify the forms of events and processes in the world? In
brief, we will be inquiring into the structure of faith and the structure
of reason and their interrelation, if any.

Ontological and Epistemological Considerations

Two basic questions, one ontological and the other epistemological,
must be dealt with before the relation of faith and reason can be properly addressed. The ontogical question is: What is the relation of
God to the world? The epistemological question is: What is the relation of symbols to reality? My position will assert that there is a participative relationship between symbols and reality and a participative
relationship between God and the world. Hence, the ontological and
epistemological questions converge in the concept of participation or
what Dorothy Emmet calls "rapport."

Miss Emmet develops her epistemological position with a special
interest in retaining the concept of "reality" or "real things" as a necessary dimension of our philosophy of science. She opposes idealist
thinkers, such as Cassirer and Eddington, who suggest that the concepts
of "things" and "causality" are no longer important for scientific purposes. Emmet makes a distinction between the adverbial and the accusative modes of perception. The adverbial mode is an "integral feeling,
qualifying a state of experience."[1] It is a physiological response to the
energetic shocks from our physical environment. This physiological
response sets up affective tones or bodily feelings which constitute the
subjective forms of the energetic processes transmitted to us from our
environment. The accusative mode of perception abstracts and differentiates certain simplified symbolic forms from the affective responses of
the adverbial mode and, in turn, projects these forms onto the external
environment.[2]

Basic to an understanding of these two modes of perception is her
concept of rapport or preanimistic relatedness. Emmet's concept of rapport points to a basic "continuity of our functions and activities with
those of the environing world."[3] She believes, with A. N. Whitehead,
that the human organism "is part of a dynamic system of nature, a field
of energetic processes of which the cerebroneural events are termi-

[1]Dorothy Emmet, The Nature of Metaphysical Thinking (London: Macmillan,
1957), 42.
[2]Ibid., 43.
[3]Ibid., 64.

nals."[4] This vague sense of interpenetrating processes constituutes the raw material out of which adverbial perception arises and is the basis for our naïve confidence that our perceptions refer to something "real" in the external world.

At the adverbial level of perception the continuity of functions between us and the world is *felt* as patterned qualities. The adverbial mode of perception must be understood as a response, a response that has some identity or correspondence with the patterned processes playing upon the organism but that, at the same time, is not unambiguously reproductive of these energetic activities.[5] Even though some originative activity may occur at this primitive level of physiological responsiveness, it is holistic in nature. It is a response of the whole organism to events in their full qualitative richness. The major abstractive and originative processes tend to occur in the accusative mode of perception.

The accusative mode of perception should be understood as a mode of construction. It differentiates the affective responses of the adverbial mode and abstracts simplified, streamlined symbolic forms from the original affective response. These forms or constructs may appear as sense or sensation such as "green" abstracted from our experience of "becoming greened."[6] In turn, the form "green" is projected on to the spatially extended world giving us the concept, perhaps, of a "green tree" instead of a "tree greening us," which, in the adverbial mode, is what we are really experiencing. It should be noted that although perceptions in the accusative mode are simplified and abstracted from the more qualified and holistic perceptions of the adverbial mode, they can still be said to have a participative relation with the organism's *response* and the energetic processes to which this response, at least in part, conforms. Only at a later and more refined level in the symbolic process can it be said that symbols become arbitrary and have no inherent or participative relation to the processes they symbolize. At this level, they are called "signs."[7]

[4]*Ibid.*, 60. As is well known, Emmet is a leading Whiteheadian interpreter. Her distinction between adverbial and accusative perception is a clarification of what Whitehead referred to as "causal efficacy" and presentational immediacy." Cf. PR 255–279. I have chosen to use Emmet's formulation of these concepts primarily because her clarifications, and, I might add, simplifications, better lend themselves to the purpose of this article.

[5]At this point it should be emphasized that I am following Emmet through this essay in her contention that the structural identity of correspondence between environmental processes and our feeling responses is not a one-to-one identity. According to her, novelty appears *before* as well as *in* conceptual transformation. Whitehead himself may have emphasized a more direct correspondence between the energetic shocks of the environment and our physiological response. Emmet, 61.

[6]*Ibid.*, 43.

[7]*Ibid.*, 58.

The Philosophy of Science

Before we can understand how Emmet's onto-epistemological position feeds into her philosophy of science, we must investigate her concepts of experience, inference, and transcendence.

Emmet defines experience to include both adverbial perceptual experience and accusative perceptual experience, that is, both the process of feeling or experiencing data and the process of ordering this data.[8] As was indicated earlier, experience at the accusative level is always a *construct* of experiencing or feeling at the adverbial level. Or to put it differently, experience at the conscious or accusative level is always an *inference* built up from experiencing on the preconscious or adverbial level. (Preconscious, as I am using it, means unsymbolized.) Hence, our conscious symbolizations of the external world do not capture what these events are in and of themselves. They only represent an inference about what they *might* be in and of themselves based on how they seem to affect us at the level of adverbial experiencing. The basis of our symbolic representation of the event is our own response to it. Since the event, at least in part, *forms* the response, the event can be said to be *in* our experience, while at the same time, transcending our experience. To "symbolize the event" means to symbolize what *transcends* our experiencing on the basis of what is *in* our experiencing. As Emmet states, "indirect inferences as to the transcendent character of these events are built up from our responses to them."[9]

She says that this inferential procedure is basically an analogical process. All attempts to know the transcendent aspect of events must be thought of as analogical in character. Emmet defends the analogical process against charges that it is primitive and crude by saying:

> But if we say that we need to keep the concept of "things" as a recognition of processes transcending our conceptual forms, and if we also allow that we have no direct knowledge of the intrinsic nature of these processes, we shall have to ask whether we are forced to try to conceive of them in concepts drawn by analogy from interpretations of experience.[10]

The planetary theory of atoms, the mechanical model, field theory, and organic models are well-known examples of interexperiential models constructed to represent realities partially transcending experience. The method of analogy rests on the assumption that there is at least a partial identity of structure between the qualitative pattern of the event and our response to it. If there is distortion between event and responses, it is, at least, Emmet suggests, a systematic distortion.[11] The very progress

[8]*Ibid.,* 19.
[9]*Ibid.,* 86.
[10]*Ibid.*
[11]*Ibid.,* 90.

of science demonstrates that this systematic distortion does not completely destroy our veridical comprehension of the structure of external events. Since there is at least a partial identity between these structures and our response, there is also at least a partial objectification of the external event in the adverbial response of the percipient. Hence, the possibility of the analogical method rests on the principle that in the concepts of rapport and adverbial response, ontology and epistemology meet. The analogy participates in the reality it represents. Further implications for what this means in terms of God's relatedness to the world will be mentioned later.

Distortions in the Symbolic Process
and the Relevance of the "Self-Concept"

With this ontological and epistemological framework in mind, let us investigate the various ways in which man fails to grasp symbolically the realities to which he is related. Our study will suggest that there are three ways in which symbolization can become distorted—through processes of selection, abstraction, and protection.

Distortions of selection and abstraction have already been discussed. Selection is a process of ordering and valuating the data of experience according to some principle of relevance and operates at both levels of perception. In the organic responses of the adverbial level, selective processes operate according to what is relevant to the fulfilment of the organism as a whole.[12] At the same time, although some selectivity may occur, adverbial responses tend to take the character of "total assertions" of the whole organism about the whole object it confronts.[13] At the accusative level, or level of conscious symbolization, whole masses of irrelevant detail are excluded according to some principle of relevance operating in consciousness at the time. The construct of the "self-concept" will help us understand how the principle of relevance operates at this level.[14]

Processes of selection involve some abstraction because selection abstracts events out of their relational context. But more directly, ab-

[12]*Ibid.*, 42. In addition, a similar principle can be gleaned from the writings of Carl Rogers in his distinction between organismic experience and self-experience. When organismic experiencing is dominant, things tend to be valuated according to what is enhancing for the organism as a whole. Cf. Carl Rogers, *Client-centered Therapy* (Boston: Houghton Mifflin, 1951), 487.

[13]Emmet, 141.

[14]The reader should be cautioned that from here on I am not confining myself to an exposition of Emmet. Her thought will be used as a resource, but her concepts often will be woven into other sources as they take shape in my own constructive thinking.

straction refers to processes of simplification and differentiation. Simplification occurs when the full richness of the qualitative pattern is reduced to a symbolic form. Differentiation occurs when the molar richness of perceptions in the adverbial mode gain heightened discreetness in the accusative mode. Both differentiation and simplification largely occur in the transition between the adverbial and accusative mode. Definiteness, simplicity, order, and consciousness are gained; wholeness, richness, and vitality tend to be lost.[15]

To talk about distortions of protection, we must set the construct of the "self-concept" into the context of this theory of perception. But first, we must ask, what is the self-concept? Second, how does it arise? And third, how does it distort the symbolization of our perceptions? In brief, the self-concept distorts the symbolization process through mechanisms of protection. Let us now elucidate.

Carl Rogers makes a distinction between the total experiencing of the organism and the self-concept. The self or self-concept (they are actually interchangeable for him) is the center of the organism's awareness of its functioning and symbolized as "me," "I," or "mine."[16] The self is the most dominating factor in consciousness and has great control over *what* and *how* experiences attain symbolization in awareness. But to understand how the self influences symbolization, we must ask how it develops.

Although Rogers believes that the self *arises* out of what Andras Angyl calls the "gradient of autonomy" (the infant's experience that certain things seem to be more under his control than other things),[17] the *elaboration* of one's self-evaluation generally reflects the "conditions of worth" introjected by the significant adults in one's environment.[18] The child tends to integrate the appraisals and conditions of worth of others into his own self-concept. In turn, the child may consider unacceptable any experiencing that contradicts the self's conditions of worth and acceptability.

This inevitably leads to a distortion of symbolization. The self establishes defensive mechanisms designed to protect the validity of its conditions of worth. These protective devices operate by either (1) denying symbolization altogether or (2) distorting symbolization, that is, symbolizing the experience as something it is not.[19] For example,

[15]Emmet, 43–46. Cf. PR 255–279. Also see Bernard Meland, *Faith and Culture* (London: Allen & Unwin, 1955) 22–36.

[16]Rogers, 497.

[17]*Ibid.*, 498.

[18]The construct of "conditions of worth" is a relatively new element in Roger's theoretical apparatus. For a discussion of this concept see his most definitive theoretical statement, " A Theory of Therapy, Personality, Interpersonal Relationships, as Developed in the Client-centered Framework," *Psychology: A Study of a Science*, Sigmund Koch, ed. (New York: Basic Books, 1958), III, 224.

[19]Rogers, *Client-centered Therapy*, 503.

what organismic valuational processes may feel as good or true may be symbolized as bad or false by the self. Or, of course, the reverse could be true. When disparity exists between organismic valuation (what Emmet would call the "adverbial mode") and the self's symbolization, incongruence with either neurotic or psychotic variations is said to exist.[20] When severe incongruence exists between the self and organismic experiencing, symbolization does not participate in the realities to which they refer. This is typical for neurotic people. Their words seem to have a hollow sound. Their symbols do not participate in the depths of their adverbial experiencing.

If, as we will attempt to do later, some correlation can be drawn between the conditions of worth of the self and the Christian concept of sin, then a ground will be laid for demonstrating the relation of sin and symbolization (reason) in a more concrete way than is usually accomplished. In addition, if some correlation can be drawn between the valuational processes at the level of organismic or adverbial experiencing and what can appropriately be called faith, then the relation between faith, reason, and sin can be specified.

The Structure of Faith

I entered into the earlier long discussion on ontology and epistemology in preparation for submitting and testing the following assumption: Let us assume that the way we come to faith in God and come to develop symbolic expressions about relationship to Him is not fundamentally different from the way we come to have certitude about and develop symbolic specificity about our other relations. This assumption is simpler and more economical than the Kantian assumption which believes that our certitude and symbolizations about God are of a different order than those referring to other relationships.

Now that this assumption has been made, we must *test* it. To test it we must determine what *sense* can be made out of the idea of "faith in God" when it is ordered by the onto-epistopsychological categories I have just set forth.

On the basis of this assumption it would follow that faith in God is grounded upon an experiencing of God in the adverbial mode of perception. Furthermore, it follows that all men experience or feel God at this level. Men are not divided between those who have this primordial faith and those who do not; they are divided between those who have symbolized their own self-concept around this primordial faith and those who have not. On the basis of our prior discussions, it can be said that coming to a knowledge about anything, be it God or other actualities, is a process of moving from depth (molar bodily valuation in the adverbial mode) to clarity (the abstracted definiteness of the accusative mode). Insofar as the more fundamental stage is characterized by total valuational responses about the good or bad, the better or worse, the trustworthy or untrustworthy, the operations of this stage are suggestive of what is commonly considered to be characteristic of faith. Faith, then, can be understood as a total valuational response to the qualitative structure of another actuality prior to any clear specification about what is in fact good or bad, trustworthy or untrustworthy about the other actuality. If this is faith, then all our cognitive operations involve a dimension of faith.[21] Within this formula we can see how it is possible to assert that all men have faith (a molar adverbial response to God), although all men have not moved to sufficient or adequate accusative clarity about this faith.

What then is the structure of faith? Faith is (1) a total valuational response resulting from (2) a partial conformation of our feelings to the pattern of feelings or qualities of another actuality (3) with which we are in some way internally related or participatively connected.

First, faith is an unreserved or total assertion as opposed to a reserved, conditioned, or partial assertion based upon a balance of probabilities. It is a response of the whole organism to the qualitative essence of the whole object confronting us. For example, we might confront a man about whom we could make several positive partial assertions but feel on the whole that he was not a good or trustworthy man. Our total response to the man would not be a balance of probabilities between possible partial assertions about the man. Balancing probabilities takes us into a theoretical and analytic attitude foreign to the character of faith or adverbial responses that tend toward an unreserved "yes" or "no."[22] Faith, understood as an unreserved "yes" as opposed to a balance of probabilities, is consistent with the Reformation view of faith. At the same time, a balancing of probable and partial assertions characteristic of accusative activity does have a place at later stages when articulation of the faith becomes the task at hand.

Second, faith is somehow self-transcending, or, as some theologians would put it, ecstatic. Although our adverbial perceptive activity is never completely without some selective influence, if our perceptive activity ever moves beyond our own self-structures, it is at the point of the adverbial mode of perception. The phenomenon of *subception*

---

[21]Scientific discourse has called these primitive judgments of importance and relevance "hunches," "intuitions," etc. But the close relationship between these phenomena and what religious discourse has called faith, has often been overlooked.

[22]Emmet, 142.

discussed by Rogers and *selective inattention* reported by H. S. Sullivan demonstrate that it is possible for the organism as a whole to conform to or experience events that the higher conscious processes will fail to detect.[23] Hence, the inhibiting and habit-ridden structures of consciousness are transcended by perception in the adverbial mode. This leads us to assert the self-transcending or ecstatic character of the unreserved response of the faith-like adverbial valuations.

Third, faith is a total or unreserved response to or assertion about something with which we have a relationship. This response arises out of an interrelation of processes, a fundamental condition of rapport between ourselves and our environment. We cannot respond to that to which we are not related. I am suggesting that our understanding of faith in God be built on the same principle. There must be some kind of interrelation or internal relation between God and ourselves if we are to have a response to God. Assuming this interrelationship, it follows that our feelings about God are rooted in our participation in God or, to put it differently, God's participation in us. It would also follow from this onto-epistemological stance that our feelings about God would have at least some continuity with the form of God's feelings, that is, the form of the quality of His own life.

Faith, then, as was stated earlier, is a total valuational response to the qualitative structure of another actuality prior to any clear specification about the definite details of the other actuality. Insofar as this is true, all perceptive activity demonstrates something of the structure of faith.

The Structure of Reason

Let us now turn to the structure of reason. For the sake of simplicity it might be tempting to associate reason solely with the abstractive, discriminating, and simplifying function of the accusative mode of perception. But it seems more appropriate to also speak of "the depth" of reason by pointing to the fact that the valuational responses of the adverbial mode contain the forms that the accusative mode abstracts and gives distinctness. Reason in its entirety includes both depth and surface dimensions, although in modern times it has often been associated more closely with the accusative mode.[24]

---

[23]For a discussion of the concept of subception, turn to Rogers, *Client-centered Therapy,* 507. For a discussion of selective inattention, refer to H. S. Sullivan, *Interpersonal Theory of Psychiatry* (New York: W. W. Norton, 1953), 233–234.

[24]The "depth of reason" is a term introduced by Paul Tillich in his *Systematic Theology.* 3 vols. (Chicago: University of Chicago Press, 1951), I, 32. Tillich contrasts this with "technical reason." We have used Tillich's term in this essay in

Verification is often considered to be a matter closely associated with the processes of reason. Verification concerns whether a particular symbolic form abstracted in the accusative mode is adequately descriptive of the event to which it refers. Of course, this statement raises the question of the criterion used in the phrase "adequately descriptive." I will contend that a symbolic form or proposition is adequate to the events it is attempting to represent if it is internally coherent (the idealist position held by Eddington and Cassirer),[25] externally coherent with other perspectives on the same events,[26] and fruitful in such a way as to give rise to further observation.[27] A satisfactory theory of verification must rely on all three. At the same time, it is my contention, as it would be Emmet's, that the validity of the first two must be based on the assumption underlying the third, that is, that our symbolic forms must be thought to refer to real "things" or events to which we must respond and to which we are related according to the concept of rapport.

The idea of internal functional coherence (the idealist's sole principle of verification) is based upon the assumption that there is no necessary connection between our symbolic forms and external reality. Hence, the concept of "things" and "causality" can be dispensed with.

The principle of external coherence asserts that the various scientific disciplines constitute different perspectives that center on the same data. Any one perspective is an abstraction and can never tell the whole truth about the event being studied. Hence, the validity of one perspective depends upon the extent to which its propositions cohere with the propositions of perspectives external to its own. Whitehead was aware of the importance of this principle for all scientific verification. It has been suggested for theological purposes by Daniel Day Williams.[28]

These two principles, when set within the context of the principle of fruitfulness as developed by Emmet, give a full and wholesome view of the process of verification. Symbolic forms are fruitful if they lead

---

order to indicate what his categories, which must be understood within the context of a more classical metaphysics, might mean in the context of a so-called process onto-epistemological position such as Emmet represents. What I am calling the "surface" dimension of reason (the accusative mode) is roughly analogous to what Tillich means by "technical reason."

[25] Emmet, 69.

[26] PR 15. In reality, Whitehead employs all three of these principles as would Emmet because of her general dependence on Whitehead. I have not found, though, a place where she explicitly mentions the principle of external coherence.

[27] Emmet, 95.

[28] Williams, "Truth in the Theological Perspective," *Journal of Religion,* XXVIII (October 1948), 242–254.

to further variations in our adverbial responses. Emmet writes, with regard to the use of analogical models, that their value "depends largely on how far they play back in suggesting further correlations and differentiations in our responses."[29] We can say that by using this or that symbolic form or proposition "the processes beyond us are so differentiated as to produce these differences of response in us. We can only indirectly conjecture their intrinsic modes of interconnection from studying the minutiae of the distinctions of our own responsive sensations."[30] Hence, verification is an endless circle of bringing the gross variations in our adverbial responses to clarity in the accusative mode and then using these more definite forms as guides for further experiencing and responsiveness in the adverbial mode.

If faith is closely related to the adverbial mode of perception, then faith may have an important role in keeping the higher symbolic processes in contact with reality, that is, the richer qualitative processes from which all experience arises. This suggests, once again, that faith is the depth of reason, and that verification involves reason in both its depth and surface dimensions. True, we have *knowledge* only when we have grasped a pattern of events with a high degree of symbolic definiteness. Some events do not yield to a high degree of symbolic specificity. But symbolic expressions referring to these events are not necessarily to be considered false. It only means that symbolic definiteness is *more difficult* to achieve with these events. It is my contention that matters of religious faith refer to events of just this character.

What does this position mean for religious discourse? Faith, when understood in its specifically religious context, refers to that total valuational response of trusting gratitude to our most fundamentally all-embracing relationship called God. From this response, then, we abstract forms with which we attempt to specify our experience of this relationship. When these symbolic forms remain at the level of dramatic imagery, faith is operating at the level of myth or confessional theology. When our symbolic forms begin to lose their dramatic quality and gain more precision, faith is operating at the level of scientific or philosophical theology. Simply because the datum "God" is more diffuse and complex than other more simple and finite structures, it does not mean that our experience of Him is unreal or that our attempt to symbolize this experience is meaningless.[31] It only means that this

---

[29]Emmet, *op. cit.*

[30]*Ibid.*, 95.

[31]It has been the tendency of modern science to believe that that which does not submit to clear and distinct specification (by which is generally meant clear and distinct experimental results according to certain laws of probability) cannot be intelligently dealt with and, therefore, either does not exist or should not be

datum does not submit to as high a degree of specification as other datum. Following Aristotle and Whitehead, it is unreasonable to expect a datum to submit to a more rigorous degree of specification than is appropriate to the complexity of the datum.[32] At the same time, some religious discourse is more meaningful than other discourse, and it is precisely the task of theology to discover the most adequate symbolic forms using the three principles of verification outlined above.

Religious discourse also needs to concern itself with the other two principles, that is, it must be internally meaningful and externally coherent with other disciplines. The presupposition behind the principle of external coherence is that as there are surface and depth dimensions to reason, there are surface and depth dimensions to reality and that God objectifies himself in the depths of every finite structure as its ground. This means that an analysis of the structure and relations of any finite actuality should, at the same time, reveal intimations about the nature of its ground. Hence, the data of all disciplines are the same except for the difference that theology attends to both depth and surface dimensions of reality, whereas other disciplines tend to concentrate more on the surface aspects. But insofar as depth and surface dimensions of reality have some continuity with one another, specification of the structures of either should tend to cohere with the other. Hence, the principle of external coherence should be operative as a criterion of verification for religious discourse.

Sin and Distortions in the Symbolic Process

Earlier in the paper, three ways were mentioned in which the process of symbolization can be distorted. The first two processes, that is, distortions of selection and abstraction, seem to be inherent difficulties in the symbolic process. They seem to be the price we pay for clearness and distinctness. Distortions of selection and abstraction become demonic when they come under the domination of the third type of distortion in the symbolic process—distortions of protection. Selection and abstraction are demonic when they become involved in the protective maneuvers of the self's conditions of worth. One of the conditions of worth of the modern mentality is the drive for clarity and specificity referred to above. The relevance of this discussion of the self in the context of the problem of faith and reason stems from the

---

taken seriously. But such an overemphasis upon the clear and distinct at the expense of the deep and complex should not be considered a fundamental challenge to the validity of religious experience or the meaningfulness of religious discourse. Cf. Meland, op. cit., p. 27.

[32]PR 11. Also see Aristotle, "Ethica Nicomachea" in Basic Works of Aristotle, Richard McKeon, ed. (New York: Random House, 1941), 936.

basic religious intuition that reason is not free to know God because of its corruption by sin and that the seat of sin is somehow in the self. It is the contention of this essay that this intuition is fundamentally correct.

Earlier it was indicated that the protective and defensive activities of the self resulted in distorted or denied symbolization for those felt experiences that seemed to contradict the conditions of worth around which the self is organized. From the perspective of Christian theology, any attempt to base one's worth or justification on something external to one's original justification in God has been understood as sin. A growing body of New Testament exegesis is interpreting sin as a matter of setting one's mind on "flesh" (sarx). Setting one's mind on sarx is attempting to use the created world as the source and justification of one's life. This is sin and idolatry because God is the sole source of both the means of life and the justification (worth) of life.[33]

Although Christians have seen their ultimate worth as derivative of their relationship to God, it is precisely the character of this relationship that there are no conditions of worth attached to it. This is the meaning of agape. It means that the giving of God's love is not conditioned by the prior worth of the recipient. Man's sin is that he thinks there are conditions of worth and proceeds to organize his self around them, thereby estranging himself from all that seems to contradict these conditions of worth. From the perspective of the conditions of worth of man's sin, God's free relationship, in which there are no conditions of worth attached, must necessarily appear as a threatening contradiction to the validity of sin's conditions of worth. The self can defend itself from its experience of God's freely given relationship by denying it altogether or by distorting it into something it is not—possibly a conditioned relationship.

An example of this can be seen in psychotherapy when the client may experience (subceive) the therapist's unconditioned acceptance at the level of organismic or adverbial feeling but, at the same time, perceive this unconditioned love as a threat to the self's conditions of worth—a threat that must be denied or distorted. Taking our clue from this, it is possible for us to understand how one might have an adverbial feeling of God's unconditioned love but distort or deny it at the level of conscious symbolization because it contradicted the self's conditions of worth.

In view of these statements, the meaning of revelation can now be stated. *Revelation is not the manifestation of God's love to those who are unrelated to it.* Revelation, at least in terms of its *subjective pole,*

---

[33]Rudolf Bultmann, *Theology of the New Testament,* trans. K. Grobel (New York: Charles Scribner's Sons, 1959), 232–246.

is the emergence of our response to this love into *conscious and appropriate symbolization*. We have already hinted as to how important symbolization is. It is only through adequate symbolization that the self becomes integrated into the deeper feelings of the adverbial mode. Anything short of some adequacy of symbolization will mean that the self will be estranged from these feelings and, hence, to some extent, be estranged from God. Revelation is always a matter of bringing depth and surface into congruence with one another. *Thus, revelation is always a matter of salvation.* In order for the self to become integrated with God's unconditional love, it must relax or repudiate the conditions of worth that are threatened by this love. The extent to which the self begins to do this is the extent to which the estrangement between self and the organism's deeper feelings about God is overcome. This is how revelation and salvation are equivalent.

But how must we understand revelation in terms of its *objective pole*? This is where the event of Jesus Christ must be considered. If sin is a matter of estrangement from our adverbial response to God because we have organized the self around certain conditions of worth taken over from the created world (*sarx*), it becomes clear that in order for the self to be redirected toward its own immediate adverbial response to God, it must be confronted by an unambiguous manifestation of God's love in the realm of *sarx* toward which it is looking for its worth and justification. One's own adverbial experience of God's unconditioned love may not penetrate the self and its conditions of worth because it is the very nature of sin to look to the created world for its justification and worth. A contingent manifestation of God's love in the figure of Jesus Christ is a divine strategy to address man at the very point his distortion has fixated him, that is, in the realm of *sarx*. This is what it means to say that in Jesus Christ, God became flesh (*sarx*).

But the objective pole of revelation in Jesus Christ does not bring us into relation with a reality to which we were earlier unrelated. Jesus Christ is the particular and unique manifestation of a general ontological reality that has objectified itself into the depths of all adverbial experiencing. Through Jesus Christ we come into conscious and appropriate symbolization of our adverbial response to God. Because of the overdetermined preoccupation of sin with *sarx*, God must manifest his love in the realm of *sarx* before he can become the occasion by which we can be reunited with our own more immediate relation to him.[34]

[34]Since Soren Kierkegaard's emergence as a significant force in contemporary Protestant theology, there has been a spirit that has tended to minimize God's real ontological relation to the world and to man. Kierkegaard repudiated the idea that Jesus Christ was the *occasion* through which we reclaimed an appropriate adjustment of our lives with God. He opposed the Socratic doctrine of

But simply because the special nature of sin demands a contingent act on the part of God to overcome it, we must not conclude that we are dependent upon this contingent act for all further verification of our faith. Because of God's general ontological relation to the world, what one becomes free to discern in Jesus Christ has an empirical validity which can transcend the biblical witness. This does not exclude the biblical witness; rather it means that the biblical witness, in fact, *makes sense with the rest of reality.* On the basis of this position, it becomes possible to come into dialogue with other positions, not just to learn what these disciplines tell us about the inauthenticity of the world, but also to learn a word of "revelation," that is, a word of truth about God. Without setting the problem of faith and reason in the context of some general ontology of events as has been done here, our dialogue can only be one-sided and imperialistic.

---

recollection because it implied that man had a prior knowledge of God which the historic event of Jesus Christ only awakened. To his thinking, this reduced the crucial character of the historic Christ event. Cf. *Philosophical Fragments,* trans. David Swenson (Princeton: Princeton University Press, 1958), 5–28. As long as Kierkegaard had no model with which to work but the Socratic doctrine of recollection, we can understand and appreciate his point. The metaphysic we are advocating is not susceptible to the same difficulties. With this metaphysic, man has no independent source of his knowledge of God that he "owns" and that must be awakened by some objective historic event. Instead, man is always dependent upon the ever constant inflow of God's ontological relationship in the depths of his adverbial experiencing. The event of Jesus Christ then makes it possible for man to adjust his historic ego (his self) to this ever newly objectified datum deep in his adverbial experience. In this system the crucial character of the historic Christ event is preserved as well as God's general ontological relation with the world.

Contemporary Analysis: 9
The Metaphysical Target
and the Theological Victim

Malcolm L. Diamond

The revival of serious work in philosophical theology that has been spearheaded by the work of Charles Hartshorne is most welcome.[1] It represents a radical change in the theological atmosphere which, for many years after World War II, was dominated by existentialism. During this period, Hartshorne's efforts to introduce logical consideration into theological discourse were constantly turned aside with variations on Kierkegaardian themes. He was accused of using an "objectifying" approach to God, that is, he was accused of excessive reliance on philosophical techniques and of excessive concern for metaphysical issues. Kierkegaard himself had scornfully dismissed the objectifying approach by saying that those who used it were bound to find themselves in the situation of the traveler who asked an Englishman if the road they were standing on led to London. The Englishman replied that it did indeed go to London. Despite this, the traveler never reached that city because the Englishman had neglected to tell him that he was proceeding in the wrong direction.[2]

We have learned a great deal from the religious existentialists, especially about the nature of faith. They contrasted the vitality and strenuousness of authentic faith with the sterility of prefabricated responses to arid dogmas. In elaborating the notion of authentic faith, religious existentialists relied heavily on categories drawn from relations between persons, for example, love, trust, and hope. In transferring these to man's relations to God, there was the obvious problem of providing a conceptual system for coping with the fact that God, by contrast with human partners of such relations, is nonsensible. How-

From *The Journal of Religion*, XLVII, 3 (July 1967). Used by permission of The University of Chicago Press and Malcolm L. Diamond.

    [1]Thirty authors contributed essays to W. L. Reese and E. Freeman, eds., *The Hartshorne Festschrift, Process and Divinity* (LaSalle, Ill., 1964).

    [2]*Philosophical Fragments*, 2d ed. (Princeton, N.J., 1962), n. 1, pp. 79ff.

ever, the religious existentialists turned this sort of theological problem aside by stressing the elements of trust and risk involved in authentic faith and by noting that a true lover does not seek "objective" validation of the worth of his beloved. As a result, for thinkers whose problem is: "How can a philosophically self-conscious individual—believer or not—*understand* what is meant by God?" the emphases of the religious existentialists are apt to seem very much beside the point. In light of the many contradictory and absurd things that have been said about God through the ages, a person worried about the *intellectual* problems has to confront the central problem of philosophical theology: the formulation of a conceptual scheme that is capable of discriminating between possible ideas of God and nonsense. No one in our time has made more significant contributions to this issue than Charles Hartshorne.

It is a tribute to Hartshorne's work that some of the best religious thinkers are dealing with these metaphysical issues. Furthermore, many of them have absorbed the lessons of the religious existentialists, which should prevent a repetition of some of the errors of the past. One of his leading disciples among contemporary philosophical theologians, Schubert Ogden, in two essays which have appeared in this *Journal,* has tried to set up ground rules for work in philosophical theology, and he has commented on the possibilities for dialogue between philosophers and theologians.[3] Much as I applaud his efforts—indeed, my own realization of some of the limitations inherent in the existentialistic approach to theology owes much to his influence—I must register a basic disagreement with one aspect of Ogden's work: his reading of the contemporary philosophical scene.

Ogden thinks that the demise of logical positivism has initiated a pluralistic era in philosophy and that this provides good grounds for hoping that fruitful discussions between theologians and philosophers are again possible. On the surface, Ogden's rather optimistic estimate of the possibilities for dialogue between theologians and philosophers is not unreasonable. Both the logical positivism which played a prominent role on the philosophical scene for a long time, and the religious existentialism that dominated the theological scene for such a long time, were vehemently anti-metaphysical. One would therefore expect their decline to enhance the prospects for the production of significant work in philosophical theology, work that would be taken seriously by post-positivistic analytic philosophers, and especially by those analysts who are again engaging in metaphysics. Therefore, Ogden chides Paul van Buren for stating (in *The Secular Meaning of the Gospel*) that a new

---

[3]"Theology and Objectivity," *Journal of Religion,* XLV (1965); "Theology and Philosophy: A New Phase of the Discussion," *Journal of Religion,* XLIV (1964).

analytic consensus has succeeded the positivistic one and that this new consensus rules out serious consideration of the concept of transcendence by those philosophers who adhere to it.[4] Despite the surface plausibility of Ogden's position, I think that his view is over-optimistic.

Positivism is dead; on that all are agreed. Furthermore, I would agree with Ogden, against van Buren, that no simple and all-embracing consensus has succeeded it. Adherents of the broad movement that might be called "philosophical analysis" displayed an intricate tangle of methodological tendencies, tentative hypotheses, and personal alliances. Nevertheless, I would side with van Buren against Ogden in maintaining that with regard to the issue of theological transcendence a consensus still prevails. Contemporary analysts are no more hospitable to this concept than were their positivistic forebears. Since analytic philosophy still dominates the scene, anyone interested in doing significant work in philosophical theology ought to have a clear picture of this analytic attitude and an understanding of the thinking that underlies it.

It was metaphysics and not theology that was the primary target of the logical positivists. They were concerned to purge philosophy of meaningless assertions and of the idle disputes that were engendered among philosophers who advanced them. Theological discourse came into the picture only by way of providing incidental illustrations of what positivists regarded as meaningless statements masquerading under the cloak of technical profundity. Contemporary analysts have turned away from the positivistic pattern by (among other things) once again engaging in an austere form of metaphysical discourse. However, this has not led them in the direction of renewed concern with transcendental concepts—theological or otherwise—but in the opposite direction. The drift of post-positivistic analysis is (as I shall try to show in Section IV) toward the ever more detailed analysis of phenomena whose character is familiar, whose reference is relatively clear, and whose operations can, at least in principle, be precisely charted.

I. The Metaphysical Target

The anti-metaphysical impetus of logical positivism was not an unprecedented chapter in the history of philosophy. It had its roots in the sense of futility engendered by the recurring cycles of speculative affirmation and skeptical criticism that have characterized the interaction of the traditional philosophical schools. The impatience felt by

[4]"Theology and Objectivity," 187ff. For the "consensus" that Ogden rejects, see P. van Buren, *The Secular Meaning of the Gospel* (New York, 1963), Part I, chap. iv.

many thinkers who compared the performance of metaphysics with that of the natural sciences was well expressed by Kant: "If it [metaphysics] be a science, how comes it that it cannot, like other science, obtain universal and permanent recognition? . . . Everybody, however ignorant in other matters, may deliver a final verdict [on metaphysical issues] as in this domain there is as yet no standard weight and measure to distinguish sound knowledge from shallow talk."[5] The logical positivists were concerned to provide this standard weight and measure. However, despairing of the prospects of advancing philosophy by making metaphysics scientific, they decided to achieve philosophical progress by eliminating it.

The positivists attempted to eliminate metaphysics by providing reliable criteria of cognitive assertions, that is, of statements which represent claims to knowledge on the part of those making them. They insisted that metaphysicians could not rival scientists in the matter of providing information about the world we live in. Metaphysicians of the past offered conceptualizations whereby they claimed to tell us some necessary truths about the world or about certain phenomena in it. The positivists initiated new departures of considerable force by means of which they tried to show that either the metaphysicians were not telling us anything about the world or they were not telling us the truth. "All men are rational" seems to be a necessary truth about a species that inhabits this earth. However, positivists claim that if it is a necessary truth, it is so only because it expresses our determination to use words in such a way that we will refuse to call anything a man unless it measures up to certain standards of rationality. Therefore, they hold that when it is understood in this way the statement does not tell us anything about what the world is like independently of our language, but only about our linguistic conventions. The other option they present is that the statement "All men are rational" is a generalization about men based on empirical inquiry. In this case, they insist that it is not necessarily true; in fact, it is not true at all, but patently false.

To gain a better understanding of what the positivists were up to in their effort to eliminate metaphysics, we must come to appreciate the way in which they assaulted metaphysics by means of two dichotomies: (1) analytic-synthetic and (2) meaningful-meaningless.

I shall introduce the first dichotomy by means of a consideration of analytic statements. They are known to be true independently of any observations, a good example being, "Either it is raining or it is not raining." Statements of this kind are necessarily true, but positivists maintained that this is the case because they are uninformative. They

[5]*Prolegomena to Any Future Metaphysics* (Chicago, 1949), 2.

merely tell us about the logical relations of the terms we use and not about any actual state of affairs. The example just given is helpful; it does not say anything about the actual state of the weather, but demonstrates the way that the logical connective "or" (disjunction) operates in the assertive context. However, not all analytic statements are (to use a term of C. G. Hempel's) so shatteringly trivial. Positivists claimed that mathematical statements are also analytic. It is obvious that the complexities of mathematical demonstration and of logical theory permit of a vast number of disclosures which are non-informative, but which are not at all trivial. They are even informative in the limited psychological sense of making us aware of things that we may not have realized such as the statement that $523 \times 1,745 = 912,635$. For this reason, analytic statements—far from being scorned by positivists— were highly valued as important sources of insight into formal aspects of thought. Statements were only dismissed by them as metaphysical nonsense if the positivists found that a smokescreen of obfuscating technical language was released by metaphysicians in the effort to suggest that some statements were informative (about some actual state of affairs in the world) as well as necessary. The "synthetic a priori" as used by Kant and subsequent philosophers is a good example of this particular *target* of positivistic analysis.

According to the positivistic dichotomy, if declarative statements are not analytic, then they are putatively synthetic, that is, they are *intended* to convey information about some actual state of affairs. However, the positivists claimed that some statements which seem to be synthetic are not really so. It is at this point that the second dichotomy —meaningful-meaningless—comes into play. Prior to the development of logical positivism, declarative statements for which synthetic status was claimed were pretty much accepted at face value, and, after investigation, they were regarded as being either true or false. The positivists regrouped these statements. If they were capable of being true or false, they were regarded as meaningful, and they were bracketed together on one side of the dichotomy. If not, they were classed as meaningless. In this context, oddly enough, the term "false" has a somewhat complimentary ring; it characterizes a meaningful assertion that really is synthetic and which, therefore, might be true. It merely *happens* to be false. By contrast, the term "meaningless" designates a statement which seems to be synthetic but which, on analysis, turns out to be masquerading. A statement of this kind cannot conceivably be true or false and is, therefore, unworthy of further serious investigation.

An obvious question arises at this point: "How does one determine whether a putatively synthetic statement is capable of being true or false?" In answering this question, the positivists sounded their most distinctive note by proposing the test of verifiability as the crucial test of synthetic meaningfulness. It is often called "the empiricist criterion of meaning." In deploying this test as an anti-metaphysical weapon, the positivists thought that they were able to determine—in advance, and without the consideration of specific metaphysical arguments—whether a metaphysical statement could be meaningful. This made the positivists' assault on metaphysics the most threatening one that had been launched in the history of philosophy. The positivists were not attempting to defeat the metaphysicians in the philosophical arena; they were trying to deny them the status of legitimate combatants.

II.   The Verifiability Principle

The story of the bold launching of "the verifiability principle" and of the sober second thoughts that succeeded it has been told many times over.[6] It is worth repeating here, even in truncated form (which, for example, omits considering the issue of specially designed empiricist languages) because:

1.   It was the main anti-metaphysical weapon in the positivist's arsenal.
2.   Ogden alluded to it without giving any details as to what was at issue.[7]
3.   In general, the authors who have contributed essays on this subject to journals of religious thought have generally given the results of philosophical reflections on the verifiability principle while noting that they do not have the time to go into the details. This procedure underscores the weaknesses of positivism while shortchanging the self-critical candor and the methodological power of the analytic thinking that succeeded it.
4.   Examination of some of the specific arguments involved will show

[6]I begin my account of the verifiability principle with the statement found in the most publicized work on the subject, A. J. Ayer's *Language, Truth, and Logic* (London, 1936), but it should be noted that in this work Ayer refined the cruder operationalistic versions of it that had been advanced by members of "the Vienna circle." The most wide-ranging historical survey of the issue is to be found in J. Passmore, *Philosophical Reasoning* (New York, 1961), chap. v. In *Logical Positivism* (Glencoe, Ill., 1959), Ayer, in the "Editor's Introduction," and C. G. Hempel, in "The Empiricist Criterion of Meaning," present historical surveys of the issue that are contributions to its advancement. A detailed survey and contribution are also to be found in Parts I and II of I. Scheffler, "Prospects for a Modest Empiricism," *Review of Metaphysics,* Vol. X (1957). In chap. v. of *Reason and Analysis* (London, 1962), Brand Blanshard presents a survey of statements of the verifiability principle and criticizes them from the standpoint of his metaphysical idealism.

[7]"Theology and Philosophy," 2.

us the kind of considerations that have led to the reformulations of the principle, and in many cases, to its abandonment.

5.   Reflection on these arguments will enable us to see just how alien the spirit and method of post-positivistic analysts are to the spirit and concerns of the philosophical theologians who employ transcendental concepts.

The bête noire of positivistic analysis is the type of metaphysical statement whose form leads us to suppose that it is telling us something about a possible state of affairs when analysis shows that it is not, and, what is more could not, be doing anything of the kind. The point was driven home by means of their most famous illustration (now as dated as the movement which spawned it), the statement, "There are mountains on the far side of the moon." The point of the illustration was that this statement, which cannot be verified in fact because of technical limitations, is *verifiable in principle*. Anyone who understood it would be clear as to just the sorts of observable phenomena that would count for and against the truth of the statement and would, therefore, know how to proceed to check it out if he were in a position to do so. The statement, "There are angels on the far side of the moon," is grammatically similar to the one about the mountains; but positivists insist that the similarity is fatally misleading. The blanket invocation of non-sensible characteristics that are used in the definition of angels renders sensible experience irrelevant to establishing the truth or falsity of the assertion. The fact that sense experience is irrelevant to it *in principle*, shows that the statement, "There are angels on the far side of the moon," is not entitled to the relatively elevated status of falsity, but, rather, it is worse off than a false statement, it is meaningless. Therefore, a philosopher who spent time examining arguments for the existence of angels, or any of the other non-sensible entities ("forms," "essences," and so on) that philosophers contrive, would be in the idiotic position of Kant's man who held a sieve underneath a male goat while another man milked it.

The sort of thing that the verifiability principle was designed to exclude was formulated succinctly by Walter Stace: "The word 'metaphysical' may, of course, be variously defined, but in this context what is meant by it is evidently any type of thought which depends upon the distinction between an outer appearance and an inner reality, and which asserts that there is a reality lying behind appearances, which never itself appears."[8] The transcendent God of the Judeo-Christian tradition is certainly an instance of "a reality behind the appearances which never itself appears." Thus the application of this seemingly reliable and quick "litmus paper test" to metaphysical assertions

---

[8]"Metaphysics and Meaning," *Mind*, XLIV (1935), 417.

seemed to eliminate this God in addition to "the absolute," "substance," "the thing-in-itself," and countless other traditional terms. Here was an unprecedented phenomenon: "Pandora's box" in reverse. The havoc that had been unleashed by the metaphysical tradition could now be rectified. Positivistic literature abounded with examples of one sort of metaphysical "howler" after the other being exposed, folded up, and packed back into a bottomless bin labeled "meaningless"! The transcendent God of the Judeo-Christian tradition was another victim of this wholesale application of the verifiability principle, but he was not the major target.

The sketch of the verifiability principle that I have presented is ample enough to serve as the basis of an examination of some of the problems associated with it.[9] They will be considered under three headings: (1) the status of the principle itself; (2) the excessive restrictiveness of the principle; and (3) the excessive permissiveness of the principle.

The problem of the status of the verifiability principle was avidly seized upon by non-positivists. They claimed that since the verifiability principle was itself neither analytic nor synthetic it should—according to the positivists' own canons—be dismissed as a piece of nonsensical metaphysics. This, of course, would destroy it as an anti-metaphysical weapon. Positivists were not overly concerned about this criticism. They felt that it showed an absence of understanding of the central issues on the part of the non-positivists who invoked it. They handled it in a variety of ways. Their most frequent defense was to concede the point that the verifiability principle was not a statement (and that it was therefore neither analytic nor synthetic), but they claimed that is was a useful *proposal* for discriminating between meaningful and meaningless assertions. The justification for it would then be that its use eliminates the inadvertent nonsense put out under the name of metaphysics, while highlighting the characteristics that endow synthetic statements with meaning.

It was precisely the ineffectiveness of this pragmatic justification of verifiability that put the principle under fire even among philosophers who were sympathetically disposed toward its anti-metaphysical intent. The application of the principle seemed, on further analysis, to be excessively restrictive because it branded as meaningless all sorts of synthetic propositions whose meaningfulness the positivists themselves had no desire to call into question. In limiting the exposition of this point, I propose to focus on the way in which the "logical" side

[9]For an examination of the important issue of "translatability" into a specially designed empiricist language, an issue that I have ignored in this essay, see, Scheffler, *op. cit.*

of logical positivism put its "positivistic," that is, anti-metaphysical, side under pressure. Consideraton of universal synthetic statements will enable us to get at the issues. "All crows are black" is not the kind of statement whose meaningfulness (as opposed to its truth) anyone, positivist or not, wants to attack. However, when tested by the verifiability principle, it turns out to be meaningless because it can never—in principle—be verified. No matter how many instances of black crows have been tallied, there is always the possibility of a yellow one turning up. And, apart from casting unwonted aspersions on the meaningfulness of statements of the kind just cited, the rampant application of the verifiability principle had the even more regrettable consequence of catching scientific laws in this same net because they too had this universal form. Positivists, because of the excessive restrictiveness of the principle, found themselves in the embarrassing situation of throwing out scientific babies with the metaphysical bath.

Karl Popper's discussion of "falsifiability" was initiated in response to this problem. He noted that although universal statements are not, in principle, verifiable, they are, in principle, falsifiable. One exception to a scientific law is enough to falsify it because it shows that the law does not hold universally (at least it shows this if the exception to the law is accepted as a genuine one; that is, as long as it is not regarded as the result of faulty experimental work or of other peculiar circumstances that rule it out as a genuine exception to the law).[10] I should note that Popper's relation to positivism and his particular purposes in pressing the issue of "falsifiability" is too complex a matter to discuss here, but the appeal to it did seem to offer positivists a chance to salvage their enterprise of formulating a clear and effective criterion for distinguishing scientific from metaphysical assertions. For some positivists insisted that, by contrast with scientific laws, such metaphysical assertions as, "The Absolute is Perfect" are not falsifiable even in principle.[11] However, the test of falsifiability suffered from a major defect with which Popper himself grappled, namely, that no existential statement, that is, no statement which asserts that something exists, is ever conclusively falsifiable. No matter how long one has gone on fruitlessly searching for the Abominable Snowman, there is always the possibility that one will turn up. In light of this discussion, the coup de grâce to both conclusive verifiability and to conclusive falsifiability is administerable by means of a statement, such as the

[10]Logic der Forschung (Vienna, 1935); revised English version, The Logic of Scientific Discovery (London, 1959), see especially, 34–42, 64–72, 78–92.

[11]A. Flew, "Theology and Falsification," in A. Flew and A. MacIntyre, eds., New Essays in Philosophical Theology (London, 1955), 96ff.

one offered by J. O. Urmson that contains both a universal ("every") and an existential ("some") element: "Every person who walks under a ladder will meet with some misfortune."[12]

One way out of the difficulty that has been suggested is the abandonment of the demand for *conclusive* verification and falsification. A statement would then be synthetically meaningful if some specifiable observation statements would tend to confirm or to falsify it.[13] The suggestion has much to recommend it, but it will not serve as a means of neatly separating scientific wheat from metaphysical or theological chaff. To appreciate this point, let us consider Basil Mitchell's parable of the partisan and the stranger.[14] In an occupied country, a partisan meets a stranger. In a night of intense communion between them, the stranger reveals himself as the leader of the resistance. The partisan, overwhelmed at this disclosure and impelled to trust the stranger, promises to keep on trusting him, whatever happens. His faith is soon put to the test because the stranger reappears as the head of the local unit of the Gestapo. The partisan keeps his trust and assures his comrades that the man is really one of them. After that, when members of the underground who have been taken into custody are unexpectedly released, the partisan's faith in the stranger is confirmed; and when members of the underground are unexpectedly taken prisoner and are then executed, the evidence seems to go against his belief in the identity of the stranger. However, persevering in his faith, the partisan assures his doubting comrades that the stranger really is one of them but that he cannot intervene too openly on the side of the underground or his role as the leader of the resistance would be discovered by the Nazis. By means of this parable, Basil Mitchell claims that events in this world do count for and against transcendental theological assertions, for example, "God loves us"; but he also claims that we can, like the partisan, retain our faith even in the face of strong evidence that counts against it. Therefore, he insists that no amount of negative evidence can ever count conclusively against it. Thus theological statements are held to be partially verifiable and partially falsifiable, but not conclusively so. However, if conclusiveness is to be jettisoned from the empiricist cri-

[12]*Philosophical Analysis* (Oxford, 1956), 113.

[13]C. G. Hempel, "Studies in the Logic of Confirmation, I and II," *Mind* (1945), reprinted in, Hempel, *Aspects of Scientific Explanation* (New York, 1964); R. Carnap, "Truth and Confirmation," in H. Feigl and W. Sellars, eds., *Readings in Philosophical Analysis* (New York, 1949); W. P. Alston, *Philosophy of Language* (Englewood Cliffs, N.J., 1964).

[14]"Theology and Falsification," in *New Essays in Philosophical Theology* (see n. 11 above), 103 ff. For comments on Mitchell's position see, W. T. Blackstone, *The Problem of Religious Knowledge* (Englewood Cliffs, N.J., 1963), 108–112; and H. R. Burkle, "Counting Against and Counting Decisively Against," *Journal of Religion*, XLIV (1964).

terion of meaning, then (if the line of thought illustrated by means of this parable is effective) theological statements ought to be included in the lists of meaningful assertions. From the standpoint of the positivists, the floodgates would then be open.[15]

Logical probing into the nature and operation of synthetic statements uncovered further difficulties. One of the basic distinctions between analytic and synthetic statements concerns their logical status. An analytic statement is necessarily true or necessarily false. If it is true, then, its negation, which is necessarily (that is, under any circumstances whatever) false, is self-contradictory. By contrast, a synthetic assertion and its negation are both possible, and both are meaningful; one is true, the other is false, and it is observation that determines the issue.

The next problem we shall consider unfolds in the following way: "There exists at least one black swan" is clearly, by any criterion, including the most stringent application of the verifiability principle, a synthetic assertion which is patently meaningful. Therefore, its negation ought to be equally meaningful. Yet, when we analyze its negation, namely, "There does not exist at least one black swan," we find that it is logically convertible to the universal proposition that "Nothing that is both a swan and black exists." However, we have noted that universal statements can never, in principle, be verified, and so this denial of an unquestionably meaningful synthetic proposition turns out to be meaningless—an utterly paradoxical result.[16]

The positivistic reaction to these difficulties was predictable enough: they qualified or "weakened" the verifiability principle in the effort to make it permissive enough to allow for the validity of scientific assertions, while still retaining enough strength (restrictiveness) to exclude metaphysical assertions. This is the theme of Ayer's Introduction to the second edition of his *Language, Truth, and Logic* (1948) which was published some twelve years after the original. With these difficulties in mind, he proposed the following, "weaker" version of the principle, "A statement is verifiable, and consequently meaningful, if some observation-statement can be deduced from it in conjunction with certain other premises, without being deducible from these premises alone."[17] The sort of thing that Ayer wanted to allow for by means of this reformulation of the principle is clear enough. A statement about electrons is not verifiable by direct observation. Nonetheless, when tied to all sorts of observations of photographic plates, meter readings, and the like, statements about electrons—functioning in the context of scientific theories—enable physicists to deduce further observation state-

[15]Alston, 72.

[16]Hempel, "The Empiricist Criterion of Meaning," 114.

[17]"Introduction," *Language, Truth, and Logic*, 2d ed. (London, 1948), 11.

ments that could not be deduced from the exclusive consideration of the empirical data. The scientist then runs experiments to see whether the deduced observation statements are experimentally verified. Here then (if for the sake of argument, we refrain from raising further difficulties), we have an example of an effective application of the weaker, that is, the more permissive version of the principle, which permits the sobriquet "meaningful" to be attached to the sort of scientific statements from which the older and tougher versions withheld it.

We have already noted the point that the logical relation of negation raised problems for the restrictive tendencies of the verifiability principle. We must now note that the logical relation of the hypothetical, "If . . . then . . . ," plays just as damaging a role with regard to the permissive tendencies of the weak version of the principle. Ayer himself (drawing on a critical essay by Isaiah Berlin) presents a *reductio ad absurdum* argument, which I shall somewhat modify.[18] The first premise is: "If the Absolute is perfect then this is white." The second premise is: "The Absolute is perfect." Taken together, they yield (by means of *Modus ponens*) the conclusion: "This is white." This conclusion is clearly a meaningful synthetic statement; indeed, it could serve as a prime example of one. By contrast, "The Absolute is perfect" might serve as prime example of the kind of metaphysical or theological statement that positivists wanted to label meaningless. Yet by the application of the weak version of the verifiability principle, the statement that "The Absolute is perfect" emerges as a meaningful instance of a synthetic assertion. Why? Because one could not deduce the conclusion, "This is white," from the first premise when taken by itself, nor could one deduce it from the second premise taken by itself; but we have seen that we can deduce the observation statement "This is white" from the two premises together. And Ayer notes that the procedure can be generalized. If we accept the weak version of the verifiability principle, any metaphysical statement which is set in a straightforward indicative form can, by conversion into the "If . . . then . . ." form, be endowed with synthetic meaningfulness.

It is now clear that no consensus regarding the verifiability principle is to be found within the broad spectrum of philosophers whose thinking may be classed as analytic; rather, there are two basic approaches to it. The first of these is to keep on modifying the statements of the principle in the effort to attain an adequate version of it. Rudolf Carnap and C. G. Hempel are outstanding representatives of this tendency. The latter, at the end of his survey of the problem has written: "Indeed, it is to be hoped that before long some of the open problems

[18]Ibid., 12; I. Berlin, "Verifiability in Principle," *Proceedings Aristotelian Society* (1938–39), 232ff.

encountered in the analysis of cognitive significance will be clarified and that then our last version of the empiricist meaning criterion will be replaced by another more adequate one."[19] His openness to criticism and his constructive efforts to uncover the principle underlying meaningful synthetic assertions make Hempel's hope a laudable one; but, insofar as it runs athwart an important emphasis of contemporary analytic thought, it is somewhat suspect. Analysts today are concerned with the formulation of ever more precise questions and with the detailed analysis of fine points that are relevant to answering them. They react strongly against large-scale generalizations that are expressed in terms of what Gilbert Ryle calls "smother words." "Reality," "truth," "experience," and the like, are words that can be misused to blanket hosts of disparate phenomena and important distinctions. Many analysts would now regard "verifiability" as a smother word because they suspect that undue rigidity is involved in the very effort to subsume the wide variety of synthetic assertions under the two categories "meaningful" and "meaningless." While no one who has read Hempel can accuse him of simplicism in his recent work on this issue, the very refinement displayed in these essays makes verifiability ineffective as the kind of instant metaphysical purgative it was originally intended to be.

The other, more common, approach to verifiability on the part of contemporary analysts is to regard it as an activity rather than a doctrine. They abandon the search for an adequate version of the principle that could be defended against all comers, and use it instead as an important move in philosophical argument. Analysts who take this tack concede the ineffectiveness of verifiability as a "litmus paper" device for eliminating metaphysics. Therefore, if a philosopher stakes out a traditional metaphysical position, such as the "substance view" of the self, analysts of this kind do not dismiss it out of hand as a species of metaphysical nonsense. Instead, they examine the arguments one by one and challenge the metaphysican to make his claim good. The nature of this challenge has been succinctly stated by Elmer Sprague, "philosophical debates are hottest between those philosophers who want to make certain entries in the list of what there is in the world and other philosophers who do not want to let them get away with it."[20]

One important feature of this story is the negative one. Positivists and their successors have not produced an adequate version of the verifiability principle. However, their ability to nail down the inadequacy of the various formulations of it provides impressive evidence of their rigor. This contrasts sharply with what goes on in theological circles where theologians cannot seem to agree as to what does not "go."

---

[19]"The Empiricist Criterion of Meaning," 126.
[20]*What Is Philosophy?* (New York, 1961), 29.

Nevertheless, there is some good news for theologians in this story of the quest for the verifiability principle, because the failure to make any particular version of it stick does mean that theology cannot be ruled out of court without examination. However, a word of caution is in order: To stand for an examination is no guaranty of passing it.[21]

III.   The Abandonment of Positivistic Dogma and the Analytic Turn to Metaphysics

An aspect of logical positivism that has carried over to the contemporary analytic scene is the orientation to the natural sciences; as manifested today, it probably owes as much to the pragmatists' emphasis on the method of scientific inquiry as it does to any of the emphases of the positivists. Earlier many philosophers were inclined to take the positivists at face value and to regard their enterprise as a vigorous manifestation of the scientific spirit within the philosophical camp; later, they began to wonder whether the positivists were not merely partisan. There was, after all, something prejudicial and dogmatic about the tortuous efforts of the positivists to achieve a version of the verifiability principle with the right combination of permissiveness ("science-in") and restrictiveness ("metaphysics-out"). A scientific inquiry into meaningfulness should have been more open-ended. In a genuine inquiry, one might well begin with a sense of the meaningfulness of certain types of statements and of the meaninglessness of other types, but one would be open to the possibility that things might not turn out just that way. The positivists, on the other hand, held their favorite metaphysical whipping boys—Platonic, Heideggerian, and theological statements—constant. These were branded as meaningless, come what may! They then tried desperately to find the broadsword that would eliminate them at one blow without injuring any innocent "scientific" or "common-sense" bystanders.

Now that we have examined the kinds of arguments that analysts have used in attacking the dogma of verifiability, it will be useful to quote an anti-positivistic polemic written by Morton White, a contemporary analyst. It strikes at a number of other dogmas as well. This will help us to appreciate the extent to which the positivistic consensus (if there ever was one outside the confines of the Vienna circle) has broken down among contemporary analysts.

> The early Platonism of Moore and Russell, the distinction between analytic and synthetic statements, the attempt to formulate a criterion

[21]For a sustained statement of the issue involved see, W. B. Bartley III, *Retreat to Commitment* (New York, 1962).

of cognitive meaning, the emotive theory of ethics, the pragmatic philosophy of science—all of them were at one time liberating forces in the philosophy of the twentieth century. They helped divert philosophical attention from a number of pseudo-problems; they increased respect for logic and exactness in philosophy; they encouraged a laudable degree of self-consciousness among philosophers which led to a healthy re-examination of philosophical methods and philosophical aims.

But . . . ideas that were once liberating and which helped puncture the inflationary schemes of traditional philosophy were soon collected and composed into a tradition. . . . The terms "analytic," "meaningless," "emotive," and "naturalistic fallacy"—to mention only some—became empty slogans instead of revolutionary tools; the quest for meaning replaced the quest for certainty; orthodoxy followed revolt. Logic, physics, and ethics were assigned special and unique methods of justification; ancient metaphysical generalizations about everything being fire or water were erased and replaced by equally indefensible universal theses, according to which all logical statements are like this, and all physical statements are like that, and all ethical statements very different from both. . . . Whereas their metaphysical predecessors, whom they regarded as benighted and befuddled, made startling generalizations about all of existence, analytically minded philosophers (and those who were pragmatically minded too) defended apparently sober but equally dubious claims about linguistic expressions or their meanings.[22]

This statement reflects the anti-dogmatic spirit that has been manifest among contemporary analysts at least since Quine published his assault on "Two Dogmas of Empiricism" in 1951.[23] It may also be taken as an earnest of the willingness of contemporary analysts to address themselves to philosophical issues that the positivists thought they had buried; metaphysics is certainly one of these. One reason for this concern with traditional issues is that once the "litmus paper" view of the verifiability principle has been abandoned there is no simple way of distinguishing what analysts of today do from that which was done by metaphysicians of the past. Traditional problems of philosophy are then found lurking in the sophisticated formulations of the present. An instructive example of this is the question of "essences." Philosophers had traditionally operated with the assumption that the use of common nouns was regulated by the essential characteristics that underlay the maze of accidental features that a given phenomenon displayed. In the effort to rid philosophers of this obsession, Wittgenstein introduced the notion of "family resemblances." He urged philosophers to abandon

[22]*Toward Reunion in Philosophy* (New York, 1963), 290ff.
[23]Reprinted in W. van O. Quine, *From a Logical Point of View* (New York, 1963).

their "essentialistic" preconceptions and to use this notion as an aid in paying the most careful attention to the nuances of words in their manifold relations to the phenomena they stand for.[24] In his well-known illustration of "games," he noted that games (board games, card games, sports, and romping children) display a complex network of crisscrossing characteristics that resemble the way characteristics of parents get scrambled among their children. There is no one "essential" characteristic which is common to all. If one applied this approach to a complex phenomenon such as religion, one would resist the temptation to search for an "essence" of it; instead, one would study as many instances as possible and map out the resemblances. This is the point of Wittgenstein's admonition: "Don't think, but look!"

The effort to eliminate fatuous quests for non-existent essences is liberating in some contexts, but the problems that exercised the philosophers of the past cannot be lightly dismissed. For one thing, to apply the technique of family resemblances to all common nouns would run counter to the resistance to dogmatic generalizations exemplified by contemporary analysts and certainly by Wittgenstein himself. Some words are inextricably tied to certain fundamental characteristics, for example, as "brother" is to "male." In addition, the conceptual considerations that agitated the "essentialists" of the past re-emerge in the context of family resemblances when one has to cope—at the fringes—with the problems of determining the limits of consanguinity.

It would, however, be a mistake to suggest that the concern with metaphysics manifest among contemporary analysts is inadvertent or that it is evoked under duress. P. F. Strawson, Wilfrid Sellars, W. van O. Quine, Gustav Bergmann, and other contemporary analysts unblushingly engage in metaphysical discourse as they tackle such traditional problems of philosophy as the metaphysics of experience (the conceptual preconditions of significant experience), the philosophy of mind, and the basic ontological questions (what there is), as well as questions of ethics. To them they bring the resources of the recent developments in formal logic, the linguistic self-consciousness induced by recent work in semantics, and an impressive mastery of the achievements and problems of the sciences.[25] Yet a qualification may be called for; in an important essay on the "Metaphilosophical Difficulties of Linguistic Philosophy," R. M. Rorty claims that these resources are employed in a way that makes it misleading to say that these analysts are doing meta-

---

[24]*Philosophical Investigations* (New York, 1953), secs. 46ff. A discussion of the broader issue is found in G. Pitcher, "The Attack on Essentialism," *The Philosophy of Wittgenstein* (Englewood Cliffs, N.J., 1964).

[25]For an important survey of American work in this field, see chap. iv of Manley Thompson's essay, "Metaphysics," which appears in R. M. Chisholm *et al.*, *Philosophy* (Englewood Cliffs, N.J., 1964).

physics, if the term "metaphysics" retains its traditional associations.[26] The issues they deal with may be traditional, but they construe their task in a radically different way. They follow the positivists in rejecting the claim—characteristic of traditional metaphysicians—that philosophy can add to our knowledge of the world. In this domain they do not believe that philosophical conceptualization can supplement scientific inquiry. They regard their job as that of providing a "clean" conceptual framework for the knowledge we actually acquire through science and common sense, that is, a framework that will be expressed in precise and controllable forms and one that will be free of the confusions of purpose and the turgid jargons that scarred the metaphysical systems of the past. If Rorty is right, then from the standpoint of philosophers who are still oriented toward the traditional approaches to metaphysics, the post-positivistic era in analysis is not all that different from its predecessor, and the analysts' turn to metaphysics is deceptive. The main difference would seem to be that contemporary analysts have been chastened by the abandonment of the dogmas that inaugurated the "revolution in philosophy," so that they ought to be less disposed to summary dismissals of metaphysical theses—regardless of the orientation of the thinkers who propose them.

In any event, whatever may be the case regarding their approach to such inescapable issues as the philosophy of mind or ontology, it is clear that contemporary analysts remain most inhospitable to transcendental metaphysics and theology. These analysts (metaphysical or not) are responsive to a point made many times over by G. E. Moore: There are all sorts of things which can be known to be obviously true but which are very difficult to analyze ("analysis" in this context means to offer a satisfactory theoretical account of *how* these obvious truths are *known* to be true). Included in the list of truisms which he regarded as certainly knowable, were such matters as the existence of his body and the contact it has with other bodies.[27] When assertions of this kind prove hard to analyze, and when scientific assertions whose truth is relatively obvious also prove hard to analyze, the analysts of today are not disposed to excursions into transcendental realms in order to analyze statements about "the Absolute," "Being-Itself," or God." In these cases, it is hard to determine just what it is that one is supposed to be analyzing, much less how one would ever agree on procedures for resolving conflicts about these transcendental matters.

Again and again, religious thinkers invoke the *Tu Quoque* in dealing with analytic philosophers. Religious thinkers point to the difficulties involved in the efforts to formulate the empiricist criterion of

---

[26]This essay is the "Editor's Introduction" to an anthology, *The Linguistic Turn* (Chicago, 1967).

[27]"In Defense of Common Sense," *Philosophical Papers* (London, 1959), 23ff.

meaning by means of the verifiability principle, or they point to the difficulties of determining the precise character of the analytic-synthetic distinction. They then say something like, "We philosophical theologians may have our difficulties, but you analysts have yours too, so that there's little to choose between us on that score. Therefore, considering the ultimate importance of the issues *we* deal with, you ought to abandon your trivial epistemological pursuits and get to work on our field."

Analysts who are confronted with this sort of appeal might well respond with the argument that Reinhold Niebuhr directed against Lewis Mumford. In one of his books, Mumford was sharply critical of the United Nations and, because of the obvious limitations of this organization, he urged that it be abandoned and that the World Federalist Program be adopted in its place. In answer, Niebuhr said that this was like a man who was crawling along the narrow ridge high up on a cliff, holding to the rocky side for dear life, being told that since the progress he was making was so tortuous and since the danger of his making a false step and plunging into the abyss was so great, the only thing for him to do was to let go and fly.

IV.   The Theological Victim

It should now be clear that philosophical theologians can take scant comfort from the revival of interest in metaphysics manifested by some philosophical analysts. To be sure, analysts are by no means the only contemporary philosophers, but they remain the dominant group among English-speaking philosophers of our day; and, if philosophical theologians are concerned to deal with the contemporary philosophical scene, they had better read them straight.

A qualification to the pessimism that I have expressed concerning the possibility of fruitful discussion between theologians and analysts is the point (already noted) that the anti-dogmatic tendencies of contemporary analysts ought to preclude the possibility of their reading any positions out of court. Yet there are special problems concerned with the theistic concept of the transcendent God that make the resurrection of this victim of philosophical analysis far less likely.[28] The problem I have in mind may be explicated by reference to J. N. Findlay's examination of the implications of worship and to Paul Tillich's examination of idolatry.

In his essay, "Can God's Existence Be Disproved?"[29] Findlay at-

---

[28]See F. Ferré "The 'Elimination' of Theological Discourse," *Language, Logic and God* (New York, 1961), for an important survey of analytic criticisms of theology, including a good number, which are not discussed here.

[29]*New Essays In Philosophical Theology*, 50ff. The fact that Findlay no longer holds the views he expressed in this essay (for his later view, see "Reflections on

tacked a dogma of the religious existentialists, namely, the dichotomy between the God of the philosophers and the God of the patriarchs. He did so by bypassing the usual philosophical point of departure, the quest for rational consistency, and by beginning instead with reflection upon the most distinctive act of religious men, the act of worship. He claimed that an implication of this act is that its object ought to be utterly unlike any being whatever that we normally encounter; a mere quantitative difference would not do because the utter adoration that characterizes the act of worship would be an inappropriate response to a being who merely differed from us quantitatively. Therefore, the God we worship must be conceived as one who does not merely happen to exist, to be good, to be knowing, or what have you. A God appropriate to the act of worship must exist necessarily and possess all attributes necessarily. This guarantees the absolute qualitative distinction between God and man, but the problem that this poses for philosophical theology is that we neither have experience of a Being of this "necessary" order nor is our conceptual apparatus equipped to handle it. Therefore, a God who is religiously appropriate would seem, "necessarily," to be conceptually contradictory.

In no other domain known to me is there as great a non-philosophical stake in setting a subject beyond the range of our conceptual apparatus. Tillich—in updating the prophetic protest against idolatry and rendering it in philosophical terms—insisted upon this point throughout his career. God cannot be treated in terms of our normal conceptual apparatus because any effort to do so results in setting God as one item alongside others, and this reduces God to the status of an idol.[30] However, there is no road from unqualified uniqueness to the language of men. To grant to God that conceptual status that the act of worship and the protest against idolatry demand is to render the concept of God transcognitive as well as transcendent; and the method of systematic silence is not one to be commended to a philosophical discipline, not even to philosophical theology.

A further barrier to fruitful discussion between theologians and analysts is that, whereas the analysts focus on method, theologians are thinkers whose major purpose is to reflect on a specific body of traditional assertions. Philosophical theologians can hardly be expected to "sit loosely" to teachings concerning God and his nature, while letting their method carry them where it will. That is one of my reasons for maintaining that, although an austere form of metaphysics has already

---

Necessary Existence," in *Process and Divinity*) does not detract from its usefulness in helping to define the task of philosophical theology in our day.

[30]*Systematic Theology* (Chicago, 1951), I, 235–241, contain a good statement of his views on this issue.

risen phoenix-like from the positivistic ashes to play a role in analytic discourse, theological discourse is still pretty much confined to the role of a horrible example of how not to proceed.

Yet we do not live by our accomplishments alone, no more in philosophy than in life. Our faith in the meaningfulness of the task at hand often derives its potency from hope. Nor are hardboiled empiricists immune to this; witness the following statement by Israel Scheffler which concludes his brilliant survey of the problem of verifiability: "It appears, in sum, that even a modest empiricism is presently a hope for clarification and a challenge to constructive investigation rather than a well-grounded doctrine, unless we construe it in a quite trivial way. Empiricists are perhaps best thought of as those who share the hope and accept the challenge—who refuse to take difficulty as a valid reason either for satisfaction with the obscure or for abandonment of effort."[31]

If analysts can take this sort of line without being branded as irrational and wishful thinkers, why cannot philosophical theologians take the same tack? After all, one thing that we should have learned from Kierkegaard's use of the "Leap" is that rational considerations regarding matters of this kind do not play the sort of clearcut and decisive role that enables us to determine with precision just when clinging to hope becomes unreasonable. An element of arbitrariness enters into decisions to say, "It is no longer reasonable to work at the task of producing an adequate version of the verifiability principle," or "It is no longer reasonable to hope that additional effort will result in the production of a conceptual scheme adequate to the task of philosophical theology." The cut-off point will vary from one individual to the next, and it will depend upon all sorts of cultural factors. With this in mind, philosophical theologians might well think that they need not be cowed by the enormity of the problems. Indeed, this attitude of "work and hope" was commended to theologians by the philosopher Richard Brandt. At a conference of philosophers (mainly analysts) and theologians, he was discussing the question of the significance of theological statements and the possibility for meaningful disagreement between skeptics and believers. He noted that we would not expect them to have the same judgments regarding the meaningfulness of a set of religious concepts because there is no mechanical routine for grading the meaningfulness of concepts.

> Furthermore, and very important, sceptics and theologians can differ on how well a system *might* score, if only it were improved in ways in which excellent minds and time might enable it to be improved. The believer will be more optimistic, the sceptic more pessimistic, on this [scoring]. . . . Even if the contemporary believer must in candor rate

[31]*Op. cit.*, p. 625.

religious concepts lower . . . than they would have reasonably been rated six hundred years ago, he might claim that they do not score too badly considering the problems, and he may construe his job to make the system clearer so that it scores better.[32]

While nothing, in principle, prevents theologians from adopting the optimistic attitude that Brandt describes, it may be useful to underscore the difficulties involved by bringing out the sort of problem to which he alludes. Let us reflect on the following sequence of problematic issues:

1. The analysis of statements about material objects, for example, a stone.
2. The scientific analysis of the phenomenon of light that leads to the paradox of the "wave" and "particle" theories.
3. The analysis of the claim, I am now in conversation with another person.
4. The moral problems involved in analyzing statements about the justice of a given set of social arrangements.
5. The problems involved in evaluating the worth of two different recordings of Mozart's "Clarinet Quintet."
6. The problem imbedded in Robert MacAfee Brown's assertion that "Christian statements will always be vulnerable, because they are such a far cry from the real thing. But the real thing is never vulnerable because the real thing is not man in his stumbling statements, but the living God himself, whose reality is not dependent upon the adequacy or inadequacy of our statements about him."[33]

In the first five cases, a common pattern prevails: Analyze as much as you like, but the phenomenon being analyzed remains palpably (i.e., "invulnerably") present to you. Dr. Johnson's crude answer to Bishop Berkeley certainly did not resolve the difficulties inherent in analyzing statements about material objects, but they could both, nevertheless, be certain that whatever the outcome of the analysis, the stone would still be there to be kicked, and the kicker would still be in danger of stubbing his toe. In similar fashion, whatever the outcome of the scientific analysis of light, the sun will still shine. Continuing down the list, we note that, regardless of the outcome of philosophical analysis, the reference to persons is inescapable. Analyses that attack the "ghost in the machine" may, if we accept them, alter our understanding of persons, but the reference for these analyses is relatively clear. Indeed it is to persons that such analyses are addressed. We may now continue to the next item and note that, regardless of the outcome of ethical analysis, people will continue to order their social arrangements in various ways

[32]In J. Hick, ed., *Faith and the Philosophers* (New York, 1964), 152ff.
[33]*The Spirit of Protestantism* (New York, 1961), 52.

and to seek moral standards for doing so. Finally, it is clear that, at the application of the stylus, records will emit their sounds and that this does not depend on the outcome of our aesthetic analysis.

The item dealing with the living God breaks the pattern. The wording suggests that here too we have a phenomenon unquestionably present over against us, a phenomenon that demands analysis in one form or another. And Brown's remarks suggest that the main difficulty is that of hitting on the right analysis. However, this is deceptive. With regard to the "living God," we can reasonably raise the issue of whether there is anything there over and above the "stumbling statements" about him. When subjected to analysis (of many kinds, and not merely of the contemporary philosophical variety), it appears that the transcendent God is "vulnerable" in ways that the other phenomena are not, because the only sensible references for theological statements about "The God who acts" are the actions of men, the regularities of the natural order, or some other wholly immanent phenomena that *are* present. Furthermore, in the other cases listed we might, on analysis, discover that what we were actually up to was a very different affair from what we had thought it was, but our jumping-off point would still be there to be pointed out. In the case of the transcendent God, when analysis induces a changed perspective, we may find ourselves unable to try for a better analysis because we would no longer be able to locate the object of it.

A final note: In cases 1–5, a person who denied the reference—in practical terms and not merely by way of pointing up the inadequacy of a particular analysis—would be a likely candidate for confinement to a mental institution. This is clearly not the case with regard to a person who denies the existence of God.

The loss of a meaningful "reference" for talk about the transcendent God, can, nevertheless, leave theologians with an obvious object of analysis: Religion in its vast ramifications. This is the sad end product of the "Death of God" theology that received its initial impetus from the work of Dietrich Bonhoeffer. His bold claim was that God so much wants men to be free and mature that he wants them to dispense with the crutch of religion, even with the crutch of the "God of religion." Bonhoeffer regarded the "God of religion" as a crutch because this "God" is the all too knowable and all too available "God" of the kind of conventional piety that treats the Ultimate as an idol. The "Death of God" theologians—aware of the challenge of contemporary analysis to the notion of transcendence, and finding themselves incapable of meeting it—claim to be following Bonhoeffer's lead when they jettison the *transcendent* God. Christianity is thus cut off from relation to the incomprehensible deity who is, as we have noted—whatever the difficulties of formulation involved—the only worthy object of worship. The "Death of God" theologians then try to convince themselves and their readers that what remains is authentic Christianity. They do this by driving an illusory wedge between Christianity and religion by means of "persuasive definitions" of both "Christianity" and "religion." These definitions are calculated to show that Christianity is not, and never really was, a "religion" and that it never essentially depended on belief in the transcendent God. Actually, what they present is that most pernicious form of idolatry: religion without God. The emergence of the "Death of God" theology, which is certainly not the best theology being done today, nevertheless well illustrates the considerations that lead me to say that the theological victim of contemporary analysis is in the worst shape of all. If you take the problem of transcendence seriously, while maintaining a Christian form of what Paul Tillich called "ultimate concern," you can be driven to this sort of thing.

V.   A Disturbing Parallel

It may well be objected that what I have presented in this essay is not an accurate description of the contemporary philosophical scene but propaganda on behalf of one particularly active segment of it. Evidence could be cited to show that not only is there an absence of consensus among contemporary analysts but that there has also been some defection from their ranks to other and more traditional philosophical approaches. Findlay, whom I have cited on more than one point in this essay, is a good example of this. His recent Gifford Lectures document his shift from philosophical analysis to his own synthesis of Hegel and Husserl.[34] In addition, many philosophers dedicated to the defense of traditional metaphysical positions are professors at important universities; they publish many books, and there are journals devoted to publishing their articles. Furthermore (to quote Findlay again), "there can be nothing really 'clinching' in philosophy: 'proofs' and 'disproofs' hold only for those who adopt certain premises, who are willing to follow certain rules of argument, and who use their terms in certain definite ways."[35] Indeed, we have noted that even among the analysts, who do pretty much adopt the same premises and standards of arguments, the central doctrines of one generation have proved to be the scornfully rejected dogmas of the next. Therefore, a theologian who rejected my account of the contemporary scene could claim that I must be surveying the prospects for meaningful confrontation between theologians and philosophers with a jaundiced eye.

I would not know how to go about refuting this charge in a conclusive way. So much depends on the perspective with which we study the material that an evaluation of the state of something as complex and variegated as the current philosophical scene is bound to be affected by

[34]*The Discipline of the Cave* (London, 1966).
[35]"Can God's Existence Be Disproved?" in *New Essays in Philosophical Theology,* 71.

all sorts of subjective considerations. In light of this, the best I can do by way of replying to the charge that I have presented a "party line" on the current philosophical situation is to call attention to a parallel that I find more than a little disturbing.

Fundamentalists today reject descriptions of the contemporary theological scene that report the triumph of the critical approach to the Bible. They claim that this judgment, which treats all modes of the literal interpretation of the Bible as passé, represents the biased view of one party to a live dispute. In advocating this position, Fundamentalists can certainly marshal a good deal of evidence. Fundamentalism, they can insist, is far from dead as a social force. Furthermore, intellectually speaking, they can point to the many schools, seminaries, and journals which are dominated by the Fundamentalist outlook, and to the many articles and books published by Fundamentalist professors.

Apart from that, Fundamentalists can press the point that there has been no conclusive disproof of the "Dictation Theory" of the verbal inspiration of the Bible or of the "Supernatural Incursion" theory of miracle. All the arguments against these views have, after all, been advanced by thinkers who assume the very point at issue, namely, the intrinsic impossibility of certain types of occurrences and the utter implausibility of the evidence on behalf of possible, but highly unlikely, occurrences (the transcendent and infinite God talking directly and audibly to men being an instance of the first sort of thing, and the instant healing of a totally paralyzed man being an instance of the second).

Furthermore, when they move to the attack, Fundamentalists point to the great changes that have taken place in higher criticism over the decades. The "Documentary Theory" of the Pentateuch and the multiplication of sources of such prophetic books as Isaiah have been replaced by theories which manifest far more conservative tendencies. What is more, no responsible higher critic could assert that a consensus on important issues, such as "The Quest for the Historical Jesus" now prevails. In light of this, Fundamentalists vehemently protest the fact that in so many great centers of theological learning the validity of the critical perspective is simply assumed and not argued for.

Higher critics used to spend a good deal of their energy arguing with Fundamentalists. Now they just get on with their work and concentrate on developing better tools, such as carbon tests, for advancing the scope of their field.

It is clear that the situation in philosophy, insofar as it pertains to the openness of philosophers to the meaningfulness of theological discourse, is not that far along, but it is well on its way. As one who is concerned (in the Tillichian sense) with philosophical theology, I find it, as already noted, a disturbing parallel.

The abandonment of the Positivistic crudities and the fluid state of analysis today open two possibilities to philosophical theologians: (1) Retreat like the Fundamentalists and say that, since analysis itself has problems, "Who are they to write us off? We can now be quite certain that no philosophy has the answers and so we can go back to where we were before, to a pre-positivistic philosophical outlook in which free-wheeling appeal to the synthetic a priori and all sorts of other devices is the fashion." (2) Work in and through the contemporary, analytically dominated, philosophical scene and struggle for conceptual adequacy.

The extent to which philosophical theologians can work in terms of the second option will determine the extent to which the parallel will prove misleading and irrelevant.

VI.   A Question for Hartshornians

One of the leading contemporary analytic philosophers has written that "our practice is a very fluid affair. If we are to speak of linguistic rules at all, we ought to think of them as rules which everyone has a licence to violate if he can show a point in doing so."[36] This might be taken as a slogan for theologians who follow through on the impetus that Charles Hartshorne has provided for philosophical theology. Hartshorne has called for, and executed, a radical revision of our conceptual apparatus in order to give to God, understood in terms of the concept of Perfection, the centrality that is his due. However, the points that Hartshorne has made in doing so have all been pretty much confined to his central theme: the adaptation of Whitehead's metaphysics to the purposes of philosophical theology.

Hartshorne's work in philosophical theology has been successful to a degree that more than justifies the interest shown in his work. He has shown that logical considerations, soberly expressed in the context of theological discourse, have a great deal to tell us about the religious impetus of theology. On logical grounds, Hartshorne maintains that the classical theistic treatment of the attributes of God is incoherent. He insists that the view that an omniscient God is nevertheless changeless in every respect whatever is a view that will not stand up under examination. In a world in which change is real, it is not conceivable that an omniscient being could know future events as *actual* in advance of their actual occurrence. Therefore, as events unfold in time, the state of knowledge of an omniscient God must change, and this is to say that *God changes* in respect of his knowledge.

However, Hartshorne also insists that the utterly changeless God of the classical theistic tradition is a religiously inadequate God. In evidence of this, he cites the fact that, within the framework of our experi-

---

[36]P. F. Strawson, *Introduction to Logical Theory* (London, 1952), 230.

ence of the contingent beings we encounter in everyday life, we find that the superior being is the being that changes in response to others, not the being that is unaffected. If a man sees a tree, the tree is not conscious of the man, whereas the man is aware of the tree and changes as a result; this is one of the things that makes the man superior to the tree. Hartshorne regards the classical view of an omnipotent and omniscient God who rules the world absolutely without being affected by the events that transpire in it as rooted in the concept—which he finds religiously unpalatable—of the Oriental view of the absolute potentate. Thus religious grounds supplement his logical ones for urging the purgation of the classical theistic view of the attributes of God.

Hartshorne's criticisms of the doctrines of classical theism are the most thoroughgoing and potently expressed since Hegel's. Furthermore, close attention to their religious content discloses the surprising phenomenon, to which Ogden has called our attention, that this theology is a startling complement to existentialistic anthropology.[37] Hartshorne's doctrine of God—expressed in logical symbols and, usually, without reference to the emotional overtones of religious language—captures the note of personal striving and creative freedom that is central to existentialistic concerns.

Yet at many points, his achievement is more a matter of pointing to the major tasks of philosophical theology than of executing them. The most important work that Hartshorne published in recent years was his lengthy essay on the ontological argument in which, placing heavy reliance on techniques of formal logic, he offered what seemed to be a "hard" proof of its validity, and so raised the hope that this statement of the proof might be the "real thing," that is, a cornerstone for the sort of conceptual revision that Hartshorne was calling for in his work. Hartshorne himself stated that this proof was not up to the job of dealing with the positivistic criticisms of religious language.[38] This ambitious and important task is, presumably, bequeathed to his followers.

The work that Hartshorne has done in adapting Whitehead's metaphysics to theological purposes and in criticizing and revising the doctrines of classical theology is an important contribution to philosophical theology but, in and of itself, this sort of thing will not evoke a new phase of the discussion between theologians and philosophers. Ogden has noted that "The 'new vision' [Hartshorne's] . . . has not yet enjoyed anything like the response—either from philosophers or from theologians—to which it is entitled."[39] As we have seen, despite the new

[37]S. Ogden, "Bultmann's Demythologizing and Hartshorne's Dipolar Theism," *Process and Divinity*.

[38]"What the Ontological Argument Does Not Do," *Review of Metaphysics*, Vol. XVII (1964).

[39]"Theology and Philosophy," 3.

openness of contemporary analytic philosophers, speculative metaphysics, in the traditional sense of the term, is still suspect, and rejected. Theological language regarding the transcendent God is even more emphatically written off. The buttressing of one questionable enterprise (theology) by means of an appeal to the insights of another questionable enterprise (Whiteheadian metaphysics) is not likely to compel attention from thinkers who are not already involved with one or the other of them. Since the analytic philosophers, who dominate the philosophical scene in the English-speaking world, are not involved with either, it would seem that prospects are not bright for discussion along the lines thus far pursued by Hartshorne and his followers.

To gain the attention of analytic philosophers, it would be necessary to come to grips with such current philosophical issues as Quine's "nominalism" and to show the fruitfulness of Whiteheadian metaphysics for areas other than theology. It might be objected that this would be equally unpersuasive. Analysts, it will be said, are so biased against speculative metaphysics that they would not pay attention to applications of it to any field whatever. Against this I would urge the example of Reinhold Niebuhr. He launched his critique of contemporary culture from the perspective of original sin, a perspective to which the climate of opinion of the day was deeply hostile. Yet he gained the attention of the non-theological and non-believing world—including many philosophers—by means of the power of his insights into politics, labor relations, international affairs, and the rest. Theologians may have been interested in his arguments with Augustine et al., over the interpretation of Christian doctrine; but if he had confined himself to this sort of thing, he would not have gained the attention of the uncommitted.[40]

In a remarkable essay on "What We Can Say about God," Fred Sommers provides a survey of the ontological options available to philosophical theologians. At the end of it, he makes a brief reference to the work of Whitehead and notes that its prospects for relevance are closely linked with work in the biophysical sciences.[41] This is the sort of extrinsic reference that would give a cutting edge to the work of Hartshorne's followers; and, if it were well done, analysts and others would listen whether they wanted to or not. In philosophy as in science, the fruitfulness of a theory is in direct proportion to the variety of kinds of circumstances to which it finds application. For this reason, I hope

[40]See W. K. Frankena, "Ethical Theory," in Philosophy, op. cit. for a statement of the way in which Reinhold Niebuhr and other Christian thinkers took over the cultural and intellectual role of James, Royce, Dewey, Santayana, and Whitehead.

[41]"What We Can Say about God," Judaism, XV (1966), 72ff. For an example of the sort of thing that I have in mind (and Sommers too, I should think), see S. Wright, "Biology and the Philosophy of Science," Process and Divinity, 101–125; 114–124 deal explicitly with panpsychism.

that the thinkers who are engaged in the revival of philosophical theology will not confine themselves to reflection on theological language. If they do so, they will wind up in a rut in which they talk to no one but themselves. This would be an irony of theological history because they would then be doing the very same things that the Barthians did; and surely one of the major factors underlying the renewed interest in philosophical theology is a reaction against the Barthian's tendency to restrict intellectual confrontations within the cozy confines of religious ingroups.

TWO

God

Toward a New Theism 10

Schubert M. Ogden

I

If anything is clear, it is that no religious tradition can long continue as a vital source of faith and life unless it is critically appropriated in each new historical situation. The importance of such tradition always lies in the precious freight of meaning it bears, not in the forms of expression through which that meaning is borne from the past to the present. All such forms are only more or less adequate to the actual occurrence of tradition, and they are to be retained, if at all, only because or insofar as they still make possible the "handing over" which the word "tradition" (*traditio*) originally signifies. Since whether any given forms of expression continue to serve this purpose is determined by our ever-changing historical situations, the more radical the changes from one situation to another, the more urgent and far-reaching the task of a critical interpretation of the tradition. There must be a winnowing and sifting of its essential meaning from its inessential forms—to the extent, indeed, implied by an Anglican bishop in the seventeenth century who remarked that "the most useful of all books on theology would be one with the title *De Paucitate Credendorum*, on the fewness of the things which a man must believe."[1]

Yet no less evident is that any such theological criticism has its bounds. What makes any religious tradition a tradition is that it has an essential meaning or motif which can be criticized as inessential only by abandoning rather than appropriating the tradition itself. Every tradition admits of critical interpretation for the simple reason that its

Revised from "Love Unbounded: The Doctrine of God," *The Perkins School of Theology Journal*, XIX, 3 (Spring 1966), pp. 5–17; and printed in *Theology In Crisis: A Colloquium on The Credibility of 'God'*, pp. 3–18, by Muskingum College. Used by permission of the publisher and Schubert M. Ogden.

[1]Quoted by W. R. Inge, *Things New and Old* (London: Longman's Green, 1933), 48.

forms of expression may always be appraised in the light of the basic motif they more or less adequately express. But no tradition may be fairly treated as a nose of wax, to be twisted and turned into whatever shape the exigencies of the present seem to demand. It will be appropriated by us only on its own terms; and we honor it more by rejecting it on those terms than by pretending to accept it on any other.

It is not the task of this lecture to attempt anything like a restatement of the Christian tradition. Yet one thing I am confident must be said, which does provide the starting-point for these reflections. The vital center of this whole tradition is its unambiguous witness to the reality of God as decisively re-presented to us in Jesus Christ. So evident is this, in fact, that it should be unnecessary even to point it out. But we live in strange times, when even the most obvious things are being called in question. I do not mean, of course, simply that ours is the so-called "age of atheism," for which the traditional Christian belief in God has become profoundly problematic for large numbers of thoughtful men. Nor am I thinking primarily of the various proposals of a "religion without God" with which all of us are familiar. Neither atheism as such nor the attempt to develop a religious outlook from the premise that "God is dead" is new to our present situation. As a matter of fact, a generation and more ago, experiments along this line were made by several prominent American philosophers of religion. In some cases—I think especially of George Santayana, John Dewey, and Henry Nelson Wieman—the results of such experiments were exceedingly fruitful and, to my mind, are still deserving of the most serious consideration. But what is in a way novel in our situation today is that somewhat similar proposals are now being put forward by certain Christian theologians. We are confronted by the strange phenomenon of a self-styled *"Christian* atheism," which maintains that the witness to God's reality has to be surrendered if there is to be anything like a tenable contemporary theology.

This position has been stated with the greatest clarity and consistency, in my judgment, by Paul M. van Buren in *The Secular Meaning of the Gospel.*[2] Van Buren argues that the attitudes of contemporary men are in every respect "secular" and that no presentation of the Christian witness can hope to be understandable which fails to reckon with this fact. Actually, what van Buren means by the word "secular" is just the outlook I should wish to distinguish as "secularist" or "secularistic." In his terms, "secular" refers to an essentially positivistic understanding of the scope of knowledge, as well as to an understanding of moral action that is exclusively humanistic. On my view, both understandings involve certain arbitrary negations which make it impossible properly

[2]New York: The Macmillan Company, 1963.

to refer to them by the essentially positive term "secular." It is one thing to affirm the validity of the scientific method and to insist on its complete autonomy within the field where it alone logically applies. But it is clearly something different to deny with the positivist that there is any other valid means to knowledge because the method of science circumscribes the limits of the whole cognitive sphere. Likewise, it is one thing to affirm that the sole standards of moral conduct are those implicit in human action itself, and quite another thing to deny with the humanist that our actions realize any will to good beyond the merely human and either require or admit of a transcendent justification. I hold that the positive affirmations here are entirely of a piece with the legitimate *secularity* of modern culture, and that no theology can fail to take them into account. Yet I equally hold that the denials in question do not follow from the affirmations and are, in that sense, arbitrary. They are the defining characteristics of that *secularism*, which seems to be becoming ever more widely prevalent among contemporary Western men, but which no theology can possibly countenance.

Terminology aside, however, van Buren is insistent that the outlook typical of men today makes any meaningful assertions about God impossible. "The empiricist in us finds the heart of the difficulty not in what is said about God, but in the very talking about God at all. We do not know 'what' God is, and we cannot understand how the word 'God' is being used."[3] Consequently, the theologian's only real option is simply to abandon any claim for God's reality and give himself to interpreting the Gospel in completely secular—or, as I should insist, secularistic —terms.

Oddly enough, van Buren holds that this choice is not only made necessary by our situation, but is also permitted as possible by the Gospel itself. Indeed, he finally assures us that the reality of God can be completely denied without in any way doing violence to the real meaning of the Christian witness. But I fear that with this assurance, his proposal ceases to be convincing and begins to appear as a not altogether ingenuous *tour de force*. However absurd talking about God might be, it could never be quite so obviously absurd as talking of Christian faith without God. If theology is possible today only on secularistic terms, the more candid way to say this is that theology is not possible today at all.

Of course, similar judgments are constantly passed by theological reactionaries, and there are many who regard a theology even on secular terms (such as I should want to defend) as equally out of the question. But the two cases, I am convinced, are at the crucial point totally unlike. Faith in God is not merely an element in Christian faith along

[3] *Ibid.*

with several other elements; it simply *is* Christian faith, the heart of the matter itself. Therefore, the very thing about the expressions of faith in the Christian tradition which makes a properly *secular* interpretation of them possible and even necessary also makes a *secularistic* theology impossible. By my lights, at least, the issue here is indeed either/or. For good or for ill, the Christian tradition stands by its witness that God is not dead but alive; and to decline to bear this witness is not simply to criticize that tradition, but to abandon it.

II

But the problem one faces in bearing this witness to God's reality is, as it were, compounded by yet another consideration. If we have regard for what may fairly be described as the "catholic" or "ecumenical" tradition in Christian theology, nothing is more striking than its repeated insistence that Christian belief in God is essentially reasonable. It is true that theologians have generally stressed the limitations of human reason, especially in things divine, and have left little question that the knowledge of God realized by Christian faith has both a scope and a certainty that reason as such is powerless to provide. Moreover, they have often invoked the distinction between a mere acknowledgement of God's reality intellectually and an actual acquaintance with him existentially, holding that the latter is impossible save where man's natural reason has been enlightened by the grace of God's own self-revelation. But, while theologians have thus emphasized that reason cannot produce faith, they have never tired of insisting that faith is always consistent with reason; and this explains why the greatest among them have again and again leaped to the defense of their Christian belief with an obvious confidence in its power to carry conviction with reasonable men. Thus almost all of the church's teachers have held that the existence of God is knowable, if not indeed demonstrable, even to reason, and that the dependence of all things on their primal cause is as definitely affirmed by the truest philosophy as by a theology whose source is the Christian revelation.

Yet it is just this confidence in the reasonableness of Christian theism that many of us today find it hard to share. In the back if not in the front of our minds, we are aware of the thoroughgoing criticism of classical theism which was so vigorously launched by Spinoza, only to be further confirmed and extended by virtually every major intellectual development since. We are forced to recognize that the form of theism which most Western men have taken for granted and have by and large made use of to explicate their understanding of faith in God is now widely held to be anything but reasonable. In fact, there are many today who make the more sweeping claim that theism as such has now been shown to be an unreasonable belief. But analysis discloses that this claim is what Kierkegaard might have called "an acoustic illusion": it is actually the negative echo of the prior claim of classical theists that theirs is the only form of Christian theism there is. Whether this claim is valid, or whether the question of theism is more complex than theists and atheists alike conventionally assume, we will presently want to ask. The important point just now is that recent announcements of the death of God are as widely received as they are largely because the God who is said to be dead is quite clearly the God conceived by a form of theism which has long since ceased to be reasonable to a vast number of contemporary minds.

How are we to account for this widespread rejection of classical theism? Without pretending to offer an exhaustive answer, I would suggest two main reasons why so many men today find the traditional form of belief in God unacceptable.

First, it seems to them that they can accept this traditional theism only by affirming statements to be scientifically or historically true without the requisite backing and warrants. Thus Christian faith in God as the Creator has usually been understood to require assent to a whole series of beliefs that are now widely regarded as false—e.g., that the creation of the world took place as recently as 4004 B.C. and that man and the various animals were all created as fixed species, in no way related to one another by any pattern of evolutionary development. Of course, it has gradually come to be agreed in the church that such beliefs are not essential to Christian faith in creation; and theologians today commonly maintain that the first two chapters of Genesis are properly interpreted as mythological. But, even from these theologians one encounters the claim that although "faith does not entail the correctness of any particular cosmological theory," some such theories "would lend the Judaic-Christian doctrine of creation a certain degree of external support."[4]

Likewise in matters of the so-called "last things," which have to do with God's action as Redeemer, men have traditionally been asked to assent to assertions that any cultivated mind today is bound to find incredible. Nineteen hundred years of unfulfilled expectations, together with our present knowledge of nature and history, have utterly discredited any notion of a near end of the world such as Christians in the past have often entertained; and even in the church the eschatological passages in Scripture are now rather generally allowed to be as mythological as those portraying creation. Yet some of the very theologians who are most insistent about this still hold that eschatological myths include a reference to "the final state of history" or "the chronological moment

[4]John Hick, *Philosophy of Religion* (Englewood Cliffs: Prentice-Hall, 1963), 9.

of the end," with which, presumably, scientific theories about the future development of the universe are also somehow concerned.[5]

Then, there is the whole matter of miracles, belief in which has traditionally been considered an integral element in Christian faith in God. According to the principal teacher of my own denomination, John Wesley, "If it please God to continue the life of any of his servants, he will suspend [gravitation] or any other law of nature: The stone shall not fall; the fire shall not burn; the floods shall not flow. . . . Gravitation . . . shall cease, that is, cease to operate, whenever the Author of it pleases."[6] Today, of course, many churchmen and theologians no longer find it necessary to take so extreme a position. They know, as Wesley did not, that many of the supposed miracles reported in Scripture can be interpreted as perfectly natural occurrences and that yet others are clearly the products of faith, instead of extraordinary happenings that somehow produced faith. Nevertheless, most of these persons would probably agree with the recent statement of a contemporary Christian philosopher that "Christian belief means accepting the resurrection of Christ, and therefore it seems to involve believing in at least one miracle."[7]

As usually presented, then, even by its more sophisticated spokesmen, classical theism requires acceptance of statements about the world, about its origin or end or the happenings within it, which men today are willing to accept, if at all, only with the backing and warrants of science or history. In the case of some of these statements, the problem is simply that our best scientific or historical knowledge clearly tells against them. In the case of others, the evidence we have either is inconclusive or else hardly even seems relevant to the question of their truth or falsity. In all cases, however, to accept such statements as true is to challenge the full autonomy of science and history within their own proper spheres; and it is this challenge to a genuinely secular outlook, rather than any particular statement in itself, which makes classical theism so widely unacceptable to contemporary men.

The second main reason for the rejection of this form of theism is that one can accept it only by affirming the entire classical metaphysical outlook of which it is integrally a part. To explain just what this means in such a way as also to do justice to the complexity and subtlety of classical metaphysics would lead us too far afield. But, al-

[5]John A. T. Robinson, *In the End God . . .: A Study of the Christian Doctrine of the Last Things* (London: James Clarke, 1950), 36, 50; cf. also p. 90: "Of course, something must actually happen to the individual, just as the world must end in one way and not another."

[6]*The Works of the Rev. John Wesley, A.M.*, ed by Thomas Jackson, (London: Wesleyan-Methodist Book-Room, 1829–1831), Vol. VI, p. 322.

[7]Ninian Smart, *Philosophers and Religious Truth*, (London: SCM Press, 1964), 26.

lowing for considerable oversimplification, I can at least try to make clear the essential point: the understanding of reality expressed in this kind of metaphysics is one for which all our distinctive experience and thought as modern secular men is negative evidence.

From its first great formulations by Plato and Aristotle, the chief defining characteristic of classical metaphysics has been its separation of what is given in our experience into two quite different kinds of reality. On the one hand, there is the present world of becoming, of time, change, and real relations, of which each of us is most immediately and obviously a part. Of this, Plato speaks in *The Republic* as "the twilight of becoming and perishing" (508). On the other hand, there is the wholly other world of timeless, changeless, and unrelated being, which is alone "real" in the full sense of the word and so alone worthy of the epithet "divine." Again, in Plato's words, this is the world of "the absolute and eternal and immutable" (479). Just how these two worlds are to be conceived, especially in relation to one another, has always been a problem for classical metaphysicians, to which they have offered a number of different solutions. Yet on one point, there has been complete consensus: the relations between the two worlds are one-way relations only, since the other divine world of pure being can be in no sense really related to this ordinary world of mere becoming. Ordinary beings are indeed related to God, whether as the formal cause which they somehow exemplify or as the final cause toward which they move in their several processes of self-development. But the converse of this statement does not hold: God is in no way genuinely related to the ordinary beings beyond himself, because for him to be thus related would involve his dependence on others and thus his participation in the time and change which are the very antithesis of his own utterly timeless and immutable being.

It is this general metaphysical outlook, bequeathed to the Western world by Greek antiquity, which provided the first fundamental concepts for the full theological explication of the Christian witness. Beginning with the church Fathers, theologians undertook to conceive the God attested by Holy Scripture as the wholly absolute Being of the philosophers. That this was a difficult, if not indeed impossible, undertaking had already been made evident by the parallel efforts of the Jewish thinker, Philo of Alexandria, who has perhaps the best claim to be the founder of classical theism. His writings leave no question that the God of Israel, whose very being is his involvement in the creatures of his love, can in no wise be simply identified with the Absolute of classical metaphysics. Even so, the whole tradition of what is usually called "Christian philosophy," whose most admirable expression is, doubtless, the imposing system of Aquinas, is but a series of attempts to make the identification; and the profound influence of that tradition, even on those who now declare its God to be dead, is proof that these attempts have enjoyed some kind of success. So far as most Western men have conceived God at all, in distinction from believing in him or merely picturing him in the manner of mythology, they have done so in the concepts of the Greek metaphysics of being.

Just this, however, enables us to understand the major stumbling-block which classical theism places in the way of many of our contemporaries. Not only have such men long since become convinced of the essential incoherence of this theism in its efforts to combine the religious insights of Christianity with the philosophical wisdom of the Greeks, but they are also deeply repelled by the central claim of Greek wisdom, that this world of time and change is somehow inferior or not fully real. Thus one of the so-called "death of God" theologians, William Hamilton, states that "in this world . . . there is no need for religion and no need for God. This means that we refuse to consent to that traditional interpretation of the world as a shadow-screen of unreality, masking or concealing the eternal which is the only true reality. . . . The world of experience is real, and it is necessary and right to be actively engaged in changing its patterns and structures."[8] I find this statement revealing in a number of ways. For one thing, it discloses how easy it is for many of us to move in our thought from the words "religion" or "God" to "that traditional interpretation of the world" in terms of which these words have usually been understood. For another, it suggests that the event the "death of God" theologians are so confusedly and confusingly summoning us to acknowledge is not the death of God but the demise of this traditional interpretation of reality. But, most important of all, this statement exposes the real nerve of modern man's profound opposition to the traditional form of Christian faith in God. Man today finds this form of faith so objectionable because it directly contradicts his profound secularity, his deep conviction of the reality and significance of this world of time and change and of his own life within it. If God must be conceived as the Absolute of traditional metaphysics, and so as in the nature of the case totally unaffected by man and the world, this can only imply that the entire secular order is in the last analysis neither real nor of any consequence. What we do or fail to do can finally make no difference one way or the other, since God is in any case a statically complete perfection, utterly independent of anything beyond himself. But simply to exist as a contemporary man is implicity to deny any such understanding of reality. The whole direction of modern culture, from the Renaissance onwards, has been away from this kind of metaphysical other-worldiness and from a Christianity which Nietzsche could plausibly dismiss as "Platonism for

[8]"The Death of God Theology," *Christian Scholar*, XLVIII, 1 (Spring 1965), 45f.

'the people.' "[9] We now realize that whatever is real and important must somehow include the present world of becoming which we most certainly know and affirm; and this means that we find the classical form of Christian theism simply incredible.

It will have become apparent from this discussion that I myself recognize the force of these two main contemporary objections to traditional Christian belief. So far as I understand the matter, the conditions of reasonableness in our situation are secular, even if not secularistic, conditions, i.e., they demand the unqualified acceptance both of the method and world-picture of modern science and critical history and of the reality and significance of this world of time and change, which is the context of our lives as secular men. Consequently, I hold that if one is to continue to affirm with the Christian tradition that faith in God is both indispensable *and* reasonable, it is incumbent on him to show that such faith may be explicated in other terms than those of classical Christian theism. By the same token, to decline this obligation seems to me in effect to abandon the Christian heritage. For, in that case, one either countenances the charge that the Christian witness is as unreasonable as its modern critics allege or else abets the claim that it can dispense with faith in God altogether as some of its own theologians are now trying to persuade us it can.

III

The crucial question, then, is whether there can be any form of genuine theistic belief other than that represented by classical Christian theology. My own clear conviction is that there can and that important recent developments both in theology and in philosophy enable us to reckon quite legitimately with a neoclassical theism. By this I mean that we already have before us a way of conceiving the reality of God, in comparison with which the theism of the classical tradition can be seen to be but a first and rather rough approximation. Moreover, while I cannot fully support it here, my belief is that this new theism may fairly claim to be reasonable in a way that the older theism in principle may not. At any rate, the neoclassical view clearly seems capable of meeting the two main objections with which classical theists today are generally confronted—as I now hope to show by briefly considering the fundamental insights from which the new view has developed.

The first of these insights derives primarily (though not exclusively) from existentialist philosophy and from the use to which this philosophy has been put in certain forms of contemporary theology.

[9]*Beyond Good and Evil*, trans. by Marianne Cowan, (Chicago: Henry Regnery, 1955), xii.

This is the discovery that the real meaning of all religious language, regardless of its terms and categories, is existential, or, if you will, metaphysical, rather than scientific or historical. Basic to this discovery is the recognition that human experience is not exhausted by the external sense perceptions of which science and history are in their different forms the critical analysis. Man also enjoys an internal awareness of his own existence and of the existence of his fellow creatures as finite-free parts of an infinite and encompassing whole. Hence the questions to which he naturally wants answers cannot be confined merely to those that seek a more reliable understanding of the variable details of reality disclosed by his senses. Beyond all such questions, he also inquires about the constant structure of reality, of himself and the world and of their ultimate ground, of which he is always more or less clearly aware insofar as he exists as a man at all.

The driving motive of this second kind of inquiry, as, indeed, indirectly of the whole of human existence, is what can only be described as an elemental confidence in the final worth of our life as men. We exist as the selves we are only because of an inalienable assurance that our lives are not merely indifferent, but are somehow both real and of ultimate significance. Thus one of the principal tasks set for human reflection right from the start is so to understand the constant structure of all our experience that this original assurance can be understood to make sense. But this is to say that the kind of meaning most fully expressed by the statements of science and history is not the only kind of meaning there is. There is also the existential or metaphysical kind of meaning which arises from this second kind of human questioning and whose most direct form of expression is the language that we ordinarily distinguish as "religious."

The importance of this discovery can be fully appreciated only if we recall a peculiarity of religious language in its primitive form as myth. It is the very nature of myth to obscure the basic human purpose it exists to serve. Although its real use is the existential or metaphysical use of clarifying our original confidence in the worth of life, the terms and categories in which it speaks are not derived from our inner awareness of our existence in relation to totality, but from our external perception of the world by means of our senses. Consequently, if mythical statements are considered in themselves, in abstraction from their actual function in human life, they can only too easily be taken as simply man's first crude attempts at what we now know as science or history. The Christian myths of creation and of the last things can then be dismissed as primitive cosmology, while all talk of miracles can be treated as a misguided effort at scientific explanation. But as soon as we recognize that mythical language has another and logically quite different use from that which its terms and categories suggest, this whole familiar situation appears in a new light. We are then able to see that a mythical assertion may be put forward as both meaningful and in a sense true without in the least challenging the full autonomy of science and history within their own proper domains. Because the meaning of such an assertion is really existential or metaphysical, the conditions of its truth are the conditions implicit in *that* kind of meaning, not those with which either the scientist or the historian is quite rightly concerned.

I noted earlier that it is rather generally conceded today that traditional Christian talk about creation and the last things has the character of myth. But, often enough, as the statements previously cited make clear, theologians still assume that mythical language is in part, at least, on logically the same footing as that of science or history. Hence, even though they acknowledge myth's existential import, they nevertheless look for support for the doctrine of creation from cosmological theorizing and suppose that eschatological myths somehow make reference to some remote "final state" of history or nature. I am convinced that this position, widespread as it is, must now be rejected as a compromise in view of our deeper insight into the real meaning of mythical language and of religious language generally. The use of such language is neither in whole nor in part a properly scientific or historical use. Rather, its entire meaning is existential or metaphysical, in the sense of expressing some understanding of our existence in its constant structure and in relation to its ultimate ground and end. This means that the reference of religious language is never to the past or to the future, but always and only to the present—to the present constituted by our own existence as selves in relation to our fellow creatures and to that circumambient reality from which we come and to which we go. Therefore, the real meaning of the Christian doctrines of creation and of the last things is to illumine each present moment of our actual existence as an existence within and under the all-embracing love of God. They teach us that the ultimate beginning and end of all our ways—indeed, of the whole finite order of which we know ourselves to be parts—is the pure unbounded love which is decisively represented in Jesus Christ. And no less clear is that the irreducible core of meaning even of miracle is wholly existential or metaphysical. Thus, rightly to believe in the central Christian "miracle" of Christ's resurrection is in no way to challenge the method of science or to suspend the warrants of responsible historical inquiry. It is to believe, rather, that the gift and demand which are re-presented to us in Jesus are none other than the very love of God himself, and so a love which is even now the encompassing mystery in which all our lives are set.

Important as this first insight is, however, it is not alone sufficient to justify speaking of a new and more adequate theism. So long as it

is assumed that classical metaphysics in some form is the only metaphysics there is, the claim that the meaning of religious language is
really existential or metaphysical in no way allows the theist to take
up a tenable position. But it is just the assumption that metaphysics
somehow has to be classical which other recent developments in philosophy give us every good reason to question. In fact, through the
work of several philosophers both in America and in Europe, our
century has witnessed the emergence of a distinctively modern metaphysical outlook which at last offers a real alternative to the *philosophia perennis* of our Western tradition. Part of the reason the new
outlook presents such a choice is that in the very philosophies in which
it has achieved its most complete and uninhibited expression, notably
in the philosophies of Alfred North Whitehead and Charles Hartshorne,
it has taken an explicitly theistic form. Hence the second insight which
permits us to reckon with a neoclassical theism is that one can clearly
arrive at a genuinely theistic conclusion without in any way presupposing the premises of classical metaphysics.

To see how this is possible, we may contrast these classical premises with the quite different ones of the new metaphysics. We saw
earlier that the main assumption of all classical metaphysicians is that
such fundamental features of our experience as time, change, and real
relations to others cannot possibly be conceived to characterize the
ultimate or divine reality. It follows, then, that, while ordinary beings
are indeed related to God, he himself is in no way related to them and
that the present world of nature and history is neither fully real nor
ultimately significant. In the case of Christian thinkers, to be sure, these
implications have usually been obscured by the presence in their
thought of another quite different understanding of reality which derives from Holy Scripture. They have spoken of God not only as the
metaphysical Absolute, whose only relation to the world is wholly
external, but also as the loving heavenly Father revealed in Christ, who
freely creates the world and guides it toward its fulfilment with tender
care. But even then, the most that can be said of these theological positions is that they are essentially incoherent, since the fundamental
premise of all their reasoning is still the main assumption of classical
metaphysics. It is just this assumption, however, that the new metaphysicians most sharply call in question. They maintain that the very
nature of reality is to be temporal and related to others and that even
the ultimate reality denoted by the word "God" can be properly conceived only in these terms. That such a conception is possible, they
argue, at once becomes clear as soon as we free ourselves from certain
arbitrary prejudices.

Thus, for example, *to be affected by* all others is evidently as unique a property as *to affect* all others, since neither property could con-

ceivably belong to any but a completely perfect or divine being. Hence there is at least as much reason to think of God as the ultimate *effect* of the world as to conceive him as its primal *cause*. And what is it, after all, that is truly admirable in one whom we consider good, even in our ordinary relations with one another? Is it a complete indifference to the being and needs of others, a stubborn independence in pursuing one's own aims? Or is it, rather, that sensitivity to others, that taking account of their being and needs as one's own which we call by the word "love"? The whole idea of moral goodness as we ordinarily make use of it clearly seems to depend for its meaning on such other basic ideas as real relation to others and capacity for change. Consequently, if we are to conceive of the truly perfect One, the One who is *eminently* good, it can hardly be otherwise than as the supreme exemplification of these very ideas, as himself the supremely social and temporal reality. So far from being the wholly absolute and immutable Being of the classical philosophers, God must really be conceived as the eminently relative One, whose openness to change contingently on the actions of others is literally boundless.

As such, of course, there is a sense in which God may be appropriately characterized by the classical attributes. Since his sociality or relativity to others is itself relative to nothing, it is quite properly spoken of as absolute. God, one may say, is absolutely relative. Likewise, the one thing about God which is never-changing, and so in the strictest sense immutable, is that he never ceases to change in his real relations of love with his whole creation. Precisely as eminently temporal, God is also of necessity strictly eternal or everlasting. But, important as it is to acknowledge this continuity with the older theism, there is no mistaking the radical difference. Although all the classical attributes contain an element of truth, they are neither the whole truth about God's nature nor the surest clue to discerning it. That clue, rather, is to be found in the ancient religious insight that the very principle of all being is love, in the sense of the mutual giving and receiving whereby each of us becomes himself only in genuine interdependence with his fellows. If to be even the least of things is somehow to be related to others and dependent on them, then the One "than whom none greater can be conceived" can only be the supreme instance of such social relatedness, the One who as the unbounded love of others is the end no less than the beginning of all that either is or can ever be.

As conceived in terms of the new metaphysics, then, God is without quibble or qualification a genuinely personal, because a genuinely temporal and social, being. Indeed, it will have become clear from even this brief summary that there is a strict analogy between God's existence as the eminent person and our own existence as men. Even as we are the selves we are only in relation to others and most directly to the others, the organs and cells, that constitute our own bodies, so God, too, exists as the supreme self only in relation to the cosmic body which is the world or the universe as a whole. For some, of course, this implication is sufficient to discredit the claim of the new view to be genuinely theistic and to provoke the charge of pantheism. But I do not think this charge need worry us very much. If we have any knowledge at all of the views that have usually (and properly) been called "pantheistic," then we should have no difficulty recognizing that the new theism is as different from them as from their traditional theistic counterparts. Both of the older types of view can be easily shown to rest on the same classical metaphysical premises, and it is just these premises which, as we have seen, a neoclassical theism is most concerned to question.

In any event, such a theism definitely seems to overcome the second main objection that reasonable men today make to the classical position. Not only does it appear free from the theoretical incoherence of the older theism, but it also removes what we saw to be the major stumbling-block to modern man's ever really hearing any witness to the reality of God—namely, the implication that this world of time and change is ultimately unreal and lacking in significance. The clear implication of the new theism, on the contrary, is that this world could not conceivably be more real or significant. Because nature and history are nothing less than the body of God himself, everything that happens has both a reality and an importance which are in the strictest sense infinite. The ultimate end of all our actions is not simply ourselves or our fellow creatures, but the everlasting life of the One to whom no thing is merely indifferent because each thing is known and valued forever for exactly what it is. Thus the *positive* motive of the "death of God" theologian cited earlier is entirely legitimate: "the world of experience *is* real, and it *is* necessary and right to be actively engaged in changing its patterns and structures." This is so, however, because anything we do to advance the real good either of ourselves or of one another is done quite literally to "the glory of God," as an imperishable contribution to God's ever-growing perfection, which is, indeed, "the true life of all."

I am well aware of the inconclusiveness of this argument. The most I can have accomplished by it is to have suggested a somewhat unconventional approach both to the problem that Christian faith in God raises today and to the way in which it might just possibly be solved. But I do hope you will have carefully noted the real nerve of this whole approach—namely, its rejection as superficial of the kind of "two-cornered thinking" which tries to reduce basic problems to the familiar dyadic formulations of philosophical and theological controversy. In my judgment, such conventional forced options as monism or pluralism, idealism or realism, determinism or indeterminism are all question-begging from start to finish, because they fail to exhaust *all* the relevant alternatives between which a reasoned choice may in fact be made. But the same is true, I have tried to suggest, of the usual discussion of the reality of God. If we are to have any hope of advancing this discussion, it is necessary to challenge *all* the answers to the theistic question, affirmative and negative alike. This is so not merely because the current formulation of this question, "Is God dead?" is as such meaningless, since it seems evident enough that the issue this formulation is intended to express is the clearly meaningful issue between theism and atheism. No, the more basic reason for the challenge is that this very issue of theism or atheism is too complex to admit of the simple either/or kinds of answers apparently called for by the question emblazoned on the cover of *Time* for Easter 1966.

Thus, in the argument I have set before you, I have been following what I take to be the only truly rational method of getting at the problem. This is the method of the "double rejection," of challenging both sides of the usual two-cornered dispute with the aim at descrying a genuinely new position in which the legitimate motives in each of the older ones are given their due. Specifically, I have ventured to challenge *both* of the simplifications whereby the problem before us is most commonly rendered incapable of solution—namely, the simplifications that one can be truly secular only by accepting modern secularism and that one can believe in God only by accepting the claims of classical theism. It is hardly surprising, therefore, that the conclusion for which I have argued unites as well as divides me from all those who represent the more conventional views. With those who contend that "God is dead" I am at one in attesting the demise of a particular form of theistic belief which not only is unreasonable to contemporary men, but has also proved incapable of doing justice to the historic witness of the Christian community. On the other hand, with those who witness that "God lives" I gladly join in what seems to me not only the central affirmation of Christian faith, but also the conclusion more or less clearly implied by all my experience and thought simply as a man.

The Formally Possible Doctrines of God

11

Charles Hartshorne

For nearly two thousand years European theology staked its fortunes upon a certain conception of divinity. In spite of the seeming variety of doctrines, one basic principle was accepted by almost all philosophical theists. Only in the last few decades has a genuinely alternative type of theology been at all widely considered—so unobtrusively, however, that many opponents of theism, even some of the most distinguished, are still fighting the older conception exclusively, convinced that if they can dispose of it the theological question will be settled. And many of those who find the idea of a godless universe incredible suppose that it is to traditional theology that they must turn. Both parties are mistaken. Today the theistic question, like many others, is a definitely new one. Many of the old controversies, in their old forms, are antiquated.

As traditional theology was a relatively well defined system, the same in certain basic respects—despite all sorts of philosophical and ecclesiastical differences—in Augustine, Thomas Aquinas, Maimonides, Leibniz, Calvin, Immanuel Kant, and some schools of Hindu thought, so the new theology which many be contrasted with the old is found more or less fully and consistently represented in thinkers as far apart as William James, . . . Henri Bergson, F. R. Tennant, . . . A. N. Whitehead, . . . Nicholas Berdyaev, . . . and in numerous others of every brand of Protestantism, besides a few . . . Roman Catholics. I have also heard a clear statement of some aspects of it from a leading Hindu thinker, Radhakamal Mukerjee. Of course, there are interesting differences between these theologians, just as there were between Bonaventura and Calvin; and in some writers now, as of old, the logical

Abridgment of "The Formally Possible Doctrines" from *Man's Vision of God*. Copyright, 1941 by Charles Hartshorne. Reprinted by permission of Harper & Row, Publishers and Charles Hartshorne.

implications are more adequately and rigorously worked out than in others. But there are some fundamental points of agreement which are rapidly becoming standard among non-Roman Catholic theologians.

To be aware of these points of convergence is essential to a liberal education today. They are as characteristic of our time as relativity physics and logical positivism are, or as medieval theology was of the thirteenth century. Ideas which until about fifty years ago were almost wholly neglected, never clearly worked out and systematized, and perhaps passed over for centuries with scarcely a mention, are now to be met in scores of theological works and in philosophical works that deal carefully with theology. The time seems at hand for attempts to state clearly the revolution of thought through which we have been passing.

What is the "new" doctrine? We shall see presently that it *must* be an expression of one of the three and only three formally possible views (including atheism and positivism as special cases of one of the three) regarding the supreme being, and that there are reasons for characterizing the new view as that one of the three which is related to the main line of the tradition as a carefully qualified assertion is to an unqualified one, and related to atheism (and certain heretical extremes of theism) as to an unqualified denial. In other words, it is related to the two other possible views as a "higher synthesis" to its "thesis" and "antithesis," as embraced and corrected in a "higher unity," or as a balanced whole truth to its two contrasting half-truths. From this standpoint traditional atheism and traditional theism are two sides of the same error, one of the most characteristic errors of human thought.

An immediate objection to the suggestion of a new idea of God will doubtless be that the term God as defined by usage properly means the God of the religious tradition. But we must distinguish, in the tradition, between religion and theology. Granting that "God" is a religious term, and that theology attempted to describe the object of religious devotion, it is one of the principal questions at issue whether or not this attempt was wholly successful. It is a belief of many today that the "new" theology is more, not less, religious than the old,[1] at least if religion means "devoted love for a being regarded as superlatively worthy of love," which is the Christian conception and to some extent the conception of the higher religions generally.

Of course theologians do not now regard as worthless and merely wrong the entire vast structure of historic theology, any more than Einstein so regards Newton's physics—to use an analogy which could

[1]One of the earliest expressions of this attitude is to be found in Otto Pfleiderer's *Grundriss der christlichen Glaubens- und Sittenlehre* (Berlin: Georg Reimer, 1888), Sections 61, 67–69, 84.

easily be pressed too far, but whose value could also be underesti-
mated. What is now being done is to distinguish two strands in the theological tradition which were not clearly held apart in the past, and to
argue that they are not only distinguishable, but so related that only
one of them can be true, and so related also that which one, if either,
is true can be ascertained from the logical relations between the two
strands alone, since one of the strands is incompatible alike with the
assertion and the denial of the other, and hence, by recognized logical
principles, is incompatible with itself and necessarily false. It is somewhat—to use another imperfect analogy—like the discovery in geo-
metry of the independence of the parallel postulate from the other
assumptions of Euclid; though in the theological case it is not really
independence but inconsistency which is involved. Thus it is not a
question of the logical possibility, merely, of what might be called a
"non-Euclidean theology," but of its logical necessity, at least if there
is to be any theology at all. (Unfortunately, there is no individual name
which can conveniently serve as the theological parallel to Euclid; but
Philo, a Jewish scholar of the first century, might be taken as the first
man to give relatively complete expression to the postulate in question,
and so we might speak of the current doctrine as non-Philonian theology, in a sense in which Aquinas, Spinoza, Royce, and orthodox
Hinduism are all Philonian.[2])

The "strand" which theologians, on the whole, still propose to
retain, and which is alone self-consistent, as judged by its relations to
the other strand, is the popularly familiar definition of God as everlasting, all-controlling, all-knowing, and ethically good or "holy" to the highest possible degree. It may seem that this is just traditional theology and
must involve the whole time-hallowed system. The extraordinary fact
is that this has been found not to be the case. None of the older theologians (unless the neglected—and persecuted—Socinians, and the
neglected Jew Gersonides, in the sixteenth and fourteenth centuries
respectively, be exceptions) were content with this popular definition of
God and the consequences which genuinely follow from it. They invariably adopted other conceptions as even more fundamental; and rather
than attempt seriously to deduce these other conceptions from the
popular definition, they treated the latter as a more or less dangerously
loose or anthropomorphic equivalent of the more fundamental definition. This more fundamental definition turns upon such terms as
perfection, infinity, absoluteness, self-dependence, pure actuality, immutability. God, for all the church writers, and for many others, in-

---

[2]The "new" theology can also be called Platonic if one interprets Plato somewhat otherwise than the Neo-Platonists and most scholars have done. See Raphael
Demos, *The Philosophy of Plato* (Charles Scribner's Sons, 1939), 120–125.

cluding Spinoza, was the "absolutely infinite," the altogether maximal, supreme, or perfect, being. All his properties, including the popular religious ones so far as philosophically valid, were to be deduced from this absoluteness or perfection, as is so beautifully explained by Thomas Aquinas. . . .

If theology is capable of rejuvenation, its hope lies, I believe, in a re-examination of the idea of infinity or perfection. Perhaps this idea is ambiguous, perhaps there is a sense in which God should be conceived as perfect, another sense in which perfection cannot apply to God, because (it may be) this sense involves an absurdity or, in other words, is really nonsense. Perhaps God is perfect in whatever ways perfection can really be conceived; but some among the traditional theological ways of trying to conceive perfection are capable of producing only pseudo-concepts devoid of consistent meaning.

To discuss God is, by almost universal usage, to discuss some manner of "supreme" or "highest" or "best" individual (or superindividual) being. As a minimal definition, God is an entity somehow *superior* to other entities. Now such superiority may be merely with respect to other actual entities, or with respect to all entities whether actual or possible. The second or more complete superiority seems to give the appropriate meaning of "perfection," and was defined long ago by Anselm in his description of God as "that than which none greater can be conceived." This definition presupposes only the ideas of *something* ("that"), *greater* or more or better (more in value) *than, negation* or none, and the conceivable or *possible*, and these ideas are secular as well as religious. Indeed, no ideas are more elementary and unavoidable in philosophy; hence it is clear that religion and philosophy can and must meet on common ground, provided the Anselmian definition successfully defines the religious object. But before we can decide whether the secular terms employed can apply to the God of religion we must be clear as to what the terms mean. Astonishingly enough, the simple phrase "none greater" involves two major equivocations, not indeed as Anselm used the phrase, but as it might reasonably be used, even though the possibility of such usage seems not to have been clearly seen by Anselm or anyone else. The neglected usages constitute, together with Anselm's usage, a complete set of possible meanings of "perfect being," choice between which meanings *is* the theistic problem, a problem not fully stated until the neglected meanings are made explicit.

"None" may mean "no entity other than *that* (the being said to be perfect) *as it actually is*," or it may mean "no entity other than *that as it either is or else could be or become*." According to the first meaning (which follows automatically if one assumes that the perfect can have no potential states—an assumption not deducible from the mere idea of "none greater," because of the latter's equivocal connotation) the perfect is *unsurpassable in conception or possibility even by itself;* according to the second meaning it is *unsurpassable except by itself.* The first or absolute unsurpassability can be called *absolute perfection,* the second may be called *relative perfection.* (We shall see in the appendix to this chapter, and the reader may have noted, that there is still a third possibility, though apparently it is of no great importance.)

"Greater" has as many meanings as there are dimensions or *respects* of more and less (or better and worse). But from a purely formal point of view (important because it is exact and non-controversial) there are just three possibilities, two positive and one negative. By "greater" we may mean, "in *some* (but not all) respects" (say in size or in ethical goodness); or we may mean, "in *all* respects whatever"; while the joint negative of these two, "in *no* respect," gives the third possibility.

Combining the two meanings of "none" with the three meanings of "greater" we derive seven possible cases, only one of which is the unequivocal negation of "none greater," or of "unsurpassability even by the conceivable." Thus it is proved that the question, Is there a perfect being? is six distinct questions rather than one. Has anyone a right to assure us, in advance of exploration of the other five, that the Anselmian (unconscious) selection of one among the six—as the faithful rendering either of the religious question or of the most fruitful philosophical one—is safely established by the fact that the choice has been repeated no less unconsciously by multitudes of theologians? If anyone asserts this, I must doubt his understanding of the elementary requirements of good reasoning.

The seven cases can be arranged, in several different ways, into three main groups. The following of the possible triadic arrangements seems the most useful:

Group	Symbol	Case	Symbol	Interpretation
I	(A)	1	A	Absolute perfection in *all* respects.
II	(AX)	2	AR	Absolute perfection in *some* respects, relative perfection in all others.
		3	ARI	Absolute perfection, relative perfection, and "imperfection" (neither absolute nor relative perfection), each in *some* respects.
		4	AI	Absolute perfection in *some* respects, imperfection in all others.
III	(X)	5	R	Absolute perfection in *no* respects, relative in all.

Group Symbol	Case	Symbol	Interpretation
	6	RI	Absolute perfection in *no* respects, relative in some, imperfection in the others.
	7	I	Absolute perfection in *no* respects, imperfection in all.

Explanation of Symbols: A stands for absolute perfection, R for relative perfection, I for the joint negative of A and R, X for the negative of A (and thus for the disjunction of R and I), and (A) or (X) for the factors occurring throughout a group.

Note: It will be shown in the appendix to this chapter that imperfection can be subdivided into two possible forms, making fifteen cases in all, though the additional eight seem of little importance—despite the fact that all eight express modes of unsurpassability, and so of perfection in the most general sense!

In a different mode of presentation we have:

Group	I			II			III	
A in	*all*			*some*			*no*	respects
	(A)			(AX)			(X)	
Case	1	2	3	4	5	6	7	
	A	AR	ARI	AI	R	RI	I	

Note: It might be thought that God's "supremacy" requires not only that he cannot conceivably be surpassed, but that he cannot even be equaled. Anyone who wishes to experiment with this conception of the *unrivaled as well as unsurpassed* is of course at liberty to do so. My reason for neglecting the concept—which might be called "incomparability"—is that I agree with the usual verdict of theologians that the unsurpassable is bound to be unique, so that if superiority is out of the question, equality is also. If good reason for doubting this verdict can be found, then "incomparability" should be substituted, at least experimentally, for "unsurpassability" in the definition of perfection.

So far as I know, this is the only rigorous *formal* classification (which as formal and a mere classification is beyond intelligent controversy) of possible doctrines about God—except mere dichotomies (e.g., God is or is not eternal, one with all reality, etc.), which are never very helpful because only one of the two classes has positive content. Yet, though formal, the classification is relevant to religion, if religion believes in an unsurpassable being. And it certainly is relevant to philosophy; for the seven cases (as formal possibilties) follow automatically from concepts which philosophy is bound to use.

At least the classification serves this purpose: it shows how hopelessly ambiguous are phrases like "perfect being," "finite God," "absolute," and the like. Six of the seven cases come under the phrase, "perfect being," if perfection means unsurpassability. At least four are compatible with the description, "finite." Four are definitely included in the class of "absolute" beings. Yet within each classification the differences are at least as important as the resemblances, indeed much more so. For it can be shown that the difference between absolute perfection in all, in some, and in no respects is the crucial difference, and yet it is neglected by all the concepts mentioned and by most generally current ones. . . .

Take, for example, the term pantheism. By any usual definition of this term, it should be possible to give a plausible interpretation of *all seven* of our cases as conforming to the definition. Thus pantheism means literally almost anything you please, and so nearly nothing. That is probably the chief reason for its popularity as a label for opponents. And it ought to be clear that to say, "God is the all," means whatever one's view of the all implies, perhaps nothing definite whatever, for offhand we have no clear notion of the all.

It is impossible to think effectively about seven possibilities at once. We think best in threes. As has been shown, the seven possibilities fall logically into three groups. God, if he exists, is *absolutely* (not relatively) perfect in all, in some, or in no respects. The usual view has been the first. Atheism is a special case of the third, in which man or some wholly imperfect thing is regarded as the nearest thing to a "supreme being" that exists. So here is the primary issue: Which group contains the truth? One of them, by absolute logical requirements, must do so. (If perfection is meaningless, this only makes case seven, that is, group three, true a priori.) When we know the answer to this question, we shall at least know whether or not the usual view of God ("usual" in philosophy and theology, perhaps not really usual in religion) is sound, and whether or not atheism or something close to it is sound, or whether, finally, the truth lies in a less explored region, the second group.

It must in all this discussion be understood that certain doubtful or trivial meanings of "perfect" or "unsurpassable" are excluded (merely to save time and energy), such as that a squirrel is perfect if it has all that is demanded by the concept (whose concept?) of a squirrel, or that a nail is as good as any other could be if it holds the building together as long and as well as is wanted. Such merely subjective or merely instrumental perfection is not what is meant by the perfection of God. It is not for this or that special purpose or point of view that God is unsurpassable. Rather it is his purpose and point of view themselves which are thought to be unsurpassable and the very standard of all other purposes or perspectives. Everything is good merely *for* something except persons, or at least sentient beings, but these are good in themselves. God (if he be an individual) must be at least sentient, or he is anything but unsurpassable.

These things being understood, it follows that *one, and only one, of the following propositions must be true:*

1. There is a being in *all* respects absolutely perfect or unsurpassable, in no way and in no respect surpassable or perfectible. (*Theism of the First Type;* absolutism, Thomism, most European theology prior to 1880.)
2. There is no being in all respects absolutely perfect; but there is a being in *some* respect or respects thus perfect, and in some respect or respects not so, in some respects surpassable, whether by self or others being left open. Thus it is not excluded that the being may be relatively perfect in all the respects in which it is not absolutely perfect. (*Theism of the Second Type;* much contemporary Protestant theology, doctrines of a "finite-infinite" or perfect-perfectible God.)
3. There is no being in *any* respect absolutely perfect; all beings are in all respects surpassable by something conceivable, perhaps by others or perhaps by themselves in another state. (Doctrines of a merely finite God, polytheism in some forms, atheism.)

This division is exclusive and exhaustive. To prove any two of these propositions false is to establish the truth of the remaining proposition; there can be no "higher synthesis" which combines the truth of any two or of all three of them, except as this synthesis amounts to accepting some one of the three as it stands and contradicting some part of each of the other two; that is, one of the three must be the higher synthesis. One may subdivide the three cases, but one cannot evade the necessity for rejecting some two and affirming some one of them as a whole, or else giving up the theistic question, the latter option being not an additional objective possibility but merely a subjective attitude toward the three possibilities. Of course one might say that there are two Gods, one corresponding to the first proposition, the other to the second proposition without the initial negative clause. But this would merely be a special case under Proposition One, and would have importance only if Proposition One is acceptable as it stands and Proposition Two false as it stands. After we have decided, if we do so decide, that there is one God wholly, partially, or not at all absolutely perfect, it will then be time enough to ask if there is also another God with another of the three characteristics.

Would it not be satisfying if the debate between atheism and theism turned out to have been so stubborn because the truth was in neither, as traditionally conceived, but in a middle ground not by any means a weak compromise between them but a clear-cut alternative as definite and legitimate, formally regarded, as any other? Without pretending here to anything like conclusiveness, I will give some reasons for taking this possibility seriously.

First of all, what does religion (not theology) say as to the three groups? Suppose the usual religious ideas of omniscience, omnipotence, and holiness or supreme righteousness be accepted. This seems to mean that God is absolutely perfect in knowledge, power, and ethical goodness. Does it follow that he is absolutely perfect in all respects? What about happiness or bliss? Surely religion is not, at any rate, so emphatic here. Is not God displeased by sin, and so something less than purely happy in beholding it? Does he not love us and therefore sympathize with our sufferings, wish that they might be removed? Do we not wish to "serve" God, carry out his purposes, contribute to his life somehow? All this must be explained as extremely misleading, if not indefensible, if God enjoys absolute bliss in eternity. But, you say, would not perfect power, wisdom, and goodness insure perfect bliss? Not at all, I answer with all the conviction I can feel about anything. To be happy is not a mere function of these three variables. For to know all that exists is not to know all that might exist, except as potentialities, and if potentialities are as good as actualities, then let us all cease to exist and be done with it. It is not even true that the omniscient must know details of the future, unless it can be proved, against Bergson, Whitehead, Peirce, James, and many others, that the future has any details to know.[3] (Of course it *will be detailed*, but this does not imply that it has detailed will-be's as parts of itself now. . . .)

Thus there is no reason why perfect knowledge could not change, grow in content, provided it changed only as its objects changed, and added as new items to its knowledge only things that were not in being, not there to know, previously. Again, to have perfect power over all individuals is not to have all power in such fashion as to leave the other individuals none. For to be individuals and to have some power are two aspects of the same thing. So even the greatest possible power (and that by definition is "perfect" power) over individuals *cannot* leave them powerless, and hence even perfect power must leave something to others to decide. And if one loves these others, and their decisions bring conflict and suffering, how can one, as loving toward them, escape a share in this sorrow? We know nothing of the nature of benevolence in ourselves if it is not a sharing, at least imaginative, in the

[3]That possibilities are real, and that the future involves open alternatives, or is indeterminate in essence, I have attempted to demonstrate in my book, *Beyond Humanism,* chaps. 9 and 10, and in an article, "Contingency and the New Era in Metaphysics," *Journal of Philosophy,* XXIX, 421ff., 457ff. Cf. Charles S. Peirce, *Collected* Papers (Harvard University Press, 1931–1935), Vol. VI, Book I A. For an elaborate defense of the opposite or deterministic view, see Brand Blanshard, *The Nature of Thought* (London: Allen & Unwin, 1939), especially Vol. II. (Blanshard virtually ignores most of what seem to me the chief arguments against determinism, but gives a fine account of the arguments which have often been thought to support it.)

interests of others, so that the partial defeat of these interests becomes in a real sense a partial defeat for us. Thus, perfect goodness is not a sufficient condition of all possible bliss. Rather, the good person suffers more than the bad at the spectacle of the badness and suffering of others. The dilemma appears final: *either value is social,* and then its perfection cannot be wholly within the power of any one being, even God; *or it is not social at all,* and then the saying, "God is love," is an error. It may be said, however, that I have confused love with desire. I reply, Love *is* desire for the good of others, ideally all others, or I have yet to be told what it is.

So religion does not decide clearly in favor of group one, and seems rather to support group two. God is absolutely perfect (and in so far "without shadow of turning") in those things that depend by their nature upon one's own excellence alone. There is, for instance, nothing in the idea of knowledge to imply that God could not know all that goes on in the bad man as well as in the good; but if he equally derives (or equally does not derive) bliss from the two, so much the worse for his alleged goodness!

Inspection of the table of seven cases reveals also interesting implications for philosophy. If there is a being corresponding to case one, then there is a being totally exempt from the possibility of decrease or increase in value, hence of *change* in any significant sense. In such a being time is not, or at least is not time, which implies certain well known philosophical paradoxes. If, on the other hand, there is no being corresponding to any of the cases except those in the third group, if, that is, even the highest being is in all respects without absolute unsurpassability, then there is no individual being not capable of change (at least improvement) in any and every respect whatever; and in that case there is no enduring individual whose identity through all time is assured, for self-identity is incompatible with "change in all respects whatever." This threatens the intelligibility of time from the opposite point of view, for time must have some identity as well as differences. And it threatens religion, for the service of a God whose permanence is not assured fails to add anything essential to the service of men; and, moreover, the perfection of God is the heart of religious thought and feeling.

From another point of view one may reach the same result. Absolute and relative are polar concepts and seem to require each other, yet only group two makes this polarity affect the nature of the basic substance or individual. In religious terms, God, according to group two, is not just the creator opposed to the creatures, nor is he just another creature, but he is the creator-with-the-creatures, his reality is not in all respects as it would be did the creatures not exist. . . .

As among the three cases under group two, it might appear that case three (ARI) is the most promising of all, since it alone combines all three fundamental categories (surpassability by nothing, surpassability by self only, surpassability by others than self). But the third category is in a sense derivative. God can very well embrace surpassability by others, but as his property only insofar as it is that of relative beings united to him by virtue of his relative aspect. Thus if x comes to be surpassed by y, then God in his total value, as first including the value of x and then the value of y, will surpass himself in a manner which will be the reality of the x and y relation as enjoyed by him. But if God were incapable even of self-surpassing, then no surpassing could contribute anything whatever to his value or mean anything to him, for to him there would be no more or less but just sheer value.

On the other hand, as between cases two and four (AR and AI), the apparent choice is in favor of two. For AI implies that a being consists exclusively of an absolute fixed perfection plus a purely changeable and surpassable imperfection; or in other words, insofar as the being changed at all there would be no ultimate limit of any sort to this change, and no guarantee that the being which in some respects was absolutely perfect would remain even superior to others in his non-absolute aspects. Even supposing that two such pure opposites could constitute one individual or entity, this entity seems to have little to do with anything that has been meant by God.

Thus we have some reason for suspecting that the second case, AR, the farthest removed from atheism or pure relativism, the closest to the theological tradition, is the truth of the whole question. Since it is five steps away from atheism out of a possible six, lovers of the letter of orthodoxy who might feel inclined to attack case two as little better than atheism, or as a blasphemous or at best a crudely inept doctrine, might pause, before indulging in such judgment, long enough to consider—and I am confident they will not have done so before—what the five steps really mean. They mean, in fact, that most of traditional theology is acceptable to AR theorists as a description of one aspect of God, the A aspect. Yet since, on the other hand, the single step separating case two from the older theory involves the entire difference between admitting and not admitting real change, growth, possibility of profit, suffering, true sociality, as qualities of the divine, along with radical differences (as we shall see) in the meanings ascribed to creation, the universe, human freedom, and in the arguments for the existence of God, those inclined to think that any view that is intimately connected with theological traditions must have been disposed of by this time should also beware lest they commit a *non sequitur*. And finally, those who think that the modern experiments with a "finite" God have proved abortive might take heed of the radical ambiguity of all such phrases, and of the logical independence of case two from all of the four or five doctrines which could most reasonably be meant by them.

It is not even to be assumed that case one, at the opposite extreme seemingly from atheism, is really in every sense "farther" from it than is case two. For the "line" connecting the seven cases may be self-returning, if more than one dimension be involved. And this condition is here fulfilled. Case one makes God no more superior than does case two in the dimensions covered by A in AR, and it makes him infinitely *less* perfect in the R dimension, if any, for these are such as to imply change, self-transcendence, for their value—as, for instance, does novelty as a dimension of value. Also, as we have seen, trying to treat these R dimensions under A might destroy even the dimensions to which A is appropriate. So the God of A might really and consistently have even less perfection than the human race, or whatever the atheist regards with such reverence as he may feel. Hume's *Dialogues* (Part IV) are one of the earliest expressions of insight into this meeting of extremes.

The formal analysis of perfection makes evident the absurdity of supposing the theistic question to be a mere product of superstition or of some "complex." The notions which define perfection are logically inevitable in philosophy. Either these notions admit consistent combination as required for the definition of perfection (in one or more of the six senses) or they do not. This depends solely upon the meanings of "greater," "none," and "possible." Hence if we do not know whether or not perfection is conceivable, and in what sense or senses, we do not know what we mean by concepts than which none could be more elementary in philosophy. . . .

Exact thinking, it is rather generally agreed among those noted for it, is mathematical, or rather has at least a mathematical aspect, however complex or simple. (In very simple cases, mathematical symbols may scarcely be required.) It will have been observed that the formally possible modes of unsurpassability are simply the mathematically possible combinations of the ideas required to render "unsurpassable" univocal in meaning. This is an application of mathematics to the greatest of human problems, an application not less legitimate or important because so elementary and simple that it seems prodigious talent must have been required, and certainly was in fact expended, to overlook it for so many centuries. As in all cases of *applied* mathematics, truth cannot be certified by the mathematics alone. What can be certified is the definiteness and completeness of the possibilities among which the truth, so far as statable through the concepts initially proposed, must lie. There is no other way whatever of insuring that the truth does lie between given alternatives, rather than in some alternative not even consciously considered. Those who may fear that the use of exact formal concepts must somehow be hostile to religion will insofar be true enemies of knowledge as well as doubtful friends of religion. But just as Bradley affected to quarrel with arithmetic, so we should expect that some will dislike the attempt to arithmetize theology. Exact thought has its enemies.

It will be noted that unsurpassability is verbally a pure negative. It can be correlated with a positive idea by the notion of totality. If a being has "all" the values that exist, then it is in all respects unsurpassed by anything actual. If it has all the values that are possible, then it is unsurpassable by anything possible. But if all values are not "compossible," cannot all coexist, as seems an almost obvious truth, then a purely final or static perfection possessing all possible values is impossible. We must then conceive perfection as partly dynamic, in some such manner as follows:

A being may have a relation to all actual values which, as a relation, has all the value possible, or as much value as possible, *in view of the relata* (the values given as actual), and the being may have a relation to all possible values as such which, as a relation to possibilities, could not be superior. Such a highest possible relation to actual and possible value might consist in this: that all possible values *would*, if and when actualized, belong to the being in question, that is, the being would always be unsurpassable, except by itself as it actualized more and more of the possibilities confronting it. Yet as possessing thus at all times the highest possible abstract *type of relation* to actuality and possibility the being would, in one aspect of itself, enjoy absolute or static perfection, be not only unrivaled but even incapable of improvement. All that is necessary to reconcile this with the religious idea is to show that such absolutes as omnipotence or omniscience or perfect righteousness or loving-kindness are abstract relational absolutes in the manner just indicated, and thus not only compatible with but inseparable from a qualitative, concrete aspect of perfection which is dynamic, since it involves inexhaustible possibilities for achievement. Is it not almost obvious, again, that the religious terms mentioned are abstract and relational precisely in the manner outlined?

One might try to make perfection positive in another way, by using the notion of surpassing all things rather than of being surpassed by none. But the reader will, I think, if he experiments with this idea, find that it leads to the same result. The importance of assuring a positive content for perfection is that otherwise one cannot well deny the contention of atheism that the word God is merely a word for what is left when we deny all that we know; that is, it represents what we know when we know nothing. This "negative theology" has often been praised, on the ground that all our knowledge is so inadequate to God that we must indeed negate it to arrive at God. But why not to arrive at non-being? Some positive content to the former idea there must be to distinguish it from the latter, and why not the utmost positive content, infinite, indeed? Surely a little dose of positivity will not suffice here. And the dilemma remains, even in the negative theology, that either all value is compossible—which seems certainly untrue, for values conflict—or else God must fail to possess some values which yet are possible—and how then can he be incapable of growth in value? Possibilities which to God represented no possible achievements would be the same to him as no possibilities. True, one can recognize values for others, say their joys, without fully possessing or expecting to possess these as one's own, but what one cannot do is to fail in such a case to derive at least some value from the joys through the act of recognition itself, and precisely the most perfect mind would derive most from the satisfactions of others. It is the imperfection of man that compels him to admit that some of the joy which he wishes others to possess may when it comes contribute nothing to him, since he may be absent, dead, or somehow cut off from participation in the joy. Only the perfect can participate perfectly, gain for himself the entire sum of all actual gains.

If all values are compossible, and are all actual in God, then it is meaningless to say that some values are only possible. Possibility in that case ceases to have any distinctive meaning. Even if you say that God has not the actuality of what *for us* are possible values but rather a value above all our possibilities, you are only saying that what we call possibility is nothing from the ultimate standpoint. It is at least a serious thing to make the idea of God the destruction of a category without which it is doubtful that we can think at all.

The question is sometimes asked, Is God a concrete individual or is he an abstraction? If there is anything in the ontological argument, it may be that God must be concrete. For that argument may perhaps amount to this, that perfection is conceivable only as the property of an existing individual, and not of merely possible individuals (whereas we may conceive the nature of Mr. Micawber, for example, as *not* in fact the nature of an existing man). But even if we grant that God is an abstraction or a Platonic form or something somehow superindividual, still this does not obviate our trichotomy of doctrines. . . . The form is in all respects, in some respects, or in none an absolute ideal, the ideal of an unsurpassable maximum. The question then is, Are the dimensions of value alike in admitting, or in not admitting, an upper limit, or are there some which do and some which do not and which yet must apply to all things having value?

Our classification of doctrines depends only upon the four following assumptions:

    p. There is a difference between actual and possible (or conceivable) things.

    q. There may be a difference between actual and possible states of an individual. (Not that God is assumed to be an individual in this sense, but that it is not assumed that he is not, in the statement of the classification, whose purpose is to state, not to answer, controversial questions.)

r. It is meaningful to say that one thing is higher or better than, or superior to (or has more of some variable property not a mere deficiency than), another; but this meaning is not simply univocal, since x may be better than y in one respect, say in ethical goodness, and not better in another, say in happiness. Thus "better than" is multi-dimensional. (The doctrine of the tradition that God is not simply better than other even possible beings, but is better than goodness itself, better than "best," since he transcends the concept of goodness altogether, does not alter the necessity that he be better-than-best in some, in none, or in all dimensions of value; or negatively, that he be surpassable in all, some, or no dimensions. The tradition spoken of clearly elected the first of the three formal cases, making God unsurpassable by anything conceivable, even by potential states of himself.)

s. The notions of "all," "some," and "none" exhaust the possible divisions of a plurality, hence of a plurality of respects of higher and lower. (Logicians distinguish between "all" and "every," but this seems of no importance here.)

These assumptions (except the last, which is clearly self-evident) are not posited absolutely. It may, you may believe, turn out that actual and possible coincide, or that the different dimensions of value or superiority are really one. The point is, we must not assume this at the outset. What we certainly must assume at the outset is that the question of such distinctions requires discussion, and that therefore every type of doctrine implied as formally possible if the distinctions are genuine must be given full and fair hearing. If two views formally distinguished turn out to be the same (since some alleged distinction separating them proves equal to zero), then that will be the conclusion reached; but it must be a conclusion, and not in any sense a formal premise, of the argumentation. There can be no harm in setting a terminological locus for alleged distinctions, admitting that they may assume every value of significance from zero to infinity; but there is very definite harm in depriving apparent distinctions of terminological and systematic locus, since their value is then determined as zero by fiat. Now the distinctions between "superior to actuality" and "superior even to possibility," or between "superior to other possible individuals" and to "other possible states of oneself" (as an individual identical in spite of changes or alternate possible states), or again, between "superior in all," "in some," or "in no" respects of value—these distinctions are urged upon us by universal experience and common-sense modes of thought. They may be overruled in the outcome, they can never validly be overruled before the outcome, of technical procedure. And we have painfully learned (all but one or two groups of philosophers) that the way to evaluate ideas is to deduce their consequences and compare these with the relevant data of experience. So we have no rightful alternative to the systematic development of the consequences of the distinctions mentioned. The discussion of the resulting doctrinal classifications is the bottleneck through which alone we can arrive, if ever, at a rational treatment of the theistic question.

This question can, it is true, be put in other initial terms than those we have used. For instance, it can be put in terms of causality. Has the world a cause, or is it self-sufficient? But this formulation is not precise. It suggests that God is nothing but causation, and the world nothing but effect; in other words, that God is in *no* sense affected by other individuals, and the world in *no* sense causal in relation to God. But the idea of God in its common-sense or religious meaning may not require this. God is of course the *supreme power* in existence, the causal influence superior to all others. It remains to be seen, however, whether superiority of power implies a purely one-way causal action, an action without reaction or interaction. That is a basic technical question, not to be decided near the beginning of discussion but toward the end. Perhaps the supreme action is also, necessarily, the supreme interaction. Nor can words like "creator" and "creation" dispose of the matter. Religion is not prima facie committed on such technicalities as the relation of creativity to various causal concepts.

In terms of causality there are, rather, three formal possibilities, corresponding to, indeed coinciding with, our basic trichotomy. The highest cause may be (1) in *every* sense or aspect "uncaused," in no sense or aspect the effect of anything else; or it may be (2) in *some* aspects uncaused, and in others causally influenced, but its manner of both acting and receiving influences may be the highest conceivable, hence absolutely "perfect," although even so its whole being *may* not in every sense be perfect, because the influences as coming from other causes, say human beings, may be less admirable than they might be; or the supreme cause may be (3) in *no* sense or aspect uncaused, independent of other powers, hence in no way wholly exempt from the imperfections of the latter. . . .

It makes no difference what concepts are used, whether "self-existent," "necessary being," "unity," "final cause," or what you will to describe the divine individuality; there are always three formally possible cases (though the boundaries between them could be variously located, and they can be subdivided) among which choice must be made openly and carefully, not surreptitiously nor by a short and easy appeal to self-evidence. A being may, for instance, be necessary in all its aspects, or not in all but in some, or, finally, in none. So with all the other concepts mentioned above. Nothing can result but endless debate (and bad feeling) from the attempt to short-cut the exploration of an irreducibly triadic situation. Dyadic formulations of the theistic problem are question-begging through and through. . . .

Naturally any view which ascribes ethical perfection and yet the "greatest possible power" to God must face the problem of evil. In its appeal to the imagination this problem will no doubt always be the most troublesome one in theology. But in pure logic it is not true that there is sheer contradiction between the joint admission of divine perfection of goodness and divine perfection of power, on the one hand, and the fact of real evil on the other, for the simple reason that the greatest possible power (which by definition is "perfect" power) may not be the same as "all the power that exists united into one individual power." For such union of "all" power may be impossible. Had God "all the power there is," he must be responsible for all that happens. But why assume that all real power could *possibly* belong to one individual? If it could not—and there is ground for this negative—then even the perfect or (by definition) greatest possible power is not all-power. Omnipotence (alas, our only word for perfection of power!) is power to the highest degree possible and over all that exists, it is "all" the power that *could* be exercised by any *one* individual over "all" that is; but it remains to be shown how much power *could* be exercised in this fashion. The minimal solution of the problem of evil is to affirm the necessity of a division of powers, hence of responsibilities, as binding even upon a maximal power. But this solution seems to imply the passivity of the supreme power, and hence not to be available to first-type theists.

Undoubtedly, "ethical" needs careful defining, but roughly it means action issuing from the fullest realization available to the individual of all the interests affected by the action. It does not necessarily mean observing the rules or codes recognized in any human society, except insofar as these represent the attempt of that society to make actions express the nearest thing to full realization of affected interests which is possible to the average human being. Being ethical does not mean never injuring anyone; for the interests of others may require such injury. Still less does being ethical mean never permitting any agency to bring injury to anyone; for not permitting this might be possible—owing to the division of power—only at the cost of greater injury through interference with other powers. Being ethical means acting from love; but love means realization in oneself of the desires and experiences of others, so that one who loves can insofar inflict suffering only by undergoing this suffering himself, willingly and fully. Those who think God cannot mean well toward us because he "sends" us suffering can prove their point only by showing that there is a way to run the universe, compatible with the existence of other real powers than just the supreme power, which would be more fully in accord with the totality of interests, or by showing that God sends us the suffering while himself remaining simply outside it, in the enjoyment of sheer bliss. Theologians themselves (first type) seem generally to have made a present of the latter notion to atheists; but the former view has its plausibility for all of us. I wish only to say here that I think neither is put beyond reasonable doubt by metaphysical necessity or empirical facts. It is poor method to try to estimate facts, especially such as are hard to measure with any accuracy, without careful survey of the logical structure of the ideas we bring to bear upon these facts. Therefore the facts of evil are not sufficient to justify dismissal of theology prior to the adequate exploration of its three main formal possibilities. Facts will never render decisions between ill-conceived alternatives; and the meaning of such terms as omnipotence or goodness depends in second-type theism upon a number of conceptions which have not been clearly considered in the classic discussions (such as the marvelous one in Hume's *Dialogues*) of the relations of such terms to the facts of evil.

One way of trying to escape a decision among the three possible views concerning God as a perfect being would be to say that perfection as "that than which nothing higher or better in a given respect is conceivable" is a meaningless concept, itself inconceivable. This, however, besides seeming tolerably dogmatic, would only be to say that Proposition Three is true by necessity; for if a predicate is nonsense, then of course nothing exists having that predicate. Hence no form of positivism can provide an evasion of the decision to be made.[4] Nor can any other doctrine do so. What we have is a non-controversial statement of what the theistic controversy is. In general, I believe, all stubborn controversies in philosophy have involved questions the very existence of which as such is itself controversial, because they have not been formulated in neutral terms, terms that avoid arbitrarily limiting the prima facie possibilities.

In particular, most philosophico-theological controversies have amounted to one of the following procedures:

A. To considering reasons for preferring one or the other of Propositions One and Three, or more probably, some special variety of One to some variety of Three;

B. To considering reasons for preferring some one variety of One (such as "theism" or "absolutism") to some other variety of One (such as "pantheism" or "deism").

A is bound, sooner or later, to involve the fallacy of inferring the truth of One from the falsity of Three, or vice versa; whereas it is for-

[4]The positivistic objections to metaphysics as such I have attempted to meet in chap. 16 of *Beyond Humanism*, and in "Metaphysics for Positivists," *Philosophy of Science*, II, 287ff. See *AI* 147f., 159–165; Peirce, *Papers*, VI, 368. . . .

mally possible, and should be held really possible, until the contrary has been shown, that both One and Three are false because Two is true. The fallacy is bound to occur so long as Two is neglected, for the reason that men do not adopt a philosophy because its proofs are beyond question and its conclusions completely satisfactory—this being never the case—but because its proofs seem to them stronger and its conclusions more satisfactory than would be true of what they regard as the alternative. It is a question of preference, not of absolute sunclear evidence and perfect understanding. In so far as this is the case, almost everything depends upon the adequacy of the philosopher's survey of the possibilities. Now there is no more rigorous trichotomy than that of "all, some, none"; hence the question, *Is God absolutely perfect in all, in some, or in no respects?* is as rigorous a division of the theological problem as can be given if any use at all is to be made of the idea of perfection—and what theology has avoided its use? Moreover, if all the formal possibilities are not controlled, we not only run the risk of fallaciously inferring the truth of one view from the difficulties of some only of its possible rivals, but also we run the risk of trying to answer a perhaps meaningless question, namely, Which of two falsehoods (or absurdities) is more false? The falsehoods may be extremes (and One and Three are clearly such), and hence one may be as false as the other, by any objective standard. In that case, the choice between them will be on subjective and variable grounds, and no agreement is to be anticipated. If then, under these circumstances, complete agreement is not reached, it does not follow that agreement could not be at least greatly increased by the accurate, exhaustive statement of the doctrines open to us, arranged in a reasonably small number of exclusive groups or types.

B is an attempt to decide upon the details of a type of theory whose admissibility as a type has not been shown, owing to the role of the fallacy mentioned (which is implicit both in traditional proofs for God's existence and in atheistic criticisms of these proofs). This does not mean that such discussions have accomplished nothing, but it does mean that no exact and reliable estimate of *what* they have accomplished (though it is, I believe, a great deal) is possible until we have granted full "belligerent rights" to second-type theism, as a no less qualified contender than either of the others. True, this type of theism has already had a good many defenders; but taking philosophers as a whole and theologians as a whole it is still far from true that the theological problem is seen in terms of its fundamental trichotomy, systematically investigated. . . .

Our basic trichotomy of doctrines may be put in still another way, which also gives a clue as to the possible validity of the neglected second type. If we define a "closed" dimension of value as one of which there can exist a supreme or maximal case, and an "open" dimension as one of which no supreme case is possible, then one of three things is true: *all* dimensions of value are closed, *some* dimensions are closed and some are open, or *none* are closed and all are open. It is indeed not formally evident that the first proposition defines first-type theism; for we have not specified or shown that the maximal case of the different dimensions must be found in the same real individual. But at least it is clear that if, and only if, the first of the dimensional propositions is true, first-type theism *may* be true; and that if the second dimensional proposition is true, second-type theism may be true, for then there may be a real case of perfection on some dimension which will not be a case of perfection upon all, because—by the assumptions—not all admit of perfection. (If the ontological argument were shown to be valid, the "may be true" would in both cases imply "is true.")

Now, is it particularly obvious that all dimensions of value must be closed dimensions, assuming some of them are? Consider the dimensions of goodness, knowledge, power, and duration. A being may perhaps be the maximal case of goodness if he guides his action by concern for *all* the interests affected by his actions. This "all" is the universe (up to the present, at least) so far as it contains values. Or, a being may be omniscient if he knows all there is to know: that is, again, the cosmos as a totality. A being may, similarly, be the maximal possible power if he controls all that exists to the greatest extent possible, that is, to the extent which is compatible with the measure of independence, if any, constitutive of the things controlled. Finally, a being may have maximal duration by being ungenerated and immortal, by enduring throughout all time. So far, our dimensions seem to admit of maxima as at least conceivable.

But there are other dimensions of value. What could be meant by maximal happiness, or beauty, or "intensity" of joy, or variety, "the spice of life"? A being may enjoy all that exists, but perhaps he longs for what does not exist; or perhaps some of what exists is not altogether enjoyable (such as the sufferings of other sentient beings). Oh, well, you say, but if the being has maximal power, he can produce such beings as he wishes to enjoy. But there is social enjoyment, and this by definition depends partly on the self-determinations of the beings enjoyed. This cannot possibly be wholly coerced by any one term of the social relation, hence not even by the maximal "possible" power. The only escape at this point is to take shelter in the doctrine of the Trinity, which offers to furnish a social relation between persons all of whom are perfect. But still, we may ask, what in this relation is enjoyed? Is it "unity in variety," as seems to be the case with us? Supposing that variety in God is really compatible with his alleged simplicity, we still have to ask, What is meant by maximal variety? Is it that all possibilities are actualized in one actual state? But there are mutually incompatible alternatives (or there is no such thing as logic, or aesthetics). Besides, if all potentiality is also actuality in God, then the distinction between potential and actual must really be an anthropomorphic illusion, invisible from his point of view. At any rate, enjoyment varies as to intensity, and what can be meant by "all possible intensity," or "absolute intensity"?

Of course one could argue that an open dimension involves an infinite regress, and is therefore impossible. But . . . the infinite regress in question is an example of the "non-vicious" type of regress, since it concerns possibilities, and these not (on one view of potentiality) as a definite multitude, whose number is infinite, but as a continuum, which in the words of Peirce is "beyond all multitude," as God was formerly described as being; and indeed, as we shall see, the continuum of possibilities is one aspect of God which may be truly so described. It has also been argued that the maximal case is required as the standard or measure for all cases (Plato). But it may be that the maximal case on the closed dimensions would suffice to furnish the standard for the open ones, that, e.g., perfection of knowledge and goodness is in some sense the "measure" of degrees of happiness, even though the latter cannot be absolutely but only relatively perfect (R but not A).

Let us return to our conceivably closed dimensions and ask if they are not really ambiguous, not really in one sense necessarily open as well as, in another sense, capable of upper limits. To "know all that exists" is, in one sense, to have perfect knowledge, it is literal omniscience (provided possibilities are also known as such, as a special class of existences or, at least, of realities). But perhaps some of what exists is not as well worth knowing as some other things would have been had they existed. This implies no error or ignorance on the part of the knower, but it does imply the possibility of an increase in the aesthetic satisfaction derived from his knowledge, should a more varied or more harmonious world come into existence and be known. Again, one might deal justly and mercifully with *all* of one's world, and still be glad should this world itself improve in some way. The justice or mercy will not be improved from the ethical standpoint, but the just and merciful one will rejoice and gain in total satisfaction should the individuals being dealt with increase in goodness or happiness. Similarly, maximal power over a good world would not be so good as maximal power over a better one, though in both cases it would be as much power as is compatible with the world to be controlled; that is, in both cases it would be maximal simply as power, though not as total value realized by the one having the power.

True, if (as we shall later see reason to question) maximal power means power to create a beginning of finite existence in time, then it would seem that God could have started with as good a world as he chose. But a "best world" may be meaningless. And besides, the very next moment he would begin to confront the results of the choices, the exercises of power, granted to the creatures, and from then on his actual state, as constituting his knowledge, goodness, and power relations, would be as we have described it.

Nor does it help to argue that since God is timeless he knows and enjoys in advance all that the world ever will become. For he cannot enjoy all that the world ever *could* become as much as he would if it actually became it; for example, he cannot enjoy all the good deeds men might have performed as much as he would have, had the good deeds been performed. At least, this must be so if any vestige is to remain of religious ethics, and even perhaps of good sense. No more does it help to suggest that God's value is wholly independent of his relations to the world, whether of knowledge or of will, for this only means that the particular characters of the objects of his knowledge, or the results of his willing, are to him totally insignificant, which is psychologically monstrous and is religiously appalling as well. . . .

Thus we have every reason to take seriously, as the tradition has plainly not done, the hypothesis (at present merely that) of open dimensions of value, even for the perfect one. Let us remember that number is incapable of a maximum, that in whatever sense God may be "beyond number," still number can hardly be in every sense without value to him—or at any rate, variety can hardly be, and there is no more reason to speak of maximal variety than of maximal number. If, however, variety is said not to be a value for God, then one asks, Why a creation at all? Why should he add to his own perfection the contrast of the purely inferior creatures, unless contrast as such is valuable? And then, how can there be a maximum of contrast? It is no use to say that God creates the creatures out of generosity or love; for if he loves the valueless, so much the worse for his love, and what but the value of contrast can the creatures add to existence? Admittedly, they do not add "unity"!

Here then is a theology that either means nothing certainly identifiable (without supernatural grace or high genius in the art of reconnecting with experience concepts carefully divested of relation to it) or else means that the world might exactly as well not have existed, or as well have existed with far more evil or less good in it than it actually presents. In short, we have the view that the world, including the theologian, is strictly valueless to God, an absolute nullity from the standpoint of ultimate truth. I submit that this is a theology to be accepted, if at all, only after all other possibilities have been carefully considered and found hopelessly untenable. If a man denies this, I only say that I scarcely believe he is thinking about what he is saying. And the writings of those who apparently do deny it show little enough evidence of thought on this aspect of the question. The very question seems, by a near-miracle of persistent looking the other way, to be passed over. Is this merely the "method of tenacity" or is there a more generous explanation?

The theological views of Philo, Plotinus, Augustine, St. Thomas, Spinoza, Leibniz, Kant, Schleiermacher, Royce, the Hindu Sankara, present differences that are striking enough, but all of them agree, or fail clearly to deny, that God is a being "absolutely infinite" (Spinoza's phrase) or every way complete and perfect, and there seems little rational place for significant variations of opinion in a doctrine so completely determined as the doctrine of complete perfection. If, nevertheless, historically endless disputes and radical disagreements over the interpretation of the doctrine have in fact arisen, this is one piece of evidence that there is probably something wrong, perhaps self-contradictory, in the basic idea. On the other hand, the proposition that God is *both* perfect and perfectible, or both statically and dynamically perfect, unsurpassable, tells us prima facie nothing as to the respects in which he is the one and those in which he is the other. Here the necessity for exploring various interpretations is obvious. The exploration, however, was left largely to the present century. The opportunity this represents will not be brushed aside too hastily by anyone trying to be scientific in philosophy, whatever his religious or philosophical tenets. . . .

Controversies between theism and atheism have generally leaped over one of the three basic possibilities. People have rejected theism because they held untenable the idea of a mind not subject to change or to interaction with other beings, or a mind omnipotent in the sense that its power was all the power in existence, or a mind having precise knowledge of details of the future (or of all times from the standpoint of eternity), or a mind creating a first state of the cosmos at a finite time in the past, or knowing all suffering although it did not itself suffer, or an all-embracing mind which in no sense could be identified with the universe, or one which could in every sense be identified with it. These and other difficulties, which may be called the absolutistic paradoxes, have force against Proposition One, but are not pertinent objections to Proposition Two. But, on the other hand, it is quite unjustified for theists to hold that we must tolerate or swallow the paradoxes or explain them away (by feats of ingenuity so subtle, and verbal methods so remote from intuitive insight or definite logical structures, that only deity could know with any assurance what was taking place), giving as justification the claim that the alternative position of atheism is even more paradoxical (lacking, it may be urged, any principle of cosmic explanation at all). The fallacy of such reasoning is clear once we see that atheism is not the only alternative to the assumptions which generate the absolutistic paradoxes. Nor, as we have seen, is the remaining alternative pantheism in any traditionally considered sense.

It might be objected to our trichotomy that there are many degrees of "some" between none and all, and that consequently nothing very definite is described by Proposition Two. However, the "some" refers to dimensions of value as significant in describing God's perfection or perfectibility, and these dimensions are so interrelated that if we could come to a decision in regard to a very few of them the decision as to the others would probably follow. Also we could agree to classify under the third proposition all views which ascribe no more perfection to the gods than did the Greeks to their Olympians, whose only point of absoluteness seems to have been their immortality. (Any finite god held to be ungenerated as well as deathless ought perhaps to be held a minimal case of the finite-infinite God of second-type theism.)

It is of some interest to note that atheism and primitive polytheism are of the same basic type. This does not prove that if polytheism is false, atheism must be; for they are subalternatives within their type. But it does suggest that the radical falsity of primitive religious ideas as they stand is not an argument for atheism, as it is rather commonly held to be. Also the fact that atheism is at least as old (as a philosophy) as theism of the second type (it was much more familiar to Plato, for instance) suggests that there is nothing philosophically very advanced or sophisticated about atheistic doctrine as such. A really clear expression even of first-type theism is apparently indefinitely later than atheism. All of which of course proves nothing except the irrelevance of certain supposed arguments for atheism, arguments more subconscious and informal than explicit and official, but still influential.

The philosophical importance of admitting some nonabsolute aspects of God is in the resulting applicability of such categories as change, passivity, complexity, and the like, to him, and for this purpose surpassability of God, as he actually is, even if only by God himself as he could or can be, is entirely sufficient. Now though the actuality of deity is, according to second-type theism, in some respects surpassable, his individuality as potentially inclusive of other than his actual predicates may be in no respect whatever surpassable, in all dimensions though not in all senses perfect. To say this is not to commit second-type theism to the view that God is an "individual." We are speaking of subalternatives which the second basic proposition admits, not of corollaries which it necessarily implies. All the proposition demands is that there be a God in some respect unsurpassable, in some other surpassable—whether self-surpassable and how, or surpassable by other entities not states of himself, or whether he has "states," being left perfectly open by the proposition. Exploration of the subalternatives may well lead to the conclusion that only one of them is really "conceivable" in the full sense (in the light of the experiential content of the ideas involved). But this again is a matter to be held in suspension until we have established some control of the relations between the basic propositions.

God, for both old and much new theology, is the being whose uniqueness consists in his unrivaled excellence, or whose amount of value defines a necessarily one-membered class (and so in a sense not a class). In some respects he is absolutely unexcelled, even by himself in another conceivable state; in *all other* respects he is (to state the view reached in this book) the only individual whose states or predicates are not to be excelled unless he excel them with other states or predicates of his own. To take an imperfect analogy, no one will ever be or can ever be so Wordsworthian as Wordsworth; but Wordsworth himself, if he (or someone about him) had made a different use of his free will, might perhaps have been somewhat "more himself," might have developed his individuality more than he did. And certainly, at any stage in his life, one could have said that he was the most Wordsworthian being that would ever exist, except as he himself might later become more so. God, however, is not simply more himself than any other can ever be; he and he alone is in all respects superior to any state that will ever characterize any individual unless it characterize him. He is the greatest conceivable actuality, except perhaps as he himself can be conceived as greater (in another, perhaps subsequent, state, or in a state he might have had in the past, had men, say, served him more faithfully).

There is a slight ambiguity in the expression "excelled by himself only." We may ourselves in the future enjoy values which God now lacks (because they are not in being). But according to AR he will not lack them when we enjoy them, so that our self-excelling will be also (infinitely magnified) his self-excelling. Thus R means that "in no possible state of affairs can there be anything in any fashion superior to God as he is in that same state of affairs."

It will be seen that the new doctrine requires careful and somewhat elaborate distinctions, and yet, if some of its supporters are right, the doctrine is nothing at all but the analysis of the simple idea that God is "the perfectly loving individual," in all respects possessed of the properties which this idea requires, even if non-perfection in some respects be among the requirements.

That God is less than he might be (though more than anything else might be) agrees with the religious conception of the free service of God. For if we had no choice but to serve God in the fullest measure, or if we could not serve him at all, then it might be held with some plausibility that he is all that he might be. But the possibility of being freely served seems clearly to imply the possibility of lacking something that better service than may actually be given would furnish. Philosophical orthodoxy has had to finesse this point, and indeed, as I believe, has fallen into sophistry of a rather revolting kind. Really there was to be no service of God, but only a service of men through the—to them—beneficial practices of religion. Sin did no real harm whatever in the universe, since the absolute perfection which the universe involves in its cause could never be more or less than absolute. To say that sin at least harmed men is beside the point; for what harm did it do to harm men, parts of a system of reality that as a whole or in its ultimate reality was incapable of loss or gain? The world plus the absolutely infinite is no more than the latter by itself. Only from a purely race-egoistic (and illusory) point of view could the harm appear as such. Thus the motivation which is the (attempted) attitude of pure atheistic humanism was the only one philosophers could approve in religion. The idea of cosmic concern, concern for the divine values, must now at last be considered on its merits. . . .

It will be seen that the God of second-type theism is not without qualification finite, or growing, or emergent; nor, without qualification, is he the contradictory of these. The traditional distrust of simple statement, and of language as applied to the religious vision, in the new theology ceases to be an inoperative or inconsistently employed formal concession, and becomes a systematic tracing of the relativity of concepts to each other and to experience as a whole. The concepts which still function as absolute are the strictly religious and experiential ones of love and goodness. God is the Holy One, the ethical Absolute, the literally all-loving Father. In these affirmations second-type theism sees no exaggeration. It holds that the distinction between God's ethical perfection (and hence ethical immutability) and his "aesthetic" perfectibility (and hence growth) fits the later Hebrew and other high religions (most of all what some of us would mean by Christianity) far more naturally and unambiguously than does the confusion of every perfection in the unchanging *actus purus* of the Scholastics (and even of Schleiermacher). Furthermore, Whitehead and others have shown that it is precisely love which must be perfect in God—and only love and what is implied by it as perfect—if either love or perfection is to serve as an explanatory concept in cosmology. . . .

What has been discovered . . . is that, on one main point at least (the choice between the three propositions), religion at its best was literally and philosophically right, and theology was but a first approximation, vitiated by ambiguities or inconsistencies. In Whitehead's cosmology—which is, in the main, simply the most fully elaborated expression of tendencies widespread in recent philosophy—all existence is "social," is "feeling of feeling," forming "societies" of interlocked experiences, and societies of societies, from electronic, almost inconceivably simple and rudimentary, societies, to the universe. In this completely social philosophy (conflict, which is not denied, being also a social relation) God is that in the cosmos whereby it is a cosmos; he is the individual case on the cosmic scale of all the ultimate categories (including those of social feeling, "subjective aim," etc.) thanks to which these categories describe a community of things, and not merely things each enclosed in unutterable privacy, irrelevant to and unordered with respect to anything else. To impute purpose to God is no dishonesty in Whitehead; for he finds no real or possible thing that is not in its degree of simplicity or complexity endowed with subjective aim. And equally, he finds nothing whose feeling and aim are without sensitivity to other feelings and aims, that is, social. Hence the cosmic individual, the cosmos as the inclusive Society of societies "with personal order" is inclusively, universally sensitive, loving, and hence decidedly not purely impassive or once for all and in all ways perfect. The sense in which conflict, as well as harmony, enters into God is just the sense to which religion refers in speaking of the grief or anger of God over our suffering or sins, the grief being symbolized by the cross. Love is not identical with harmony, though it includes a measure of it. God conflicts, however, only with what he also participates in through his sensitivity or "tenderness." If Whitehead said less than this, it is the logic of his system that would collapse, and not merely its religious applicability.

A Whiteheadian Doctrine of God   12

John B. Cobb, Jr.

1. God as Actual Entity

. . . Whitehead's philosophical reasons for affirming God and his attempt to show that God is not an exception to all the categories appear to me philosophically responsible and even necessary. Nevertheless, at several points questions occur that Whitehead seems to answer in ways which create more problems than would some alternative answer. Whitehead has succeeded in interpreting God in such a way that, with very minor exceptions, he exemplifies the categories necessary to all actual occasions.[1] However there are other features characteristic of all actual occasions but not included among the strictly necessary categories. Whitehead's philosophy would be more coherent if he had interpreted God as conforming to these features of actual occasions as well.

In this chapter, I undertake to develop a doctrine of God more coherent with Whitehead's general cosmology and metaphysics than are some aspects of his own doctrine. This project presupposes that there are elements of incoherence in Whitehead's doctrine of God. This incoherence does not amount in most cases to strict inconsistency. But Whitehead holds before philosophers an aim at something more than mere logical consistency. Consistency is only freedom from contradiction.[2] Undoubtedly Whitehead's writings also include points of self-contradiction, but these are minor and easily remedied. The further criticism of a philosophy as incoherent has to do with its "arbitrary dis-

[1] William A. Christian, *An Interpretation of Whitehead's Metaphysics* (New Haven: Yale University Press, 1959), chap. 15.

[2] *PR* 5.

connection of first principles."[3] To the extent that the four ultimate elements of his system (actual occasions, God, eternal objects, and creativity) are arbitrarily disconnected, to that extent some measure of incoherence remains in Whitehead's own philosophy. It is my intention to show both that Whitehead moved far toward overcoming such incoherence and also that one can go, and therefore should go, farther yet.

Lest this appear unduly pretentious, a few further words of justification are in order. . . . When Whitehead first introduced God as a systematic element into his philosophy, he made no attempt to assimilate this principle to any other category.[4] God was to be viewed as a unique attribute of the substantial activity alongside of eternal objects and actual occasions. Further, there is direct continuity between what is said of God in *Science and the Modern World* and what is said of the primordial nature of God in *Process and Reality.*[5] In the latter book it is explicitly recognized that the primordial nature of God is an abstraction from God as actual entity,[6] yet most of the references to God in that book are references to this abstraction. When in the end Whitehead discusses more fully the consequent nature, he tells us that, unlike the primordial nature, this is fully actual.[7] Yet he cannot strictly mean this, for again and again he tells us that actual entities are the only finally concrete individual things.[8] He means to say that God is concrete by virtue of his consequent nature, and even that is not precise. Unless God is much more of an exception than Whitehead intends, God is concrete by virtue of being an actual entity, and being an actual entity involves both the primordial and the consequent natures. The reason Whitehead introduces concreteness with the consequent nature is that at this point he takes for granted the primordial nature and that the consequent nature is its complement, whereas when he previously discussed the primordial nature, the consequent nature was not in view.

The objection to Whitehead's formulation, then, is that too often he deals with the two natures as though they were genuinely separable. Further, he frequently writes as though God were simply the addition of these two natures. Thus God's primordial nature performs certain functions and his consequent nature others. But according to White-

---

[3]*PR* 9.

[4]See *A Christian Natural Theology* (Philadelphia: Westminister, 1965), 140ff. (hereafter referred to as *CNT*).

[5]Whitehead equates the primordial nature of God with the principle of concretion. (*PR* 373–374, 523.)

[6]*PR* 50.

[7]*PR* 524.

[8]For Whitehead's acknowledgment of the misleading character of his language on this subject, see Appendix B in Johnson, *Whitehead's Theory of Reality* (Boston: Beacon, 1952), esp. 215, 216.

head's own understanding, this cannot be the precise and adequate formulation. Actual entities are unities composed of a synthesis of their mental and physical poles, but they are not exhaustively analyzable into these two poles. In such analysis we would omit precisely the subjective unity, the concrete satisfaction, the power of decision and self-creation. It is always the actual entity that acts, not one of its poles as such, although in many of its functions one pole or another may be primarily relevant. Whitehead must certainly have meant to say this also about God, but his separate and contrasting treatment of the two natures is misleading—indeed, I believe that he was himself misled into exaggerating their separability.

That Whitehead wrote much of the time, even in *Process and Reality*, without holding clearly in view his own doctrine of God as an actual entity, is illustrated by the extraordinary treatment of the category of reversion, the category that explains the emergence of novelty in the actual occasion. It has to do with the way in which the prehension of an eternal object derived from objectification of an antecedent occasion gives rise to the prehension of a related but novel eternal object. In the initial statement of the categories, this prehension is understood as a new conceptual feeling.[9] However, in the course of his fuller exposition in the second part of the book, Whitehead realizes that the prehension of the novel eternal object must be an objectification of that possibility as envisioned in God, hence a hybrid prehension of God. At this point he states that "by the recognition of God's characterization of the creative act, a more complete rational explanation is attained. The category of reversion is then abolished; and Hume's principle of the derivation of conceptual experience from physical experience remains without any exception."[10] To carry through the process of rethinking the account of actual occasions and eternal objects in the light of the full doctrine of God will be in line with the direction in which Whitehead's own thought was moving at this point and will also alter in subtle, but at times important, ways the precise form of the doctrine of God.

My aim at each point is to achieve "a more complete rational explanation" in just the sense meant by Whitehead in the preceding quotation. This is the same goal as that of achieving greater coherence of first principles. The attempt is to explain the way in which God is related to actual occasions, eternal objects, and creativity, in such a way that at no point do we attribute to him a mode of being or relation inexplicable in terms of the principles operative elsewhere in the system.

This program may well begin with reference to the perplexing problem as to how the eternally unchanging primordial nature of God

[9]*PR* 40.
[10]*PR* 382.

can provide different initial aims to every occasion.[11] That each occasion has its unique, appropriate aim given to it, Whitehead is clear. God's aim at universal intensity of satisfaction determines a specific aim at the appropriate satisfaction of each individual occasion. But it is very difficult to imagine how these individual aims can be wholly timeless and yet become relevantly effective at particular moments of time. . . .

The initial aim can be conceived as a feeling of a proposition clothed with the subjective form of desire for its actualization.[12] A proposition is a togetherness of some actual entity or nexus of actual entities with some eternal object. For example, "The stone is gray," is a sentence that expresses a proposition of which the subject is a nexus of molecular actual occasions and the predicate is the eternal object gray. Many propositions are felt without being expressed in language. The initial aim would almost always be the feeling of an unexpressed proposition. In this case, the subject of the proposition would be the occasion itself, and the predicate would be that form of actualization which is ideal in that situation.

In temporal occasions the initial aim is always an aim at some intensity of feeling both in the occasion itself and in its relevant future.[13] . . . The relations of an individual's own future and those of others introduce tensions that are highly relevant to man's ethical thinking.[14] In God, however, there are no such tensions because the ideal strength of beauty for himself and for the world coincide.[15] Hence, we may simplify and say that God's aim is at ideal strength of beauty and that this aim is eternally unchanging. On the other hand, even in God there must be tensions between immediate and more remote realizations of intensity.

Assume a similar situation in man. . . . The man aims at the realization of some ideal satisfaction in the present occasion and in his future occasions. His subjective aim in the strictest sense is a propositional feeling about himself in that immediate moment of becoming, but this aim is determined in part by propositional feelings about future occasions of his own experience. He aims at actualizing himself in the present in such a way that these future occasions will have the possibility of enjoying some measure of beauty. Instrumental to this goal must be the behavior of occasions of experience other than his own, for example, occasions in his body and in other persons. He must entertain

[11]See CNT 155ff.
[12]See CNT 156–157.
[13]PR 41.
[14]See CNT 110ff.
[15]In PR Whitehead uses "intensity" to refer somewhat loosely to what is analyzed in AI as strength of beauty. See PR 134–135, 160–161, 373, 381.

propositional feelings about them also. There will be a large complex of such propositional feelings, entertained with an appetite for their becoming true, synthesized in the one propositional feeling of his own satisfaction. He aims at so actualizing himself that other occasions will actualize themselves as he desires. His aim at ideal satisfaction for himself will be unchanging, but it will take a different form according to every change in his situation.

In God's case there is nothing selfish about the constant aim at his own ideal satisfaction, since this may equally well be described as an aim at universal satisfaction. But in other respects there is no reason not to see the situation as analogous. Certainly God's aim is unchangingly directed to an ideal strength of beauty. In this unchanging form it must be indifferent to how this beauty is attained.[16] But if God's aim at beauty explains the limitation by which individual occasions achieve definiteness, then in its continual adaptation to changing circumstances it must involve propositional feelings of each of the becoming occasions as realizing some peculiar satisfaction. God's subjective aim will then be so to actualize himself in each moment that the propositional feeling he entertains with respect to each new occasion will have maximum chance of realization.[17] Every occasion then prehends God's prehension of this ideal for it, and to some degree the subjective form of its prehension conforms to that of God. That means that the temporal occasion shares God's appetition for the realization of that possibility in that occasion. Thus, God's ideal for the occasion becomes the occasion's ideal for itself, the initial phase of its subjective aim.

If the dynamic of the relation between God and man can be understood in this way, it is analogous to the dynamic of the relation between at least some temporal occasions and some occasions in their future. For example, the human actual occasion frequently so actualizes itself as to aim at influencing other occasions in the body. This may be a matter of raising the hand or swallowing food, or it may be far more complex. In general, the body is highly responsive to this influence, although not absolutely so. One may also attempt to actualize himself so as to influence future occasions of his own experience, as when he determines not to forget an appointment or to resist a particular temptation in the future. These decisions also have some real influence on the future, although still less perfectly so. Finally, one attempts by his self-actualization to influence future occasions in other persons, with some, although much less, success.

A new occasion, then, may feel past occasions in the temporal world in terms of their aim for it, and it will be affected to some degree

___

[16]PR 160–161.

[17]This is at least a possible interpretation of Whitehead's statements. (PR 134, 343; AI 357.)

in the formation of its subjective aim by these feelings. If this is so, then Whitehead's sharp distinction within the initial phase of an occasion between the initial aim and the initial data may be modified. The new occasion prehends all the entities in its past. These entities include God. All the entities will be positively felt in some way, some by simple physical feelings, others by hybrid physical feelings. These hybrid physical feelings will include feelings of propositional feelings about the new occasion, and these in turn will include propositional feelings whose subjective forms include desire for realization. In its prehension of these propositional feelings, the subjective form of the new occasion will at least partly conform to that of the past occasions it prehends. Hence, its aim for itself will always partly conform to the aim that past entities have entertained for it. Among the entities so felt, God will always be by far the most important one and, in some respects, prior to all the others.[18] The subjective aim of the new occasion will be some synthesis and adaptation of these aims for it, which it also feels conformally.

It would be possible to support this analysis in some detail by citation of passages from Whitehead that point in this direction. However, I resist this temptation. The analysis as a whole is not found in this form in his writings, and it deviates from the apparent implications of some of his statements in at least two ways. First, it rejects the association of God's aim exclusively with the primordial nature, understood as God's purely conceptual and unchanging envisagement of eternal objects; this rejection is required if we deny that God's immutable aim alone adequately explains how God functions concretely for the determination of the events in the world. Second, it interprets the subjective aim of the actual occasion as arising more impartially out of hybrid feelings of aims (propositional feelings whose subjective form involves appetition) entertained for the new occasion by its predecessors. In other words, it denies that the initial phase of the subjective aim need be derived exclusively from God.

In *Process and Reality,* much more sharply than in *Religion in the Making,* Whitehead treats the causal efficacy of the consequent nature of God for the world quite separately from that of the primordial nature.[19] I believe that this is a mistake. If God is an actual entity, God will be prehended by each new occasion. We will assume that God's aim for it, a propositional feeling for which the new occasion is the logical subject and some complex eternal object the predicate, will in every case be prehended and play a decisive role in the determination of the sub-

---

[18]Probably the function of determining the locus and extension of the new standpoint must be assigned exclusively to God. See CNT 153.

[19]PR 532.

jective aim of the occasion. But the occasion's feeling of this propositional feeling in God need not exhaust the objectification of God in the
new occasion.

In my feeling of my immediate past I may feel conformally the intention of that immediate past that in this moment I shall carry out some
project. But my feeling of that past also feels many other aspects of
that past, perhaps its discomfort or its hope for some more distant future. Similarly, there is no reason to suppose that the prehension of
God's aim for the occasion will exhaust the prehension of God in that
occasion. Hence, Whitehead was right to insist that in addition to deriving the initial aim from God, men also prehend God in some other
way.[20] But just as he was wrong to identify the derivation of the initial
aim wholly with the primordial nature, so also he is wrong to identify
the other prehensions of God solely with the consequent nature if this
is simply identified with God's physical prehensions of the world.
Whitehead's own writings about the consequent nature seem to attribute to it a synthesis of the physical prehensions with the conceptual
ones.[21] If so, there need be no quarrel—only an insistence that there
can be no sharp distinction between the reception of the initial aim and
the other prehensions of God.

According to my view, the actual occasion is initiated by a prehension of all the entities in its past, always including God. Some of
these entities, always including God, have specific aims for this new
occasion to realize. The subjective aim of the new occasion must be
formed by some synthesis or adaptation of these aims for which it is
itself finally responsible. In addition, the past entities, including God,
will be objectified by other eternal objects. What these other eternal
objects will be, complex or simple, is determined partly by the past
entities and partly by the new subjective aim.

2.   God and Time

Whitehead's discussion of the relation of God to time, like much of
what he says about God, is primarily focused on the primordial nature
of God. For this reason, the emphasis is on the nontemporality, pri-
mordiality, and eternity of God. God's envisagement of pure possibility is
beyond the influence of events. When Whitehead does discuss the consequent nature of God, he necessarily introduces some kind of process
into God, for the consequent nature is affected by what occurs in the
world. Whitehead never tries to solve this problem by denying the reality of the temporality of the world. On the contrary, he accepts the

[20]PR 532.
[21]PR 524.

doctrine that there is real becoming in God. Still, he refuses to say that God is temporal.[22] How is this possible?

Whitehead distinguishes between two types of process. "Time," he reserves for physical time, the transition from one actual occasion to another.[23] It is an abstraction from that process. This means that time is not, as in the Newtonian scheme, there prior to actual occurrences. Nor is it, as in the Kantian scheme, a way in which the mind necessarily orders the phenomenal flux. What is given ultimately are actual occasions with real internal relations to past occasions. Time is an important aspect of these relations.

From the point of view of physical time the actual occasions are temporally atomic. That is, they are indivisible into earlier and later portions, but they are not, like points, indivisible because unextended. Each actual entity has temporal extension, but the temporal extension happens all at once as an indivisible unit.[24]

However, one can analyze the process of becoming of the actual occasion, and indeed, Whitehead develops an extremely elaborate analysis.[25] Each occasion begins with an initial phase constituted by its initial data and its initial aim. It ends in its satisfaction through which it becomes a datum for further occasions. Between the indeterminateness with which it begins and the determinateness with which it ends, each occasion passes through a succession of phases in which complex syntheses of data replace the mere data.

There is, clearly, some continuity between the physical time derived from transition from one occasion to another and the process internal to the becoming occasion. In terms of physical time the occasion must be said to become all at once, yet it is eminently clear that some phases of the becoming presuppose others;[26] and Whitehead does not hesitate to use such temporal terms as earlier and later.[27]

The complexities of the relation between time as an aspect of the succession of occasions and the process internal to occasions need not be resolved here, since the basic principles necessary for understanding God's relation to time have already been noted. However, some further effort to explain Whitehead's meaning will not be amiss.

Physical time is observed or measured time. Observation and measurement presuppose objective occurrences. The absolute unit of objective occurrences is the becoming of an occasion of experience. This occasion is related to other occasions only at its initiation (as

---

[22]Note the partial exception in *AI* 267.
[23]Cf. *PR* 107, 196, 442–444.
[24]*PR* 434.
[25]*PR*, Part III.
[26]*PR* 225, 234.
[27]E.g., *PR* 132, 337.

prehender) and at its consummation (as datum for prehension). Hence, in principle, its own inner process of becoming is irrelevant to its observable relations. For every perspective other than its own, the occasion either is not at all or is completed. One cannot observe, from without, an occasion in the process of becoming. From the perspective of the becoming occasion, of course, the situation is different. It does experience itself as a process of becoming, and indeed only as such.

We are now prepared to ask how Whitehead relates God to time. We have already noted that his most frequent formulations seem to deny temporality to God altogether. God is the nontemporal actual entity. However, in the brief treatment of God as consequent as well as primordial in the concluding pages of *Process and Reality,* Whitehead introduces a threefold distinction.

Actual entities other than God are temporal. This means that they perish as soon as they have become. For Whitehead, "time" is physical time, and it is "perpetual perishing." The primordial nature of God is eternal. This means that it is wholly unaffected by time or by process in any other sense. The primordial nature of God affects the world but is unaffected by it. For it, before and after are strictly irrelevant categories.

The consequent nature of God is "everlasting."[28] This means that it involves a creative advance, just as time does, but that the earlier elements are not lost as new ones are added. Whatever enters into the consequent nature of God remains there forever, but new elements are constantly added. Viewed from the vantage point of Whitehead's conclusion and the recognition that God is an actual entity in which the two natures are abstract parts, we must say that God as a whole is everlasting, but that he envisages all possibility eternally.

It is then quite clear that the description of God as nontemporal does not mean that there is no process in God. Before and after are relevant terms for describing this process. There is God before he has prehended a given human occasion and God after he has prehended that occasion. Time and history are real for him as well as for temporal occasions. God's being as affected by temporal events also, in turn, affects subsequent temporal events.[29]

The easiest way to understand this would be to regard God, like human persons, as a living person.[30] A living person is a succession of moments of experience with special continuity.[31] At any given moment I am just one of those occasions, but when I remember my past and anticipate my future, I see myself as the total society or sequence of

[28]PR 524ff.
[29]PR 532.
[30]See CNT 50. Hartshorne prefers this doctrine (e.g., Kline, p. 23).
[31]See the discussion of personal identity in CNT, chap. II, sec. 4.

such occasions. God, then, at any moment would be an actual entity, but viewed retrospectively and prospectively he would be an infinite succession of divine occasions of experience. It is clear that Whitehead himself thought of God as *an* actual entity rather than as a living person. The thesis I wish to develop is that, despite this fact, the doctrines he formulated about God compel us to assimilate God more closely to the conception of a living person than to that of *an* actual entity.

The argument begins with the fact that Whitehead recognizes process in the consequent nature of God. Such process must be conceived either as the kind of process that occurs between occasions or as that kind which occurs within an occasion. Whitehead's position that God is *an* actual entity requires the latter doctrine. But the chief distinction between internal process and physical time is that the process occurring within an occasion has no efficacy for other occasions except indirectly through the satisfaction in which it eventuates. If the process in God's consequent nature is thought of in these terms, it cannot affect the events in the world. Yet Whitehead explicitly affirms just such an influence. Furthermore, if in the light of the discussion in the preceding section, we recognize the indissoluble unity of the primordial and consequent natures of God even in God's function as principle of limitation, then we must acknowledge that what is involved is not only the special case of the causal efficacy of God's consequent nature, but also the basic efficacy of God in the provision of the initial aim for each occasion. God's causal efficacy for the world is like the efficacy of completed occasions for subsequent occasions and not like that of phases of the becoming of a single occasion for its successors.

It may be objected that it is my development of Whitehead's thought in the preceding section that is in trouble here rather than Whitehead's usual formulations. If only the primordial nature of God were causally efficacious for the world, and if it were indifferent to time, then the problem would not arise. But if, as I hold, God can function as principle of limitation only by entertaining a specific aim for each becoming occasion, that aim must take account of the actual situation in the world. In that case, the problem does arise. Furthermore, since Whitehead unquestionably affirms the causal efficacy of the consequent nature of God, the problem also occurs for his explicit formulation. We must either reject this doctrine of the causal efficacy of the consequent nature and also affirm that an entirely static God can have particularity of efficacy for each occasion, or else we must recognize that the phases in the concrescence of God are in important respects more analogous to temporal occasions than to phases in the becoming of a single occasion.

The same problem may be posed in terms of God's satisfaction. In all other entities satisfaction is not attained except as the completion of the entity. If God is a single entity who will never be completed, then on this analogy, he can never know satisfaction. It would be odd that God should eternally aim at a goal that is in principle unreachable, and Whitehead explicitly refers to God's satisfaction as something real.[32] Apparently, satisfactions are related to the successive phases in God's becoming as they are related to temporal actual occasions, and not as they are related to successive phases of the becoming of such occasions.

In at least these two respects Whitehead's account of God is more like an account of a living person than of an actual entity. Yet Whitehead never suggests this position. Are there any systematic reasons for affirming that God is *an* actual entity rather than a living person? First, it is clear that as long as the primordial nature is chiefly in view, God would be thought of as a singular entity. If this were the only reason, we could easily set it aside. But we have seen that even when the consequent nature is in view, Whitehead avoids speaking of God as temporal. Unless we speak of him as temporal, we cannot speak of him as a living person, for the living person is defined by a temporal relationship among actual occasions.

There are two closely related characteristics of living persons that Whitehead wishes to deny with respect to God. They are, first, lack of complete self-identity through time and, second, loss of what is past. God must, without qualification, be self-identically himself, and in him there must be no loss. Whether or not these are strictly philosophical requirements of his system, they are powerful intuitions one must hesitate to set aside.

In my earlier discussion of the personal identity of living persons, I suggested that such identity is attained to the degree that there are immediate prehensions by each new occasion in the person of the occasions constituting the past of that person.[33] I recognized there that this did not entirely solve the problem since there would also be prehensions of the temporally noncontiguous experiences of other persons that would complicate the picture. In God's case, however, prehensions of all earlier entities would not be something other than his prehension of his own past, since they would all be included in his consequent nature. Therefore, his unity must be complete. Similarly, loss in the temporal world is the result of the very fragmentary way in which past occasions are reenacted in the present. The vast majority of such prehensions are unconscious and even in

[32]PR 48, 135.
[33]See CNT 77-78.

the unconscious we assume that the past is only fragmentarily effective. At any rate, the unconscious memory of a conscious experience
loses a very important part of the remembered experience. In God we
may suppose that no such loss occurs. He vividly and consciously
remembers in every new occasion all the occasions of the past. His
experience grows by addition to the past, but loses nothing.

One may still object that the concrete individuality of the past
in its own subjective immediacy is lost. That is true. But if the same
living person now enjoys a new experience that includes everything
in the old and more, this loss seems to be no loss of value. While
we humans are alive, the passing of time entails loss in two ways.
First, the beauty of most past occasions seems to be gone beyond
recall. Second, we move on toward the time when as living persons
we will be no more.[34] This means that all the beauty we have known
will have only the most trivial value for the future.[35] It also means
that the compensation of novel experiences is nearing its end. But the
passage of time in God would entail none of this loss.

The final objection to identifying God as a living person is that the
envisagement of the eternal objects is a primordial and unchanging
act and not an endless succession of acts. There is a certain plausibility to this argument, yet it is essentially arbitrary. When I gaze
at an aesthetic object for one minute, I might well describe this as a
single act. Yet Whitehead speculates that as many as six hundred acts
may have taken place. Insofar as what is enacted in each successive
act is the same, we may well conceive it as a single act. In our continually fluctuating experience no such absolute identity obtains from
moment to moment, but in God's one unfettered envisagement of all possibilities, the absolute identity from moment to moment means that
in our normal language it is a single unchanging and eternal act.

Specific problems remain, but for the most part they are already
raised by Whitehead's formulation and should not be regarded as
peculiar difficulties of this interpretation. For example, we may ask
how many occasions of experience would occur for God in a second.[36]
The answer is that it must be a very large number, incredibly large
to our limited imaginations. The number of successive electronic
occasions in a second staggers the imagination. God's self-actualiza-

[34]I am assuming here that we are not destined to live again beyond death. If
we believe that we are, the sense of loss is greatly mitigated. For my discussion of
this possibility, see CNT chap. II, sec. 3.

[35]I am omitting from consideration here the preservation of these values in
God, so important to Whitehead at just this point. See CNT 219–220.

[36]Hartshorne asks this question of Whitehead with respect to the phases of
becoming in God and suggests a similar answer. See his "Whitehead's Idea of God,"
in Paul A. Schilpp, ed., The Philosophy of Alfred North Whitehead (New York:
Tudor, 1951), 545–546.

tions must be at least equally numerous if he is to function separately in relation to each individual in this series. Since electronic occasions are presumably not in phase with each other or with other types of actual occasions, still further complications are involved. Obviously, this is altogether unimaginable, but since all the dimensions of our world revealed to us by physical science are also quite beyond imagination, in this sense, we should not be surprised that this is true of God.

My conclusion, then, is that the chief reasons for insisting that God is *an* actual entity can be satisfied by the view that he is a living person, that this view makes the doctrine of God more coherent, and that no serious new difficulties are raised.

3. God and Space

It is possible in Whitehead to consider time in some abstraction from space without serious distortion. Successiveness is a relation not dependent upon spatial dimensions for its intelligibility. I understand Whitehead to say that time, in the sense of successiveness, is metaphysically necessary whereas space, or at least anything like what we mean by space, is not. There might be one dimension or a hundred in some other cosmic epoch. Since God would remain unalterably God in any cosmic epoch, his relation to space must be more accidental than his relation to time. Nevertheless, space, or rather spacetime, is a real and important factor in the only world we know, and we may legitimately inquire how God is related to space-time. Since in this section we will not be focusing upon successiveness, we will for convenience often speak simply of space.

Every occasion of experience actualizes a spatiotemporal region that then constitutes its standpoint. In this connection we must note that what is fundamentally given is not space but actual entities. Space is affirmed only because the way in which actual entities prehend each other has a dimension that produces in us the experience of spatial extension. This idea allows us to say further that although real space is constructed by the actualization of just those occasions that do become, space could have been divided up in other ways, indeed, in an infinity of other ways. Thus, we may treat the space occupied by occasions in abstraction from the occasions that occupy it, and consider its properties—properties which then also characterize whatever occasions, in fact, occur in our spatial cosmic epoch.

Space and time conjointly constitute the extensive continuum in our cosmic epoch. Every occasion occupies as its standpoint some region within this extensive continuum. In an epoch lacking spatiality, this region would be temporal only, but in ours, again, it is spatiotemporal. Now the question is whether the fact that in our epoch occasions occupy spatiotemporal regions means that God also occupies a spatiotemporal region. There seem logically to be only three possible answers. Either God occupies some particular region, or his mode of being is irrelevant to regions, or he occupies the entire continuum.

The first of these alternatives may be rather readily dismissed on philosophical grounds. Since God's functions as philosophically identified are related with equal immediacy to every occasion, any special spatial location is impossible. The choice between the remaining alternatives is far more difficult. Since God's own being is independent of spatiality, it is clear that there is an important sense in which God transcends space. But that does not settle the question as to whether in a spatial epoch he is characterized by spatiality.

To deal with this problem in the face of Whitehead's silence, we must begin with the relevant principles that he does provide us. God does prehend every spatiotemporal actual occasion and he is prehended by it, both in his primordial nature and in his consequent nature. Furthermore, these prehensions in both directions are unmediated.

Normally we think of unmediated prehensions as prehensions of occasions immediately contiguous in the spatiotemporal continuum. This suggests the doctrine of God's omnispatiality. Indeed, if contiguity were essential to unmediated prehensions, it would be necessary to posit God's omnipresence throughout space. However, even apart from consideration of God, we have seen that Whitehead qualifies this principle. He holds that in our cosmic epoch, prehension of the physical poles of other occasions seems to be dependent on contiguity, but that prehensions of the mental poles of other occasions may not be dependent on contiguity.[37] By this principle we could explain our prehension of God's primordial nature and God's prehension of our mental poles quite apart from any spatial relations. Further, since no metaphysical problem is involved in affirming that physical experience may also be prehended apart from contiguity, the doctrine of the radical nonspatiality of God is compatible with all the functions attributed to God by Whitehead. Indeed, since his thinking about God was largely formed with the primordial nature in view, it is probable that nonspatiality was assumed by him.

If the nonspatiality and omnispatiality of God are both equally allowed by Whitehead's metaphysics, we can choose between them only on the basis of coherence. My own judgment is that that doctrine of God is always to be preferred which, other things being equal, interprets his relations with the world more, rather than less, like the

[37]*SMW* 216; *PR* 469; *AI* 318.

way we interpret the relations of other entities. If we adopt this principle, there is prima facie support for the doctrine that God, like all actual occasions, has a standpoint. Since that standpoint could not be such as to favor one part of the universe against others, it must be all-inclusive.

The only serious philosophical objection to this doctrine arises from the rejection of the possibility that actual standpoints can include the regions that comprise other actual standpoints. This problem [has been] considered in some detail [elsewhere],[38] and the arguments in favor of the affirmation of such regional inclusion of standpoints will here be only summarized. The argument is that whereas Whitehead neither affirmed this relation nor developed its implications, it does seem to be implied by the most natural reading of some of his cosmological assertions. It is compatible with his metaphysical doctrines and his understanding of the relation of space-time to actual occasions. Further, it is compatible with the doctrine that contemporaries do not prehend each other, since each of the entities participating in this special regional relationship would still prehend the other only when that other entity had passed into objective immortality. Finally, the doctrine that the regions that constitute the standpoint of actual occasions of human experience include those of subhuman occasions in the brain has several specific advantages.[39]

If we can think of the spatiotemporal regions of the occasion of the human person as including the spatiotemporal regions of numerous occasions in the brain, then we may think analogously of the region of God as including the regions comprising the standpoints of all the contemporary occasions in the world. If we follow the argument of the previous section, there would be some difference, for whereas the occasions of human experience have considerable temporal breadth in relation to the electronic occurrences in the brain, we have seen that the occasions of God's experience must be extremely thin in their temporal extension. The regions of other occasions would be included, not in that of a single occasion of the divine experience, but in the regions of a succession of such experiences.

Once again we have a choice of treating God as an exception or of speculating that he is more like other actual entities. If God occupies no region, yet is related to all equally, it is as if he were regionally contiguous with all regions. Whitehead may deny this and intend that, unlike all other actual entities, God's immediate physical prehensions of other entities do not involve him in having a regional standpoint. Since regional standpoints are not introduced into the cate-

[38]See CNT 82–91.
[39]See CNT 83–85.

gorial scheme, no self-contradiction is entailed. However, if God is related to every occasion as if he were physically present, it seems more natural and coherent to affirm that he *is* physically present. That could only mean that his region includes all other contemporary regions.

4. God and the Eternal Objects

In *Religion in the Making*, we read that "the forms (i.e., eternal objects) belong no more to God than to any one occasion."[40] God is seen as envisaging all the eternal objects as well as all actual occasions, but Whitehead does not see this envisagement as fundamentally different in kind from that possible to other occasions. No problem of coherence arises.

Further reflection led Whitehead, in *Process and Reality*, to make a more radical differentiation between the way in which God prehends the eternal objects and the way actual occasions prehend them. According to the ontological principle he affirmed: "Everything must be somewhere; and here 'somewhere' means 'some actual entity.' Accordingly the general potentiality of the universe must be somewhere; since it retains its proximate relevance to actual entities for which it is unrealized. . . . This 'somewhere' is the non-temporal actual entity. Thus 'proximate relevance' means 'relevance as in the primordial mind of God.'

"It is a contradiction in terms to assume that some explanatory fact can float into the actual world out of nonentity. Nonentity is nothingness. Every explanatory fact refers to the decision and to the efficacity of an actual thing. The notion of 'subsistence' is merely the notion of how eternal objects can be components of the primordial nature of God."[41]

This passage seems virtually to deny the eternal objects any status apart from God's envisagement of them. On the other hand, Whitehead is very clear that God does not create the eternal objects;[42] they *are* for him eternally. Still, Whitehead seems to assign to God a relation to eternal objects wholly different from that possible to any other entity. That is, does not God have an unmediated relation, whereas all other entities have only a mediated relation? If so, is there not again a danger of a final incoherence? Have we not introduced God to solve a problem without providing any clue whatever as to how it is done?

[40]RM 157.
[41]PR 73.
[42]PR 392.

This seems to be parallel to the weaknesses that Whitehead points out in other philosophers.[43]

It may not be necessary, however, to understand Whitehead in this sense. What the ontological principle demands is that no agency be attributed to eternal objects in themselves. It does not forbid that they be classified as one of the categories of existence.[44] Nor does it demand that their sheer existence be regarded as dependent upon God. Let us take as our point of departure the formulation of the ontological principle to the effect that "every explanatory fact refers to the decision and to the efficacity of an actual thing." On the basis of this formulation I suggest that the relation between God and the eternal objects can be restored to the situation we found in *Religion in the Making,* namely, that it belongs to no totally different mode from that of other actual entities to the eternal objects.

The apparent incoherence with respect to eternal objects arises at two points. First, it seems that God renders eternal objects effective for actual occasions in a way *radically* different from that in which temporal occasions make them effective for each other. Second, God seems to envisage eternal objects in a way for which the conceptual prehensions of actual occasions provide no analogy. It is my contention that the first of these areas of incoherence can be rather easily resolved into coherence if the conclusions of preceding sections of this chapter[45] are accepted, but that much greater difficulty attaches to the second. We will treat the problems in that order.

Whitehead appeals to the principle of universal relativity to argue that there are physical prehensions of the world by God and of God by the world. He has in mind the consequent nature of God, but I have argued that God as actual entity is involved. When we recognize the indissoluble unity of the mental and physical poles in God as in other actual entities, we have no difficulty in seeing that even when the mental pole of God is primarily involved, God as actual entity is involved. Whitehead's recognition of this led him to note that some of the feelings he usually called conceptual prehensions (prehensions of eternal objects) are really hybrid prehensions (objectifications of an actual entity by an eternal object derived from its mental pole).[46] In this way Whitehead moves in the direction of assimilating the relation of actual occasions to God to the relation of actual entities to each other. This is a step toward coherence.

[43]*PR* 78, 219, 289; *FR* 24; *AI* 171.

[44]They are so classified, *PR* 32. However, Christian correctly calls attention to Whitehead's wavering on this point. See Christian, 265–266.

[45]See especially sec. 1.

[46]*PR* 343, 377.

However, two points remain at which God seems to function in presenting eternal objects to actual occasions in a way *radically* different from that in which they present eternal objects to each other. These two points are the provision of the initial aim and the provision of relevant novel possibilities. The analysis of the becoming actual occasion in which these occur should be briefly reviewed.

Every occasion of experience arises in an initial phase in which there are initial data and the initial phase of the subjective aim. The initial data are all the actual occasions in the past of the becoming occasion. The initial aim is the desire for the achievement of a definite value allowed and made possible by the initial data. In accordance with the initial aim, the initial data are severally objectified by the new occasion in terms of eternal objects realized by them. The new occasion then reenacts these eternal objects as now constitutive of its own subjective immediacy.[47] But in addition to this reenactment of what is given in the initial data, there is also a "secondary origination of conceptual feeling with data which are partially identical with, and partially diverse from, the eternal objects" derived from the initial data.[48] Here novelty enters the new occasion. In subsequent phases of the becoming of the occasion, complex syntheses of conceptual and physical prehensions occur, but these are not our concern at this point.

In Whitehead's presentation God seems to be the sole ground of (1) the initial aim and (2) the relevant novel eternal objects. In section 1 above, it has already been argued that, without detracting from God's supreme and decisive role, we can think of past actual occasions as also contributing to the formation of the initial aim.[49] That argument will not here be repeated. If it is accepted, then there is no incoherence at this point. Here we must consider whether in the origination of novelty, also, God's role can be coherently explained.

Whitehead already goes far toward a coherent explanation. He holds that God so orders the realm of otherwise merely disjunctive eternal objects that the prehension of one eternal object suggests that of another. The prehension of the novel eternal object is in fact a hybrid prehension of God.[50]

However, it is impossible to rest with Whitehead's brief and almost incidental statements on this point, for they raise additional problems to which he did not address himself. Let us consider in somewhat more detail the apparent meaning of his position.

A past actual occasion is objectified by eternal object X. This eternal object is then reenacted in the new occasion by a conceptual prehen-

---

[47]PR 39–40.
[48]PR 40.
[49]See CNT 182–183 (reprinted above, pp. 219–220).
[50]PR 377.

sion of X. In addition, eternal object Y is also enacted in the new occasion. This means that God has been objectified by Y. Presumably the objectification of God by Y was triggered by the prehension of X derived from the past actual occasion. The dynamic by which this triggering occurs is not explained. Perhaps the objectification of a past occasion by X leads to the objectification also of God by X and this in turn leads to the objectification of God by Y because of the close association of X and Y in God. Already this seems somewhat farfetched.

In addition, it introduces two further problems. Whereas in relation to other actual occasions their causal efficacy for the new occasion functions only in the initial phase, this interpretation of the rise of novelty requires that God's causal efficacy function also in subsequent phases since "conceptual reversion" occurs after the initial phase of the occasion.[51] Second, if the prehension of the novel eternal object is, in fact, a hybrid prehension of God, then the new occasion should deal with it as it does with other hybrid prehensions. This would mean that it not only would reenact the eternal object in its own subjective immediacy but also that there might again be "secondary origination of conceptual feeling" introducing new novelty. This would lead to a regress that is clearly vicious and completely unintended by Whitehead.

A much simpler theory, more coherent both in itself and with Whitehead's general position, is as follows. According to this theory, there is just one hybrid prehension of God, the prehension that includes the feeling of God's aim for the new occasion. This aim includes not only the ideal for the occasion but alternative modes of self-actualization in their graded relevance to the ideal.[52] It certainly includes God's conceptual feeling of eternal objects X and Y together with his feeling of relevance of Y to X. Hence no new hybrid prehension of God is required in subsequent phases. Although the new actual occasion may not actualize itself according to God's ideal aim for it, it will not include any possibility not provided as having some relevance for it in the initial hybrid prehension of God.

This interpretation also allows us to see that the difference between God's function in providing novelty and that of past occasions, although great, need not be total. Some ordering of eternal objects is possible also in temporal occasions and in principle may have some effectiveness for future occasions. The difference, the vast difference, is that God envisages and orders *all* eternal objects, whereas temporal occasions can order only an infinitesimal selection of eternal objects. But this kind of difference threatens no incoherence.

[51]PR 378.
[52]That this is Whitehead's intention is indicated in PR 74, 75, 342, 343.

I assume, therefore, that the explanation of the derivation from God of the initial aim and of novelty, need not attribute to God's causal efficacy for temporal occasions a function *radically* different from that exemplified in the interrelationships of other actual entities. If this is correct, there is no danger of incoherence, a danger that arises whenever an inexplicable mode of functioning is attributed to God. However, the second major problem noted above remains unsolved. Is God's envisagement of eternal objects totally discontinuous with the conceptual prehensions of temporal occasions?

The problem may be explained as follows. According to the ontological principle, eternal objects cannot be effective for actual occasions except by the decision of some actual entity. That seems to mean that the conceptual feelings of an actual entity always derive from its physical and hybrid feelings. An eternal object not given for the new actual occasion in some other actual entity cannot enter the new occasion. But in the case of God we seem to confront a total exception. Here all eternal objects are effective without the mediation of any other actual entity.

Either the ontological principle is simply inapplicable to the relation of eternal objects to God (in which case incoherence threatens) or the decision to which the effectiveness of eternal objects for God is to be attributed is God's primordial decision. If we adopt the later position, as I believe we should, then we must ask whether in the case of temporal occasions as well the ontological principle allows that their own decisions can be explanatory of conceptual prehensions not derived from physical prehensions.

The question is not really whether such decisions occur or even whether there are actually any occasions capable of making such decisions. The question is whether in principle the kind of decision by which eternal objects become relevant for God is categorically impossible for all other actual entities. I see no reason to insist upon this absolute difference, and could even suggest that at the highest levels of their intellectual functioning human occasions *may* be able to conceive possibilities directly. Such a claim would supplement rather than contradict Whitehead's analysis of novelty in actual occasions as arising from hybrid prehensions of God. He focuses on the emergence of novelty as it precedes and is presupposed by all conscious reflection and decision, whereas I am speaking of new possibilities introduced by highly reflective consciousness.[53] However, I do not wish to press any claim beyond this: Whitehead should not preclude *in prin-*

[53]Whitehead thought that "in our highest mentality" we may have clues to the kind of order that will be dominant in a future cosmic epoch (*ESP* 90). This indirectly suggests some openness to my speculation.

ciple the possibility that a temporal occasion may have toward some eternal object the kind of relation God has toward all.

If we may modify Whitehead's apparent position to this extent, then we can affirm with *Religion in the Making* that in principle "the forms belong no more to God than to any one occasion." The apparent incoherence introduced into Whitehead's thought by the application of the ontological principle to the role of the eternal objects can be removed.

5.   God and Creativity

In Whitehead's analysis, God's role in creation centers in the provision to each actual occasion of its initial aim.[54] This role is of such importance that Whitehead on occasion acknowledges that God may properly be conceived in his philosophy as the creator of all temporal entities.[55] Yet, more frequently, he opposes the various connotations of the term "creator," as applied to God,[56] and prefers to speak of God and the temporal world as jointly qualifying or conditioning creativity,[57] which then seems to play the ultimate role in creation.[58] In this section I will attempt to clarify both the role in creation attributed to God by Whitehead and the relation of God to creativity. The process of clarification will lead to the attribution to God of a more decisive role in creation than Whitehead himself intended.

The contribution to an occasion of its initial aim is not simply one among several equally important contributions to its actuality and nature. The initial aim is in reality the initiating principle in the occasion. Whitehead says that along with the initial data it constitutes the initial phase of the occasion. In some of his statements he seems to imply a general equality of functioning between the initial aim and other elements in the initial phase. But in fact in his detailed analyses no such equality obtains.[59]

In the first place, the initial aim determines the standpoint that

[54]In section 1 above, I have argued that past temporal occasions may also contribute to the formation of the initial aim. Some support for this is found in Whitehead's emphasis on the creative role of all actual entities (*PR* 130) and in the doctrine that an enduring object "tends to prolong itself" (*PR* 88). But the decisiveness of the role of God remains unquestioned.

[55]*PR* 343.

[56]He especially resists any appeal to the will of God because of its suggestion of arbitrariness. (*PR* 344; *AI* 215. See also *RM* 69–70; *PR* 519–520, 526.)

[57]*PR* 30, 47, 130, 134, 135, 344, 374.

[58]Both God and the world "are in the grip of the ultimate metaphysical ground, the creative advance into novelty" (*PR* 529).

[59]*PR* 343.

the occasion will occupy, its locus and extent in the extensive continuum. This, in turn, determines what occasions will be in its past, in
its present, and its future. That means that the initial aim determines
which occasions will constitute the past and therefore, the initial data
of the new occasion.[60]

In the second place, the initial data are not a part of the becoming
occasion in the same sense as the initial aim. The initial data are the
occasions in the past of the becoming occasion as they were in themselves in their own subjective immediacy. They are appropriated by the
becoming occasion as it objectifies them. But how it objectifies them is
determined by the initial aim.[61]

For these reasons we may properly think of the initial aim as the
originating element in each new occasion. Since Whitehead regards
God as the sole ground of the initial aim, he systematically attributes
to God the all-decisive role in the creation of each new occasion, although he draws back from so strong a formulation.

However that may be, Whitehead does restrict the creative role of
God in such a way that his sole responsibility for what happens is
effectively and properly denied. First, the initial aim is the aim that is
ideal for that occasion *given its situation.*[62] It is not God's ideal for the
situation in some abstract sense. It is the adaptation of God's purposes
to the actual world. Second, the initial aim does not determine the
outcome, although it profoundly influences it. In subsequent phases
the occasion adjusts its aim and makes its own decision as to the outcome it will elicit from the situation given to it. The actual occasion is
its own creator, *causa sui,* Whitehead likes to say.[63] In the third place,
God does not create the eternal objects. He presupposes them just as
they, for their efficacy in the world, presuppose him.[64] In the fourth
place, Whitehead envisions no beginning of the world, hence no first
temporal creation out of nothing.[65] In every moment there is given to
God a world that has in part determined its own form and that is free
to reject in part the new possibilities of ideal realization he offers it.
This is certainly a different understanding of God as creator from that

[60]*PR* 104. For exposition of this, see *CNT* chap. IV, sec. 3.

[61]*PR* 342, 420. Cf. Donald W. Sherburne, *A Whiteheadian Aesthetic* (New Haven:
Yale University Press, 1961), 48.

[62]*PR* 373. Whitehead strongly opposes the Leibnizian doctrine that this is the
best of all possible worlds (*PR* 74).

[63]E.g., *PR* 131, 228, 338, 339.

[64]*PR* 392.

[65]*PR* 521. Cf. Leclerc, *Whitehead's Metaphysics* (New York: Macmillan,
1958), 194–195. I am not sure that the *possibility* "that creativity originally had
only a single instantiation" is strictly ruled out by Whitehead's metaphysics, but I
am not interested in arguing this question here.

which has been customary in many Christian circles, but it is never-theless a doctrine of God as creator.

The problem on which I wish now to focus is that of the relation of God as creator to creativity. There are passages in which the dom-inant role in creation is apparently assigned to creativity, such as where God is spoken of as the accident or creature of creativity.[66] This seems to suggest that even if God creates individual occasions, God is him-self created by creativity. However, this is a misunderstanding. The way in which Whitehead conceives of creativity as related to God is not analogous to the relation of God to temporal occasions. To make this clear we may have recourse to Aristotle's terminology of the four causes, of which Whitehead also makes use.[67]

According to the ontological principle, only actual entities can have efficient or final causality for other actual entities.[68] God as an actual entity does have such efficacy for other entities, but creativity is not an actual entity and hence, cannot function as an efficient (or final) cause of anything. Therefore, if we mean by creator an efficient (or final) cause, creativity is not a creator, certainly not the creator of God. Similarly, creativity is incapable of functioning as the formal cause of any actual entity, since it is totally neutral as to form.

Whitehead explicitly explains that creativity is in his system what prime matter is in Aristotle, namely, the material cause.[69] This sug-gests, correctly, that the problem of a doctrine of creation in Whitehead is much like that in a philosophy based on Aristotle: the role of the creator is to provide form for a reality given to him. The creator does not create the reality as such. It is my thesis, however, that the role of the creator in Whitehead must be more drastic than in Aristotle, more drastic also than Whitehead recognized. To support this thesis, a brief consideration of the role of prime matter in Aristotle and of creativity in Whitehead is required.

The philosophical problem in Aristotle may be explicated by ref-erence to the distinction between *what* things are and *that* things are. When Aristotle is explaining *what* things are, he never refers to prime matter. Since it is subject to any form whatsoever, it cannot explain the particular form of anything. However, if one asks why it is that there is anything at all, the answer must be that prime matter is eternal and demands some form.

[66]PR 11, 135.

[67]PR 129, 320, 423. See also notes 68 and 69 below.

[68]PR 36–37.

[69]PR 46–47. Elsewhere he identifies the Category of the Ultimate, which in-cludes "many" and "one" along with "creativity," as Aristotle's "primary substance" (PR 32).

Thinkers divide on the question as to whether that is an adequate answer. First, is it intelligible? It is at least sufficiently suggestive that one who thinks in terms of matter can have some dim intuition as to what is meant. One can see that the same matter takes different forms, as in ice, water, and steam, and that that which takes these several forms must have much less definite form than any of these individual forms of it. This suggests a relatively formless state of matter. If that which can be ice, water, and steam differs from that which can be wood or paper, this must be because it has some difference of form, however primitive. In that case, some still less definitely formed matter must be subject to alteration between these forms, since rain appears to be part of what enters into the formation of trees. At the end of such a hierarchy of less-formed matter we can posit prime matter, enduring unchanged through all the forms imposed upon it. This matter neither increases nor decreases, it is in no way affected by time, hence it must be conceived as eternal. Let us assume that this is intelligible, at least given the science of Aristotle's day or perhaps any science down into the nineteenth century.

Second, if it is intelligible, does it answer the question? Prime matter does not explain why there is prime matter. Only if one first posits prime matter can one explain why there will always be material things. But this may mean only that the question is meaningless. The question "Why?" in this case cannot be asking for a material or a formal cause, since that would be ridiculous. Prime matter is its own material cause and it has no form. It must be asking either for an efficient cause or for a final cause. The final cause of prime matter might be said to be the forms that can be actualized, but this is of doubtful meaning. And prime matter requires an efficient cause only if it came into being at some point in time or if it lacks in itself the power to sustain its own being.

Christian Aristotelians have developed the idea that prime matter and all the entities composed of it cannot be conceived as having in themselves the power to exist. They depend for their existence on a power beyond themselves. This power, or its ground, must be a necessary existent, or a being such that its essence involves its existence. Prime matter cannot be a necessary existent since it can be conceived as not existing. Hence, the necessarily existent is the efficient cause of the being of everything that is. It explains *that* there are things as well as what they are. It can then be assimilated to Aristotle's God who thus becomes both the efficient and the final cause of the world. Once this is done, there is no philosophical objection to asserting a temporal beginning of the creation, or perhaps better, a beginning of time itself.

This argument may be rejected on the grounds that there is no reason to go beyond the beginning of things to a ground of their being.

Certainly Aristotle never intended to raise the question as to why there is anything at all. He asked only for an explanation of what in fact is. Many moderns sympathize with Aristotle at this point and refuse to accept the more ultimate question as an appropriate topic for inquiry. The being of things in their eyes simply is; it does not point beyond itself to a ground.

This rejection of the radical question as to why there is anything at all is also characteristic of Whitehead. Sometimes it almost sounds as if "creativity" is intended as an answer to that question,[70] but it can be so even less than Aristotle's prime matter. We must ask to what "creativity" refers and whether in the context of Whitehead's thought it is an intelligible concept.

Creativity, for Whitehead, does not "exist." This is clear in that it cannot be understood in terms of any of his categories of existence.[71] Creativity is specifically described as one of the ultimate notions that along with "many" and "one" are "involved in the meaning of the synonymous terms 'thing,' 'being,' 'entity.' "[72] We cannot think of an entity except as a unit of self-creativity in which the many factors of the universe become one individual thing which then becomes a part of the many for creative synthesis into a new one.

These "notions" are not treated by Whitehead as eternal objects[73] because, unlike eternal objects generally, they are necessarily referent to everything that is. The eternal objects express pure possibilities. These notions express absolute necessities. Hence, they jointly constitute the "Category of the Ultimate and are presupposed in all the more special categories."[74]

Focusing now specifically upon creativity, we see that it is that

[70]For example, he speaks of "the creativity whereby there is a becoming of entities superseding the one in question" (PR 129).

[71]The categories of existence are listed in PR on pp. 32–33.

[72]PR 31.

[73]Johnson interpreted creativity as an eternal object in pages submitted to Whitehead, and Whitehead did not challenge this. If we follow Johnson here, the thesis that I am arguing, namely, that creativity cannot answer the question why occasions occur, is self-evidently established. See Johnson, op. cit., Appendix B, p. 221. But creativity should not be understood as an eternal object. Eternal objects are forms or formal causes, and creativity is not. An eternal object is "neutral as to the fact of its physical ingression in any particular actual entity of the temporal world" (PR 70), but there can be no actual entity apart from creativity. There is a sense in which "creativity," like any other idea whatsoever, is an eternal object. That is, I can think about Whitehead's idea of creativity, and when I do so, I am thinking of an eternal object. Similarly, "actual entity" and "prehension" are eternal objects when thought of as ideas. But the entities to which Whitehead intends to refer us when he uses these terms are not eternal objects.

[74]PR 31.

apart from which nothing can be. It is not in the usual sense an abstraction,[75] for whatever *is* is a unit of creativity. Creativity is the actuality of every actual entity. We may think of all the forms embodied in each instance of creativity as abstractable from it, since creativity might equally have taken any other form so far as its being creativity is concerned. But it is confusing to speak of creativity as being itself an abstraction from its expressions, since it is that in virtue of which they have concreteness. Nevertheless, creativity as such is not concrete or actual.

Once again, as with Aristotle's prime matter, we may say that this is fundamentally intelligible. Whitehead knows that he can only point and hope that we will intuitively grasp that at which he points. But this is the method of philosophy everywhere. It must appeal to intuition.[76] The next question is as to whether this intelligible idea can answer the question as to why there is anything at all. Despite Whitehead's own failure to raise this question in its radical form, I now propose to give it serious consideration.

My contention is that "creativity" cannot go even so far in the direction of an answer as did "prime matter." Once we have intuited the idea of prime matter we see that from the Aristotelian perspective there must be something eternally unchanging at the base of the flux of things. But creativity is another word for the change itself. Whitehead constantly denies that there is any underlying substance which is the subject of change. Does the notion of change, or becoming, or process include in it some sense that this changing must have gone on forever and must continue to do so? On the contrary, it seems just as possible that it will simply stop, that there will be then just nothing. There is a radical and evident contingency about the existence of new units of creativity (actual entities) that is not characteristic of new forms of prime matter.

Whitehead, of course, was convinced that the process is everlasting. Creativity will always take new forms, but it will always continue to be unchangingly creative. My point is only that the notion of creativity in itself provides no grounds for this faith. Hence, as an answer to the question of why there is and continues to be anything at all, creativity cannot play in Whitehead's philosophy quite the role prime matter plays in Aristotle. In Whitehead every actual occasion is a novel addition to the universe, not only a new form of the same eternal stuff.

---

[75]At times Whitehead makes statements that seem to imply that creativity is an abstraction (e.g., *PR* 30), but in the absence of explicit statements to this effect, these passages should not be pressed.

[76]Indeed, all language requires an imaginative leap for its understanding. (*PR* 20.)

Creativity is inescapably an aspect of every such entity, but it cannot be the answer to the question as to why that entity, or any entity, occurs. The question is why new processes of creativity keep occurring, and the answer to this cannot be simply because there was creativity in the preceding occasions and that there is creativity again in the new ones. If occasions ceased to occur, then there would be no creativity. Creativity can explain only ex post facto.

Creativity as the material cause of actual entities, then, explains in Whitehead's philosophy neither what they are nor that they are. If the question as to why things are at all is raised in the Whiteheadian context, the answer must be in terms of the decisions of actual entities. We have already seen that the decisive element in the initiation of each actual occasion is the granting to that occasion of an initial aim. Since Whitehead attributes this function to God, it seems that, to a greater degree than Whitehead intended, God must be conceived as being the reason that entities occur at all as well as determining the limits within which they can achieve their own forms. God's role in creation is more radical and fundamental than Whitehead's own language usually suggests.

If this is the "correct" Whiteheadian position, in what sense can we understand those passages that seem to subordinate God to creativity? Fundamentally they mean that God also is an instance of creativity. For God to be at all is for him to be a unit of creativity. In this respect his relation to creativity is just the same as that of all actual occasions. Creativity does not explain why they occur or what form they take, but if they occur at all and regardless of what form they take, each will be an instance of creativity, a fresh unity formed as a new togetherness of the antecedent many and offering itself as a member of the multiplicity of which any subsequent occasion must take account.

Like the Christian Aristotelians, I have stressed God's responsibility for the being as well as the form of actual entities. It may be wise to stress also the points of difference between the Whiteheadian doctrine developed here and this Aristotelian one. I am not claiming for God either eminent reality or necessary existence in contrast to contingent existence. Since God does exist, and since he aims at the maximum strength of beauty, he will continue to exist everlastingly. The necessity of his everlasting existence stems from his aim at such existence combined with his power to effect it. But I am more interested in God's power to cause actual occasions to occur than in the "necessity" of his existence. It is no objection to my mind that if that which has the power to give existence requires also that it receive existence, then we are involved in an infinite regress. I assume that we are indeed involved in an endless regress. Each divine occasion (if, as I hold, God is better conceived as a living person rather than a single actual entity[77]) must receive its being from its predecessors, and I can image no beginning of such a series. It is true that I also cannot imagine an infinity, but this problem obtains in any philosophy which supposes that something, whether God, prime matter, or creativity, has existed without a beginning. It is no special problem here.

In concluding this argument for God as the cause of the being as well as of the form of actual occasions, I want to suggest that Whitehead's thought moved in the *direction* I have developed. When the metaphysical questions were raised in *Science and the Modern World,* they were answered in terms of substantial activity and its three attributes. Comparison with Spinoza was specifically invited. Substantial activity seems to be thought of as an explanation of the universe in a way that would participate in efficiency as well as in passive materiality, but in fact the Aristotelian categories of causality do not apply to Spinoza's vision of infinite substance. In *Religion in the Making,* . . . two of the attributes, God and temporal occasions, were grouped together as actual entities, leaving only substantial activity and its two attributes of eternal objects and actual entities. But beyond this, it is significant that the analogy to Spinoza disappears[78] and with it the term "substantial activity." In its place is creativity, which is ranked with actual entities and eternal objects coequally as an ultimate principle.[79]

In *Process and Reality,* there was introduced the ontological principle that denies efficacy to whatever is not an individual actual entity. The eternal objects were shown to depend for their efficacy upon God's envisagement. Creativity is interpreted as an "ultimate notion." Nevertheless, the connotations associated with substantial activity in the earlier work still find expression in a number of passages. These passages can be interpreted in terms of the doctrine that creativity is an ultimate notion of that apart from which no actual entity can occur; but when they are interpreted in this way, their force is altered, and one suspects that Whitehead meant more than this. My own conclusion is that although Whitehead was compelled by the development of his thought to recognize that creativity is not an agent[80] or explanation of the ongoingness of things, nevertheless, his feeling for its role continued to be greater than his definitions allowed. My suggestion is that

[77]See above, sec. 2.

[78]Cf. PR 125.

[79]Indeed, creativity is subordinated to actual entities in their self-constitution as, e.g., in the following passage: "But there are not two actual entities, the creativity and the creature. There is only one entity which is the self-creating creature" (RM 102).

[80]PR 339.

if we adhere to the definitions and principles formulated with maximum care, we will be left with the question as to what causes new occasions to come into being when old ones have perished, and that when that question is clearly understood, the only adequate answer is God. This doctrine increases the coherence of Whitehead's total position.

In section 1, . . . I introduced a qualification with respect to God's sole agency in the provision of the initial aim. I there argued that past occasions with aims for the new occasion might also contribute to this initial aim. In that way the role of creator may be understood as shared between God and past occasions along with the self-creation of the new occasion. Nevertheless, the radical decisiveness of God's role cannot be denied. In the absence of any aim for the new occasion on the part of past temporal occasions, God's aim is quite sufficient, whereas apart from God's efficacy the past must be helpless to procure a future.

If now we combine this conclusion of section 1 with the discussion of creation in this section, we may say in summary that God always (and some temporal occasions sometimes) is the reason *that* each new occasion becomes. God, past occasions, and the new occasion are conjointly the reason for *what* it becomes. Whatever it becomes, it will always, necessarily, be a new embodiment of creativity.

God for Today and Tomorrow

13

and Tomorrow

Walter E. Stokes, S.J.

The problem of the philosophy of religion involves the question of the relation between philosophy and religion. On the one hand, as Henry Duméry points out: "We should not speak of a God peculiar to philosophers, but of a God that religion worships and that philosophy must take into consideration, as it does any other value."[1] In fact, the idea of God is not invented by the philosopher but encountered in human history so that it cannot be sustained by merely logical construction. On the other hand, there is no God of a religious tradition cut off from critical reflection so that "it is wrong for religion's advocate to confound the object of this affirmation with the modalities of the affirmation; it is wrong for him to believe that the transcendence of the divine mystery is extended to the materiality of the expressions that it takes on in human consciousness; with greater reason it is wrong for him to consider that his problematic is canonized by this transcendence."[2] Therefore, philosophy of religion must balance itself between the extremes of a philosophy that cuts itself off from religious experience and a religious stance that segregates itself from philosophical reflection.[3] The search for a philosophy of religion is a search for a total world-view in which the idea of God encountered in human history is thoroughly integrated.

Today many different philosophical voices in a variety of idioms question whether this search is possible any longer. They ask: Can God's existence be reconciled with man's deepened experience of himself as a free creator of the world? Can God's existence be accepted

---

[1] Henry Duméry, *The Problem of God in Philosophy of Religion*, tr., Charles Courtney (Evanston: Northwestern University Press, 1964), 7.

[2] *Ibid.*, 9.

[3] This point is supported by James Collins's study, *The Emergence of Philosophy of Religion* (New Haven: Yale University Press, 1967).

without destroying man's dignity in his free creative role in the universe? Can God's existence be affirmed as transcendent without making God a functional element in an abstract scheme? These questions are concerned with the possibility of reconciling God's presence in experience with God's transcendence; with preserving both the uniqueness of God's actuality and the uniqueness of man's freedom.

In one popular study of the problem of God today, John A. T. Robinson questions the relevance of a theism that would think of God as a heavenly, completely perfect person who resides above the world and mankind.[4] The same issue is raised by Harvey Cox, who writes: "The willingness of the classical philosophers to allow the God of the Bible to be blurred into Plato's Idea of the Good or Aristotle's Prime Mover was fatal. It has resulted in a doctrine of God which in the era of the secular city forces men like Camus to choose *between* God and human freedom, between Christian faith and human creativity."[5] This polarity between man's freedom and God's transcendence also appears in Gabriel Vahanian's reflection on Macleish's theme in *J.B.*, viz., that a God of justice has nothing to do with life because life is moved by love: "Why try to prove God, if all that man needs is to be himself? Why seek God, if all that man wants is love?"[6] In still another idiom it is dramatized by Jean-Paul Sartre in *The Devil and the Good Lord:* "Silence is God. Absence is God. God is the loneliness of man. There was no one but myself. I alone decided on evil, I alone invented Good. It was I who cheated. I who worked miracles, I who accused myself today, I alone can absolve myself; I, man. If God exists, man is nothing; if man exists. . . ."[7] And Maurice Merleau-Ponty recalls that Jacques Maritain rejected a notion of God as "the absurd Emperor of the world" who would finally sacrifice man to the cosmos. But Merleau-Ponty goes on to ask whether or not the concept of God as necessary being is not so bound up with this notion that without it God would cease to be the God of theism. "Yes, *where* will one stop the criticism of idols, and *where* will one ever be able to say the true God actually resides if, as Maritain writes, we pay tribute to false gods 'every time we bow before the world.' "[8]

In a contemporary form of Marxism, Roger Garaudy stresses the two essential dimensions of man: both subjectivity and transcendence. Man's task is to stretch man's creative energies to the maximum for

[4]John A. T. Robinson, *Honest to God* (Philadelphia: Westminster, 1963), 39.

[5]Harvey Cox, *The Secular City* (New York: Macmillan, 1965), 77.

[6]Gabriel Vahanian, *The Death of God* (New York: Braziller, 1957), 127.

[7]Jean-Paul Sartre, *Le diable et le bon Dieu* (Paris, 1951); tr. Kitty Black, *The Devil and the Good Lord* (New York: Knopf, 1962).

[8]Maurice Merleau-Ponty, *In Praise of Philosophy,* tr. John Wild and James M. Edie (Evanston: Northwestern University Press, 1963), 47.

the sake of realizing man's dynamic totality. In the area of knowledge, religion's weakness is not in questions it raises but in its attempt to give dogmatic answers: "Beyond the myths about the origin, end and meaning of life, beyond the alienated notions of transcendence and death, there exists the concrete dialectic of finite and infinite, and this remains a living reality as long as we remain aware *that it is not in the order of answer but in the order of question.*"[9] In the realm of action, this creation will be the fulfillment of the specifically human need to create and to create oneself so that the infinite is *absence* and *exigency* rather than *promise* and *presence*. Accordingly, Garaudy asks: "Is it to impoverish man, to tell him that he lives as an incomplete being, that everything depends upon him, that the whole of our history and its significance is played out within man's intelligence, heart and will, and nowhere else, that we bear full responsibility for this; that we must assume the risk, every step of the way, since, for us atheists, nothing is promised and no one is waiting?"[10]

Finally, Thomas Altizer expresses this tension between man's creative subjectivity and a transcendent reality: "Once the Christian has been liberated from all attachment to a celestial and transcendent Lord, and has died in Christ to the primordial reality of God, then he can say triumphantly: God is dead! Only the Christian can speak the liberating word of the death of God because only the Christian has died in Christ to the transcendent realm of the sacred and can realize in his own participation in the forward-moving body of Christ the victory of the self-negation of Spirit."[11]

Although their perspectives differ widely, these thinkers share a preoccupation with the tension between the dignity intrinsic to man's creative freedom, on the one hand, and, on the other, the threat to that dignity posed by a God who is wholly transcendent. In the Lowell Lectures of 1926, years before the "death of God theology," Alfred North Whitehead sensed this tension and remarked: "The modern world has lost God and is seeking him."[12] Since Whitehead anticipated the current dilemma so early, it may be worthwhile to explore his approach to the philosophy of religion.

A Whiteheadian treatment of the problem of God starts with the experience of discovery which opens up a cyclic process of rhythmic growth in the knowledge and experience of God. This growth process begins with the stage of romance wherein the experience of God has

[9]Roger Garaudy, *From Anathema to Dialogue,* tr. Luke O'Neill (New York: Herder & Herder, 1966), 89.

[10]Garaudy, 95.

[11]Thomas J. J. Altizer, *The Gospel of Christian Atheism* (Philadelphia: Westminster, 1966), 102.

[12]RM 62.

the freshness of novelty combining realizations not yet explored with "possibilities half-disclosed by glimpses and half-concealed by the wealth of possibilities."[13] This naturally leads on to the stage of precision which adds to man's experience the coherence and adequacy of a scheme of interrelated notions. Since no determinate meaning can be given to expressions of our notion of God as personal, individual and actual apart from the framework provided by such a scheme, this stage in man's knowledge of God depends on the previous stage of romance: "It is evident that a stage of precision is barren without a previous stage of romance: unless there are facts which have already been vaguely apprehended in their broad generality, the previous analysis is an analysis of nothing."[14] Still, lest God become a counter in an abstract scheme, another stage is required: the stage of synthesis. This final stage is "nothing else than the satisfactory way in which the mind will function when it is poked up into activity."[15] But, of course, though this represents momentary final success, each of the stages must be continually revivified, recreated, and developed in an unending process if man is to know the living God; if man's knowledge of God is to be real it must grow in an unending cyclic process even though attention may focus now on precision, now on synthesis, once more on romance. But man must continuously press on toward knowledge and experience in the indeterminate future and not rest with the notion of a God caught somehow in the net of concepts at some moment in his past.

Dimension of Experience

Even though the growth process in man's discovery of God is not linear and irreversible from stage to stage, it is useful to consider these stages in turn. The first is the level of experience. In this stage man's situation in the world raises for him the question: "What, in the way of value, is the attainment of life?"[16] This stage begins with three fundamental concepts unified in one moment of self-consciouness. These concepts are:

1. the value of an individual for itself.
2. the value of the diverse individuals of the world for each other.
3. the value of the objective world which is a community derivative from the interrelations of its component individuals and also necessary for the existence of each of these individuals.[17]

13 *AE* 28–29.
14 *AE* 29.
15 *AE* 37.
16 *RM* 49.
17 *RM* 48.

Man's consciousness of God begins with self-valuation, broadens into the intuition of the character of the universe as a realm of interrelated values, and finally, of adjusted values. Man's discovery of God in this stage is very similar to the way in which a man grasps the character of a friend. Drawing on experience described in the philosophy of Berkeley and Bacon, concretized in literature, especially the Romantic poets, and abstracted in the formalized viewpoints of science, especially quantum physics, relativity and evolution, Whitehead gives the experiential base for his intuition into the character of the universe. One principal source is poetic expression in Shelley who concretizes the flux of things, and in Wordsworth who captures the intuition of enduring permanence. Together they express the solidarity of the universe of real novelty with enduring permanences. "Both Shelley and Wordsworth emphatically bear witness that nature cannot be divorced from its aesthetic values; and that these values arise from the cumulation, in some sense, of the brooding presence of the whole unto its various parts."[18] Here Whitehead discovers first of all the value of the individual: "Remembering the poetic rendering of our concrete experience, we see at once that the element of value, of being valuable, of having value, of being an end in itself, of being something which is for its own sake, must not be omitted in any account of any event as the most concrete actual something."[19] But this individual is not self-sufficient; it unifies the larger universe in which it finds itself because it grasps nature *in solido*. In this way it raises the question: "What is the status of the enduring stability of the order of nature?"[20] Because stable order implies limitation there must be a source of limitation which cannot in turn have a further explanation of its definiteness. In this sense God is the ultimate irrationality: the principle of limitation and the ground of rationality. But this is a stage in man's rhythmic growth in the knowledge of God. This unsystematic affirmation must find a systematic context unless its meaning is to remain thoroughly indeterminate.

The experiential dimension does not involve immediate intuition of a personal God even though God is directly present within human experience.[21] For if religious experience consists exclusively in such an immediate encounter, then there is no broad foundation of agreement to which one could appeal. Such an encounter belongs to a private world which is reducible to whatever may have been the origin of this

---

[18]*SMW* 127.
[19]*SMW* 136.
[20]*SMW* 134.
[21]John E. Smith, *Experience and God* (New York: Oxford, 1968), 81–89, discusses revelation in terms of this distinction.

heightened emotional state. Accordingly, reason is necessary in order to maintain the objectivity of man's encounter with God. The religious experience has to do with man's direct but mediate experience of permanence with novelty within the intelligible unity of his life: "But there is a large consensus, on the part of those who have rationalized their outlook, in favour of the concept of the rightness of things, partially conformed to and partially disregarded. So far as there is conscious determination of actions, the attainment of this conformity is an ultimate premise by reference to which our choice of immediate ends is criticized and swayed."[22] Man's valuing experience involves the intuition of permanence with novelty grounded in the presence of a transcendent source of order in the world.

The Dimension of Formulation

In a recent interpretation of Hegel's philosophy of religion Emil L. Fackenheim rejects Kierkegaard's view that Hegel's philosophy is destructive of religion, and argues that Hegel seeks to penetrate "the relation between rational self-activity and religious receptivity to the divine and the relation of philosophical self-activity to both."[23] Similarly Whitehead insists that the philosophical reflection that aims at formulating a coherent and adequate account of the wholeness of experience is neither a reduction of experience to its categories nor a rationalization of the wholeness of human life and activity. Philosophical reflection is the process of the humanization of religion. Man must try to give adequate and coherent systematization to romantic experience. Therefore, the stage of romance must find completion in the stage of precision.

The notion of God, especially, requires metaphysics, because there are no "floating statements," but only answers to questions. And, as we have seen, the notion of God arises in "the question whether the process of the temporal world passes into other actualities, bound together in an order in which novelty does not mean loss."[24]

Now the central task of philosophy is "to conceive a complete (panteles) fact."[25] Philosophy tries to clarify the fundamental beliefs that finally determine the emphasis of attention that lies at the base of character.[26] It seeks the general ideas that are indispensably relevant to everything that happens and judges them in terms of their place in

[22]RM 55.
[23]Emil L. Fackenheim, The Religious Dimension in Hegel's Thought (Bloomington: Indiana University Press, 1967), 37 footnote.
[24]PR 315.
[25]AI 203.
[26]AI 125.

and contribution to what we find credible, reliable, humanly important. Philosophy is concerned with what really matters, and is orientated toward the complete fact in its concreteness.

Accordingly, interrelatedness or "solidarity" is the key to Whitehead's metaphysics.[27] "Solidarity," for Whitehead, means that the universe is a dynamic whole, a plurality of individual entities which in their interaction produce the one single result that is the complete fact. But in so doing, the divergent and diverse activities produce the single result without losing their individuality. For the universe is a unity constituted by the interaction of a plurality of interrelated individual entities—each individual is essentially what it is by its relation to the 'other', the entire universe.

In this way Whitehead formulates the poetic grasp of nature *in solido*. Its technical statement is Whitehead's Ontological Principle: "apart from things that are actual, there is nothing—nothing either in fact or efficacy. . . . Everything is positively somewhere in actuality, and in potency everywhere."[28] This principle expresses Wordsworth's experience of "that mysterious presence of surrounding things, which imposes itself on any separate element that we set up as individual for its own sake."[29] It involves the discovery that the universe is made up of entwined interconnected unities that are suffused with the modal presence of others. In this way Whitehead restores the interconnectedness of things to a universe shattered by the abstractions of Cartesian substance. Whitehead takes seriously Wordsworth's warning that:

> Our meddling intellect
> Misshapes the beauteous forms of things.
> We murder to dissect.

In this movement away from disconnected abstractions to the interrelatedness of concrete fact, Whitehead agrees with Bergson. But Whitehead does not agree that "spatialization" of things is an error bound up with man's intellectual grasp of reality. Man can use his

---

[27]This notion, borrowed from the legal notion *in solido,* has for its direct source H. W. Carr who used it to describe the interrelation of soul and body in man: "The term which seems best adapted to express the interaction of the mind and body is solidarity. The old legal meaning of this term fits the notion. It was originally a term of Roman and Civil law to express the character of a contract which in a single matter involved several obligations on the part of the debtors, with corresponding rights to the creditors. . . . The term solidarity means that diverse, even divergent, activities together bring to pass a single common result to which all the activities contribute without sacrificing their individual integrity." (See H. W. Carr, *"The Interaction of Mind and Body,"* Proceedings of the Aristotelian Society, XVIII (1917–1918), 32.)

[28]PR 64.

[29]SMW 121.

intellect properly, he can overcome the tendency to mistake abstractions for concrete reality, and so he can avoid the fallacy of misplaced concreteness.

Accordingly, Whitehead holds that each element within his metaphysical scheme requires each of the others for its own intelligibility. The elements are meaningless in isolation from one another. These coherent notions are: the actual entities of the temporal world, together with their formative elements—eternal objects, God and Creativity. *Together* they interpret every element of human experience. This means that metaphysics grasps the concrete existents of the universe in their interrelatedness. In this scheme, God is not a mere counter within a scheme but God's transcendence is encountered within experience.

Whitehead believes that Plato discovered those general ideas which are relevant to everything that happens: The Ideas, the Physical Elements, The Psyche, The Eros, The Harmony, The Mathematical Relations, The Receptacle.[30] In adapting Plato's seven basic notions Whitehead takes "the notion of actuality as in its essence process"[31] as his starting point. Here he is taking over Plato's Receptacle: "The community of the world, which is the matrix for all begetting, and whose essence is process with retention of connectedness—this community is what Plato terms the Receptacle."[32] More precisely, Creativity is that "ultimate principle by which the many which are the universe disjunctively, become the one actual occasion, which is the universe conjunctively."[33] Creativity is conditioned by the actual world relative to each novel coming-to-be of individual actual entities in the temporal world. Each actual occasion is a unique synthesis of the actual world relative to its becoming. There is no completed set of actual things that make up the universe. The set of all actual occasions is the initial situation for the novel actual occasion so that the "actual world" is always a relative term. This actual world provides the "data" for each novel actual entity in process. But this data is not passive but active precisely because Creativity is with the actual world. This initial datum with Creativity is the "real potentiality" of the novel actual occasions. It is real in the sense that Plato affirms the reality of nonbeing in the *Sophist*.

The counterpart of Plato's Ideas are Whitehead's Eternal Objects. In abstraction from actual entities, including God, the eternal objects together with Creativity constitute unlimited, abstract possibility. Accordingly, the very meaning of actuality is "decision" whereby unlim-

---

[30] *AI* 203.
[31] *AI* 355.
[32] *AI* 192.
[33] *PR* 31.

ited possibility is limited and so attains actuality. Just as potentiality
for process is the meaning of the more general term "entity" or "thing,"
so "decision" is the added meaning of the word "actual" in the term
"actual entity." This means that all forms of realization involve limitation. Each actuality is this, and not that. Each involves negation and exclusion, because mere omission is characteristic of confusion. To be is
to be finite; only the finite can be actual and intelligible. Infinity is on
the side of undetermined, abstract possibility.

The primordial limitation of Creativity is God in his contemplation
of the eternal objects in a harmony of conceptual valuation. The order
and harmony of the universe indicate that there is a "givenness" of relevant eternal objects for each actual occasion in the temporal process.
For this reason, there must be a nontemporal actual entity to account
for this graded relevance of eternal objects: "The limitation whereby
there is perspective relevance of eternal objects to the background is
characteristic of decision. Transcendent decision includes God's
decision."[34]

There is an unending interaction of God on the world, the world on
God, each requiring the other for its own completeness. Since the powers of human knowledge are limited, and God is without limit, this
process has no end. (There is no closed and fixed goal to-be-achieved).
The notions of God and the world require one another for their own
intelligibility, so that it is equally true to say that the world creates God
as it is to say that God creates the world. This conclusion means that
there is mutual immanence between God and the world, which, according to Whitehead, is very much in accord with "the Galilean origins of
Christianity."[35]

Whitehead's position here opposes several strains of thought combined in traditional theism: the divine Caesars that lead to fashioning
God in the image of an imperial ruler; the Hebrew prophets that lead to
fashioning God in the image of moral energy; and Aristotle's "unmoved
mover" that leads to the fashioning of God in the image of an ultimate
metaphysical principle. Together these strains produce the idea that
God is "an aboriginal, eminently real, transcendent creator, at whose
fiat the world came into being, and whose imposed will it obeys."[36] By
contrast, Whitehead's natural theology "dwells on the tender elements
in the world, which slowly and in quietness operates by love; and finds
purpose in the present immediacy of a kingdom not of this world."[37] In

---

[34]PR 248.
[35]PR 520.
[36]PR 519.
[37]PR 520.

Whitehead's metaphysics God by his very nature enjoys maximum free-dom.[38] To be is to be free, but God enjoys maximum freedom because his is totally unconditioned and has the total initiative. From this view-point it follows that God is no exception to the requirements of metaphysics.

To be not only is to be free, but also it is to be related. Religious in-tuition tells us that God loves all beings and is related to them by a sympathetic union surpassing any human sympathy. And all our experi-ence supports the view that knowing and loving constitute the knower or lover, not what is known or loved. According to the traditional the-ism, however, God's knowledge and love of this world are an enormous exception to the rule. For divine knowledge and love make a real differ-ence in the creature, but cannot make any difference to an immutable and necessary God. The traditional view maintains that God is not re-lated to the world but that God in knowing and loving himself knows himself as Creator of the world. But God is not really related to this world in knowledge and love, and so "it follows that God does not know or love or will us, his creatures. At most, we can say only that we are known, loved and willed by Him."[39]

Classical formulation of this view is given by St. Thomas: "God's temporal relations to creatures are in Him only because of our way of thinking of Him; but the opposite relation of creatures to Him are reali-ties in creatures."[40] And St. Thomas's reasoning is equally clear and sound.[41] God's real relation to the world could only be either a predica-mental relation or a transcendental relation. However, a predicamental relation would mean that God acquired a new accidental relation;[42] and a transcendental relation would mean that God depended on creatures. Rejection of accidental perfection is deeply rooted in St. Thomas's metaphysics of God as *esse subsistens* and provides no way of articulating God's relation to the world. However, even St. Thomas's own argument against a real transcendental relation of God to the world indicates that not all possibilities have been considered. Basic to this argument is the position that what by its nature is related to something else, depends on it, since without it this being can neither be nor be thought of. Accordingly, God could not be transcendentally related to creatures by a real relation without essential dependence on this world.

[38]This is developed by William A. Christian, *An Interpretation of Whitehead's Metaphysics* (New Haven: Yale University Press, 1959), 371–372.

[39]C. Hartshorne, *The Divine Relativity*, 2nd ed. (New Haven: Yale University Press, 1964), 16. The question is discussed thoroughly on pages 1–59.

[40]*S. T.*, I. 13, 7 ad 4. Also see *S. C. G.*, 11, chs. 11–14; *De Pot.*, q. 7 art. 8–11.

[41]The basic argument is given in *S. C. G.*, 11, 12.

[42]*S. C. G.*, 1, 23; *S. T.*, 1, 3, 6 resp.

For God's nature could neither be nor be thought of apart from this world. But this dependence would make him a radically contingent being.[43]

In a discussion of Paul Weiss's Whiteheadian approach to God's relation to the world, Kenneth L. Schmitz[44] rightly sees that in this question the nature of relation is the central philosophical question: "the modal philosophy sees the margin of being of creatures to lie within their being a non-reciprocal relation to a perfect God. The philosophical issue, then is between conceptions of relation."[45] I wish to argue that the development of the philosophy of relation within Whiteheadian metaphysics would make it possible to move between these alternatives.

Concerned primarily with categories proper to "things," theists have traditionally stressed God's liberty of indifference—God's perfection as an incommunicable supposit rather than as person in outgoing self-relation. St. Augustine's theology of the Trinity has enabled modern man to think of a person as constituted by his self-giving to another.[46] For Augustine, a person is at once self-subsistent yet essentially ordered to others, so that the person constitutes himself in a relation of opposition to the other. To understand the Persons in the Trinity, Augustine used the analogy of man, mind, and soul rather than the analogy of the cosmos. Memory, intellection, and that love of self which is identical with the ecstatic love of God—man seen as related to God, proceeding from God, and constituted in his personality by a pre-awareness of God as the source of his being—such is the analogy that enables Augustine to develop his theology of the Trinity. This philosophy of the person as self-relating which transforms the notion of "person" also transforms the notion of "freedom." For the Augustinian notion of liberty contrasts the personal autonomy of the free man with the bondage of a slave. What it excludes is not necessity but coercion from without. A being who enjoys this liberty acts for its own good without being coerced. This contrasts the unique personal value of an individual's power of self-determination or auto-finality, whereby he has dominion over himself, with the slave who is merely a means for obtaining goals set by others. Although God cannot but love himself, God loves himself freely. In this sense, too, if God wills to extend his love to creatures, in doing so he is free. The significant aspect is the personal dimension: God in self-giving, in self-relating to the world, placed himself in a state of gift. St. Thomas, similarly, in his theology of the Trinity insists that relation en-

[43]*S. C. G.*, I. 13.
[44]K. Schmitz, "Weiss and Creation," *Review of Metaphysics*, 18 (1964), 147–169.
[45]*Ibid.*, 162.
[46]For an excellent summary of this point, see P. Henry, *St. Augustine on Personality* (New York, 1960).

ters into the very notion of person; the Persons are subsistent relations. Within the Trinity the Persons are constituted distinct subsistent relations: subsistent because of their identity with God's absolute essence, and distinct because of their relative opposition.

The notion of Augustine and Thomas, in their theology of the Trinity, that persons are constituted in relation of opposition or mutual immanence is made a general principle in the Whiteheadian philosophical scheme. First, God's freedom may be understood as self-determination, self-relation or self-giving without external coercion. Second, person is understood to have two aspects, the incommunicability of a rational supposit and the communicability of the relation of opposition which constitutes persons. Both together provide a new dimension to the doctrine of relations—a dynamic, self-relating outgoing personal relation.[47]

From this perspective, God's relation to the world is real but God is not a "thing" which essentially depends on another. Because God is a personal, self-relating being, God can be understood to be Creator by an everlasting, free decision which could have been other than it is. It is true that God's nature and personal being as infinite actuality also determine him to be what he is. So that God can be known to be the ultimate source of order. This primordial aspect of God is eternal and essentially transcends the temporal process. But creation reveals that God is also what he is everlastingly by a free decision to create the world, so that not everything that is true about God is due to the necessity of his very nature. By deciding to create, God everlastingly becomes a being in a way which could not be realized apart from that historical situation with these particular relations in all their concreteness. This relation does not imply imperfection in God any more than the relations of mutual immanence among the Persons of the Trinity in classical theology implied any imperfection in the Father, Son and Holy Spirit. Rather it is the perfection of God's personal being freely choosing history and the actuality and risks of human freedom. God's free self-giving, or self-relating, adds no perfection to him; rather it gives rise to a real distinction based on the reality of a new relation of opposition. If relation can be active-self-relating, it can be identical with directing one's powers in love. Such a relation based on the relative opposition of God and this world is God's actuality loving *this* world and these men, rather than another world or no world at all.

Through this relation God reveals himself to us in time and history as other than he could have been. This means that God is not the perfect Being of the Greek world wherein immutability and eternality are associated with perfection. The Greek notion of perfection has its roots in considering man's mind as the measure of intelligibility. Without

[47]AI 205–225.

doubt man has a tendency to associate intelligibility with necessity. Once the Supreme Reality is discovered to be a personal being, however, the human mind, with its imperious demand for the intelligible to be "the one same thing," can no longer be the measure of what is ultimately real and valuable.

We discover the contingent aspects of God's living reality in time and history. The evolving universe gives testimony to the totality of that gift. So that God's gift may achieve its fullness in free beings who are themselves capable of placing themselves in return in a state of gift, the universe is ordered to become a universe-with-man. To bring about a universe in which God's love can attain its fullness in man's free response, all the forces of nature interact. Time, history, and freedom make a difference because through them God reveals that he is a living God in man's future waiting for man's free return of self. God wills to be a lover responding to man's free return of love. The paradox is that the autonomy of man's free response is God's gift of self to man. And that gift increases as man's return gift of self increases, for man's life is a project to be achieved in time and through history. In this way, God through his own act of self-giving constitutes man whose genuine free response completes God's gift. Without freedom, man could not place himself in a state of gift in return; without it God's love of the world would be without the fullness that freedom makes possible. In community, man can strive for those social conditions that can make man's free response to God possible. Aware of God's call to a share in his creative activity, man grows in the consciousness of his responsibility to make that response possible. Since God wills to give himself in personal love, risk becomes a necessary element in creation, for only free self-giving creatures can give personal love in return.

To be free and responsive and yet be time oriented, man has to be spirit-matter, capable of assimilating the past and appropriating it for the future. When we look at man we see that he is spirit essentially ordered to fulfilling his creative responsibility in time. *To be* a man is *to be creating self* in personal history. For man as spirit-ordered-to-time, time becomes a necessity for placing self in a state of gift in return of God's love. Time does make a difference, for it is only in time that man completes God's love. In choosing to give self in love to a spirit-in-flesh, God makes time valuable.

Since Whitehead himself holds that God has no temporal priority over the world, so that God is not before all creation but with all creation, the impression may be given that in no sense is God creator of this world. But the notion of creation is not bound to the notion of the world having a beginning in time. Certainly, the traditional phrase "creation out of nothing" seems to imply that the created world has a beginning in time. But the phrase, "out of nothing" means only that the creator makes the world neither from pre-existing material nor from his own being. Therefore, the notion of creation is indifferent to the world being eternal or having a beginning in time. Creation means that God has a radical and fundamental initiative in the coming-to-be of each temporal process.

Once causality is conceived of as personal and not merely as a mechanical force, this radical initiative need not threaten the creature's own autonomy. In fact, in interpersonal relations the causal activity of a person on another does not diminish one's autonomy but actually does increase it. One person can act on another without constricting the other because the causal power calls the other to create himself. God's initiative is a call to man to create himself freely and not a threat to man's freedom. From this viewpoint, there is nothing about man or any other creature that does not radically depend on God's initial causal activity, but also everything of importance to man depends on man's creative response. There is lawfulness because each creature has real potentialities limited by its historical situation; there is room for spontaneity because each creature freely responds to God's call.

Once this creative activity is thought of in the analogy of person rather than the analogy of things, it is possible to understand that God's creative activity is a call to the creature to create itself. Since this involves interpersonal activity, the intensity of God's activity does not diminish but enhances the autonomy of the creature. Certainly it is true that the more a mechanical force acts on a thing in a purely mechanical way, the more the autonomy of the thing is diminished. But a person acting on another need not lessen the freedom of the person acted upon; he can even intensify the creative freedom of that person. Furthermore, since the creature depends totally on the creator for its creative aim, the creature's autonomy is in direct, not inverse, proportion to God's creative activity.

We have now seen how, between a philosophy of creative act which excludes the possibility of the real relation of God to the world and a modal philosophy which demands reciprocal relations between God and the world, it is possible to posit a "third position"—a philosophy of creative act with real but asymmetrical relations between God and the world. In this stage of precision, the metaphysical scheme has in an important, reformable way interpreted the final opposites of experience in terms of God and the world: "In our cosmological construction we are left with the final opposites, joy and sorrow, good and evil, disjunction and conjunction—that is to say, the many in one—flux and permanence, greatness and triviality, freedom and necessity, God and the World. . . . God and the World introduce the note of interpretation."[48] At this stage experience has been enriched by philosophical reflection.

Dimension of God's Presence in Life and Activity

Not only is this interpretation of experience in terms of God and the world itself capable of reformulation, the rhythmic process demands to be completed in the further stage of synthesis. The work of precision leads back to the concrete historical experience of man as he moves to build civilization through art, its sublimation in the pursuits of truth and beauty, the impetus towards adventure beyond perfection realized, and, finally, the sense of peace, because only a return to life and activity can mediate the empirical dimensions of the stage of romance and the schematic formulations of the stage of precision.

In the study of the creating of civilization, the four interrelated factors: art, truth, beauty, and adventure are involved. "We have found the growth of Art: its gradual sublimation into the pursuit of Truth and Beauty: the sublimation of the egotistic aim by its inclusion in a transcendent whole: the youthful zest in the transcendent aim: the sense of tragedy: the sense of evil: the persuasion towards Adventure beyond achieved perfection: the sense of Peace."[49] Now the Whiteheadian reflection moves to the level of life and action and now calls on "those exceptional elements in our consciousness"[50] as we build a civilization of art, truth, beauty, and adventure. Art sublimates man's drive to enjoy the vividness of life which first springs from sheer necessity, yet points beyond itself. "It exhibits for consciousness a finite fragment of human effort achieving its own perfection within its own limits."[51] But this embodiment of beauty tends toward shallowness because it concentrates on adapting immediate appearance for immediate beauty. In both science and art man seeks beauty and truth so that "the finite consciousness of mankind is appropriating as its own the infinite fecundity of nature."[52] And both are exercising a healing role as they reveal absolute truth about the nature of things: "Churches and Rituals, Monasteries with their dedicated lives, Universities with their search for knowledge, Medicine, Law, methods of Trade—they represent that aim at civilization, whereby the conscious experience of mankind preserves for its use the sources of Harmony."[53] In this way art, truth and beauty beget civilization which is the relentless pursuit of the major perfections of

[48]*PR* 518.
[49]*AI* 386.
[50]*AI* 379.
[51]*AI* 348.
[52]*AI* 350.
[53]*AI* 351.

harmony. But the very essence of real actuality is *process* so that it is impossible to maintain perfection statically; actualities of civilization must be understood to be becoming and perishing. Moreover, to be is to be finite in the sense that all actualization excludes other possibilities which might have been and are not. And art must create individuals that are immortal in their contribution to the whole: "Thus civilization in its aim at fineness of feeling should so arrange its social relations and the relations of its members to its natural environment, as to evoke into the experiences of its members Appearances dominated by the harmonies of forceful enduring things."[54] Art, truth, beauty, and adventure each point beyond themselves to a permanence which transcends them.

This element is the harmony of harmonies, peace. Although it is difficult to put into words, peace is ever at the fringe of man's consciousness: "It is a broadening of feeling due to emergence of some deep metaphysical insight, unverbalized and yet momentous in its co-ordination of values. Its first effect is the removal of the stress of acquisitive feeling arising from the soul's preoccupation with itself."[55] This element excludes the pursuit of beauty and truth, art and adventure in hungry egotism and so involves the transcendence of the self. Peace is "primarily trust in the efficacy of beauty. It is a sense that fineness of achievement is, as it were, a key unlocking treasures that the narrow nature of things would keep remote. There is thus involved a grasp of infinitude, an appeal beyond boundaries."[56] Peace is at once the understanding and the preservation of tragedy since it is the intuition of the permanence of things in the face of fading beauty, pain, and sudden death. Peace "keeps vivid the sensitiveness to the tragedy; and it sees the tragedy as a living agent persuading the world to aim at fineness beyond the faded level of surrounding fact. Each tragedy is the disclosure of an ideal:—What might have been, and was not: What can be."[57] But youth as yet untouched by tragedy is especially sensitive to the harmony of the soul's dynamism with ideals which go beyond self-gratification.

This sense of peace habitually at the fringe of consciousness implies something more than itself. No argument could possibly prove that this gap exists because all such demonstrations are only helps for man to come to reflective consciousness of what is intuitively present within man's consciousness. At this point he "is seeking, amid the dim recesses of his ape-like consciousness and beyond the reach of dictionary language, for the premises implicit in all reasoning."[58] In this reflec-

[54]*AI* 363.
[55]*AI* 363.
[56]*Ibid.*
[57]*AI* 369.
[58]*AI* 380.

tion, the incompleteness is in the area of transcendence which is essential for adventure and peace. This requires that the notion of God as Eros, the persuading force in the world, be complemented by the notion of God as final Beauty: "This Beauty has always within it the renewal derived from the Advance of the Temporal World. *It is the immanence of the Great Fact* including the initial Eros and this final beauty which constitutes the zest of self-forgetful transcendence belonging to Civilization at its height."[59] This immanence is the key to understanding how the world is lured toward perfection that is really possible for its individual entities: "This is the secret of the union of Zest with Peace:— That the suffering attains its end in a Harmony of Harmonies. The immediate experience of this Final Fact, with its union of Youth and Tragedy, is the sense of Peace."[60] This same insight is expressed in other terms in *Religion in the Making*:

> The order of the world is no accident. There is nothing actual which could be actual without some measure of order. The religious insight is the grasp of truth: that the order of the world, the value of the world in its whole and in its parts, the beauty of the world, the zest of life, and the mastery of evil, are all bound up together—not accidentally, but by reason of this truth: that the universe exhibits a creativity with infinite freedom, and a realm of forms with infinite possibilities; but that this creativity and these forms together are impotent to achieve actuality apart from the complete ideal harmony, which is God.[61]

In this last stage of synthesis, Whitehead returns to the history of man's effort to create civilization and shows the presence of God as Eros and Beauty present within man's consciousness, effectively directing man's pursuit of civilization even in the face of tragedy.[62]

The experience central to the human situation is value-affirmation. In this reflection, man knows himself as situated in the world faced by a variety of values-to-be-realized in time. Man recognizes that some values are real possibilities and others are not. He also realizes that some values are compatible with his historical situation and some are not, some are compatible with each other and others are not. In the project of self-creation throughout his life, man must strive to bring these values into aesthetic harmony aiming at intensity of feeling both

---

[59]*AI* 381.
[60]*Ibid.*
[61]*RM* 105.
[62]Cf. Aime Forest, "St. Anselm's Argument in Reflexive Philosophy," *The Many-faced Argument*. Eds. John Hick and Arthur C. McGill (New York: Macmillan, 1967) for an informative exposition of Blondel: "In the very depths of the act in which we become conscious of what we are, we recognize an interior beyond, since this is constitutive of the dynamism of our souls" (p. 281). A comparison between Blondel and Whitehead in this area remains to be done.

in its subjective immediacy and in the relevant occasions beyond itself to achieve objective immortality.[63] And man realizes that to achieve his individual destiny he must create civilizations which embody truth and beauty. At any moment of his life-project a man can know that he must choose among values which aim at intensity of feeling. And choose he must, because not to choose would itself be activity.

In order to achieve values, one must freely enter into communities of knowledge and love. In entering such a community, man implicitly affirms that he knows and loves beauty and truth. In this way, man affirms that he knows and loves something as true, or as good, or as beautiful, and at the same time knows and loves truth, goodness and beauty to-be-realized. What is actually known and loved is limited and recognized as limited compared to what is as yet unrealized and re-mains to be realized. Furthermore, the drive for truth, goodness, and beauty which led to joining the community can be recognized to be be-yond the goals already achieved. This means that there is a dynamism in the valuing process that cannot be satisfied with any succession of temporal values or any intensification of these temporal values. For man discovers within his life-process a non-temporal factor that tran-scends all temporal realization and yet is immanent to each temporal process. For example, a man's drive for truth and beauty can be satis-fied by no limited truth whatsoever. To recognize limited truth as lim-ited is to be already beyond limited truth through one's dynamism of knowledge and love for unlimited truth. Each new discovery of truth and beauty is recognized for what it is—limited truth and beauty un-able to still man's drive for unlimited truth. This recognition of truth as limited implies that the drive for truth transcends its temporal embodi-ment. Moreover, no temporal truth added to temporal truth could sat-isfy this drive. In fact, man's self-creative process reveals the presence yet absence of an unconditioned non-temporal source of value which man can value without reservation or qualification. Since this answers to man's finer religious instincts, it can be called God, the source of all value in the temporal world.

The Dialectic of the Discovery of God, Today and Tomorrow

The dialectic of the discovery of God, today and tomorrow, begins with the realization that there is a human dimension to religious experience open to critical philosophical reflection. Accordingly, a fully developed philosophy of religion becomes desirable to achieve a properly human grasp of religious experience. This unfolds in three stages which contin-

[63]PR 41.

ually require one another in an unending process of growth from the dimension of experience to the dimension of schematization, from the dimension of formulation in a metaphysical scheme to reflective consciousness of God's presence in human life and activity as the condition of possibility of the other stages. So that not only do these stages require one another, they in turn complement one another and stimulate their further growth.

Each of these interrelated and interdependent dimensions opens onto the others. The initial reflection concerns the possibility and necessity of a philosophy of religion. On the one hand, it might seem that a philosophy of religion must necessarily reduce religion to the level of naturalistic concepts which must destroy it; on the other, philosophy appears to be recklessly entering the realm of the superhuman. According to the first alternative, religious experience would be destroyed and lose its autonomy. According to the second, philosophy itself would lose its own autonomy and critical powers. But the key is that religion concerns man's own relation to a being to whom man commits himself without reservation and without qualification. In this experience, religion arises in human intelligence, imagination, and emotion and uses symbols of human discourse. For this reason, religion can be subject to the laws of logic and man's critical reflective powers. Moreover, since God is not merely a construct of the philosopher but is actually encountered by the philosopher, philosophy must take this into account. There then is the possibility that philosophy can be the completion of human religious experience without naturalizing it. There is the necessity that philosophy through reason complete religious experience.

In its experiential dimension, the subjectivity of reflection on personal experience has the strength of vividness and immediacy. But its weakness is that its informality and subjectivity does not present itself for criticism by the community of men. On this level, what does it mean to say that God is a personal being, a uniquely transcendent being, or for that matter, 'God exists'?

This experiential dimension demands the development of a framework to enable man to possess in a thoroughly human way what he grasps in religious experience. This leads to the formulation of the cosmological and teleological arguments for God's existence. Now the strength of this dimension is the rigor of its logic and the precision achieved by placing notions such as God within the context of a coherent and adequate scheme. Apart from such a scheme, these notions can have a meaning that is so indeterminate that it is equivalent to no meaning at all.

But arguments, no matter how well-formulated, raise still other questions. For, each of these arguments appears to suppose somehow that the universe is intelligible. But if one were merely to suppose that

God exists because otherwise the universe would not be intelligible, is not the philosopher presupposing what he is attempting to prove? In these proofs, the world is recognized as a sign of the direct but mediate presence of God. But what enables man to read his own experience as the sign of God's presence? What framework could make such a reading of the sign of God's presence in the world possible?

The dimension of formulation and schematization calls man to return to his interior life and activity and reflect that God's presence yet absence is the condition of possibility of any intelligibility at all. For it would seem that the arguments from order and from contingency either rest on a misunderstanding of what an explanation is, or more likely, on an arbitrary supposition that man's experience is intelligible precisely in this way. But in fact reflection on man's consciousness of his interior drive to build civilization through art and science embodying beauty and truth manifests God's concrete presence yet absence in man's valuing process. This means that an ontological approach, but not the ontological argument as an argument, reveals that God's presence in consciousness is the condition of possibility of any humanization of religious experience.

In conclusion, we can sum up some of the resources of a Whiteheadian approach to meet the contemporary problem of God. If man today is asking, can God's existence be reconciled with man's deepened experience of himself as free creator of the world, the Whitheadian approach with its notion of God's persuasive personal action in the world, with its discovery of God's presence yet absence in man's creative activity, with its stress on the mutual immanence of God and the world, offers pathways for further development. If man today is asking, can God's existence be accepted without destroying man's dignity in his free creative role in the universe, the Whiteheadian approach with its unwillingness to make God an exception to metaphysics, with its rejection of God as an eminently real despotic ruler of the universe, with its view that God and man are the responsible co-creators of the universe, shows that man is not forced to choose between man's dignity and God's existence. If man today is asking, can God's existence be affirmed as transcendent without making God a functional element in an abstract scheme, it may be fruitful to realize that knowledge and experience of God involve a cyclic growth process from experience to schematization, from formulation to God present in the dynamism of man's life and activity. Finally, if man today is searching for a living God of the future rather than an anthropomorphic God of frozen history, the growth process has begun. The Whiteheadian approach offers man a living God for today and tomorrow.

Ely on Whitehead's God   14

Bernard M. Loomer

This article is a discussion and evaluation of a recent book on White-head's religious philosophy.[1] It is hoped that some of the questions raised by the discussion will stimulate others to propose constructive solutions. The problems dealt with in Ely's analysis are important for three reasons: first, because of the stature and increasing appeal of Whitehead's general philosophic position; second, because the religious implications of this framework of thought are still in the pioneer stage; and, third, because of Ely's conclusions in regard to the unsatisfactoriness of Whitehead's religious philosophy.

Ely's book consists of a nontechnical exposition of Whitehead's metaphysics and his philosophy of religion, together with a critical internal analysis of the latter.

I

The exposition, although limited to bare essentials and necessarily restricted for the most part to *Process and Reality,* is excellent. It probably contains the best summary statement of Whitehead's general position now in print. Its definitiveness is qualified, however, by two basic errors, the implications of which would necessitate serious changes in Whitehead's philosophy.

1. The first is his statement that "there are, strictly speaking, no external relations" (pp. 14–15). The grounds of Ely's contention on this point are not clear, because assuredly Whitehead does hold to the notion that there are external relations. The first instance is found in the relations between mutually contemporaneous occasions. It is a doctrine

From *The Journal of Religion,* XXIV, 3 (July 1944). Used by permission of The University of Chicago Press and Bernard M. Loomer.

[1] Stephen Lee Ely, *The Religious Availability of Whitehead's God: A Critical Analysis* (Madison: University of Wisconsin Press, 1942). All references will be from this book unless otherwise stated.

continuously reiterated in *Process and Reality* and in the last half of *Adventures of Ideas* that contemporary events happen in causal independence of each other. (*Science and the Modern World* is ambiguous on this point.) The freedom of events is due partly to the external relatedness of contemporaneous events. Also this sort of external relation is exemplified in the distinction between nonsensuous perception ("causal efficacy") and sense perception ("presentational immediacy"). The second example of external relation is found in the bearing of eternal objects upon events—although from the standpoint of the event the relation is an internal one. This doctrine is found in all his major works. A third case is the relation of the past to the present or the present to the future. As far as I know, this last is not an explicit doctrine in Whitehead's system, but it seems to be a possible implication of the theory of "objective immortality." The past is externally related to what succeeds it in the sense that the past, as past, remains unalterably what it was. The concept of "negative prehensions" constitutes a fourth illustration of external relations.

2. In dealing with the arguments that underlie the primordial nature of God and/or the principle of concretion, Ely states that they are based "on a fundamental postulate of Whitehead's—that the possible is prior to the actual, not only logically but metaphysically" (p. 14). This interpretation seems to be involved in the following statements:

> Whence comes this order? It cannot be a metaphysical character of the underlying activity, for any type of order is too special, too arbitrary. . . . Yet order must be in some sense prior to the events, for the events comply with it. We must therefore have recourse to a realm of possibility. . . . If then, there were order in the realm of possibility, . . . we should have a possible explanation of order in the active world [pp. 17–18].

> Before any order could enter the world there must have been some mental power to accomplish a complete ordering of the entire realm of possibility. . . . God is the "aboriginal creature" of the underlying activity, because he must have been produced before any order could appear. This does not mean that God was created in time. God as "aboriginal" or "primordial" means that he is logically and metaphysically posterior to the underlying activity [p. 20].

> As primordial, God is timeless and eternal. He is, however, not a mere ideal or a cosmic trend; he is a real fact, just as much as any event. The ultimate reasons for anything, says Whitehead, must be ultimately traceable to something in the actual make-up of a real existent, not to a mere unrealized ideal or to an abstract possibility. . . . This being is the Primordial Nature of God [p. 21].

Now the difficulties and ambiguities in these quotations may be due, in part at least, to the inadequacies of language—on the part both of Ely and of Whitehead. But if the priority of the possible over the actual is a fundamental postulate in Whitehead's system, it is not obviously or explicitly so. Ely appears to be saying that, metaphysically speaking, we have creativity and then the primordial nature of God and lastly order. From Ely one gets the picture of a God who somehow (being uncreated in time) stands back of the order in the world—a primordial God who exists apart from the order and/or the ordered events which make up the actual world.

But such is not the case. God, seen purely as primordial, is not a real fact that has its being apart from the order that obtains between possibilities. God as primordial *is* the order between possibilities; he is a universal structure or pattern that has ingression in every event. He is a metaphysical order that is exemplified in all orders of less generality than its own. In a sense, God as primordial is the most inclusive eternal object that binds all other eternal objects together so as to make them relevant to every occasion. As such this primordial order has no reference to any particular or *specific* events whatsoever.[2] In this sense, and in this sense only, possibility is prior to actuality. But, while the primordial nature of God has no reference to any specific creative processes, it has reference to whatever processes do and must occur. "The *particularities* of the actual world presuppose *it,* while *it* merely presupposes the *general* metaphysical character of creative advance, of which it is the primordial exemplification. The primordial nature of God actually is the acquirement by creativity of a primordial character."[3] Stated otherwise, God "is not *before* all creation, but *with* all creation."[4] This is to say that there is no such thing as creativity apart from a principle of concretion or limitation which conditions the creativity. Thus, "God is at once a creature of creativity and a condition for creativity."[5] One could interpret "primordial" to mean "no matter when or where." Thus no matter when or where creativity occurs, it occurs under the most general condition or limitation which *is* the changeless structure or character of God. And this character of God (his primordial nature) is the most general order of the realm of possibility graded in relevance to any and all particular events that occur. The conclusion remains: even considering the primordial nature of God alone, possibility is not prior to actuality.

But this is only half the picture. The same conclusion holds when we consider the "consequent nature" of God. Ely says that God as pri-

---

[2]Ely says that God as primordial is religiously inadequate because he "is not only unconscious and impersonal, but he has no concern for us as individuals" (p. 31).

[3]*PR* 522.

[4]*PR* 521.

[5]*PR* 47.

mordial is "an actually existing being" (p. 21). But God as primordial is
not "an actually existing being"; he is a "real fact," but he is *not* as real
"as any event." To say that he is, is to violate Whitehead's "ontological
principle" (which is one of the bases of his speculative empiricism, and
helps to distinguish his philosophy from a formalistic or disembodied
idealism). As eternal structure (i.e., as primordial), God is found in all
events (because, as Ely states, every ideal aim is derived from God). But
God's concrete or physical nature is his consequent nature. Ely acutely
points out a basic difference between *Science and the Modern World*
and *Process and Reality*. In the former the realm of possibility is ordered (is a realm) in itself and apart from God as the orderer. But, in
terms of Whitehead's later thought, this theory violates the ontological
principle which states that the ultimate reasons for things are found in
actual events and their relations. There are no disembodied principles,
explanations, or universals. So in *Process and Reality* Whitehead states
that the realm of possibilities is a realm because God envisages or feels
these possibilities. But apparently Ely does not see that the ontological
principle involves one further step, namely, that the ontological status
of God as primordial is ultimately traceable to God as consequent, to
God as concrete actuality. Unless this step is taken, the ontological principle is truncated.[6]

It might be objected that possibly Whitehead himself does not
clearly see and assert this as an explicit doctrine. The vacillation on this
point even in *Process and Reality* forces us to acknowledge the justice
of the objection. There are grounds for Ely's interpretation, but the interpretation given above seems to be the one that ties in most coherently
with Whitehead's basic philosophy, even though he may not have realized all its implications.

The conclusion of our interpretation is that possibility is not prior
to actuality in Whitehead's system because there is possibility only in
reference to some actuality, and the basic *concrete actuality* is God as
consequent. The fact that, in terms of explanation, God is logically subordinate to the category of creativity, does not weaken the contention
that, if there is any creativity whatsoever, there is a consequent nature
of God. Nor is this contention weakened by Whitehead's statement that
God's experience originates from conceptual feelings while the experience of finite occasions originates from physical feelings. For God and
the world, while contrasted opposites, are "mutual necessities." That is,
there is no world of events without the primordial nature of God; but,
conversely, there is no primordial order without God as physical—that
is, without a world of events. (For the moment we are avoiding the

[6]There is no conception of God as concrete in *Science and the Modern World*.
In fact, this notion is explicitly denied: "God is not concrete, but he is the ground
for concrete actuality" (p. 257).

problem whether God as physical or consequent is identical with the world of events.)

These considerations do not imply that the present consequent nature of God was inevitable. Rather, as Whitehead says: "In all philosophical theory there is an ultimate which is actual in virtue of its accidents. . . . In the philosophy of organism this ultimate is termed 'creativity'; and God is its primordial, non-temporal accident."[7] That is, it may be necessary that there be a consequent nature of God, but its specific concrete nature is accidental: it could have been otherwise than what it in fact is. Just what will be the content of God's physical nature is, in part at least, contingent upon the freedom of the particular creative events which constitute the world of process. But any contingent content of God's nature will illustrate his primordial structure or nature. Thus there is no temporal or metaphysical interval between creativity and God, whether God be considered as primordial or consequent. And since the distinction within God is one of reason only (God's two natures are not correlative), and in keeping with the ontological principle, there is no metaphysical interval between God's two natures.

The question as to whether this whole conception necessarily implies the eternality (in the sense of "everlastingness") of time and the world, is perhaps debatable. Ely alludes to one reference wherein Whitehead speaks of the "everlasting—that is, consequent—nature of God, which in a sense is temporal."[8] This seems to mean that God is temporal in the sense that he grows and nontemporal in the sense that he does not perish.

II

Ely's general conclusion of his analysis is stated in this way:

> The God that Whitehead derives from metaphysical analysis is not the God of religions. Whatever religious value Whitehead's God may have depends on aspects of God that lie beyond reason—aspects that Whitehead either intuits, guesses at, or has faith in. And if this is the upshot, why should not religionists intuit, or guess at, or have faith in a God who is more of a God? [p. 57].

But, philosophically speaking, this situation leaves us in a predicament.

> The only God that metaphysics can attain to has no religious value and presumably ought not to be called God, whereas the only Being who has a possible right to be called God can be reached only by religious and moral intuitions. Philosophers . . . . have been taught to view such intuitions with a certain distrust [p. 56].

[7]*PR* 10–11.
[8]*AI* 267.

Ely's more detailed analysis and discussion of the religious aspects of Whitehead's God pertain to three central problems as they function in Whitehead's thought: (1) the preservation of values (God's consequent or concrete nature); (2) the transmutation of evil into good (which includes the problems of evil and God's goodness); and (3) the problem of the relation of God's goodness and the preservation of the individual as such. We shall deal with each of these problems in the order named.

III

All of Ely's three criticisms either center in or stem from the concept of God's consequent nature. Admittedly, this is one of the most complex and obscure aspects of Whitehead's thought, delineated only in the last short chapter of *Process and Reality*. Yet this concept is one way of stating a basic distinction between religious humanism and religious theism. The issue between the humanists and the theists is not primarily concerned with God as some kind of abstract order. It has to do with God conceived as an actual concrete entity or process—whether God be considered as personal or impersonal.

To some readers of Whitehead, it may seem that the consequent nature of God is something of an addendum, something that was "stuck on" as an afterthought and which is not essential to his system. But Whitehead's ontological principle should lead us to think otherwise, even though this aspect of God is not developed and clarified in his thought. Epistemologically speaking, the ontological principle emerges in the doctrine of "causal efficacy" whereby, Whitehead holds, we actually perceive individual and particular events. That is, we do not infer the existence of particular concrete individuals on the basis of our perception of universals or abstract qualities or essences. Rather, we actually perceive the former by means of the mediating function of the latter (the "relational character of eternal objects"). The eternal objects partly constitute the character of concrete existents. In terms of Whitehead's concept of God, the primordial nature is the unchanging character or structure of an ontological concrete individual—God as consequent.

The problem of God's consequent nature is, in one sense, the problem of the "concrete universal." It is the problem of God's unity as a concrete individual. The problem of God's unity as an abstract universal, as a principle, as a structure or character, is the problem of God's primordial nature. God as consequent is God as one concrete physical process. There are two basic issues in this conception which should be considered.

In the first place, Whitehead has never clearly stated in what sense

and how God is an organic unity or a concrete individual. Is he one concrete individual among others, or is he a "compound individual" inclusive of all other concrete existents? Is "the one" in whom "the many"
inhere of such a nature that "the many" refers to all or only some of the
component individuals? As an organic unity, as "the one," God is always in the past, the immediate past. (Does this include *all* of the remote past?) This unity does not include the present processes of
becoming because of the mutual independence of contemporaries. If
God is all of the past, both immediate and remote, how is the past *as one*
known? How is the past as one distinguished from its component parts?
As the whole is distinguished from its parts? The difficulty in Whitehead's undeveloped theology is that he never speaks of knowledge of
God as consequent. God appears to be perceived by means of "hybrid
physical feelings," never by "pure physical feelings." In Whitehead's
system a physical feeling is the perception of a past event as distinguished from a "conceptual feeling" which is the entertainment of an
eternal object. A hybrid physical feeling is the perception of an actual
entity by means of that entity's projected conceptual feelings. Apparently, this latter type of feeling can apply equally to our perception of
God and also lesser individuals. But the two situations are not quite
analogous because we can check our hybrid perceptions of lesser occasions with our pure physical perceptions of them, while in the case of
God we have only our hybrid feelings of him.

This distinction appears to be necessary in Whitehead's system
(as it now stands) because we must conform to what we physically feel.
In Whitehead's emphasis, God is almost exclusively defined as final
cause and not as efficient cause; he is conceived of as love or persuasion or lure. This emphasis is more characteristic of God as primordial,
of God as form, structure, order, and vision. God is not felt physically
in the pure sense because (apparently) many of our conformable physical feelings are not compatible with our ideal aims which are derived
from God as primordial. That is, we know God in terms of his vision
(his ordering of relevant possibilities), and this ordering or vision is
constituted by the conceptual or mental feelings of a physical process.

But the point is that, while we must conform to what is already
achieved and settled (i.e., the past as physically inherited), we can reject more or less the "lure" of God's vision. We can refuse to be persuaded. Apparently, God will not coerce us to conform to his purpose.
Yet, if God is physical, he must exert efficient power over us. This efficient action on us should be compatible with God's persuasive lure unless God is a "split personality." It may be that Whitehead's weakness
in regard to the consequent nature of God stems from his implicit assumption that God is identical with all of creativity (all of the past). On
this view, and because of the fact that much of our past molds us in

ways that are not consonant with the vision of God, Whitehead may be forced to emphasize only the primordial nature of God. But the consequence is that Whitehead is not able to justify the concrete nature of God. Actually, on this view God as consequent seems to be an inference and not a perceivable actuality. Further, it becomes difficult if not impossible to distinguish the creativity of the past as one from the creativity of the past as many. Of course, each event feels the past as one, but this involves perspectives of the past.

One possible solution would consist in breaking down Whitehead's concrete monism into a concrete pluralism whereby God as consequent is not identical with all of the immediate past or with all of the concrete processes of the world. God as concrete would be that process whose efficient causation is compatible with his primordial order and vision. Furthermore, God as concrete could be perceived physically and not merely inferred.

The second related problem has to do with the "saving function" of God, or the preservation of all values. Ely claims that this function of God, while it has great religious significance, is not deducible from Whitehead's principles and cannot be attained by metaphysical analysis; this attribute of God, especially, is what Whitehead "either intuits, guesses at, or has faith in." Others would say that the question of the preservation of values is the chief argument for the existence of God.

On the one hand, Ely seems to imply that the whole notion of God as consequent is unjustified. Yet he admits that in Whitehead's system it is necessary that God have a consequent nature, even though he feels that the preservation of all values does not logically or empirically follow from this admission. Ely's qualification may be true; but, if God is to be concrete at all, he must preserve some values, because, for one reason, in Whitehead's system contemporary actualities do not form a concrete unity. Therefore, and to this extent at least, God's "saving function" is deducible from Whitehead's principles. Even though one does not establish the concept of the preservation of all values, one has not thereby disproved the validity of the idea of a God who is in some sense concrete and consequent—even though this God may not be Whitehead's.

Of course, the basic issue is whether Whitehead's consequent God is identical with all of the past, whether God is ultimately synonymous with creativity as such or whether God is one kind of creativity. These statements merely restate the problem of the saving of all values. If God as concrete is constituted by all of the past, both immediate and remote, then it might be argued that God preserves all values (although some would deny the empirical and logical validity of this implication). One of God's functions is the preservation of values already achieved in the actual world. But lesser individuals also preserve some values insofar as the present is partly constituted by the past. Therefore, one version of this problem concerns the question as to what God does over and above what is accomplished by these lesser temporal processes. Some statements in Whitehead seem to imply that God as consequent is not free and is a mere recipient of the experiences of other processes. As a recipient he may preserve all values but still lack efficacious power to realize other possible values.

But the solution to the problem of whether the preservation of *all* values is a logical implicate of Whitehead's principles (and whether the idea is empirically valid) is at least partly dependent on the answers that are given to these concepts: (A) "elimination" (which involves "negative prehensions"); (B) "objective immortality"; and (C) the "incompatibility of values." We shall deal with each in turn.

A.   One interpretation of "elimination" supports Ely's claim that all values are not preserved and seems to involve Whitehead in a contradiction; and, also, God becomes an exception to metaphysical first principles. Finite individuals perceive or feel the past in terms of perspectives or abstractions. Some elements in our past are eliminated because of the very nature of actuality itself. "In the temporal world, it is the empirical fact that process entails loss: the past is present under an abstraction."[9] Of course, the whole point involved in the contradiction centers around the meaning of the words "abstraction" and "elimination." Both of these terms have to do with the fact of negative prehensions. One of the basic questions in regard to the problem of negative prehensions has to do with the further question as to whether they exclude only eternal objects, or feelings as well. In this interpretation of "elimination" we are assuming that negative prehensions refer to the exclusion of feelings as well as eternal objects. Whitehead seems to mean that finite individuals preserve only *some* of the values of the past. Others are lost or discarded. This is "the empirical fact." But, continues Whitehead, "there is no reason, of any ultimate metaphysical generality, why this should be the whole story."[10] Therefore in God there is no loss of values. This would seem to imply that God does not perceive in terms of perspectives or abstractions. (Of course, God does not know the present events as present anyway.) Yet, in elucidating the consequent nature of God, Whitehead states that God "inherits from the temporal counterpart according to the same principle as in the temporal world the future inherits from the past. Thus in the

[9]PR 517. It should be kept in mind that the loss involved in "abstraction" is not identical with the loss involved in "perpetual perishing." The latter concept refers to the death of the individual as a subject enjoying its component experiences. The former concept refers to the preservation of those values which the individual achieved and enjoyed.

[10]PR 517.

sense in which the present occasion is the person *now,* and yet with his own past, so the counterpart in God is that person in God."[11] The contradiction involved here consists in holding that there is a loss of values and that there is not a loss of values—when God is supposed to have his past incorporated into his present according to the same principle by which finite individuals inherit their pasts. The contradiction is denied, on this interpretation, only by exempting God from those principles by means of which we can attain any knowledge of him in the first place. On this interpretation we would have to agree with Ely that Whitehead's concept of the consequent nature of God as saving all values is not justified in terms of the system.

This interpretation of "elimination" has been questioned. An alternative view would hold that elimination does not mean sheer obliteration but rather that an individual feels all of his past with greater or less intensity or vividness. Those aspects of his past which are very dimly and vaguely felt might be said to be insignificantly present, or irrelevant to an almost absolute degree, and thus "eliminated" for all "practical" purposes. That is, relevance and elimination would be end-points on the dimension of vivid experience. Then there would be no loss except in terms of intensity of feelings. And God as consequent would be that individual for whom there is *full vividness* of all values or feelings. As a cosmic individual he would not be subject to perceptual abstractions in our sense because a perspective is a characteristic only of local individuals. As a matter of fact, finite individuals would not be subject to perspectives in the sense that some feelings in their pasts had been forgotten or that some actualities in their pasts had been forgotten. They would remember all of their pasts, but mostly subconsciously.

However, this latter interpretation is contrary to many explicit passages in Whitehead. Also, it makes unclear the reasons for his doctrine of the "divisible" character of individual existents (whereby "causation is the transfer of a feeling and not of a total satisfaction"), and his discussion of the "medium." Furthermore, this interpretation lacks empirical support. Psychoanalysis has shown that we preserve more past values than we are conscious of, but this is still a matter of degree.

B. On the other hand, Whitehead's conception of the consequent nature of God seems to be theoretically supported by his discussion of the larger context of the problem which centers around the concept of "objective immortality." This idea is both epistemological and religious in its scope. Epistemologically, it means that the past as past remains what it was—unchangeably so; that the present does not alter

[11]PR 531–532.

what the past was when the past was present. This is the past as "stubborn fact" making the present partially conform to what the past is as past. This theory may be only an unverifiable inference considered from the point of view of a "perspective" theory of knowledge ("objective relativism"), since we can know the past only through the eyes of the present. It may be trying to know the "thing-in-itself" when a thing is known only by means of its relations. Yet the alternative view, that the past as past actually changes, seems to raise havoc with our notions of time. If one accepts Whitehead's definition of time as "the conformation of state to state, the later to the earlier," and if one assumes that the past really changes, then we would have no conception of time because there would be nothing definite or determinate for the present to conform to.[12] The distinction between the past and the future seems to be at least partly defined in terms of determinateness and indeterminateness. God, as preserving the past in its unalterable state, becomes the "measure of reality"; that is, by preserving the past "as it actually happened" (whatever that might mean), God makes possible our various perspectives and interpretations of it.

Ely interprets Whitehead as saying that evil disappears as far as God is concerned. But Whitehead's concept of objective immortality renders this interpretation invalid. (Ely's criticism will be treated more fully later on, but the groundwork of our reply to it can be set forth here.) Now it is true that Ely can cite references which seem to assert or imply that evil is nonexistent for God. At times, Whitehead's consequent God seems to refer to some completely transcendent realm where all evil is transmuted into good in spite of the enduring stubbornness of evil in the concrete world. It is true that Whitehead does not seem to have developed fully the relations between the concepts of God and objective immortality. The reason for this seeming transmutation of evil into good in another-worldly consequent God lies in the fact that Whitehead has not really developed the idea of God as efficient cause. This development would result in an explicit formulation of the idea of transmutation and redemption as processes which occur in the concrete world of events. But in fairness to Ely it must be recognized that there is ambiguity in Whitehead on this point.

At least one interpretation of the concept of objective immortality does not break down the distinction between good and evil but rather acts as its preservative. The immortality of the past includes the preservation of past evil as evil. The fact that future developments may take what is now an undeniable evil and utilize it for the creation of some good does not alter its character as a present evil. It is evil

[12]Of course, one could take the middle ground—which may be the position of objective relativism—and say that the question whether the past changes is a meaningless question because we have no way of verifying the proposition.

now because it obstructs the realization of a greater good than is being realized. At a future time the present evil will still be an evil (in spite of the fact that it will then be an aspect of some good) precisely because greater possibilities of good could have been realized in the present and would have been realized in the future.

The present character of an evil (that is, its mutual obstructiveness) endures, and this is its objective immortality. If evils were not preserved as such, we would not be subject to their continuing destructive influences. It is the means by which we still recognize a past evil as evil. The fact that some good may have come out of the first World War does not alter the other present fact that the war was evil and that it is still recognized as evil because it involved elements of mutual obstructiveness. Whitehead's doctrine of objective immortality means that the evil endures as evil and the good as good, that present achievements do not alter a past evil as past and as the past lives in the present and makes the present conform to it. To say that evil endures everlastingly as evil means that a present good is less valuable than it might have been if the past evil had been less evil. However, this does not make a present good any less valuable than it actually is in relation to possible lesser goods that might have been actualized.

However, these connections between Whitehead's concepts of the consequent nature of God and objective immortality should be noted. If *every* actual entity is objectively (not subjectively) immortal (and immortal in terms of its concrete objective individuality or *totality*, and not merely in terms of *some* of its aspects or feelings), then God as consequent would save *every* value. God would not feel the world in terms of perspectives. There would be no negative prehensions in God's consequent nature (regardless of whether negative prehensions apply only to rejected eternal objects or to rejected feelings as well). Then, in order to make God consistent with other concrete individuals or vice versa (a principle which Whitehead is committed to, with one basic and necessary exception), these lesser individuals must also feel and preserve *all* of *their* pasts. And the perceptual abstractions of these lesser individuals will consist in feeling most of their pasts very dimly (and subconsciously). In their feelings of the past, negative prehensions could refer only to rejected eternal objects and not to feelings.

On the other hand, if these lesser individuals do not preserve all of their pasts but really feel in terms of selected abstractions, and if God feels the world in a like manner (as he would have to in order to be consistent with our first principles), then he will not save all values. In this case, not all values would be objectively immortal. God would still be consequent or concrete, but it would be a different God than if all values were saved. Then the question would be: On what basis are some values preserved and others lost? Also, what becomes of the objective immortality of "forgotten" or lost events? Is it possible for events of the past to be lost and yet "condition" or "be present in" the immediate present? Is it necessary to distinguish between (1) the idea that all of the past inheres in the present because the present is what it is because of what the past was, and (2) the preservation of all "values"? Is the unchangeableness of the past synonymous with the preservation of all values?

C. The problem in regard to the incompatibility of ideals is directly related to the preceding. Whitehead has said that some incompatible ideals or values cannot coexist in one individual. This notion is grounded in the doctrine that all actualities are aesthetic syntheses. Finitude is a necessary qualification of actuality, and all realization of the good involves aesthetic limitation. The basis of tragedy lies in the fact that all ideals are not mutually compatible. God as primordial envisages all ideals, even incompatible ones, but he is "the urge to their finite realization, each in its due season. Thus a process must be inherent in God's nature, whereby his infinity is acquiring realization."[13] Various incompatibilities may be transcended in the process of development, but this higher inclusion must occur at the proper time. "Insistence on birth at the wrong season is the trick of evil."[14] And evil in a positive sense denotes the presence of mutually obstructing elements. Thus the *process* is necessary to God as well as man if good is to be achieved.

But these metaphysical principles appear to be transcended in the notion that God as consequent preserves all values. If some ideals are incompatible, how can God feel them all in a living immediacy? Why is the principle of a value's realization different from that of its preservation in God? One answer to this question would be that values which are not compossible as contemporaries may be compossible as earlier and later. But since values which are compossible as earlier and later are felt in God's immediacy, that is, as contemporaries, one might ask why they were not compossible as contemporaries in the first place. One answer might be that the experiencing of values first in temporal sequence and then in immediate togetherness adds to the richness of the values experienced.

IV

Ely's second basic objection to Whitehead's God centers around God's complementary function whereby actual evils are confronted with their "ideal complements" and actual values are enhanced by their complements.

---

[13]*AI* 357.
[14]*PR* 341.

Ely is right in holding that the "complementary" function of God is a necessary deduction from Whitehead's principles. But Ely's implications are not necessarily deducible. His interpretation of Whitehead's concept of transmutation reduces Whitehead's theology to an absurdity. Ely states that God is not good because he "integrates the achieved evils of the world with their ideal complements in a system in which the evil character disappears as far as God is concerned" (p. 39). He says that God perceives the evils of the world not as final but as transient, because "he sees them in such a setting that what is itself evil performs a good function and hence helps to make up a valuable whole" (p. 38). Ely seems to be saying that, in preserving the past everlastingly, God automatically turns evil into good, black into white, the incomplete good into the perfect and complete good. Yet Ely also states that "the evil is not really transcended in the world, for what is done is done, and God cannot unmake the past" (p. 38).

Now, ultimately, Ely cannot have it both ways: if God cannot unmake the past, then it is not true, in any simple sense, that God causes the evil to disappear by changing it into a good. Ely's interpretation implicitly presupposes, as we noticed before, that the consequent nature of God is some kind of a nontemporal transcendent being for whom every evil is seen as a good. And there is ambiguity on this point in Whitehead's writings. For example, the following would seem to support Ely's contention: "The perfection of God's subjective aim, derived from the completeness of his primordial nature, issues into the character of his consequent nature. . . . The wisdom of subjective aim prehends every actuality for what it can be in such a perfected system."[15] We suggest that this ambiguity is caused by the failure to develop the notion of God as creative power, and to relate more coherently this notion with the concepts of objective immortality and efficient causation. "God's role is not the combat of productive force with productive force, of destructive force with destructive force; it lies in the patient operation of the over-powering rationality of his conceptual harmonization."[16] Thus at times Whitehead appears to say, as Ely contends, that evil remains evil in the world of events ("God cannot unmake the past") but that in God's experience evil is transmuted into goodness. This results in a basic and inexplicable dichotomy whereby transmutation and redemption are regarded as nontemporal achievements.[17] But if transmutation is a fact, and if God as con-

[15]PR 524–525.

[16]PR 525–526. Whitehead says that the *primary* action of God on the world is defined by God's primordial nature. The creative and more compulsive power of God as a concrete process is not emphasized (see *ibid.*, p. 523).

[17]Ely expresses this negatively by saying that "evil is not really transcended in the world." This seeming transcendentalism is the basis for Ely's later point that Whitehead's God may will what is evil for man.

sequent is a concrete actuality, transmutation must be a temporal affair—even though it has a nontemporal element.

If Ely's interpretation were the true one, it would mean that (for Whitehead) it would not make any difference to God how we acted. If all evil is seen as good in God's eyes, what's the difference what we do? This is nothing but value-chaos where good and evil are indistinguishable. But this contradicts Whitehead's whole conception of God as process, as growth of values. Ultimately, it destroys the unchanging character of God. God then becomes (as Ely says) a cosmic fiend whose delight consists in devising new tortures for man to endure, because for man the evil is really evil. God would then have a "Diabolic Nature."

But this is not the case. Rather, as Ely points out, God's primordial nature gives him a vision of how an evil event can be turned to good account. But this can only mean that God does the best he can with what he has—under the circumstances. "The initial aim is the best for that *impasse*."[18] His primordial nature is such that evil events *can* be related to other events in such a way that *some* value can result. In one sense, this constitutes the "forgiveness" (unmerited "grace") of the love of God in traditional theology. God forgives the sinner not in the sense that the sinner's past is changed, not in the sense that the consequences of his sin (to himself and others including God) are obliterated and past evils are no longer evils, but in the sense that possibilities for good are ever present in spite of the evils.

There is tragedy in God even though it be a tragic peace. The redemption of evil through suffering includes the suffering of God (even though the fact of suffering in itself is not sufficient to produce redemption—a more creative element is needed). Considering only the primordial character of God, evil can be transformed into good because of God's vision—because of his conception of the ideal whole. But evil is real and endures because the actualized "whole" would have been different if the evils had not been evils. The fact that a whole is valuable does not entirely validate the character of the parts because there are good wholes and there are better wholes. God does not love sinners because they are sinners but in spite of the fact. The transformation of a past evil into a good does not change the character of the past evil as past. It changes the direction of a tendency whereby a greater good (or a lesser evil) may result than will be the case if the tendency persists in its evil ways.

If Whitehead had developed the efficient and creative aspect of God, we would be able to see more clearly that the transformation of evil, as conceptually seen by God and apart from the transformation

---

[18]PR 373.

as it occurs in the actual world, is only a possibility for realization. God feels the past world as it occurred with whatever character it possesses. But he feels it also through the eyes of his "perfect vision"; that is, he sees the past as surrounded with relevant possibilities for a greater realization of value. The past, as felt by God, is reflected back into the world. Thus the present is conditioned by the past with the past's character (the past, as felt by God and by the present, remains unchanged), but the basic unchanging character of creativity is such that the past as evil has possibilities of resulting in some good. The past as good has possibilities of enhancement. This is the *initial* aim which may be more or less blocked. But the freedom of events, both good and evil, is a necessary character of their being.

The "superjective nature" of God (another distinction of reason within the concept of God) refers to God's efficacious power whereby what is felt by God conditions the world of becoming. Whitehead speaks of the past as felt by God in terms of "perfected actuality" which qualifies the temporal world of process.[19] And Ely seems to give a value connotation to this term:

> The actualities of the world are received into God, where they are purified and perfected (as far as possible) by God's vision of an ideal complement. But this integration, though it takes place only in God's mind, is itself a perfectly definite fact of the universe [p. 42].

But Whitehead's own statements seem to carry a different meaning. "Perfected actuality" is attained when "the many are one everlastingly, without the qualification of any loss either of individual identity or of completeness of unity."[20] In other words, the phrase is synonymous with "everlastingness" wherein "immediacy is reconciled with objective immortality."[21] Everlastingness has reference to the preservation of values, but it does not necessarily mean that evils are automatically transmuted into goods. And by means of the living immediacy, the past is felt by God and as potent with possibilities of greater value is passed back into and qualifies the world of living experience. In other words, God never presents a past evil to us as final and incorrigible. Therefore, the nontemporal element in the process of transmutation is the eternal (in the sense of "unchanging") character of God whereby possibilities of growth are relevant to both good and evil events. This is transmutation as an ever present characteristic of God's nature, of his ordering of possibilities. Whitehead's "kingdom of heaven" is a conceptual, not a physical, fact. But transmutation as an accomplished fact is the product of the present

---

[19]*PR* 532.
[20]*Ibid.*
[21]*Ibid.*

events' reactions to the objective creative world of the past as it is qualified by God's ordering of possibilities. This is God functioning both as lure and as creative compulsion. And evils remain and endure as evils because of the stubbornness of the past and the "great refusal" of the present.

But the ambiguity in our interpretation persists. Because we try to discuss God as creative power, and not only as persuasion, and because Whitehead seems to identify God and creativity, we appear to be saying that God is responsible for the endurance of evil as well as presenting to us persuasive lures of greater value. This basic difficulty has been implicit in our whole discussion. The solution may reside in a distinction between creativity as such and creativity which refers to God as propulsive in accordance with his unchanging structure.

But Ely says there is another reason why Whitehead's God is not good. The "tremendous doubt" that plagues us in his writings is the notion that God's values may not be our values. We cannot be sure that "what God considers a greater good would be so in my standard of values" (pp. 44–45). And while God may not will what is evil from his point of view, he may will what is evil from man's point of view. Therefore, Whitehead has not shown that God is good "in any sense resembling that in which a man is good" (p. 47). In God's vision of the whole, everything (no matter how ugly or evil) can assume a good function because of the nature of the whole. What appears as an evil to us may be beautiful to God by virtue of its inherent contrast with something else. "Perhaps World Wars are the black spots necessary for the perfection of the divine painting" (p. 51). Thus Ely says that Whitehead's theory of evil "is a variant of the old conception that evil is an illusion of our shortsightedness; given . . . God's view . . . what seems to us evil is really not evil" (p. 51).

This criticism is organically related to and partly dependent upon Ely's interpretation of transmutation. To the extent of dependence, this criticism is negated by the previous discussion. But there is more involved.

It would seem that a meaningful theism must avoid the extremes of humanism and complete transcendence on this question. If God's standard of value bears no relation to our own, then God's function in man's life is unknown and unknowable—and it can be dispensed with. On the other hand, if God's goodness is identical with our own, what is the function of God? If God merely symbolizes or echoes our present or even our ideal notions of goodness, why not forget God and keep the ideals? Nothing important will have been left out. Nor would we find anything worthy of worship or commitment except man's ideals. If there is to be a God in any meaningful sense of the term, he must transcend at least to some degree human ideals of goodness.

Ely seems to imply that the most important problem in theology is to justify the ways of God to man. This is essential, but it is just as important and perhaps more so to justify the ways of man to God.

If Whitehead's God were completely transcendent, there might be some grounds for doubting whether God wills what is good for man. But Whitehead's God is a naturalistic one, meaning that he exemplifies our first principles. Thus we have some basis for thinking that God's standard of value is compatible with our own—in principle. This standard of value is defined by the concept of the primordial nature of God, a structure which is exemplified to a greater or less degree in every kind of experience. This structure is the secular equivalent of the religious concept of "love." This structure or standard may be roughly described as the greatest diversity, contrast, and intensity consonant with the greatest unity. Or, again, that the various feelings within one actual occasion or the activities of several occasions are so related that they intensify one another by means of compatible contrasts. "What is inexorable in God, is valuation as an aim towards 'order'; and 'order' means 'society' permissive of actualities with patterned intensity of feeling arising from adjusted contrasts."[22] God attempts to avoid both the obstructiveness of chaos and the triviality and deadness of monotony.

Now insofar as we have found that this value pattern has resulted in human satisfaction and good, we have empirical grounds for trusting God's standard of value. In fact, some would say that there is no human value or goodness unless this value pattern is exemplified in our activities; that the capacity to realize this structure of relations in our lives (to a greater extent than can the other animals) is what largely constitutes our humanity. God's willing evil from man's point of view could only mean (in Whitehead's system) that man was unwilling to realize a growth in value experience. The willingness to commit one's self to a process which exemplifies this value structure (on the grounds that greater human values would be achieved thereby) is what constitutes faith in God. Only if it can be shown that human values exemplify a basically different structure from that defined by the primordial nature of God is it true that Whitehead's God is irreconcilable with human goodness.

This does not mean that God's goodness is identical with our own. It does not mean that some particular situation which certain men at a given time hold to be good would necessarily be "acceptable to God." Nor does it mean that some particular situation which certain men at a given time hold to be evil would necessarily be as evil from God's point of view. In Whitehead's system there really is no problem of

22PR 373–374.

justifying the ways of God to man because whatever God wills for man would be recognized by man as good if man (in the most inclusive sense) were to realize his greatest potentialities. If one accepts as valid Whitehead's general criterion of value, and if one defines God as the most inclusive generalization of this value pattern (as Whitehead does), then how could God will evil for man? What was "really" good for man, from man's highest interest, could not be an evil for God. God's self-interest and his altruism coincide by virtue of the dependence of God on the world as his internal parts. God is supreme value for man. God's will might seem evil to us in our baser moments; it often does. But commitment to God defined as supreme worthfulness for all men implies a faith which trusts that a finer approximation to God's goodness on the part of men in general will result in a situation that men will call good. If the attainment of God's will involves the destruction of my present standard of values, it means that my criterion of goodness is inadequate to the best interests of myself and others.

Is this a blind and irrational faith, an ultimate prejudice that is unsupported? In the history of Western culture we have usually defined God in terms of supreme value. Even when God has been pictured as a wholly transcendent being whose goodness was as superior to ours as the reach of the zenith, the implication was not that God's goodness would be evil from man's highest standpoint. God judged man and found him evil in terms of man's own implicit standard of goodness. Men have thought themselves to be good, and God has called them evil because of their inhumanity to man—and thus of their unhumanity to God. In Western culture it has usually been the case that even those who defined God in terms of the greatest power thought of this power as being consonant with or identical to the greatest good.

Ely's criticism is really ambiguous: "If God's values are not my values, I shall not rejoice at finding God's love 'flooding back again into the world' " (p. 45). Does Ely mean by "my values" those values I cherish now, or those I cherished as a child, or those values I cherish when I am most sensitive to my fellow-men and try to take the "role of the other"? Or does he mean more than just myself? If so, whom and how many? Or does he refer to the value pattern on the basis of which I try to decide whether a given situation is good or evil? Even though (in some instances at least) a parent knows what is better for the child than the child himself knows, and even though the parent acts accordingly, the child may not rejoice. People conflict and war with one another because both their standards of value and their sensitivities differ. Those whose standard includes what is involved in "the century of the common man" and those whose standard extends only to the perpetuation and furtherance of existing inequalities and injustices constitute a case in point. If God's standard of value corresponds more with the former's than with the latter's and if the former's prevails, the latter will not rejoice, and they will define the situation as evil. And from their viewpoint the latter will say that God willed "what is evil to humanity."

Ely claims that Whitehead's God is not good because he "does not will the good. He wills the beautiful" (p. 52). Ely seems to interpret Whitehead's concept of beauty as meaning that which is indifferent to goodness. But Whitehead is not talking about God as an amoral aesthete. Whitehead does speak of that kind of love which "is a little oblivious as to morals,"[23] and of perspectives of the universe to which morality, logic, art, and religion are irrelevant. But they are irrelevant in contrast to "importance" or "worth" conceived of in terms that transcend narrow and conventional categories. That which transcends does not thereby and necessarily deny—in the small sense. That which transcends can also include and improve. It is the denial of certain moral standards in the interest of a more sensitive morality or a finer beauty. Certain kinds of love transcend the bounds of justice, but can one thereby say that a finer and nobler beauty or goodness has not been attained? Ultimately, Ely's criticism loses its force in the light of a different interpretation of the fact of transmutation.

V

Ely's third basic objection to Whitehead's God centers in the problem of the preservation of the individual and his values. Ely complains that even if God triumphs over the evil of "perpetual perishing" (which is the "ultimate evil in the actual world"), the ultimate evil is still ultimate for us humans because we do perish as individuals. Even if God does preserve my values, but does not preserve me, I receive no benefit; the final enjoyment is God's and God's only. Even if God can see how an evil can be transmuted into a good, and can see how my suffering can be redeemed, all this does not help me in my evil and suffering. Furthermore, the individuality of finite things does not count because they are all merely transient instruments for God's enjoyment —and even God, in preserving my individual values, preserves and enjoys them only as parts of a system. Therefore, even for God their individuality has perished. These considerations suck "all the vital juices from Whitehead's basic metaphysical contention that every ac-tuality is something for its own sake" (p. 50). And so again: "White-head does not give a satisfactory solution to the problem of evil because

[23]PR 521.

he has not shown that God is good in the important sense that he cherishes individuals and their values" (p. 50).

Some of Ely's criticisms of Whitehead's God, in this connection, lose some of their relevance in the light of the foregoing analysis. For example, the concept of objective immortality does furnish some basis for believing that God preserves an individual's values for whatever worth they may be and yield. But this need not include the preservation of the individual as such.

But why should God's goodness be correlative to or dependent upon the preservation of individuals as such, that is, on immortality? Or why is the redeeming of my suffering and tragedy and the transformation of my evil into a good meaningful only if I am present to share in the redemption and transformation? To hold these two ideas as inseparable is to cling to a type of "reward" theology which implies that there is no such thing as altruism or a disinterested love for God. This means that at best there is only an enlightened self-interest. Humanism, in order to maintain a respectable ethic, must insist on the notion of altruism. The inclusion of God in the picture by the theists does not change the fundamental principle involved. Whether God alone is the ultimate benefactor of my suffering, or whether its redemption is shared by later finite individuals like myself (and perhaps including myself), the issue at stake is the same. If the humanists can find it meaningful to suffer for the sake of a finer society which they may never share, why cannot theists suffer for "the glory of God" which they may never fully inherit? Ely's position is really ironical: he implies that it would be religiously justifiable for God to serve man and his values and to preserve them both indefinitely but that the saving of our values by God for his own enjoyment would be evidence of God's ultimate selfishness. This is equivalent to remonstrating with God for his being God. The difference between God's "selfishness" and our own is that in God's nature his selfishness and his altruism coincide for the reason previously given. This relationship between self-interest and altruism does not seem to hold necessarily for lesser individuals.

Ely might ask: Why could not both man and God together enjoy man's achieved values indefinitely? Why should an individual's span of existence be finite? If God really loves individuals and shares with them their sufferings and triumphs, why does not his love extend to the preservation of these individuals as well as to their values? Whitehead might reply that creativity (as distinguished from God) holds the answers. If Whitehead's God had created the world and all its conditions, these questions would be relevant. But such is not Whitehead's God, for, as Ely says God "cannot repeal fundamental metaphysical laws." The perishing of individuals in their immediate subjectivity appears to be a condition necessitated by a world of process. In this respect Whitehead's "event philosophy" differs from the more traditional "substance philosophies." The indefinite or ever-lasting prolongation of an individual might add to the monotony of the world and thereby decrease value. Old age is not synonymous with adventure and increase of novelty. In this sense it is true to say that God's abstract or primordial nature has no regard for specific individuals. It is concerned with any individuals who can add to the growth of value—both for themselves and for God.

Furthermore, Ely's statement that "the very notion of 'redemption through suffering' implies a divorce between suffering as a means and as an end" and his contention that the individuality of finite things does not count are both denied in Whitehead's system by the notion that the meaning of existence is "now"—for God and man. (And both of Ely's statements rest upon an incorrect version of the fact of trans-mutation.) Ely's statements really imply that the only real end is a final, perfect, and complete state. But, as Whitehead says, there is no one far-off divine event to which the whole creation moves. There is no perfection beyond, which there is no greater perfection. We are not merely means to the end of God's enjoyment. We are means for his enjoyment, yes, but we are also ends for God and ends for ourselves. Every means is an end and every end is a means—for God and men. If I have hope that my sufferings can lead to the increase of another's value, this present hope of a future eventuality qualifies my present suffering. If I do not have that hope, my suffering is all the more tragic. In either case my suffering, whether qualified or not, is at that time my end, my meaning. It is my suffering as an end (whether later redeemed or not, but especially when not) which helps to make evil so tragic, because it could have been otherwise.

Therefore, every actuality is something for its own sake in two senses. First my experience, whether of good or ill, is all that I have. It is its own reward. And for that reason it then becomes a "stubborn fact" for all future actualities (including my own future states and God's future states). It becomes a fact which must be reckoned with. For in a sense God can only enjoy what lesser temporal actualities give him to enjoy. If we experience suffering, so does he; if we experience tragedy, so does he; if we benefit by someone else's suffering, so does he; and if some later individuals reap the reward of our sufferings now, so does God. For God has only his present experience, which includes his memories and his anticipations. The future may contain more of value than the past or the present, but in any event White-head's God lives in terms of adventure. And since there is no final end, is it not true that "to travel hopefully is better than to arrive"? Since there is no final arriving, the meaning of the adventure for Whitehead's God is "now."

VI

Our conclusion is that Ely's interpretation of Whitehead's theology brings out into the open the basic ambiguity existing in his God-concept. But the ground of the ambiguity does not consist in the idea that Whitehead's theological doctrines are false; rather the whole position is not fully developed in terms of coherently interrelated religious categories. In other words, Ely has not been sufficiently just to the richness of Whitehead's thought. There is a more positive and constructive interpretation and development of Whitehead's religious philosophy that can be made. This pioneer work is one of the tasks for the present philosophic and religious generation.

Divine Persuasion and the Triumph of Good

15

Lewis S. Ford

In Archibald MacLeish's *J. B.*, Nickles hums a little tune for Mr. Zuss:

> I heard upon his dry dung heap
> That man cry out who cannot sleep:
> "If God is God He is not good,
> If God is good He is not God;
> Take the even, take the odd,
> I would not sleep here if I could . . ."

These words epitomize the unyielding difficulty confronting classical theism, for it cannot seem to reconcile God's goodness with his power in the face of the stubborn reality of unexplained evil. The process theism of Alfred North Whitehead and Charles Hartshorne was clearly designed to circumvent these persistent difficulties. The time has now come, perhaps, to probe the adequacy of this solution. While it may handle the problem of evil, does not process theism's critique of classical omnipotence open up a Pandora's box of its own? If God lacks the power to actualize his own ends in the world, how can we be certain that the good will ultimately be achieved? In a recent article, Edward H. Madden and Peter H. Hare contend that process theism lies shipwrecked in the very same shoals it sought to avoid.[1] If God's power is curtailed in order to absolve him of re-

From *The Christian Scholar*, L, 3 (Fall 1967). Used by permission of the National Council of the Churches of Christ and Lewis S. Ford. Lines from Archibald Mac-Leish's "J. B." by permission of Houghton Mifflin Company.

[1]E. H. Madden and P. H. Hare, "Evil and Unlimited Power," *The Review of Metaphysics*, XX, 2 (December 1966), 278–289. This article has been revised and reprinted in Hare and Madden, *Evil and the Concept of God* (Springfield: Chas. C. Thomas, 1968). Throughout the revision the original phrase "triumph of good" has been softened to "growth of value." In the present essay we shall quote from the original article, adding in parentheses a reference to the corresponding passage from the book.

sponsibility for evil, they suggest, then the guarantee for the ultimate triumph of good has been undermined. The process theist may say that

> natural events do not thwart [God] but are the occasions for his exercise of creative power, but he still must admit that on his view of the matter God is still limited in the sense that he neither creates nor wholly controls actual occasions. Moreover, if God does not wholly control actual occasions, it is difficult to see how there is any real assurance of the ultimate triumph of good. The two elements of traditional theism reinforce each other. The unlimited power of God insures the triumph of good, and the latter requires the notion of God's unlimited power. The mutual reinforcement, however, is wholly lacking in Whitehead's system. The absence points up a fundamental difficulty with his quasi-theism.[2]

Madden and Hare implicitly construe divine power to be coercive, limited by the exercise of other coercive powers in the world. We contend that divine power is neither coercive nor limited, though we agree that God does not wholly control finite actualities. This means we must recognize their contention that process theism does preclude any *necessary* guarantee that good will triumph on the stage of worldly endeavour. Yet should there be such a guarantee? Far from being required by theism, we shall argue that such a philosophical guarantee would undermine genuine religious commitment, and that the ultimate redemption from evil moves on a very different plane. With respect to any such guarantee we find, as Kant did on another occasion, that it becomes "necessary to deny knowledge, in order to make room for faith."[3]

I

Now clearly, if power is exerted only to the extent that control is maintained, then Whitehead's God is limited. But power may be defined more broadly as the capacity to influence the outcome of any process of actualization, thereby permitting both persuasive and coercive power. Coercive power directly influences the outcome, since the process must conform to its control. Persuasive power operates more indirectly, for it is effective in determining the outcome only to the extent that the process appropriates and reaffirms for itself the aims envisioned in the persuasion. Thus the measure of control introduced differs; coercive power and control are commensurate, while persuasive power introduces the additional variable of acceptance by the process in actualization. That God's control is in fact limited by the existence

---

[2]*Ibid.*, 281f. (117).

[3]Immanuel Kant, *Critique of Pure Reason,* B xxx. Norman Kemp Smith, trans. (London: Macmillan, 1929), 29.

of evil would signify a limited coercive power, but it is compatible with unlimited persuasive power.

Whitehead's thesis is that God possesses no coercive power at all. Whether limited or unlimited, such power is incompatible with divine perfection. In the official formulation of Christian doctrine, Whitehead complains, "the deeper idolatry, of the fashioning of God in the image of the Egyptian, Persian, and Roman imperial rulers, was retained. The Church gave unto God the attributes which belonged exclusively to Caesar" (PR 520). The concept of divine coercive power, both in its pure and modified forms, has led to grave difficulties.

Consider the extreme instance in which God is conceived as exerting unlimited coercive power, thereby controlling and determining all things. God is the master potter, moulding the clay of the world by the force of his creative activity, except that God has no need of any clay with which to work; he makes his own. On this exception the analogy breaks down, for the potter's vase asserts it own reality apart from the human potter precisely because it had already existed separately as clay. Could a world moulded completely by God's coercive power assert any independent existence of its own? To do so the world must possess some power. Pure coercive power transforms *creatio ex nihilo* into *creatio ex deo,* with the world possessing no more independent actuality than an idea in the divine mind would have. Even if it were to exist apart from the divine mind, it could not enrich God's experience, for he fully experiences in imagination any world he could completely determine.

Most views of divine power are less extreme, but they all share the same basic defects insofar as they ascribe coercive power to God. To the extent that God exercises such power, creaturely freedom is restricted, the reality of the world is diminished, and the divine experience is impoverished. Creaturely freedom is all important, for without it God is deprived of the one thing the world can provide which God alone cannot have: a genuine social existence. Abandoning the angelic marionettes who merely echo his thought as further extensions of his own being, God has elected to enter into dialogue with sinful, yet free, men.

Divine persuasive power maximizes creaturely freedom, respecting the integrity of each creature in the very act of guiding that creature's development toward greater freedom. The image of God as the craftsman, the cosmic watchmaker, must be abandoned. God is the husbandman in the vineyard of the world, fostering and nurturing its continuous evolutionary growth throughout all ages; he is the companion and friend who inspiries us to achieve the very best that is within us. God creates by persuading the world to create itself. Nor is this persuasion limited by any defect, for as Plato pointed out long ago, the real good is genuinely persuasive, in contrast to the counterfeit of the apparent good we confront on all sides.

This vision appears to many as too bold, for its seems to ascribe mind and consciousness to all beings. In ordinary discourse only those who are consciously sensitive to the directives and promptings of others can be persuaded, although we are beginning to recognize the subliminal influence of the "hidden persuaders." Whitehead is urging us to broaden our understanding of persuasion, for otherwise we lack the means for penetrating the nature of creation. Without the alternative of divine persuasion, we confront two unwelcome extremes: divine determinism or pure chance. In neither instance can God create. If determined by God, the world lacks all ontological independence. It makes no difference even if God only acts through the secondary causes of the natural order. To exist apart from God, either the world as a whole or its individual parts must possess a self-activity of its own. This self-activity is denied to the world as a whole if God is its primary (coercive) cause, and it is denied to the individual parts if they are determined by the secondary causes of the natural order acting in God's stead. Chance, on the other hand, ignores God's role in the evolutionary advance entirely and renders this advance itself unintelligible. We need not anthropocentrically imagine the evolutionary process to culminate in man, for it is quite conceivable that in time it might bypass man and the entire class of mammals to favor some very different species capable of a greater complexity than man can achieve; if not here on earth, then in some other planetary system. Nevertheless it seems impossible to deny that there has been an evolutionary advance in the sense of increasing complexity of order over the past several billion years. This increasing complexity cannot be satisfactorily accounted for simply in terms of the chance juxtaposition of component elements, and calls for a transcendent directing power constantly introducing richer possibilities of order for the world to actualize. God proposes, and the world disposes. This response is the necessary self-activity of the creature by which it maintains its own existence. The creature may or may not embody the divine urge toward greater complexity, but insofar as that ideal is actualized, an evolutionary advance has been achieved. Any divine power which so influences the world without violating its integrity is properly called persuasive, while the necessary self-activity of the creature insures the spontaneity of response. This spontaneity may be minimal for protons and electrons, but in the course of the evolutionary advance, sustained until now, it has manifested itself in ever richer forms as the vitality of living cells, the conscious activity of the higher animals, and the self-conscious freedom of man. Spontaneity has matured as freedom. On this level it becomes possible for the increasing complexity of order to be directed toward the achievement of civilization, and for the means of divine persuasion to become ethical aspiration (see *RM* 119). The devout will affirm that in the ideals we envision we are being persuaded by God, but this self-conscious awareness is not necessary for its effectiveness. Not only we ourselves, but the entire created order, whether consciously or unconsciously, is open to this divine persuasion, each in its own way.

II

The model of divine coercive power persisted so long primarily because God's activity is usually conceived in terms of efficient causality. The effect must conform to its cause; this is the basis for all causal law. Yet Aristotle's insight that God influences the world by final causation is more insightful, though it must be reformulated so that God can *act* to provide each actuality with its own final cause, and not just inspire the world as a whole through the perfection of his *being*. Whitehead suggests that God experiences the past actual world confronting each individual occasion in process of actualization, and selects for it that ideal possibility which would achieve the maximum good compatible with its situation. The occasion's past actual world consists in the totality of efficient causal influences impinging upon it which it must take into account and integrate into its final actualization. The efficient causal influences provide the means whereby actualization occurs, but the way in which they may be integrated can vary, depending upon the complexity of the situation. God's directive provides an initial aim for this process of integration, but unlike the efficient causal influences, that aim can be so drastically modified that its original purpose could be completely excluded from physical realization in the final outcome.[4] Insofar as the occasion actualizes its initial aim, the divine persuasion has been effective. God furnishes the initial direction, but the occasion is responsible for its actualization, whether for good or for evil.

In presenting this theory of divine activity, Whitehead unfortunately concentrated his attention upon the primordial nature of God as the locus of possible values to be presented to individual occasions,

---

[4]The subjective aim cannot be rejected in the sense that the aim could be excluded (i.e. negatively prehended) in its entirety at some phase in concrescence, thereby leaving the occasion bereft of any direction whatsoever. There must be continuity of aim throughout concrescence, for the process of unification is powerless to proceed in the absence of some direction. Nonetheless it is possible for the subjective aim to be so continuously modified in concrescence that the final outcome could express the contrary of the initial aim. Though genetically related to the initial aim, such a final outcome has excluded that initial purpose from realization.

at the expense of the consequent nature's role in determining which possibility would be most appropriate for the particular contingent situation. As John B. Cobb, Jr. has convincingly demonstrated,[5] Whitehead's "principle of concretion" only gradually takes on flesh and blood as he subjects his conception of God to the categoreal obligations of his own metaphysical vision during the years 1924–1929. Any statements taken from *Science and the Modern World* or *Religion in the Making* about the nature of God are systematically worthless unless proleptically interpreted in terms of Whitehead's mature position. Taken in isolation they only serve to muddy the waters.[6] Even in *Process and Reality* the transformation of God into an actual entity is not wholly complete, and to that extent there is some truth in the assertion that "what little influence Whitehead's God has on the actual world . . . he has as a principle, not as a being or person, and insofar as God is a personal being, he is without any effect on the actual world."[7] On the other hand, it is possible to modify Whitehead's presentation in the direction of greater consistency with his own categoreal scheme, indicating the very active role the consequent nature plays in providing the initial aim. William A. Christian recognizes the interweaving of the primordial and consequent natures when he writes:

> As prehended by a certain actual occasion, God is *that* unity of feelings which result from the integration of his primordial nature with his prehensions of the past actual world of *that* actual occasion.[8]

Cobb also develops this point:

> Whitehead speaks of God as having, like all actual entities, an aim at intensity of feeling. . . . This aim is primordial and unchanging, and it determines the primordial ordering of eternal objects. But if this eternal ordering is to have specified efficacy for each new occasion, then the general aim by which it is determined must be specified for each occasion. That is, God must entertain for each new occasion the aim for its ideal satisfaction.[9]

[5]John B. Cobb, Jr., *A Christian Natural Theology* (Philadelphia: Westminster, 1965), 135–185.

[6]*Contra* Madden and Hare, 282f. (118).

[7]*Ibid.*, 285f. (121).

[8]William A. Christian, *An Interpretation of Whitehead's Metaphysics* (New Haven: Yale University Press, 1959), 396; italics his. See also pp. 268, 275.

[9]Cobb, 156. He continues: "Such an aim is the feeling of a proposition of which the novel occasion is the logical subject and the appropriate eternal object is the predicate. The subject form of the propositional feeling is appetition, that is, the desire for its realization." We agree, except for the identification of the logical subject, which we take to be the multiplicity of actual occasions constituting the past actual world of the novel occasion, as reduced to the status of bare logical subjects for God's propositional feeling.

Cobb recognizes that his account goes "a little beyond the confines of description of Whitehead's account in *Process and Reality* in the direction of systematization,"[10] but he is prepared to defend his interpretation in detail.[11] What is important for our purposes is the fact that the involvement of God's consequent nature in divine persuasion renders that activity intensely personal. For God thus serves as a dynamic source of value, personally responding anew to the concrete situation confronting each creature in turn, and providing it individually with its own particular initial aim. Through this ever ongoing activity God becomes the ultimate source for all value, though not one which is static and impersonal like Plato's Form of the Good.

III

If there is no fixed, final end towards which God and the world are moving, what governs God in his choice of the good? Socrates once asked Euthyphro (10 A), "whether the pious or holy is beloved by the gods because it is holy, or holy because it is beloved of the gods?" In response to the corresponding ethical question, Duns Scotus declared that what God wills is good because God wills it, rather than that he wills it because it is good. If in affirming God as the dynamic source of value we agree with Scotus, what prevents our God from being utterly capricious in what he chooses to be good?

In order to grapple with this question we must first appreciate Whitehead's analysis of the good. Because he subordinates goodness to beauty, he runs a serious risk of being misunderstood. He has been accused of a general aestheticism which fails to take seriously the tragic conflict between good and evil, though his own motives are quite different. He does not seek to trivialize the good, but to enhance it by placing it in relation to an all-embracing value which would not be restricted to the limited context of human conduct. Beauty, the name of this all-embracing value, cannot be interpreted simply in terms of aesthetic categories. It is evoked by natural occurrences and by works of art, to be sure, but also by conduct, action, virtue, ideas, and even by truth (*AI* 342f.).

Goodness is essentially subordinate to beauty for two reasons. As Whitehead uses these terms, goodness is primarily instrumental while beauty is intrinsically valuable, actualized in experience for its own sake. It is a quality of experience itself, while that which occasions our experience of beauty (such as the good) is more properly called "beautiful" (*AI* 328). Moreover, goodness is rooted in Reality, the to-

---

[10]*Ibid.*, 157.

[11]*Ibid.*, 157–168, 176–185. (The latter section is reprinted in this volume, pp. 215–221.)

tality of particular finite actualizations achieved in the world, while beauty pertains also to Appearance, our interpretative experience of Reality:

> For Goodness is a qualification belonging to the constitution of reality, which in any of its individual actualizations is better or worse. Good and evil lie in depths and distances below and beyond appearance. They solely concern interrelations within the real world. The real world is good when it is beautiful (*AI* 345).

We are apt to dismiss appearance as unimportant in contrast to reality, regarding it as largely illusory. Appearance need be neither unimportant nor illusory. It is presupposed by truth, which as "the conformation of Appearance to Reality" (*AI* 309) could not exist without it. It is the basis for the intelligibility of our experience, and as we shall see in the final section, appearance plays a crucial role in the establishment of the kingdom of heaven. In any event, whether appearance is significant or trivial, that value which includes it along with reality is clearly the more inclusive.

The good, therefore, is to be understood in terms of its contribution to beauty. Beauty, in turn, is described as "the internal conformation of the various items of experience with each other, for the production of maximum effectiveness" (*AI* 341). This effectiveness is achieved by the conjoint operation of harmony and intensity. Harmony is the mutual adaptation of several items for joint inclusion within experience, while intensity refers to the wealth and variety of factors jointly experienced, particularly in terms of the degree of contrast manifest. In effect, then, actuality is good insofar as it occasions an intrinsic experience of harmonious intensity.

By the same token, evil is the experience of discord, attesting to the presence of destruction. "The experience of destruction is in itself evil" and in fact constitutes its meaning (*AI* 333). This definition is fully serviceable, once we realize that what is destroyed is not what is but what might have been. We tend to think of existence only in terms of continued persistence of being, but whatever has once achieved actual existence remains indestructible as determinate fact, regardless of the precariousness of its future continuation. In like manner, we ordinarily restrict destruction to the loss of anticipated continuing existence. Such continuing existence, however, if destroyed, never was but only might have been. As such it is merely a special case of what might have been, along with lost opportunities, thwarted experiences, disappointed anticipations. Whenever what is is less than what might have been there is destruction, no matter how slight.

Whitehead is emphatic in insisting upon the finitude of actuality, which in its exclusiveness affords the opportunity for evil.

> There is no totality which is the harmony of all perfections. What-
> ever is realized in any one occasion of experience necessarily excludes
> the unbounded welter of contrary possibilities. There are always 'others',
> which might have been and are not. This finiteness is not the result of
> evil, or of imperfection. It results from the fact that there are possibili-
> ties of harmony which either produce evil in joint realization, or are
> incapable of such conjunction. . . . History can only be understood by
> seeing it as the theatre of diverse groups of idealists respectively urging
> ideals incompatible for conjoint realization. You cannot form any his-
> torical judgment of right or wrong by considering each group separately.
> The evil lies in the attempted conjunction (*AI* 356f.; see *AI* 375, *MT* 75).

This conflict of values in attempted actualization is experienced as
discord, and engenders destruction. "There is evil when things are at
cross purposes" (*RM* 97). "The nature of evil is that the characters of
things are mutually obstructive" (*PR* 517).

While evil is the disruption of harmony, it need not detract from
intensity. In fact, the intensity of evil may be preferred to the triviality
of some dead-level achievement of harmony, for the intense clash may
be capable of resolution at a much higher level of complexity. The
unrelieved "good life" may be rather dull, yielding no more zest of
value than the perfectly harmonious repetition of dominant fifth chords
in C major. "Evil is the half-way house between perfection and triviality. It is the violence of strength against strength" (*AI* 355).

In his consequent nature God experiences both the good and the
evil actualized in the world. His own aim, like that of the creature, is
at beauty. "God's purpose in the creative advance is the evocation of
intensities" (*PR* 161), but these intensities must be balanced to overcome the mutual obstructiveness of things. God therefore seeks in his
experience of the world the maximum attainment of intensity compatible with harmony that is possible under the circumstances of the
actual situation. In order to insure this richness of experience for his
consequent nature, God therefore provides to each occasion that initial
aim which, if actualized, would contribute maximally to this harmonious intensity. This is the aim God wills as good for that creature in his
role as the dynamic source of value. It is not capricious for it seeks the
well-being both of the creature and of God. Were God to select any
other aim for that occasion he would be frustrating his own aim at
beauty.

Because of the intrinsic unity of the divine experience, all the
finite actualities of the world must be felt together in their measure of
harmony and discord. Insofar as they are individually intense and vivid,
these occasions contribute to the maximum intensity of experience for
God. Insofar as the several occasions are mutually supportive of one
another, they also contribute, but should they clash, or be individually

trivial, they detract from this final unity of all actuality within God. Divine love and justice may serve as primary symbols for God's aim at the harmonious intensity of beauty. Love expresses God's concern and appreciation for the particular intensity achieved by each individual, who finds ultimate significance in this divine feeling of appreciation for its particular contribution. Justice, on the other hand, expresses God's concern for the social situation of the togetherness of all occasions, since his experience of the world necessarily includes all the harmonies and clashes between individual achievements. Human justice tends to be cold and impartial, because our own partiality is so imperfect and limited to permit fair adjudication. Our sympathy and participation in the needs and claims of one party usually precludes any adequate participation in the rival needs and claims of others, particularly if the rival claimant is "society as a whole." Divine justice, on the other hand, is not abstract, following inexorably from the character of the primordial nature, but is concrete, the natural and spontaneous activity of the consequent nature integrating God's individual appreciations of the several occasions. Far from being impartial, God is completely partial, fully participating in the needs and claims of every creature. But because he is partial to all at once, he can judge the claims of each with respect to all others, valuing each to the extent to which this is consonant with all rival claims. Justice is ultimately the divine appreciation for the world, that is, the divine love simply seen in its social dimension.

This analysis of divine activity as the source of human value enables us to make sense out of the competing claims of rival ethical theories by assigning each a subordinate role within a wider explanation. Hedonistic and emotivistic theories emphasize the necessity to locate intrinsic value solely in subjective experience, though they tend to ignore the divine experience in this connection. Utilitarian theories stress the need for individual achievements of value to support and enhance one another. Their rule of "the greatest happiness for the greatest number" is strictly applicable, but it is spontaneously and non-calculatively calibrated to balance the claims to individual experience both qualitatively and quantitatively in the divine experience. Theories of duty, including Plato's vision of the Forms, see both the ideal character of the initial aim for each individual as well as the transcendent character of its source.

Religion seeks to enhance the role of ethical aspiration embodied in initial aims by concentrating upon their source in God. God is supremely worthy of worship because he is the ultimate source of value, as well as being that actuality in which all other actualities achieve their ultimate significance. The metaphysical description of God serves to purify the religious tradition of accidental accretions, while the religious experience of God gives concrete embodiment to these philosophical abstractions.

IV

Is there then any ultimate triumph of good? The Christian and the Jew alike wait with confident expectation for that day when the wolf shall lie down with the lamb. Classical theism, construing omnipotence in terms of coercive power, provides a philosophical guarantee that that day will in fact come to pass, or argues that it is already taking place (Leibniz' best of all possible worlds). This guarantee, however, transforms a confident expectation into a determinate fact, whether that fact be regarded as present or future. From the standpoint of faith, this appears to be nothing more than an emphatic underscoring of an intense trust in God. From the standpoint of logic, however, the fact of the triumph of good vitiates all need to strive for it. As in the case of the Marxist vision of a classless society, if its coming is inevitable, why must we work for it?

In process theism the future is an open risk. God is continuously directing the creation toward the good, but his persuasive power is effective only insofar as the creatures themselves affirm that good. Creaturely evil is an ever-present contingency, unless Origen is correct that we cannot resist the grace of God forever. On the other hand, the absence of any final guarantee now makes it genuinely possible for the expectation of the good to become a matter of faith. By faith I do not mean its rationalistic counterfeit: a belief based upon insufficient evidence. Rather I mean what Kierkegaard meant by truth for the existing individual: "an objective uncertainty held fast in an appropriation-process of the most passionate inwardness."[12] Faith is belief in spite of doubt, sustained by trust, loyalty, and devotion. The future is now doubtful, risky, uncertain. Yet the theist is sustained by his confident expectation that if we as creatures all have faith in God, that is, if all rely upon his guidance (given in the initial aim of each occasion), trusting him sufficiently to actualize the good which he proposes as novel possibility, then the good *will* triumph. The continued persistence of evil, both in man and in the natural order, testifies to the very fragmentary realization of creaturely faith in God. Nonetheless we may hope that the grace of God may be received and permeate all beings, and in that hope do our part in the great task. Such hope prohibits

---

[12]Soren Kierkegaard, *Concluding Unscientific Postscript,* David F. Swenson, trans., (Princeton: Princeton University Press, 1944), 182.

other worldly withdrawal, but calls upon us to redouble our efforts to achieve the good in this world with all its ambiguities for good and evil.

Faith in this sense is reciprocal. Just as the world must trust God to provide the aim for its efforts, so God must trust the world for the achievement of that aim. As Madden and Hare point out, "he is apparently so weak that he cannot guarantee his own welfare."[13] This is true to the Biblical image of God's vulnerability toward man's waywardness. We read that "God repented that he had made man, and it grieved him to his heart."[14] Israel remembers God's suffering and anguish over his chosen people,[15] a suffering most poignantly revealed to the Church in the crucifixion of Jesus of Nazareth. The world is a risky affair for God as well as for us. God has taken that risk upon himself in creating us with freedom through persuasion. He has faith in us, and it is up to us to respond in faith to him.

[13]Madden and Hare, *op. cit.*, 288 (125). In *Evil and the Concept of God,* 121f., Madden and Hare insert three paragraphs summarizing and criticizing the argument thus far of this paper (except for the discussion of evil in section II). Their summary is succinct and accurate, and they introduce the interesting analogy that Whitehead's God is like "an especially effective leader of an organization . . . who is powerful enough to guarantee the success of the organization *if* most of the members pitch in and help." They propose two objections to the existence of such a conditional guarantee of the triumph of good. "First, if cases can be found in which there has been widespread human cooperation and yet there has been no success, these cases would count as evidence against the existence of such a conditional guarantee. Such cases seem easy to find." Yet none are mentioned. I suspect all such instances would turn out to be problematic, for the theist and the naturalist would evaluate "widespread human cooperation" and "success" rather differently. Only widespread human cooperation *with* God can count as the proper fulfillment of the condition attached to the guarantee. Here the Christian might point to the rise of the early church, and the Muslim to the initial spread of Islam, both of which were eminently successful. Ancient Israel always understood her success in terms of her obedience to God, and her failures in terms of a widespread lack of cooperation with him. Secondly, they argue that the amount of evil in the world suggests that God is not a very persuasive leader. "It is a little too convenient simply to attribute all the growth to God's persuasive power and all the evil to the world's refusal to be persuaded." Now convenience, by itself, is not objectionable; in this instance, it may indicate that we have hit upon a proper solution. The measure of persuasion, moreover, is not how many are actually persuaded at any given time, but the intrinsic value of the goal envisaged. The only really satisfactory motive for action must be the achievement of the good, which alone is purely persuasive. All other "persuasion" is mixed with apparent, counterfeit goods and with indirect coercion. Divine persuasion may be a "still, small voice" amid the deafening shouts and clamourings of the world, but it is most effective in the long run—it brought this mighty universe into being out of practically nothing.

[14]Genesis 6:6.

[15]Hosea 11:8, Jeremiah 31:20, Isaiah 63:15. See also Kazoh Kitamori, *Theology of the Pain of God* (Richmond: John Knox Press, 1965), and Abraham J. Heschel, *The Prophets* (New York: Harper & Row, 1962), chaps. 12–15.

V

Thus far we have spoken concerning the actualization of the good in the world. Here the good will not triumph unless we achieve that victory. Nevertheless there is an ultimate consummation, not in the world but in the divine experience, that accomplishes our redemption from evil.

Whitehead provides an extremely detailed analysis of experience as a process of integration whereby an initial multiplicity of direct feelings of other actualities fuse together with the help of supplemental feelings to achieve a unified outcome. This distinction between initial, physical, conformal feelings and supplemental, conceptual feelings can be significantly applied to the divine experience. In this initial phase God experiences each actuality just as it is for itself, with all its joy and/or suffering. As Christian documents so well, God's initial conformal feelings are perfect, re-enacting the same feeling with all of the intimacy and poignancy that the creature felt, without any loss or distortion.[16] Here God is completely vulnerable, completely open to all the evil and the tragedy that the world has seen. "God is the great companion—the fellow-sufferer who understands" (PR 532). Moreover, the early phases in his integration of these several conformal feelings introduce dimensions of suffering the world has not known. God experiences fully the discord between incompatible achievements of value, since he honors and appreciates the value of each wholeheartedly, refusing to moderate the cause of any party in the interests of easy compromise. He also faces the disappointment of the disparity between the initial ideal he proposed for any occasion and its subsequent faulty actualization. God is a most sensitive individual, with the highest ideals, constantly thwarted at every turn, yet who resolutely refuses to give up his grip on either ideality or actuality. At the same time, however, he is also a most imaginative being, whose unlimited conceptual resources enable him to transmute this suffering into joy and peace.

In his analysis of beauty and evil, Whitehead discusses four ways of dealing with the suffering of disharmony (AI 334f.). The first three are inhibitory, directly or indirectly, excluding and rejecting some elements for the sake of the final harmony. Since God is hospitable to all, refusing none, none of these approaches is finally satisfactory. Yet there is hope in the final approach.

> This fourth way is by spontaneity of the occasion so directing its mental functionings as to introduce a third system of prehensions, relevant to both the inharmonious systems. This novel system is such as

[16]Christian, 351–353.

radically to alter the distribution of intensities throughout the two given systems, and to change the importance of both in the final intensive experience of the occasion. This way is in fact the introduction of Appearance, and its use to preserve the massive qualitative variety of Reality from simplification by negative prehensions [i.e. by inhibitory exclusions] (*AI* 335).

Here we can best understand Whitehead's point by analogy with works of the imagination, since this fourth way calls upon the resources of conceptual possibility to heal the wounds inflicted by actuality. Art and poetry transform the dull, ugly, irritating commonplaces of life into vibrant, meaningful realities by inserting them within fresh and unexpected contexts. Dramatic insight at the hands of Sophocles can suffuse the tragic deeds and suffering of Oedipus the King with dignity and honor by skillfully weaving these actions into an artful whole. Imaginative reason in the form of a speculative philosophy such as Whitehead's can surmount the interminable conflicts between man and nature, mind and body, freedom and determinism, religion and science, by assigning each its rightful place within a larger systematic framework. The larger pattern, introduced conceptually, can bring harmony to discord by interrelating potentially disruptive elements in constructive ways. Since God's conceptual feelings as derived from his primordial nature are inexhaustible, he has all the necessary resources to supplement his initial conformal feelings perfectly, thereby achieving a maximum harmonious intensity from any situation.

As the last sentence of our quotation indicates, the shift from initial conformal feelings to supplemental conceptual feelings marks a shift from reality to appearance. The objective content of conformal feelings constitutes reality as experienced, for it embodies our direct confrontation with other actualities (*AI* 269). The difference between this objective content and the content arising out of the integration of conformal feeling with supplemental conceptual feelings (the "mental pole") is felt as "appearance."

> In other words, "appearance" is the effect of the activity of the mental pole, whereby the qualities and coordinations of the given physical world undergo transformation. It results from the fusion of the ideal with the actual—The light that never was, on sea or land (*AI* 270).

Appearance plays little or no role in simpler actualities, for they tend simply to conform to the realities of the immediate situation. Appearance becomes of the utmost importance with the emergence of sensory perception, for this complex mental functioning provides the means whereby the bewildering bombardment of causal influences can be reduced to a vivid awareness for perceptive discernment. We tend to despise appearance for its occasional lapses from reality, but this is short-sighted thinking. Appearance, Whitehead argues, is the locus for perception, novelty, intelligibility, and even consciousness. We constantly strive to encounter reality directly, but such an effort simply takes us back to a preconscious physical interaction with our surroundings. What is needed is not reality but truthful appearance, that is, conscious perceptive experience which is directly derived from and rooted in reality. Appearance becomes illusory only to the extent that the final integration achieves completion by the inhibitory exclusion of some elements of reality.

Clearly, divinely experienced Appearance is thoroughly truthful, incorporating all Reality within its comprehension, yet infusing it with an intensity and harmony that Reality failed to achieve for itself. Goodness, as pertaining solely to the achievement of Reality, is left behind in this final experience of Beauty, though its contribution forms its necessary basis. In this way Truth, as the conformation of Appearance to the Reality in which it is rooted, enhances Beauty (see AI 342f.). In Beauty the goodness of the world is saved and preserved whole, while its evil is redeemed and purged of all its wickedness.

Hopefully this technical analysis will illuminate Whitehead's lyrical words towards the end of Process and Reality:

> The wisdom of the divine subjective aim prehends every actuality for what it can be in such a perfected system—its sufferings, its sorrows, its failures, its triumphs, its immediacies of joy—woven by rightness of feeling into the harmony of the universal feeling. . . . The revolts of destructive evil, purely self-regarding, are dismissed into their triviality of merely individual facts; and yet the good they did achieve in individual joy, in individual sorrow, in the introduction of needed contrast, is yet saved by its relation to the completed whole. The image—and it is but an image—the image under which this operative growth of God's nature is best conceived, is that of a tender care that nothing be lost.
>
> The consequent nature of God is his judgment on the world. He saves the world as it passes into the immediacy of his own life. It is the judgment of a tenderness which loses nothing that can be saved. It is also the judgment of a wisdom which uses what in the temporal world is mere wreckage (PR 525).

(The last two sentences recall to mind the ancient vision of a law-giver, the leader of a second exodus, who humbly fulfills the task of the suffering servant:

> A bruised reed he will not break,
> and a dimly burning wick he will not quench;
> he will faithfully bring forth justice.)[17]

[17]Isaiah 42:3.

George F. Thomas, while most sensitive to the metaphorical power of these words of Whitehead, offers a searching critique which must be answered:

> The nature of the process by which God "saves" the world is not entirely clear. "He saves the world," says Whitehead, "as it passes into the immediacy of his own life." This means that in some way the values realized by actual entities are saved by being included in the experience of God as a "completed whole." But does it mean that the world is transformed and the evil in it overcome, or only that it is included in the harmony of God's experience? The method by which it is "saved" is said to be rationality rather than force. . . . But the "over-powering rationality of his conceptual harmonization" (PR 526) seems to be effective not in transforming the *world* and overcoming its evil but in harmonizing its discords in the experience of God.[18]

Yet is it God's task to transform the world? Clearly the ancient Hebrew looked to Yahweh to bring about the prosperity of his nation. Thomas reaffirms that hope, but is it a realistic and justifiable expectation?

Samuel H. Beer argues that this expectation was transformed by the proclamation of Jesus:

> The gospel of the kingdom is that there is another order beyond our earthly existence. Things of the world as we find it are mortal and so without consequence and meaning, except as they may be preserved in that saving order. Here the covenant with man is not that he and his children shall thrive and prosper in history. It is rather that they shall sooner or later die in history but that they shall yet live in an order which transcends history. The meek, the merciful, the pure in heart, shall inherit it, not on earth, but in heaven.[19]

We are to seek "a kingdom not of this world" (PR 520), a kingdom which both Beer and Whitehead find exemplified in the consequent nature of God (PR 531).

Were God to transform the world, he would usurp our creaturely function in the moral economy. Yet suppose he were to usher in a perfected world tomorrow, the fulfillment of all our wishful dreaming. That would certainly redeem the world from all the evil which it would otherwise fall heir to tomorrow, but would it purge the world of today's

---

[18]George F. Thomas, *Religious Philosophies of the West* (New York: Charles Scribner's Sons, 1965), 368.

[19]Samuel H. Beer, *The City of Reason*, (Cambridge: Harvard University Press, 1949), 131. Beer is Professor of Government at Harvard and very distinguished in that field, yet quite versatile. In this remarkable book he sought "to state a philosophy of liberalism based on A. N. Whitehead's metaphysics of creative advance" (p. vii). See particularly chap. 12, "A Saving Order," which considers most of the themes of this final section.

evil? Remembering Ivan Karamazov's words, would such a perfect world even compensate for the innocent suffering of one baby in to-day's world? For what has already happened is past and cannot be altered; no future transformation can affect it. Nevertheless it can be transformed in the divine experience of the world, and this is where its redemption is to be sought. Finite actualization is necessarily transient. Far from saving and perfecting the past, the present blocks out the immediacy of the past by its own presence. If "the nature of evil is that the character of things are mutually obstructive" (PR 517), then the constant displacement and loss of the past through the activity of the present is most evil, however unavoidable, and no present or future achievement of the world can remedy that situation. "The ultimate evil in the temporal world . . . lies in the fact that the past fades, that time is a 'perpetual perishing' " (PR 517). This perishing can only be over-come within a divine experience which savors every occasion, no matter how distantly past with respect to ourselves, as happening now in an everlasting immediacy which never fades.

> Each actuality in the temporal world has its reception into God's nature. The corresponding element in God's nature is not temporal actuality, but is the transmutation of that temporal actuality into a liv-ing, ever-present fact (PR 531).[20]

Finally, however, it may be objected that this ultimate consum-mation of all things is fine for God, but has no value for us. Thomas argues that Whitehead's God is not "the Redeemer of the world who transforms His creatures by the power of His grace and brings new life to them."[21] In response Whitehead speaks of "four creative phases in which the universe accomplishes its actuality" (PR 532),[22] which cul-minates in the impact of God's consequent experience upon the world.

> For the perfected actuality passes back into the temporal world, and qualifies this world so that each temporal actuality includes it as an im-mediate fact of relevant experience. For the kingdom of heaven is with us today (PR 532).

This follows from his general 'principle of relativity,' whereby any actuality whatever causally influences all subsequent actualities, how-ever negligibly (PR 33). As it stands, this brief description of our intuition of the kingdom of God in the last two paragraphs of Process

---

[20]For a detailed development of this point, see my article, "Boethius and White-head on Time and Eternity," International Philosophical Quarterly, VIII, 1 (March 1968), 38–67.

[21]George F. Thomas, 389.

[22]The first three phases are (a) God's originating activity in providing initial aims, (b) finite actualizations in the world, and (c) God's complete experience of the world in his consequent nature.

and Reality is exceedingly cryptic, and must be explicated by means of the final chapter of *Adventures of Ideas* on "Peace." In this chapter, however, there is a tentativeness, a suggestive inarticulateness struggling with a far wider vision than we can possibly do justice to. Whitehead tells us he chose "the term 'Peace' for that Harmony of Harmonies which calms destructive turbulence and completes civilization" (*AI* 367). "The experience of Peace is largely beyond the control of purpose. It comes as a gift" (*AI* 368). I take it to be the way in which we participate in the divine life through an intuitive foretaste of God's experience. "It is primarily a trust in the efficacy of Beauty" (*AI* 367), presumably that Beauty realized in God's perfected experience of all actuality. It is here that the good finally triumphs in all her glory—or, more precisely, as engulfed by all the divine glory as well.

Whitehead Without God 16

Donald W. Sherburne

"When a human being tries to formulate a general concept of the universe, he is bound to use his favorite preconceptions in his descriptive generalizations of experience. Whitehead's preconceptions were largely Platonic and religious. . . . The experiment of naturalizing Whitehead's metaphysics of nature might well be tried. The idea has long been attractive to a few students of Whitehead, but I know of no attempt to carry it out full-scale."

Victor Lowe*

I had been tempted to perform the experiment of naturalizing Whitehead's metaphysics before I read these sentences. They encouraged me to continue my reflections and I have now arrived at the point where I believe that the experiment can be conducted successfully. I am engaged in working out the myriad details of the enterprise and I expect that, sooner or later, the results will appear in book form. On the present occasion, a journal issue devoted to exhibiting the implications for theology of post-Whiteheadian metaphysics, it is my function to point out that post-Whiteheadian metaphysics, in one of its developments, points towards a radical theology in the sense made popular by the Death of God movement. The body of this article will present some of the issues which lead to my disillusionment with the concept "God" in the framework of Whitehead's system and will adumbrate some of my suggestions for recontouring that system. But before I enter into that discussion, I will say a brief word about where my project leaves me in regard to the whole religious enterprise.

Exorcising the concept "God" from the system leaves me in a stance very similar to that of Paul van Buren, who holds that the essence of Christianity is an ethical message about how to live a life and

Revised from *The Christian Scholar*, L, 3 (Fall 1967). Used by permission of the National Council of the Churches of Christ and Donald W. Sherburne.

Understanding Whitehead (Baltimore: The Johns Hopkins Press, 1962), 87f.

that "God" talk is a dated, misleading, unhelpful, obscure way of saying what Christianity wants to say about what it is to be a man and to live a moral life. To slip into Whiteheadian technical terminology, I understand Jesus as a figure the story of whom we objectify with peculiar vividness as a result of his power to grasp the successive subjective aims of generations and generations of men by the sheer massiveness and compelling weight of the ideal vision which he has presented as a lure promising richness and depth of feeling in human satisfactions. Those who have been grasped and oriented in their life values by this lure have been called Christians. "God" talk and the language of miracles, immortality, and saving grace have created a good bit of the aesthetic compulsion behind this lure in past generations. In our generation there is danger and hope—*danger* that these noncognitive accoutrements will lose their aesthetic harmony and hypnotic power when integrated with the basic prehensions of science, and be reverted into impotent and empty symbols, jarring, ugly, and without force in final satisfactions: *hope* that the power of Jesus as lure will reassert itself in an aesthetic context devoid of supernaturalism, a context such that (the language now picks up echoes of van Buren) the vision of Jesus, the free man, free from authority, free from fear, "free to give himself to others, whoever they were"[1]—such that this vision in its earthly, human purity will lure our aims to a harmonious concrescence, integrating scientific insight and moral vision and producing a modern, intensely fulfilling human satisfaction.

What role does the concept "God" play in Whitehead's system? There are three main roles: (1) God preserves the past and in so doing creates significance, meaningfulness, and also provides the ontological ground for the claim that truth is immortal; (2) God provides the ontological ground, the "somewhere," for eternal objects; (3) God is the source of subjective aims in temporal occasions, and in this role is the principle of limitation productive of order, the source of novelty, and the source of the real perspective standpoint within the extensive continuum for each occasion. A naturalistic reinterpretation of Whitehead's scheme has to show (1) that in some one, at least, of these roles the concept "God" violates the fundamental metaphysical principles of the system and thereby introduces incoherence into the scheme, and (2) that the system can be so interpreted and modified that each of these roles is superfluous. In this essay I shall concentrate on the issue of the past. My first concern, in Part A below, will be to show that on either the orthodox interpretation of Whitehead (as presented in Whitehead's writings and expounded by William Christian), or on the interpretation offered by Charles Hartshorne and John Cobb, there is

[1]Paul van Buren, *The Secular Meaning of the Gospel*, (New York: Macmillan, 1963), 123.

incoherence. This will require some detailed textual analysis, but when accomplished it will meet the first requirement. I will then adumbrate, in Part B, the manner in which I intend to resolve the problem of the past. Finally, in Part C, I will introduce considerations designed to show not only that God, viewed as ground of the past, is superfluous, but that his other roles, the role of ontological ground for eternal objects and the role of providing subjective aims, are also superfluous.

A

The question of the status of the past is crucial in Whitehead's thought as a result of his systematic account of the nature of a full fact. That which is fully and finally real for Whitehead is termed an actual entity, or actual occasion. An actual entity is a microcosmic entity, and, as microcosmic, analogous to the atoms of Democritus or the monads of Leibniz; macrocosmic things of ordinary experience such as trees, mountains, people, are conceived as societies, or nexūs, of actual entities, and more specifically as four-dimensional societies, and societies of societies stretched out in space and time. The enduring things of the universe are societies; individual actual entities do not endure, but are momentary drops of experience that become, concresce, by synthesizing into a fully definite unity of feeling the elements provided by their environment. Their becoming is also their perishing. They do not linger over their feelings when completed but perish in handing on the synthesizing vitality of subjective feeling to subsequent generations of actual entities.

This brief summary of fundamental notions is sufficient to permit the introduction of the problem of the status of the past.[2] The universe is a realm of perpetual perishing, a realm where actual entities enjoy their brief moment of subjective immediacy and then quickly slip into the status Whitehead refers to as objective immortality. The key question is this, what does it mean to say that an actual entity is objectively immortal? These objectively immortal actual entities are the past, and one is tempted to ask with Francois Villon, "Où sont les neiges d'antan?" Where are the snows of yesteryear and how are they related to the present? In terms of what scheme of ideas is their efficacy on the present to be understood? The Whiteheadian answer to these questions is simply that the past is preserved as objectively immortal in the consequent nature of God and has what efficacy it has on the present as a result of the role played by God at the birth of every actual occasion.

[2]The account of technical Whiteheadian terminology is here kept to a bare minimum. The reader wishing to refresh his understanding of Whitehead's scheme is urged to consult my recent study, A Key to Whitehead's Process and Reality (New York: Macmillan, 1966).

There are problems with this Whiteheadian answer, however, and we must approach this account with the aim of making these problems apparent.

The key problem concerns how God gets to perceive occasions in the first place so that they can be taken up as objectively immortal into his consequent nature. But how this is a problem can be seen only after we first descend to the level of an ordinary temporal occasion, A, and ask how it can prehend a past occasion, X, which is part of A's actual world. William Christian analyzes this question with great care in his book, *An Interpretation of Whitehead's Metaphysics*,[3] and, since his analysis seems to me an eminently fair and accurate account, I will draw upon it heavily. Christian notes that Whitehead doesn't seek to prove that the past is given, he rather assumes the obvious fact that the past *is* given and then asks, How is it possible that the past is given now? (Christian, 320). To ask this question is to ask for a reason, and Whitehead has a basic principle, termed the ontological principle, which asserts that "actual entities are the only *reasons*" (PR 37). The reason we give to explain how the past can be given now must be a reason which refers ultimately to an actual entity or entities as ontological ground for the past. Christian argues that the grounding actual entity cannot be the past actual occasion X because "X has now perished and is no longer actual, whereas the only 'reasons' according to the ontological principle are *actual* entities" (Christian, 321) and also cannot be the concrescing occasion A because "the occasion for which the data are given cannot be the reason why the data are given" (Christian, 322). God is the only actual entity available to do the job. Christian holds that God, who prehends all occasions, has prehended X, and since God, unlike X, does not perish but endures everlastingly, God presents to A, for A's prehension, an aspect of himself whch includes his (God's) prehension of X. In this way the past is given for A to prehend.

This is the account I find compatible with Whitehead's often tantalizingly imprecise discussions, but I find it quite unacceptable. *If* God, has prehended the past occasion X, then, since God endures everlastingly, God can be the ontological ground, the reason, explanatory of how X can be given as datum to a concrescing actual occasion A. But this is a big "if," for how is it possible for God to prehend X? It is an integral part of Christian's argument to say, "God in his consequent nature prehends X" (Christian, 327). But now all the problems that clustered about the ontological ground of X when we thought of A prehending X come back to haunt us when we rise back up to the level of God and raise the question how it is possible for God to prehend X.

---

[3]New Haven: Yale University Press, 1959, 319–330, hereafter referred to as "Christian."

Christian, as noted above, argues that it is not possible that the presently concrescing entity be the ground of the givenness of the past. In the present instance God is the concrescing entity, so God cannot be the ground of the givenness of X when God is prehending X. God is in unison of becoming with every occasion (cf. Christian, 333–334), but it is the definition of contemporary occasions, occasions in unison of becoming, that neither of them prehend the other (cf. *PR* 102). Therefore, even though God was around and prehending something when X was becoming, and hence was actual, God could not then have been prehending X. When X was past, then the possibility was open for God to prehend X. But, of course, X was then not actual, not *formaliter,* but *objective,* drained of subjectivity. So the problem of the ontological ground for X, when X was prehended by God, remains unsolved. Any way that this problem is approached is going to make God an exception to principles governing and limiting normal, temporal, actual entities. To say that God in his consequent nature can prehend a contemporary actual entity, a then-concrescing occasion, is to provide a ground for the datum (viz. the actuality of the then-concrescing occasion) but is to make an exception of God in order to prevent the collapse of the system. To say that God can prehend datum occasions when they have no ground, or to say that God, as prehending subject, can somehow provide a ground for occasions he prehends in a way that temporal actual entities cannot, is again to make an exception of God. Nowhere in Christian or in Whitehead do I find a way out of this impasse. Hence I offer this specific difficulty as the first systematic reason why I find Whitehead's system *with God* incoherent.

One possible position, held in the past by Charles Hartshorne, is to affirm an alternative I have rejected, i.e., to affirm that God does prehend actual occasions as they are concrescing. If this were an acceptable view, then there would be no problem about the availability of the past. I must argue in more detail that this alternative is unacceptable. I shall begin by expanding the argument, already adumbrated, that it is a violation of the principles of Whitehead's system to suggest that contemporary actual entities can prehend each other. I shall then show that this view rests on the assumption of the omnispatiality of God, the assumption that God is everywhere, and I shall attack this assumption, particularly as it is defended by John Cobb, in some detail.

It is a violation of the principles of Whitehead's system to suggest that contemporary actual entities can prehend each other. It is a clear-cut principle of his system that "so far as physical relations are concerned, contemporary events happen in *causal* independence of each other" (*PR* 95). Whitehead adds in a footnote. "This principle lies on the surface of the fundamental Einsteinian formula for the physical

continuum." In *PR* 102 Whitehead provides what amounts to a definition of "contemporary": "Actual entities are called 'contemporary'
when neither belongs to the 'given' actual world defined by the other."
But Hartshorne, whose purpose was to find a way of preserving the past
everlastingly in its full *subjective* immediacy, insisted that God prehends
contemporaries as they are concrescing so that what God will know and
preserve will be those entities in the immediacy of their becoming, so
that he will know and preserve them *formaliter* and not *objectivé* (the
way ordinary temporal entities know and preserve occasions in their
past). Occasions prehended, however, are occasions in the actual world
of the prehending subject. Therefore, since God prehends contemporaries, contemporary occasions are in the actual world of God, a result
which contradicts the *PR* 102 definition of "contemporary." In this instance God is not exemplifying what Whitehead calls "the principle of
contemporary independence" (*PR* 96); rather, he is treated as an exception to this principle invoked to save the collapse into nothingness of
the past. In this sentence I have been recalling against Hartshorne one
of the most well-known passages of *Process and Reality*: "In the first
place, God is not to be treated as an exception to all metaphysical principles, invoked to save their collapse. He is their chief exemplification"
(*PR* 521).

It might be helpful at this point to enlarge upon the view held by
Hartshorne so that his assumptions will emerge more clearly. Hartshorne warns us at one point that, "the poetic majesty of the conception
of unfading everlastingness of all occasions in God (down to the *de
facto* present) should not blind us to the simple, cogent reason for the
idea."[4] The reason for the idea is the doctrine of the immortality of
truth; holding a correspondence view of truth, Hartshorne feels he requires the unfading everlastingness of all occasions in God to make the
notion of truths about the past intelligible. The end is to ground a theory
of truth; the immediate means to this is the doctrine of the unfading
everlastingness of all occasions in God; the proximate means then becomes the doctrine that God prehends actual occasions as they are becoming, as they are contemporary with the appropriate moment in his
developing consequent nature; finally, the remote assumption grounding this proximate means, and hence the whole edifice of Whiteheadian
interpretation at stake here, is the assumption that God is everywhere
and hence includes the regional standpoint of every temporal actual
entity. It is this ground floor assumption that must be examined very
closely.

As I read Hartshorne, he maintains that "God is not spatially lo-

[4]"Whitehead's Idea of God," in Paul A. Schilpp, editor, *The Philosophy of
Alfred North Whitehead*, (New York: Tudor, Second Ed., 1951), 543, hereafter referred to as "Schilpp."

calized" (Schilpp, 545) and the meaning of this phrase is that God is everywhere—"God is not spatially separated from things" he has written (Schilpp, 545), and in a recent book he claims that deity, the universally immanent, is everywhere.[5] Given this assumption Hartshorne is then able to say that since God, being everywhere, includes the regional standpoint of every temporal actual entity, "he must intuit all occasions wherever they are as they occur" (Schilpp, 545). This puts Hartshorne where he wants to be, because to intuit (prehend) actual occasions *as they occur* is to intuit (prehend) them *formaliter,* as they exist in the immediate subjectivity of concrescence, and since God is everlasting, and experiences all actual occasions *formaliter,* actual occasions are preserved everlastingly (in their full, warm, subjective immediacy) in the consequent nature of God.[6] This interpretation resolves the question of the status of the past, the problem of how the past is given as datum for concrescing actual occasions, and the question of a ground for truth claims about the past. It is an impressive accomplishment and certainly exhibits why Hartshorne has become a leading interpreter among many theologically inclined neo-Whiteheadians. But I am myself unhappy with the interpretation, as I have already indicated to some degree, and we must turn now to a more careful analysis of the basic assumption of the omnispatiality of God.

This doctrine of the omnispatiality of God assumes that "it is possible for the region that constitutes the standpoint of one occasion to include the regions that constitute the standpoints of other occasions." This quote is from John Cobb,[7] and since Cobb has presented the clearest, most sustained defense of this assumption underlying the interpretation of his mentor (he dedicates his book to Hartshorne), I shall attack the assumption as it is presented and defended by Cobb.

1. My first point is that there already exists a carefully documented set of arguments which shows that within the Whiteheadian system it is impossible for there to be any relation of overlapping or inclusion among standpoints of actual occasions. This set of arguments occurs in Chapter 4 of Christian (especially pp. 92–103) and, in order to repudiate the Hartshornian interpretation, marshals a great deal of evidence from (1) the theory of coordinate division, (2) the doctrine of the solidarity of the extensive continuum, (3) Whitehead's explanation of the physical transmission of energy, (4) the epochal theory of time, (5) the doctrine of durations, and (6) Whitehead's analysis of the con-

---

[5]*Anselm's Discovery* (LaSalle: Open Court, 1965), 125–126.

[6]This last point emerges clearly in Hartshorne's article, "Whitehead's Novel Intuition" in *Alfred North Whitehead: Essays on His Philosophy,* George L. Kline, editor (Englewood Cliffs: Prentice-Hall, 1963), 22.

[7]*A Christian Natural Theology,* (Philadelphia: Westminster, 1965), 83, hereafter referred to as "Cobb."

temporary world. Cobb acknowledges these arguments (Cobb, 86, fn. 77) and in the accompanying text states that he will, implicitly, be directing his paragraphs against Christian's objections. I do not find that Cobb has met Christian's objections at all adequately, and I count this failure my first point against the Hartshorne-Cobb assumption that there can be a sharing of standpoints.

2.   My second point is that I do not see how one who adheres to the doctrine of regional inclusion can avoid affirming that one prehension has two subjects and this implication of the doctrine constitutes a *reduction ad absurdum*.[8] That if established, it would be a *reductio* is clear from passages such as the following: "A feeling is in all respects determinate, with a determinate subject, determinate initial data . . ."; ". . . no feeling can be abstracted either from its data, or its subject" (*PR* 338 and 355). My view here hinges on my understanding of the nature of a concrescence and its relationship to its region.

A concrescence is a growing together into a unity of feeling (a satisfaction) of a mass of feelings, or prehensions, which all have one and the same subject. This growing together is a quantum phenomenon with temporal and spatial dimensions. The concrescence arises out of a past, a past that limits the possibilities open to that concrescence. The most general limitations of all placed on the concrescence by the past have to do with the extensive characteristics which structure the past. The past, the actual world at that instant, in virtue of its actual structure, limits the pure potentiality of the realm of eternal objects in regard to extensive relationships that might have obtained for that concrescence and converts that pure potentiality into the real, limited potentiality facing that, and any other, concrescence that is to arise out of just that world (Cf. *PR* 102). The only possibilities that are real possibilities in the unfolding of the extensive character of the actual world are those that are compatible with the realized extensive character of the objectively immortal past. "The extensive continuum" is the name for this set of extensive relationships exemplified in the past and limiting the future:

> . . . the real potentialities relative to all standpoints are coordinated as diverse determinations of one extensive continuum. This extensive continuum is one relational complex in which all potential objectifications find their niche. It underlies the whole world, past, present and future. . . . It is not a fact prior to the world; it is the first determination

[8]Although I continue to believe that this second point is valid, I now recognize that it is expressed inadequately. In response to John Cobb, I have more recently argued that the doctrine of regional inclusion commits one to just those elements of the Newtonian position most explicitly rejected by Whitehead. Cobb's criticism of my position on this issue and my response will appear in *Process Studies*, I, 2 (1971).

of order—that is, of real potentiality—arising out of the general character of the world. . . . This extensive continuum is 'real,' because it expresses a fact derived from the actual world and concerning the contemporary actual world (PR 103).

These passages should make it clear that the extensive continuum is not a container sitting there waiting for actual occasions to happen in it; it is not an analogue to the notion of absolute space and time; it is not a fact prior to the world. It is a set of conditions exemplified in the past which condition any future which is to arise out of that past. It is a vast society, the widest of all societies, which lays down the obligation on everything which is that it conform to its very general sort of social order; it socializes into its extensive mold all the individuals which arise within it, just as we in our culture "Americanize" all the children born into it. When Whitehead writes, "The concrescence presupposes its basic region, and not the region its concrescence" (PR 434), I understand this phrase to mean that the actual presupposes that which is potential, that which is possible for it. This interpretation is compatible with the following passages: "The reality of the future is bound up with the reality of this continuum. It is the reality of what is potential, in its character of a real component of what is actual. . . . With the becoming of any actual entity what was previously potential in the space-time continuum is now the primary real phase in something actual" (PR 103 and 104).

Now this compressed account of the nature of the extensive continuum must be brought back to the point at hand, the point that the doctrine of regional inclusion cannot avoid affirming that one prehension has two subjects. There is no region, actually, until a mass of feelings emerge and concresce; these feelings actualize the region. The becoming of the actual occasion constituted by these feelings is a quantum phenomena; it is a drop of experience which, as a quantum, is so related to other quanta as to constitute a space-time continuum. A region doesn't become actual until a mass of feelings concresces to create one subject. Suppose, now, regional inclusion were to occur—what would have to be the case for this to be possible? Since a region is not a bucket-like container that is there before it is filled, but, rather, is actualized by the emergence of a group of prehensions, it would have to be the case that these prehensions belonged to more than one subject. But this, as we have seen, is a reductio. But perhaps it might be argued that in this region prehensions which were to grow into two different subjects were intertwined. To this suggestion I would reply that, no matter how complex and involuted the boundaries, there would be two regions, one actualized by each of the concrescing subjects. Cobb suggests, in passages that will be analyzed in detail shortly, that "the regions occupied by some electronic occasions are entirely included in the

regions occupied by some molecular occasions" (Cobb, 90). I suspect he
may have in mind an image of overlapping, as a layer of cold air and a
layer of warm air may both overlay the same geographic region. But
that image won't do here; as I have argued, there is no region, actually,
before a mass of prehensions concresces. But once that mass of prehensions has concresced, it *is* a region: "There is a spatial element in the
quantum as well as a temporal element. Thus the quantum *is* an extensive region" (*PR* 434, italics mine). Any other mass of prehensions could
only constitute another region. Hence the only alternative left open to
Cobb, as he argues that two actual occasions occupy the same region,
is to hold that one prehension can have two subjects, and this is a
suggestion which is incompatible with Whitehead's doctrine of
prehensions.

    3.   My third point is that Cobb is very seriously misleading in his
argument that Whitehead considers molecules, electrons and protons to
be enduring objects. An enduring object is a personally ordered society,
a society that is purely temporal in the sense that it is a mere thread of
continuous inheritance containing no two actual entities which are contemporaries. If a molecule were such a society, and if, as is clearly the
case, electrons are contained inside molecules, then it would follow that
"the regions occupied by some electronic occasions are entirely included
in the regions occupied by some molecular occasions" (Cobb, 90—the
argument begins on p. 89). The thrust of the cumulative argument of
Cobb's book is that since Whitehead wrote statements that clearly imply that regional inclusion obtains between molecular and electronic
occasions, we ought to be receptive to the suggestion that "soul" occasions include the regions of brain occasions and God includes the regions of all temporal occasions, because there is no principle involved
in these latter two instances which has not been acknowledged by
Whitehead himself in the case of the relations holding between molecular occasions and electronic occasions. Since this analogy gives Cobb's
defense of the Hartshornian interpretation of God a good deal of the
persuasiveness that it has, it is very important to recognize that the
analogy is highly suspect since it is based upon a questionable reading
of the Whiteheadian texts. I must now show in some detail how this
is the case.

    Cobb prepares for this analogy early in his book; during his first
discussion of societies (p. 41) he uses a molecule as his example of an
enduring object. Then later, when he really settles in to argue his interpretation, Cobb claims (p. 89) that Whitehead explicitly gives molecules, electrons, and protons as examples of enduring objects. Cobb
footnotes his claims. The passages concerning molecules are given as
PR 124–125 and 151. These references must be examined carefully. In
PR 124–125 Whitehead writes:

An event is a nexus of actual occasions interrelated in some determinate fashion in some extensive quantum: it is either a nexus in its formal completeness, or it is an objectified nexus. One actual occasion is a limiting type of event. The most general sense of the meaning of change is "the differences between actual occasions in one event." For example, a molecule is a historic route of actual occasions; and such a route is an "event." Now the motion of the molecule is nothing else than the differences between the successive occasions of its life-history in respect to the extensive quanta from which they arise; and the changes in the molecule are the consequential differences in the actual occasions.

Obviously, Whitehead does not in this passage say directly or indirectly that a molecule is an enduring object. He merely says it is an historic route of actual occasions and that such a route is an event. Now if it could be shown that Whitehead means the same thing by "event" that he means by "enduring object," then Cobb would have his point, but (a) there are no grounds I can find at all to ground such an equivalence, and (b) quite to the contrary, "events" can be, though they need not be, spatially extended. For example, the life span of the tree outside my window is an event, and the tree is not an enduring object in the technical sense, but rather a very complex structured society. Speaking of events, Christian writes, "An event has temporal thickness (duration) *and spatial spread*. Within its unity are temporal and spatial 'parts' " (Christian, p. 177—italics mine). Christian is here speaking of the concept "event" as used in Whitehead's earlier works; the term doesn't change its reference in the later works, though it practically drops out of the picture as being a less than ultimate concept (corresponding to the notion of a structured society) which gives way to the category of "actual entity" as the term descriptive of ultimate, concrete reality. In this passage, then, we do not find Whitehead, even by inference via "event," giving a molecule as an example of an enduring object.

Is Cobb's claim substantiated any more adequately in PR 151? The passage is set in the context of a discussion of structured societies and the two types of component groups that may be included in them, "subordinate nexūs" and "subordinate societies."

The distinction arises because in some instances a group of occasions, such as, for example, a particular enduring entity, could have retained the dominant features of its defining characteristic in the general environment, apart from the structured society. It would have lost some features; in other words, the analogous sort of enduring entity in the general environment is, in its mode of definiteness, not quite identical with the enduring entity within the structured environment. But, abstracting such additional details from the generalized defining characteristic, the enduring object with that generalized characteristic may be conceived as independent of the structured society within which it finds it [itself?]. For example, we speak of a molecule within a living cell, because its general molecular features are independent of the environment of the cell. Thus a molecule is a subordinate society in the structured society which we call the "living cell." [Whitehead then goes on to say that a subordinate nexus cannot sustain itself apart from the special environment provided by that structured society.]

The first point to be made about this passage is that a given subordinate society may, or may not, be an enduring entity. In the first sentence Whitehead picks "an enduring entity" as an example, but he could just as well have picked a structured society with spatial spread. Structured societies may be very complex indeed, with their subordinate societies themselves containing subordinate societies: "The Universe achieves its values by reason of its coordination into societies of societies, and into societies of societies of societies" (*AI* 264). We could start with a society like a tree and then a cell would be a subordinate group within the tree and a molecule would be another subordinate group within the cell. The point, then, is that a society, B, subordinate to another, A, may yet itself host further subordinate societies, C, D, E, who may in turn etc. etc. In short, a subordinate society is not necessarily an enduring object, though, of course, a subordinate society *may* be an enduring object. Secondly, we must note that Whitehead gives two examples of a subordinate society in this passage. The first example is an enduring object, and Whitehead discusses this example for three sentences. His second example of a subordinate society, introduced in the fourth sentence as a new example by the phrase "for example," is a molecule. *It is an example of a subordinate society, however, and not an example of an enduring object.* The two examples are on coordinate levels; it is *not* the case that the second example is an example of the first example. But this is how Cobb must read the paragraph. If the analysis so far has not clinched my case, no question at all can remain when we note that on the very next page, in the context of this same discussion, Whitehead writes: "Molecules are structured societies, and so in all probability are separate electrons and protons" (*PR* 152). This is no casual, careless statement; two sentences later Whitehead writes: "But gases are not structured societies in any important sense of the term; although their individual molecules *are* structured societies" (*PR* 152, italics mine). Since a structured society cannot be an enduring object, Cobb cannot use the *PR* 151 discussion of subordinate societies to justify his claim that molecules are enduring objects.

At this point Cobb might be tempted to make one last ditch stand, arguing that I have begged the question by merely assuming that a structured society cannot be an enduring object, whereas what he is saying, when he says that one regional standpoint can include another, is that one enduring entity, one nonspatial, serially ordered society, can still be a structured society in that its temporally successive occasions can include the regional standpoints of the "narrower" actual entities which make up its subordinate societies and/or nexūs. If Cobb attempts to argue this way, then the issue boils down to what is meant by a structured society and I am convinced that if Cobb attempts to argue this way he would be misreading the nature of a structured society. The following passage clearly rules out the interpretation of "structured society" which, I have suggested, Cobb might like to hold: "A structured society *consists in* the patterned intertwining of various nexūs with markedly diverse defining characteristics" (PR 157, italics mine). A structured society is not an entity above and beyond its component groups, anymore than a baseball team is some kind of entity above and beyond the sum of its players; rather, it "consists in" (or "consists of," as we would put it on this side of the Atlantic) the patterned relations holding among its component entities. This passage effectively rules out any attempt to argue that an enduring entity could be a structured society, and consequently blocks the only possible counter-argument that I can see which Cobb might bring against my position.

So much for molecules; now we can turn to the PR 139–141 passages where, Cobb tells us (Cobb 89, fns. 83 and 84), Whitehead asserts that electrons and protons are enduring objects. We have already seen that Whitehead says that "in all probability" electrons and protons are structured societies—this warns us both that (1) he is not ready to die in the last ditch over this issue, but (2) he is pretty certain that at the level of electrons and protons we have not yet gotten down to personally ordered, serial strands of actual occasions. The first relevant passage, PR 139–140, occurs in the context of a discussion of what a "cosmic epoch" is, and more particularly, what the character of our cosmic epoch happens to be.

> This epoch is characterized by electronic and protonic actual entities, and by yet more ultimate actual entities which can be dimly discerned in the quanta of energy. Maxwell's equations of the electromagnetic field hold sway by reason of the throngs of electrons and of protons. Also each electron is a society of electronic occasions, and each proton is a society of protonic occasions.

This passage clearly does *not* say or imply that electrons and protons are enduring objects. It says that an actual occasion which finds itself within an electron is called an electronic occasion and one which finds itself within a proton is called a protonic occasion. It also says that electrons and protons are societies, but it gives no indication as to whether they are spatially thick, structured societies (my view) or enduring objects (Cobb's view) except where Whitehead speculates about the dimly discerned "yet more ultimate actual entities"—this could be taken to imply that electrons and protons are complex, made up of distinct types of subordinate entities, and this would support my claim that electrons and protons are structured societies. It seems to me quite

possible that Whitehead had the likely existence of these dimly discerned entities in mind when he wrote, as we have seen, that "in all
probability" electrons and protons are structured societies. The final
relevant passage spans PR 140–141.

> In speaking of a society—unless the context expressly requires an-
> other interpretation—'membership' will always refer to the actual occa-
> sions, and not to subordinate enduring objects composed of actual
> occasions such as the life of an electron or of a man. These latter so-
> cieties are the strands of 'personal' order which enter into many societies;
> generally speaking, whenever we are concerned with occupied space, we
> are dealing with this restricted type of corpuscular societies; and when-
> ever we are thinking of the physical field in empty space, we are dealing
> with societies of the wider type. It seems as if the careers of waves of
> light illustrate the transition from the more restricted type to the wider
> type.
> Thus our cosmic epoch is to be conceived primarily as a society of
> electromagnetic occasions, including electronic and protonic occasions,
> and only occasionally—for the sake of brevity in statement—as a society
> of electrons and protons. There is the same distinction between thinking
> of an army either as a class of men, or as a class of regiments.

The message of this passage, clearly stated at the beginning and the end,
is that when Whitehead speaks of the membership of a society, he is
referring to its component actual entities and not to its component subordinate societies. Again, it is the examples Whitehead uses which seem
to be the source of Cobb's confusion: "membership" does not refer to
subordinate enduring objects "such as the *life* of an electron or of a
man." I have italicized the word "life" here because it is the key to understanding the examples. Now a man, the total man, is not an enduring
object. He is, rather, a very complex structured society which sustains,
among many other societies, a regnant, personally ordered, subordinate
society (an enduring object) which Whitehead refers to as "the soul of
which Plato spoke" (AI 267—see also pp. 263–264 for a clear statement
of the distinction between "the ordinary meaning of the term 'man,' "
which includes the total bodily man, and the narrow sense of "man,"
where "man" is considered a person in Whitehead's technical sense,
i.e., as the regnant, personally ordered society which he identifies as his
equivalent of Descartes' thinking substance and Plato's soul). Now this
"soul" is the "life" of the man, and it is an enduring object, a personally ordered, purely temporal, continuous, subordinate society within
the total, bodily man. So the point of Whitehead's example in the above
passage would be that in talking about the membership of the complex
structured society which is a total man, in the ordinary sense of the
term, one is referring not to a subordinate society, such as the enduring
object which is the life, or soul, of the man, but to all the individual ac-

tual occasions in all the subordinate societies and subordinate nexūs which make up the man. Now the situation with the electron is exactly the same. The membership of the complex structured society which is the electron is not, properly speaking, any of the subordinate societies or nexūs of the electron, such as the personally ordered society, the en-during object, which constitutes the "life" of the electron, but, rather, the individual actual occasions of which these subordinate entities are composed. It should be very clear now that to speak of the enduring object which constitutes the life of an electron is *not* by any stretch of the imagination to identify electrons as enduring objects, as Cobb claims, which is the sole point that needs to be made about this passage.

We have now examined the passages in *Process and Reality* which, Cobb claims, exhibit Whitehead identifying molecules, electrons and protons as enduring objects and we have found that in none of the pas-sages is Cobb's claim substantiated. Whitehead does *not* identify mole-cules, electrons and protons as enduring objects; he, rather, explicitly identifies them as structured societies, and I have defended with argu-ments and citations the pretty obvious point that a structured society cannot be an enduring object. The conclusion from this examination of the texts is that the analogy between molecules and electrons on the one hand and God and actual occasions on the other is without founda-tion and very misleading, since it lulls the unwary reader into feeling that since Whitehead at least implicitly acknowledges overlapping re-gional standpoints in the first instance (which we have seen to be false) then to say that God is omnipresent, meaning that the standpoint of God includes the regions which constitute the standpoints of all actual occa-sions, is merely an extension of a general principle which Whitehead at least implicitly endorses.

Now that this analogy has been seen to be without foundation, what should we conclude about Cobb's efforts to support Hartshorne's position? We should conclude that the effort to show that the Hart-shorne-Cobb conclusions are really just below the surface in White-head's own writings must be abandoned. But showing that this analogy must be abandoned does not, I am the first to admit, conclusively show that the Hartshorne-Cobb development itself ought to be abandoned. But it does, I believe, cause us to recognize their position *as* a develop-ment and to have real reservations about that development; it causes us to ask, what is the relationship between this development of the theol-ogy of *Process and Reality* and the underlying principles and categories which constitute the metaphysical substructure for that theology? My own answer to this question is that they do not fit together very well. Hartshorne himself writes with large strokes, with sweeping insight—his concern is to state his vision of God and then to look outward to other traditions and show the superiority of his own conception of God to alternative conceptions. This has resulted in polemics of a high order, in argumentation which is original and subtle. Cobb, on the other hand, has undertaken a task which is not so dramatic, but nevertheless badly needs doing, the task of relating Hartshorne's theological vision to the ordinary, everyday categories of the process metaphysics which supports that vision. The point of my textual arguments is to show that Cobb's effort doesn't come off very well; the job is not easy, perhaps impossible to do. I understood Professor Hartshorne to say in conversation recently that he is now at work on a book setting forth his own metaphysical categories; it might be that with the publication of this book we will see that the process metaphysics involved has undergone a sea-change commensurate with, and integrated into, the sea-change that Hartshorne has wrought in Whitehead's concept of God. But until we have a chance to evaluate this new development we have to conclude, for the nonce, that there is an incompatibility between the Hartshorne-Cobb conception of God and the metaphysical categories and principles of *Process and Reality*.

In Part A I have exhibited some of the reasons which have led me to conclude that Whitehead's system, *with* God, is incoherent. The account of God which seems most compatible with Whitehead's categories, and which is presented in detail by Christian, was shown to involve incoherence in that it explains how ordinary temporal actual entities can experience the past as given but includes no account which shows how God can experience the past without making God an exception to the principles of the system, a *deus ex machina*. Hartshorne's interpretation of God resolves the problem of the past, granted, but it does so only by violating the principle of contemporary independence and assuming that it is possible for the region that constitutes the standpoint of one occasion to include the regions that constitute the standpoints of other occasions, an assumption which I trust by now has been seen to be quite incompatible with Whitehead's scheme of ideas. I turn now to Part B, where my task will be to outline briefly how I would deal, in a neo-Whiteheadian system which lacks the concept "God," with the problems and issues that have been raised in Part A.

B

There is an issue in connection with the past about which Whitehead is vague and ambiguous, and we must be precise in how we deal with that issue. The question is, (a) do actual occasions immediately prehend only contiguous actual occasions, prehending all other, noncontiguous occasions mediately (i.e., as mediated by a string of actual occasions, such that each member of the string inherits immediately from another member of the string), or (b) do actual occasions, in some instances at least, immediately prehend noncontiguous actual occasions (e.g., actual occasions in their remote past)? *PR* 345–346 and 435 imply clearly that (b) is the alternative Whitehead had in mind, for in each passage he presents a situation where a given occasion, X, inherits from another occasion, Y, in its past, which in turn inherits from Z, which is in its past—the point of each passage is to say that X inherits doubly from Z, both immediately and as mediated by Y. Z is not in the immediate past of X, and yet X is exhibited as prehending Z directly. In *PR* 183, however, Whitehead's very similar example is presented in such a way that it is pretty clear he is thinking of the distant occasions as being given only mediately. *PR* 468–469 is the most candid and conclusive discussion of this issue. Whitehead presents the immediate-mediate distinction, replaces "the notion of continuous transmission in science" with "the notion of immediate transmission through a route of successive quanta of extensiveness," and then reflects as follows:

> It is not necessary for the philosophy of organism entirely to deny that there is direct objectification of one occasion in a later occasion which is not contiguous to it. Indeed, the contrary opinion would seem the more natural for this doctrine. Provided that physical science maintains its denial of 'action at a distance,' the safer guess is that direct objectification is practically negligible except for contiguous occasions; but that this practical negligibility is a characteristic of the present cosmic epoch, without any metaphysical generality (*PR* 468–469).

In our cosmic epoch, Whitehead opines, direct, immediate objectification is confined, for all practical purposes, to contiguous occasions. Whitehead refers to "the evidence for peculiar instances of telepathy" and "the instinctive apprehension of a tone of feeling in ordinary social intercourse" as giving possible support for the view that hybrid physical prehensions can execute immediate objectification of noncontiguous actual occasions, but his tone here is very tentative. Though he doesn't refer to God in these passages, the system would require that God undergird any such immediate prehension of noncontiguous occasions by being the ground for the givenness of the remote past.

My own move here would be to generalize metaphysically the doctrine that Whitehead is willing to extend only to our cosmic epoch, i.e., I would insist in my version of the philosophy of organism that it is a categoreal demand that all prehensions be immediate prehensions of contiguous occasions. As Whitehead acknowledges, this suggestion is compatible with the experience and categories of the scientist. The few psychologists with whom I have discussed telepathy seem confident that if and when more is learned about telepathy it will not be necessary to assume "action at a distance," and my own experience assures me that what Whitehead refers to as "the instinctive apprehension of a tone of feeling in ordinary social intercourse" is explicable in empirical terms, in terms of past experience and unconscious memories. After all, we do make mistakes; many of us misread social feelings and commit gaucheries with alarming regularity, something one would be surprised at if our prehensions were as direct as Whitehead suggests might be the case. Immediate prehension of noncontiguous actual occasions, if accepted, also renders the functioning of God arbitrary and *ad hoc,* another good reason for reformulating Whitehead's position. For example, if true, it would imply that God *could* present as a direct datum for an occasion in my stream of consciousness an occasion of the stream of consciousness of Cheops the pyramid builder. And this doesn't mean a ghostly revisitation of the shade of Cheops; this means my immediate feeling now of Cheops making a specific decision in, say, the year 2900 B.C. Now God doesn't do this sort of thing. There are times in the life of an archeologist or historian when such immediate feeling would give great satisfaction to the man and hence to God through his consequent nature, yet still God doesn't make it available. Rather than, Berkeley like, explaining this as a result of the whim of God, it seems eminently more rational to me to eliminate the possibility of immediate prehension of noncontiguous actual occasions categoreally, which is what I propose. All of our knowledge of the past is quite explicable in terms of a doctrine which limits immediate prehension to contiguous actual occasions.

Having eliminated the need for God to be ground for the remote past, by eliminating categoreally the possibility of prehending the remote past, we must now ask whether God is necessary to enable an actual occasion to prehend a contiguous past occasion. Here my answer is no—the past contiguous occasion is still actual, is still its own ground, as the concrescing occasion initiates its primary phase. Whitehead makes statements which strongly imply that he would accept this view. In *AI* 233 he writes: "The present moment is constituted by the influx of *the other* into that self-identity which is the continued life of the immediate past within the immediacy of the present." In *AI* 234 he again explicitly refers to the immediate past: "The immediate past as surviving to be again lived through in the present is the palmary [primary] instance of nonsensuous perception." Again, "There is a continuity between the subjective form of the immediate past occasion and the subjective form of its primary prehension in the origination of the new occasion" (*AI* 235). Much work needs to be done in clarifying the relationship between creativity on the one hand and inheritance from the immediate past on the other —I have begun this clarification in section I of Chapter 2 of my *A Whiteheadian Aesthetic.*[9] It has been a characteristic of the Hartshornian

9New Haven: Yale University Press, 1961; Hamden, Conn.: Archon Books, 1970.

group to play down the notion of creativity at the same time that they augment the importance of God—God has encroached on the role Whitehead assigned to creativity. It is a bizarre image, but it sometimes seems to me that the Hartshornians conceive of God as a rickshaw boy rather than a charioteer, as Whitehead himself saw it. The charioteer image is more proper because God is only one of several formative elements: creativity is the motive power, the horses, of the system and God the power of persuasion which struggles to direct the ongoing surges of power, which are autonomous from, coordinate with, God. But the Hartshornians don't dwell much on creativity and seem to want to get God down front where he pulls as well as guides. My position is that the concept "creativity" is adequate to provide a rational account of the process from an immediately past occasion to the presently emerging occasion contiguous to it.

We have shown that both the orthodox interpretation of Whitehead and the Hartshornian interpretation flirt with incoherence in their discussion of the past. My own approach has been to turn to a naturalistic development of the scheme and suggest that by distinguishing between the remote past and the immediate past (a distinction other commentators, surprisingly, have not insisted upon) and dealing with each separately, a coherent account can be obtained. Two issues are now left which I must address myself to briefly: the orthodox Whiteheadians and the Hartshornians would want to know, (a) how I handle the problem of truth, which Hartshorne, as we saw, indicated was one of the key issues which led him to his position, and (b) how I handle the question of significance, or meaning, on my naturalistic interpretation of Whitehead.

(a) Hartshorne's objection to my position on truth would be that I assume that there are truths about the past and that truth is real now as involving a relation of correspondence with an object, the past; however, the past on my view is not real now, is not preserved in its full subjective immediacy in the consequent nature of God. Hartshorne considers this paradox (see Schilpp, 543). I don't view the situation as a paradox. Truth is a property of propositions. In a proposition a predicative pattern is asserted either to be, or not to be, in whole or in part, exhibited in some logical subject or subjects. Every occasion, as it completes its concrescence, is (1) located in a specific region of the space-time continuum, and (2) is perfectly definite in regard to the inclusion of every eternal object. A proposition about the past asserts that in a given region of the space-time continuum a certain pattern of eternal objects either was or wasn't exemplified. In fact, that pattern either was or wasn't exemplified, hence the proposition is either true or false—this is what the words "true" and "false" mean in this context. (I would hold, however, in agreement with Hartshorne, that one could not say this concerning propositions about the future.) It is indeed the case that there are many propositions about the past of which I do not know the truth value, and many, the truth values of which are completely unknown to anyone, and could not become known to anyone. I see no paradox in holding that truths are immortal and also holding that many truths are unknown. Correspondence, in the sense specified, is the nature of truth, the meaning of truth; yet the test of truth that we most frequently employ in connection with the past is the test of coherence: historians and archeologists have nothing available to them that is not given in the present—this book, the reliability of which must be evaluated; this artifact, the significance of which must be construed—and coherence is the final test of their theories about the past built up from the givens of the present. The historian and archeologist know what truth of fact is even though they may be perfectly aware that their accounts are only highly probable and that there is no conceivable way for anyone to know conclusively how closely their accounts approximate the truth.

(b) Hartshorne's uneasiness in connection with truth may well be just one manifestation of his general concern with meaningfulness, or significance, a concern shared by Cobb and especially by Schubert Ogden. Significance and the question of the past are related for the Hartshornians because by "ultimate meaning" they seem to mean "God preserves the past." If God did not preserve the past, they would find existence meaningless, absurd. The Hartshornians can do without the conventional notions of subjective immortality and a scheme of supernatural rewards and punishments,[10] and can also do without a belief in a final order, in Tennyson's "far-off divine event to which the whole creation moves" (PR 169). But God has to feel, to sympathize and to preserve: this "makes possible 'a general confidence about the future,' an assurance of the final worth of our life which will not be disappointed" (Ogden, 64). As Cobb puts it, God doesn't "assure the success of the good in the world," but "the vision of God nevertheless guarantees the worthwhileness of present life whatever may be its temporal outcome. In part it seems to be the sheer fact that there is a permanence 'beyond, behind, and within, the passing flux of immediate things' [SMW 275] that inspires the sense of the worthwhileness of these things themselves. . . . But primarily Whitehead's treatment of this theme, that values are after all worth achieving despite their transience, is associated with his doctrine of the consequent nature of God [i.e. the preservation of the past]" (Cobb, 218–219). Since I eliminate

---

[10]Cf. Ogden, *The Reality of God and Other Essays* (New York: Harper and Row, 1966), 36, hereafter referred to as "Ogden."

God, what do I do about significance, about "the worthwhileness" of the "passing flux of immediate things"?

In answering, I look closely at Whitehead's theory of value. It is an axiology which makes aesthetic value primary. What is valuable is intensity and depth of feeling. Value arises in, is present in, "the passing flux of immediate things." Take God away and you don't take away all value—there will still be the value, the significance, of experience as immediately felt by temporal subjects. The worthwhileness of occasions is in the richness of the experience of occasions. As agents we can make that experience either richer or poorer; there lies the ground of our obligation, whether there be a God to enjoy this realized value at second hand or not. Personally, I find the second hand experiencing of God superfluous and redundant; God is a supernumerary. If one were the type to be depressed at the thought that the sun will run out of energy some day and our planet become an empty chunk of rock, then I should think one would derive cold comfort in the thought that even at that time God will prehend the present as objectified in his consequent nature! Ogden writes that in the consequent nature of God "we have a final standing or security that can nevermore be lost" (Ogden, 179). I find this a strange kind of security; my past is already there, supposedly, but I have no awareness of this at all, no knowledge at all of its "final standing," and that fact militates, or seems to me should militate, against security. Since Whitehead wrote, Camus and Sartre have appeared on the scene. I feel that what must be done is to bring the "absurd hero" within the context of a revised, naturalistic, neo-Whiteheadian ontology—this merger will dispel the harshness of bleak despair from the one position and the remnants of parsonage Victorianism from the other as it links creative insecurity, adventure, with a more penetrating metaphysical analysis than the existentialists were ever able to achieve. There is a need, however, that in the process the existentialists' insights into the human condition fill the psychological gaps in Whitehead's philosophizing.

C

In this final section I will suggest in a tentative manner how the two remaining roles of God (as ontological ground for eternal objects and as source of subjective aims in temporal occasions) could be rendered superfluous in a naturalistic, neo-Whiteheadian, system.

In connection with eternal objects my move is to play Aristotle to Whitehead's Plato by giving forms of definiteness their ontological grounding in the concrete world of flux. Whitehead consciously recognizes that his ontological principle—the principle that apart from actual entities there is nothing, bare nothingness—is a restatement of the general Aristotelian protest "against the Platonic tendency to separate a static spiritual world from a fluent world of superficial experiences" (PR 319—see also PR 64). My criticism of Whitehead would be that while he makes token acknowledgement of the Aristotelian principle, his concept of God as a non-temporal entity ontologically grounding the realm of eternal objects shows that his heart basically remains with Plato. In making the full Aristotelian move I am really drawing much of my insight from *Science and the Modern World,* a book four years earlier than the full-blown theory of *Process and Reality.* It seems to me at least somewhat plausible to suggest that in the earlier work Whitehead did not feel he needed God as an ontological ground, but only to function as the principle of limitation, which is the role referred to in *Process and Reality* as "presenting the subjective aim." So my twofold task is first to show what it is about the treatment of eternal objects in *SMW* which makes the Aristotelian move possible, and then secondly to suggest a way of handling the source of subjective aims without there being any need to implicate God in the procedure.

In *SMW* Whitehead says that "every occasion is a synthesis of all eternal objects under the limitation of gradations of types of entry" (*SMW* 252). Whitehead can say this because in his chapter on "Abstraction" he has so conceived eternal objects that to have *one* involved in a concrescence is really to have *all* involved in a concrescence. This is the case because no eternal object can be divorced from its reference to other eternal objects, a conclusion which follows from the assertion that the relationships holding between any given eternal object, A, and other eternal objects are internal relationships, i.e., the relationships of A to other eternal objects stand determinately in the essence of A, are constitutive of A. This leads Whitehead to say:

> Accordingly there is a general fact of systematic mutual relatedness which is inherent in the character of possibility. The realm of eternal objects is properly described as a 'realm,' because each eternal object has its status in this general systematic complex of mutual relatedness (*SMW* 231).

The conclusion I want to pull out of these considerations is this: if there is at least one actual entity in the world characterized by at least one eternal object, one specific form of definiteness, then this actual entity provides all the ontological ground required for the realm of eternal objects—an appeal to God is not necessary.[11] And, indeed, in Whitehead, as in Aristotle, there is an eternity and an abeternity of becoming so that within the terms of the system it is inconceivable that

---

[11]It is interesting to note that at RM 141 Whitehead writes: "The forms belong no more to God than to any one occasion."

there be any region of the extensive continuum, no matter how far it be extended fore or aft, where there is not a generation of actual entities exhibiting concrete forms of definiteness. Each actual entity is, viewed from this perspective, a process of emerging definiteness where the process is the decision whereby the essence of each and every eternal object is either included or excluded from positive aesthetic feeling—is either positively or negatively prehended, to use the terminology of *Process and Reality*.

There is at least one problem visible at the surface level of this account. An eternal object is supposed to bestow or withhold a specific, precise form of definiteness, but how can this be if every eternal object drags along with it, so to speak, the whole choir of eternal objects in virtue of the fact that its relationships to other eternal objects are internal relations? The response lies in making it clear that the essence we have been talking about is the relational essence of A. In addition, A has an individual essence which is its own peculiar character, its own unique definiteness, which is self-identical wherever it is ingredient in actual entities. Let me try to make this clear and to illustrate the point with a simple example. The relational essence of an eternal object specifies a particular *how* relationship. This means, as Whitehead puts it, that "a particular determination can be made of the *how* of some definite relationship of a definite eternal object A to a definite number n of other eternal objects, without any determination of the other n objects, $x_1, x_2, \ldots x_n$, except that they have, each of them, the requisite status to play their respective parts in that multiple relationship" (*SMW* 237). Now to present an example of this relationship. Every shade of color has a definite "how" relationship to every four-sided plane figure. This definite "how" relationship is a component of the relational essence of each shade and each figure, and binds all the shades and all the figures together internally. These possible relationships are, however, expressible without reference to the individual essence of any particular shade of blue or to the individual essence of any particular right-angled parallelogram. The relational essence of turquoise blue vis-à-vis any four-sided plane figure is not unique to turquoise blue, but is the same as that of pea green and jet black. Thus the individual essence of turquoise blue is quite aloof from the relational essence of turquoise blue and can characterize the specific definiteness of a particular actual entity without involving necessarily the specific individual essence of any particular geometrical shape, though through its relational essence it does specify the range, and the "how" relationship, of all possible geometrical figures, $x_1, x_2 \ldots x_n$, which have the requisite status to possibly merge with that individual essence turquoise blue in constituting the complex synthesis of forms which is the peculiar, concrete definiteness of an individual actual entity. In this way there is individual, unique determination of actual entities while there is also the tight welding of relational essences into a realm of pure potentialities.

Let us turn now to the second systematic role filled by God, viz. the provision of a subjective aim. In *SMW* God in this role is described as providing an antecedent, ordering limitation upon values prior to any given concrescence and is referred to as the principle of limitation. Whitehead correctly notes that there cannot be an emerging value without there being antecedent standards of value. Here I find the past, and there is always a past for Whitehead as for Aristotle, adequate to perform this function. There is always a past condition of limitation with its frustrations and narrowness, or its depth and eagerness for reiteration, out of which a present arises. Introducing two new non-Whiteheadian technical concepts will enable us to understand, in the terminology of *PR*, both the origin of subjective aims and the origin of creative modifications of subjective aims. The two concepts are (1) that of an actual entity in the immediate past of a concrescing entity which I will call the dominant past actual entity for that concrescing entity, and (2) a group of past actual entities which I will call the obliquely influential past actual entities of the concrescing entity in question. The physical prehension of the dominant past actual entity will constitute the subjective aim of the emerging entity. In a simple, unstructured environment oblique occasions will offer no significant alternatives to the aim presented by the dominant past entity and concrescence will be essentially reiteration of prior forms of definiteness—experience will be at the level of what Whitehead calls, technically, physical purposes. In a complex, structured environment, however, the brain of a man for instance, there would be myriad oblique entities which, for example, might be themselves the termini of routes of inheritance from all over the body, which would introduce to the concrescing central entity all sorts of new data from the complex supporting organism (such as hunger pangs, visual impressions, memory traces, sounds, etc.) which were not directly inherited from the dominant past entity. In these circumstances the possibilities for creative novelty in the synthesis of feeling which constitutes the satisfaction of the concrescing actual entity are great indeed.

Brief as they are, these remarks should indicate to someone familiar with Whitehead's scheme of ideas how I would propose to deal with the topics of order, novelty, and subjective aim in a Whiteheadian scheme stripped of the concept "God."

THREE
Christ

A Christological Assessment 17
of Dipolar Theism

Thomas W. Ogletree

For over forty years, Charles Hartshorne has been clarifying and defending a conception of God which he has variously termed "panentheism," "surrelativism," "dipolar theism," or "neoclassical theism,"
depending upon which aspect of his understanding he has been concerned to emphasize. The distinctive feature of his viewpoint is the contention that notions of relativity, contingency, and change, rather than
being incompatible with the nature of deity, must themselves be
essential components in an understanding of God which is both coherent and religiously adequate.

Hartshorne's work has long received appreciative attention from
persons who interpret reality in terms of a metaphysic of process,
especially along the lines worked out in Whitehead's *Process and
Reality.* Doubtless this general perspective does provide the most
natural "home" for interpreting and assessing his achievement. However, it is the contention of this essay that Hartshorne's thought has
a significance which cannot be limited to the confirmed "Whiteheadians," but which also has relevance for styles of thinking that are
more explicitly historical and self-consciously theological, including
even the anti-metaphysical attempts of the "secular" theologies to
speak of God in a political fashion.

In arguing this thesis I will first describe the most salient features
of Hartshorne's neoclassical or dipolar understanding of God. Consideration will be given to the method he characteristically uses in
establishing his case. Stated briefly, I will show that he identifies abstractly the various conceptions of God which are logically possible
and argues by means of a rigorous analysis and criticism of the alternative views that his own position is the one which handles most coherently the elements that belong to any adequate understanding of

Reprinted from *The Journal of Religion,* XLVII, 2 (April 1967), by permission of The
University of Chicago Press and Thomas W. Ogletree.

God. Second, I will seek to defend Hartshorne's conclusions by means of a reasoning process that is at variance with the one he develops in his own writings. In essence, it will consist of a critical explication of the peculiar logic of the Christian's confession of Jesus Christ—the primordial source of the distinctively Christian vision of God. I will contend that such a procedure not only confirms Hartshorne's basic understanding but also that it enables us to assess more adequately the nature of the truth claim which can appropriately be made for that understanding.

I

Of the various terms Hartshorne uses to describe his position, the one which is immediately most revealing is "dipolar theism."[1] Hartshorne argues that the most coherent and adequate way to conceive of God is to view his being in terms of two contrasting aspects or poles, one abstract and the other concrete. The abstract pole embodies the being of God insofar as he is the absolute. It concerns that which God necessarily is, regardless of the particular course of the world process. Special attention is given in Hartshorne's writings to the necessity that pertains to God's existence, a necessity which excludes not simply his non-existence but even the possibility of his non-existence.[2] Though this pole points to that aspect of God which is independent of all contingencies whatever, its significance is not to isolate God from the world, but to interpret his reality with reference to the "neutral universally common element of meaning" in all propositions whatever, ordinary and scientific.[3] Hence, it identifies God with those ultimate metaphysical presuppositions which make possible a rational interpretation of reality.

---

[1]The basic features of this position are given careful formulation in a number of Hartshorne's writings, among them *Man's Vision of God* (Chicago: Willett, Clark, 1941), *The Divine Relativity* (New Haven: Yale University Press, 1948, 1964), and the introductory and concluding essays of *Philosophers Speak of God,* edited by Charles Hartshorne and William L. Reese (Chicago: University of Chicago Press, 1953), 1–25, 499–514. The essays referred to in the last volume, both by Hartshorne, are entitled: "Introduction: The Standpoint of Panentheism" and "The Logic of Panentheism." Two recent volumes embodying his attempt to restate and defend the ontological argument for the existence of God also include careful statements of his conception of God: *The Logic of Perfection* (LaSalle, Ill.: Open Court, 1962), especially the title essay, pp. 28–117; and *Anselm's Discovery* (LaSalle, Ill.: Open Court, 1965).

[2]This is the key issue in Hartshorne's analysis of the ontological argument for the existence of God (see *The Logic of Perfection,* 49–57, 58–61; and *Anselm's Discovery,* 33–36, 41–44, 88–98).

[3]*Anselm's Discovery,* 43.

The concrete pole points to the aspect of God's being that is dependent on the world process. It is in connection with this pole that contingency, relativity, mutability, and multiplicity are attributed to God. Hartshorne's view involves not simply the idea that God in one of his aspects is shaped and conditioned by the world, but also that God incorporates the totality of the world into his being at each stage of process. The term Hartshorne uses to identify this conception is "panentheism," which conveys the idea that God, though more than the world, includes the world as an element in his own reality. Hartshorne summarizes his position by saying that God is being in both its opposite aspects: "abstract least common denominator, and concrete de facto maximal achieved totality."[4]

It should be noted that there is a sense in which the concrete pole of God's being can be identified with his totality. Hartshorne's concern is to make clear that God in his concrete actuality, as including the particularity and determinateness of the world process, is not less than the absolute. While the absolute is that which God necessarily is, independently of the world, it is as such a pure abstraction, having no reality apart from its embodiment in the concrete reality of God. So God in his concreteness includes both these absolute and necessary principles which are the precondition for everything whatever and also the actual, contingent realities which have in fact emerged in the course of the world process.[5]

How does Hartshorne justify his conclusions? To what does he appeal for support, and what precisely is the structure of argument he uses? In his numerous writings on this subject, many different lines of thought have entered into his work at one point or another. His most concise and rigorous defense of his position, however, is contained in the essay, "The Logic of Panentheism," an essay which embodies the style of reasoning upon which his case most fundamentally rests.[6] The initial task of the essay is to construct a rigorous system of logical possibilities. Such a system is particularly crucial for Hartshorne's purposes since the dipolar theism he advocates has usually lost out by default, by failing to receive consideration even as a possibility. We are in no position, he contends, to judge whether theism is true or even meaningful until we first know its possible forms.[7]

In this particular essay, Hartshorne classifies the various conceptions of God in terms of two considerations: God's independence or dependence with respect to the world and the nature of his perfection,

---

[4]The Divine Relativity, 88.

[5]Ibid., 83, 86–87.

[6]Philosophers Speak of God, 499–514. Also published in an earlier form under the title "A Mathematics of Theism," Review of Religion, VIII (1943), 20–38.

[7]Philosophers Speak of God, 499.

the former of which receives further analysis by means of the categories of causality and totality (i.e., the sense in which God does or
does not include the world in his own being). The result is a scheme
containing nine basic possibilities ranging from a view of God as the
independent cause of the world, absolutely perfect in all respects, to
a view of God as pure relativity, wholly bound up with the world
process and having no element of independence, necessity, or self-
existence.[8] Hartshorne's position proves to be the perfect embodiment
of the "golden mean," incorporating all the positive features of the
various possibilities, but excluding their (arbitrary) negations. Thus,
there is one sense in which God is an independent cause of the world
and another in which he is an effect of the world. He is an independent cause, because he embodies those common elements which
are the precondition for any world whatever. He is an effect, because
his concrete actuality is always in part a consequence of the fact that
the world in its particularity and determinateness enters into his being.
There is also a sense in which he can be called a dependent cause of
the world, for his function as a concrete causal agent in the forward
movement of process is itself shaped by the way he has appropriated
previous stages of the developing world into his own reality. Likewise,
there is one sense in which God is absolutely perfect or unsurpassable
and another in which he is only relatively perfect and, hence, ever able
to surpass himself. Where the qualities which express the perfection
of God are given an abstract form, they direct our attention to the
sense in which God's perfection is absolute. Where our concern is with
the concrete actualization of these qualities in relation to the world
process, our attention is directed to the sense in which God's perfection
is relative to each stage of process, for God continually surpasses previous states of his being, as new developments in the world become a
part of his concrete actuality.[9]

Hartshorne's discussion of the divine knowing can illustrate the

---

[8]*Ibid.*, 512. In *Man's Vision of God*, Hartshorne's classification is made with
sole reference to the idea of perfection. By listing the various combinations of
absolute perfection, relative perfection, and imperfection, he identifies seven possible views, three of which have serious claim to consideration. See especially pp.
8–12, though the entire first chapter is aimed at developing and analyzing the basic
scheme. In *Philosophers Speak of God*, Hartshorne's classification of the various
conceptions is based on five questions: Is God eternal? Is he temporal? Is he conscious? Does he know the world? Does he include the world? On the basis of these
considerations, Hartshorne identifies nine views as in need of careful attention. Of
course, many others are logically possible in terms of the five principal factors, but
the nine all have one or more significant historical spokesmen (see pp. 16–17). The
interesting thing to note is the increasing precision and sophistication which Hartshorne's successive schemes of classification have.

[9]*Philosophers Speak of God*, 512.

last point. Abstractly considered, God's knowledge is perfect, that is, completely adequate to its object. God knows the possible as possible and the actual as actual. Since this assertion holds regardless of the particular nature of the known object, it states something which is true of God absolutely. However, concretely considered, God's actual knowing is dependent on the specific character of what is known. As more and more possibilities are actualized in the course of the world's development, what God once knew as possible he comes to know as actual. The result is the continual enrichment of the divine knowing, and hence also of the divine being.[10]

Hartshorne's basic claim is that his own position constitutes a synthesis of the positive features of the logically possible conceptions of God. He finds in contrast that the remaining alternatives get into logical difficulties at one point or another, usually because they are ill equipped to handle some of the positive elements that have been a part of man's thinking about God. Dipolar theism emerges, therefore, as the conception which is able to handle most coherently the features which are essential to an adequate view of God. It should be added that Hartshorne's highly formal analysis gains added weight from his careful examination and criticism of the writings of actual spokesmen for the most important among the logical possibilities he identifies.[11]

Hartshorne undergirds his basic argument by an appeal to what Morris Cohen calls the "Law of Polarity."[12] The law states that ultimate contraries, such as being-becoming, actuality-potentiality, necessity-contingency, are mutually interdependent correlatives, so that nothing real can be described by an exclusive reference to only one of the contraries. Hartshorne's contention is that classical forms of both theism and pantheism violate this "law," since they characteristically attribute one side of the basic polarities to God while wholly denying him the contrasting term. The assumption seems to be that one of the poles in each set of contraries is superior to the other and, hence, more appropriate for interpreting deity. Hartshorne raises two basic questions about this procedure. First, he suggests that it is far from apparent that any single pole in the various sets of contraries is even intelligible without reference to the other. Second, he challenges the assumption that either of the poles can legitimately be considered superior to the other. To be specific, he argues vigorously that we have erred in depreciating notions of contingency and relativity to a status unworthy of God.

---

[10]See *The Divine Relativity*, 120–124.

[11]*Philosophers Speak of God*, 512. The book consists of selections from major philosophers, Eastern and Western, dealing with the nature of God. Hartshorne and Reese subject the materials they include to searching analysis and criticism. In each case, they argue the panentheist position in evaluating their sources.

[12]*Ibid.*, 2.

Rightly understood, such notions can indicate God's responsiveness and sensitivity to the world. Indeed, if we attribute to God the "categorical ultimate" of relativity ("surrelativism"), it distinguishes God from finite creatures just as decisively as the notion of absoluteness, for it expresses the conviction that God relates himself to the world and appropriates the contingent actualities of the world into his own being with such complete adequacy that the significance of all things is fully appreciated and preserved.[13]

Clearly Hartshorne's dipolar theism represents his attempt to embrace both aspects of the "ultimate contraries" in conceptualizing God. It is noteworthy that his extensive use of the *via eminentia* for interpreting the meaning of divine perfection likewise embodies the "law of polarity." The *via eminentia* involves attributing to God the "categorically ultimate," or at least the categorically superior," form of the positive qualities and attributes used in interpreting experience.[14] Since Hartshorne insists that all the qualities we value in human experience be utilized in the attempt to describe the nature of God, notions of relativity, contingency, becoming, complexity, etc., figure just as prominently in his thinking as absoluteness, necessity, being, and simplicity.

Before leaving the direct consideration of Hartshorne's viewpoint, some brief comment is in order regarding the role of religious experience in his thought. Though Hartshorne has never given a great deal of attention in his writings to concrete religious phenomena, he has always been concerned about the religious significance of his work. He advocates the neoclassical conception of God partly because he believes it is more in keeping with religious experience than classical formulations of either theism or pantheism. In his recent attempts to interpret and defend the ontological argument for the existence of God, he has stated explicitly that his thought requires for its cogency some sort of intuitive element beyond "mere formal reasoning."[15] His study of the ontological argument has convinced him that the only defensible alternative to theism is positivism, a view which denies the intelligibility of the idea of God. Presumably, if the idea of God is to be even minimally significant, some sort of religious experience is necessary.[16] This appeal to religious experience is itself a qualified one, since Hartshorne is prepared to argue that positivism cannot exhibit a coherence in its basic life principles that is comparable to a theistic position.[17]

[13]See *The Divine Relativity*, 49–51.
[14]*Philosophers Speak of God*, 4–5. See also *The Divine Relativity*, 77.
[15]*Anselm's Discovery*, 54.
[16]*Ibid.*, 53.
[17]*Logic of Perfection*, 112. Hartshorne does not claim to have demonstrated the truth of this assertion. He realizes that his case for theism requires a fully developed speculative philosophy or metaphysics (*ibid.*, p. xiii). He promises to undertake a systematic statement of his total perspective in a later volume.

So he operates in general on the assumption that the crucial issues involved in man's attempts to conceptualize God can and must be adjudicated by a rigorous analysis and criticism of the various views of God which are logically possible. His judgment seems to be that, even though some kind of faith or intuition is a formal requisite for critical reflection on the nature of God, the specific content or character that faith has as a concrete, historically conditioned phenomenon does not materially affect the reasoning process which is both possible and appropriate in such reflection. Not surprisingly, where he does speak of the religious basis of his thought, he is usually content to do so in terms of the rather abstract idea of a being "worthy of worship."[18] Even this idea does not receive its content from a careful description and analysis of concrete religious phenomena. Rather, it gains its meaning from his use of the *via eminentia,* where qualities judged to be valuable in human beings are attributed to God in the supreme degree. Hartshorne does not give much weight to the fact that men can and do diverge significantly in their understanding of what is worthy of worship. Nor does he consider the possibility that these divergencies may have roots more elemental than human rationality so that they cannot be resolved or overcome by a critique that is purely logical. It is at this point that the thesis to be developed in the remainder of this essay is most sharply at issue with Hartshorne's work.

To sum up, Hartshorne advocates a dipolar conception of God in which the being of God is interpreted in terms of an abstract and a concrete pole. The abstract pole refers to the fact that God embodies the universal common element in all experience whatever. The concrete pole refers to the actuality which results from God's appropriation of the world process into his own being. While Hartshorne recognizes the presence of an intuitive element in his understanding, he bases his case primarily on the contention that his position among the various logical possibilities expresses most adequately the positive elements that have been present in man's thinking about God.

II

Assuming the adequacy of this sketch of Hartshorne's understanding of God, the present task is to examine his conclusions in light of the Christian's confession of Jesus Christ. The intent is to show that a critical explication of the central motif of Christian faith confirms in general the results of his own inquiry. If this intent is successfully realized, it will in part lend support to Hartshorne's claim that the dipolar conception of God is more compatible with religous experience

[18]*Logic of Perfection,* 91, 113, esp. 113. Cf. also *Anselm's Discovery,* 26.

than views which conceive God primarily in terms of the category of the absolute, or pure actuality, or being, etc. At the same time, the present discussion is aimed at challenging Hartshorne's views about the style of reasoning that is appropriate for critical reflection on the nature of God. Instead of believing with Hartshorne that man's convictions about the ultimate character of reality can and should be determined by allegedly neutral logical principles, the understanding here being argued is that man's thinking about God is and should be governed by a vision emerging in the context of faith, a vision that is itself decisively conditioned by its rootage in history and in the pre-reflective levels of consciousness.

It must be emphasized that the latter view does not necessarily imply an assault on reason, though in actual practice it has often been understood in that fashion. Instead, it implies that on the question of God reason properly functions, not neutrally or independently of a faith commitment, but in the service of the explication of the vision of faith which makes thinking about God possible. The assumption is that the vision of faith always has a particular and determinate form which materially conditions the way we think about God.[19]

In order to clarify this point, it is necessary to make some comment about the kind of situation that gives rise to a notion of God. A notion of God emerges because a certain happening or complex of happenings in ordinary experience undergoes a transfiguration that gives it a paradigmatic role in man's perception of reality. To say that a happening functions paradigmatically is to say that it provides the determinative clue for man's interpretation of what reality is all about. The assumption is that the fundamental character of reality, which is not apparent in ordinary experience as such, not even in its totality, has become manifest in this happening. Because this happening discloses what is most essential for our understanding of reality, it enjoys an importance in human thought and behavior that sets it apart from all other happenings, for it is precisely in relation to the real that man finds fulfilment in his own being. At the same time, because this hap-

---

[19]In view of Hartshorne's extensive discussion of the ontological argument for the existence of God, it must be emphasized that I am not suggesting that faith affects the operation of formal logic. Where the validity of an argument is in question, formal considerations alone are relevant. It should be clear, however, that the focus of this essay is not on the ontological argument as such—though I do find Hartshorne's defense of that argument illuminating and, within limits, convincing. The issue for us is the reasoning process by which we arrive at our basic understanding of the nature of God. Since an understanding of God provides the key premise of the ontological argument, this process is prior in signficance to the logic of that argument. I am suggesting that we do not and cannot establish and defend our view of God by a neutral and detached use of reason. At this point, the way we think is materially conditioned by non-rational factors.

pening has the power to illumine the totality of experience, it has a positive relation to all other happenings, involving and encompassing their reality, too.

The term "transfiguration," or we might say "transformation," points to the process by which a phenomenon that is a part of ordinary experience comes to assume a controlling interpretative role in man's understanding of himself and his world. This process is complex and highly variable, and it is beyond the range of this essay to analyze it in detail. It should be emphasized, however, that it does not come about simply because a conscious and rational decision has been made to elevate a given happening to a paradigmatic status. The transfiguration of experience with which we are concerned itself precedes critical reflection, even making that reflection possible. The point is not that we decide or act blindly, but that we find ourselves claimed by the reality disclosed in a certain set of happenings—perhaps because of its manifest relevance to issues which are of immediate concern to us—before we have begun to grasp all that it means or implies.

It is in relation to happenings that function paradigmatically in our experience that we are obliged to deal with a notion of God. The term "God" at least means that reality or dimension of reality which cannot simply be equated with ordinary experience, but which yet discloses itself concretely in ordinary experience as the source of its reality and value. This formulation taken by itself is highly abstract, encompassing a variety of contrasting views of God. It is an attempt to indicate the minimal implications of granting paradigmatic significance to given phenomena in human experience. The possibilities of saying more about God come largely from the concrete character of the happenings that disclose his reality. In the specific case of Christianity, the happenings in question are those bound up with the name Jesus. Christian thinking about God is, therefore, christologically determined. It grows out of the attempt to interpret the significance of the confession of Christ for man's understanding of himself and his world.[20]

The role of reason in critical reflection on the meaning of God is to unfold the basic understanding of reality expressed in the paradigmatic happening and to explore that understanding in relation to the totality of experience. Though the primary function of reason is ex-

---

[20]Cf. Gordon Kaufman's *Relativism, Knowledge, and Faith* (Chicago: University of Chicago Press, 1960), 105–110, with the line of thought here being developed. See also Van Harvey's discussion of "paradigmatic events" in *The Historian and the Believer* (New York: Macmillan, 1966), 253–258. While the Christian's confession of Christ has provided the principal model for the present analysis, it also finds support in Mircea Eliade's discussion of theophanies or hierophanies in archaic religion, especially in their function as ontophanies, manifestations of the "real." See *The Sacred and the Profane* (New York: Harper Torchbook, 1959), 21–22, 64–65, 94, and 117.

plication, the critical comparison of different views of reality is not ruled out, for it is by setting our own perspective alongside of others that we come to the clearest awareness of its distinctive meaning and significance. Besides, living perspectives are never so well defined or fixed as to exclude the possibility of their modification or enlargement in a process of interaction with one another. The construction of a scheme of logical possibilities, such as those found in Hartshorne's writings, can perhaps facilitate the comparison and interaction of different positions. Even so, it is doubtful that schemes of this kind can ever be neutral. Invariably they embody the vital concerns of one particular viewpoint, so that positions having a different focus of interest suffer some distortion in the scheme.[21] By definining the role of reason in relation to paradigmatic happenings, we take clear cognizance of the fact that we do not think about God in a neutral and detached fashion but in a way that is conditioned by our own particular history and by our total experience as selves.

Man's thinking about God, in spite of its historicity, has within it a thrust toward universality. The very logic of a paradigmatic happening pushes us in that direction, for such a happening embodies the claim to illumine the totality of experience. Since this is the case, it should not be surprising that men generally tend to absolutize their own position as the only true one, or at least as the one superior to all others. However, by keeping in view the historicity of our own perspective, we are able to acknowledge that other perspectives may have equally serious claims to a totality of understanding. We need not assume, as Hartshorne seems to do, that differences in understanding reflect differences either in the capacity to reason or in the degree of respect accorded to reason.[22] Such disagreements may simply indicate differences in the basic visions which inform the reasoning process. Where this is recognized, conversation between contrasting viewpoints can take place in an atmosphere of mutual respect with genuine open-

[21]Hartshorne's discovery that his own position is the "golden mean" in his scheme of possibilities does not necessarily indicate the rigorous neutrality of his reasoning; it may simply show that his scheme embodies the considerations which are most crucial for his particular vision of God. It is far from evident that the scheme he presents can adequately represent all possibilities; for example, classical expressions of mysticism or the highly dialectical position of Hegel. Hartshorne does not discuss Hegel, but it is noteworthy that the questions he presses against Sankara reflect a preoccupation with issues which Sankara considered so ephemeral and lacking in substance as to be unworthy of the term "real." It is beside the point to argue that Sankara's treatment of these questions is irrational, since from Sankara's standpoint the very putting of the questions reflects an even more profound expression of irrationality. Hartshorne merely proves that he is unable to entertain seriously a conception of God like Sankara's (cf. *Philosophers Speak of God*, 173–175).

[22]See, e.g., *Logic of Perfection*, ix, 29.

ness on both sides to the possibility that the conversation will lead to a mutual enrichment in understanding, or even to the development of a common understanding.

Though Hartshorne's conception of the reasoning process appropriate to reflection on the nature of God has been challenged, his labors are, nonetheless, relevant to the attempt to think about God christologically. They are relevant because his formulation of dipolar theism seems to express the understanding of God that is implied in the distinctive logic of the Christian's confession of Christ. My present task is to justify this claim. If the attempt is successful, the way can be opened for a fuller theological appropriation of Hartshorne's exploration of the idea of God.

The most striking thing about the Christian's confession of Christ is the thoroughgoing way in which it links God with flesh, earth, time, process, history. Old Testament materials prepare the way for this understanding by naming the name of God in connection with historical events and by interpreting his reality, partly at least, in terms of his involvement in the fortunes of Israel. Indeed, it would not be amiss to characterize the whole of the Old Testament as incarnational in its basic thrust. Yet it is in the affirmation that the Word became incarnate in Jesus of Nazareth that time and flesh are most decisively related to the being of God. Mircea Eliade's studies of archaic religion have highlighted the uniqueness of the biblical perspective at this particular point. The characteristic orientation of the myths and rituals of archaic religion, he notes, is toward a primordial time and a primordial reality. To be sure, these myths are expressed in a spatio-temporal form. They also presuppose hierophanies that utilize the materials of ordinary experience. At the same time, their logic is to surpass time and flesh in order that men may participate more immediately in that reality which is prior to the earthly and the historical. The result is a devaluation of the earthly and the historical to a kind of second-level reality or even to unreality.[23] In contrast, biblical faith, but especially Christianity, "valorizes" historical time. In Eliade's words: "Since God was *incarnated*, that is, since he took on a *historically conditioned human existence*, history acquires the possibility of being sanctified."[24] In this frame of reference, flesh and history are not simply transparent media for linking us to a primordial reality. They are rather disclosed

---

[23]Eliade's studies may help explain the strong association which is commonly observed, even among Christian theologians, between the notion of God and ideas of immutability and absoluteness. The more characteristic religious vision apparently portrays reality in precisely these terms! As a result, the high valuation placed upon the concrete and the temporal both by Hartshorne and biblical faith calls for a reorientation in fundamental attitudes which men cannot easily achieve.

[24]*The Sacred and the Profane*, 111. Italics Eliade's.

as constitutive factors in the nature of the real.[25] Thus, the paradigmatic happening which governs the distinctively Christian vision of God prohibits us from perceiving God as a self-contained, immutable Absolute. Whatever the term "God" means, it must encompass the reality of the historical process, which means it must encompass contingency and relativity. While Hartshorne's analysis of the place of contingency and relativity in the divine being may not reflect a neutral and universal reason, it still expresses a view which is compatible with biblical faith, especially the notion of incarnation.

It must be granted that Christian theologians have repeatedly denied the logic of their central conviction, as if the happenings which disclosed for them what reality is all about could not be trusted. They have spoken of how the Word became flesh, but in such a way that God in no sense becomes other than what he has been from eternity—a "becoming" which does not "become."[26] Or they have spoken of how Jesus Christ took on flesh but in a manner that did not influence or condition his being in the least.[27] Such assertions cannot, however, be considered expressions of the meaning of the paradigmatic event upon which the Christian understanding of God is based. Rather, they suggest an uncritical acceptance of the assumption that to be God means to be immutable and independent of all contingencies and relativities. Hartshorne rightly shows that this assumption cannot be held without qualification if we are to speak of God's love for the world, an affirmation which is at the center of the Christian's celebration of the Incarnate Word.[28]

It is no longer unusual for Christian theologians to portray the God of the Bible as a changing God. However, much less attention has been given to the possibilities of using Hartshorne's conception of panentheism for unfolding the biblical understanding of God. Yet there is good reason to suppose that the logic of the Incarnation can be most adequately grasped if God is perceived as one who appropriates the

---

[25]It is for precisely this reason that Christian faith cannot relieve itself of the agony of dealing with the problem of the historical Jesus. While the paradigmatic happening that shapes the Christian perspective cannot be reduced to the life of a historical figure, it always includes that life as an essential element in its own reality. For a fuller discussion of this issue, see my *Christian Faith and History* (New York: Abingdon, 1965), 202–219.

[26]Cf. Karl Barth's *Church Dogmatics,* trans. G. T. Thompson and Harold Knight (Edinburgh: T. & T. Clark, 1956), I, part 2, 136, 159–160.

[27]Martin Kähler, for example, asserts that Jesus in his "kingly character" was "complete in Himself." He lives out of Himself and takes nothing from His environment but only gives" (*Der sogenannte historische Jesus und der geschichtliche biblische Christus,* ed. E. Wolf [2d enlarged ed.; München: Chr. Kaiser Verlag, 1956], 77).

[28]Cf. *The Divine Relativity,* 14, 16–17.

totality of the world process into his own being. In part this suggestion simply reflects the way a paradigm functions. If a happening is genuinely paradigmatic, constituting the decisive point of reference for interpreting the totality of experience, the reality it discloses in some sense encompasses the reality of all things. Where the paradigm which shapes man's vision of God has the effect of reducing the actualities of the world to a status of unreality, their participation in the being of God implies their dissolution as concrete phenomena. However, where it expresses an affirmation of the earthly and the historical, the reality it discloses can encompass all things only if the actualities of the world so shape and condition its being that their full significance is preserved in the divine life. The latter position is essentially what Hartshorne means by panentheism.

There are some New Testament passages, especially in Colossians and Ephesians, which explicitly present Christ as one who encompasses all things. Paul's statement that Christ "is before all things, and in him all things hold together" has certain affinities with Hartshorne's contention that God is both the "supreme source" and the "supreme result" of process.[29] More to the point is the assertion in Ephesians that the purpose of God set forth in Christ is a "plan for the fullness of time to gather all things together in him, things in heaven and things on earth" (Eph. 1:9–10). The key word is *anakephalaiosasthai*, literally, recapitulation or, we might say, a "summing up" of all thing. If all things have a share in Christ, then we cannot speak of the fullness of Christ's reality apart from the actualities that have their being in him. It is noteworthy that the writer of Ephesians later speaks of the church as the "fullness of him who fills all and all," suggesting not only that all things have a share in Christ, but also that the community of faith, if not the whole world, contributes something to his fullness.[30] In this respect, the last thing to be fully known and understood is Christ, for knowing Christ involves knowing the world. Then it is no longer enough to say that Jesus Christ is the interpretative key for our understanding of the totality of experience; our understanding of worldly actualities also enriches and completes our grasp of who he is. Following Hartshorne's terminological suggestions, we might classify this viewpoint as "panenChristism," keeping in mind that the term Christ accents the concreteness of God, his involvement with the world, his activity of drawing the world unto himself.

---

[29]*Ibid.*, 59. See Colossians 1:17. Passages having a somewhat similar force might include I Cor. 15:20–28, esp. 25–28; Eph. 1:15–23; Phil. 2:9–11.

[30]Eph. 1:23. It is striking that the *New English Bible* completely inverts the clear meaning of this text. It speaks of how the church receives the fullness of Christ. Apparently the translators could not bring themselves on dogmatic grounds to suggest that the church somehow "fills up" the reality of Christ!

The confession of Christ equally points us to considerations that correspond roughly with Hartshorne's analysis of the "abstract pole" of the divine being, the pole that expresses God's independence of process. Interestingly enough, it is this pole rather than the concrete one which has become problematic at the present time. Thomas J. J. Altizer, for example, has vigorously argued that the Incarnate Word attests the total self-emptying of God into flesh and history. As the transcendent, immutable, and sovereign Lord, God is "dead." Henceforth, the Word has its being solely in flesh, undergoing continual transformation in the forward movement of process. Since the Word now has only a fleshly being, any suggestion that the divine transcends the world is wholly negated.

Altizer's position represents his attempt to grasp the inner logic of the Incarnation, though he is fully conscious of the fact that the profanity of contemporary culture plays an essential role in his formulation of a radically immanental interpretation of Christ.[31] He presents a telling case against attempts in Christian theology to conceive God as an immutable Absolute wholly unaffected by the contingencies of history. However, it is not so clear that he has dispensed with all meanings of transcendence whatever, provided these are positively related to the forward movement of process. When Hartshorne speaks of the absolute pole of the divine being, his intent is not to isolate God from process, but to identify one of his aspects with those factors which are the precondition for there being anything whatever. Abstractly considered, God is the "reason" that there is something and not nothing. In this function, he is independent of the contingencies of process, even while he is embodied in them.

To confess Christ as the paradigm for interpreting the totality of experience is to link him positively with the elemental principles which make possible the actualities of the world. This connection is made explicit in the prologue to the fourth Gospel: "All things were made by him, and without him was not anything made that was made."[32] The significance of understanding Christ in this fashion is not that we find in him some ready-made clues about the nature of the elemental principles underlying the reality of the world. In this respect the Christian's confession of Christ does not provide much specific assistance in the construction of a metaphysic. The point is, rather, that the concrete meanings and purposes disclosed in Christ are not incompatible with

---

[31]Cf. Thomas J. J. Altizer, *The Gospel of Christian Atheism* (Philadelphia: Westminster, 1966), 46–47, 82–83, 103–105, 113, *et al.* Cf. also his "Word and History," *Radical Theology and the Death of God* (Indianapolis: Bobbs-Merrill, 1966) 121–138. For my analysis of Altizer's work, see *The Death of God Controversy* (New York: Abingdon, 1966), 75–108.

[32]John 1:3. Cf. also Col. 1:15–16 and Heb. 1:3, 10–12, 2:10.

the actualities of the world process. The unequivocal way the Word is actualized in flesh directs us to see that the Word, far from being fundamentally alien to flesh, is itself the source and ground of fleshly realities within which we find ourselves. As a result, the world, regardless of its particular shape at any given place or time, is disclosed as a suitable context within which man can enter into the possibilities of existence set forth in Jesus Christ.

The divine transcendence or independence of the world has a second meaning that is even more central to the Christian's confession of Christ. It indicates that God, though he is continually being shaped and conditioned by the world, nevertheless remains sufficiently free of the world so that he can ever be true to himself in the fulfilment of his purposes for the world. Apart from this element of transcendence, God would be so completely bound to process as to be unable to be a creative factor in it. The "transcendental" symbols used in celebrating Christ, especially the resurrection and the ascension, dramatize this aspect of the meaning of Christ. These symbols have at times been understood as indications of Christ's removal from the travail and humiliation of the flesh, of his restoration to an immutable and transcendent realm of glory. Viewed in that manner, they unquestionably reverse the force of the divine movement into flesh.[33] They must, rather, be interpreted in relation to the positive involvement of God with the world. In that relation they express the divine freedom from the world process which enables God to be effectively and steadfastly present in it. Jesus' going away, the writer of John reminds us, is for our advantage, for it frees him to come to us in ever new forms, ones not so restricted by the particularity of Jesus' spatio-temporal existence.[34] In short, the positive significance of God's responsiveness to the contingencies of the world and his appropriation of the world into his own being requires that he be sufficiently free of the world to be a creative and constructive factor in it regardless of the actual contingencies that may arise. Here too, Hartshorne's analysis of the abstract pole of the divine being contributes to an elucidation of the Christian's confession of Christ.

I have been arguing for the fruitfulness of Hartshorne's dipolar conception of God. I found it necessary to challenge his attempt to justify his conclusions on the basis of an allegedly neutral and detached analysis of the logically possible doctrines of God. I contended instead that reflection on the meaning of God grows more properly out of the attempt to explicate critically the import of certain happenings

---

[33]Altizer interprets the resurrection and ascension in this fashion (*The Gospel of Christian Atheism*, 39, 43–46).

[34]John 16:7–8.

having a paradigmatic significance in human experience. With the latter approach, we remain more cognizant of the historicity and relativity of our own perspective even while we attend seriously to its implications for the totality of human experience. As a result, we are less tempted to make undue claims for our own "rationality" in contrast to the supposed "irrationality" of others.

Even so, I found Hartshorne's work to be highly suggestive for unfolding the distinctively Christian vision of God, perhaps because his own value assumptions have been significantly conditioned by the impact of biblical faith on Western thinking about God. I argued that the attempt to explicate the Christian's confession of Jesus Christ points in the direction of dipolar theism. On the one hand, it suggests that God is conditioned by the relativities and contingencies of the world process, even to the point of appropriating that process at each of its successive stages into his own being. On the other hand, it indicates that God also has a relative independence of the world, so that he is able to remain true to himself and his purposes even in his involvement with the changing world. Insofar as this argument is convincing, it presents a challenge to process philosophers and theologians to be more sensitive to the historicity of their own thought processes. At the same time, it opens the way for theologians more decisively guided by the distinctive character of biblical faith and of Christian symbols and images to appropriate the achievements of process thinkers into their own understanding.

Schubert Ogden's Christology and the Possibilities of Process Philosophy

18

David Griffin

Schubert Ogden's theology as a whole is best characterized as an attempt to correct the "one-sidedly existentialist character" of Bultmann's theology[1] by combining existentialist analysis with process philosophy in such a way that they mutually complement each other.[2] This characterization applies likewise to Ogden's treatment of Christology in particular. He believes there is some point to the criticisms that Bultmann dissolves Christology into soteriology,[3] for he has been unable "to express in an adequate way the 'objective' reality of the revelatory event Jesus the Christ,"[4] even though he does "intend a divine act in the fully real and 'objective' sense."[5] Ogden means to overcome this christological inadequacy by employing insights of process philosophy.

Little attention has been given to Ogden's employment of process philosophy to this end. Almost all criticism has been devoted to his interpretation of Bultmann,[6] and to the soteriological side of his Christology, i.e. to the question of whether Jesus is necessary to the Chris-

From *The Christian Scholar*, L, 3 (Fall 1967). Used by permission of the National Council of the Churches of Christ and David Griffin.

[1]Schubert M. Ogden, *The Reality of God and Other Essays* (New York: Harper & Row, 1966), 170; cf. also *Christ Without Myth: A Study Based on the Theology of Rudolf Bultmann* (New York: Harper & Brothers, 1961), 151, and "Bultmann's Demythologizing and Hartshorne's Dipolar Theism," in William L. Reese and Eugene Freeman, eds., *Process and Divinity: The Hartshorne Festschrift* (LaSalle, Illinois: Open Court, 1964), 501.

[2]*The Reality of God,* 172; *Process and Divinity,* 498f., 508f., 511f.: *Christ Without Myth,* 151.

[3]*Christ Without Myth,* 159.

[4]*Ibid.,* 158.

[5]*Ibid.,* 91.

[6]Cf. Thomas C. Oden, "The Alleged Structural Inconsistency in Bultmann," *Journal of Religion,* XLIV (1964), 193–200; John Young Fenton, "The Post-Liberal Theology of Christ Without Myth," *Journal of Religion,* XLIII (1963), 93–104.

tian mode of existence.[7] Hence it seems appropriate to focus attention directly on Ogden's Christology proper, that is, on its "objective" side, as opposed to its subjective, existential, or soteriological side. Therefore, although implications for the soteriological issue will be briefly mentioned, the task of this essay is to determine whether Ogden's employment of process philosophy has enabled him adequately to explicate the objective intention of Christian faith in regard to Jesus, i.e., to explain how one can speak of Jesus as God's decisive act.

The first part of the essay will give a brief analysis of Ogden's Christology, centering on the question of how we are to understand the affirmation that Jesus is God's decisive act. The second section will suggest in what way Ogden's explanation of this affirmation is not adequate. The third section will indicate that process philosophy contains possibilities for more adequately accounting for this affirmation. The fourth section will suggest why Ogden has not availed himself of these possibilities, and will also mention other implications which the employment of these possibilities might entail.

I

Ogden holds that Jesus is God's decisive act because he is the decisive revelation or re-presentation of a certain possibility for human existence on the one hand, and of God's being and action on the other.[8] Since this essay is concerned with the question of how Jesus is God's act, the concentration will be upon affirmations based on that side of the revelation which is concerned directly with God and his action.[9] God's being is love,[10] and his action can be summarized as creation

[7]Cf. James M. Robinson, *Theology Today*, XIX (1962), 439–444; William O. Walker, Jr., "Demythologizing and Christology," *Religion in Life*, XXXV (1965–1966), 67–80; Robert W. Funk, *Language, Hermeneutic, and Word of God: The Problem of Language in the New Testament and Contemporary Theology* (New York: Harper & Row, 1966), 87–108; Daniel L. Deegan, *Scottish Journal of Theology*, (March 1964), 83–89; Harold H. Ditmanson, *Dialogue*, I (1962), 75–78; Rudolf Bultmann, *Journal of Religion*, XLII (1962), 225–227. The articles by Oden and Fenton also deal with this issue. The only treatment of Ogden's Christology in reference to his use of process philosophy which I have seen is that by Eugene H. Peters, *The Creative Advance: An Introduction to Process Philosophy as a Context for Christian Faith* (St. Louis: Bethany, 1966), 112–117. The present critique takes a completely different approach from that of Peters.

[8]The point of saying re-present is Ogden's doctrine that what is manifested of God in Jesus is no different than what is presented to man in God's "original revelation." The content is the same as what is expressed everywhere in the events of nature and history. Cf. *Christ Without Myth*, 156.

[9]*The Reality of God*, 178. Ogden also states that Christian faith could be explicated as a doctrine of God just as well as it could as a certain possibility of self-understanding, *ibid.*, 170; *Christ Without Myth*, 148.

[10]*The Reality of God*, 177.

and redemption.[11] God's activity as Creator does not refer to a particular time in the past, nor is his redemptive activity something which will take place only in the future. Rather, God's constant, universal activity is creation and redemption.[12]

The constant, universal nature of God's action as Creator and Redeemer is emphasized by Ogden's view of the nature of theological language. Because of God's transcendence it would be mythological to refer to God's action in terms appropriate only to objects available, in principle at least, to ordinary sense perception.[13] This especially means that one cannot speak of God in terms of the categories of time and space;[14] i.e., whatever is predicated of God cannot apply only to some particular time and space, but must apply equally to all times and spaces.[15] Thus the implication of Ogden's criterion for non-mythological language about God corresponds to his statement of several years ago, that "there is not the slightest evidence that God has acted in Christ in any way different from the way in which he primordially acts in every other event."[16] If God acts the same way in relation to the event of Jesus as he acts in relation to every other event, and if theology can only make statements about God which apply to his relation to every event, it would seem that Ogden had made it doubly impossible to assert that Jesus is the decisive act of God. For would this assertion not presuppose that God had acted somehow differently here? Would one not have to say something about God's action which did not hold true anywhere else? The key to Ogden's attempted solution to this apparent dilemma lies in the idea that Jesus is the decisive re-presentation of God's being and action. By means of this idea he attempts to explain how we can say that Jesus is God's decisive act without saying that God acted at all differently in this situation.

Ogden stated in *Christ Without Myth* (1961) that he intended to express the "objective" reality of the event Jesus Christ more adequately than Bultmann had succeeded in doing, but that this would have to come in a later work.[17] His fullest treatment of the problem thus far appeared in 1963 in his essay, "What Sense Does it Make to

---

[11]*Ibid.*, 178f., and *passim.*

[12]*Ibid.*, 168.

[13]*Ibid.*, 76, 104.

[14]*Ibid.*, 76, 166f., 175f.

[15]*Ibid.*, 173. This is one basis for saying that Bultmann's treatment of the decisiveness of Jesus Christ is mythological. Ogden says that to imply that God redeems men only in the history of Jesus Christ is mythological because it "subjects God's action as the redeemer to the objectifying categories of time and space."

[16]"Bultmann's Project of Demythologization and the Problem of Theology and Philosophy," *Journal of Religion*, XXXVII (1957), 169.

[17]*Christ Without Myth*, 159.

Say, 'God Acts in History' "?[18] The second part of this essay is explicitly directed toward answering "the question of the sense, if any, in which one can still say with the historic Christian community that the event of Jesus Christ is the decisive act of God."[19] The chief resource Ogden employs is Hartshorne's idea that "God is to be conceived in strict analogy with the human self or person."[20] God's relation to the world is to be understood as analogous to the relation of the human self to its body. On the basis of this insight Ogden means to explain how all historical events are acts of God, how some of these can be called "special" acts of God, and how one of these can in turn be called God's decisive act.

First one must understand two senses in which "human act" can be intended. On the one hand, it refers to the act of word or deed whereby the self expresses itself through the instrumentality of the body. On the other hand, it can refer to the act by which the self constitutes itself as a self; the public acts of word and deed are just ways of expressing this inner act which corresponds to the more primary meaning of "human act."[21] Applying this distinction to God we can see that the primary meaning of an "act of God" would refer to "the act whereby, in each new present, he constitutes himself as God."[22] In this act God responds to the previous stage of the world and, in constituting himself, thereby lays the ground for the next stage of the creative process. Just as the primary meaning of human action does not refer to a public, historical act, the primary meaning of God's action does not refer to any act in history.[23] However, since the relation of the world to God is analogous to that of the body to the self, then in the secondary sense of God's action, every event is to an extent an act of God. Of course, every creature has its freedom, so it is not solely a result of God's action, but its freedom has limits ultimately grounded in God's creative action, and so it is partly an expression of God's act in the primary sense.[24]

Having established how, although God's action in its primary sense transcends history, we can still say that all historical events are acts of God, Ogden must now show how some events can be "special" acts of God. Although every action of our body is ours in one sense, there are certain actions which we say are "peculiarly ours in a way that the

[18]*Journal of Religion*, XLIII (1963), 1–19; reprinted in The *Reality of God*, 164–187.
[19]The *Reality of God*, 174.
[20]*Ibid.*, 175.
[21]*Ibid.*, 176f.
[22]*Ibid.*, 177.
[23]*Ibid.*, 179.
[24]*Ibid.*, 180.

others are not."[25] These are the acts of word and deed which give peculiarly apt expression to our inner beings and understandings. We call these our "characteristic" actions, since through them "the persons we are, are uniquely re-presented or revealed to others."[26] Analogously, insofar as an historical event reveals or re-presents God's characteristic action as Creator and Redeemer, this event is his act in a special sense.[27] Any event has the possibility of becoming such an act, since every event expresses God's being and action.[28] However, those uniquely human events in which man expresses his understanding of existence are especially adapted to becoming special acts of God.[29] If one expresses his understanding in such a way that God's being and action are appropriately re-presented, then this event is a special act of God.

Finally, if the foregoing is granted, there is no problem as to a "decisive" act of God. This would be an event which not only re-presented God's being and action appropriately, but also normatively.[30] In this way Ogden believes one can assert that Jesus is the decisive act of God without implying that God acted in any way differently in relation to him. He acted, as always, as Creator and Redeemer, as transcendent love. Since, as Creator, he was the ultimate ground of every word and deed of Jesus, Jesus was to some extent an expression of God's decisions, thus an act of God. Of course, this is true of every word and deed of every person. But Jesus is special in that his words and deeds (e.g. his preaching and acts of healing, his fellowship with sinners and his death[31]) represent God's being and action in a decisive or normative fashion. Thus he is the normative or decisive act of God.

II

Now I propose to show in what way Ogden's explanation of how Jesus can be called God's decisive act is not adequate. But first some terms need to be discussed. The notion of one's "inner being" will be central to the following argument. Ogden treats this notion in terms of two basic possibilities, which are his equivalents for authentic and inauthentic existence. A self "can open itself to its world and make its decisions by sensitively reponding to all the influences that bear upon

---

[25]Ibid., 181.

[26]Loc. cit.

[27]Ibid., 182.

[28]Ibid., 183.

[29]Ibid., 182, 184.

[30]Ibid., 184. When I say there is "no problem," I am not referring to the question as to how one would establish which special act was the normative one. I refer only to the formal description of what an event would have to be in order to be, in fact, God's decisive act.

[31]Ibid., 186.

it, or it may close itself against its world and make its decisions on the basis of a much more restricted sensitivity than is actually possible for it."[32] These two possibilities describe respectively a self who loves and one who hates. I assume that the word "character" (also a problematic term) might also point to what is intended by the expression "inner being," and that such words as unselfish and selfish, helpful and unhelpful, friendly and hostile, open and bigoted, would be more particularized variations of the more basic notions of loving and hating.

The term "special act" is synonymous with the notion of an act of a person which is "peculiarly his." The difference between Ogden's and my use of this term is central to the following discussion and hopefully will become clear as the essay develops. However, I will here summarize the difference. For Ogden, a person's special act is one which "reveals" or "represents" his inner being to another person. The emphasis tends to be placed on the reception of the act by the other person. In my usage the emphasis is on the causal relation between the inner being of the person and the nature of the outer act. Hence, rather than "reveal" or "represent," I prefer the term "express." This word, especially when its root is considered, places the emphasis on the fact that something is "pressed out" from the inner being of the person. Thus, while Ogden's usage equates a special act and a revelatory one, mine implies a distinction. A special act would be only *potentially* revelatory; a revelatory act would be a special act which is in fact received in such a way that it does reveal the inner being of the person to the one receiving it. A revelatory act would have both an objective and a subjective aspect; the objective aspect of it would be the special act.[33]

What I feel to be the inadequacy of Ogden's treatment is already suggested by the foregoing terminological remarks. According to his interpretation, one of my special acts would be a word or deed which represents to someone else the person I really am. This would mean that the action is, as all my actions are, an *expression* of my inner being, but not necessarily any more so than any other of my actions. However, it is *interpreted* by someone in such a way that this act does in fact represent my inner being, i.e., the interpretation of my inner being on the basis of this action *corresponds* to what I in fact am like. With this understanding of what makes an act peculiarly mine, the act *becomes* a special act of mine *if* someone interprets my inner being *accurately* on the basis of this act.

In view of the emphasis I am placing on this point, one passage which might seem to belie this interpretation of Ogden's position

[32]*Ibid.*, 177.
[33] Cf. Ogden's discussion of this subject, *ibid.*, 185.

should be examined. He says that certain acts are revelatory both because they do in fact express one's being and because they are received as doing so.[34] However, the first part of this needs refer only to the fact that *every* outer act of a person is *to some extent* an expression of his inner being. For Ogden, this seems to be enough to establish the "objective" side of a "revelatory" act. The point I am making is that for him the "specialness" of a special act is entirely a function of someone other than the person whose special act it is.

Everyone has, of course, the right to define his terms as he wishes. However, I believe that Ogden's explanation of a special act does not do justice to the "objective intention" implied in saying that a certain action is peculiarly someone's, in a sense that other of his actions are not. For, objectively speaking, according to his explanation a special act does not *express* the person's inner being any more than his other actions do; it does *reveal* his inner being more than other actions do, but this is due to its being received in a certain way by others. I believe a more adequate understanding of a special act is needed, and can be given. When we say that a particular outer action is peculiarly ours we mean that the act is such that it in fact is an *expression* of our inner being, and thus we mean to imply something about the intentionality of the act. Some examples should make this clear.

Say that Jones is an unselfish person. When people infer from his selfless actions that are motivated by a real concern to help that he is unselfish, they are right. And they are right not only about his inner being, but they are also right in taking these particular actions as his "characteristic" actions, those which especially express the person he is. However, there are all sorts of things which he may do which might be interpreted by others as manifestations of his unselfishness which in fact are not. His motivation for some of his contributions to charities might be related to tax considerations rather than to his unselfishness; his allowing another motorist to have the last parking place might be due solely to the fact that his own engine had died. If someone had observed these acts and then said, "Jones is unselfish," he would still be right. But he would not be right insofar as he took these particular items to be manifestations of Jones' unselfishness, and thus "peculiarly his." For an action to be ours in this special sense requires more than (a) that it be thought to be this by someone and (b) that the trait attributed to us on the basis of this interpretation actually describes us. Rather, the most essential point is that it really *expresses* our inner being more than most of our actions do. What this entails (the element of intentionality has already been mentioned) will be discussed in more detail in the next section. For the present purposes, the important factor is that the

[34]*Ibid.*, 185.

specialness of a special act is partially a *function of the person* whose special act it is.

Now we must see how this discussion relates to the question of special acts of God. For an event to be a special act of God, the specialness of it would have to be partially a function of God.[35] However, according to Ogden's explanation of what constitutes a special act, this is not the case. Of course, a special act of God is *to some extent* an expression of God, but so is every event; the thing that differentiates a special act of God from an ordinary one is not at all due to anything done by God.

That this is Ogden's understanding can be readily seen. He says that *any* event can *become* a special act of God "insofar as it is received by someone as a symbol of God's creative and redemptive action."[36] And, even in the case of the types of events which are uniquely adapted to becoming special acts of God, i.e. human words and deeds, the specialness is still due only to human doing. Man is uniquely the creature of meaning, and thus is "able to grasp the *logos* of reality as such and to represent it through symbolic speech and action."[37] Thus, whether the specialness of an event is due only to an interpreter of the event, or whether it is due to both a person who is speaking and acting and to someone receiving this as a special act, it is man who turns an ordinary act of God into a special one. There is no talk of God's doing anything different in relation to his special acts.

This corresponds, of course, to Ogden's requirement for nonmythological talk about God, as explained in the previous section. If it were implied that God did something different at one point in space and time, one would be involved in mythological talk. Thus, Ogden's position is here completely self-consistent—only its adequacy is at issue. If my understanding as to what would constitute an act which is peculiarly someone's is accepted, then Ogden's explanation of a special act of God is not adequate. For one condition of an adequate explanation would be that it *somehow* attribute the specialness of a special act of God partially to God. It follows by the same reasoning that his explanation of Jesus as the "decisive" act of God is not adequate. An adequate account would have to make the "deciveness" of Jesus partially a function of God's initiative. But in Ogden's account the deciveness is solely a function of human doing, i.e. of Jesus and his disciples. Jesus

----

[35]"Partially" is added because the specialness is also partially a function of the creature, since the creature has a certain freedom in regard to actualizing God's intention for it. The same is true in regard to the human analogue, since, when by "person" we mean the "self" as opposed to its body, the specialness of an act will be due partly to the person and partly to how well the body carries out the person's intention for it. This should become clearer in the third part of the essay.

[36]*Ibid.*, 183.

[37]*Ibid.*, 37.

was able to "grasp the *logos* of reality as such and to re-present it
through symbolic speech and action," and this in a normative fashion.
He became the decisive act of God in that he did this and has been received as having decisive revelatory power.[38]

III

My verdict in the previous section was that Ogden's use of process philosophy in order to give an adequate account of Jesus as the decisive act
of God has not been successful. However, I believe that there is a notion in process philosophy by which one could, using the same self-body
analogy, more adequately explain what would constitute a "special" act
of God, and thereby better explain how Jesus could be God's decisive
act. By using this notion Ogden could attribute the decisiveness of Jesus
partly to God, and still say that *in one sense* God acted no differently
here than he acts elsewhere.

This is Whitehead's concept of the "ideal aim." According to this
notion, every event has its origin in God's specific purpose for it. Every
creature or event is initially constituted by God's ideal aim for it.[39] The
ideal aim is the goal or possibility which, if actualized by the creature,
would be best, given all the relevant circumstances.[40] This notion is implicit in Ogden's theology, in that it lies behind his discussion of God as
"Creator." For instance, the notion of the ideal aim entails that God
"limits" the possibilities which are relevant to a particular occasion.
Ogden mentions that the freedom of each creature "has definite limits
ultimately grounded in God's own free decisions."[41] However, there are
a couple of distinctions which can be made which Ogden does not employ, and which can be applied to the christological problem.[42]

---

[38]*Ibid.*, 184f.

[39]*PR* 374. This side of Whitehead's thought has been developed by John B.
Cobb, Jr., *A Christian Natural Theology* (Philadelphia: Westminster, 1965), cf. esp.
96, 128f., 151–157, 182ff., 203–214.

[40]*Ibid.*, 373.

[41]*The Reality of God,* 180. The notion of the ideal aim is not often directly
discussed by Hartshorne, upon whom Ogden is more immediately dependent than
upon Whitehead. However it is discussed quite explicitly in at least one place. Hartshorne mentions that "God can set narrow limits to our freedom." He speaks of
God's presenting himself so as "to weight the possibilities of response in the desired
respect." God presents at each new moment a "partly new ideal or order of preference." He inspires us with "novel ideals for novel occasions." Charles Hartshorne,
The Divine Relativity: A Social Conception of God (New Haven: Yale University
Press, 1948), 142.

[42]These distinctions have already been made, and in connection with Christology, by John B. Cobb, Jr., in "The Finality of Christ in a Whiteheadian Perspective," *The Finality of Christ,* Dow Kirkpatrick, ed. (New York-Nashville: Abingdon
Press, 1966), 144.

The first distinction concerns the *degree* to which a creature actualizes the ideal aim given him by God. In terms of the self-body analogy,
this would correspond to how well one's body carries out what one intends it to do. We perhaps do not normally think of this factor since, in
relation to the parts of our body over which we have conscious control,
the degree of our control is quite high and rather constant. However,
there would be a rather significant difference in this regard between a
champion gymnast and a spastic person. So, in a different sense than we
have employed the idea thus far, we would say that the athlete's bodily
actions were more fully *his* acts than is true for the spastic person, for
they more adequately express his intentions. And there would be, in between these extremes, all degrees of control and agility. Also, even in
regard to one and the same person there will be differences in this respect, especially when alcohol, drugs, fatigue, and old age are factors.
Thus, we can see that, in one sense, the question of whether some actions of a person are more fully "his" than others is a matter of degree.

This distinction can be applied to the relation of God and the world
in a way which indicates how some events can be "acts of God" to a
higher degree than others are. In Whitehead's view, the initial or ideal
aim given by God includes alternatives;[43] these are "graded" according
to their relevance;[44] the creature can modify his initial subjective aim,
i.e. the ideal aim given by God.[45] Thus, a creature could use his freedom
in order to actualize the ideal aim given him, or he could modify this
aim to such an extent as to choose the worst alternative open to him, or
his actualization could fall anywhere in between. Ogden mentions that
"every creature is to some extent God's act," and that each creature has
a certain freedom;[46] but he does not make use of this notion to point out
that different creatures will be acts of God to *different* degrees depending upon how they actualize their freedom. That is, in terms of this first
distinction a certain event would be an act of *God* only to the degree
that the creature actualized God's will for it.

A second distinction that can be made in regard to God's creative
activity, seen in terms of his supplying of the ideal aim for each creature, regards the "whatness" of the aim. Here again the human analogy
can be used. Some of our outward acts are of a type which do not do
much toward expressing our inner being no matter how well our body
responds to our wishes for it. For example, say that you are a helpful
person; your act of tying your shoelaces will generally not do much toward expressing this fact, no matter how nimbly your fingers respond
to your intentions for them. Only certain types of actions have the po-

[43]PR 342.
[44]*Ibid.*, 248.
[45]*Ibid.*, 374f.
[46]*The Reality of God*, 180.

tentiality for expressing helpfulness, such as stopping to help a stalled motorist. In a case like this, the situation is such that your helpfulness can be expressed (assuming that your intention is really to be helpful and not, say, to impress a companion). Thus, for your helpfulness to be expressed, the event must be of an appropriate nature, and your intention must be appropriate. (Also—to bring in the previous distinction— your body must also respond to your intentions to an adequate degree; e.g., if you intended to stop to help the motorist but ran over him instead, this would not do much toward expressing your helpfulness. This is why the specialness of a special act is partly a function of one's inner being, and partly a function of the body.)

This analogy can be applied rather strictly to God. Whitehead clearly intends that God's ideal aim for any particular occasion is relevant to the situation—it is the best possible aim given the conditions. Since God's aim for a certain person at a certain time and place will be determined not only by God's general purpose for the world, but also by the genetic and environmental past of the person, and also by the particular situation he faces, the "whatness" of God's aims at different times and places will vary considerably. Thus, one would expect that many human events would not do much toward expressing God's being, no matter to what degree his will is actualized by the person at that moment. God's aim for some human events, on the other hand, will be such that, if his will is actualized to a high degree by the person, the event will effectively express God's being. As in the human example, not only must the nature of the event be appropriate in order to have a special act of God, God's intention must also have a sufficiently large influence in determining the nature of the action. As mentioned before, the specialness will be only partially a function of God's doing; the creature must actualize God's aim for it to a sufficient degree, so the specialness will also be partly a function of the creature's free response.[47]

[47]These proposals of a constructive nature must here remain highly formal, and can be, at best, only vaguely suggestive. A fuller explication must await a later work. For example, in talking about an "act of God" I have discussed God's intentionality, and the degree to which his intention is actualized by his creature. But to discuss this adequately, the problem of the intentionality of the person involved would have to be explored. Thus, the whole question of Jesus' intentionality, his "self-understanding," would come into the issue. Ogden, not wanting to make any assertions about Jesus which are not historically demonstrable, believes one can remain neutral on this issue; cf. *Christ Without Myth*, 161; "How New is the 'New Quest of the Historical Jesus' "? (with Van A. Harvey), *The Historical Jesus and the Kerygmatic Christ*, Carl E. Braaten and Roy A. Harrisville, eds. (New York: Abingdon, 1964), 230f., 232, n. 103. However, if one said, for example, that the question of Jesus' own intentions were a matter of total indifference, so that he possibly was deliberately deceptive in everything he did and said, could one still say in any meaningful sense that he was the decisive *act of God*? In other words, can one really *completely*

Whereas the previous distinction gave us a means for seeing how different events could differ in *degree* in regard to being an "act of God," this latter distinction provides a basis for making *qualitative* differentiations. Some events will be "peculiarly" acts of God not only because his will is realized to a high degree in the event, but also because his ideal aim for the event was such as to be especially expressive of his being. Thus, different events can be different "in kind" as well as in degree.

In terms of the twofold distinction discussed in this section we can now formally state what a "decisive" act of God would be. This would be an event (a) for which God's aim was such that, if the aim were actualized, the event would optimally express God's being, and (b) which did in fact actualize God's aim or will for it to an optimal degree. With this understanding God has, formally speaking, acted in the same way he always acts, i.e., by supplying the ideal aim for the event. Yet the decisiveness of the act is partially a function of God's activity, which is in one sense different here than in other places, for the particular ideal aim given here is such as to give particularly apt expression to his being. Thus, by making a formal-material distinction, one can combine a certain particularity and avoid the kind of conception of "decisive act" which Ogden would have to judge mythological.

IV

If employing the suggested possibilities would actually help Ogden with his stated intention of being more adequate to the "objective" side of faith assertions about Jesus, and if these possibilities are inherent in the process philosophy which Ogden employs, the question raises itself as to why Ogden has not developed his position along the suggested lines. The reason is probably that the major influences on his thought are such as to militate against this. Heidegger's presentation of the possibilities of human existence suggests that they are applicable to man as such, and not, say, only to modern European man. There is no suggestion that persons formed by different histories have different possibilities open to them. Bultmann has said that philosophical reflection alone can discover and describe the nature of authentic, i.e., Christian existence: "Philosophy all by itself already sees what the New Testament says."[48] Hartshorne's discussion of philosophy also has quite an ahistorical quality about it; one gains the impression that he believes that

---

isolate the question of *"what God did* through the man Jesus in his vocation or office" (*ibid.*, 232, n. 103, italics mine) from the issue of the *"existentiell selfhood"* of Jesus?

[48]*Kerygma und Mythos,* I (Hamburg: Herbert Reich Evangelische Verlag, 1951), 33, translated by Ogden, *Christ Without Myth,* 69.

there is no *necessary* connection between his doctrine of God and the Christian tradition. Ogden himself has approved Hartshorne's distinction "between a philosophical theology developed from 'the standpoint of the minimal common faith or experience of men in general' and a theology grounded in 'revelation' and thus developed from 'the standpoint of the faith or religious experience of a person or group.' "[49] Finally, there is the idea, derived mainly from the first two chapters of *Romans,* that all men are responsible for their sin, since the truth of God has been given them. Ogden seems to take this to mean that all are *equally* responsible for not actualizing authentic existence, since the primordial revelation of God already contained the content of the revelation in Jesus the Christ.[50] This is, of course, the basis for Ogden's well-known rejection of the distinction between Christian existence as a "possibility in principle" for all men but a "possibility in fact" only for some.[51]

All of these factors militate against accepting an idea which suggests that God, in his creative activity, presents different possibilities to different men, depending upon various circumstantial factors, paramount of which would be the historical situation. Such a notion would mean, for example, that an Australian aborigine would not be responsible for not having actualized the type of existence which has appeared in history through the Judeo-Christian tradition. Thus, if Ogden were to employ the suggested means for making his Christology more adequate, this would imply a change in his soteriology. Ogden has confronted the issue of the two types of possibility as it is presented by Bultmann. As William Walker has pointed out, Bultmann's remarks suggest that the event of Jesus Christ is "somehow objectively different in principle as well as in fact from all other events and thus constitutes an invasion into the normal course of history."[52] The way Bultmann has employed the distinction between an "ontological" and an "ontic" possibility does suggest a type of supernaturalism which Ogden justifiably wishes to avoid.[53] However, a misuse of a distinction does not necessarily invalidate it. One can very well agree that Christian existence has always been an ontological possibility for man, in the sense that it does not entail "changing human nature into a supernature,"[54] and yet say that it

---

[49]*Journal of Religion,* XLIV (1964), 15f., n. 18, quoting from Charles Hartshorne, *Man's Vision of God and the Logic of Theism* (Hamden, Conn.: Archon Books, 1964), 73.

[50]*Christ Without Myth,* 142, 154.

[51]Cf., e.g., *ibid.,* 117ff.

[52]Walker, 73.

[53]Cf. *Journal of Religion,* XLII (1962), 225–227.

[54]John Fenton has emphasized this meaning of an ontological possibility, *op. cit.,* 97.

is an ontic possibility only for those in a certain historical situation. One could thus affirm the "necessity" of Jesus for Christian existence as a purely historical fact. This kind of "particularism" should give no offense.

A few of Ogden's remarks suggest that he recognizes the validity of the distinction between the two types of possibilities. For example, in one place he himself gives an example of such a distinction, pointing out that the "possibility of man's encircling the globe by air has always been a 'possibility in principle,' although only quite recently has it also become a 'possibility in fact.' "[55] Also, Ogden affirms that the possibility of authentic existence "has especially been given to the Jew."[56] Would this not mean that the Jew was "especially" responsible, that possibilities and therefore responsibilities of different men are different? Furthermore, Ogden recognizes that there is a definite historical connection between the Christian tradition on the one hand, and existentialism and process philosophy on the other.[57] Would one not have to say that both of these forms of philosophy *became* possibilities in fact only as a result of the emergence of Christian faith in history, and of the particular direction the theological tradition developed?[58] I am suggesting that if the implications of this side of his thought were developed along with the aspect of process philosophy that he has not yet employed, Ogden would have a way of stating more adequately that Jesus was "objectively" the decisive act of God, without making this event different in principle from other acts of God. And this christological position would be correlative with a soteriological position which would insist on the necessity of Jesus for Christian existence, and yet not in any dogmatic or supernaturalistic sense.

Some other implications of the christological approach suggested here can only be touched upon. In regard to the nature of theological language, it would mean avoiding a position which limited meaningful

[55]Ogden, 118. But Ogden then rejects an application of this to the problem of the necessity of Jesus to authentic existence on the grounds that this would imply a "quasi-Gnostic conception in which man is understood as the helpless and irresponsible victim of fate" and would deny man's freedom and responsibility, *ibid.*, 119. But to equate dependence upon historical circumstance with being "at the mercy of powers whose agency is independent of [man's] own responsible decisions" and thus to call such talk mythological seems to stretch the meaning of myth beyond any justifiable limits.

[56]*Ibid.*, 154; cf., also 156, and *The Reality of God,* 203.

[57]*Christ Without Myth,* 71.

[58]*The Reality of God,* 69, 96. Ogden seems reluctant to put it this strongly for fear that this admission would weaken the claim for validity which one can make for these philosophies. For instance, while admitting with Bultmann that existential philosophy is *historically* connected to the New Testament, he still wants to say that "the claim of philosophy that the true nature of man can be discovered and known apart from the New Testament is not to be disputed."

or nonmythological theological statements to assertions about God's activity which apply universally. That is, besides ontological statements about how God always is and acts, there will be room for ontic or historical assertions about what God has in fact done. This would mean that not every theological assertion could be *completely* interpreted as a statement about man and his possibilities, for the ontic statement that God's love was especially revealed in a certain historical figure adds nothing, in terms of possibilities for self-understanding or ethical intention, to a statement about God's love.[59]

Also, with the possibilities of process philosophy discussed in this essay one could develop a more "active" meaning to God's love. In Ogden's discussions God's love is described in purely passive terms (partly justifiable as a reaction to a theological tradition which disallowed any element of passivity in God's love). God is love in that he can perfectly sympathize with, participate in, the being of his creatures.[60] The emphasis is totally on God's receptivity, on his action as Redeemer. However, if one emphasized God's providing of individualized ideal aims for each occasion, God's love could be conceived in a creative sense, as his "active goodwill" toward each of his creatures. God would be seen as not only fully understanding and appreciative of what his creatures in fact are, but also as willing their good and influencing them toward it. . . .

[59]See Walker, esp. 78f., for a criticism of Ogden which is based on the view of language that I am here opposing. It would be strange if, after all the recent discussion as to how much Christianity is a "historical faith," Christian theologians would adopt an understanding of theological language which ruled out all historical statements.

[60]*The Reality of God*, 178.

Some Proposals for a Modern Christology

19

Peter N. Hamilton

The term Christology is used in two senses. It can be confined to the doctrine of the *Person* of Christ; but for reasons that will soon emerge I take it in the wider sense of the *Shorter Oxford English Dictionary*: 'that part of theology which relates to Christ.' 'Christ' is, of course, a title: used on its own, it lacks a referent. I therefore prefer to speak of 'Jesus' or 'Jesus Christ,' bearing in mind Paul Tillich's precise but cumbersome phrase, 'Jesus whom men call the Christ.' As Tillich thus reminds us, this combination of proper name and title must include in its scope the *response* to Jesus as well as his personality, teaching, and manner of life—and at least those aspects of the history and religion of Israel that are relevant to Jesus, to this response, and to the title Christ. And since the response includes the belief in his resurrection and ascension, the scope of the term 'Jesus Christ' must include the coming into being of this resurrection-faith and of the Church. Indeed this entire sequence of events possesses a unity such that we can meaningfully speak of it as 'the event Jesus Christ.' I here largely confine myself to its central core: the life, death, and resurrection of Jesus, and the initial response to this.

I shall seek to distinguish three constituents alike of the wider event and of this central core: history, mythology, and divine activity. These interpenetrate and overlap, but the main burden of this lecture is the assertion that the third constituent cannot be wholly subsumed under the other two. Theists who speak of God acting in or through some event often qualify this by saying that since God transcends both space and time he cannot be said to 'act' in any literal sense. We cannot here embark on the doctrine of God, but I would wish to affirm both God's transcendence in one aspect of his being and his temporality in

From *Christ for Us Today*, ed. Norman Pittenger. Copyright 1968, SCM Press. Used by permission of SCM Press and Peter Hamilton.

another aspect, and to say that God does act within our temporal history, and that the response of faith—itself a part of history, affecting what follows—is a response to the *ontological reality* to which it points in saying *God has acted.*[1] I affirm that God so acted within the wider event 'Jesus Christ,' and in particular in his resurrection.

It may be helpful to begin by considering this claim in connexion with an event that we can perhaps view more dispassionately, the escape from Egypt under Moses. We need not concern ourselves with the mechanics of this, but rather with its religious status and sequel. For the atheist, the escape must have been due to good luck, good leadership, or Egyptian incompetence. The theist can say that God acted, either by a physical miracle or by so guiding the Jews that they benefited unwittingly from a sudden change of wind and tide; or he can deny that God acted and say rather that God's strengthening influence upon the Jews and their leaders—for example, as they turned to him in prayer—inspired but did not arrange their escape. *Any* of these views, including the atheist one, is an admissible interpretation of the evidence: a tribal nationalism, belief in their tribal god, and an unexpected and improbable escape *could* account for the rise of the exodus-faith and its subsequent centrality in the religio-political history of the Jews.

I do *not* believe that a parallel statement can be made about the birth of the resurrection-faith among the disciples of Jesus. Unlike the Jews on the East side of the Sea of Reeds, the disciples were not confronted with a sudden improvement in their fortunes—precisely the reverse. It may be that we sometimes exaggerate the disciples' despair at their master's death, and that in its very nature this despair was only temporary. It is also undeniable that a person's closest friends often see him in a new light immediately after his death. It may be possible to develop these and similar lines of thought to establish what for brevity's sake I will call a self-generated or psychological theory of the disciples' belief that their leader was in some sense still alive and present with them.

My first difficulty is that this runs counter to elements in the New Testament which seem to survive rigorous critical analysis and 'demythologizing'; I have particularly in mind the disciples' *surprise,* their experience of being unexpectedly *accosted* by the risen Lord: neither the evangelists nor their sources had any motive for introducing this element, which is also found in Paul's own references to his experience of the risen Christ. Secondly, any naturalistic explanation of the rise of the Easter faith raises the further question why such a belief should have arisen once, and only once, in all recorded history. I believe that any modern Christology must be very wary of asserting claims to

[1]On being-ful reality: ontology is the study of being.

uniqueness, and I shall decline to affirm traditional uniqueness-claims as to the nature of God's indwelling in the person of Jesus. But the birth and continuance of the resurrection-faith is a historical phenomenon so strikingly unique as to query the adequacy of any naturalistic explanation, and to suggest that that faith includes what I have called an ontological element and was, and is, a *response* to a unique act and presence of God.

In thus presenting a theistic interpretation of Jesus and his resurrection, insisting upon an ontological element where others see only myth, I will be held by some to have abandoned all claim to offer proposals for a *modern* Christology. If in this connexion modern be synonymous with atheistic, and if the scope of Christology includes the resurrection-faith, then—for the reasons just given—I have no proposals to offer.

I continue this lecture because I do not accept—and I sincerely hope that many of you would not accept—so narrow an interpretation of the adjective 'modern' in this connexion. I regard a Christology as modern if it uses every relevant insight of modern knowledge to differentiate the historical element in its interpretation of the event Jesus Christ from the mythological, and remembers that the actual event comprises only history and the ontological reality of God's presence and action within that history—whilst the mythology expresses that reality in ways which may indeed convey deep truth, yet have in themselves the status not of ontological reality but of poetry. In saying this I assume that the starting-point for such a Christology will be, not the historic creeds and formularies of later centuries, but the attempts of the New Testament writers both to describe and to interpret the life, death, and resurrection of Jesus.

Our starting point is the New Testament, but this itself needs to be interpreted if it is to point us, as I believe it can, to the person of Jesus and the initial response first to him and later to his resurrection. These form the datum; the later insights, including the proclamation or *kerygma* in the New Testament itself, are highly significant for Christology, but must be assessed in relation to our attempts to reconstruct that datum. In the words of Ernst Fuchs: 'Formerly we interpreted the historical Jesus with the help of the kerygma. Today we interpret the kerygma with the help of the historical Jesus.'[2]

I must here quickly re-tread ground covered in previous lectures. I take the view that the principles of form criticism have been established beyond question, but that some of the more negative conclusions draw from them are unjustified. Detailed comparative analysis of individual sections or pericopae in the synoptic gospels has confirmed the

---

[2]From the foreword to his collected essays, which is unfortunately omitted from the English edition.

hypothesis that during the lengthy period before the writing of our earliest gospel individual sayings and incidents in Jesus' ministry were —note the verb—*used*: as they were worked over and adapted, their context and wording may have been altered beyond recall. This analysis shows all the gospels to be deeply theological interpretations of Jesus. They are all so impregnated with belief in Jesus as Messiah, and as eschatological and pre-existent Son of Man, that it seems probable that these beliefs arose early in the pre-New Testament period. Indeed the evangelists and their source-material are alike so suffused with this post-Easter faith as to make impossible any attempt to construct either a biography of Jesus or a 'definitive edition' of his teaching.

The methods of form criticism help us to pick out aspects of the gospel accounts of Jesus' conduct and teaching which are in sharp contrast to the current practice and teaching of his day, and which it would not have been in the earliest church's interest to introduce into the material: for example, Jesus' attitude to women, his table-fellowship with 'tax collectors and sinners', his refusal of the epithet 'good', and Mark's comment—altered by Matthew—that in Nazareth 'he *could* do no mighty work'. That the gospel narratives do include actual historical memories is most clearly seen in their treatment of the disciples. Consider first the repeated references, particularly in Mark, to their lack of understanding. Of course the cynic can say that in attributing prodigious miracles and claims to the earthly Jesus, Mark is forced to exaggerate the disciples' failure to understand: to insert the messianic secret in order to compensate for unhistorical messianic claims. (He could add that the disciples' lack of understanding is most pronounced in the Fourth Gospel, where Jesus is portrayed as virtually identifying himself with the divine 'I AM.') But it would have been just as easy—indeed more likely, if the evangelists and their sources paid no regard to historicity —to describe Jesus' immediate entourage as being swept along on this flood-tide of claims to, and acts of, divine authority, whilst emphasizing the lack of understanding of everyone else. There was no need to emphasize the *disciples'* failure to understand, nor their surprise at the resurrection, nor to record that one of the twelve betrayed Jesus, that they all fled at his arrest, and that Peter denied him to a servant-girl.

Such honest reporting shows that the synoptic evangelists and their sources did attach some value to history. This makes it the more significant that there is no hesitation in attributing to the lips of Jesus sayings that can only belong historically to the post-resurrection period. I see this as evidence that 'the early Church absolutely and completely identified the risen Lord of her experience with the earthly Jesus of Nazareth.'[3]

The tentative nature of the findings of form criticism has already

[3]N. Perrin, *Rediscovering the Teaching of Jesus*, 15.

been stressed. But these findings are valuable in precisely those areas which most concern us if we seek the *same* sort of understanding of the historical Jesus as we have come to have of man in general—an understanding or image succinctly expressed in Dr. Dillistone's lecture: 'This image is a "dynamic, temporal one that sees man as first of all an agent, a self," who stands self-revealed only in the midst of the density of temporal decisions.'

We are sometimes told by New Testament scholars that we are in no position to enter into—let alone to psychoanalyse—the mind of Jesus in order to establish the primary motivation for certain decisions or sayings, in particular the decision to go to Jerusalem at Passover-time which led to his death.[4] I am myself uncertain how sharply one can differentiate between a person's decisions and the motivation that lies behind them. In any case this does not affect the point I wish to make as to the application of Dr. Dillistone's words to Jesus. For even if analysis of the individual pericopae in the gospels does not reveal the primary motivation of Jesus, such analysis does reveal his decisions, some at least of the competing pressures between which these decisions were made, and the still greater pressures they engendered. We find a striking unity between Jesus' decisions and actions and his teaching. He not only practised what he preached but also preached or proclaimed his own practice: *'Jesus' conduct* was itself the real framework of his proclamation.'[5]

I would agree with Fuchs and others that it was Jesus' conduct, thus closely reinforced by his proclamation, that led the Jewish leaders to destroy him. Jesus both proclaimed God's love and forgiveness and lived this out in his repeated table-fellowship with 'tax collectors and sinners,' Jews who were regarded as having 'made themselves as Gentiles.' This must have been bitterly resented, as the gospels record. Is it fanciful to see a close parallel between this resentment and that of the prodigal son's elder brother, as also of the labourers who had borne the burden and heat of the day in the vineyard? Both parables proclaim that God loves and forgives all men, including the idler and the waster who becomes a swineherd, and precisely in thus proclaiming God's universal love they also justify Jesus' own conduct, grounding this in the very nature of the love of God. Here indeed is cause for the hierarchy to take strong offence: here also, as yet only by implication, is deep ground for the later belief that 'God was in Christ.' 'There is a tremendous personal claim involved in the fact that Jesus answered an attack upon his conduct with a parable concerned with what *God* does![6] Some find a similar claim in his characteristic *opening* 'Amen, I say unto you.'

[4]See Bultmann's recent essay in *The Historical Jesus and the Kerygmatic Christ*, eds. C. E. Braaten and R. A. Harrisville, (New York: Harper and Row, 1964).
[5]E. Fuchs, *Studies of the Historical Jesus*, 21.
[6]E. Linnemann, *Parables of Jesus*, 87.

In analysing the gospel accounts of Jesus' teaching, form criticism attributes greatest reliability to those elements that contrast with the outlooks of both Judaism on the one hand and the early church on the other. It must suffice to mention one complex of such elements, all closely inter-related. The Kingdom (or Reign) of God, Jesus' 'comprehensive term for the blessing of salvation,' is an eschatological concept which shows that 'Jesus stands in the historical context of Jewish expectations about the end of the world and God's new future'[7]—yet his teaching also contrasts with that context. He dispenses with the customary apocalyptic 'signs of the end' (found only in secondary material). The Kingdom of God—the phrase itself is distinctive, being rare in the contemporary literature—is 'at hand,' quietly and unobtrusively breaking through in the everyday situations of life. Jesus' emphasis is not on nations or groups (as in the Old Testament prophets), but on the *individual* as confronted *in and through his daily life* by God's demand upon him as summed up in the two commands 'love God' and 'love your neighbour as yourself.'

This direct relating of God to everyday situations is epitomized by the way Jesus addresses God, not as 'O Lord God, Creator of the Universe,' but simply as 'Abba,' 'Daddy.' The relating of *God to* particular situations is also seen in Jesus' words of healing and exorcism: 'Your sins are forgiven'; 'Your faith has saved you.' In all of this Jesus stands in sharp contrast to his contemporaries.

In what has been so briefly outlined we find Jesus *proclaiming* the concern and love and forgiveness of God and *living out* that same concern and love and forgiveness amongst those he met, and those he went out of his way to meet. As Jesus called men to 'radical obedience,' so he lived out that obedience, 'intensifying his obedience to the call of God as every successive challenge in life makes its impact upon him.'[8] To Dr. Dillistone's description of the historical Jesus intensifying his obedience to God's call must be added St. John's 'the Word became flesh and tabernacled among us'. Personification of the *Logos* belongs not to history but to mythology: the immense significance of this way of expressing that power of God which men sensed in Jesus—even if they sensed it only dimly before his death and resurrection—is perhaps brought home to our modern minds by Norman Pittenger's fine paraphrase 'the Word or *Logos* or Self-Expressive Activity of God.'[9]

We have now reached a point at which, in my view, the 'philosophy of process' of Alfred North Whitehead and others has something of value to contribute: I therefore make an apparent digression in order to

[7]R. Bultmann, *Theology of the New Testament*, Vol. I, 4.
[8]From an earlier paper in *Christ for Us Today*, 96.
[9]*The Word Incarnate*, 187.

give the briefest outline of that philosophy. Whitehead is best known in English academic circles for his work with Bertrand Russell in the field of mathematical logic. For the nonspecialist, the most prominent feature of Whitehead's philosophical writings—like those of Teilhard de Chardin—is their fundamentally evolutionary viewpoint. But Whitehead was a mathematician, not a biologist: he was acutely aware of the two great discoveries in physics made while he was teaching mathematics, the theories of relativity and the quantum. Whitehead was also greatly concerned with aesthetics. As his mind turned increasingly to philosophy, the physicist in him sought to understand the whole of reality and not only man, whilst the aesthete in him interpreted all reality by extrapolation from human experience, thus finding aesthetic value in all actuality.

I here make two comments: that the resulting interpretation of the nature of the world is far easier to reject than to make one's own; and that it is peculiarly vulnerable to attack by linguistic-analysis philosophy. (This because it extrapolates the usage of such terms as 'feeling' and 'mind' even into the inorganic realm.) Both comments apply equally to Christian theology, which also stretches the meanings of words.

Charles Hartshorne resembles Whitehead in having had the privilege, or the misfortune, to be the son of an Anglican clergyman. He has certainly had the misfortune of being too often labelled the 'leading exponent of Whitehead,' whereas in fact Hartshorne is a significant philosopher-theologian who evolved his own principal positions prior to his contact with Whitehead. Hartshorne's main importance for Christian theology is his application of modern logic to the doctrine of God. The discipline of rigorously logical thinking has proved its value in many philosophical fields and should be more used—less feared, perhaps—in Christian theology. Highly significant for Christology are these two quotations from Hartshorne's The Divine Relativity.[10] In the first he refuses to allow 'paradox' to cover up illogicality: 'A theological paradox, it appears, is what a contradiction becomes when it is about God rather than something else. . . .' In the second he applies this to the relation between God's power and our human decisions: 'For God to do what I do when I decide my own act, determine my own concrete being, is mere nonsense, words without meaning. It is not my act if anyone else decides or performs it.'

Throughout this lecture I have assumed that whatever else we may believe about Jesus we accept that he was, inwardly as well as outwardly, a man: I need not spend time showing that this assumption is to be found in every part of the New Testament. Hartshorne's statement

[10]Pp. 1, 134.

about human acts and decisions applies, therefore, to Jesus: we must not say that *his* acts and decisions were 'also'—still less, that they were 'really'—*God's*. If we feel that the concept of Jesus intensifying his obedience to God's call does not adequately express the divinity of Jesus, then we must seek to express this in ways that neither compromise his humanity nor rely upon contralogical paradox.

One such way is suggested by Whitehead's philosophy of nature and in particular its central feature, which he calls 'the theory of prehensions.' Whitehead sees all actuality in terms not of substance but of process, not of being but of becoming. The process *is* the reality: every entity *is* the process of growing together into a unity of its 'prehensions' or 'impressions' of everything in its environment. But 'impression' is primarily a passive term, and therefore not a good paraphrase for 'prehension': 'grasping at' is better.[11] A novel entity 'becomes' by grasping at the influences surrounding it: in grasping at each such influence it incorporates something of its environment into itself, so that the novel entity *is* the growing together into a unity of all its graspings at the influences comprising its environment. Thus a viewer's impression of a painting is the growing together into a single unified experience of his impressions of all its elements, impressions which he does not passively receive like incoming telephone calls, but grasps at in his own distinctive manner.

As has been said, Whitehead interprets *all* actuality by extrapolation from human experience, and is thereby peculiarly vulnerable to linguistic criticism. Whilst some of this criticism must be accepted, I myself find aspects of this extrapolation from experience both meaningful and valuable. But it is precisely human experience and its relation to God—the human experience of the historical Jesus and the Easter experience of his disciples—with which we are here concerned; we need not consider this extrapolation and the criticisms of it, except to note that Whitehead sees his theory of 'prehensions' as also applying to God, emphasizing that 'God is not to be treated as an exception to all metaphysical principles. . . . He is their chief exemplification.'[12]

In what follows, the person and resurrection of Jesus Christ are treated *not* as exceptions to, but as the chief exemplifications of, metaphysical principles. The principle applicable to the person, the divinity, of Jesus is that of immanence: *incarnation*; '*in* him all the fullness of God was pleased to dwell.' Whitehead's theory of 'prehensions' here offers a significant contribution: it attempts to describe the manner in which one entity is actually, not just metaphorically, immanent in an-

----

[11] I prefer 'grasping at' to Whitehead's own usage of 'feeling' as an alternative to 'prehension.'

[12] *PR* 521.

other—actually immanent in that it contributes to and is constituent in the other's subjectivity. For Whitehead there *is* actual immanence, yet each entity, each experience, retains its own subjectivity. He saw experience—and therefore everything—as divisible, not continuous: drops of experience, like the frames of a cinematograph film. (There is a clear parallel here with the quantum theory, the discovery that radiant or electromagnetic energy consists of minute, discrete pulses or *quanta* of energy.) Each drop of experience enjoys its own subjectivity during its brief 'process,' the growing together of its constituent 'prehensions.' Only thereafter, when it has 'perished' as a subject, moved away from in front of the lens, is it available as an object to be grasped at by other subjects. Thus when a new subject, a new moment of experience, 'A,' grasps at an object 'B' (itself, so to speak, an ex-subject, a moment of experience that has perished), what happens is that A makes its own an element or 'feeling' which formerly belonged to the subjectivity of B, wherein it was perhaps an insignificant, perhaps a decisive, element. Thus a part of B's moment of experience becomes objectively immanent in the experience of A.

This is so crucial to one of my Christological proposals that I venture the personal illustration of my relationship with my wife. In common parlance, in so far as I am a good husband I enter into her joys and sorrows—as she certainly enters into mine. To take an instance that is perhaps unimportant, and certainly infrequent, consider my wife's first wearing of a new dress. As I 'prehend' her evident enjoyment of this I enter into her joy—or rather, I make something of her joy my own. At that moment my wife's enjoyment is central to her experience, to her *self,* and in so far as I make this my own I make an element of her—strictly, of the 'she' of a moment ago, since my senses are not instantaneous—to become an element constitutive of me. Thus she becomes partially and objectively immanent in me. The more *sympatique* I am, the more vivid, and accurate, will be my impression of her enjoyment, making her—her experience—more fully immanent in me.

In general, the extent to which the experience of one person, A, enters into that of a new subject, B, depends both upon how *sympatique* B is to A and how compatible A is to B. Thus the belief that God's self-expressive activity was supremely present in the person and the decisions of the historical Jesus implies the belief that Jesus was supremely *sympatique* to God, and that God is supremely compatible to Jesus.

We are for the moment still concerned with the ministry of Jesus: we turn shortly to his resurrection. It may be that during Jesus' ministry his disciples did *not* fully or consciously think of him as divine, as Son or Servant of God, as Son of Man, or as Messiah: it may also be that Jesus did not explicitly see himself in any of these terms. Indeed there are a small number of very significant passages in the New Testament which depict Jesus as completely human up to his death, at or after which God raised him to superhuman dignity: 'descended from David according to the flesh and designated Son of God in power . . . by his resurrection from the dead.'[13]

I shall suggest that the resurrection-faith may have begun as the *God-given* awareness, both individual and corporate, that in some intensely significant sense Jesus was still alive and present with his disciples. I shall emphasize this awareness as God-given, not self-generated: but in our present experience God works in and through our thoughts and aspirations—inspiring new ideas, certainly, but building these upon the foundations of previous ideas, not out of a vacuum. It therefore seems more probable, to say the least, that the disciples' later insights arose out of their *earlier* feeling—perhaps at the time only half-formed and largely subconscious—that in being with Jesus they were in some extremely special sense in the very presence of God's love and power.

The belief that 'in Christ God was reconciling the world to himself' belongs to mythology: however significant they may be, sin and reconciliation are mythological terms. The four opening words perhaps should not be separated from the rest of Paul's sentence, but if they are so separated the phrase 'God was in Christ,' still more 'God was in the historical Jesus,' is *not* a mythological statement: it corresponds to what I earlier called ontological reality. The further statement that Jesus' disciples were at least dimly aware of that reality *during his ministry* belongs, as I have just suggested, to history—as does the fact that Jesus was fully human.

Christian theology has always sought to affirm these three statements: process philosophy offers a framework within which they can be affirmed without either impairing their true status or resorting to paradox. God's indwelling in Jesus is the chief exemplification of this philosophy's principle of immanence: as Jesus intensified his obedience to the call of God so, without impairing Jesus' humanity and human freedom, God was supremely, yet objectively, immanent in Jesus. Thus the two 'natures' of Jesus Christ are affirmed, whilst Jesus remains—as logic insists—the one subject of his own decisions: Jesus the subject, yet God objectively present in such high degree that Jesus' decisions and actions supremely reveal, through the self of the historical Jesus, the 'Self-Expressive Activity of God.'

What has just been said may be regarded as true, but inadequate: inadequate firstly in failing sufficiently to affirm the *priority* of God's will and act in the whole event Jesus Christ, and secondly in failing to maintain the *uniqueness* of Jesus. These may well be two ways of saying the same thing, but it is convenient to consider them separately.

[13]Romans 1.3, 4 (RSV).

The divine priority in the Incarnation is symbolized both by the Annunciation, God's messenger announcing his plan in advance, and by the virgin birth—more precisely, the virginal conception—of Jesus; also by the concept of the pre-existence of Christ, whether as *Logos* or Son of Man.

Even if he regards all of these as mythological, the Christian will find deep value in them and will wish to affirm them just as far as he can: the limiting factor is that nothing must impair our accompanying belief in the manhood of Jesus. One aspect of the Annunciation narrative is significant here: it depicts God's messenger, and therefore God's purpose, waiting upon Mary's consent: 'Be it unto me according to thy word,' God's will indeed has priority, but seeks to elicit Mary's consent rather than override her human freedom.[14]

A facet not yet mentioned of Whitehead's philosophy of process makes the same point. If each bud of experience *is* a growing together of its constituent elements, its own subjectivity arising with the process and not the precursor of it, then the process needs an initial aim or purpose, which must be *given* to it. Whitehead sees God as giving this 'initial aim.' Thus we are free in each moment of experience either to conform to that initial aim or—within the limits of our freedom—to diverge from it. Once again, God's will has priority, but seeks to elicit our co-operation.

If one follows Whitehead in extrapolating from human experience, one can find in this interpretation of the divine priority a doctrine of creation that is compatible with biological evolution: in the concept of God supplying a 'lure' to evolution, 'process' thinking approximates to that of Teilhard de Chardin.

But we are here concerned to apply this concept of the priority of God's will and purpose, which however waits upon—and may be thwarted by—human free will, to the whole event Jesus Christ, including its Old Testament background. I do not claim that God determined the course of that event in every detail: God did not foreordain the worship of the golden calf. But I do see the divine priority, God's prevenient guidance, in the event as a whole—the history of Old Testament Israel, the birth, ministry, death and resurrection of Jesus, and the coming into being of his church—and in its effect, which we variously describe as the supreme revelation of God's love, the redemption of the world, the coming into being of the church.[15] Indeed it is precisely God's prevenient guidance that makes of this entire historical sequence, including its climax in Jesus, one single event, producing one single effect. I here quote from John Knox:

[14] I owe this insight to Dr. Norman Pittenger.
[15] The coming into being of the church can be regarded either as the effect or as part of the event. See John Knox, *The Church and the Reality of Christ*, 71, 121–129.

The event was a whole event and its effect was a whole effect. We cannot break the event into parts and attribute the whole effect to one part, nor can we ascribe any particular part of the effect to any particular part of the event. Both event and effect are one and indivisible and . . . belong indissolubly together.[16]

We now turn to the charge of having failed to maintain the uniqueness of Jesus. Those who feel strong *religious* reasons for affirming this uniqueness may not appreciate that there are others, and other Christians, for whom claims to uniqueness are an inevitable barrier to relevance. Proclaimed as the chief exemplification of the potentiality of human life lived in utter obedience to God, the life and resurrection of Jesus could become meaningful for some who find them utterly irrelevant when proclaimed as unique acts of God.

Thus there are also strong *religious* reasons for not exaggerating the difference between Jesus and the rest of mankind: this is best avoided by not isolating Jesus from his historical context. I prefer to avoid the word 'unique,' with its several shades of meaning, but if it is to be used I wish to affirm the uniqueness of the whole event Jesus Christ, the whole Judaeo-Christian 'salvation-history,' as the supreme revelation and enactment of God's redeeming love: a unique event, with a unique effect. (To affirm this is not to deny that God also both acts and reveals himself in other ways and in other religions.) Within this whole unique event the life, death and resurrection of Jesus occupy a uniquely central, indeed pivotal, position. In his historical context Jesus is thus doubly 'unique.'

Claims for the uniqueness of Jesus often take two forms not covered by the above. God's presence and indwelling in Jesus is said to differ not only in degree but in kind from his indwelling in the greatest of his saints, or in us. I can find no way of accepting this claim that does not impair, indeed deny, Jesus' manhood. If religion has any meaning, a man's conscious and unconscious relationship with God is a vital aspect of his *self*. If this aspect differed in kind in the case of Jesus from every other member of the species man, then *in the present state of our knowledge* it would seem impossible rightly to describe Jesus as a man.[17] It may be the case that most Christians (and most Christian theologians) in most centuries *have* accepted this claim: but most have not shared either our modern sensitivity to the difference between history and mythology or our concern for the principles of logic. I emphasize the phrase 'in the present state of our knowledge,' because it may well be that in the future new insights will enable us to affirm this claim: we

---

[16]*The Death of Christ*, 159.

[17]This 'difference in kind' is also expressed by saying that Jesus is 'sinless' or 'perfect' man. Sin and sinlessness are mythological terms. I agree with John Knox that 'a perfect historical event is a contradiction in terms.'

should never assume that what now seems impossible will always be so. But at this present time I cannot affirm a difference in kind between Jesus and other men; indeed I find important religious reasons for wishing to deny this.

The Christology of this lecture may also be attacked on the ground that it sees every constituent of the event Jesus Christ as *contingent*: Jesus' obedience to God is a contingent concept, whereas it may be claimed that God's redemption of the world in Christ is not contingent but foreordained. My reply is as before: if Jesus' obedience was not contingent, it was not human obedience. I would add that I see no need for this claim. That Napoleon was defeated at Waterloo is a contingent fact, and also true. Where religious truth is found enacted within history it cannot avoid contingency, and loses nothing thereby. As we now consider Jesus' resurrection, I would just add that there is contingency in the disciples' response to this.

As has often been pointed out, the resurrection narratives in the gospels—like the infancy narratives—have the characteristics of myth, while the tradition in Luke and John that the first resurrection appearances were in Jerusalem cannot satisfactorily be combined with the Galilee tradition of Mark and Matthew. Furthermore, neither tradition agrees at all readily with Paul's list of appearances in I Corinthians 15. Neither there nor elsewhere does Paul refer to the empty tomb, and his emphatic 'flesh and blood cannot inherit the kingdom of God' certainly suggests that when Paul wrote First Corinthians he did not know of the empty tomb tradition. In any case the main emphasis in the New Testament as a whole, and even in Matthew and Luke, is not on the empty tomb but on the *appearances* of the risen Lord, again present with his disciples and continuing to instruct them. This ties in with a point made near the beginning of this lecture—the extent to which the early church identified the risen Lord with the historical Jesus.

It seems that the earliest preaching of the resurrection made no attempt to describe the appearances, but rather proclaimed the *fact* of the resurrection as God's reversal of the disgrace of crucifixion: 'the death of Jesus is interpreted as Israel's No to the proclamation of Jesus and the resurrection as God's Yes, his validation of Jesus' message.'[18] This No-Yes pattern is found in the Marcan passion predictions, whose detailed form is almost certainly editorial; in Philippians 2, where Paul may be quoting a very early Christian hymn; and in Peter's speeches or sermons in Acts. Whilst these speeches are presumably Lukan compositions, many scholars believe that they

[18]R. H. Fuller, *The New Testament in Current Study*, 152.

include traces of the earliest Easter proclamation, preserved because they were remembered as being apostolic, and in spite of their 'adoptionist' tone: that God has raised his *pais* (child) Jesus; that God has *made* him both Lord and Christ.

Thus Paul begins I Corinthians 15 with a list of resurrection appearances, each limited to the bare verb 'he appeared to.' By this repetition Paul places his own resurrection experience on a par with that of the original disciples. Neither his own brief references nor the more detailed, but secondary, accounts of Paul's conversion in Acts suggests a publicly visible appearance of the risen Christ. Thus the quest of the historical Easter, in the sense of the *initial* nature of the disciples' Easter faith, suggests that this began with the conviction 'that Jesus was somehow alive among them and that, if this was so, God had indeed acted and had raised him and exalted him.'[19]

All this would seem to imply that—I quote from Professor Lampe's recent essay[20]—'the Easter appearances were not dissimilar in kind from other phenomena in the history of religious experience.' However, as Dr. Lampe says in the same paragraph, 'this does not imply that these men were not confronted with the Lord's presence as an eternal reality.' It is precisely this *external reality* of the Lord's presence which I wish to affirm for the first disciples, for Paul, and for ourselves.

Professor Lampe draws a parallel between the disciples' Easter experience and Isaiah's vision in the Temple. There is, however, a crucial difference. Isaiah was confronted by, and in his vision 'saw' God. But the Christian experience of the risen Lord is of being confronted by an external reality that is both of God (and not simply from God), yet also *distinct* from God the Father: as he cries 'my Lord and my God,' the Christian feels—as all the New Testament writers emphasize—that the living presence which confronts him is that of Jesus. This distinctively Christian experience differs from Isaiah's vision of God; from Mary's vision of Gabriel the messenger from God; and from that other Christian experience of being confronted by St. Mary or one of the saints.

If one accepts that the disciples were confronted by the Lord's presence as an external reality, the question remains whether the risen Jesus was—and is—encountered as an individual distinct from God, and is therefore to be thought of as living on with his own subjectivity. The resurrection narratives in the gospels clearly imply *encounter* with Jesus, who both 'speaks' to the disciples—perhaps

---

[19]Robert M. Grant, *The Early Christian Doctrine of God*, 43.
[20]In G. W. H. Lampe and D. M. MacKinnon, *The Resurrection*, 27–60.

through visionary experience—and also responds to their response to him. The same is probably implied in I Corinthians 15. But whilst every chapter of the epistles is suffused and inspired by the resurrection-faith, few others—if any—use actual encounter-language. I cannot avoid the conclusion that by the time they were written—and the Pauline epistles are the earliest of the New Testament writings— Christians no longer thought in that way of their present experience of the risen Jesus; but reserved such language for the initial Easter period (extended by Paul to include his own formative experience). Indeed the ascension narratives imply such a distinction between initial and subsequent resurrection-experience.

I cannot survey Christians' experience of the risen Christ down the centuries, nor discuss its relationship to their other beliefs. In our own day, many Christians do indeed speak of their awareness of the living presence of Jesus in terms that imply encounter; but it by no means follows that, if asked to choose their words carefully, they would describe their experience of the risen Jesus as more like an encounter with another human being than like our encounter in prayer with God. Both I myself and most Christians of my own limited acquaintance would, I think, choose the second as being the closer parallel. Consider, for example, the difference between entering the Lady Chapel of a church to kneel for ten minutes in prayer before the reserved sacrament, and calling at a friend's house for a ten-minute conversation. There are a number of Christians for whom the former is often the deeper and more vivid experience. But many of these would regard their experience in the Lady Chapel as a vivid form of *prayer,* in which they may have prayed to Jesus, but about which they would *not* employ the encounter-language that we use to describe a conversation, and which Luke used of the walk to Emmaus. They would, I suggest, be content to describe their experience as one of being 'confronted with the Lord's presence as an external reality,' a reality distinct from, yet part of, the reality of God.

Process philosophy offers a framework within which one can affirm precisely this. It sees experience as consisting of discrete 'buds,' each of which enjoys its own subjectivity during its brief growing together into a unity; it then perishes as a subject, 'living on' *only* in so far as its influence is felt by other moments of experience which make it ingredient—'objectively immanent'—in themselves.

God is the chief exemplification of both aspects of this principle of immanence. We have so far considered only one aspect in this connexion: that the more we open ourselves to God and intensify our obedience to his call, the more God becomes objectively immanent in us, and supremely so in Jesus. But God also 'prehends' or grasps at us—at everything—in each moment of our experience. The more our thoughts and actions are compatible with God's loving will and purpose, the more fully he will incorporate them as objectively immanent in one aspect of his nature.[21] We earlier emphasized the divine priority in the whole event Jesus Christ: we also thought of Jesus intensifying his obedience to the call of God in each situation that confronted him. These alike suggest that the thoughts, actions, and experiences comprising Jesus' life and person will have been supremely compatible with God's loving purpose, with which ours are only sometimes compatible; and that they will have been supremely incorporated by God into himself.

We can now attempt to interpret both the similarity and the difference between Isaiah's vision in the temple and the Christian's awareness of his risen Lord. Both experience the external reality of God,[22] but in this experience the Christian also meets with the risen Christ, the total action of the life and ministry and death of Jesus, which has been raised or 'prehended' into the Godhead, into that external reality which confronts us in prayer and sacrament and accompanies and sustains us throughout our lives. Process philosophy envisages God 'prehending' aspects of everything—more precisely, of everything not utterly alien to his will—and making these ingredient in himself. But it is God in relationship to us and our cultural heritage of whom we are made aware in religious experience. God 'prehends' aspects of everything into himself, but our awareness lacks his universality: it has often been remarked that it is usually Roman Catholics who have visions of the Blessed Virgin Mary. Similarly, both now and in the initial Easter period, it is those within the community of his followers, and perhaps some on its fringes, who experience the presence of Christ. And just as those who had known and accompanied Jesus identified the risen Lord with their master and friend, so we—less confidently, perhaps—identify the risen Christ whose presence we experience with the Jesus whom we meet through the gospels. And if modern criticism enables us to get a little way behind the Christ of the New Testament proclamation towards the historical Jesus, then the identification we make will the more nearly resemble that made by the first disciples.

What has been said may be criticized as failing to maintain the

[21]It is a fundamental tenet of this philosophy that God's nature has two inseparable aspects distinguishable only for purposes of thought: an absolute or 'primordial' aspect, absolutely unchanging and unaffected by the world; and a related or 'consequent' aspect, which is affected by the world. (See the great final chapter of Whitehead's *Process and Reality* or, for a brief summary, my article on Whitehead in *Theology*, April 1965.)

[22]I here assume without discussion the meaningfulness of 'the external reality of God.' We are concerned with the *Christological implications* of the New Testament witness to the Resurrection, and of our own sense of Christ's presence. That *God* is experienced as external reality is, to my mind, both the *theological* implication of this and also its presupposition.

uniqueness of the resurrection of Christ; this can be answered in much the same way as the parallel criticism in relation to the person of Christ. But two further criticisms of this interpretation of the resurrection did not apply in the earlier case. It may be said that to speak of Jesus' thoughts, actions, and individual experiences being raised into God is not the same as to speak of *Jesus* being so raised. But 'nothing is more personal about a man than his concrete experiences':[23] inasmuch as Jesus lived a life of 'perfect' or 'supreme' obedience to God, so his experiences will have been wholly or supremely raised into the Godhead.[24]

This leads into the deeper criticism that in this interpretation the risen Christ is not *alive,* whereas the coming into being of the Easter faith was earlier described as 'the disciples' experience that Jesus was somehow alive among them.' In one sense this criticism is indeed valid, for in this interpretation of his resurrection it is not Jesus but *God* who is the subject, God having raised the concrete experiences of Jesus into 'objective immortality' in himself. These 'live,' objectively, in God analogously to the manner in which my wife's joys and sorrows 'live,' objectively, in me. But of course, my wife also lives subjectively. And the critic may well ask whether what I have said does or does not affirm that the risen Jesus also lives subjectively. This requires a careful answer.

The interpretation I have proposed sees the resurrection of Jesus as the supreme instance, the 'chief exemplification,' of its general concept of resurrection as 'objective immortality.' In these terms, the proposition that Jesus lives on subjectively is the supreme instance of some more general proposition as to individual survival after death: to reach a decision as to this supreme instance one would first have to investigate the general concept of resurrection, which lies beyond our present task.[25] It must here suffice to answer that these proposals neither affirm nor deny the doctrine that both Jesus and the 'souls of the righteous' live on subjectively. Indeed I commend them for your consideration largely because they offer a meaningful interpretation of the resurrection of Jesus, and of ourselves, *which does not depend upon that doctrine.*

By contrast, Paul makes the resurrection of Christ *dependent* upon a general concept of resurrection: 'For if the dead are not raised, then Christ has not been raised.'[26] Clearly, some members of the Corinthian church had rejected the Pharisaic doctrine of res-

---

[23]C. Hartshorne and W. L. Reese, *Philosophers Speak of God,* 285.
[24]See footnote 17, above.
[25]See my *The Living God and the Modern World,* 108–141.
[26]I Cor. 15.16. (See also v. 13, and the chapter as a whole.)

urrection (or its Greek equivalent)—a doctrine that was accepted by Jesus, by Paul, and by the evangelists. Whilst this doctrine often forms perhaps the most cherished item of belief, I believe that there are many today, both inside and outside the churches, who follow the Corinthians in rejecting any such doctrine. In my own ministry I have talked with a number of thoughtful people—mainly young people—who accept belief in God as giving meaning and joy and hope to *this* life but reject, or are at best highly doubtful about, any concept of personal resurrection or immortality. Similarly, when using the Psalter, I am frequently struck by the note of *joy* and *hope* in psalms that rank high among the greatest religious poetry ever written, although their authors—in common with most of the Old Testament —quite clearly did not believe in any concept of individual resurrection.

This matter is far too important to be judged by comparing numbers for or against—whether of ancients or of moderns. But our modern, indeed very recent, understanding of the psychosomatic unity comprising a person, and of the deep influence of environmental factors upon personality, raises in acute form the question whether our present personality *can* be raised individually and clothed upon with a resurrection-body in a resurrection-environment. I ask myself whether it may not be *this* concept, and not the 'death' of God, that God himself is gently but firmly leading us to think out afresh. All I can do here is to suggest that there is a place today for a general concept of resurrection that sees permanent meaning and value in our lives without *depending upon* belief in individual life after death.

But my proposals as regards resurrection are neither wholly nor mainly negative. This interpretation of the resurrection of Jesus rests upon a general concept of resurrection as 'objective immortality' that I believe to be no mere metaphor. The aspect of process philosophy to which I have most particularly drawn your attention is its concept of immanence, whereby it affirms an *actual* sense in which one entity is immanent in another; a sense in which the experiences of one individual 'live on' in those of another, the subjectivity of these experiences passing from the former to the latter. We applied this to the case of God's indwelling in—God 'living in'—Jesus, seeing this as the supreme instance, the 'chief exemplification,' of his universal indwelling in his creatures. Process philosophy affirms that there is a *mutual* relationship between God and the world in that each affects, and is affected by, the other: its concept of immanence applies, therefore, to our indwelling in God as well as to God's indwelling in us; thus it is as meaningful to speak of Jesus raised into God and 'living on' in God as it is to speak of God 'prehended' into and indwelling in—'living' in—Jesus. The first is the supreme instance of resurrection, the second the supreme instance of incarnation.

The difference between the two is that the living God becomes incarnate afresh in each moment of the life of Jesus (or of ourselves), whereas the experiences of Jesus 'prehended' by God into himself —Jesus' resurrection and ascension—form a finite sequence that terminated on Calvary. This sequence lives on in God, continually re-created afresh in God's living memory and re-presented to Christ's followers as they turn to God in prayer and sacrament. But it is the sequence as a whole that is re-presented; no new subjective experiences are added—or if they are, that is another story. That is why *this interpretation* of Jesus' resurrection cannot take literally the encounter-language of the gospel narratives, but stands much closer to the epistles, and to much of our own experience of our risen Lord.

By way of illustration I take two key verses from Luke's beautiful narrative of the walk to Emmaus: 'And beginning with Moses and all the prophets, he interpreted to them in all the scriptures the things concerning himself.' 'Then they told what had happened on the road, and how he was known to them in the breaking of the bread.'[27] These symbolize two ways in which we are especially conscious of the presence of the risen Christ. As we seek prayerfully to interpret the gospels, either publicly or alone, we feel his living presence, objectively immortal in God and revealed to us as we search the scriptures. Some of us have this experience more vividly when we meet together for the breaking of the bread, as in our moving and memorable evening communion just now. As we turned in prayer to God, as we focussed our thoughts upon that Last Supper which so perfectly sums up Jesus' life of love and his obedience into death, as we remembered and re-presented his words and actions, so we sensed his presence with us—not the presence of another subject wholly distinct from God and from ourselves, but rather the living presence of his words and actions and the love that they convey; the risen and ascended Lord Jesus, objectively immortal in God, and revealed to us, in and through the whole action of the Eucharist, as of God and in God, yet also distinct from God.

The detailed framework of Whitehead's philosophy is far less known than his aphorisms, for example: 'Christianity has alway been a religion seeking a metaphysic'[28]—with the implication that it never rests in any one metaphysic, or philosophy. Whilst our understanding of Christ can be deepened through insights of process philosophy,

[27]Luke 24.27, 35.
[28]*Religion in the Making*, 50.

Christology can never rest in this philosophy, any more than in that accepted by the early Fathers. In summing up, therefore, I would remind you of those parts of this lecture which do not rest upon process philosophy. The primary raw material of Christology is the New Testament documents. To study these I used the methods of form criticism. To interpret the results of that study I relied first upon logic. Hartshorne's criticism of paradox, and Whitehead's insistence that God is not an exception to all metaphysical principles but their 'chief exemplification,' are products of logical thought that in no way depend upon process philosophy: indeed the converse is the case, for this philosophy is largely built upon such principles of logic.

It is logic, not process philosophy, which insists that one cannot both describe Jesus as a man and also say that God's indwelling in him differs in kind from his indwelling in other men: since a study of the raw material confirms the first statement, logic demands a modification of the second. The further insight I then derive from process philosophy is that of seeing God's indwelling in Jesus as the supreme instance, the chief exemplification, of God's indwelling in his creatures—a divine indwelling which is itself the chief exemplification of this philosophy's concept of immanence. This insight closely corresponds to the disciples' experience—perhaps fully explicit only after the resurrection—that when they were with Jesus they were in some special sense in the presence of God. I suggested a like correspondence between the original Easter faith and the insight that the resurrection of Jesus is the chief exemplification of God's raising into himself of everything compatible with his loving purpose —an insight that is itself compatible with our experience of the risen Jesus as of God, and in God, yet also distinct from God.

A Whiteheadian Christology

20

John B. Cobb, Jr.

Classical Christology focused upon the question of the unique relation between God and Jesus. It dealt of course also with the work of Jesus. Modern Christology has tended to focus on the work of Jesus and to avoid metaphysical questions about his nature and his relation to God. The most radical Christologies dispense altogether with the question of God.

This paper is an attempt to return to the classical problem. This return does not assume that the modern focus on soteriology is misplaced, but it does assume that much of the discussion of soteriology is consciously or unconsciously determined by ideas about Jesus' nature. The major reason for concern about Jesus' nature is his work, but beliefs about his nature affect the understanding of the work.

One can approach the question of Jesus' nature from two standpoints. On the one hand, modern historical study has attained a limited but important knowledge of Jesus that is relatively reliable. On the other hand, as Christians we confront traditional creeds and confessions which are still officially recognized as somehow normative. It is no secret that the historical picture and the creedal picture accord poorly with one another. The historical picture presents Jesus as an entirely human figure. The creedal picture offers a rather abstract humanity combined with deity in a paradoxical manner.

Nevertheless, there is a historical connection between Jesus and the metaphysical claims about him, and the fundamental grounds of this connection in the human figure are as clear now as ever. Jesus was certainly a man conditioned by his time and place. But he was a strange figure for any time and place. His teaching and action involved an implicit assumption or claim of authority that was different in kind rather than degree from the claim of other teachers of his time or of ours. The authority he implicitly claimed rested in himself rather than in received teachings or a fresh word from God. It was closely con-

nected with a sense of relatedness to God such that he saw the response
of men to his message and himself as decisive for their response to
God or even identical with it. The disciples' experience of the resur-
rected Christ heightened and transformed their perception of the
authority of Jesus, but historical research confirms the rootedness of
the claim of authority in Jesus himself.

The process of the church's theorizing on the meaning of this claim,
which led to the creedal formulations, is not one we should or even
can follow today. Acceptance of the creeds today can only be in the
form of recognizing the sound elements of their intention and attempting to be faithful to that intention insofar as our present historical
knowledge encourages this. The creeds were sound in their intention
to insist both that Jesus was fully man and that in accepting his authority and responding to his call men are accepting the authority
and call of the one God and not simply of a man or of some demigod or
inferior divine being. This meant for the early church and for orthodoxy in general that God was genuinely present in Jesus in a unique
way. That is a legitimate and even an essential implication of acceptance of Jesus' claim of authority.

This paper is an attempt to explain how we can intelligibly affirm
the unique presence of God in Jesus in such a way as to avoid detracting from his humanity and yet explain his strange authority. Like the
classical debates and creeds, the whole procedure is speculative. The
results of such speculation are binding on no one. Nevertheless, they
should show the possibility of a style of thinking potentially more
meaningful to us than the traditional formulations and yet in greater
continuity with the tradition than modern radicalism. It may prove
useful today to demonstrate that Christians *can* think of Jesus' relation to God as decisively unique without involving themselves in
absurdity, or irrational acceptance of dogma.

The paper is divided into three sections. The first reviews the
varied possibilities provided by Whitehead for conceiving of the
presence of one entity in another and considers how these might apply
to God's varied modes of presence in different men. The second approaches the uniqueness of Jesus from the standpoint of his self or
"I" and relates the result of this approach to the discussion of the
varied modes of God's presence in men. The third briefly indicates
the implications of this discussion for consideration of Jesus' work.

I.   How God is Present

Every conception of how God was present in Jesus has presuppositions
and implications that are subject to philosophical discussion. Most
philosophies, however, render thought about this subject very difficult

and obscure, and this situation has been reflected in the highly paradoxical character of the church's historic affirmations. In classical
philosophy it is possible to understand how a form is present in a
human being without distorting or destroying his humanity, but it is
unintelligible how one substance can enter into another without displacing some part of that other substance. Substances, including human
beings are seen as occupying space, and two substances can not be conceived as occupying the same space. When the images are psychological,
much the same results are reached. For God to be present and active in
Jesus means in classical conceptualities that some aspect of what would
otherwise have been the human Jesus was replaced by God. This aspect
could be the soul as a whole or some element in the soul such as the will.

It is remarkable that despite the pressure of its conceptuality the
church refused to sanction any view of Jesus that curtailed his full
humanity in this way. The church insisted that Jesus had a human soul
and a human will. However, the pressure of the conceptuality remained,
and we find down to our own time the view that if not the soul or will,
then the ultimate "I" of Jesus was not human but divine. The doctrine
that Jesus' humanity was impersonal has much support in orthodox
circles, and it reflects the fact that, given the traditional conceptuality,
there is no other way of conceiving God's presence in Jesus than by
displacing some aspect of the human Jesus. Nevertheless, the view
makes mockery of the Christian conviction of the *full* humanity of
Jesus and it runs counter to the picture of Jesus provided us by New
Testament scholarship.

Whitehead certainly did not develop his philosophy for the purpose of assisting Christians to re-think the relation of God to Jesus,
but he nevertheless provided us with a far richer conceptuality for
conceiving the presence of one entity in another; and this conceptuality
can be used also for christological reflections. It will not be possible
here to give a complete account of Whitehead's doctrine of relations,
but a brief highlighting of the relevant points will be in order.

Let us consider the mode of presence of one actual entity in another. For convenience we can take as our example two successive
occasions of human experience, A and B. A is present in B. This
does not mean, of course, that B is less an independent entity than
was A. A had also in its moment of immediacy incorporated past
entities within itself without sacrifice of its unique and self-determining
identity. The presence of A in B does not conflict with the subjective
unity and actuality of B. No aspect of B's own being is displaced by
A's presence.

At the same time the presence of A is an ultimately real feature
of B. It canot be reduced to the fact, also true, that B actualizes many
of the same eternal objects as A. A as A is also prehended and thus

incorporated into B. A is genuinely and effectively present in B, and B would not be what it is apart from this presence. B does not first exist and then incorporate A; rather this incorporation is constitutive of B's coming into existence.

Thus far only one point is being made. That is, whereas in classical philosophy the idea of one entity being present in another carries with it the notion of displacement, in Whitehead's philosophy this is not the case. This is an important point because of the havoc wreaked in traditional Christology by this tendency to displacement, but by itself it does not solve the problem of Christology. We must proceed to ask two additional questions. (1) Does or can this mode of presence apply to God's relation to men? (2) If so, can we meaningfully speak of differences in the mode of God's presence in different men?

1. Interpreters of Whitehead differ in the extent to which they differentiate God from actual occasions and the relation of God to actual occasions from the relation of actual occasions to each other. On the one hand, Whitehead contrasts God with actual occasions as the one nontemporal actual entity. On the other hand, he stresses that God is not an exception to the categories and uses much of the same language about him as he uses about actual occasions.

My own judgment is that, despite the difficulties, the greatest coherence and intelligibility can be obtained when we think of the ontological structure of God as much as possible in terms of the structure of actual occasions. God's relations with actual occasions will then be understood as resembling in most respects their relations with each other. I will not argue this view here and will try to carry on the discussion presupposing as little as possible my own peculiar proposals for a doctrine of God, proposals which depend upon, but differ from, Whitehead's own position. He certainly writes as if actual occasions prehend God, and I will proceed on the assumption that the word prehend has the same meaning here as elsewhere.

The answer to the question whether God can be present in a man as actual occasions are present in subsequent occasions is, therefore, affirmative. The mode of presence of one occasion in another is as prehended datum. God is also a prehended datum, and he is therefore present in actual occasions in the way in which prehended data generally are present. This is an ultimately real presence which involves no displacement.

2. Not only *can* we say that God is present in actual occasions, but, on my understanding, we *must* say that he is present in every actual occasion whatsoever. Hence, whereas we are freed by Whitehead to think of God as present in Jesus without reducing his full humanity, by itself this does not enable us to see any distinctiveness in God's presence in him. We must, therefore, ask the second question,

Can we meaningfully speak of differences in the mode of God's presence in different men?

If the mode of prehension of God by all entities were identical, then the mode of God's presence in all entities would be identical, and there would be no possibility of asserting that the mode of God's presence in Jesus is unique. But such identity should not be assumed. Prehensions by one actual occasion of others are highly differentiated. Hence the modes of presence of past actual occasions in becoming ones differ greatly. It is my belief that something of this diversity is present also in the prehension of God by actual occasions. This belief rests on the general assumption that Whitehead is best understood and his thought best developed when the structure and relations of God are assimilated as far as possible to the structure and relations of actual entities generally. In light of this assumption, a somewhat detailed account of diverse types of prehensions by one actual occasion of others is relevant to the question of the possible diversity of modes of God's presence in man.

Since the concern is with prehensions of other occasions, the focus of attention is on physical feelings. However, an important distinction immediately presents itself between pure physical feelings and hybrid physical feelings. Pure physical feelings objectify the entities felt by their physical feelings, whereas hybrid physical feelings objectify by conceptual or impure feelings. Most of the following discussion will have hybrid feelings in view. Further distinctions of this type can be made but they are not needed here.

A second major way of distinguishing prehensions is less stressed by Whitehead. However, he holds that the statement that B prehends A also means that A has causal efficacy for B. The relation of A and B can be viewed from either end. Whitehead is also clear that A does not rigidly determine *how* it will be present in B, but that B must take account of A, and how it takes account of A is influenced by what A in fact has become. The actual mode of A's presence in B is partly determined by A's decision and partly by B's. Of course, it is also influenced by many other decisions.

Now let A and B again represent two successive occasions of human experience. The role of A in B is partly determined by A and partly by B. Furthermore, the respective importance of the decisions of A and B for the outcome varies. Sometimes A is relatively passive with respect to how B takes account of it, and B is the chief actor; sometimes A's decision is largely determinative of B.

Consider the case in which A represents the last occasion in a daydreaming sequence and B involves an abrupt decision to return to work. Here A's role in determining B is minimized, and that of B is maximized. Consider, on the other hand, the case in which A represents the occasion in which a decision is made to attend carefully to what another person is saying. The content of B may be largely determined by that decision.

This latter example has peculiar importance as highlighting a special mode of relation between occasions. Whitehead makes the sweeping assertion that all occasions aim at some intensity both in their own satisfaction and in the relevant future. This implies that every decision includes some decision about what its successor occasions should be. However, for the most part the successors are envisioned only as sets of possible occasions dimly anticipated, in the case of man primarily a decision about the content of subsequent moments of his own experience. It does not remove the freedom of its successors, for these are not compelled to acquiesce in the decision made about them. But the later occasions probably cannot eliminate the decision made about them from their objective data or avoid some conformity with the subjective form of the deciding occasion. In other words, when A's self-actualization is determined by an aim to have a definite influence on B, it can bind B to a significant degree.

When A's aim for B plays a major role in its self-actualization, that aim may vary indefinitely. Only one distinction among possible aims is sufficiently important to require statement here. A's aim for B (1) may be that B reenact significant features of A or it (2) may lack this reflexive element. For example, (1) I may now decide that I will evermore nurse and retain the anger I now feel toward one who has betrayed me, or (2) I may make a resolution to be different in the future, a resolution whose carrying out will not entail reference to the initially resolving occasion.

Now let us consider possible applications of this variety to the problem of God's presence in men. According to Whitehead every occasion derives from God its initial aim. This suggests that God entertains an aim for each occasion to which that occasion's feelings conform in its initial phase. Whitehead associates this aim with the primordial nature or mental pole of God. He may mean that in the initial aim each occasion objectifies God by one of God's pure conceptual feelings. I prefer the view that the mental pole of God, like the mental pole of actual occasions, includes also propositional feelings and that it is by a propositional feeling that God is objectified in the initial phase of every becoming occasion. In either case, the derivation of the initial aim from God is common to all occasions.

Diversity is introduced, however, in three ways. First, God's aim for each occasion differs. In this sense God's presence in every occasion is concretely unique and there is no specifiable limit to the diversity of aims or to the importance of what is distinctive in particular cases. Second, the prehensive objectification of God need not be restricted to the initial aim. Third, the degree to which God's aim for an occasion is realized in that occasion's self-actualization differs. These three points require brief elaboration.

Since no two occasions have identical worlds, the self-actualization that is ideal for each must be unique. This is a metaphysical requirement. Furthermore, there are different kinds of occasions ranging from electronic to human ones with differing capacities such that, for example, the aim for an electronic occasion cannot include consciousness, whereas the aim for a human one normally does. Similarly, the aims for most living occasions include no (or few) hybrid prehensions, whereas the aim for a dominant occasion in an animal organism is heavily weighted toward hybrid prehensions of past dominant occasions, which in the case of higher organisms jointly constitute the soul or living person. Whitehead does not discuss the diversity of initial aims experienced by different men, but such a diversity clearly exists. Unless we are to suppose that there is little or no correlation between the initial aim and the final form of the subjective aim—a very strange supposition—we must assume vast differences in the initial aims derived from God by a primitive man and by an Einstein, or for that matter, between myself as I drop off to sleep in the evening and as I write these words.

The aim for most occasions seems to be that the aim be experienced as a possibility for actualization without reference to its source, but in some instances realization of the reference to the source may be a part of the aim. This leads to the second point—that an occasion may prehend God in ways other than the derivation of its initial aim. The initial aim of a human occasion might be that the occasion prehend wider purposes of God or enjoy a peculiar sense of intimacy or oneness. There might be pure physical feelings of God as well as hybrid feelings, or hybrid feelings other than the initial aim.

Third, in the relation of God and a human occasion the relative importance of the divine and the human decisions may vary. God's decision for an occasion cannot be ignored, but it can be accepted or resisted. The human response to one aim influences God's aim for the following occasion.

II.   The Unique "I" of Jesus

Whitehead concentrated attention upon the common features of actual entities. He also showed how increasing complexity in the structure of actual entities introduces radically new structures culminating in intellectual feelings of several kinds. In less technical treatises he proceeded to discuss human history and peculiarly human problems—science, religion, morals, education, reason, art, and so forth. These discussions are generally compatible with his ontology and cosmology, but they are not readily translatable into the technical vocabulary of *Process and Reality*. For example, in *The Function of Reason*, reason is defined as "the self-discipline of the originative element in history." This originative element is "reversion" in the technical language of *Process and Reality*, but how reversion disciplines itself is not technically explained. I do not state this as a criticism. Perhaps it points to one of the unfinished aspects of Whitehead's systematic position, but I mention it to indicate the sense in which Whitehead was aware that the discussion of human and historical problems required the introduction of new concepts only loosely related to the categoreal scheme.

The formulation of a Christology also requires that one go far beyond the general ontological questions to a discussion of what man is like. In what follows the influence of Whitehead should be apparent, but the thought is parallel to, rather than derived from, Whitehead's humanistic writings.

One little recognized factor in the usual formulations of Christology is a certain assumption about the meaning of the word "man." This word is treated as if it referred to a fixed and definite mode of being. It is assumed that when we say—surely we must—that Jesus was fully man, we know just what we mean. It is supposed that to be a man is to fall under certain clearly defined categories such that we know quite well the structure of the existence so designated.

Against this view some implications of evolution should be affirmed. However clearly those beings we designate as men are now marked off from all others, the difference came into being gradually. Among our ancestors were creatures that spanned the gap now existing between ourselves and our simian relatives. The term man must either be reserved to a very late arrival on the planet or be extended to include many creatures very different from ourselves.

These differences include physiological ones, but our primary concern is with the dominant or psychic occasions rather than with the organism as a whole. The structure of psychic existence with which we are familiar in ourselves did not appear suddenly but evolved and developed over hundreds of thousands of years. Furthermore, since the peculiarity of the human psyche is indeterminateness or openness to diverse determination, developments in different cultures are markedly diverse. Occasions of human experience everywhere exhibit the structures described by Whitehead's categories and, in addition to that, the special forms described as intellectual feelings. But beyond these and other elementary structures shared with at least some subhuman occasions, there is no one structure of existence to be designated as human.

This means that the statement, Jesus was fully human, while entirely true, is less informative than it seems. Human beings differ from one another not only superficially but also profoundly, in the very structures of their existence. My common humanity with Jesus does not guarantee that I can understand what it was like to be Jesus any more than a primitive man's co-humanity with Einstein—to return to that example—guarantees that he can understand what it is like to think Einstein's thoughts.

That Jesus was fully human does mean that the actual occasions constituting Jesus as a living person were not in any instance the actual entity God or, if God is conceived as a living person, the actual occasions constituting the divine life. Strict identity of Jesus with God is simply nonsensical. But it is not nonsensical that God's presence in Jesus played a structural role in the actual occasions constituting his personal life which it has played nowhere else.

A useful way of approaching the varied structures of human existence is through reflection on the meaning of "I." The use of the first person singular in some way is probably coterminous with language, but its meaning varies widely. It may refer, first, to the speaker as a physical organism in the public world. Each man learns to differentiate himself from others and from the environment in this way. He becomes aware of himself through becoming aware of others' awareness of him.

Many men become aware of a distinction between psyche and body. A second use of the word "I" is to designate the former. The body is then perceived as an instrument, a context, or a limitation of the self. Further, the psyche may be understood in a variety of ways, thus altering the meaning of "I." For example, it may be seen as a self-identical entity underlying the flow of experience. This allows for a third use of "I," to refer to a transcendental ego, a mental substance, or an atman, and it reflects a definite structuring of human existence. Having thus identified the "I," its existence may be either affirmed or denied, and the Whiteheadian must share with the Buddhist in the denial of its existence. But for the Whiteheadian this denial can mean only that a more accurate understanding of "I" is needed. This could return to the identification of "I" with the psyche along with the recognition that the psyche is exhaustively constituted by a succession of experiences. Or it could recognize that the psyche is a highly differentiated actuality within which the "I" is one factor or element. This latter approach, by no means limited to Whiteheadians, points to a fourth meaning of "I," the one requiring the most discussion.

Most of us do in fact use the term "I" in this way because we participate in structures of existence in which differentiation of aspects of the psychic life is important, as we do not identify ourselves equally with all of them. For example, some men identify themselves with the rational aspect of psychic activity and perceive passions and emotions as something to be controlled, whereas others identify themselves with this affective aspect and perceive the claim of reason as a heteronomous demand. "I" means something different in these two instances, and this difference expresses itself in quite different structures of existence, but in each case "I" refers to that center which tries to organize the whole psychic life.

The notion of "I" in this sense is inseparable from some element of self-identity through time. Unless the organizing center of one occasion of experience has continuity with its predecessors and successors, it cannot usefully be designated as "I." If the dominant occasions of animal experience are, as seems likely, organized around purposes determined by changing organic needs, the requisite continuity does not occur. To whatever extent in primitive men or young children dominant occasions of experience are determined more by new stimuli received through the body than by continuity with past dominant occasions, the requisite identity through time is lacking. And to whatever extent the Buddhist succeeds in extirpating the peculiar continuity of the occasions constituting the living person, he succeeds also—as he intends—in destroying the "I."

The "I" then is a relatively continuous center within human experience around which the experience attempts more or less successfully to organize itself. Human existence can occur without any "I" even in this broad sense. But the variety of structures of existence can be further clarified by defining the "I" more strictly. If the organizing center of experience is in the unconscious aspect of experience, as is true for those whose world of meanings is primarily mythical, then the term "I" in the strict sense is inappropriate. And even when the center is identified with conscious aspects of emotion or reason, the "I" in the strictest sense does not occur. A man becomes an individual "I," rather than a peculiar mixture of universal forces or principles, only as he inwardly transcends both emotion and reason, accepting responsibility for the outcome of the struggle between them. This involves detaching the self from the several given functionings of the psyche which then become instrumental to the self. At this point a man knows himself unequivocally as an "I" who, by bearing his own responsibility and making his own decisions, ceases to be fundamentally a part of a biologically defined species or a culturally defined tribe or community. With the emergence of the "I" in this full sense a radically new structure of existence appears. Such a structure gained effective entry into the human scene first in Israel and is most clearly represented by Jeremiah.

The prophetic "I" was formed in relation to the divine "I." Israel knew God as "I" before individual Hebrews entered into this structure of existence. The prophet knew himself addressed by the divine "I" and as he became aware of the tension between the requirements of that "I" and his own thought and feelings, he found himself called to responsibility for his actions in a new way. He thus became an "I" in relation to the divine "I." The relation was one of encounter, or demand and response.

The prophetic "I" embodied no authority. It exercised freedom in response to the authoritative command of the divine "I." The prophet's word had authority only insofar as it articulated the divine word.

Here the contrast of Jesus with the prophets is most clear. He spoke on his own authority which was at the same time the authority of God. The "I" of Jesus, rather than standing over against the divine "I," identified its authority with that of God. Among the religious leaders of mankind this is a unique role. It differs from the mystics and ecstatics as much as from the great Hebrew prophets. The "I" of Jesus was neither merged with the divine nor replaced by the divine. On the contrary it retained its autonomous existence but in such a way as to identify its perceptions with God's.

Serious claim of Jesus' uniqueness today arises chiefly from the uniqueness of the relation to God implicitly claimed in his mode of teaching and acting. Our task now is to speculate as to how Jesus' "I" could have been so related to God as to explain this unique claim. The problem can be approached by returning to consideration of the variety of modes in which a prehension makes its object A present in the subject B. The assumption here is that the prophets and Jesus, like all men, prehended God, but that they prehended God in unusual and in distinct ways.

B may prehend A in such a way that although important aspects of A are re-enacted, the source of these eternal objects has no importance. For example, we might judge that much about the personality of B reflects the influence of A, whereas B is virtually oblivious to that dependence. Or we may hear important news over the radio without being interested in the personality of the newscaster. On the other hand, B may prehend A in such a way that the fact that it is A which it is prehending is of paramount importance for the subjective form of B rather than the particular aspect of A by which A is objectified. For example, a child may experience inner tranquility because of the presence of a parent apart from anything peculiar to the present experience of the parent. A third possibility is intermediate to the other two. In this case both the specific content of the prehension and the fact of its source in A are important to B.

In general, men embody the first of these three possibilities in their relation to God. The initial aim is derived from God, but although the character of the initial aim is of crucial importance to the becoming occasion, the fact that it is derived from God usually plays but a small

role in its conscious subjective form. What is important is the urge to actualization of a particular sort, not the source of the urge. On the other
hand, for some men some of the time the sense that they are being urged
or called or guided by God becomes a very important part of the experience of the initial aim.

In the case of the prophets this dual importance of content and
source obtained. But for them the content of the prehension of God was
not only that of the initial aim. It was also some meaning of much
broader relevance than the private ideal for a particular moment of the
prophet's life. We may conjecture that the divine aim for such occasions of the prophet's experience included the prophet's objectification
of God by other aspects of God's total actuality than his aim for that
private occasion. The fact that the meaning by which God was objectified had God as its source was of equal importance with the content
of the meaning.

The obligation to bear and communicate such meanings against his
natural feeling and thinking was the ground of Jeremiah's discovery of
his selfhood as "I." Not the reception of the Word as such but the
necessity to decide about it was crucial to the formation of this structure of existence and to its preservation and strengthening in the Jewish
community. The "I" was thus formed in the prehensions of two imaginative propositions together with the valuation of one as identical
with God's will.

This kind of experience may not have been alien to Jesus, but it
did not constitute his uniqueness. In his case the prehension of God was
one for which specific content was of secondary importance. God's aim
for Jesus was that he prehend God in terms of that which constitutes
him as God—his lordship, his love, and his incomparable superiority of
being and value. This prehension was not experienced by Jesus as
information about God but as the presence of God to and in him. Furthermore, and most uniquely, it was not experienced by him as one
prehension alongside others to be integrated by him into a synthesis
with them. Rather this prehension of God constituted in Jesus the
center from which everything else in his psychic life was integrated.
This means that at least in some decisive moments of his life he perceived the world, his own past and future, his emotions and reason, in
terms of the presence of God in him. At least in such moments Jesus'
weighting of values—his perception of the relative importance of things
and persons, of the self and others, of motives and actions, of past,
present, and future—was from the perspective given in his prehension
of God. This does not mean, of course, that Jesus was privy to God's
knowledge of possibilities or that he shared God's prehensions of the
world. But it does mean that the "I" of Jesus was constituted by his prehension of God.

A separate question must be raised as to the relative roles of God and Jesus in determining the unique structure of Jesus' existence. The two extreme answers are: one, that God simply determined that he be uniquely present in Jesus; or two, that God offers to all men essentially the same relation to himself which Jesus realized. Orthodoxy has tended to the former answer; liberalism, to the latter. But the analysis above of the respective weight of the decisions of occasions A and B suggests that these two extremes must be rejected.

No entity, including God, finally determines exactly how it will be prehended by any other entity. The final decision always remains with the prehending entity. But high-grade occasions can and do actualize themselves with a view to uniquely influencing other entities. Such actualization, on the one hand, provides new possibilities to the subsequent entities otherwise lacking and, on the other, compels the later entities to take account of particular aspects of the earlier. Assuming that God's causal efficacy for becoming occasions is analogous to that of past actual occasions, we should think both of God's offering differentiated opportunities and of the free response to those opportunities on the part of the recipient. Then the possibility offered Jesus, or the call to Jesus, was distinctive, and apart from it Jesus could not have been what he was. The initiative was with God. But the call did not compel the response. We can never know whether others may not have been called before Jesus to more or less similar modes of existence.

To summarize, we can intelligibly and with some indirect historical justification assert that God's presence in Jesus constituted Jesus' essential selfhood. The one God was thus uniquely present in him. At the same time, Jesus was fully human and no aspect of his humanity was displaced by God. It was a thoroughly human "I" that was constituted by God's presence in Jesus.

III.   The Work of Jesus

Speculation about the mode of God's presence in Jesus would have minimal interest unless it threw light upon the question of how we now are, or should be, related to Jesus. Hence, although the objective question about Jesus himself is central to his study, some indication of its implications for us is appropriate. These implications can be considered briefly under four headings: (1) authority, (2) revelation, (3) example, and (4) salvation.

1.   The view here presented warrants the attribution of authority to Jesus. This does not mean that one can or should argue from a speculative doctrine as to how God was present in Jesus to the fact of his authority for us. The warrant of the speculative doctrine is the implicit claim of authority in Jesus' message. The fact of the claim gives reason

to ask whether it *could* be justified, that is, whether it is possible that a man have that kind of relation to God which could ground such a claim. But the fact of the claim plus the demonstration of the possibility of the requisite relationship in no sense substantiates the claim. The substantiation can consist only in the inherent power of the claim and the church's experience of it and testimony to it. Being a Christian has to do directly with being grasped by the claim, not with some speculation about how God was present in Jesus. Yet in the long run, the power of the claim is weakened when no conceptuality is available to support it, and it is to offer such a conceptuality that this paper has been prepared.

The question is not simply whether Jesus' claim to authority is thus rendered intelligible but also just what kind of authority this is. The theory here developed provides no basis for the older view that Jesus' message was infallible either because it was the direct word of God himself or because God revealed these truths to Jesus in such a way as to preserve him from error. We may assume that God provided Jesus with no peculiar conceptuality, that he guaranteed no freedom from sharing in the errors and misconceptions of his time. The presence of God in Jesus in no sense entailed the presence in Jesus of the divine knowledge.

Jesus spoke with an authority uniquely related to that of God because Jesus' existence was uniquely related to God's. The center from which he perceived his world was determined by and given in his experience of God. The reality of God and his will dominated his perception of the world in such a way that he saw all else in relation to this supreme reality. The result was an intensification and transformation of Jewish understanding of both God and his creatures.

For most men the world is very real. If they believe in God at all, they accept the idea that his reality is prior and incomparably superior to that of the world. This belief modifies their perceptions to some degree, but intellectual belief remains in some tension with perception. Effective belief is much more a function of perception than of the assent to the idea of God's superior reality. That means that what one really cares about is himself and his world, and that his real interest in God is limited largely to how he hopes or fears that God may impinge upon that world. The weighting of concern, the attitude toward the neighbor, the valuation of possessions and power, all arise out of the perception which is in tension with the acknowledgment of God's superior reality. This acknowledgment introduces certain obligations felt as heteronomously imposed burdens.

For Jesus the situation was quite different. His perception conformed with his belief. Hence he could speak directly out of his perception. His preaching was not proclamation of an ought that stood overagainst him supported by beliefs that were heteronomously grounded. It was a description of what he saw from a perspective that could not be transcended. Whereas others recognize that man should live from God and for God, Jesus embodied that life.

When we are encountered by Jesus' message we recognize a final claim upon us. It presents us with the world as we acknowledge the world must be from a perspective truer than our own and itself not subject to further transcending. We see what it would mean to believe effectively what we, to some extent, already admit to be true.

2. The nature of Jesus' authority leads directly into the question of revelation. What does Jesus reveal and how? What has been said about authority implies that he reveals what it means to live in terms of the way reality actually is. Although Jesus' life, like his beliefs, were conditioned by his time and place in history, at a deeper level we see in him what it is like for a man to exist in a manner appropriate to what God is and what man is. This is fundamental.

Christians often speak of Jesus as the revelation of God or of God revealing himself in Jesus. Such language means different things to different speakers, and in some of these meanings it is to be affirmed. It can be another way of saying what has already been said above. But it can also refer to more direct modes of revealing God.

The God whom Jesus revealed was the God already known by those to whom he spoke. Hence it is not meaningful to think of his revelation of God as something wholly new. But his teaching about God, both explicit and implicit, altered the balance and weighting of the ideas already held about God in such a way as to change the total understanding. Furthermore, reflection about Jesus' message and life has led to still further reconsideration of the nature of God, to beliefs that were probably absent from Jesus' own consciousness. When history is read in terms of the centrality of Jesus, the total understanding of God is affected. Paul's theology illustrates this mode of revelation. Since this reading is new in every generation according to the situation in which it occurs, we can say that Jesus even now continues to reveal God to us in new ways.

Christians are also wont to say that Jesus reveals to us what man really is. This can be a restatement of the claim made above that in him we see what it means to exist in an objectively appropriate relationship to the real. The perceptions which determine our responses to the ever new situations of life are narrow and distorted. Since at the same time we are able to transcend these perspectives in the recognition of their distortion, we acknowledge in principle an ideal limit of such transcendence which would fulfill our ultimate potentiality. In Jesus we recognize the embodiment of that ideal limit and hence of what man "really" or rather ideally is.

3. The doctrine that Jesus reveals the reality of man can be understood to mean that in him we have an example to follow. Although such a view should not be totally rejected, the basic implication of the theory developed in this paper cuts against it. There is no indication that God provides all of us with the peculiar aim or possibility with which he endowed Jesus. Jesus was fully human, but that does not mean that what he was called to be and to become is what I am called to be or to become. Perhaps I am even called to be a theologian, and that is something very different from Jesus.

In a much more abstract sense one may speak of Christian discipleship as imitation. If we assume that Jesus was obedient to God's call in his situation, we can try to imitate him by being obedient to God's very different call to us in our very different situation. Also, if Jesus shows us fundamentally what it means to live from God and for God, we can seek to find what it means in our situation to live from God and for God. But it is important to recognize that the structure of existence embodied in Jesus is not ours and that hence the translation into our situation is a very radical one.

4. The most important and universal categories for acknowledging Jesus' importance for Christians are "lord" and "savior." The discussion thus far has dealt more directly with the former. Jesus as lord is authoritative for life and belief. Some Christians have understood that Jesus' saviorhood is a function of this lordship. For example, they have believed that we are saved by acceptance of his teaching or by following his example. And in the sense now explained this must play an important part in Jesus' saving work.

However, most Christians have believed that Jesus affected a change in the human situation not only by instruction and example but also in some other way. This additional way is vaguely and variously understood. Some have supposed that he changed God's attitude toward man or effected some alteration in the power of evil over the world. Others have felt him as a mystical or sacramental presence.

Nothing in the account offered in this paper either supports or opposes theories of this latter sort, and for this reason it would be inappropriate to discuss them here. However, one dimension of Jesus' work is suggested by the foregoing which deserves more attention than it has yet received.

I have urged that we should recognize the radical diversity among men even at the level of the structures of their existence. The distinction of Jesus' structure of existence from that of other men has been central to the above discussion. This at least suggests that Jesus' message and work may have introduced into human history a new structure of existence different from his own in which Christians participate. A new structure of existence opens up new problems and new possibilities for man. The existential problem of Socrates differed radically from that of Neanderthal man. If salvation means wholeness, then salvation has a different meaning for each structure of existence.

It is my conviction that Jesus brought into being for those who responded to him a final and unsurpassable structure of existence. This structure was the solution of the problem posed in the Jewish structure of existence and in that sense was salvation. It in its turn, however, has introduced new possibilities of sickness and fragmentation as well as new possibilities of health. Hence Jesus as savior is not only the ground of the new structure of existence but also the one in relation to whom the health of that structure can be attained.

Process Cosmology and Theological Particularity

21

Ralph E. James, Jr.

Current theological interest in process philosophy sets the stage for a new confrontation between what might be called the cosmological perspective of philosophy and the historical perspective of theology. The cosmological perspective derives, at least in part, from the philosopher's determination to be comprehensive; the historical perspective arises out of the theologian's conviction that it is his task to elucidate and defend one unique particular, namely, the event of Jesus Christ. Of course the degree to which philosophies are cosmological and theologies historical, varies. The present confrontation is sharpened because process philosophy is highly cosmological in its perspective as is suggested by the title of Whitehead's key work, *Process and Reality, An Essay in Cosmology*. Theological interest in this "essay in cosmology" comes at a time when theological writing is markedly historical in perspective. Ironically, the confrontation between process cosmology and theological historicity appears at a time when theologians are noticing the compatibility between process thought and historical thinking. Whitehead's metaphysical system pictures dynamic occurrences, and historically minded theologians like to speak of dynamic events. The confrontation is, therefore, not over dynamics, change, or becoming. Rather, the confrontation is between the general cosmic process and one particular historical event.

Obviously the cosmological vision available to modern man transcends any one metaphysical description. Moreover, what is described is constantly enriched and "filled in." When Loren Eiseley describes the process of evolution of plant and animal life struggling through the hot, red winds of the young earth, and when space shots send back data from the Moon and Mars, our cosmic vision expands. Paleontological and astronomical findings daily stretch the horizons of human imagination beyond former boundaries. The term *cosmos* itself fails to be satisfactory as a way of describing recent findings. The original Greek word, *kosmos*, meant order of harmony and could hardly encompass the post-enlightenment discovery of oceans of cosmic dust and debris floating randomly in space. In the present discussion the term *cosmology* will signify not only Whitehead's philosophical vision but a vision of a process enriched by very recent discoveries in the physical sciences.

Whitehead himself was quite explicit about cosmology: "The theme of Cosmology, which is the basis of all religions, is the story of the dynamic effort of the World passing into everlasting unity, and of the static majesty of God's vision, accomplishing its purpose of completion by absorption of the World's multiplicity of effort."[1] In a sense, the "historical captivity" of Christianity means theology has abandoned cosmology as "the basis of all religions." Process theology may well provide a way to return theology to a cosmic basis: a modern cosmological theology, a post-historical theology, that is nevertheless aware "of the dynamic effort of the World passing into everlasting unity."

I think the present confrontation between Whiteheadian cosmology and Christian theology can be best focused in terms of the traditional problem of particularity. In this context the problem of particularity is two problems in one: it is the problem of the relationship between one historical event, the event of Jesus Christ, and all other particulars in the universe; it is also the question of the relationship between human history and the cosmic process in general. The latter form of the problem emerges with the space age; the former has surfaced before in the argument about "the two natures of Christ" and in the more recent "scandal of particularity" (it is scandalous to think God is uniquely incarnate in Jesus, but nevertheless true). The problem is renewed by theological appropriation of process philosophy because of theological interest in the preservation of the uniqueness of one historical particular in the general scheme of unique particulars. A process theology true to the cosmic scope of Whitehead's philosophy must be a cosmological theology embracing both history and nature. Indeed, the distinction between history and nature as a methodological device loses force in process ontology. Rejection of the history/nature dichotomy ushers the question of the particularity of theology's subject to the fore. Process theology assigns uniqueness to every finite particular but special uniqueness to none.

The practical importance of an inclusive cosmological theology for the future increases in proportion to growing cosmic awareness. Two thousand years of Christian history become decreasingly venerable when confronted by the findings of radioactivity dating techniques which date the hardened crust of the earth at three billion years. Even Professor Leakey's recent extension of possible humanoid remains as

[1]PR 529–530.

far back as 2,000,000 B. C. leaves man (if this be man) with but a brief
history compared to earth time, to say nothing of the general cosmic
process. The relative size of the earth and the significance of the human
race shrinks before extragalactic distances exceeding a billion light
years. The reach of the cosmos now measurable by radio astronomy
exceeds the wildest dreams of those who formulated traditional Christian beliefs in terms of the particularity of Christ and human history.
In their way, for example in the *logos* theology of John, early Christians
also attempted to relate Jesus to the cosmos, but the sheer scope of this
undertaking is now vastly enlarged.

I do not intend to argue that truth claims based upon historical particulars cannot logically be cosmic in scope. Rather, the issue is whether
theology expressed in the particular form of one historical perspective
is more convincing than a general cosmic perspective. Whitehead's cosmological orientation seems to offer some hope as a way to pose a theological alternative to the historical tendency in Western theology just
because it is not limited to one particular, though it may be found to do
justice to that particular within a cosmic context. There are several
areas for discussion in developing such an alternative:

History and Metaphysics. Since the Kierkegaardian and Nietz-
schian revolts against the Absolute with its component metaphysical
difficulties, theologians have preferred the meaningfulness of personal
subjective experience to abstract and dehumanizing metaphysics. Historical thinking has been distinguished from metaphysical thinking in
order to preserve the personal and unique content of faith. Neo-reforma-
tion theologians (with the exception of Paul Tillich) have been particularly gratified by the belief that historical thinking somehow restored
the uniqueness that had been so viciously attacked by nineteenth century skepticism, rationalism, liberalism and historicism. At least in the
earlier decades of the twentieth century the split between theology and
philosophy, the problem of hermeneutics and the problem of language,
emerging from christological historical thinking, seemed a fair price to
pay for protecting the uniqueness of the theological subject. But with
the intensification of the later problems in the second half of this century the price of historical thinking has risen.[2]

It is against the background of increasingly costly historical thinking that process theology appears as a solution to current theological

[2]One series of volumes particularly relevant to the problem of history is *New
Frontiers in Theology, Discussions Among Continental and American Theologians*,
Vol. I; *The Later Heidegger and Theology* (1963), Vol. II; *The New Hermeneutic*
(1964), Vol. III; *Theology as History* (1967). Edited by James M. Robinson and John
B. Cobb, Jr. (New York: Harper and Row). The latter volume focuses most sharply
upon the present discussion, but the first two volumes illuminate the development
of the problem of history in recent theology.

difficulties. Basically, it approaches the problems associated with historical thinking by rejecting the existential historical (and positivistic) attitude toward metaphysics that helped to bring these problems to their present form. An example of how one might employ the process rejection of the dichotomy between history and metaphysics can be found by looking at the methodology of the contemporary theologian, Friedrich Gogarten. Gogarten holds that the Christian faith is historical "and not to be harmonized with traditional metaphysical thinking—an impossible task!"[3] Of course, process thinkers can agree with the rejection of traditional metaphysics. But Gogarten seems to imply that historical thinking somehow escapes being metaphysical in any sense. He argues that reality, experienced through faith, is "that to which man's freedom for God and his independence toward the world correspond."[4]

Presumably such a claim about reality is not metaphysical, but is this true? Does knowledge of reality, whether experienced through faith or not, fail to give us a specific metaphysical description of reality? Describing Gogarten's position, Theodore Runyon writes, "faith is itself a kind of relativity, man relative to God in every moment."[5] Since the process theologian makes the definite claim that God is also relative to man, is it not true that this becomes an argument between two kinds of religious metaphysical positions?

Contrast Gogarten's understanding of metaphysics with that of Charles Hartshorne who thinks of metaphysics as a "descriptive science" which, among other functions, aids one's understanding of his participation in the love of God. Hartshorne's understanding of God can be communicated through abstract, relatively nonhistorical metaphysical symbols. This does not mean such symbols do not characterize history. By rejecting such an understanding of metaphysics, Gogarten leaves himself at a strategic disadvantage in attempting to elucidate his theological subject. One suspects that Gogarten would more clearly see the problem of the particularity of his subject if he admitted that he takes a metaphysical position if only by implication. An implicit metaphysic is just as real as an explicit one, but its very implicit character hides metaphysical problems.

Wolfhart Pannenberg evidences more concern for the problem of

[3]*The Reality of Faith*, trans. Carl Michalson and others. (Philadelphia: Westminster, 1959), 24. The significance of this distinction between historical and metaphysical thinking in Gogarten's theology of secularization is glimpsed in its influence on the theologies of Harvey Cox, Carl Michalson, Gehard Ebeling, and Ernest Fuchs. See Larry Shiner, *The Secularization of History, An Introduction to the Theology of Friedrich Gogarten.* (Nashville and New York: Abingdon, 1966), 18–19.

[4]*The Reality of Faith*, 111.

[5]Gogarten, *A Handbook of Christian Theologians*, eds. Martin E. Marty and Dean G. Peerman (Cleveland and New York: World, 1965), 430–431.

the particularity of his theological subject by basing his theology in historical revelation *as universal*. (See *Offenbarung als Geschichte*.) But how universal is Pannenberg's understanding of universal history when he speaks of "the Kingdom of God in which alone human destiny can find its ultimate fulfillment"?[6] The test from the perspective of a Whiteheadian cosmology is how much such ultimate fulfillment is dependent upon one contingent historical event. This is the question of the relationship between the general cosmic process and one finite particular. Pannenberg's answer to the crucial question is clear: "The eschatological event of the appearance of Christ is the summation of the universe from its end in that this event has consummating power in the fullness of time."[7] I see no logical conflict between Pannenberg's claim that one event is the summation of the universe and Whitehead's metaphysics so long as existential language is employed, i.e. "consummating power," "fullness of time." The question is the ontological status of the finite particular upon which he bases his existentially worded case. If, in reality, all power is in one particular, all other particulars cease to have power. If not, how are we to take Pannenberg's language?

Pannenberg's failure to clarify the ontological status of the finite particular which he claims consummates the whole universe is only part of the problem. The deeper question is how intuitively convincing is this claim when confronted by the fact that the whole earth is one fleeting speck in the observable space-time continuum of the cosmic process? Is not Pannenberg's universal history unnecessarily restricted by finite historical thinking centered in his desire for salvation through Jesus Christ? Certainly theology cannot escape finitude in its perspective, but I am convinced that it could now broaden its perspective (1) by admitting the metaphysical implications of its "historical" claims, (2) by thinking through the ontological status of the particular upon which it rests its case, and (3) by placing its historical thinking in cosmic perspective.

Anthropology and particularity. A second area that should be explored in the confrontation between Whiteheadian cosmology and historical particularity is the doctrine of man. Process theology is well known as a determined program to rethink the doctrine of God so that the understanding of God is not limited to ontological categories of being. Process theologians insist that God is dipolar; both eternal and temporal, absolute and relative, necessary and contingent. Since God is in part temporal, relative, and contingent, man can actually change reality through his finite decisions—his existence has ontologial significance.

    [6]*Jesus—God and Man*, trans. Lewis L. Wilkins and Duane Priebe (Philadelphia: Westminster, 1968) 377.
    [7]*Ibid.*, 388.

Such an emphasis upon the role of man with the rejection of the monopolar classical understanding of God, means that process theology has much in common with the theological intention of Thomas J. J. Altizer's radical theology. Process theology differs sharply, however, from radical theology's solution to the problem of God and its eschatological and apocalyptic view of man. Altizer writes, "A new humanity is created by the death of God in Jesus, a humanity that is a direct contrary of the natural man who is isolated in his own selfhood and imprisoned by the brute contingency of time."[8] In effect, such a new humanity involves movement from contingency to noncontingency so that noncontingency (God is all in all) becomes the triumphal status. Radical theology's "new forms of faith may be seen to have an apocalyptic form: the new humanity that they proclaim dawns only at the end of all that we have known as history; its triumph is inseparable from the disintegration of the cosmos created by historical man, and it calls for the reversal of all moral law and the collapse of all historical religion."[9]

Again, process theology can applaud "disintegration of the cosmos created by historical man." Certainly process theology is open to a possible reversal of moral law, perhaps even the collapse of historical religions. But noncontingent existence in the time of triumph for the new man is another matter. Eschatological visions (such as Altizer's) are challenged by the question of the meaning of basic beliefs such as noncontingent times of triumph, which seems to require the end of cosmic process. A few years ago a bitterly satirical movie, *The Victors*, suggested the hollowness of the meaning of military victory in modern warfare. The notion of victory in warfare, like the ideas of an apocalyptic triumph, seems to have meaning only within the historical contexts which produce them. Thus, it is not surprising to find apocalyptic thinking decreasingly adequate for modern life. This becomes especially evident as the doctrine of the second coming of Christ continually wanes as a cultural force. The interim before the Kingdom, the time of triumph proclaimed by Jesus, stretches itself until the ongoing process becomes more meaningful than the postponed Kingdom.

Apocalyptic thought implies an epoch, a period of time, before the triumph. What then? Perhaps this is an unfair question because "then" is a time word. Nevertheless, what if the universe as an ongoing process will continue forever? Without giving up its doctrine of God or man, process theology appears to imply that the process simply continues as both necessary and contingent in different respects. The notion of an

---

[8]*The Gospel of Christian Atheism* (Philadelphia: Westminster, 1966), 72.
[9]"Theology and the Contemporary Sensibility," *America and the Future of Theology,* ed. William A. Beardslee (Philadelphia: Westminster, 1967), 23.

expected future eschaton gives way to the satisfactions of particular occasions before an immediate vision of God. The reference point of satisfaction is not necessarily tied to one past holy event pointing to *human* salvation. Releasing a tradition or a man from a particular reference point in time may well have a salutary effect upon that tradition or individual. The process alternative seems better equipped to accomplish such a release from human particularity, indeed, Whitehead once defined religion as that which "is directed to the end of stretching individual interest beyond its self-defeating particularity."[10]

Evolution and God. A third area in which the confrontation between process cosmology and theological particularity arises is the relationship between evolution and God. Largely due to the influence of Teilhard de Chardin, Catholic theologians have recently done considerable work in this area. [11] Under the influence of Whitehead, process theology holds out a parallel promise within but not limited to Protestantism or even Christianity. One can make a historical case that Whitehead's metaphysic is in some sense a systematic metaphysical description of evolution. Whitehead's philosophy would certainly be less intelligible if the idea of evolution were not generally known and accepted. Of course this does not mean that non-Whiteheadian concepts such as determinism, sometimes associated with evolution, are required by process philosophy.

One reason process theology harmonizes well with evolution is that in process theology God himself evolves in one aspect of his nature. Being in one respect relative, contingent and free, God can relate to and include the universe in process. Emphasis upon history in recent theology salvaged something of evolving process, but failure to work out the ontological relationship between history and God has been a serious problem. Theologians have attempted to protect the special uniqueness of one historical event, but have not satisfactorily shown how that event relates to general evolution or to God. Process theology offers an alternative by insisting on real process in God. This means that every particular contributes its uniqueness (not special uniqueness) to the becoming of cosmic evolution. Evolving particulars become the dynamic events of time. God is literally "timeful."

Process and Hope. In proposing a Christian theology of hope Jürgen Moltmann agrees that theology cannot live with the Parmenidean god of being who renders the reality of time empty. "The contemplation of this god does not make a meaningful experience of history possible, but only the meaningful negation of history. The *logos* of this being liberates and

---

[10]PR 8.

[11]See, for example, Christopher F. Mooney, *Teilhard de Chardin and the Mystery of Christ.* (New York: Harper and Row, 1966).

raises us out of the power of history into the eternal present."[12] Moltmann sees that the loss of an open future removes the basis of hope.
From the perspectives of both Whitehead and Moltmann one can notice
more than casual connections between Greek philosophy of being and
the Greek sense of tragedy, despair and fate.

Whitehead and Moltmann are in agreement in assigning ontological
primacy to temporal history instead of eternal being; each accepts the
basic premise of evolution in God. But even when there is agreement
that hope requires an open future, the question of the *basis for hope*
remains unsettled. For Whitehead hope is grounded in the continuing
process of reality toward its potentialities in God. Such process includes human history but includes also the dim past studied by the
paleontologist and the distant space of the astronomer. Dinosaurs, men,
and stars participate in the cosmic process as the basis of life and hope
for creatures in all possible times and galaxies. Moltmann, on the other
hand, insists that the only basis of true hope for the future is a particular event in history: "This realm of the future which lies before us cannot be turned into mere 'futurity' by reflecting solely on its relation to
existence, but it is the future of Jesus Christ and can therefore be inferred only from the knowledge and recognition of that historic event
of the resurrection of Christ which is the making of history and the key
to it."[13] Utilizing this particular event as the criterion of *all* true hope,
Moltmann rejects romantic and Marxist utopian ideas for attempting to
establish hope in human community. These, he thinks, are false hopes.
Process theology can, however, produce a doctrine of hope that avoids
both romantic and Marxist utopianism and the problem produced by
founding hope in one particular historical event. Whitehead's metaphysic could describe a third kind of utopia, just as one *can* declare one
event in human history final for the universe. Nevertheless, in process
theology, it is not necessary to take either of these steps in order to
have a useful doctrine of hope. Hope can be based upon components of
process itself: (1) the generally available vision of God; (2) the openness
of the future; (3) the everlastingness of the past in the memory of God;
(4) freedom to create novel experience at all levels of the cosmic process; (5) aesthetic enjoyment of existence, and (6) the *possibility* of a
better society through intelligent use of the first five elements.

Obviously, because of the reality of freedom, these elements can also
function to produce evil and despair. In the sense that process theology
may not operate under the "necessity" of hope founded by the Christ
event, it is less hopeful than the theology of hope. But in the sense in

[12]*Theology of Hope, On the Ground and the Implication of a Christian Eschatology* (New York: Harper and Row, 1965), 29.
[13]*Ibid.*

which it is more universal, and not necessarily tied to a particular event, it is more hopeful. If world society is ever to evolve, and social evolution is at least as important to man as biological, it will require a common base such as "being-before-the-cosmos," i.e., a cosmic common denominator. Social evolution, like biological evolution, is checked by the compartmentalization of traditions. Recent research on the human brain indicates how much more adequately the flexible young brain is able to cope with problems than the more compartmentalized older one.[14] Similarly, transcending traditional compartmentalization with the cosmic vision may be just what is required to give fresh life to human society. What Whitehead might call *adventure* may be reborn just because evolution speeds out of its present forms, forms inadequate for the novelty of the future.

Hope for the future includes but does not depend upon one event or one tradition alone. A vision of cosmic process raises human horizons above traditional divisions based in the particulars of history, and above divisions based in the absolutization of many kinds of particulars in addition to theological ones. In this vision, hope begins with a declaration that men are immediately together before one unifying vision and potentially brothers in a future that is really open. I think such a vision will endure beyond the epochs of revised traditional theology through which we are now rapidly passing. Just as Copernicus lifted us out of Ptolemaic anthropocentricism, process cosmology may help us beyond the particularity of the religious traditions of our time. It is especially well equipped to do this as *A Natural Theology for Our Time* (Hartshorne);[15] it will take much longer as *A Christian Natural Theology* (Cobb).[16] Our hope lies in the general cosmic process Hartshorne described when he wrote, "God is the cosmic 'adventure' (Whitehead) integrating all real adventures as they occur, without ever failing in readiness to realize new states out of the divine potency. . ."[17]

[14]Eric H. Lenneberg, *Biological Foundations of Language* (New York: John Wiley & Sons, 1967), 142ff.

[15]LaSalle, Ill.: Open Court, 1966.

[16]Philadelphia: Westminster, 1965.

[17]Hartshorne, *Man's Vision of God and the Logic of Theism* (New York: Harper & Row, 1951; Hamden, Conn.: Archon Books, 1964).

FOUR

Man and Society

Evolution and the Imagery of Religious Thought: from Darwin to Whitehead

22

Bernard E. Meland

In the spring of 1926 an incident occurred at the University of Chicago which may well be considered symbolic of the shift in perspective about which I am to speak in this chapter. Whitehead's book, *Religion in the Making,* had just appeared. From the title of the book and its chapter headings one had every reason to assume that it would speak directly to the concerns of any student or scholar in the field of religion for whom the evolutionary point of view had become basic. Yet, to the dismay and irritation of many who were then with the Divinity School of the University of Chicago, including such students of the history and development of religious doctrine and institutions as Shailer Mathews, Edward Scribner Ames, and Shirley Jackson Case, this book was wholly unintelligible. Shailer Mathews was heard to remark, "It is infuriating, and I must say, embarrassing as well, to read page after page of relatively familiar words without understanding a single sentence." The fact that other members of the Divinity faculty and their colleagues in other theological schools who had read the book felt likewise lessened the embarrassment, but it hardly lessened the irritation. Shirley Jackson Case was able to set the book aside as being another instance of a metaphysically burdened philosopher stumbling through unfamiliar terrain, creating problems and giving explanations where no real problems existed. Shailer Mathews, however, was less inclined to dismiss it so readily. At one moment he would bristle with indignation at being put in such a predicament; but then as the humor of the situation seized him his face would light up with a marvelous smile and he would say, "Of course, 'the fault could be in ourselves.' Whitehead may be telling us something we ought to know about."

From Bernard E. Meland, *The Realities of Faith,* Chapter Four. (New York: Oxford University Press, 1962). Used by permission of Bernard E. Meland.

It was this hunch that led Mathews to invite Henry Nelson Wieman to the Chicago campus to interpret Whitehead's book. Wieman had just broken into the field of philosophy of religion with an equally startling book, *Religious Experience and Scientific Method*. He had been attentive to Whitehead's writing long before the latter had addressed himself to problems of religion or metaphysics. He had read Whitehead's *Inquiry into Principles of Natural Knowledge* (1919), and *The Concept of Nature* (1920), and through these and other works[1] had become acquainted with what was occurring in the new physics. He had adopted the principles of Gestalt psychology as being especially relevant to current issues and problems in religion. He was aware also of the theories in emergent evolution that were then appearing,[2] and considered these to be of a piece with the configurative thinking which the new physics and modern metaphysics were employing. In short, Wieman was attuned to the very notions which had been shaping the imagery of Whitehead's thought, and thus words which appeared to be mere abstractions, or awkward combinations of otherwise familiar words to some readers, conveyed significant new depth of meaning which Whitehead was at pains to present to his readers.

The occasion of Wieman's interpretation was a meeting of the Theology Club of the Divinity School in the Swift Common Room. Edward Scribner Ames, Shirley Jackson Case, Gerald Birney Smith, and Shailer Mathews, and their colleagues were all there, most of them in the front row, and behind them a packed audience extended to the rear of the room, all awaiting the miracle of interpreting "this book." The miracle was performed. With deftness and patience, and with occasional sallies in poetic imagination, Wieman took the key phrases and their basic concepts and translated them into the more familiar imagery of the pragmatic Chicago school. It was as if shuttered windows in one's own household had been swung open, revealing vistas of which one had hitherto been unmindful. Needless to say the act of interpretation in this context was impressive, and the response of the audience was equally so.

[1]Notably *Principia Mathematica* (with Bertrand Russell), 3 vols. (Cambridge University Press, 1910–1913); *The Principle of Relativity* (Cambridge University Press, 1922); *Science and the Modern World* (Macmillan, 1925).

[2]S. Alexander, *Space, Time, and Deity* (Macmillan, 1920), and C. Lloyd Morgan, *Emergent Evolution* (Henry Holt, 1923). In 1926 three more significant studies in emergent evolution were to appear: C. Lloyd Morgan, *Life, Mind, and Spirit;* J. C. Smuts, *Holism and Evolution,* and Edmund Noble, *Purposive Evolution.* Behind these works and underlying their organismic philosophy were Bergson's *Creative Evolution,* which had made a deep impression on Wieman, and the radical empirical writings of William James, especially *Pluralistic Universe* and *Essays in Radical Empiricism.*

I

Now it is what underlies this memorable occasion that is my concern at the moment. I would venture to say that it marked the coming together of two distinct eras of imagery and their consequent perspectives. The Chicago School of Mathews, Ames, and Case was essentially shaped, both in imagery and interest, by the biological notions that had come into general usage through the stimulus of Darwin's *On the Origin of Species*. In fact, one may say that the issue between science and religion had been posed for these men within the ethos of thought which Darwinian evolution had largely created. Not that they depended in any immediate sense upon biological science for their concepts or method, or that they had any conscious concern with Darwin, but the "modernism," "environmentalism," and "functionalism" that were explicit in their methodology and emphasis had been implicitly derived from the Darwinian theory of natural selection. For while, to the popular mind, natural selection conveyed a sanctioning of competitiveness and assertiveness in the interest of survival, to the more specialized mind in psychology and sociology and in the study of religion, it revealed the decisive role of environment and the importance of functional adaptation. Modernism can be understood best, I think, as a blanket term covering the gamut of functional adaptations in response to the demands of a changing environment and the forward-moving perspective consequent to it. And I would claim that modernism, in the technical sense of that term, began with Darwin. Or perhaps one should say that Darwin's theory of evolution gave it its essential impetus precisely in the way that Rousseau sparked the romanticist era and Descartes and Newton launched seventeenth-century rationalism.

To be sure, it took more than a biological theory to set in motion all the cultural forces which were beginning to reshape the ethos of the West in the mid-nineteenth century. The industrial age was in the ascendancy, ready to take full advantage of technical contributions from the physical sciences then coming into their maturity. Through the creation of "invention factories," of which Thomas Edison's laboratory was the precursor, scientific invention was being consciously correlated with industrial needs. The opportunities, both for industrial and for scientific advance, were of such magnitude that nothing, not even the surviving sensibilities of an idealistic age and a mature artistic sense (in retrospect, least of all, these), could restrain the accelerating drive to bend human energy to the task of meeting the immediate demands for adaptation in the service of function, either elicited by opportunities of a changing environment or imposed by current demands. The times were ripe for precisely what did happen in Europe and America in 1859.

Darwin's theory did not create the era; it provided it with the rationale that enabled it to give "full speed ahead" to the process of adaptation, accentuating the concern with practical demands and function. It brought to fruition, or at least to a period of full growth, the bent of mind which had been initiated by Francis Bacon,[3] directing inquiry as well as cultural effort to the idea of achieving mastery over the forces of nature, and turning the concern for knowledge into a zest for power. Pragmatism was to be the philosophy best suited to serve this awakening power culture, and it can be said to have been evoked by the issues which were brought to light by its problems. Similarly, functional psychology was the mode of inquiry into human behavior calculated to yield understanding of the human response to environmental demands, replacing introspective or subjective psychology whose interests were more internal and even mystical. The earlier Chicago School of Theology availed itself of both pragmatism and functional psychology and made these determining factors in its methodology.

Harry Overstreet has said that "there are two kinds of challenge that life makes to us, the challenge of needs and the challenge of the unknown."[4] The imagery of thought provided by the era of modernism, following from the stimulus of Darwinism, clearly expressed a response to the challenge of needs. It would be misleading to say that the challenge of the unknown was wholly absent from this modernistic mode of thought. Even in the Darwinian theory of evolution something of this challenge was acknowledged. In nineteenth-century philosophies elaborating the evolutionary theory it appears as an overtone of agnosticism, as in Herbert Spencer's reference to the Unknowable.[5] Even in modernist theologies like that of Shailer Mathews one senses this agnostic note accompanying the formulation of its practical or functional rationale, as when he wrote,

> Like a vast parabola, the personality-evolving activities of the cosmos touch our little circle of experience. We know not whence they come or whither they go; but we cannot evade them. *We set up relations with them* similar to those which we set up with persons. And thus we derive new strength and courage and moral motive for facing the tasks of life.[6]

The modernist, whether scientist, philosopher, or theologian, was content to confine observation and inquiry to the immediate data at hand and to offer judgment based upon experimentation within these limits. All concern with ultimates was to be excluded from such inquiry, for these lay outside the scope of the method.

[3]Cf. *The Advancement of Learning*, 1605.
[4]*The Enduring Quest* (Chautauqua Press, 1931), vii.
[5]Cf. his *First Principles*. (Appleton, 1862).
[6]*Growth of the Idea of God* (Macmillan, 1931), 230.

This understanding of the limited scope of scientific method had been generally accepted since Kant's *Critique of Pure Reason* (1781); but in nineteenth-century evolutionary parlance it took on the specific meaning that "all beginnings and endings are lost in mystery," a phrase that became commonplace in the sciences and social sciences as a way of dismissing or circumventing probing questions that sought to assess the larger implications or consequences of scientific analysis. What this meant was that, as long as the sciences or any related form of inquiry attended to the immediacies of nature or experience, no ultimate question need intrude or be considered. One can see now that this was a judgment dictated by the modernistic imagery which a confirmed trust in evolution provided. Sanguine modernists could accept this dismissal of ultimate questions because their faith in the evolutionary process was such that they need have no fear of its implications. Usually in such instances there was imported into the scientific view something of the ethos or sensibilities of modern idealism. The mode of thought described as "theistic evolution"[7] which came into prominence in America during the late nineteenth century simultaneously with a resurgence of Hegelianism, spoke of evolution as "God's way of doing things." This was tantamount to identifying God and evolution, which had the effect of insulating the man of faith from whatever dire effects might seem to follow from the scientist's study of the process in the immediate data at hand. Certain scientists, too, were ready to adopt this assumption as an "over-belief," either as men of faith or simply as scientists at work, only too glad to subscribe to whatever might keep the issue between science and religion in a state of quiescence. For many other scientists, however, and for people of a modernistic bent of mind who saw in the sciences "a new messiah," or at least a directive of life displacing both religion and philosophy, this preoccupation with the immediacies to the exclusion of ultimates meant frankly a secularizing of life, that is, a relinquishing of all ideal or transcendent aspects which hope and wonder might evoke. Preoccupation with practical problems and present needs, as science and industry pursued them, offered a way of life that provided incentive and zest enough. This, I should say, is the true meaning of secularism—living shorn of its ultimate dimension and sensibilities. It would not be too farfetched or inaccurate to say that Darwinism in its deeper and persistent effects, as these became manifest in science and industry of the nineteenth and twentieth centuries, and, through them, in other cultural disciplines

[7]John Fiske was one of the earliest exponents of this view. His most substantial work was *Outlines of Cosmic Philosophy* (1874), though smaller works such as *The Destiny of Man* (1884), *The Idea of God* (1885), and *Through Nature to God* (1899), were more influential. Other works contributing to this view were Newman Smyth, *Old Faiths in New Light* (1879), Henry Drummond, *Natural Law in the Spiritual World* (1883), and Lyman Abbott, *The Theology of an Evolutionist* (1897).

and activities, contributed to, if in fact it did not create, a new ethos in Western society, dedicated to the task of dealing with the immediacies of existence in their practical aspect.

II

Now the shift in mode of thought and sensibilities which has marked our recent thinking as a post-Darwinian era has to do chiefly with the reconception of this preoccupation with immediacies. I am not concerned here with detailing corrections and modifications of the Darwinian theory of evolution. There have been many such changes,[8] so significant, in fact, that one wonders if Darwin must not be regarded, even by the biologists themselves, more as a precursor of developments leading to present-day evolutionary thinking rather than as a continuing historical source of our scientific understanding of man. But this may be putting the matter in the extreme. However that may be, it is Darwinism as the scientific sanction of the modernistic ethos with which I am now concerned. The shift in thought and sensibilities to which I refer reveals, not an abandonment of immediacies, but a reconception of them. In this reconception ultimacy and immediacy are seen to be inseparable, as inseparable as space and time. Ultimacy is seen to be in the immediacies of existence, not a remote aspect which is to be designated by the mystery of beginnings or endings. This is what is meant by the much-used phrase in our present discourse, "the dimension of depth." For many of our day, of course, this phrase has only the connotation of a mystifying irrationalism. Actually, however, it stems from serious renovations in the mode and structure of modern thinking.

It all began with modern physics, we are wont to say. In large measure this is true. That is, it is true for many of our most influential thinkers such as Einstein, Planck, Eddington, Millikan, Whitehead, and others. The discoveries and scientific creations of recent years in the field of nuclear energy, transforming our period into a new power age, are directly traceable to the discoveries of radioactive elements by Becquerel and the Curies, inaugurating the new physics.[9] A new depth

---

[8]These revisions of the Darwinian theory of evolution have been interestingly summarized for the general reader in George Gaylord Simpson's *The Meaning of Evolution* (Yale University Press, 1949), and in 1958 published as a Mentor Book in a paper-bound edition.

[9]A full account of these developments leading to the new physics is given in Ernst Zimmer, *The Revolution in Physics* (Harcourt, Brace, 1936), and C. D. Broad, *Scientific Thought* (Routledge & Kegan Paul), 1923. See also Max Planck, *The Universe in the Light of Modern Physics* (W. W. Norton, 1931); Albert Einstein, *Essays in Science* (Philosophical Library, 1934); and Albert Einstein and Leopold Infeld,

of relations and energy revealed in both earlier and more recent experiments has routed the world-view of mechanism which Newton and his followers through the nineteenth century had come to take for granted. Writing in 1927, Robert A. Millikan reported,

> I was present in Berlin on Christmas Eve, 1895, when Professor Roentgen presented to the German Physical Society his first X-ray photographs. Some of them were of the bones of the hand, others of coins and keys photographed through the opaque walls of a leather pocket-book, all clearly demonstrating that he had found some strange new rays which had the amazing property of penetrating as opaque an object as the human body and revealing on a photographic plate the skeleton of a living person.
>
> Here was a completely new phenomenon—a qualitatively new discovery and one having nothing to do with the principles of exact measurement. As I listened and as the world listened, we all began to see that the nineteenth century physicists had taken themselves a little too seriously, that we had not come quite as near sounding the depths of the universe, even in the matter of fundamental physical principles, as we thought we had.[10]

But while physics has been the most formidable source of this sense of depth, developments in other areas of modern thought have also contributed to the new ethos. At the very time that Roentgen and Becquerel were bringing to a close the Newtonian era in science, Henri Bergson and William James were introducing, into philosophy and psychology respectively, the notion of relations as being internal and experienceable; and this was to alter radically the terms of philosophy laid down by Descartes, Kant, and Hegel.

Bergson has often been dismissed by scientists[11] and philosophers[12] alike, possibly for different reasons; but in most instances he has been criticized for his irrationalism and his vitalism. In my judgment both these criticisms have been overdone to the point of neglecting what Bergson was really about. I shall not delay the discussion here to defend Bergson against his critics, except to point out that what is frequently termed "irrationalism" in Bergson is precisely what he has in common with all modern disciplines that take the dimension of depth seriously. Concern with internal relations means, not that

_____

The Evolution of Physics (Simon & Schuster, 1938). Readable accounts of the general situation leading to these developments are given in J. E. Boodin, Three Interpretations of the Universe (Macmillan, 1934), 144ff., and in W. C. Dampier, A History of Science and Its Relations with Philosophy and Religion., 3rd ed. (Macmillan, 1946).

[10]Evolution in Science and Religion (Yale University Press, 1927), 7ff.

[11]Cf. George Gaylord Simpson, 131.

[12]Cf. W. T. Jones, A History of Western Philosophy (Harcourt, Brace, 1952).

one disavows structured meaning to which intelligible inquiry can address itself, but that, to attend to it with any sense of reality, one must employ a mode of inquiry that is appropriate and adequate to deal with structure that is living, that is, dynamic in an organic sense. Bergson distrusted intellect as it was commonly conceived and employed in scientific and philosophical circles precisely because of its abstractive procedure in forming any cognitive judgment. What he was seeking for was a way of apprehending any fact within the living situation so as to capture what was wholly its reality in that living situation. That he chose intuition as a mode of apprehension best calculated to seize such true images of things as they are in their living context simply meant that, of the tools available, this, in his judgment, was best suited to accomplish the intellectual task in its most realistic and vital sense. He was vulnerable at many points, as we are now able to see; for the art of thinking forward, as we live forward,[13] or of perceiving holistically, or relationally, not only was as yet undeveloped but hardly acknowledged as being legitimate in Western thought during Bergson's earlier years when he wrote *Creative Evolution* (1911). What has since become commonplace in modern psychology as field theory under the influence of the Gestalt school and subsequent modes of holistic psychology, and in the new metaphysics since Whitehead,[14] was scarcely manageable or even definable, except as one associated it with the intuitive act.

It must be said, of course, in order not to blur the fallacy in Bergson's method, that he chose intuition as being a mode of apprehension most appropriate to a concern with internal relations precisely because he failed to note or to acknowledge the structural or contextual character of such relations as an external pattern of existence as well. His insistence that that which defied abstraction was simply internal within the living experience precluded a satisfactory conception of the thought process and led him to employ what was available as the antithesis to abstractive cognition, namely, intuition, or, as it is sometimes put, imagism. William James, who sensed the importance of Bergson's effort and shared his impatience with abstract metaphysics and scientism, saw the problem with more proportion. For him relations were experienceable in a way that could make them designative as well, as

[13]This observation that we live forward but think backward was first made by Kierkegaard, and quoted by Harold Hoffding in an article in *The Journal of Philosophy, Psychology, and Scientific Methods.*, II (1905), 85–92. James took up this notion of Kierkegaard's and advanced the notion of thinking forward as we live forward in his *Essays on Radical Empiricism*, p. 238.

[14]Cf. also Dorothy Emmet, *The Nature of Metaphysical Thinking* (Macmillan, 1945), and *Function, Purpose and Powers* (Macmillan, 1958); Susanne Langer, *Philosophy in a New Key* (Harvard University Press, 1958).

in speaking of an experience of transition, or the flux of experience.[15] A persisting positivism in his thinking, however, prevented James from doing full justice to the rich perceptions he had, in his effort to convey the "thickness of experience." What he and Bergson failed to do, Whitehead undertook to accomplish through his method of rational empiricism. However, Whitehead was brought to his metaphysics of relations through the revolution in the new physics; this fact has given to his thought, in designating the nexus of events, more externality than he really means to convey, or should imply. Nevertheless, a close study of his doctrine of prehension will reveal that he is really struggling with the same problem that challenged and excited Bergson and James in their insistence upon relations being experienceable. In Whitehead, the sense of structured meaning in the creative flow or living situation is more marked, and thus less suspect of being a detour into mysticism. One needs the corrective of Bergson and James at times in reading Whitehead, however, lest the formative notions of the new physics implicit in his imagery render one's understanding of this creative nexus more external and rationalistic than it actually can be. There is a depth in the living situation that resists formulation. It was this that Bergson knew well and meant to take with the utmost seriousness and realism. The followers of Whitehead who take his imagery literally without pondering this important insight are inclined to be more rationalistic than Whitehead intended, and than the method of rational empiricism requires.

Again, to speak of another criticism which modern biologists often make of Bergson, I think that we are not to take his formulation of *élan vital* simply as a statement of a vital principle to explain the history of life, as George Gaylord Simpson seems to assume.[16] It is his way, not only of depicting the evolutionary character of all existence, but of accentuating the dynamic context in which all existence is cast, in contrast to the mechanical space-time imagery of pre-evolutionary science and philosophy. It is, as George Herbert Mead has said, a way of "taking time seriously"[17] to the point that no definable space in the mechanistic sense can be designated, or fixed, except as a supposition for purposes which require one to arrest the process, which is to assume that time does not matter or that it does not exist. Bergson's term "duration" is a space-time notion which implies that space can be conceived only in the context of time; and this means that every point of space is in process of passing into a subsequent point, etc. *Elan vital,*

---

[15]Cf. his *Psychology,* Vol. I., esp. chap. IX, and chap. VII, and *Essays in Radical Empiricism,* Chap. VI.

[16]Op. cit., 131.

[17]George Herbert Mead, *Movements of Thought in the Nineteenth Century.* Merritt H. Moore, ed. (University of Chicago Press, 1936), 311ff.

then, is no catchall phrase to explain evolution, in Simpson's sense of that term, but a notion lighting up the dynamic or process character of reality.

The notion of depth as a dimension of the living situation resisting abstract thought, or at least qualifying its relevance to every situation, which we find so dominant in Bergson and in subsequent forms of organismic thinking, is traceable also to other anti-Hegelian developments. The one that has received most attention in our time is that stemming from Soren Kierkegaard and issuing in modern existentialism.[18] I shall not develop this point beyond suggesting that here, too, concern with the ultimate import of the immediate situation associates ultimacy with immediacy in its concreteness. In existentialism the living situation is no mere center of practicality, shorn of ultimate concern. It is the vivid arena of decision and act, carrying the risks and burden of their ultimate meaning. Although the mode of thinking here is radically different from that of modern metaphysics, by following the lead of the new physics, it converges toward the latter in countering the positivism and the practically oriented modernism following from Darwinian evolution, with its stress upon "environmentalism" and "functionalism" as modes of adaptation within a secularized immediacy, an immediacy shorn of depth and ultimacy.

III

There is yet a further aspect to be noted in contrasting creative evolution, as it has taken form within the newer ethos, with evolutionism in its Darwinian and modernistic meaning. Darwin was in every respect indentified with what is now designated *nineteenth-century science*. Now nineteenth-century science is to be understood as the summit of the scientific movement which had begun in the seventeenth century, fulfilling its vision of a mechanistic world order and its dream of the human conquest of nature through measurement and predictability. The success with which physicists particularly had been able to expand, verify, and utilize the image of a world machine provided by Newton led more and more to an assumption of a dependable mech-

---

[18]Important as Kierkegaard is in the recent history of Western thought, especially in theological thought, it is a mistake, I think, to single him out exclusively as if he alone stemmed the tide of abstract thought and opened the way for the "existential" stance. This is to exaggerate his role. The critics of Hegel were legion, and their contributions took a variety of directions. The scope of this variety can be indicated by the mere mention of the names of men who figured in this historical revolution in fundamental notions, for example, Schelling, Herbart (a contemporary of Schelling), Schopenhauer, Feuerbach, Marx, Hartmann, Nietzsche, Freud, Bergson, and William James.

anism underlying every natural phenomenon including man and society. The notion of orderliness in nature had become a dogma. And this at once gave assurance of a wholly rational interpretation of its processes and the growing conviction that mechanism and materialism as a final reading of the nature of reality were indisputable. Darwin's theory certainly followed within this tradition. In fact it was said to exemplify it decisively in the human realm.

We have already noted what happened in physics late in the nineteenth century to upset this dogma of orderliness and to shatter the imagery of mechanism as a controlling notion. "The childish mechanical conceptions of the nineteenth century," declared Millikan in recalling his eyewitness account of Roentgen's report on his experiments, "are now grotesquely inadequate."[19]

The new vision of science to which modern physics was forced to come was not to be universally accepted throughout the sciences. The imagery of mechanism proved to be useful to sciences, such as biology in the late nineteenth century, which were only beginning to achieve measurability and predictability. The younger sciences, bent on attaining precision in these matters, were reluctant to give up the very facilities that assured them such results. It must be said in their defense that often the kind of problem being investigated could be well served by assuming an imagery of mechanism. Modern physics abandoned this imagery precisely because it no longer enabled this science to explore the kind of problem that presented itself, once radioactivity was envisaged. Nevertheless, the lag between other sciences and physics in these matters and the persistence of (the) mechanistic imagery in psychology and the social sciences have been real obstacles to taking this revolution in fundamental notions seriously throughout the various disciplines.

Such a notion as emergence, for example, which is closely allied with the principle of indeterminacy and uncertainty and which was later to develop in physics, actually assumed more credence in physics before it took root in biology and psychology; yet it has more significant implications for the data of the organic and social sciences than for physics. But here again measurement and prediction were at issue. When biologists could see that emergence and structure go together, that the one is present wherever the other appears, there were grounds for seeing that emergence did not preclude measurability, though predictability was to a degree radically lessened. Yet the notion of emergence opened the way for biology really to take the living character of its data seriously.

[19]*Evolution in Science and Religion* (Yale University Press, 1927).

Harry Overstreet wrote in *The Enduring Quest*:

> Professor Jennings has hailed the doctrine of emergent evolution as
> "the declaration of independence of biology." It is not difficult to under-
> stand why. As long as biology was headed for a complete predictability,
> it was necessary to believe that "the only method of learning about the
> organic is to study the inorganic." In short, biology was forced to become
> physics. Every living creature had to be studied, not in terms of its own
> unique configuration, but in terms of its constitutent physicochemical
> parts.[20]

IV

The contrast between Darwinian evolution and the creative or emergent
evolution of recent years may be sharpened if we look more closely at
the decisive notions which are seen to be formative in each case. It was
common in the nineteenth century and even later to set Darwin over
against Lamarck or vice versa, and by this means to point up the contrast
between the inner and the outer orientation of evolutionary thinking.
Lamarck was supposed to have ascribed to the internal condition of
the organism itself, its inheritable side, a good deal of the initiative in
the variations observed. Thus evolution could be said to be inherent
in the organisms of life themselves. Environmental conditions could
be said to be the occasions of change in the activities of the organism;
but the decisive thrust of evolutionary change was internal process of
a sort. One can see how vitalism could draw upon such an orientation
and why Bergson preferred Lamarck to Darwin. Lamarck believed in
a single life process which expressed itself in many forms. Organisms
behaved in certain ways under the pressure of circumstances in the
environment. Every activity of the organism, as Mead has observed,
"altered the form of itself, and the form then handed on the change to
the next generation."[21] The effort of the organism to adapt itself to
these circumstances may, as Bergson has said, be simply mechanical
and external; but it may also involve consciousness and will. Thus
Bergson was moved to say that "Neo-Lamarckism is therefore, of all
later forms of evolutionism, the only one capable of admitting an internal and psychological principle of development, although it is not
bound to do so."[22]

Darwin, on the other hand, tended to look solely at the external
phenomenon of the organism's response to conditions in the environment and to ascribe to such response the initiation of change or varia-

[20]Op. cit., 61–62.
[21]*Movements of Thought in the Nineteenth Century* (University of Chicago
Press, 1936), 159.
[22]Henri Bergson, *Creative Evolution* (Henry Holt, 1911), 77.

tion in the species. All internal factors were set aside, for these presumably, according to Darwin, played no significant role in the evolutionary process.

The issue between these two orientations was not so much discussed as acted upon. The scientist assumed one or the other stance, and, accordingly, moved in the direction of a mechanistic naturalism or in the direction of a more organic view of evolution, often veering toward mysticism or vitalism.

The orientation which best describes the stance of emergent evolution is neither internal nor external but a subtle interplay of both aspects; but this can make sense only if one takes into account the whole discussion of form and structure which has dominated the holistic thinking of those who speak of emergence and field theory. The imagery of organism in relation to environment seems altogther too simple and external to express what is envisaged in these various formulations of a dimension of depth. As Boodin has said, the new intellectual renaissance into which physics has led us in the twentieth century is marked, not only by the emancipation from mechanism, but "the discovery of form or structure as fundamental in reality."[23] In this context, variation, or let us say emergence, is no mere chance response to a condition in environment, as if miscellaneous parts were going their own way, conditioned only by incidental or accidental factors in environment. To quote Boodin again, "Nature is not a mere random collection of parts, but a whole-making activity is manifest in nature."[24] Thus it is emergence with structure.

Now this, I should say, points up the basic difference between the way evolution was conceived in Darwinism and the way in which it is understood by the emergent evolutionist. In Alexander's words, it is nature as a whole that manifests the "nisus toward deity,"[25] deity here being simply the level beyond any presently established structure, and thus the lure toward which the evolutionary thrust is directed. In less metaphysically motivated disciplines the nisus, or the movement toward novelty, is simply expressive of the Gestalt itself. This is a way of saying that relationships carry within themselves a potency that is creative of new situations. They yield a "More," in William James's words, that is not the sum of the parts but a new creation, an emergent quality or character.

Here one will see that the external and the internal have merged, as it were. Or one may say that mechanism has yielded to organism, to the creativity of relationships which are at once internal and external, yet neither one nor the other at any one given moment of time.

[23]Op. cit., 178.
[24]Ibid.
[25]Op. cit. Vol. II, Book IV.

V

The implications of this shift in perspective for theology are quite marked. Darwinian evolution, we noted earlier, created a serious problem for all religious inquiry in the nineteenth century, and, to some extent, continued to do so beyond the turn of the century. A perusal of the literature in religious and theological journals following 1859 throughout the 'sixties will reveal a resounding sense of despair and denunciation. The linkage of man with an animal heritage on grounds of variation dictated simply by his response to environmental changes introduced a dominance of physical influences which could in no way be squared with the Christian doctrine of man. What ultimately turned the tide in a direction which could accommodate theological thinking to the evolutionary view was a resurgence of personal idealism which purported to see the entire process of evolution, animal as well as human, in the context of a cosmic drama presupposing a Creator God. Hermann Lotze's philosophy in *Microcosm*,[26] provided many a theologian and churchman of this period with the key to resolve the issue between religion and evolution. For while he took mechanism seriously as a physical base for all phenomena, including man and society, he was able to show that even the formation of this physical base in each instance took place within the cosmic ground of a higher purpose. Thus the material was a function of the spiritual and, to a degree, a manifestation of it, not its ultimate ground or directive.

It would be difficult to find any one individual of the nineteenth century whose thought proved more basic in resolving the issue between evolutionism and religion than Hermann Lotze. In philosophical circles, especially in nineteenth-century America, the resurgence of Hegelian idealism was to have wider influence in dealing with this problem. Among theologians, however, Lotze's thought, either directly or as mediated through the Ritschlians and the personalists, had the greater impact. Lotze, in placing emphasis upon the disclosure of the spiritual reality in its effects, cut a path between a mechanistic science and an abstract metaphysics and thus was more immediately available to the religiously motivated mind of the period, say from 1880 to the early nineteen twenties. He was the basic source for the American personalist movement founded by Borden P. Bowne; and the frequency with which he was quoted in the writings of other liberal theologians would indicate that his influence was pervasive. I would even claim

[26]Rudolf Hermann Lotze, *Microcosm,* 3 vols. (Leipzig, Verlag von G. Hirzel, 1872). (This work was actually written between the years 1856–1864.) Eng. trans. 1884. Lotze's work was in medicine before he turned to philosophy, and in these writings as well as in the early volumes of *Microcosm* he actually anticipated Darwin's theory.

that the procedure by which Shailer Mathews resolved the issue between evolution and religion, in which he conceived evolution to be a personality-producing activity in the universe continually making the world more personal, partakes of this personal idealistic vein. Mathew's "Noble Lectures," published under the title *The Spiritual Interpretation of History*, were an eloquent account of the march of human history toward this personal end. And in his "Ingersoll Lectures," *Immortality and the Cosmic Process*, he saw this movement of life toward the personal continuing beyond death. Immortality was itself another stage in the fulfillment of personality.

Edward Scribner Ames was more cautious than Mathews about injecting so tenuous a metaphysical notion as "personality-producing activities" into the empirical discussion of religion. He was willing to settle for what he called "practical absolutes,"[27] that is, visions of the mind or idealizations which, at any given time, had the value of an ultimate directive in decision or action, but which were clearly to be understood as being a piece with man's own nature and experience. It was man acting with full commitment to idealized dimensions of his experience. One will see, even here, the shadow of idealism. And this was generally true of the pragmatist when he expressed himself even tentatively in the ontological vein. For it must be said that, while the pragmatist considered himself to be departing from Hegel and from any explicit ontology, it was generally the abstract, universal notions from which he was departing. The process of idealization remained intact at the empirical level. Thus pragmatism must be seen as a truncated idealism. The superstructure of the Absolute or of a personal God may have been relinquished, but the idealization of the human equation, consonant with such a superstructure, was as decisive as ever. This was as evident in Dewey as it was in Ames and Mathews.

The Chicago School of Theology made much of its opposition to philosophical idealism; but its strategy of thought in transmuting evolution into something other than mechanistic naturalism was actually dictated and directed by the vestigial remains of its own personal idealism. It could hardly be otherwise, with "environmentalism" and "functionalism" playing so large a role in the formulation of its critical method. There was nothing in the method itself to justify a religious or a Christian resolution of problems that emerged. Some recourse to idealism, as a counterpart or corrective of the mechanism implied in its environmental and functional method, was demanded, whether implicitly or explicitly employed.

The change that has come about in theologies that partake of crea-

[27]Cf. his "Religious Values and the Practical Absolute," *International Journal of Ethics*, XXX (1922), 347–365.

tive and emergent evolution can be described in this way: since mechanism is no longer the base of their evolutionary thinking, idealism is no longer essential as a strategy of thought in resolving the tension between science and faith. The relinquishment of the dichotomy implied in the issue between mechanism and idealism has been followed by a reformulation of the meaning of man and nature. Whether one speaks of this as a new naturalism or a religious naturalism, or abandons these terms altogether, choosing to see the world of reality in its dynamic and creative character as being "dimensional," and expressive of many stages of creative emergence, the correlation of man and nature, in contrast to their antithesis in earlier evolutionary and idealistic thinking, seems evident.

The notion of dimensions or levels of reality within nature has introduced into this later mode of evolutionary thinking qualitative distinctions which alter one's understanding of the conditions under which evolution occurs; such a concept also alters the implications of the notion itself. To put it sharply, discontinuities appear between levels or structures by reason of the something new that has occurred to create the one level which transcends the other. "Emergence with structure" thus implies structural change and qualitative innovations which, as it were, set the one apart from the other, even as their continuity in nature is acknowledged. The novel event is never reducible to its antecedents, once emergence has occurred; it is not simply the sum of its parts, but real innovation. Spirit, personality, community individuality, psychical qualities, organic processes, each in its own way manifests a *More,* a novelty in quality and in structure by which it transcends its antecedents. Yet transcendence is never separation or alienation, for the higher subsumes the lower. Thus dimensional thinking provides a context of continuity within which discontinuities are constantly occurring.

This more complex evolutionary picture reduces mechanism and fixity to the minimum, yet retains them in forms appropriate to the level or dimension of emergence. It accentuates the role of freedom, thus extending the range of flexibility; yet it sees all freedom and flexibility as being within a field or structure of relationships.

Such a complexity at once alters the fundamental imagery from which implications or consequent meanings are formed. For example, the notion of automatic progress, which seemed to follow rather naturally from nineteenth-century evolutionism, cannot be deduced so readily from this context. The simultaneity of continuity and discontinuity within any dimension or level, of mechanism and freedom, of moral and rational qualities of personality and the grace and forgiveness of spirit, of individuality and community, bring to each event or existing situation the tension and contradiction inherent in the complexity of each structure. What Kant perceived as "radical evil," rendering the freedom of man subservient to the mechanisms of nature that persisted in him, takes on an even darker and more subtle turn in this emergent situation. For the issue is not simply between freedom and mechanism, as in the Kantian view, or between the personal and man's vestigial animal heritage, as nineteenth-century personal idealists viewed it. Rather, it is a variation of these along with the demonry of personality itself, of man's moral and rational capacities in tension with the sensitivities of spirit as a higher dimension of freedom and goodness which grasp him as a novelty of grace within his human structure, judging him, yet summoning him to that which is beyond his own human order of good.

This sense of tension and contradiction is not of necessity a movement onward and upward. It is fraught more with frustration, dissipation, pride, and pretension, and the anxiety which must inevitably ensue from these human failings demanding resolution in a doctrine of redemption.

Or again, it does not follow from this emergent reading of the human situation that the structure of man, that is, "personality," is dominant and sovereign in value. Moral and rational good, expressive of man's ideal aspects and thus characteristic of this human dimension, stands under the judgment of a sensitivity more consonant with the freedom of spirit, a structure of sensitivity and grace transcending man's level. The grace of the spirit evident in acts of love and forgiveness, though present in the human structure, is not to be subsumed under its category. Thus any idealization of the human equation or projection of it as an absolute or ultimate good becomes a voluntary act of illusion, making absolute a level of reality which is patently relative and thus insulating the characteristically human structure of personality from its sensitive frontier where it might otherwise encounter the dimension of spirit, expressive within its own structure, yet not of it.

The Darwinian theory of evolution took form in a period of history when individuality was itself at a premium. It was often expressed as the "primacy of the person," a dictum which had been affirmed since the time of Descartes. Obviously, some of the qualitative overtones of this liberal dictum were seriously threatened by the evolutionary theory, principally because its ideal aspects appeared to be dissipated under the disclosure of man's animal antecedents. Furthermore, in its concern with the species, the priority of the individual person tended inevitably to be obscured. Nevertheless, the virtues of individuality as such were enhanced. Individualism, in fact, gained a new status, encouraging aggressiveness, if not ruthlessness, in the pursuit of individual enterprise as adaptability and the competitiveness it entailed. What natural science stimulated, industry furthered in the very mode of activity it promoted and the ethos it tended to generate within communities and within culture as a whole.

What has followed from the creative evolution of emergence and the accompanying notion of field theory, on the other hand, is a radically different view of individuality and of human fulfillment. It would be a mistake to say that it reverses matters, setting up community in opposition to individuality. To some extent this has followed; though when it occurs, it represents an exaggeration or even a perversion of what is implied in this newer image of man. For while relations are real and can be experienced, forming the context of man's being and providing resources of energy and power which are greater and other than he, himself, can effect, they are also expressive of what he, in himself, represents. The truer imagery is the one formulated by Whitehead, in saying that the topic of religion is "individual in community,[28] which is to see individual values empowered through relationships, and the community expressive of freedom and qualitative differences. In this context the meaning of men enlarges because selfhood itself widens and deepens its bounds. Freedom also changes in meaning. In addition to connoting a measure of independent judgment or decision as well as flexibility, it means, in this context, freedom to have relations, freedom to avail one's self of the grace and power which relationships can bestow. The atomism of the autonomous self thus gives way to a sound sense of the community of being and the responsibility, as well as the opportunity, of being fulfilled within such a creative nexus.

One can see, then, that the theological significance of this reorientation of evolutionary thinking could be considerable. However, the relevance of the imagery provided by such notions as emergence and field theory to the theological task will be judged variously. Those theologians who are persuaded by present discussions in analytical philosophy will insist that even a consideration of the problem of their relevance to theology is misguided; for this is to confuse two different areas of discourse, the scientific and the religious. Others, open to the suggestion that some interrelation between discourses is permissible, will object to intruding these particular notions into current theological thinking on the grounds that they are not significant or even legitimate notions in the biological sciences themselves. Again, theologians who are persuaded of their usefulness in conveying theological meaning to the contemporary mind may have gone so far as to claim emergent evolution to be a theological symbol by which biblical events

---

[28]*RM*. Whitehead, in using this phrase, was reaffirming a notion well known in classical Christian thinking, as expressed in the Covenant and in the *Imago Dei*. But his metaphysics sets forth a new rationale for it, giving it added contemporary force.

of history as well as subsequent doctrinal formulations may be explicated. This view was implicit in the theological writings of the late Archbishop William Temple, particularly in his volume on *Nature, Man, and God.* It has been explicity set forth by another British theologian, L. S. Thornton, in his trilogy on *The Form of the Servant,*[29] in which he virtually equates the terms "emergence" and "revelation." A more recent exposition of this position appears in a paper by John Hayward entitled "Evolution as a Theological Symbol."

The problem of how scientific, philosophical, or even common-sense notions are to be employed in bringing intelligibility to the Christian faith intrudes here. I would venture to suggest that to apply them so directly and completely as to subsume all theological meaning under these notions is to make too much of them. They are at best analogies that can help the modern mind to take such Christian concepts as "revelation," "grace," and "spirit" more seriously than is possible within the monolithic discourse which our contemporary disciplines provide. This applies particularly to many of our time who have been schooled in the thought of Western culture, say from the period of the enlightenment through nineteenth-century philosophy and science. The imagery of thought provided by this period literally closed the modern mind to dimensions of meaning which such terms as "revelation," "spirit," and "grace" convey. The aversion to supernaturalism or to any appearance of dualism that seemed to threaten or to undo the assumption of "one-world order of meaning" has rendered the modern consciousness peculiarly insensitive to the great themes of Christian faith that have meant to point beyond man's own human powers and resources. And with no imagery available, other than that of supernaturalism, to suggest such nuances or sensitive ground for pointing toward dimensions of grace or spirit, Christian faith could mean for the modern consciousness only confidence in the resources of man's moral idealism. The radical turn of Protestant thought in recent years, motivated largely by a rediscovery of Kierkegaard's critique of modern idealism, represents one serious reaction within Western culture against this impasse and self-enclosure. But the protest extends beyond specifically theological literature. For example, what has come about in the shift of imagery exemplified in the new physics and in emergent thinking generally represents not so much a reaction as a radical reconception of fundamental notions, altering the modern consciousness itself. Insofar as one partakes of this deepened mode of modern consciousness, one is made aware of depths and nuances in the complexities of man's existence which at once sober one with the limits of

[29]This trilogy includes I, *Revelation and the Modern World,* 1950; II, *The Dominion of Christ,* 1952; and III, *Christ and the Church,* 1956).

man's reason and perceptive powers, and awaken one to the very dimensions of experience to which the themes of the Christian faith bear witness.

It is quite possible that, when one has been awakened to the import of the Christian witness through a distinctive imagery, partaking of specific philosophical or scientific notions, these notions will affect one's speech and even condition one's understanding of the witness to faith. It was so with Augustine, for whom Neoplatonism served such a role, enabling him to take the Gospels seriously, whereas previously they had offended his disciplined taste. But it does not follow that one is necessarily subjected to these thought-forms in his effort to understand the witness to faith. Insofar as they are assumed to be "instruments of vision," lighting up realities of the spirit which would otherwise remain obscure, or even nonexistent, they will be understood to be subservient to the realities disclosed. What is thus seen and heard within this more sensitive stance will bring its own occasion of judgment and understanding.

To speak specifically on this point, the fact that form and relationship have been restored to the current image of man, both in the new metaphysics and in the sciences of man, enables us to be more understanding in our anthropology of what is being conveyed in such historically biblical notions as the Covenant and the *Imago Dei*. Care needs to be exercised, lest we make the correlation between these biblical notions and contemporary ideas too complete and simple. There are differences to be noted, respected, and seriously pondered. Nevertheless, the recovery of these valued notions in the current discourse is a decided gain. Where the dialogue between this newer modern consciousness and the biblical witness is sensitively pursued, it can yield the kind of critical insight into our understanding of man which we desperately need in this age of yearning and conflict.

Religion and Science   23

Alfred North Whitehead

The difficulty in approaching the question of the relations between
Religion and Science is, that its elucidation requires that we have in
our minds some clear idea of what we mean by either of the terms,
'religion' and 'science.' Also I wish to speak in the most general way
possible, and to keep in the background any comparison of particular
creeds, scientific or religious. We have got to understand the type of
connection which exists between the two spheres, and then to draw
some definite conclusions respecting the existing situation which at
present confronts the world.

The *conflict* between religion and science is what naturally occurs
to our minds when we think of this subject. It seems as though, during
the last half-century, the results of science and the beliefs of religion
had come into a position of frank disagreement, from which there can
be no escape, except by abandoning either the clear teaching of science,
or the clear teaching of religion. This conclusion has been urged by
controversialists on either side. Not by all controversialists, of course,
but by those trenchant intellects which every controversy calls out
into the open.

The distress of sensitive minds, and the zeal for truth, and the
sense of the importance of the issues, must command our sincerest
sympathy. When we consider what religion is for mankind, and what
science is, it is no exaggeration to say that the future course of history
depends upon the decision of this generation as to the relations between
them. We have here the two strongest general forces (apart from the
mere impulse of the various senses) which influence men, and they
seem to be set one against the other—the force of our religious intui-

Reprinted with permission of the Macmillan Company and Cambridge University
Press from *Science and the Modern World* by Alfred North Whitehead. Copyright
1925 by The Macmillan Company; renewed 1953 by Evelyn Whitehead.

tions, and the force of our impulse to accurate observation and logical deduction.

A great English statesman once advised his countrymen to use large-scale maps, as a preservative against alarms, panics, and general misunderstanding of the true relations between nations. In the same way in dealing with the clash between permanent elements of human nature, it is well to map our history on a large scale, and to disengage ourselves from our immediate absorption in the present conflicts. When we do this, we immediately discover two great facts. In the first place, there has always been a conflict between religion and science; and in the second place, both religion and science have always been in a state of continual development. In the early days of Christianity, there was a general belief among Christians that the world was coming to an end in the lifetime of people then living. We can make only indirect inferences as to how far this belief was authoritatively proclaimed; but it is certain that it was widely held, and that it formed an impressive part of the popular religious doctrine. The belief proved itself to be mistaken, and Christian doctrine adjusted itself to the change. Again in the early Church individual theologians very confidently deduced from the Bible opinions concerning the nature of the physical universe. In the year A. D. 535, a monk named Cosmas[1] wrote a book which he entitled, *Christian Topography*. He was a travelled man who had visited India and Ethiopia; and finally he lived in a monastery at Alexandria, which was then a great centre of culture. In this book, basing himself upon the direct meaning of Biblical texts as construed by him in a literal fashion, he denied the existence of the antipodes, and asserted that the world is a flat parallelogram whose length is double its breadth.

In the seventeenth century the doctrine of the motion of the earth was condemned by a Catholic tribunal. A hundred years ago the extension of time demanded by geological science distressed religious people, Protestant and Catholic. And to-day the doctrine of evolution is an equal stumbling-block. These are only a few instances illustrating a general fact.

But all our ideas will be in a wrong perspective if we think that this recurring perplexity was confined to contradictions between religion and science; and that in these controversies religion was always wrong, and that science was always right. The true facts of the case are very much more complex, and refuse to be summarised in these simple terms.

Theology itself exhibits exactly the same character of gradual development, arising from an aspect of conflict between its own proper

---

[1]William E. H. Lecky, *The History of the Rise and Influence of the Spirit of Rationalism in Europe* (London: Longmans, Green, 1910), Chap. III.

ideas. This fact is a commonplace to theologians, but is often obscured in the stress of controversy. I do not wish to overstate my case; so I will confine myself to Roman Catholic writers. In the seventeenth century a learned Jesuit, Father Petavius, showed that the theologians of the first three centuries of Christianity made use of phrases and statements which since the fifth century would be condemned as heretical. Also Cardinal Newman devoted a treatise to the discussion of the development of doctrine. He wrote it before he became a great Roman Catholic ecclesiastic; but throughout his life, it was never retracted and continually reissued.

Science is even more changeable than theology. No man of science could subscribe without qualification to Galileo's beliefs, or to Newton's beliefs, or to all his own scientific beliefs of ten years ago.

In both regions of thought, additions, distinctions, and modifications have been introduced. So that now, even when the same assertion is made to-day as was made a thousand, or fifteen hundred years ago, it is made subject to limitations or expansions of meaning, which were not contemplated at the earlier epoch. We are told by logicians that a proposition must be either true or false, and that there is no middle term. But in practice, we may know that a proposition expresses an important truth, but that it is subject to limitations and qualifications which at present remain undiscovered. It is a general feature of our knowledge, that we are insistently aware of important truths; and yet that the only formulations of these truths which we are able to make presuppose a general standpoint of conceptions which may have to be modified. I will give you two illustrations, both from science: Galileo said that the earth moves and that the sun is fixed; the Inquisition said that the earth is fixed and the sun moves; and Newtonian astronomers, adopting an absolute theory of space, said that both the sun and the earth move. But now we say that any one of these three statements is equally true, provided that you have fixed your sense of 'rest' and 'motion' in the way required by the statement adopted. At the date of Galileo's controversy with the Inquisition, Galileo's way of stating the facts was, beyond question, the fruitful procedure for the sake of scientific research. But in itself it was not more true than the formulation of the Inquisition. But at that time the modern concepts of relative motion were in nobody's mind; so that the statements were made in ignorance of the qualifications required for their more perfect truth. Yet this question of the motions of the earth and the sun expresses a real fact in the universe; and all sides had got hold of important truths concerning it. But with the knowledge of those times, the truths appeared to be inconsistent.

Again I will give you another example taken from the state of modern physical science. Since the time of Newton and Huyghens in the seventeenth century there have been two theories as to the physical nature of light. Newton's theory was that a beam of light consists of a stream of very minute particles, or corpuscles, and that we have the sensation of light when these corpuscles strike the retinas of our eyes. Huyghens' theory was that light consists of very minute waves of trembling in an all-pervading ether, and that these waves are travelling along a beam of light. The two theories are contradictory. In the eighteenth century Newton's theory was believed, in the nineteenth century Huyghens' theory was believed. To-day there is one large group of phenomena which can be explained only on the wave theory, and another large group which can be explained only on the corpuscular theory. Scientists have to leave it at that, and wait for the future, in the hope of attaining some wider vision which reconciles both.

We should apply these same principles to the questions in which there is a variance between science and religion. We would believe nothing in either sphere of thought which does not appear to us to be certified by solid reasons based upon the critical research either of ourselves or of competent authorities. But granting that we have honestly taken this precaution, a clash between the two on points of detail where they overlap should not lead us hastily to abandon doctrines for which we have solid evidence. It may be that we are more interested in one set of doctrines than in the other. But, if we have any sense of perspective and of the history of thought, we shall wait and refrain from mutual anathemas.

We should wait: but we should not wait passively, or in despair. The clash is a sign that there are wider truths and finer perspectives within which a reconciliation of a deeper religion and a more subtle science will be found.

In one sense, therefore, the conflict between science and religion is a slight matter which has been unduly emphasised. A mere logical contradiction cannot in itself point to more than the necessity of some readjustments, possibly of a very minor character on both sides. Remember the widely different aspects of events which are dealt with in science and in religion respectively. Science is concerned with the general conditions which are observed to regulate physical phenomena; whereas religion is wholly wrapped up in the contemplation of moral and aesthetic values. On the one side there is the law of gravitation, and on the other the contemplation of the beauty of holiness. What one side sees, the other misses; and vice versa.

Consider, for example, the lives of John Wesley and of Saint Francis of Assisi. For physical science you have in these lives merely ordinary examples of the operation of the principles of physiological chemistry, and of the dynamics of nervous reactions: for religion you have lives of the most profound significance in the history of the world.

Can you be surprised that, in the absence of a perfect and complete phrasing of the principles of science and of the principles of religion which apply to these specific cases, the accounts of these lives from these divergent standpoints should involve discrepancies? It would be a miracle if it were not so.

It would, however, be missing the point to think that we need not trouble ourselves about the conflict between science and religion. In an intellectual age there can be no active interest which puts aside all hope of a vision of the harmony of truth. To acquiesce in discrepancy is destructive of candour, and of moral cleanliness. It belongs to the self-respect of intellect to pursue every tangle of thought to its final unravelment. If you check that impulse, you will get no religion and no science from an awakened thoughtfulness. The important question is, In what spirit are we going to face the issue? There we come to something absolutely vital.

A clash of doctrines is not a disaster—it is an opportunity. I will explain my meaning by some illustrations from science. The weight of an atom of nitrogen was well known. Also it was an established scientific doctrine that the average weight of such atoms in any considerable mass will be always the same. Two experimenters, the late Lord Rayleigh and the late Sir William Ramsay, found that if they obtained nitrogen by two different methods, each equally effective for that purpose, they always observed a persistent slight difference between the average weights of the atoms in the two cases. Now I ask you, would it have been rational of these men to have despaired because of this conflict between chemical theory and scientific observation? Suppose that for some reason the chemical doctrine had been highly prized throughout some district as the foundation of its social order:—would it have been wise, would it have been candid, would it have been moral, to forbid the disclosure of the fact that the experiments produced discordant results? Or, on the other hand, should Sir William Ramsay and Lord Rayleigh have proclaimed that chemical theory was now a detected delusion? We see at once that either of these ways would have been a method of facing the issue in an entirely wrong spirit. What Rayleigh and Ramsay did was this: They at once perceived that they had hit upon a line of investigation which would disclose some subtlety of chemical theory that had hitherto eluded observation. The discrepancy was not a disaster: it was an opportunity to increase the sweep of chemical knowledge. You all know the end of the story: finally argon was discovered, a new chemical element which had lurked undetected, mixed with the nitrogen. But the story has a sequel which forms my second illustration. This discovery drew attention to the importance of observing accurately minute differences in chemical substances as obtained by different methods. Further researches of the most careful accuracy were undertaken. Finally another physicist, F. W. Aston, working in the Cavendish Laboratory at Cambridge in England, discovered that even the same element might assume two or more distinct forms, termed *isotopes,* and that the law of the constancy of average atomic weight holds for each of these forms, but as between the different isotopes differs slightly. The research has effected a great stride in the power of chemical theory, far transcending in importance the discovery of argon from which it originated. The moral of these stories lies on the surface, and I will leave to you their application to the case of religion and science.

In formal logic, a contradiction is the signal of a defeat: but in the evolution of real knowledge it marks the first step in progress towards a victory. This is one great reason for the utmost toleration of variety of opinion. Once and forever, this duty of toleration has been summed up in the words, 'Let both grow together until the harvest.' The failure of Christians to act up to this precept, of the highest authority, is one of the curiosities of religious history. But we have not yet exhausted the discussion of the moral temper required for the pursuit of truth. There are short cuts leading merely to an illusory success. It is easy enough to find a theory, logically harmonious and with important applications in the region of fact, provided that you are content to disregard half your evidence. Every age produces people with clear logical intellects, and the most praiseworthy grasp of the importance of some sphere of human experience, who have elaborated, or inherited, a scheme of thought which exactly fits those experiences which claim their interest. Such people are apt resolutely to ignore, or to explain away, all evidence which confuses their scheme with contradictory instances. What they cannot fit in is for them nonsense. An unflinching determination to take the whole evidence into account is the only method of preservation against the fluctuating extremes of fashionable opinion. This advice seems so easy, and is in fact so difficult to follow.

One reason for this difficulty is that we cannot think first and act afterwards. From the moment of birth we are immersed in action, and can only fitfully guide it by taking thought. We have, therefore, in various spheres of experience to adopt those ideas which seem to work within those spheres. It is absolutely necessary to trust to ideas which are generally adequate, even though we know that there are subtleties and distinctions beyond our ken. Also apart from the necessities of action, we cannot even keep before our minds the whole evidence except under the guise of doctrines which are incompletely harmonised. We cannot think in terms of an indefinite multiplicity of detail; our evidence can acquire its proper importance only if it comes before us marshalled by general ideas. These ideas we inherit—they form the tradition of our civilisation. Such traditional ideas are never static. They are either fading into meaningless formulae, or are gaining power by the new lights thrown by a more delicate apprehension. They are transformed by the urge of critical reason, by the vivid evidence of emotional experience, and by the cold certainties of scientific perception. One fact is certain, you cannot keep them still. No generation can merely reproduce its ancestors. You may preserve the life in a flux of form, or preserve the form amid an ebb of life. But you cannot permanently enclose the same life in the same mould.

The present state of religion among the European races illustrates the statements which I have been making. The phenomena are mixed. There have been reactions and revivals. But on the whole, during many generations, there has been a gradual decay of religious influence in European civilisation. Each revival touches a lower peak than its predecessor, and each period of slackness a lower depth. The average curve marks a steady fall in religious tone. In some countries the interest in religion is higher than in others. But in those countries where the interest is relatively high, it still falls as the generations pass. Religion is tending to degenerate into a decent formula wherewith to embellish a comfortable life. A great historical movement on this scale results from the convergence of many causes. I wish to suggest two of them which lie within the scope of this chapter for consideration.

In the first place for over two centuries religion has been on the defensive, and on a weak defensive. The period has been one of unprecedented intellectual progress. In this way a series of novel situations have been produced for thought. Each such occasion has found the religious thinkers unprepared. Something, which has been proclaimed to be vital, has finally, after struggle, distress, and anathema, been modified and otherwise interpreted. The next generation of religious apologists then congratulates the religious world on the deeper insight which has been gained. The result of the continued repetition of this undignified retreat, during many generations, has at last almost entirely destroyed the intellectual authority of religious thinkers. Consider this contrast: when Darwin or Einstein proclaim theories which modify our ideas, it is a triumph for science. We do not go about saying that there is another defeat for science, because its old ideas have been abandoned. We know that another step of scientific insight has been gained.

Religion will not regain its old power until it can face change in the same spirit as does science. Its principles may be eternal, but the expression of those principles requires continual development. This evolution of religion is in the main a disengagement of its own proper ideas from the adventitious notions which have crept into it by reason of the expression of its own ideas in terms of the imaginative picture of the world entertained in previous ages. Such a release of religion from the bonds of imperfect science is all to the good. It stresses its own genuine message. The great point to be kept in mind is that normally an advance in science will show that statements of various religious beliefs require some sort of modification. It may be that they have to be expanded or explained, or indeed entirely restated. If the religion is a sound expression of truth, this modification will only exhibit more adequately the exact point which is of importance. This process is a gain. In so far, therefore, as any religion has any contact with physical facts, it is to be expected that the point of view of those facts must be continually modified as scientific knowledge advances. In this way, the exact relevance of these facts for religious thought will grow more and more clear. The progress of science must result in the unceasing codification of religious thought, to the great advantage of religion.

The religious controversies of the sixteenth and seventeenth centuries put theologians into a most unfortunate state of mind. They were always attacking and defending. They pictured themselves as the garrison of a fort surrounded by hostile forces. All such pictures express half-truths. That is why they are so popular. But they are dangerous. This particular picture fostered a pugnacious party spirit which really expresses an ultimate lack of faith. They dared not modify, because they shirked the task of disengaging their spiritual message from the associations of a particular imagery.

Let me explain myself by an example. In the early medieval times, Heaven was in the sky, and Hell was underground; volcanoes were the jaws of Hell. I do not assert that these beliefs entered into the official formulations: but they did enter into the popular understanding of the general doctrines of Heaven and Hell. These notions were what everyone thought to be implied by the doctrine of the future state. They entered into the explanations of the influential exponents of Christian belief. For example, they occur in the *Dialogues* of Pope Gregory,[2] the Great, a man whose high official position is surpassed only by the magnitude of his services to humanity. I am not saying what we ought to believe about the future state. But whatever be the right doctrine, in this instance the clash between religion and science, which has relegated the earth to the position of a second-rate planet attached to a second-rate sun, has been greatly to the benefit of the spirituality of religion by dispersing these medieval fancies.

Another way of looking at this question of the evolution of religious thought is to note that any verbal form of statement which has been before the world for some time discloses ambiguities; and that often such ambiguities strike at the very heart of the meaning. The effective sense in which a doctrine has been held in the past cannot be deter-

[2]*Cf.* F. A. Gregorovius, *History of Rome in the Middle Ages* (London: G. Bell & Sons, 1894), Book III, Ch. III, Vol. II, English trans. by Annie Hamilton.

mined by the mere logical analysis of verbal statements, made in ignorance of the logical trap. You have to take into account the whole
reaction of human nature to the scheme of thought. This reaction is of
a mixed character, including elements of emotion derived from our
lower natures. It is here that the impersonal criticism of science and of
philosophy comes to the aid of religious evolution. Example after example can be given of this motive force in development. For example,
the logical difficulties inherent in the doctrine of the moral cleansing of
human nature by the power of religion rent Christianity in the days of
Pelagius and Augustine—that is to say, at the beginning of the fifth century. Echoes of that controversy still linger in theology.

So far, my point has been this: that religion is the expression of one
type of fundamental experiences of mankind: that religious thought develops into an increasing accuracy of expression, disengaged from adventitious imagery: that the interaction between religion and science is
one great factor in promoting this development.

I now come to my second reason for the modern fading of interest
in religion. This involves the ultimate question which I stated in my
opening sentences. We have to know what we mean by religion. The
churches, in their presentation of their answers to this query, have put
forward aspects of religion which are expressed in terms either suited
to the emotional reactions of bygone times or directed to excite modern
emotional interests of nonreligious character. What I mean under the
first heading is that religious appeal is directed partly to excite that instinctive fear of the wrath of a tyrant which was inbred in the unhappy
populations of the arbitrary empires of the ancient world, and in particular to excite that fear of an all-powerful arbitrary tyrant behind the
unknown forces of nature. This appeal to the ready instinct of brute
fear is losing its force. It lacks any directness of response, because modern science and modern conditions of life have taught us to meet occasions of apprehension by a critical analysis of their causes and
conditions. Religion is the reaction of human nature to its search for
God. The presentation of God under the aspect of power awakens every
modern instinct of critical reaction. This is fatal; for religion collapses
unless its main positions command immediacy of assent. In this respect
the old phraseology is at variance with the psychology of modern civili-
sations. This change in psychology is largely due to science, and is one
of the chief ways in which the advance of science has weakened the
hold of the old religious forms of expression. The non-religious motive
which has entered into modern religious thought is the desire for a comfortable organisation of modern society. Religion has been presented as
valuable for the ordering of life. Its claims have been rested upon its
function as a sanction to right conduct. Also the purpose of right conduct quickly degenerates into the formation of pleasing social relations.

We have here a subtle degradation of religious ideas, following upon their gradual purification under the influence of keener ethical intuitions. Conduct is a by-product of religion—an inevitable by-product, but not the main point. Every great religious teacher has revolted against the presentation of religion as a mere sanction of rules of conduct. Saint Paul denounced the Law, and Puritan divines spoke of the filthy rags of righteousness. The insistence upon rules of conduct marks the ebb of religious fervour. Above and beyond all things, the religious life is not a research after comfort. I must now state, in all diffidence, what I conceive to be the essential character of the religious spirit.

Religion is the vision of something which stands beyond, behind, and within, the passing flux of immediate things; something which is real, and yet waiting to be realised; something which is a remote possibility, and yet the greatest of present facts; something that gives meaning to all that passes, and yet eludes apprehension; something whose possession is the final good, and yet is beyond all reach; something which is the ultimate ideal, and the hopeless quest.

The immediate reaction of human nature to the religious vision is worship. Religion has emerged into human experience mixed with the crudest fancies of barbaric imagination. Gradually, slowly, steadily the vision recurs in history under nobler form and with clearer expression. It is the one element in human experience which persistently shows an upward trend. It fades and then recurs. But when it renews its force, it recurs with an added richness and purity of content. The fact of the religious vision, and its history of persistent expansion, is our one ground for optimism. Apart from it, human life is a flash of occasional enjoyments lighting up a mass of pain and misery, a bagatelle of transient experience.

The vision claims nothing but worship; and worship is a surrender to the claim for assimilation, urged with the motive force of mutual love. The vision never overrules. It is always there, and it has the power of love presenting the one purpose whose fulfillment is eternal harmony. Such order as we find in nature is never force—it presents itself as the one harmonious adjustment of complex detail. Evil is the brute motive force of fragmentary purpose, disregarding the eternal vision. Evil is overruling, retarding, hurting. The power of God is the worship He inspires. That religion is strong which in its ritual and its modes of thought evokes an apprehension of the commanding vision. The worship of God is not a rule of safety—it is an adventure of the spirit, a flight after the unattainable. The death of religion comes with the repression of the high hope of adventure.

Time, Progress, and the Kingdom of God

24

Daniel Day Williams

The Christian faith that God works creatively and redemptively in human history does not contradict the facts of history. It is required by
those facts when we see deeply enough into them. So we have asserted.
We have argued that man's bond with the ultimate structure of God's
good, and man's dependence upon the working of God's power is disclosed in the midst of the turmoil of our existence. We can discern the
presence of the ultimate order of love even in the political orders where
compromise, clash of interests, and warfare seem to prevail in disregard
of the divine law. God's Kingdom, which is the assertion of His love
with power, does "press upon" the world at every moment. Yet even as
we make this assertion we recognize that we live in actual estrangement
from God. There is a dark reality of evil which sets the creation against
God's love, and turns the human heart upon itself. We are left therefore
with the perplexity which we must examine in this chapter. Can we believe in the progress of the reign of God in history or is the ultimate
conflict between His Kingdom and the kingdoms of this world unre-
solved to the end of time?

I

The question of progress involves the problem of the nature of time
which has been hovering on the edge of our discussion and which must
now be brought to the center of attention. Our life passes from birth to
death. The world moves into its future, and moment by moment dies
away. What is lost and what is saved in this everlasting passage? Does
God's Kingdom really grow in depth and fulfillment through the long
sweep of the ages, or is that merely an outworn liberal notion which has
brought liberal theology to its present extremity?

There are some who say that all attempts to speak of the course of events in relation to an indeterminate future are speculative and fruitless. Had we not better say "it doth not yet appear what we shall be" and go about our business unafraid and untroubled? Certainly humility and reserve are appropriate. No questions lead us so quickly beyond our depth as those concerning time. There is a certain practical wisdom in refusing to allow the fulfillment of today's task to depend upon answers to obscure questions about tomorrow.

Yet to leave the matter there is not only superficial, it is paralyzing to action, for hope has practical consequences. Hope in the human spirit means its relation to the future before it, the eternity above it, and the saving of the precious values of its past. The depth and range of hope qualifies our sense of the worth of the present. I am in part what I hope for; for what I am is what I am willing to commit myself to, and that depends upon what I believe finally counts. As Professor Whitehead observes, "The greater part of morality hinges upon relevance in the future."[1] I encounter my neighbor as one who shares with me the fate of death. If death destroys for me my hope, it also destroys my valuation of my neighbor. I can treat him as a bit of earth dust, to be exploited for whatever momentary benefit I can secure from him. But if my hope for all of life involves the belief that the good of life has eternal stature then I see my neighbor in a different light. Berdyaev is profoundly right in insisting that all ethics needs eschatology.[2] One factor in the sickness of the modern world is the loss of confidence in any abiding significance of the transitory goods of life. For evidence we may cite the contemporary existentialist philosophy in which nothing matters but the moment of experience. Its consequence is the hell depicted in Sartre's *No Exit*. The possibility that our civilization and perhaps even the human race itself might be destroyed in atomic warfare has but given new intensity to the problem which has always haunted man the creature.[3]

If hopelessness breeds paralysis of will, hope releases human energies. The causes which enlist men always give some assurance that what is to be sacrificed for will bear fruitful consequences in some new order. The dynamic of fascism, communism, and democracy is in each case related to a faith in which each individual can see his life linked with a significant future. Hitler promised the thousand year Reich, the Marxists believe in the inevitability of the classless society, Democrats proclaim the century of the common man.

The Christian interpretation of man's pilgrimage in time cannot be

[1]PR.

[2]N. Berdyaev,*The Destiny of Man* (New York: Charles Scribner's Sons, 1937), 317ff.

[3]Cf. Joseph Haroutunian, *Wisdom and Folly in Religion* (New York: Charles Scribner's Sons, 1940), 35–36.

put into a simple parallelism with these political philosophies. Christianity does not ignore the vision of a redeemed political order but it sets all political hopes in a perspective which relates each person and each historical fact to the ultimate community of all life with God. A Christian view of time and history which preserves the truth and rejects the illusion in man's vision of history can organize and release human energies today as it did in the days of St. Augustine, and as it did in the bright days of the nineteenth century when the prospect of a reborn society on earth seemed to light the way.

If a new vision of man's destiny is to come it will have to be founded on something different from the liberal theory of progress, and also something different from the complete rejection of that idea in contemporary theology. In this chapter I shall state the reasons for saying that the liberal doctrine will not do, and then try to save out of the liberal perspective the valid concept which it possessed. We can then examine the views of history of those who reject entirely the concept of the progress of man toward the Kingdom of God. Finally, we shall state the key concept by which a Christian conception of history can maintain fidelity to the facts and yield a more sobered but still hopeful view of the long pilgrimage of man.

II

The notion of a cumulative achievement of good in history which brings about in the world a more complete embodiment of the divine order was an integral part of the liberal Christian theology. What is often overlooked in the reaction against this doctrine is that the liberals formulated it in more than one way. Actually the conception of a cumulative achievement in our moral and religious experience is not easy to discard. Reinhold Niebuhr, for example, carefully insists that there are cumulative achievements on the plane of history.[4] Paul Tillich, in his discussion of the idea of progress, distinguishes several spheres to which the idea may be related: the first is that of technical progress, the second, that of political unification, and the third, "the gradual humanization of human relationships." In these, he agrees, progress has actually taken place. But there are two areas where the idea of progress does not apply: There is no progress with respect to the creative works of culture or with respect to the morality of mankind. The first is impossible because creativity is a matter of grace, not of growth; the second is impossible because morality is a matter of free decision, and consequently not a matter of delivery and tradition.[5]

[4]Reinhold Niebuhr, *The Nature and Destiny of Man*, Vol. II, *passim*, New York: Charles Scribner's Sons, 1941).
[5]*The Kingdom of God and History*, ed. J. H. Oldham (Chicago: Willett, Clark, 1938), 113-114.

These distinctions are clarifying, yet if they are held without qualification they deny the truth that the liberal theology was groping for, even though it never set it free from an untenable doctrine of the progressive elimination of evil from human life. This judgment may be sustained by examining briefly some of the formulas by which liberals sought to interpret the progress of the Kingdom of God in history.

Professor Case's *The Christian Philosophy of History* shows clearly the difficulties of interpreting history as the simple triumph of good men over evil men. His pattern is the liberal one:

> God is working within history where he has willed that men should learn to be the efficient instruments of the divine energy. Upon their shoulders has been placed the responsibility for learning and pursuing God's designs for bringing his Kingdom to realization on earth.[6]

History resolves itself into a conflict of good men with bad men. Badness is the result of a beastly strain "inherited perhaps from a Neanderthal man."[7] Case does not quite say the complete eradication of evil will ever be accomplished but still "the accumulations of the years mount ever upward toward the goal of the good man's desire."[8]

The moralism which makes possible such a neat separation between good and evil men, and which implies subtly that we who make the distinction are to be counted among the good cannot be refuted by argument. But once this simple removal of our own consciences from the sphere of judgment has been shaken, once we see the conflict between good and evil in its true depth in every human heart, a deeper view of history must be found if we are to have a hope based on solid foundations. Even on Case's terms the question of the meaning of the whole process remains unsolved. What is the meaning of the life of an individual with all its suffering and frustration if it be but a stage on the way to some future consummation in an infinitely removed time? In what sense is life fulfilled now? The problem is especially acute when we recognize as Case himself does that "a closer scrutiny of the historical process shows that disasters overtake equally the righteous with the wicked."[9] Christian liberalism must rewrite its philosophy of history with this fact given its full value. If we make a less simple distinction between the righteous and the wicked, and treat the problem of fulfillment in relation to the mystery of temporal flux and its relation to the abiding realities, then the Christian philosophy of history will stand upon the belief in a redemptive activity of God which wins its strange

[6]S. J. Case, *The Christian Philosophy of History* (Chicago: University of Chicago Press, 1943), vi.

[7]*Ibid.*, 213–215.

[8]*Ibid.*, 218.

[9]*Ibid.*, 211.

victory in spite of the continuing tragic character of the course of events.

The interpretation of cosmic progress which Whitehead offers in his *Adventures of Ideas* is not subject to quite the same criticism. He takes the fundamental conflict to be that between force and persuasion.

> The history of ideas is a history of mistakes. But through all mistakes it is also the history of the gradual purification of conduct. When there is progress in the development of favorable order, we find conduct protected from relapse into brutalization by the increasing agency of ideas consciously entertained. In this way Plato is justified in his saying, "The creation of the world—that is to say, the world of civilized order— is the victory of persuasion over force."[10]

The progress of mankind can be measured by this yardstick. Note Whitehead's insistence that conduct is "protected from relapse." The fact of progress was symbolized for Whitehead in the year he wrote, 1931, by the achievement of a peaceful settlement between Gandhi and the Viceroy of India.[11]

Waiving for the moment the far from settled question of the extent that Gandhi's techniques of nonviolence were adapted to the particular social and cultural situation in which he found himself, we still must ask whether we can really see the vindication of hope for the higher values in a cumulative and secure achievement of orders of persuasion over brute force. Certainly the experience of the twentieth century confirms the fear that cultures of high moral sensitivity may yet relapse into incredible cruelty. Whitehead's doctrine does not seem to square with his own view that there is an element of conflict and exploitation in the very structure of life. "Life is robbery."[12] Nor does his view square with the contemplation of the tragic element in the vision of God with which his *Process and Reality closes.*[13]

The case may be put this way. If new configurations of power are always to be expected in the ongoing march of creativity, what reason have we to believe that the persuasive elements in life will not forever have to maintain a precarious existence amidst the formidable march of more ruthless powers? We must not discount the significance or worth of the "tendernesses" of life.[14] We may well account them more

---

[10]*AI* 30–31.

[11]*AI* 205.

[12]*PR* 160.

[13]*Ibid.,* "We are therefore left with the final opposites joy and sorrow, good and evil . . ." (518). "Thus the universe is to be conceived as attaining the active self-expression of its own variety of opposites" (531).

[14]For a development of this theme of Whitehead's see B. E. Meland, *Seeds of Redemption* (New York: Macmillan, 1947).

valuable just because they are precious amidst staggering forces. Yet the evidence seems slim indeed that the history of the cosmos exhibits a universal and progressive taming of the elemental forces. Whitehead himself has called for the cleansing of dogma by the recourse to critical analysis of the evidence. His view of history has a romantic overtone which goes beyond the facts.

A similar difficulty is presented by John Macmurray's attempt to combine a Christian-Augustinian doctrine of God's sovereignty with a Marxist interpretation of the structure of historical development as leading inevitably toward the fulfillment of the good society. Macmurray gives content to the doctrine that man is created in the image of God by saying this means we are created for freedom and for equality. The community defined by these two concepts is what our human nature really craves, and what it must have if it is not to be in conflict with itself both within the individual and within society. Therefore, any social structure which separates men into classes produces overt conflict between classes. Out of these conflicts the more adequate order of freedom and equality must certainly emerge, for it represents the embodiment of the real structure of historical forces which possess ultimately irresistible power. In his *Clue to History* in 1939 Macmurray wrote:

> It is the inevitable destiny of fascism to create what it intends to prevent—the socialist commonwealth of the world. The fundamental law of human nature cannot be broken. "He that saveth his life shall lose it." The will to power is self-frustrating. It is the meek who will inherit the earth.[15]

Macmurray himself seems to allow some sort of qualification of this determinism. He says that "unless progress can be stopped altogether" his prediction stands.[16] But if stopping progress is a real possibility then the view that history is simply the carrying out of the intention of God must be restated.

All the paradoxes and difficulties of determinist views of history appear in Macmurray's treatment of freedom. The achievement of the divine intention is inevitable; yet men are called upon to "make the effort" on which depends the future of Western civilization.[17] If men must be rallied to "make an effort" in our historical period, an effort which they may fail to make, why may it not be so in every historical period? Macmurray's interpretation of the course of history has the advantage which comes from a realistic acceptance of the fact of conflict and tragedy in history. Yet like its Marxist counterpart his view is utopian in outcome, and falls into the error of all utopianism, that of en-

[15]New York: Harper & Brothers, 1939, 237.
[16]*Ibid.*, 220.
[17]*Ibid.*, xi.

dowing some particular historical movement or group with a moral significance and purity which it does not rightfully possess. So Macmurray says:

> Soviet Russia is the nearest approach to the realization of the Christian intention that the world has yet seen, for the intention of a universal community based on equality and freedom, overriding differences of nationality, race, sex, and "religion," is its explicit and conscious purpose.[18]

One does not have to indulge in hysterical anticommunist sentiment to detect the exaggeration and illusion in this statement.

Let us summarize the three difficulties which all theories of historical progress toward the Kingdom of God inherently involve, and at the same time try to extract from the liberal doctrine the element of truth which it certainly embodies.

There is, first, that aspect of the passage of time which makes it a threat to the enduring worth of all the particular carriers of value which we know. "Time is perpetual perishing," says Whitehead following Locke. If the worth of life is to be secured, we must find some sense in which, again in Whitehead's words, the occasions of experience "live for evermore."[19] No matter how we try to tell ourselves that each moment has its value regardless of its endurance, we cannot be indifferent to the fact that the running stream of time bears away all that we cherish. Unless religious faith faces the possibility that the human race on this earth is not a permanent fixture in the scheme of things, its hope must be forever based on concealment. The humanist Max Otto closes his survey of the human enterprise with words of ringing promise:

> Oh, walk together children,
> Don't you get weary,
> There's a great Camp Meeting in the Promised Land.[20]

It is noteworthy that the humanist turns to the language of the religious tradition to express this conclusion. But on what basis does he hold out such a promise? We do not know what may be the fate of humanity in the course of cosmic history. The question of what may happen to life some billions of years from now is perhaps too remote to have any consequence in our thinking, except as it reminds us of the precarious situation of all life. Professor Gamow, the physicist, says our scientific knowledge gives us reason to expect that within some billions of years life will have been ended by the increasingly intense heat of the sun unless technical development may have made it possible to trans-

[18]Ibid., 206.
[19]PR 126, 533.
[20]The Human Enterprise (New York: Appleton-Century-Crofts, 1940), 369; cf. his Natural Laws and Human Hopes (New York: Henry Holt, 1926).

port the race to some cooler portion of the universe.[21] This speculation takes on grim present significance when we contemplate the possibility that humanity now may have in biological and atomic weapons the means to make earth uninhabitable.

Religious hope clings to something deeper than the continuing chance that something will turn up to keep life going. It also rests on something deeper than speculation about an infinitely prolonged life in the form of what is often meant by immortality of the soul. It depends upon the insight that the value of life is conserved by an enduring and healing fact, the fact of God. How this truth is to be expressed is indeed a perplexing problem.

Though the liberal doctrines of progress did not squarely face the fact that "nature intends to kill man," there was an element in the liberal view of the meaning of the temporal character of life which is valid. It is that the risk and adventure in the process of life is itself a meaning and a value. As Winfred E. Garrison has suggested, "being on the way" in some sense forms part of the goal of life.[22]

The passage of time is not wholly a sentence of death upon value; it is also the form of creative effort and moral achievement. Life in time is life in decision. Without decision there can be nothing of the spiritual stature which gives to our existence its real worth. If our life is merely an imitation of eternity then it is but a game, and of no consequence. Involvement in process is itself an enduring value. We cannot imagine any good without it. Certainly it is an error to suppose that process and progress are synonymous. But it is a valid insight to see process as integral to the spiritual character of our existence. It is significant that there are an increasing number of those who believe that God's life itself must be conceived as having an element of adventure and movement into an open future, else we cannot conceive that He enters sympathetically into our human experience.[23]

The second problem in the theory of progress is involved in the fact of freedom. Reinhold Niebuhr points out the dilemma of liberal thought which has insisted on the freedom of man to guide his own life, and yet which has tried to imagine that this freedom will be progressively used only for the good. But moral freedom is freedom to rebel against the moral claim, and freedom of the spirit is freedom to rebel against God. The conclusion is inescapable that so long as man is free the risks of freedom must be admitted with all the possibilities of its misuse.

Even the most individualistic liberalism we may still say clung to

[21]*The Birth and Death of the Sun* (New York: Penguin Books, 1945), 104–105, 154.

[22]Reflections on the Goal of History," *The Christian Century*, LV, 2 (1938), 959.

[23]This truth has been most clearly expressed in Charles Hartshorne, *Man's Vision of God.*

an important insight in its conception of the meaning of freedom. The use of freedom is the participation of one life in the lives of others. Freedom means the opportunity to decide how one's life shall enter into the continuum of conditions and consequences. We have no freedom to decide whether we shall "give our lives away" in the continuing social process. We are always giving them away either constructively or destructively. The meaning of life is participation in an ongoing flow of activities in which the good of all participants is either served or blocked.

In the philosophic tradition it is the idealists rather than the naturalists who have made the fullest place for this insight into the essentially social character of human existence, though contemporary naturalism as in Mead, Dewey, and Wieman has achieved a similar perspective. There is now emerging a reconciliation of the emphasis on individual freedom and the fact of the involvement of every creature in social structures. My life is not my own. It is the result of the creative activity of God in a stream of conditions and events far beyond the range of my knowledge. My conscious life is but a faint light shining out of a background of powers, processes, events, and memories. In every moment of life, I give my being back into the stream. I am actually in large measure what others can take me to be. My own self is completed only as others are affected by my being. I am passive to the social process in every moment and yet an active creator of it. Within this taking and giving the marvelous fact of free, responsible reflection and decision appears. Now this self which decides freely is not apart from the social process, but rather embedded in it. Yet in some degree it can in its own integrity freely choose what it shall accept and reject from the whole, and thus it chooses in part the way in which it shall enter into the experience of others. What I decide becomes a datum for others and the consequences of my decision a part of their objective world.

In some such fashion we can do justice to the elements of determination and freedom in our experience. Only individuals have minds, but each mind is what it is in large part because of what it has received from the group. Hence the group is something more than a collection of individuals' minds; the group is a process in which individual minds are woven together in a dynamic pattern which tends to impose itself on each one.

The liberal gain in the interpretation of freedom can still be held. Freedom means the possibility to allow ourselves to be determined by that which is deepest in the process of life; and to relate our own lives to the ongoing whole in decisions made out of faith, hope, and love. Freedom is the opportunity to qualify the structure of life for ourselves and for others. It is the possibility of maintaining integrity by serving first the good of God and all other things second. To affirm this possibility is not to claim that in human experience it is ever perfectly actualized. But it is to recognize that our human decisions are made possible by our appropriation of the meanings, memories, hopes, and possibilities which become available to us in the history in which we live.

The judgment that there can be no progress in the moral realm is not defensible. Unless there be some cumulative and progressive development of the community of freedom, equality, and love among men it is impossible to give any adequate account of our common experience of sharing in the spirit and insight which comes to us from others. It is this sharing which makes our own moral decision possible. We are members one of another, even in moral experience. Every parent's concern for the kind of environment in which his child grows up is testimony to this fact, even though we know that we can never *guarantee* the quality of life which will emerge in any free person.

The final problem for the progressive view is that of the actual fact of the persistence of evil in all the structures of human history. There are varieties of Christian experience with the evil in the self. For some the break with sin appears to be possible; for others, there is the continuing experience, "that which I would I do not, and that which I would not that I do." But in either case we cannot say that any life is beyond the power of temptation and sin. We know of no social order which does not show exploitation and injustice, none in which tragic choices do not have to be made. There is a rent in existence, and its name is evil. All that it means we cannot know. The Christian theologian, John Bennett, has powerfully stated this truth in his *Christian Realism*.[24]

While the belief in the cumulative processes of life permits us no superficial optimism, it does require the acknowledgment that the final meaning of evil cannot be known until all things are done. There is, we do know, a redemptive work of God through which past evil, while it remains evil, can enter into the creation of present good by qualifying our moral sensitivity, and deepening our valuation of life. There can be moral maturing through tragic experience both for individuals and for whole peoples. Out of the suffering of the Hebrew people has come the moral power of the prophets and the spiritual reality of reconciliation between man and God.

Liberal theology made its contribution to theology through its affirmation of process as the most fundamental category of being. The Christian interpretation of the meaning of history becomes transformed when this conception is allowed to replace the metaphysics of static being. It should be possible to restate the Christian hope for God's work with man in history from this new perspective without falling into the

[24]New York: Charles Scribner's Sons, 1941, Appendix.

errors of those who allowed process to become too simply identified with progress.[25] But before we come to our constructive statement, it is necessary to examine the alternative treatment of this problem in neo-orthodox thought today.

III

An alternative to the interpretation of history as process is offered to-day in those Christian theologies which have been influenced by existential philosophy which has its primary source in Kierkegaard. It is argued that process metaphysics takes the measured or clock time of physics and identifies it with the time which is relevant to human decisions and to freedom. This identification is said to be untenable. The time form of freedom is another structure, related in some way to clock time, but never to be identified with the sequential order of natural processes. Nicolas Berdyaev who affirms the existential point of view summarizes the position: "There are three times: cosmic time, historical time; and existential time." Cosmic time is symbolized by the circle, it is calendar or clock time. Historical time is that of memory and prospect. It is always broken. The moments pass away and are not fulfilled. Its symbol is the line. Berdyaev says:

> Existential time must not be thought of in complete isolation from cosmic and historical time, it is a break-through of one time into the other. . . . Existential time may be best symbolized not by the circle or by the line but by the point. . . . This is inward time . . . not objectivized. It is the time of the world of subjectivity, not objectivity. . . . Every state of ecstasy leads out from the computation of objectivized mathematical time and leads into existential qualitative infinity.[26]

These distinctions appear in various forms in Kierkegaard, Cullman, Minear, Niebuhr, and Tillich, and in each case they are used for the interpretation of the Biblical world view. And in each case the history of salvation is interpreted as belonging to a superhistory which is something superimposed upon the cosmic process.

Let us try to formulate as accurately as possible what is being affirmed in this existential theory. When man confronts the question of the meaning of his life he finds that the question can only be answered if he sees that he is related to a transcendent reality, a God whose being is of a different order from that of all creatures and processes in our experience, who is the "unconditioned" ground of all being, to use Tillich's phrase. Since the meaning of life lies in man's relation to God so

[25]This confusion seems to me patent in W. H. Sheldon, *America's Progressive Philosophy* (New Haven: Yale University Press, 1942).

[26]*Slavery and Freedom* (New York: Charles Scribner's Sons, 1944), 257, 260–261.

conceived, the dimension of our being with which religion is concerned involves something other than any experienced process immanent in existence. The meaning of life cannot be measured in relation to a structure of value discoverable in our existence. When we speak therefore of Creation, of God's purposes, of the times in which God reveals Himself, and when we speak of the end of all things, the coming of the Kingdom, we use temporal terms but we are not speaking of events to which a date can be assigned. To be sure in the case of the revelation in Jesus Christ, to take the most important example, the time of salvation is intimately connected with an actual historical period and date. But we are speaking of a realm of meaning which is not bound by the categories of historical experience. We can apprehend the meaning of what we say only in the moment and in the act of decision or, as Berdyaev says, in ecstasy. The ultimate reality upon which our hope depends is therefore the eternal truth and power of God, breaking into the flow of historical events, qualifying it, transforming it, yet always to be understood as giving meaning to life through its relation to that which is beyond the time form of the world process.

So far at least I understand Kierkegaard and his followers. This standpoint represents the sharpest possible challenge to the liberal theology with its affirmation that the natural processes are the locus of God's redemptive work; and that the meaning of life is organically involved in the emergence of orders of value in history.

This problem is so fundamental to the whole question of the nature of Christian hope and the existential analysis is so widely influential that I propose to examine Kierkegaard's formulation more closely and to offer a criticism of it.

Soren Kierkegaard is the most important source and the magnificent genius of existential philosophy. If a reconstruction in theology which is neither liberal nor neo-orthodox is to emerge it will have to define itself against Kierkegaard even as Kierkegaard defined himself against Hegel. And it will, I believe, learn much from Kierkegaard as he learned much from the great idealist.

Hegel's philosophy is a thoroughgoing and grandiloquent attempt to conceive the whole of world history as a process exhibiting a rational structure. It is the spirit coming to self-consciousness, God realizing Himself in human society. That Hegel badly overstated and overworked his thesis is universally recognized. He did have a profound sense of the tragic and the ironic in human affairs. He was not a naïve optimist; but he did not avoid the idolatry of identifying the absolute will of God with the Prussian state in which he happened to live and work.[27]

---

[27]For incisive criticism see Reinhold Niebuhr, *The Nature and Destiny of Man*, Vol. I, 116–118.

Kierkegaard's work is a sustained and passionate protest against the Hegelian system, and against what Hegel made out of human history, and out of Christianity. Where Hegel saw continuity and rational pattern, Kierkegaard saw discontinuity and paradox. Hegel and his followers felt intellectually secure in the logical structure which underlay the System. Kierkegaard attacked this complacency with savage irony and invective. When Hegelianized theology became the means of fortifying the complacencies of the established Christian Church, Kierkegaard literally poured out his life in a struggle to expose what to him was a betrayal of the Christ who suffered and died that men might repent.

For Kierkegaard the human soul is poised on the knife edge of lostness. He tried to break through Hegelian objectivity to the inwardness and suffering of personal existence. No Christian before him, and perhaps none since, has so profoundly expressed the desperation of the soul's search for a rock of faith which will hold firm in the midst of the complete insecurity of human existence. These things Kierkegaard felt, and he said them with a penetration of the human heart and a consummate artistry rarely equaled in either philosophical or theological writing. I do not see how one can read him and remain the same person. We turn eagerly to learn the secret of that leap of faith which gains assurance of God and through which a man becomes a disciple of the Christ who is contemporary with every age.[28]

Just here the perplexities begin. Kierkegaard describes this movement toward God, or this being met by God, in terms which remove it from any recognizable human experience. He insists that his philosophy makes a place for real becoming where Hegel's "becoming" is all shadow play.[29] Becoming is defined by Kierkegaard as "a change in actuality brought about by freedom."[30] But this becoming takes place in the moment of existential time. It is no process in the time sequence of human events. "If a decision in time is postulated then . . . the learner is in error, which is precisely what makes a beginning in the moment necessary."[31] The knife of existential analysis cuts cleanly between the past and present in describing the new birth. "In the Moment man also becomes conscious of the new birth, for his antecedent state was one of non-being."[32]

What is this movement which takes place outside of time; which is a leap from non-Being to Being without even so much as the Hegelian dialectical logic to connect the two stages? The closest Kierkegaard

[28]Philosophical Fragments (Princeton: Princeton University Press, 1942), 44ff.
[29]Repetition (Princeton: Princeton University Press, 1941), 29.
[30]Philosophical Fragments, 64.
[31]Ibid., 41.
[32]Ibid., 15.

comes to giving a philosophical answer is his notion of repetition. The Socratic "recollection" will not do, for that is recall of something temporally past. There must be a movement toward eternity which is movement toward realization but not in a temporal sense. This he calls repetition. This concept never received very clear definition from Kierkegaard but we are perhaps not far wrong if we say that repetition is man's free enactment of his relationship to eternity. For example, Kierkegaard is "repeating" Abraham's sacrifice of Isaac in his renunciation of his fiancée. In any case this conception cannot be made intelligible. Kierkegaard himself says that this category is the "interest upon which metaphysics founders."[33] The whole continuum of conditions and consequences in time is set aside. For the religious movement it does not exist.

Four unhappy consequences flow from Kierkegaard's doctrine of time. They have not been escaped in the neo-orthodox movement which he has greatly influenced, though some of his exaggerations have been sharply qualified. We should consider in our time of theological ferment what price must be paid for the existential doctrine that ultimate meaning belongs only to the Moment, that is, to a time which is other than the time of the world-historical process. It is, I suggest, too high a price, both in the loss of rational coherence, and in loss of the relevance of religious faith to human problems.

The first consequence is Kierkegaard's extreme individualism. He declared his category was "the solitary individual" and desired these words inscribed on his tomb.[34] It is, to be sure, something of a relief in the midst of today's sentimentalities about "fellowship" to hear Kierkegaard affirm that fellowship is a lower category than the individual.[35] But he overshot his mark. He practically ignored the significance of life in the social process, and in the religious community. This was not accidental. Our common-sense view of time regards it as the form of social process. It is the order which links past with future in the continuum of influences and consequences. But Kierkegaard's "Moment" is apart from all this. In the crisis of decision a man may think of himself as freed from all external relations. So Kierkegaard apparently thinks. But this is an illusion. It is a distortion of the facts to say that "the disciple who is born anew owes nothing to any man but everything to his Divine Teacher."[36] We are not solitary individuals, even in the moment of decision. What happens in the moment of choice owes much to our inheritance from the communities in which our lives are lived.

---

[33]*Repetition*, 34.
[34]*Training in Christianity* (New York: Oxford University Press, 1941), 57.
[35]*Ibid.*, 216.
[36]*Philosophical Fragments*, 14.

Kierkegaard's own individualism is partly explicable in relation to his experience of discovering that he was not "like the others."[37]

The issue here joined with existential philosophy involves much more than philosophical technicalities. It is a matter of life and death to our civilization that we recover what it means to possess freedom in community. Real freedom belongs not to the isolated individual, but to the person who can maintain his individuality and integrity even as he accepts his interdependence with other life. If theology is to illuminate the life of the human spirit it must interpret both the fact of man's capacity to judge society from a point of view which transcends all achieved cultural values, and also the fact of that social solidarity which in the religious community makes the prophetic critic possible. Isaiah and Jeremiah spoke for their people Israel even as they spoke against them.

The second consequence is that the time-form of religious decision is divorced from the time-form of political and social effort. Kierkegaard confesses he knows and cares nothing about politics. Amusingly he says his acquaintances charge him with being politically "a nincompoop who bows seven times before everything that has a royal commission." It is not altogether a satisfactory answer that he is serving the kingdom which "would not at any price be a kingdom of this world."[38] The question of responsible decision in the political order remains. To say that "there exists only one sickness, sin,"[39] and to pour scorn on all political movements produces a simplification of human problems, and in some instances prophetic judgment; but it also leaves the manipulation of social and political institutions which do make and break lives of people to whatever shrewd and ruthless schemers may get social power.

A third consequence follows inevitably. Kierkegaard denies all meaning to moral progress in history. The sharpness of his analysis enables us to recognize the real problem but it also discloses the inadequacy of his answer. He holds that all ages and times stand under the same judgment of God. "Every generation has to begin all over again with Christ."[40] He contrasts the idea of the Church Militant in which the Christian stands in opposition to his culture, with the idea of the Church Triumphant (on earth), in which the Christian is honored and rewarded for being a Christian. The first he believes is Christianity,

[37]*The Point of View*, trans. W. Lowrie (New York: Oxford University Press, 1939), 81.

[38]*The Attack upon "Christendom"* (Princeton: Princeton University Press, 1944), 44.

[39]*Training in Christianity*, 65.

[40]*Ibid.*, 109.

the second hypocrisy.[41] Therefore, "if the contemporary generation of believers found no time to triumph, neither will any later generation, for the task is always the same and faith is always militant."[42]

Now in one sense the task is always the same. It is to transform men who try to live life apart from God into men who begin to trust God. No human progress can change the fundamental necessity of that movement in every age and time. But it does not follow that all societies and cultures offer equally adequate contexts for making the transformation possible for more and more persons. The Church grows in a time of persecution. But we do not therefore work for the creation of a society so inhuman and unjust that any who seek justice and love will be cast into prison, tortured and killed. Let us substitute our own paradox for Kierkegaard's. The task of serving the Kingdom of God will always be the same. But that task includes the everlasting effort to bring decency and justice into human society. While that aspect of the task is never finished, it is not without its real successes, or its hope for greater ones.

A final consequence of Kierkegaard's view is that it becomes inconceivable how God can share in the actual processes of human experience. "The eternal . . . has absolutely no history."[43] Therefore, we can make nothing of the conception of God as patient and suffering worker. The meaning of our existence as unfinished creatures in a life which has its times of planting and its times of reaping becomes an insoluble riddle. I do not say Kierkegaard accepts this conclusion in all respects. But it is inherent in his view of time.

Many of the extreme consequences of Kierkegaard's position are avoided by those contemporary theologians who have gone through existentialism to the reconstruction of Biblical theology, and who have sought to discover, usually with Kierkegaard's help, the "unique time-consciousness" of the Bible.[44]

This assertion that there is a distinctive time-consciousness in the Biblical world view is made by Professor Paul Minear. His studies in Biblical theology show that there is in the Bible the basis for a corrective of the exaggerated individualism of Kierkegaard. The Bible grows out of historical experience and its world view involves a profound

[41]*Ibid.*, 205 ff.

[42]S. Kierkegaard, 91.

[43]*Ibid.*, 62.

[44]Paul S. Minear, "Time and the Kingdom," *The Journal of Religion*, XXIV, 2 (April, 1944), p. 85. Cf. his *Eyes of Faith* (Philadelphia: Westminster, 1946), Oscar Cullmann, *Christus und die Zeit* (Zurich: 1946), and Karl Barth, *Credo.* For analysis of contemporary literature on the eschatological problem see Amos Wilder, "The Eschatology of the Gospels in Recent Discussion," *The Journal of Religion*, XXVIII, 3 (July, 1948).

sense of the meaning of the life of peoples, their hopes and expectancies, their time of crisis, and their ultimate destiny. But Professor Minear's interpretation of the Biblical outlook falls short just at the point where he insists on reading the Bible through the eyes of Kierkegaard.

Minear points out that the Bible speaks of time in two senses, which are usually designated by two different words, *chronos* and *kairos*.[45] *Chronos* refers to calendar time, *kairos* to historical and eschatological time. The *"kairos"* is the "crucial stage in destiny." It is the time of decision which involves man's ultimate destiny.

It is characteristic of the tendency of neo-orthodox thought, even when it returns to the Biblical conception of time, to make the distinction between *kairos* and *chronos* too sharp. The distinction is made in such a way that *chronos*, the day-by-day time which is the form of our human existence, is either treated as irrelevant to the issues of man's salvation, or else it is regarded as the sphere of death and frustration from which we must be saved. Minear seems to be imposing a metaphysical distinction on the Bible when he says that the coming of Christ means that "the tyranny of *chronos* has been broken once and for all. It stands under the all-encompassing negation of God's judgment. Its boundary has been set by the manifestation of a 'wholly-other order of reality.' "[46] But why, we ask, must *chronos* be negated? Is it wholly evil in God's sight or man's experience that there should be times and seasons? Does the Bible really separate a calendar time which is the sphere of tragic frustration from a time which is wholly different? It appears rather that the Bible views the history of the Hebrew people, the life of Jesus, and the life of the Church as sharing in one continuous working of God in which every aspect of human life and its natural environment has its necessary and fruitful role to play. There are difficulties indeed with the Biblical eschatology; but some of them arise precisely from the fact that the Biblical world view did not contemplate a distinction between two orders of time. The world, it is said, was created in six days. The end of the world is an event expected before those now living pass away. When the Apostle Paul says, "It is far on in the night the day is almost here," and when John says, "It doth not yet appear what we shall be,"[47] they transcend the distinction between *chronos* and *kairos*. Both are within the sphere of God's redemptive purpose. It is difficult to see how, if God's relationship to the world is "wholly other" than the relation of creative spirit to its actual working in time (chronos), we can

[45]*Ibid.*, 81.
[46]*Ibid.*, 83.
[47]I John 3:2; Romans 13:12.

avoid discounting the Christian significance of creative effort, patient workmanship, and that careful assessment of conditions and consequences which make up so large a part of the wisdom of life.

Such an outcome which is both un-Biblical and irrational can be avoided by a restatement of the meaning of time. The concrete reality of life is the community of created beings in their individuality and their togetherness. This community moves in a continuous stream from the past into the future. God is the supreme and uncreated member of this community. We are therefore members of Him and of one another. The time structure of this interweaving of processes is duration. This is time as the order characterizing the flow of process.

Chronos, then and *kairos* are abstractions. They are structures which our minds can distinguish in the concrete reality for the purpose of speaking intelligibly about it. *Kairos* abstracts the elements of meaning, valuation, purpose, and expectation. Both terms designate something less than the full meaning of duration which escapes adequate interpretation. Yet on this view we can say that God enters into the experience of man. Both *chronos* and *kairos* have meaning for God. Professor Hartshorne's statement of the relation of God to time saves what is intellectually and religiously meaningful in the Biblical conception.

> God is the cosmic "adventure" (Whitehead) integrating all real adventures as they occur, without ever failing in readiness to realize new states out of the divine potency, which is indeed "beyond number" and definite form, yet is of value only because number and form come out of it.[48]

It follows that one dimension of the meaning of the Christian life is our share in world-building. It means we accept the process of becoming with all the tasks of politics, education, and reconstruction, as the area where some of God's work gets done. We may thus preserve a unity in life. Such unity is lost if we say that the time in which we prepare today for tomorrow is of another and lesser order from the time in which we encounter God.

IV

When we attempt to do justice to all aspects of the problem of the nature of progress in human history we discover we must try to hold two truths together. The first is that our life is a process. Every moment of experience enters into and qualifies the continuous stream of life in and through which God works. The second truth is that there is a cleft which runs through the whole of our existence. Possibilities

[48]*Man's Vision of God,* 227–228.

remain unrealized. There is real evil, and real loss. We live on the boundary line between the actual and the potential good. We cannot see the whole, or the end. Life resembles a poem the last line of which has not been written. Yet the meaning of the whole depends upon it. We know what it is to participate in God's cumulative victory over the chaos of existence. Yet the victory is not yet won. We know that God works creatively and redemptively to overcome all that estranges us from Him. Yet we continually cry out, How long, O Lord how long?

It is absurd to think that a simple formula can interpret the mystery of man's pilgrimage. But the discussion so far suggests the possibility that a new Christian perspective on history may be emerging which will hold together the truth in the liberal doctrine of progress and the truth in the neo-orthodox affirmation of the judgment of God upon all existing things. We have now reached the point in our argument where the proposed synthesis can be formulated. Every interpretation of the meaning of history has its guiding image. We need a key concept with which to draw together the many strands of truth about one history. There is such a concept in the New Testament. Both liberalism and neo-orthodoxy have done it less than justice. It is the concept of our present history as proceeding under the reign of Christ. But the Christ who reigns in our history is embattled with his enemies. The Biblical source of this image is Paul's word in the eschatological passage of I Corinthians 15. "He must reign till he hath put all his enemies under his feet. The last enemy that shall be destroyed is death."[49] He has already despoiled the principalities and powers in the victory of the cross yet he remains the embattled Christ, contending with all things which stand in the way of God's fulfillment of His redemptive work.[50] Professor John Knox summarizes the Biblical view of our human situation after Christ has entered our history in the life and death of Jesus:

> Sin is doomed and its power is weakened, but it has not been actually destroyed: salvation has already been bestowed in Christ, but the fulfillment of that salvation awaits Christ's return in glorious power to bring to completion his victory over sin and death and to inaugurate fully and finally the Kingdom of God.[51]

Biblical concepts should not be strait jackets for the mind, but wings for it. They guard in metaphorical terms the fundamental insights which have come through God's revelation to the prophets, and through the impact of Jesus upon the world. We can use the conception of the embattled reign of Christ as a guide to a reformulation of the Christian

[49]I Corinthians 15:25-26.
[50]Colossians 2:15.
[51]*Christ the Lord* (New York: Harper & Brothers, 1945), 123. Cf. W. A. Visser 't Hooft, *The Kingship of Christ* (New York: Harper & Brothers, 1948).

view of history. In the end this symbolic expression can have just so much meaning for us as we can give it through specifying that in our experience which bears it out. It is a Christian symbol which can form the key to a more realistic theology than that which conceived of "building the Kingdom of God in history." It is a symbol which can be the basis for understanding between the American social gospel and the Continental insistence that God's Kingdom cannot be identified with human schemes. It can be the basis for a realistic expression of the Christian hope. We know that we live as sinners in social structures and spiritual climates which corrupt our souls, and which plunge us toward horrible catastrophe. But we know also that these powers have not the last word. They can be broken. They have been exposed through the revelation culminating in Jesus Christ. We could not even recognize them for what they are if we were not living in the beginning of a new order where love dwells.

Let us be specific about what it means to say we live in that history which is determined by the reign of Christ in conflict with his enemies.

We mean, first, that through what God has accomplished in the events which came to their climax in the life of Jesus our human existence has been given a new structure. Creative and redemptive power has been released in it which was not wholly released before. We see a meaning in life which was not so fully discerned before. There is a new community in history. Members of that community begin to live on the basis of what has taken hold of them through the life of Jesus.

The reign of Christ, then, is that period in human history which is interpreted by Christians through what God has done in the life of Jesus to disclose the ultimate meaning of our existence. That meaning is life in the community of love. It is the *logos* of our being. The *logos* is God Himself known to us under the form of the Christ-figure.[52] There is an endless variety of ways in which men respond to this disclosure of God. They may ignore it, reject it, despise the view of life to which it gave rise. Or they may begin to live life in response to the truth and power there given. What is given to us through God's revelation includes the ethic of outgoing and forgiving love. It includes the knowledge of our radical dependence upon God's grace which goes out to those who are not worthy of it. It includes the depth and mystery of the suffering of God known to us through the suffering of Jesus upon the cross. And it includes the new life of the Christian as the enactment of the way of love in a community of those who live in this faith. It is possible to speak of such a life only because we acknowledge that it depends wholly upon our participation in the working of God which is infinitely

[52]John 1:1.

deeper than anything we can define or control. Only as Christ reigns can we serve one another in love.

While we affirm the release of the power of God as the meaning of the reign of Christ it must be understood that that power is no arbitrary and ruthless force. Certainly it is true that God does exercise coercive power. We cannot escape that fact when we look at the way in which the structures of life coerce us, smash our plans, seize us in the grip of their inevitabilities. God is not identical with those structures but His wrath is in them as they are related to the ultimate structure of value which is His own being. But God also works persuasively; and His supreme resource is not coercive force, but the compelling power of His revelation in the Suffering Servant of all. The Christ who reigns asserts God's power as truly in the washing of the feet of the disciples as in the condemnation of the Pharisees. He transforms the world as he dies upon the cross, even as he transforms it in expelling the money-changers from the temple. We should not absolutize any one event in the life of Jesus as disclosing the way in which God's love must work. The ethical implications of this position we shall shortly examine. But here it is necessary to point out that when we speak of the reigning Christ we do not mean the monarchical concept of an arbitrary exercise of power. Christ reigns supremely because he reigns from his cross.[53]

This conception of the reign of Christ includes the universality of his meaning for human existence. Here is the bridge between the social gospel and the neo-orthodox theology. There are not two kingdoms, one an inner kingdom of Christ related only to believers, and another a kingdom of this world which God has left to other powers, and upon which His love makes no immediate demands. That conception was destroyed long ago by the social gospel with its affirmation of the Christian concern with the structure of human society. It is also being vigorously criticized by the continental theologians today. Karl Barth himself perhaps even fell into an exaggerated identification of a political cause with the cause of Christ in some of his writings during the war.[54] In any case the Christian affirmation is that the reign of Christ involves a demand for justice and freedom throughout the whole of life. Nothing less than the whole is the field of God's redemptive work.

In the second place, to live in the reign of Christ means to share in an actual and continual victory of good over evil. It is one thing to recognize that evil is never eradicated from the self or from society.

---

[53]Visser 't Hooft, The Kingship of Christ, 17.
[54]See a comment on Barth's interpretation of the war in a letter by E. G. Homrighausen in The Christian Century, LVI (May 24, 1939), 678.

But it does not follow that good never triumphs over evil. The fact is quite the contrary. There would be no world at all, if there were not a continual realization of good. Every achievement of good is in so far a victory over evil, either over the evil of chaos and meaninglessness, or the evil of actual obstructions to the growth of the real good. Christians ought always to take heart. It is not true that there are no historical gains making for a humanity which more nearly exemplifies the image of its creator. There is always something to be done in the service of God under the reign of Christ. While we have admitted we cannot from our human point of view guarantee the permanence of any created good we know; we do know that wherever conditions of slavery, ignorance, and established privilege have been broken there is a gain which man can surrender only at the cost of denying that which is deepest in himself.

Perhaps men will deny their own will for life in community. The reign of Christ is always an embattled reign. Our third assertion is that we know nothing of the working of God in the world except in relation to real opposition. Christ's reign is embattled in the human spirit, in the social structures, and in the Church which is his own body in the world. Protestant hope for the Church is not based upon any notion of its freedom from the corruptions of sin. It is based on the fact that in the Church among all human communities men can most directly appeal to the reigning Christ's judgment upon the community itself. The Church is not the Kingdom of God. It is the people who live by faith in the Christ who reigns against an opposition which exists even in those who have begun to serve him.

Christ is embattled with untruth. Our perspective applies in the realm of knowledge. "Now we see through a glass darkly."[55] We speak of the very essence of God's being. We know He is love. Yet we know that all human constructions in which we try to grasp this essence are inadequate.

The struggle with evil goes on "until Christ has put death under his feet." So far as we know human history will always be the scene of contending powers. But the conception of the reign of Christ contains a hope which looks beyond all the particular victories which God continues to win. This is our fourth assertion. Our hope is that the good which comes to be is not lost, but participates in the continuing life of God and thus shares in His ultimate victory. A consummation of history in which evil is finally purged and destroyed is beyond our power even to imagine. Hope does not depend upon it, though it may include it. But we do know that it means to share in a victory of God over the world in the sense that through faith in Him and His ultimate

[55]I Corinthians 13:12.

mercy we are reconciled to the conflict in which we stand. We believe that not only our present victories but even our failures can be transmuted into good. We believe that good is everlasting in God.

The question of the ultimate outcome of history involves the meaning of the Kingdom of God. We distinguish between the reign of Christ and the Kingdom of God. God's Kingdom is always present in history for it is His assertion of His love with power. It has come among us in Jesus Christ, whose reign is God's reign. But the Kingdom of God is also a symbol for the fulfillment of love in all things. That fulfillment is beyond the reign of Christ. It is an eschatological concept. It symbolizes an ultimate victory which we can know only as promise and share only in hope. Thus the concept of the reign of Christ enables us to make a clear distinction between what our human works achieve in history and the community of God's love in its perfect fulfillment. His Kingdom is always judgment upon our works, even while it is manifest in His power in our midst.

To live as a believer in the reign of Christ means to live within the battle not apart from it. It is no sham battle. But to believe that Christ reigns within the battle is to find peace. We know that God has His own strategy for bringing good out of evil. As believers we begin to live in a new history where love is accomplishing its perfect work, though this new history is never separate from the old. Again Paul's words express both the continuing struggle and the everlasting victory:

> We are pressed on every side, yet not straitened; perplexed, yet not unto despair; pursued, yet not forsaken; smitten down, yet not destroyed; always bearing about in the body the dying of Jesus, that the life also of Jesus may be manifested in our body.[56]

With this interpretation of the Christian philosophy of human history we have reached the affirmation upon which our entire argument rests. Christian hope which gathers up all particular human hopes and yet is deeper than they is founded upon the fact of the present creative and redemptive working of God in human life. It remains to show what this implies for individual ethics, for social ethics, and for the progress toward spiritual maturity of the Christian.

[56]II Corinthians 4:8-12.

The Aims of Societies and the Aims of God

25

George Allan

This paper defends the view that human institutions have aims not reducible to, yet inextricably bound up with, the aims of individuals. Human and institutional behavior both exhibit the formal characteristics of purposiveness; in particular, both have aims they seek to actualize. On the one hand, these aims are distinguishable: institutional goals are not simply the sum of individual ones. But, on the other hand, they are inseparable in the sense that personal goals are shaped by the purposes of the institutions which environ them while community ends are molded by the aims of the individuals who comprise them.

It follows that a theology of God's activity in history is inadequate if it denies or slights the question of his purposes for nations and institutions. It will be argued that the divine aims are substantially the same for societies as for persons, and consequently that such qualities as sinful, wayward, moral, and redeemed characterize institutions as truly as they do men. In short, the question to which this article addresses itself might be phrased: "Is there any salvation apart from the salvation of the social order—or, for that matter, apart from the salvation of the world?"

I

Almost all activity is oriented activity. There is a given state of affairs and there are the real possibilities for the immediate future. What activity there is in the present is oriented toward at least one of those

From the *Journal of the American Academy of Religion*, XXXV, 2 (June 1967). Copyright 1967 by the American Academy of Religion. Used by permission of the publisher and George Allan.

possibilities, and the new state of affairs that comes to occupy the present expresses the success or failure of that orientation.

I shall call this structure within which action occurs a "teleological ordering" of the situation. Teleologically structured activity is to be distinguished, however, from purposive behavior as genus is distinguished from species. A "purposive" order is teleological, but with the added factor that the possibilities orienting activity are consciously envisioned and desired by the actor. In other words, purposive situations involve values, the entertainment of which functions causally to orient action toward specific goals.

The heliotropic movement of a plant illustrates a teleogical but non-purposive orientation. Its direction of growth is not random, but rather oriented toward a state of affairs initially unactualized. Yet the plant certainly does not behave purposively; the end for the sake of which it moves is not envisioned and valued by the plant itself. However, I shall pass over this obviously Whiteheadian claim that all activity is teleological, and instead limit the discussion to that particular kind of orientedness I have termed "purposive."

Teleological purposive ordering can be analyzed in terms of the five necessary and sufficient conditions of its occurring. (1) There is the completed present, a created temporal accomplishment slipping into the status of the freshly past, and leaving its legacy of attainments and of problems. Thus, for example, after a hard hour's work I find my throat parched: I stand on the threshold of the present, and I am thirsty. (2) There are the *teloi* or ends that deploy themselves as possibilities for the present. A situation in which I am no longer thirsty is a possibility I, as thirsty, might entertain. These possible future states-of-affairs include, in the short run, my having drunk a glass of water or, more mediately, the possession of a new well or the diverting of a river. (3) There are those values that determine one from among the presented possibilities as a goal to be realized, and transform an end into an end-in-view. It is because I crave the quenching of my thirst that the drinking of a glass of water becomes no longer a mere possibility but a goal-for-me. (4) There is an activity that defines the method by which the end is actualized. To attain my goal I drink water, or hire a drilling rig, or organize a lobby for a federal dam. (5) There is the new world that is born out of this flux of activity, incorporating with characteristic success and failure the ideals and possibilities that called it forth.

Hence a structure of goals, values, and means characterizes the behavior of certain of the entities in our world. Quite obviously, individual human actions are in this sense purposive. But not only human actions. Social institutions are phenomena with a unity and stability sufficient to qualify as effective agencies with identifiable activities and patterns of behavior. I suggest that it is a valid application of our thesis to attribute to them also purposive structures of activity.

Men, being social animals, find their behavior inescapably infecting and infected by the behavior of other men. Thus, the structure of goals, values, and means that describes their activity will of necessity include description of the clash and agreement of ends, goods, and methods. The clash is the locus of individuality; it is in decisions made among competing claims to one's loyalty and energies that the individual emerges as a center of value and accomplishment in the midst of his environment. But, conversely, agreement on ends, goals, and methods celebrates the birth of transpersonal purposes. The harmonization of activity in virtue of shared values and common goals marks the emergence of institutions—ephemeral ones such as social cliques and pressure groups, enduring ones such as churches and empires.

An institution is not merely a convenient tool in the kit of instrumentalities by means of which an individual makes his way toward a plethora of destinations. It has a life of its own in the sense that it shapes individual activity as well as serving as an outlet for it, entertains goals and affirms goods as well as being the empty form on which they may be hung. In the subordination of idiosyncratic ends or values to ones held in common, a transformation occurs in which mere agreement among individuals gives way to what can only be described as trans-individual goals and goods. In short, collective ends can and do become the ends of collectives; commonly held values can and do become values of the commonwealth.

As the goals of diverse individuals come to converge and to be routinized and directed in terms of institutional structures, an institutional purpose becomes visible alongside individual purposes. The institutional purpose is transcendent to the purposes of individuals, even though dependent upon them and inseparable from them. The national purpose is not merely the purpose of the president or premier; in fact, one criterion of greatness in a national leader is his ability to subordinate his own interests to those of the commonweal or, better, to identify the former with the latter. This presupposes that institutional ends are not reducible to those of its spokesmen. Nor are societal goals and values merely the sum of those of its constituency. Public opinion polls may shed light on societal values, for citizens express and influence institutional aims and goods. But it would be false to contend that the polls describe those values in their statistical summaries.

Certain ends and norms cannot, in fact, be coherently understood except as transpersonal. It is the university and not some one of its officers that incurs debts and grants degrees. If the United States is said to have pursued an inconsistent foreign policy over the past hundred years, it is the nation that is being accused of inconsistency. While each secretary of state may have been himself consistent, the inconsistency requires a referent transcendent to any single policy maker. The locus of the inconsistency is institutional rather than individual.

It is extremely difficult, however, to speak about institutional aims without either reifying or reducing their reality. An institution is conspicuously dependent upon individual human beings for its existence. For instance, if an organization may be said to have an articulated aim, the articulation rests ultimately upon the expenditure of human energy. The muscles of a human throat or hand are the inescapably necessary conditions for such expression. A given foundation may grant a million dollars to a certain college, but it is a particular representative who speaks for the foundation and it is a human counterpart who graciously accepts the gift in behalf of the college. In this sense an institution is the creation of persons. It expresses their attitudes much as a smile expresses happiness; it exhibits the attainment or the ruin of their desires in the same way as any human artifact.

However, it is equally obvious that an individual is dependent upon institutions for the way in which he exists. One's goals are in large part derived from and sustained by the social structures that impinge upon him. It is a commonplace of sociological theory that a person defines himself in terms of the social roles he plays, out of either necessity or choice. Although it would be false to reduce an individual to the societal forces that shape his behavior, it would be an act of blindness to ignore their influence. In this sense a person is the creation of the societies to which he belongs. They orient his activity both from without and by means of the phenomenon of internalization. They provide him with his aims and attitudes much as parents provide their child with food and clothing.

To talk of the activity of institutions apart from the men who create and sustain them is a useful abstraction susceptible to the dangers of reification. Philosophers of history of the mold of a Spengler or a Hegel tend to commit this fallacy of misplaced concreteness. But to talk about the life of men apart from the societies that shape and constitute them is similarly an abstraction which borders on the reductionist fallacy, which sees social wholes as merely summaries of individual behavior. Positivistic philosophers and historians are open to a fallacy of misplaced concreteness in this different sense.

On the one hand, attention to the widespread presence of societal forces obscures the reality of autonomous individuality; on the other hand, a concern for the fact of idiosyncratic action beclouds awareness of the reality of social wholes. An adequate theory must do full justice both to the claim that culture is an expression of human aims and understandings and to the claim that persons are expressions of institutional forces and structures.[1]

The conclusion seems trivially true, and in fact almost anyone will readily admit that social interaction is a compromise between *Walden One* and *Walden Two*, between freedom and order, the individual and the collective. But everyone is not so ready to accept the ontological conclusions that this middle-of-the-road solution entails. In particular, it is typically difficult to accede to the grand assertion that an institution has as much ontological claim to the approbative status of "purposive entity" as does an individual. However, such equality of status can be shown by referring to institutions as individuals, as in legal theory concerning corporations. Or it can be done, as in Whitehead, by referring to human beings as societies. It is enough for the purposes of my argument to show that societies exhibit in their behavior the same five necessary and sufficient conditions for purposiveness that I applied at the outset to individual behavior. This behavioral isomorphism, despite all other obvious differences, elects societies as well as persons to membership in the select club of entities that, amid the multitudinous teleologies of the universe, are also purposive in their activity.

Whether the institution be a nation or a garden club, a business corporation or a family unit, the pattern is the same: (1) There is the contemporary generation, whose members exhibit in their being the traits peculiar to that society: the Frenchman with his linguistic artistry, the executive with his immaculate grooming. There are also the babies about to be born and the young men about to enter the world of business, bearers of future possibilities. (2) There are ideal possibilities for attainment—perhaps expressed in some archetype or paradigm of the relevant qualities already embodied brokenly in present attainment; perhaps expressed only by unreasonable hopes and the dim awareness of worlds beyond imagining. There is the possibility of reasserting the grandeur that is the "rightful" possession of France; there is the vision of corporation expansion and success. (3) There is a reciprocity of "care" or intentionality that defines the valuational woof upon which the disparate threads of individual activity are woven into a social fabric. The activities of both the seasoned corporation officer and the bright new initiate are oriented in terms of common values, shared judgments concerning the desirability of certain ends. For the present generation there is the aim of transforming the environment so as to

[1]These polarities can be suggestively associated with the sociological theories of, respectively, Max Weber and Emil Durkheim. Cf. Peter Berger and Stanley Pullberg, "Reification and the Sociological Critique of Consciousness," *History and Theory*, IV, 3 (1965), 196–211.

mold the future closer to the heart's desire; for the rising generation there is the aim of embodying that perfection. The executive seeks young men who will be effective servants of the business, and young men present themselves as the answer to his needs. (4) There are the activities undertaken in the light of these orienting goals that effect their attainment, in part or in whole. Through the mediation of a commonly envisioned and valued ideal, characteristics qualifying the present generation come to qualify its successors. The young man buys his proper suit of clothing; there grows upon the child a dawning awareness of himself as citizen of a nation and partial custodian of its destiny. (5) There is the dawn of the new day or age—a world in which French grandeur is a bit more evident, in which corporation profits are a little higher; or a world that marks the failure of such ideals and the triumph of other dreams. Here are the visible signs of that kind of purposive ordering that defines an institution: acquired characteristics commonly qualifying a number of individuals in virtue of the goals and values they collectively share.

II

So far I have argued three points: that persons engage in behavior patterns which can be characterized as purposive, i. e., as exhibiting a structure of aims, values, and methods of attainment; that individuals and institutions are interrelated, with each side influencing and being influenced by the purposes and activities of the other, although with neither being in any way reducible to or explicable solely in terms of the other; and that the institutional pole in this interaction shares with the individual as its opposite those characteristics that define its behavioral patterns as purposive. If this line of interpretation is at all adequate, it raises some interesting and important theological issues, to which we may now turn.

Christian thought has usually placed an emphasis upon the revelance of God to the question of aims and values. It is characteristic of Christianity, and even more so of the Hebraic heritage in which it is grounded, to assert that one of the few qualities shared by men and God is purposefulness. In the hands of the theologians this trait has often been intellectualized at the divine level into the qualities of omniscience and foreordination. But for the anthropomorphizing poets and prophets of the Bible it means the conviction that God wills and acts, that Yahweh grows angry or tenderly gives succour, that the father of Jesus Christ directs his love toward men and prepares them for the closing of the ages.

However, human social activity—that is, historical activity—is inescapably purposeful. If it is asserted that God acts in history, then the claim is being made that God is caught up in the structures of purposefulness. Such divine involvement should, I suggest, be seen as twofold. First, to believe that God acts in history is to assert that the aims, values, and methods of an individual's activity are influenced by the divine presence. This may find expression in such existential language as "encounter," "confrontation," "I-Thou." Second, one claims that the divine reality itself considers certain things valuable, entertains ideal ends, and engages in behavior aimed at the actualization of those ends. It is this latter claim that underlies the contemporary attacks on the doctrine of God's aseity. To biblical theologians and followers of Charles Hartshorne alike, the structures of purposiveness preclude the notions of classical perfection and of the God who, in his eternal completeness, lacks nothing. It is not my concern here to argue this point but, having assumed it, to draw out a few of its implications in relation to the prior discussion. If God has aims and men have aims, interaction among these aims finds expression in the further assertion that God has aims for men and that the true or authentic aim for a man is at ends and activities that accord with God's aim.

The structure of the divine purposings can be analyzed apart from any presumptive claim to private knowledge of what God's purposes in fact are. To act in history is to have purposes, no matter what they are, and consequently to exhibit the characteristics of teleological order strictly defined. Since biblical faith involves the further belief that these purposings include purposes for men—or, put existentially, for me—three things follow immediately. First, some potential, though not now actual, state of affairs, involving my self, my being-in-the-world, is a part of the divine vision. Second, this possibility is valued by God for me on the basis of criteria of value that he entertains or creates or is. Third, certain activity, engaged in by God, aims at transforming the realizable into the realized. Whether this activity is inexorable in its accomplishment of the divine intention or whether it can be thwarted by human activity is open to argument. I favor the latter view, primarily on the basis of its greater adequacy to the facts.

A right relationship, as understood by the religious individual, is similarly threefold. Among the possibilities for my life are those entertained by God. If I come to appropriate these divine goals-for-me as my goals-for-me, then the orientation of my behavior is, in terms of ends, identical with God's. This orientation will be achieved, presumably, only to the degree that I also appropriate God's system of values as my own. From this, appropriate activity should issue as a means to attain the valued end-in-view.

Any suggestion here of an overly simple piety or optimistic works-righteousness is blocked by an insistence upon the ideality of the model just constructed. The human situation is such that it frustrates at every point the ideal's full accomplishment. God's purposes are in part, and more often than not in whole, inscrutable. In their hiddenness they compel the individual to act without the assurance that he acts as God wills. Only in retrospect may one say with Paul, "Not I but Christ in me"; in the existential moment, decision is shot through and through with risk and hence is carried out in faith. Moreover, the individual's intentions are never so pure as always to quicken him into compatible activity for the sake of divinely given goals, even when he has or thinks he has full knowledge of God's will. Men are sinners as well as fools.

Having spoken against some particular heresies, I shall say no more of them. The task at hand is to extend this individualistic analysis to the social order. I have suggested that Christianity makes a claim concerning God's activity that is susceptible to analysis in terms of the interpenetration of divine and human structures of purposings. But I argued earlier that individual values, goals, and activities are inextricably bound up with the social order, and that one of the results of this is the emergence in history of institutions, of transindividual realities that exhibit as literally as do individuals the threefold qualities of goods, goals, and methods. I am now ready to argue that the Christian belief in a God who acts in history entails the belief that God has aims for institutions and that a nation or a church, or even a garden club, is in right relationship to God only when its aims are identical with his.

The conviction that God has a purpose for the nations is well grounded in biblical thought and accordingly reiterated in Christian theology, most notably by Augustine. The phrase "God's purpose for the nations" is equivocal, however. It can be taken to mean that God *has a use* for nations, that they have a role to play in the divine economy. His purposes for institutions are in this sense akin to his purposes for other inanimate or nonhuman portions of the creation. They are necessary conditions instrumental for the fulfillment of human aims and of the divine aims for human beings. On the other hand, the phrase can be interpreted as asserting that God *provides a purpose* to the nations, that with respect to an institution, God entertains a goal-for-it just as he entertains a goal-for-me. He confronts the institution with that goal as a possibility for it to actualize.

The first of these two meanings requires no reinterpretation of the ontological nature of social structures. The familiar idea of the "fullness of time," for example, reflects an instrumental view of institutions. Thus, the function of the Roman Empire has been identified as making possible the proclamation of the Christian message to "all" men, so that the particularity of final revelation might be given a universality akin to natural revelation and "all" men might be left without excuse. Or, heuristically speaking, the rise and fall of empires might be construed as means by which men are brought to a realization of the vanity of their earthly, God-thwarting purposes. In this sense, however, a natural event or thing can serve as readily as an institutional event or structure as a catalyst for a person's conversion or chastisement. Martin Luther was caught at one time in a thunderstorm and at another in a controversy over indulgences. But the acts of Pope Leo X were no different than the flashes of lightning: simply stimuli to occasion individual choice.

One difficulty in this approach is that it inadequately explains the meaning of man's social existence. That the fall of a nation is on the same level as the withering of a fig tree—functioning merely as a sign of the divine intentions—makes arbitrary the social quality of human life. Society, like food and sex, is seen as a given pre-condition for the fulfillment of purposes but not as itself purposive. Nor does it appear even necessary: like sex, if not like food, it can be foresworn by those saints who would follow the higher pathways to salvation. What is amazing is how such tendencies of thought could survive as they did in the face of both biblical and philosophical evidence of their inadequacy.

The second interpretation of the assertion that God has purposes for societies is at the same time more in harmony with Hebraic and Christian insights and more adequate to philosophical reflection. Institutions, as purposive structures, have ends that orient their behavior, guide their policy, and inform their obligations. God purposes to influence these social aims just as much as he seeks to influence the aims of the individual members of the social fabric. When God is said to will that Israel be a light to the nations (Isa. 49:6), it is Israel and not just the Israelites with whom he is concerned. And the demand is not simply that the nation be a showpiece that lights the way to God as a beacon lights the way to harbor. Rather God's purpose is revealed as intending that Israel's national purpose—its very national and cultic policies—be such that it leads the other nations to God. Israel's role is an active one, not a passive one. It should be noted that Israel is identified here as a light to *nations,* not just to individual people. The subjects of the whole passage are institutions, and the revelation concerns the relationship of the purposings of these institutions to the purposings of God.

The interpenetration of self and society requires such a conclusion. If men will evil and if society is shaped by human ideas and actions, then social purposes will be molded in evil ways. But it is equally true that if societies are oriented toward evil ends and men are influenced by ideologies and customary patterns of behavior, then individual goals will gain an evil tone. In this sense men are a product of their societies, just as societies are a product of the beliefs and practices of their citizenry.

Hence, if God aims at the salvation of men, at transforming in-dividual lives so that they are lived in transparent harmony with the divine purposes, he must also be said to aim at transforming the social order in similar fashion. A man can be forgiven his failure to hear or heed God's will in an evil and wicked age. The achievement of an I-Thou relation is difficult in the absence of a We-Thou relation. Whereas it is anachronistic to condemn Aristotle for recommending slavery, it is morally right to criticize a contemporary Westerner for merely condoning racial segregation. So also an institution can be for-given for its actions when it is under the control of evil and wicked men. The attitudes of victorious nations to the vanquished may at times reflect this last point—as, for instance, in the Allied inclination to "forgive" Germany for its Nazism.

My argument would be lost, however, if the above reasoning were taken to mean that men have no social responsibilities and that states have no moral responsibilities. For a person to see himself as the wholly innocent observer of institutional atrocities beyond his control either implies the very bifurcation I am attempting to deny or else entails a deterministic view of social and individual behavior that is equally opposed to the view I am defending. For example, granted that the evil acts of the Third Reich may have molded the moral beliefs of its citi-zens so that they became literally incapable of seeing the evil as evil, it is also the case that Nazism was itself possible only because of the willingness of individual Germans to have the nation's policies trans-lated into fact. The choice between condemnation and forgiveness rests on judgments concerning the freedom of the parties involved. Was the individual sufficiently free from the influences of anti-Semitism to be able to oppose it? Was the ethos of the nation such that it could pro-vide reasonable instrumentalities for effective opposition to Nazism? The tragedy of human history is exemplified in the ever recurrent am-biguity of the answer: yes and no.

The relation of God's purposings to the historical situation suggests his role as source of the power that makes for creative transcendence of the given. In an evil world, communication of the divine vision of a better order of the ages can lead an individual to entertain goals contrary to those of his environment and empower him to act for their accomplishment. Of such stuff are heroes and martyrs made. Similarly, an institution can come to reaffirm old values or en-vision new goals, and in this way come to alter its wicked course. Israel may repent for its violation of the Covenant; a college newly seeking excellence may positively transform faculty, student, and alumni at-titudes in ways that amaze both outside observers and those within.

However, God can fail, just as individual men or societies can. There are triumphs of evil over good as well as the victories of light over darkness. Most frequently, there is inertial preservation, with only minor modifications of what is neither wholly good nor wholly evil, neither totally conformed to God's aims nor totally athwart them.

III

If societal institutions are objectifications of human subjectivity, then their aims and the values in which they are rooted express the goals and goods of the individual saints and sinners who populate them. The divine aim to raise up persons whose goals and values are identical with God's goals-for-them and whose actions are complementary to the divine activity succeeds, therefore, only in so far as social ends and cultural traditions are also in harmony with the divine. For if the objective situation be alienated from God, the subjective activity which it expresses must also be alienated from him. And conversely, since individuals are subjective distillates expressing the wider social forces that environ and mold them, their private aims and personal beliefs are as cryptograms, wherein the trained eye can read the workings of the era or locale that brought them forth. The divine aim to call forth civilizations whose meanings and purposes are at one with God's purposes-for-them and whose histories accord with the divine activity succeeds, therefore, only where individual human beings, citizens of those societies, act and believe in ways transparent to the ways of God. For if men act evilly, the times are put out of joint.

The God who acts in human history acts for the salvation of his children. But since these children are inseparable from the social meanings and structures within which they move, God's aims for men imply and are implied by his aims for societies. Sin and waywardness, rightness and righteousness, characterize, therefore, the activities of civilizations and civic groups as well as citizens. Both have ends-in-view, orienting their behavior in accord with the divine ends, or out of accord with these ends. Both accept and embody structures of value and meaning that either reflect or blur the values and meanings that God creates and is. Both employ methods, successfully or not, for translating desired ends into present realities. Thus, in the midst of the multifarious, cachophonous activities of men and nations, God works to bring the goods and goals of individuals and societies nearer to the inscrutable purposes he holds for each. The salvation therein hoped for is the world's, apart from which no man is saved.

Bibliography

The intent of this bibliography is to present, as far as possible, a complete listing of significant works on Whiteheadian process theology. It includes all of the works by Whitehead and Hartshorne that have obvious theological importance, works on theological topics that have been significantly influenced by Whiteheadian philosophy, and essays that are critical of process theology. It does not include unpublished articles and dissertations, most book reviews, or journal articles that have been subsequently published in books (including the present volume). Neither does it include a complete bibliography for any individual philosopher or theologian, since the philosophers have written material that is not directly relevant to theology and the theologians have written material that does not especially reflect the influence of process philosophy.

Allan, George and Merle Allshouse. "Current Issues in Process Theology," *The Christian Scholar*, L (1967), 167–175.

Ames, E. S. "Humanism Fulfilled," *The Christian Century*, LIV (1937), 1075–1167.

Aubrey, Edwin E. "The Naturalistic Conception of Man," *The Journal of Religion*, XIX (1939), 189–200.

————. *Present Theological Tendencies*. New York: Harper and Brothers, 1936.

Azar, Larry. "Whitehead: Challenging a Challenge," *The Thomist*, XXX (1966), 80–87.

Barbour, Ian. *Issues in Science and Religion*. Englewood Cliffs, N.J.: Prentice-Hall, 1966.

————. "Teilhard's Process Metaphysics," *The Journal of Religion*, XLIX (1969), 136–159.

Barnhart, J. E. "Incarnation and Process Theology," *Religious Studies*, II (1967), 225–232.

Beer, Samuel H. *The City of Reason*. Cambridge: Harvard University Press, 1949.

Bennett, John C. "Three Levels of Persuasiveness," *Christendom*, VII (1942), 102–104.

Bidney, D. "The Problem of Substance in Spinoza and Whitehead," *The Philosophical Review*, XLV (1936), 574–592.

Birch, L. Charles. "Creation and the Creator," *The Journal of Religion*, XXXVI (1957), 85–98.

————. *Nature and God*. Philadelphia: Westminster, 1965.

Bixler, J. S. "Whitehead's Philosophy of Religion," *The Philosophy of Alfred North Whitehead*, P. A. Schilpp, ed. New York: Tudor, 1941.

Bodkin, M. "Physical Agencies and Divine Persuasion," *Philosophy*, XX (1945), 148–161.

Boodin, J. E. *Three Interpretations of the Universe*. New York: Macmillan, 1934.

Braham, E. G. "The Place of God in Whitehead's Philosophy," *London Quarterly Review*, CLXIV (1939), 63–69.

Brown, Delwin. "God's Reality and Life's Meaning: A Critique of Schubert Ogden," *Encounter*, XXVIII (1967), 256–262.

————. "Recent Process Theology," *Journal of the American Academy of Religion*, XXXV (1967), 28–41.

Browning, Don S. *Atonement and Psychotherapy*. Philadelphia: Westminster, 1966.

————. "Whitehead's Theory of Human Agency," *Dialogue*, II (1963–1964), 424–441.

Buehrer, Edwin T. "Mysticism and A. N. Whitehead," *Mysticism and the Modern Mind*, Alfred P. Stiernotte, ed. New York: Liberal Arts Press, 1959.

Burgers, J. M. *Experience and Conceptual Activity*. Cambridge: M. I. T. Press, 1965.

Burkle, H. R. *The Non-Existence of God*. New York: Herder and Herder, 1969.

Burrell, David B. "The Possibility of a Natural Theology," *Encounter*, XXIX (1968), 158–164.

Campbell, Harry M. "Emerson and Whitehead," *Proceedings of the Modern Language Association*, LXXV (1960), 577–582.

Capps, W. H. " 'Being and Becoming' and 'God and the World': An Analysis of Whitehead's Account of their Early Association," *Revue philosophique de Louvain*, LXIII (1965), 572–590.

Cauthen, Kenneth. "Process and Purpose: Toward a Philosophy of Life," *Zygon*, III (1968), 183–204.

————. *Science, Secularization, and God*. New York: Abingdon, 1969.

Cesselin, Felix. *La Philosophie organique de Whitehead*. Paris: Presses Universitaires de France, 1950.

Chappell, V. C. "Whitehead's Metaphysics," *The Review of Metaphysics*, XIII (1959), 278–304.

Christian, William A. "The Concept of God as a Derivative Notion," *Process and Divinity*, William L. Reese and Eugene Freeman, eds. LaSalle, Ill.: Open Court, 1964.

————. "God and the World," *The Journal of Religion*, XXVIII (1948), 255–262.

————. *An Interpretation of Whitehead's Metaphysics.* New Haven: Yale University Press, 1959, 1967.

————, and others. "A Discussion On the New Metaphysics and Theology," *The Christian Scholar,* L (1967), 304–331.

Clarke, Bowman L. *Language and Natural Theology.* The Hague: Mouton, 1966.

————. "The Language of Revealed Theology," *The Journal of Bible and Religion,* XXXII (1964), 334–341.

————. "Whitehead's Cosmology and the Christian Drama," *The Journal of Religion,* XXXIX (1959) 162–169.

Clarke, W. F. "The Idea of God in a Philosophy of Events," *The Monist,* XXXVIII (1928), 620–629.

Cobb, John B. Jr. "Can Natural Theology be Christian?" *Theology Today,* XXIII (1966), 140–142.

————. *A Christian Natural Theology.* Philadelphia: Westminister, 1965.

————. "Christian Natural Theology and Christian Existence," *The Christian Century,* LXXXII (1965), 265–267.

————. "Christianity and Myth," *The Journal of Bible and Religion,* XXXIII (1965), 314–320.

————. "The Finality of Christ in a Whiteheadian Perspective," *The Finality of Christ,* Dow Kirkpatrick, ed. Nashville: Abingdon, 1966.

————. "Freedom in Whitehead's Philosophy: A Response to Edward Pols," *The Southern Journal of Philosophy,* VII (1969-1970), 409–413.

————. "From Crisis Theology to the Post-Modern World," *The Centennial Review,* VIII (1964), 174–188.

————. *God and the World.* Philadelphia: Westminster, 1969.

————. *Living Options in Protestant Theology.* Philadelphia: Westminster, 1962.

————. "Nihilism, Existentialism, and Whitehead," *Religion in Life,* XXX (1961), 521–533.

————. "Ontology, History, and Christian Faith," *Religion in Life,* XXXIV (1965), 270–287.

————. "Perfection Exists: A Critique of Charles Hartshorne," *Religion in Life,* XXXII (1963), 294–304.

————. "The Philosophical Grounds of Moral Responsibility: A Comment on Matson and Niebuhr," *The Journal of Philosophy,* LVI (1959), 619–621.

————. "The Possibility of Theism Today," *The Idea of God: Philosophical Perspectives,* Edward Madden, Rollo Handy, and Marvin Farber, eds., Springfield, Ill.: Charles C. Thomas, 1968.

————. "A Process Systematic Theology," *The Journal of Religion,* L (1970), 199–206.

————. "Some Thoughts on the Meaning of Christ's Death," *Religion in Life,* XXVIII (1959), 212–222.

————. "Speaking About God," *Religion in Life,* XXXVI (1967), 28–39.

————. *The Structure of Christian Existence.* Philadelphia: Westminster, 1967.

————. "Theological Data and Method," *The Journal of Religion* XXXIII (1953), 212–223.

————. "What is Alive and What is Dead in Empirical Theology," The Future of Empirical Theology, Bernard E. Meland, ed. Chicago: University of Chicago Press, 1969.

————. "Whitehead's Philosophy and a Christian Doctrine of Man," The Journal of Bible and Religion, XXXII (1964), 209–220.

Comstock, W. Richard. "Naturalism and Theology," Heythrop Journal, VIII (1967), 181–190.

Connelly, G. E. "Whitehead and the Actuality of God in His Primordial Nature," The Modern Schoolman, XLI (1964), 309–322.

Connelly, R. J. "The Ontological Argument: Descartes' Advice to Hartshorne," The New Scholasticism, XLIII (1969), 530–554.

Cooper, Robert M. "God as Poet and Man as Praying: An Essay on the Thought of A. N. Whitehead," The Personalist, XLIV (1968), 474–488.

Cotton, J. Harry. "The Meaning of 'God' in Whitehead's Philosophy," Encounter, XXIX (1968), 125–140.

Cousins, Ewert. "Truth in Saint Bonaventure," Proceedings of the American Catholic Philosophical Association, XLIII (1969), 204–210.

Crosby, Donald A. "Language and Religious Language in Whitehead's Philosophy," The Christian Scholar, L (1967), 210–221.

Curtis, J. C. "Ecumenism and Process Theology," The Hartford Quarterly, VII (1967), 34–42.

————. "God and the World in Process," Dialog, V (1966), 112–117.

————. "Philosophy and Ecumenical Dialogue," The Ecumenist, IV (1966), 76–78.

————. The Task of Philosophical Theology. New York: Philosophical Library, 1967.

de Laguna, Grace A. On Existence and the Human World. New Haven: Yale University Press, 1966.

Dresch, P. "The Transcendence of God in Whitehead's Philosophy," Philosophical Studies, XI (1961–1962), 7–27.

Ely, Stephen Lee. The Religious Availability of Whitehead's God. Madison: University of Wisconsin Press, 1942.

Emmet, Dorothy M. Whitehead's Philosophy of Organism. London: Macmillan, 1932; New York: St. Martin's, 1966.

Eslick, Leonard J. "God in the Metaphysics of Whitehead," New Themes in Christian Philosophy, Ralph M. McInerny, ed. Notre Dame: University of Notre Dame Press, 1968.

Farley, Edward. The Transcendence of God. Philadelphia: Westminster, 1960.

Fenton, John Young. "The Post-Liberal Theology of Christ Without Myth," The Journal of Religion, XLIII (1963), 93–104.

Ferré, Nels F. S. "Beyond Substance and Process," Theology Today XXIV (1967), 160–171.

————. Review of Charles Hartshorne, The Divine Relativity, in The Journal of Religion, XXIX (1949), 304–305.

Fitch, Frederick B. "The Perfection of Perfection," *Process and Divinity*, William L. Reese and Eugene Freeman, eds. LaSalle, Ill.: Open Court, 1964.

Flew, Antony. "Reflections on 'The Reality of God,'" *The Journal of Religion*, XLVIII (1968), 150–161.

Foley, L. A. *A Critique of the Philosophy of Being of Alfred North Whitehead in the Light of Thomistic Philosophy*. Washington: The Catholic University of America Press, 1946.

Ford, Lewis S. "Boethius and Whitehead on Time and Eternity," *International Philosophical Quarterly*, VIII (1968), 38–67.

————. "Can Whitehead Provide for Real Subjective Agency? A Reply to Edward Pols," *The Modern Schoolman*, XLVII (1970), 209–225.

————. "Is Process Theism Compatible With Relativity Theory?" *The Journal of Religion*, XLVIII (1968), 124–135.

————. "On Genetic Successiveness: A Third Alternative," *The Southern Journal of Philosophy*, VII (1969–1970), 421–425.

————. "Whitehead's Conception of Divine Spatiality," *The Southern Journal of Philosophy*, VI (1968), 1–23.

Forsyth, T. M. "Creative Evolution in its Bearing on the Idea of God," *Philosophy*, XXV (1950), 195–208.

Foster, A. Durwood, Jr. "The Resurrection of God," *Religion in Life*, XXXVIII (1969), 131–147.

Fries, Horace. "The Functions of Whitehead's God," *The Monist*, XLVI (1936), 25–58.

Funk, Robert W. *Language, Hermeneutic, and the Word of God*. New York: Harper and Row, 1966.

Garland, Williams J. "The Ultimacy of Creativity," *The Southern Journal of Philosophy*, VII (1969–1970), 361–376.

Gentry, G. V. "The Subject in Whitehead's Philosophy," *Philosophy of Science*, XI (1944), 222–226.

Gibson, A. Boyce. "The Two Strands in Natural Theology," *The Monist*, XLVII (1963), 335–364.

Gilkey, Langdon B. *Maker of Heaven and Earth*. New York: Doubleday, 1959, 1965.

————. Review of John B. Cobb, Jr., *A Christian Natural Theology*, in *Theology Today*, XXII (1966), 530–545.

————. "A Theology in Process," *Interpretation*, XXI (1967), 447–459.

Gray, Wallace. "Whitehead and Ferré Discuss God," *Hibbert Journal*, LVI (1957–1958), 262–272.

Gruenler, Royce Gordon. *Jesus, Persons and the Kingdom of God*. St. Louis: Bethany, 1967.

Gustafson, D. F. "Christian on Causal Objectification in Whitehead," *International Philosophical Quarterly*, I (1961), 683–696.

Guthrie, Shirley C., Jr. "Theology and Metaphysics," *America and the Future of Theology*, William A. Beardslee, ed. Philadelphia: Westminster, 1967.

Guy, Fritz. "Comments on a Recent Whiteheadian Doctrine of God," *Andrews University Seminary Studies*, IV (1966), 107–134.

Hall, David. "The Autonomy of Religion in Whitehead's Philosophy," *Philosophy Today,* XIII (1969), 271–283.

Hamilton, Peter. *The Living God and the Modern World.* London: Hodder and Stoughton, 1967.

Hanna, Thomas. "The Living Body: Nexus of Process Philosophy and Existential Phenomenology," *Soundings,* LII (1969), 323–333.

Hare, P. H., and E. H. Madden *Evil and the Concept of God.* Springfield, Ill.: Charles C. Thomas, 1968.

―――――. "The Theological Importance of A. N. Whitehead," *Theology,* LXVIII (1965), 187–195.

Hart, Ray L. "Schubert Ogden on the Reality of God," *Religion in Life,* XXXVI (1967), 506–515.

Hartshorne, Charles. *Anselm's Discovery.* LaSalle, Ill.: Open Court, 1965.

―――――. *Beyond Humanism: Essays in the New Philosophy of Nature.* Chicago: Willett, Clark, 1937, Lincoln: University of Nebraska Press, 1968.

―――――. "The Buddhist-Whiteheadian View of the Self and the Religious Traditions," *Proceedings of the IXth International Congress for the History of Religions.* Tokyo, 1960, 298–302.

―――――. "Criteria for Ideas of God," *Insight and Vision: Essays in Philosophy in Honor of Radoslav Andrea Tsanoff,* Konstantin Kolenda, ed. San Antonio: Principia Press of Trinity University, 1966.

―――――. "The Dipolar Conception of Deity," *The Review of Metaphysics,* XXI (1967), 273–289.

―――――. "Divine Absoluteness and Divine Relativity," *Transcendence,* Herbert W. Richardson and Donald R. Cutler, eds. Boston: Beacon Press, 1969.

―――――. "The Divine Relativity and Absoluteness: A Reply," *The Review of Metaphysics,* IV (1950), 31–60.

―――――. *The Divine Relativity: A Social Conception of God.* New Haven: Yale University Press, 1948, 1964.

―――――. "Efficient Causality: A Comment," *The Journal of Religion,* XXVI (1946), 54–57.

―――――. "Ethics and the New Theology," *The International Journal of Ethics,* XLV (1934), 90–101.

―――――. "God and Man Not Rivals," *The Journal of Liberal Religion,* VI (1944), 9–13.

―――――. "The God of Religion and the God of Philosophy," *Talk of God: Royal Institute of Philosophy Lectures,* II, 1967–1968. London: Macmillan, 1969.

―――――. "God's Existence: A Conceptual Problem," *Religious Experience and Truth,* Sidney Hook, ed. New York: New York University Press, 1961, 211–219.

―――――. "The Immortality of the Past: Critique of a Prevalent Misinterpretation," *The Review of Metaphysics,* VII (1953), 98–112.

―――――. "Is Whitehead's God the God of Religion?" *Ethics,* LIII (1943), 219–227.

―――――. *The Logic of Perfection and Other Essays in Neoclassical Metaphysics.* LaSalle, Ill.: Open Court, 1962.

_____. "Man's Fragmentariness," *Wesleyan Studies in Religion*, LVI (1963–1964), 17–28.

_____. *Man's Vision of God and the Logic of Theism*. Chicago: Willett, Clark, 1941, Hamden, Conn.: Archon Books, 1964.

_____. "The Modern World and a Modern View of God," *The Crane Review*, IV (1962), 73–85.

_____. *A Natural Theology for Our Time*. LaSalle, Ill.: Open Court, 1967.

_____. "Necessity," *The Review of Metaphysics*, XXI (1967), 290–296.

_____. "The New Pantheism," *The Christian Register*, CXV (1936), 119–120, 141–143.

_____. "Panpsychism," *A History of Philosophical Systems*, V. Ferm, ed. New York: Philosophical Library, 1950.

_____. "A Philosopher's Assessment of Christianity," *Religion and Culture: Essays in Honor of Paul Tillich*, Walter Leibrecht, ed. New York: Harper and Row, 1959.

_____. "The Philosophy of Creative Synthesis," *The Journal of Philosophy*, LV (1958), 944–953.

_____. "Process Philosophy as a Resource for Christian Thought," *Philosophical Resources for Christian Thought*, Perry LeFevre, ed. Nashville: Abingdon, 1968.

_____. *Reality as Social Process: Studies in Metaphysics and Religion*. Glencoe and Boston: Free Press and Beacon Press, 1953.

_____. "Redefining God," *The New Humanist*, VII (1934), 8–15.

_____. "Religion and Creative Experience," *The Unitarian Register and the Universalist Leader*, CXLI (1962), 9–11.

_____. "Tillich and the Nontheological Meanings of Theological Terms," *Religion in Life*, XXXV (1966), 674–685.

_____. "Tillich and the Other Great Tradition," *Anglican Theological Review*, XLIII (1961), 245–259.

_____. "Whitehead and Berdyaev: Is There Tragedy in God?" *The Journal of Religion*, XXXVI (1957), 71–84.

_____. "Whitehead's Idea of God," *The Philosophy of Alfred North Whitehead*, P.A. Schilpp, ed. New York: Tudor, 1941.

_____. "Whitehead's Metaphysics," *Whitehead and the Modern World* by Victor Lowe, Charles Hartshorne, and A. H. Johnson. Boston: Beacon Press, 1950.

_____. "Whitehead's Novel Intuition," *Alfred North Whitehead: Essays on His Philosophy*, George L. Kline, ed. Englewood Cliffs: Prentice-Hall, 1963.

_____ and William L. Reese. *Philosophers Speak of God*. Chicago: University of Chicago Press, 1953.

Hartt, Julian. "The Logic of Perfection," *The Review of Metaphysics*, XVI (1963), 749–769.

Harvey, Van Austin. *The Historian and the Believer*. New York: Macmillan, 1966.

Hatchett, Marion J. "Charles Hartshorne's Critique of Christian Theology," *Anglican Theological Review*, XLVIII (1966), 264–275.

Hazelton, Roger. "Time, Eternity and History," *The Journal of Religion*, XXX (1950), 1–12.

Henry, Carl F. H. "The Reality and Identity of God: A Critique of Process Theology," Christianity Today, XIII (1969), 523–526, 580–584.

Henry, Granville C. "Mathematics, Phenomenology, and Language Analysis in Contemporary Theology," Journal of the American Academy of Religion, XXXV (1967), 337–349.

Herzog, Frederick. Understanding God. New York: Charles Scribner's Sons, 1966.

Hocking, Richard. "The Polarity of Dialectical History and Process Cosmology," The Christian Scholar, L (1967), 177–183.

Hocking, William E. Science and the Idea of God. Chapel Hill, N.C.: The University of North Carolina Press, 1944.

Hooper, Sydney E. "Whitehead's Philosophy: Eternal Objects and God," Philosophy, XVII (1942), 47–68.

Hopper, Stanley R. "Whitehead: Redevivus? or Absconditus?" in America and the Future of Theology, William A. Beardslee, ed. Philadelphia: Westminster, 1967.

Huckle, John J. "From Whitehead to Ogden: Possibility in Contemporary Theology," Dunwoodie Review, VII (1967), 177–198.

Hutchison, John A. "The Philosophy of Religion: Retrospect and Prospect," The Journal of Bible and Religion, XXX (1962), 12–17.

James, Ralph E., Jr. The Concrete God. Indianapolis: Bobbs-Merrill, 1967.

————. "Hot Theology in a Cool World," Theology Today, XXIV (1968), 432–443.

————. "A Theology of Acceptance," The Journal of Religion, XLIX (1969), 376–387.

Johnson, A. H. Whitehead's Philosophy of Civilization. Boston: Beacon Press, 1958, New York: Dover, 1962.

————. Whitehead's Theory of Reality. Boston: Beacon Press, 1952, New York: Dover, 1962.

Johnson, Joseph A., Jr. "A Comparative Study of the Idea of God in the Philosophy of Alfred North Whitehead and Henry Nelson Wieman," The Center, II (1961), 16–37.

Jordan, Martin. New Shapes of Reality: Aspects of A. N. Whitehead's Philosophy. London: Allen and Unwin, 1968.

Kaufman, Maynard. "Post-Christian Aspects of the Radical Theology," Toward a New Christianity: Readings in the Death of God Theology, Thomas J. J. Altizer, ed. New York: Harcourt, Brace and World, 1967.

Kuntz, Paul G. "Religion of Order or Religion of Chaos?" Religion in Life, XXXV (1966), 433–449.

————. "What Do You Mean By 'God,' " The Personalist, L (1969), 393–397.

Kuspit, Donald. "Whitehead's God and Metaphysics," Essays in Philosophy, (no ed. named). University Park, Pa.: Pennsylvania State University Press, 1962.

Lafleur, Lawrence J. "If God Were Eternal," The Journal of Religion, XX (1940), 382–389.

Lamont, Corliss. "Equivocation on Religious Issues," The Journal of Religion, XIV (1934), 412–427.

Lawrence, Nathaniel. "The Vision of Beauty and the Temporality of Deity in Whitehead's Philosophy," The Journal of Philosophy, LVIII (1961), 543–553.

Leclerc, Ivor, ed. The Relevance of Whitehead. New York: Macmillan, 1961.

————. Whitehead's Metaphysics: An Introductory Exposition. New York: Macmillan, 1958.

————. "Whitehead and the Problem of God," The Southern Journal of Philosophy, VII (1969–1970), 447–455.

Levi, Albert William. Philosophy and the Modern World. Bloomington: Indiana University Press, 1959.

Lintz, Edward J. The Unity of the Universe According to Alfred North Whitehead. Baltimore: J. H. Furst, 1939.

Loomer, Bernard M. "Empirical Theology Within Process Thought," The Future of Empirical Theology, Bernard E. Meland, ed. Chicago: The University of Chicago Press, 1969.

————. "Neo-Naturalism and Neo-Orthodoxy," The Journal of Religion, XXVIII (1948), 79–91.

Lowe, Victor. Review of Stephen Lee Ely, The Religious Availability of Whitehead's God, in The Review of Religion, VII (1943), 409–415.

————. Understanding Whitehead. Baltimore: The Johns Hopkins Press, 1962.

Lyman, Eugene W. The Meaning and Truth of Religion. New York: Charles Scribner's Sons, 1933.

MacCormac, Earl R. "Indeterminacy and Theology," Religion in Life, XXXVI (1967), 355–370.

Macintosh, D. C. Review of Charles Hartshorne, Man's Vision of God, in The Review of Religion, VI (1942), 443–448.

Macquarrie, John. Studies in Christian Existentialism. Philadelphia: Westminster, 1965.

Madden, Edward H., and Peter H. Hare. "Evil and Unlimited Power," The Review of Metaphysics, XX (1966), 278–289.

Martin, Oliver. "Whitehead's Naturalism and God," The Review of Religion, III (1931), 149–160.

Martland, T. R. "Is A Theology of Dialogue (of Process) Permissible?" The Christian Scholar, L (1967), 197–209.

Mascall, E. L. He Who Is. London: Longmans, Green, 1943.

————. "Three Modern Approaches to God," Theology, XXX (1935), 18–35.

Mays, W. The Philosophy of Whitehead. New York: Macmillan, 1959.

Meland, Bernard E. "Can Empirical Theology Learn Something from Phenomenology?" The Future of Empirical Theology, Bernard E. Meland, ed. Chicago: University of Chicago Press, 1969.

————. "The Empirical Tradition in Theology at Chicago," The Future of Empirical Theology, Bernard E. Meland, ed. Chicago: University of Chicago Press, 1969.

————. *Faith and Culture.* New York: Oxford University Press, 1953.

————. "For the Modern Liberal: Is Theology Possible? Can Science Replace It?" *Zygon,* II (1967), 166–186.

————. "The Genius of Protestantism," *The Journal of Religion,* XXVII (1947), 273–292.

————. "How Is Culture a Source for Theology," *Criterion,* III (1964), 10–21.

————. "Interpreting the Christian Faith Within a Philosophical Framework," *The Journal of Religion,* XXXIII (1953), 87–102.

————. "Modern Protestantism: Aimless or Resurgent?" *The Christian Century,* LXXX (1963), 1494–1497.

————. "The Mystic Returns," *The Journal of Religion,* XVII (1937), 146–160.

————. "New Dimensions of Liberal Faith," *The Christian Century,* LXXIV (1957), 961–963.

————. "New Perspectives on Nature and Grace," *The Scope of Grace,* Philip J. Hefner, ed. Philadelphia: Fortress Press, 1964.

————. "The Perception of Goodness," *The Journal of Religion,* XXXII (1952), 47–55.

————. "The Persisting Liberal Witness," *The Christian Century,* LXXIX

————. *The Realities of Faith.* New York: Oxford University Press, 1962. 1962), 1157–1159.

————. *The Reawakening of Christian Faith.* New York: Macmillan, 1949.

————. "The Religious Availability of a Philosopher's God," *Christendom,* VIII (1943), 495–502.

————. *The Secularization of Modern Cultures.* New York: Oxford University Press, 1966.

————. *Seeds of Redemption.* New York: Macmillan, 1947.

————. "The Structure of Christian Faith," *Religion in Life,* XXXVI (1968), 551–562.

Michalson, Carl. *The Hinge of History.* New York: Charles Scribner's Sons, 1959.

Miller, Randolph Crump. "Theology In Transition," *The Journal of Religion,* XX (1940), 160–168.

Milligan, Charles S. "Religious Values of Whitehead's God Concept," *The Iliff Review,* IX (1952), 117–128.

Morgan, G. "Whitehead's Theory of Value," *International Journal of Ethics,* XLVII (1937), 308–316.

Morrison, C. C. "Thomism and the Re-birth of Protestant Philosophy," *Christendom,* II (1937), 110–125.

Moxley, D. J. "The Conception of God in the Philosophy of Whitehead," *Proceedings of the Aristotelian Society,* XXXIV (1933–1934), 157–186.

Murphy, Arthur E. "The Anti-Copernician Revolution," *The Journal of Philosophy,* XXVI (1929), 281–299.

Neville, Robert C. "Neo-Classical Theology and Christianity: A Critical Study of Ogden's 'Reality of God,'" *International Philosophical Quarterly,* IX (1969), 605–624.

————. "Whitehead on the One and the Many," *The Southern Journal of Philosophy,* VII (1969–1970), 387–393.

Niebuhr, H. Richard. *The Meaning of Revelation.* New York: Macmillan, 1941, 1962.

Niebuhr, Reinhold. Review of Charles Hartshorne, *Man's Vision of God,* in *Christianity and Society,* VII (1942), 43–44.

————. "Science and the Modern World," *The Christian Century,* XLIII (1926), 448–449.

Norman, Ralph. "Steam, Barbarism, and Dialectic: Notations on Proof and Sensibility," *The Christian Scholar,* L (1967), 184–196.

O'Brien, John A. "God in Whitehead's Philosophy," *The American Ecclesiastical Review,* CX (1944), 444–450, CXI (1944), 124–130.

Oden, Thomas C. "Bultmann As Lutheran Existentialist," *Dialogue,* III (1964), 207–214.

Ogden, Schubert M. "Beyond Supernaturalism," *Religion in Life,* XXXIII (1963–1964), 7–18.

————. "Bultmann's Demythologizing and Hartshorne's Dipolar Theism," *Process and Divinity,* William L. Reese and Eugene Freeman, eds. La-Salle, Ill.: Open Court, 1964.

————. "Bultmann's Project of Demythologization and the Problem of Theology and Philosophy," *The Journal of Religion,* XXXVII (1957), 156–173.

————. *Christ Without Myth.* New York: Harper and Row, 1961.

————. "The Christian Proclamation of God to Men of the So-Called 'Atheistic Age,' " *Is God Dead?* Concilium Volume 16, Johannes B. Metz, ed. New York: Paulist, 1966.

————. "Faith and Truth," *The Christian Century,* LXXXII (1965), 1057–1060.

————. "God and Philosophy: A Discussion with Antony Flew," *The Journal of Religion,* XLVIII (1968), 161–181.

————. "How Does God Function in Human Life," *Christianity and Crisis,* XXVII (1967), 105–108.

————. "Love Unbounded: The Doctrine of God," *The Perkins School of Theology Journal,* XIX (1966), 5–17.

————. "The Possibility and Task of Philosophical Theology," *Union Seminary Quarterly Review,* XX (1965), 271–279.

————. "Present Prospects for Empirical Theology," *The Future of Empirical Theology,* Bernard E. Meland, ed. Chicago: University of Chicago Press, 1969.

————. *The Reality of God.* New York: Harper and Row, 1966.

————. "The Significance of Rudolf Bultmann for Contemporary Theology," *The Theology of Rudolf Bultmann,* Charles W. Kegley, ed. New York: Harper and Row, 1966.

————. "Theology and Metaphysics," *Criterion,* IX (1969), 15–18.

————. "Theology and Philosophy: A New Phase of the Discussion," *The Journal of Religion,* XLIV (1964), 1–16.

Otto, M. C. "A. N. Whitehead and Science," *The New Humanist,* VII (1934), 1–7.

Overman, Richard H. *Evolution and the Christian Doctrine of Creation.* Philadelphia: Westminster, 1967.

Pailin, David A. "Some Comments on Hartshorne's Presentation of the Ontological Argument," *Religious Studies,* IV (1968), 103–122.

Parker, Francis H. "Head, Heart, and God," *The Review of Metaphysics,* XIV (1960), 328–352.

Parmentier, Alix. *La philosophie de Whitehead et le problème de Dieu.* Paris: Beauchesne, 1968.

Parsons, Howard L. "History as Viewed by Marx and Whitehead," *The Christian Scholar,* L (1967), 273–289.

————. "Religious Naturalism and the Philosophy of Charles Hartshorne," *Process and Divinity,* William L. Reese and Eugene Freeman, eds. La-Salle, Ill.: Open Court, 1964.

Peters, Eugene H. *The Creative Advance.* St. Louis: Bethany Press, 1966.

Pittenger, W. Norman. "Bernard E. Meland, Process Thought, and the Significance of Christ," *Religion in Life,* XXXVII (1968), 540–550.

————. *Christology Reconsidered.* London: SCM Press, 1970.

————. "A Contemporary Trend in North American Theology: Process-Thought and Christian Faith," *Religion in Life,* XXXIV (1965), 500–510.

————. "A Fresh Look at Christian Moral Theology," *Religion in Life,* XXXVIII (1969), 548–554.

————. *God in Process.* London: SCM Press, 1967.

————. *Process Thought and Christian Faith.* New York: Macmillan, 1968.

————. "Some Implications, Philosophical and Theological, in John Knox's Writing," *Christian History and Interpretation: Studies Presented to John Knox,* W. R. Farmer *et al,* eds. Cambridge: Cambridge University Press, 1967.

————. *Theology and Reality.* Greenwich, Conn.: The Seabury Press, 1955.

————. "Toward a More Christian Theology," *Religion in Life,* XXXVI (1967), 498–505.

————. *The Word Incarnate.* New York: Harper and Brothers, 1959.

Platt, David. "Some Perplexities Concerning God's Existence," *The Journal of Bible and Religion,* XXXIV (1966), 244–252.

Pols, Edward. "Freedom and Agency: A Reply," *The Southern Journal of Philosophy,* VII (1969–1970), 415–419.

————. *Whitehead's Metaphysics.* Carbondale: Southern Illinois University Press, 1967.

Purtill, R. L. "Hartshorne's Modal Proof," *The Journal of Philosophy,* LXIII (1966), 397–409.

————. "Ontological Modalities," *The Review of Metaphysics,* XXI (1967), 297–307.

Reck, Andrew J. "The Fox Alone is Death: A. N. Whitehead and Speculative Philosophy," *American Philosophy and the Future,* Michael Novak, ed. New York: Charles Scribner's Sons, 1968.

————. "The Philosophy of Charles Hartshorne," *Studies in Whitehead's Philosophy* (Tulane Studies in Philosophy, Vol. X). New Orleans: Tulane University, 1961.

Reese, William L. and Eugene Freeman, eds. *Process and Divinity: Philosophical Essays Presented to Charles Hartshorne.* LaSalle, Ill.: Open Court, 1964.

Reeves, Gene. "God and Creativity," *The Southern Journal of Philosophy*, VII (1969–1970), 377–385.

Reinelt, Herbert R. "Whitehead and Theistic Language," *The Christian Scholar*, L (1967), 222–234.

Richmond, James. "God, Time, and Process Philosophy," *Theology*, LXVIII (1965), 234–241.

Robinson, John A. T. *Exploration Into God*. Stanford: Stanford University Press, 1968.

Roth, Robert T. *American Religious Philosophy*. New York: Harcourt, Brace and World, 1967.

Sarkar, A. K. "Whitehead's Conception of God," *Prabuddha Barata*, XLIV (1939), 397–403.

Schilling, S. Paul. *God in an Age of Atheism*. Nashville: Abingdon, 1969.

Schilpp, Paul Arthur, ed. *The Philosophy of Alfred North Whitehead*. New York: Tudor, 1941.

Shahan, Ewing P. *Whitehead's Theory of Experience*. New York: King's Crown Press, 1950.

Sheen, F. J. "Professor Whitehead and the Making of Religion," *The New Scholasticism*, I (1927), 147–162.

Sherburne, Donald W. *A Key to Whitehead's Process and Reality*. New York: Macmillan, 1966.

————. "Responsibility, Punishment, and Whitehead's Theory of the Self," *Alfred North Whitehead: Essays on His Philosophy*, George L. Kline, ed. Englewood Cliffs: Prentice-Hall, 1963.

————. *A Whiteheadian Aesthetic*. New Haven: Yale University Press, 1961.

Sisson, Edward O. "Whitehead's Mysticism: A Review Article," *The Review of Religion*, VIII (1944), 150–153.

Skutch, Alexander F. *The Quest of the Divine*. Boston: Meador, 1956.

Slater, R. H. L. *God and the Living*. New York: Charles Scribner's Sons, 1939.

Smith, Gerald Birney. "Science and Religion," *The Journal of Religion*, VI (1926), 308–315.

Smith, John E. "Philosophy of Religion," *Religion*, Paul Ramsey, ed. Englewood Cliffs: Prentice-Hall, 1965.

Stokes, Walter E. "Freedom as Perfection: Whitehead, Thomas and Augustine," *Proceedings of the American Catholic Philosophical Association: Justice*, XXXVI (1962), 134–142.

————. "Is God Really Related to This World," *Proceedings of the American Catholic Philosophical Association*, XXXIX (1965), 145–151.

————. "Recent Interpretations of Whitehead's Creativity," *Modern Schoolman*, XXXIX (1962), 309–333.

————. "Whitehead's Challenge to Theistic Realism," *The New Scholasticism*, XXXVIII (1964), 1–21.

Taubes, Jacob. "Philosophers Speak of God," *The Journal of Religion*, XXXIV (1954), 120–126.

Taylor, A. E. "Dr. Whitehead's Philosophy of Religion," *Dublin Review*, CLXXXI (1927), 17–41.

Temple, William. *Nature, Man and God*. London: Macmillan, 1934.

Thomas, George F. *Religious Philosophies of the West.* New York: Charles Scribner's Sons, 1965.

Thompson, E. J. *An Analysis of the Thought of Whitehead and Hocking Concerning Good and Evil.* Chicago: University of Chicago Press, 1935.

Thornton, Lionel S. *The Incarnate Lord.* London: Longmans, Green, 1928.

Van Nuys, Kelvin. *Science and Cosmic Purpose.* New York: Harper and Brothers, 1949.

Weingart, Richard E. "Process or Deicide?" *Encounter,* XXIX (1968), 149–157.

Welch, Claude. "Theology," *Religion,* Paul Ramsey, ed. Englewood Cliffs: Prentice-Hall, 1965.

Westphal, Merold. "Temporality and Finitism in Hartshorne's Theism," *The Review of Metaphysics,* XIX (1966), 550–564.

Whitehead, Alfred North. *Adventures of Ideas.* New York: Macmillan, 1933, The Free Press, 1967.

————. *The Aims of Education and Other Essays.* New York: Macmillan, 1929, Free Press, 1967.

————. *Dialogues of Alfred North Whitehead.* As recorded by Lucian Price. Boston: Little, Brown, 1954, New York: New American Library, 1956.

————. *Essays in Science and Philosophy.* New York: Philosophical Library, 1947.

————. *The Function of Reason.* Princeton: Princeton University Press, 1929, Boston: Beacon Press, 1958.

————. "Immortality," *The Philosophy of Alfred North Whitehead,* P. A. Schilpp, ed. New York: Tudor, 1941.

————. *Modes of Thought.* New York: Macmillan, 1938, Free Press, 1968.

————. *Process and Reality.* New York: Macmillan, 1929, Free Press, 1969.

————. *Religion in the Making.* New York: Macmillan, 1926, World, 1960.

————. *Science and the Modern World.* New York: Macmillan, 1925; Free Press, 1967.

————. *Symbolism: Its Meaning and Effect.* New York: Macmillan, 1927, Capricorn, 1959.

Whittemore, Robert C. "Time and Whitehead's God," *Studies in American Philosophy* (Tulane Studies in Philosophy, Vol. IV). New Orleans: Tulane University, 1955.

Wieman, Henry Nelson. *Religious Experience and Scientific Method.* New York: Macmillan, 1926.

————. Review of Charles Hartshorne, *The Divine Relativity,* in *The Philosophical Review,* LVIII (1949), 78–82.

————. *The Source of Human Good.* Chicago: University of Chicago Press, 1946, Carbondale: Southern Illinois University Press, 1964.

————. "A Waste We Cannot Afford," *Unitarian Universalist Register-Leader,* CXLIII (November 1962), 11–13.

————. *The Wrestle of Religion With Truth.* New York: Macmillan, 1927.

———— and Bernard E. Meland. *American Philosophies of Religion.* Chicago: Willett, Clark, 1936.

Wilcox, John T. "A Question from Physics for Certain Theists," *The Journal of Religion,* XLI (1961), 293–300.

Wild, John. "The Divine Existence: An Answer to Mr. Hartshorne," The Review of Metaphysics, IX (1950), 61–84.

_____. Review of Charles Hartshorne, The Divine Relativity, in The Review of Metaphysics, II (1948), 65–77.

Williams, Daniel Day. "Brunner and Barth on Philosophy." The Journal of Religion, XXVII (1947), 241–254.

_____. "Christianity and Naturalism: An Informal Statement," Union Seminary Quarterly Review, XII (1957), 47–53.

_____. "Deity, Monarchy, and Metaphysics: Whitehead's Critique of the Theological Tradition," The Relevance of Whitehead, Ivor Leclerc, ed. New York: Macmillan, 1961.

_____. God's Grace and Man's Hope. New York: Harper and Brothers, 1949, 1965.

_____. "How Does God Act? An Essay in Whitehead's Metaphysics," Process and Divinity, William L. Reese and Eugene Freeman, eds. LaSalle, Ill.: Open Court, 1964.

_____. "John Knox's Conception of History," Christian History and Interpretation: Studies Presented to John Knox, W. R. Farmer et al, eds. Cambridge: Cambridge University Press, 1967.

_____. "Moral Obligation in Process Philosophy," Alfred North Whitehead: Essays on His Philosophy, George L. Kline, ed. Englewood Cliffs: Prentice-Hall, 1963.

_____. "The New Theological Situation," Theology Today, XXIV (1968), 444–463.

_____. The Spirit and Forms of Love. New York: Harper and Row, 1968.

_____. "Suffering and Being in Empirical Theology," The Future of Empirical Theology, B. E. Meland, ed. Chicago: University of Chicago Press, 1969.

_____. "Theology and Truth," The Journal of Religion, XXII (1962), 382–397.

_____. "The Theology of Bernard E. Meland," Criterion, III (1964), 3–9.

_____. "Tillich's Doctrine of God," The Philosophical Forum, XVIII (1960–1961), 40–50.

_____. "Truth in the Theological Perspective," The Journal of Religion, XXVIII (1948), 242–254.

_____. "The Victory of Good," The Journal of Liberal Religion, III (1942), 171–185.

Williams, Ronald L. "The Types of Christology: A Neoclassical Analysis," The Journal of Religion, XLI (1969), 18–40.

Williamson, Clark M. "God and the Relativities of History," Encounter, XXVIII (1967), 199–218.

_____. "A Response to Professor Cotton," Encounter, XXIX (1968), 141–148.

Wilson, Colin. Beyond the Outsider. Boston: Houghton Mifflin, 1965.

_____. Religion and the Rebel. Boston: Houghton Mifflin, 1957.

Wyman, Mary A. The Lure for Feeling. New York: Philosophical Library, 1962.

Index